HMH

GO MATH!

Middle School
Advanced 2

Edward B. Burger • Juli K. Dixon

Timothy D. Kanold • Matthew R. Larson

Steven J. Leinwand

Martha E. Sandoval-Martinez

COMMON
CORE
EDITION

Authors

Edward B. Burger, Ph.D., is the president of Southwestern University, a former Francis Christopher Oakley Third Century Professor of Mathematics at Williams College, and a former vice provost at Baylor University. He has authored or coauthored more than sixty-five articles, books, and video series; delivered over five hundred addresses and workshops throughout the world; and made more than fifty radio and television appearances. He is a Fellow of the American Mathematical Society as well as having earned many national honors, including the Robert Foster Cherry Award for Great Teaching in 2010. In 2012, Microsoft Education named him a "Global Hero in Education."

Juli K. Dixon, Ph.D., is a Professor of Mathematics Education at the University of Central Florida. She has taught mathematics in urban schools at the elementary, middle, secondary, and post-secondary levels. She is an active researcher and speaker with numerous publications and conference presentations. Key areas of focus are deepening teachers' content knowledge and communicating and justifying mathematical ideas. She is a past chair of the NCTM Student Explorations in Mathematics Editorial Panel and member of the Board of Directors for the Association of Mathematics Teacher Educators.

Timothy D. Kanold, Ph.D., is an award-winning international educator, author, and consultant. He is a former superintendent and director of mathematics and science at Adlai E. Stevenson High School District 125 in Lincolnshire, Illinois. He is a past president of the National Council of Supervisors of Mathematics (NCSM) and the Council for the Presidential Awardees of Mathematics (CPAM). He has served on several writing and leadership commissions for NCTM during the past decade. He presents motivational professional development seminars with a focus on developing professional learning communities (PLC's) to improve the teaching, assessing, and learning of students. He has recently authored nationally recognized articles, books, and textbooks for mathematics education and school leadership, including *What Every Principal Needs to Know about the Teaching and Learning of Mathematics*.

Matthew R. Larson, Ph.D., is the president of the National Council of Teachers of Mathematics (2016-2018) and served on the Board of Directors for NCTM from 2010-2013. He is a past chair of NCTM's Research Committee and was a member of NCTM's Task Force on Linking Research and Practice. He is the author of several books on implementing the Common Core Standards for Mathematics. He has taught mathematics at the secondary and college levels and held an appointment as an honorary visiting associate professor at Teachers College, Columbia University.

Steven J. Leinwand is a Principal Research Analyst at the American Institutes for Research (AIR) in Washington, D.C., and has over 30 years in leadership positions in mathematics education. He is past president of the National Council of Supervisors of Mathematics and served on the NCTM Board of Directors. He is the author of numerous articles, books, and textbooks and has made countless presentations with topics including student achievement, reasoning, effective assessment, and successful implementation of standards.

Martha E. Sandoval-Martinez is a mathematics instructor at El Camino College in Torrance, California. She was previously a Math Specialist at the University of California at Davis and former instructor at Santa Ana College, Marymount College, and California State University, Long Beach. In her current and former positions, she has worked extensively to improve fundamental pre-algebra and algebra skills in students who have historically struggled with mathematics.

Program Reviewers

COMMON CORE

UNIT 1

Expressions, Equations, and Inequalities

MODULE 1 Expressions and Equations

CLUSTER

MAJOR CLUSTERS ■
SUPPORTING CLUSTERS ■
ADDITIONAL CLUSTERS ▦

MODULE 2 Inequalities

CLUSTER

MAJOR CLUSTERS ■
SUPPORTING CLUSTERS ■
ADDITIONAL CLUSTERS ▥

UNIT 2 Geometry

MODULE 3 Modeling Geometric Figures

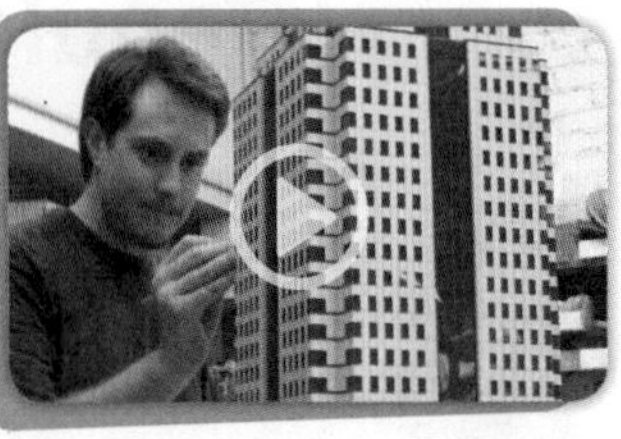

CLUSTER

MODULE 4 Circumference, Area, and Volume

CLUSTER

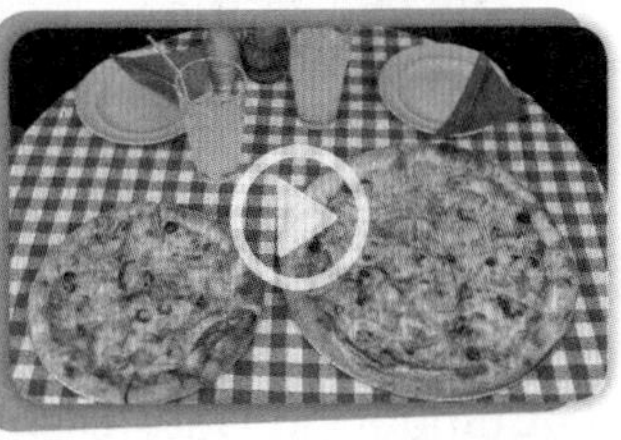

MAJOR CLUSTERS ■
SUPPORTING CLUSTERS ■
ADDITIONAL CLUSTERS ▦

UNIT 3 Statistics

MODULE 5 Random Samples and Populations

CLUSTER

MODULE 6 Analyzing and Comparing Data

CLUSTER

MAJOR CLUSTERS ■
SUPPORTING CLUSTERS ■
ADDITIONAL CLUSTERS ▥

UNIT 4 Probability

COMMON CORE

MODULE 7 Experimental Probability

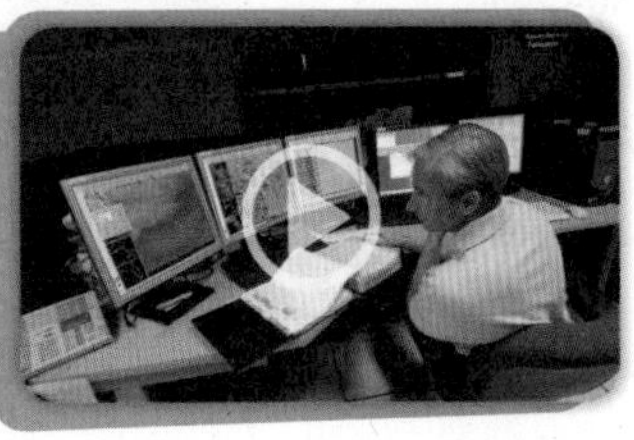

CLUSTER

MODULE 8 Theoretical Probability and Simulations

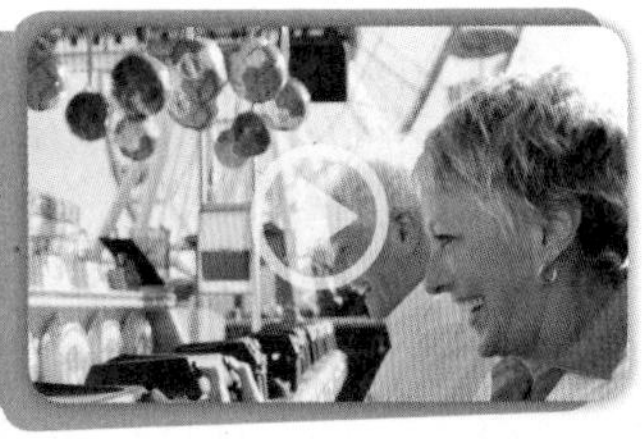

CLUSTER

MAJOR CLUSTERS
SUPPORTING CLUSTERS
ADDITIONAL CLUSTERS

UNIT 5 Real Numbers, Exponents and Scientific Notation

 MODULE 9 **Real Numbers**

MODULE 10 **Exponents and Scientific Notation**

MAJOR CLUSTERS ■
SUPPORTING CLUSTERS ■
ADDITIONAL CLUSTERS ■

UNIT 6
Proportional and Nonproportional Relationships and Functions

MODULE 11 Proportional Relationships

CLUSTER

MODULE 12 Nonproportional Relationships

CLUSTER

MAJOR CLUSTERS ■
SUPPORTING CLUSTERS ■
ADDITIONAL CLUSTERS ▥

MAJOR CLUSTERS ■
SUPPORTING CLUSTERS ■
ADDITIONAL CLUSTERS ■

UNIT 7

Solving Equations and Systems of Equations

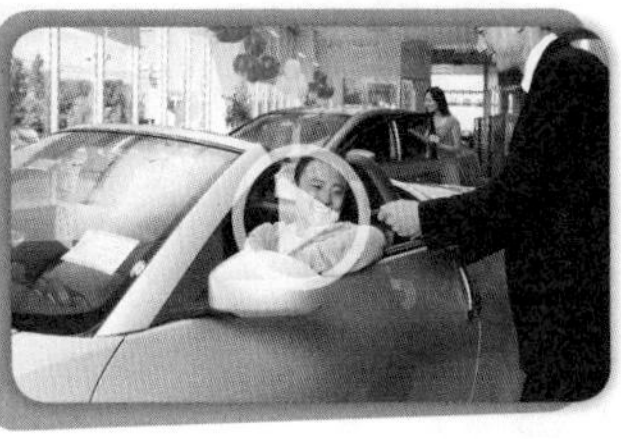

MODULE 15   Solving Linear Equations

MODULE 16   Solving Systems of Linear Equations

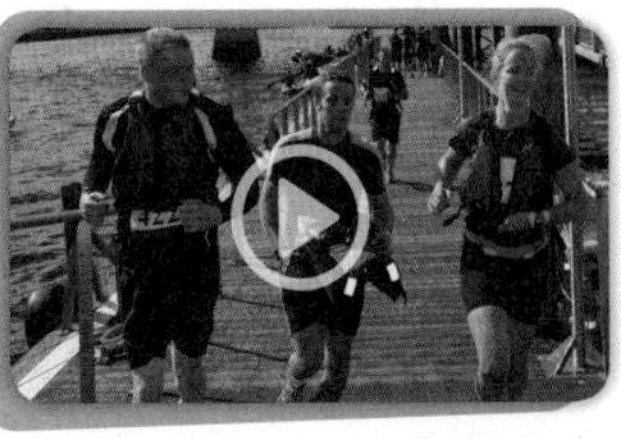

MAJOR CLUSTERS ■
SUPPORTING CLUSTERS ■
ADDITIONAL CLUSTERS ■

MODULE 17 Transformations and Congruence

MODULE 18 Transformations and Similarity

MAJOR CLUSTERS ■
SUPPORTING CLUSTERS ■
ADDITIONAL CLUSTERS ▨

Measurement Geometry

MODULE 19 Angle Relationships in Parallel Lines and Triangles

CLUSTER

MODULE 20 The Pythagorean Theorem

CLUSTER

MAJOR CLUSTERS ■
SUPPORTING CLUSTERS ■
ADDITIONAL CLUSTERS ▦

MODULE 21 Volume

MAJOR CLUSTERS ■
SUPPORTING CLUSTERS ■
ADDITIONAL CLUSTERS ■

Common Core Standards for Mathematics

Correlations for *HMH Go Math* Advanced 2

Standard	Descriptor	Taught	Reinforced
7.RP RATIOS AND PROPORTIONAL RELATIONSHIPS			
Analyze proportional relationships and use them to solve real-world and mathematical problems.			
■ CC.7.RP.2	Recognize and represent proportional relationships between quantities.	SE: 71, 74, 76A, 150A; *See also below.*	SE: 76B, 93–94, 150B; *See also below.*
■ CC.7.RP.2a	Decide whether two quantities are in a proportional relationship, e.g., by testing for equivalent ratios in a table or graphing on a coordinate plane and observing whether the graph is a straight line through the origin.	SE: 99–100	SE: 104
■ CC.7.RP.2c	Represent proportional relationships by equations.	SE: 153, 221–224	SE: 155, 164, 225–226
■ CC.7.RP.3	Use proportional relationships to solve multistep ratio and percent problems.	SE: 71, 74, 76A, 150A, 221–224, 245–248	SE: 75–76, 76B, 93–94, 150B, 225–226, 227–228, 249–250, 258
7.NS THE NUMBER SYSTEM			
Apply and extend previous understandings of operations with fractions to add, subtract, multiply, and divide rational numbers.			
■ CC.7.NS.3	Solve real-world and mathematical problems involving the four operations with rational numbers.	SE: 221-224	SE: 225-226
7.EE EXPRESSIONS AND EQUATIONS			
Use properties of operations to generate equivalent expressions.			
■ CC.7.EE.1	Apply properties of operations as strategies to add, subtract, factor, and expand linear expressions with rational coefficients.	SE: 7–10, 12A	SE: 11–12, 12B, 31–32
■ CC.7.EE.2	Understand that rewriting an expression in different forms in a problem context can shed light on the problem and how the quantities in it are related.	SE: 7–10, 107, 117	SE: 11–12, 12B, 31–32, 110

■ MAJOR CLUSTERS ■ SUPPORTING CLUSTERS ■ ADDITIONAL CLUSTERS

Standard	Descriptor	Taught	Reinforced
Solve real-life and mathematical problems using numerical and algebraic expressions and equations.			
■ CC.7.EE.4	Use variables to represent quantities in a real-world or mathematical problem, and construct simple equations and inequalities to solve problems by reasoning about the quantities.	SE: 13–16, 19–22, 25, 41–42, 45–48, 56A; *See also below.*	SE: 17–18, 23–24, 28, 29–30, 31–32, 43–44, 49–50, 56A–56B, 57–58; *See also below.*
■ CC.7.EE.4a	Solve word problems leading to equations of the form $px + q = r$ and $p(x + q) = r$, where p, q, and r are specific rational numbers. Solve equations of these forms fluently. Compare an algebraic solution to an arithmetic solution, identifying the sequence of the operations used in each approach.	SE: 25–28, 30A, 88–90	SE: 29–30, 30B, 30C–30D, 31–32, 91–92, 93–94
■ CC.7.EE.4b	Solve word problems leading to inequalities of the form $px + q > r$ or $px + q < r$, where p, q, and r are specific rational numbers. Graph the solution set of the inequality and interpret it in the context of the problem.	SE: 37–42, 51–54, 56A	SE: 43–44, 44A-44B, 55–56, 56A–56B, 57–58

7.G GEOMETRY

Standard	Descriptor	Taught	Reinforced
Draw, construct, and describe geometrical figures and describe the relationships between them.			
■ CC.7.G.1	Solve problems involving scale drawings of geometric figures, including computing actual lengths and areas from a scale drawing and reproducing a scale drawing at a different scale.	SE: 71–74, 76A	SE: 75–76, 76B, 76C–76D, 93–94
■ CC.7.G.2	Draw (freehand, with ruler and protractor, and with technology) geometric shapes with given conditions. Focus on constructing triangles from three measures of angles or sides, noticing when the conditions determine a unique triangle, more than one triangle, or no triangle.	SE: 77–79, 80A–80B	SE: 79–80, 80A–80B, 93–94
■ CC.7.G.3	Describe the two-dimensional figures that result from slicing three-dimensional figures, as in plane sections of right rectangular prisms and right rectangular pyramids.	SE: 81–82	SE: 83–84, 93–94
Solve real-life and mathematical problems involving angle measure, area, surface area, and volume.			
■ CC.7.G.4	Know the formulas for the area and circumference of a circle and use them to solve problems; give an informal derivation of the relationship between the circumference and area of a circle.	SE: 99–102, 105–108	SE: 103–104, 109–110, 129–130

■ MAJOR CLUSTERS   ■ SUPPORTING CLUSTERS   ■ ADDITIONAL CLUSTERS

Standard	Descriptor	Taught	Reinforced
CC.7.G.5	Use facts about supplementary, complementary, vertical, and adjacent angles in a multi-step problem to write and solve simple equations for an unknown angle in a figure.	SE: 85–90	SE: 91–92, 93–94
CC.7.G.6	Solve real-world and mathematical problems involving area, volume and surface area of two- and three-dimensional objects composed of triangles, quadrilaterals, polygons, cubes, and right prisms.	SE: 111–114, 117–120, 123–126	SE: 115–116, 121–122, 127–128, 129–130

7.SP STATISTICS AND PROBABILITY

Use random sampling to draw inferences about a population.

Standard	Descriptor	Taught	Reinforced
CC.7.SP.1	Understand that statistics can be used to gain information about a population by examining a sample of the population; generalizations about a population from a sample are valid only if the sample is representative of that population. Understand that random sampling tends to produce representative samples and support valid inferences.	SE: 145–148, 151–154	SE: 149–150, 163–164, 155–156, 163–164
CC.7.SP.2	Use data from a random sample to draw inferences about a population with an unknown characteristic of interest. Generate multiple samples (or simulated samples) of the same size to gauge the variation in estimates or predictions.	SE: 151–154, 157–160	SE: 155–156, 161–162, 163–164

Draw informal comparative inferences about two populations.

Standard	Descriptor	Taught	Reinforced
CC.7.SP.3	Informally assess the degree of visual overlap of two numerical data distributions with similar variabilities, measuring the difference between the centers by expressing it as a multiple of a measure of variability.	SE: 170, 172, 176, 178, 181–182, 184	SE: 173–174, 179–180, 185–186, 187–188
CC.7.SP.4	Use measures of center and measures of variability for numerical data from random samples to draw informal comparative inferences about two populations.	SE: 169, 171–172, 175, 177–178, 183–184	SE: 173–174, 179–180, 185–186, 187–188

Investigate chance processes and develop, use, and evaluate probability models.

Standard	Descriptor	Taught	Reinforced
CC.7.SP.5	Understand that the probability of a chance event is a number between 0 and 1 that expresses the likelihood of the event occurring. Larger numbers indicate greater likelihood. A probability near 0 indicates an unlikely event, a probability around $\frac{1}{2}$ indicates an event that is neither unlikely nor likely, and a probability near 1 indicates a likely event.	SE: 201–202, 205–206	SE: 207–208

Standard	Descriptor	Taught	Reinforced
■ CC.7.SP.6	Approximate the probability of a chance event by collecting data on the chance process that produces it and observing its long-run relative frequency, and predict the approximate relative frequency given the probability.	SE: 209, 211–212, 221–224, 235–236, 245–246	SE: 213–214, 225–226, 249–250
■ CC.7.SP.7	Develop a probability model and use it to find probabilities of events. Compare probabilities from a model to observed frequencies; if the agreement is not good, explain possible sources of the discrepancy.	SE: 235–236; *See also below.*	SE: 237–238; *See also below.*
■ CC.7.SP.7a	Develop a uniform probability model by assigning equal probability to all outcomes, and use the model to determine probabilities of events.	SE: 203–206, 233–234, 247–248	SE: 207–208, 227–228, 237–238, 249–250, 257–258
■ CC.7.SP.7b	Develop a probability model (which may not be uniform) by observing frequencies in data generated from a chance process.	SE: 209–211, 212	SE: 213–214, 227–228
■ CC.7.SP.8	Find probabilities of compound events using organized lists, tables, tree diagrams, and simulation.	SE: 215–218, 239–242, 252–254; *See also below.*	SE: 219–220, 227–228, 243–244, 255–256, 257–258; *See also below.*
■ CC.7.SP.8a	Understand that, just as with simple events, the probability of a compound event is the fraction of outcomes in the sample space for which the compound event occurs.	SE: 215–218, 239, 242	SE: 219–220, 227–228, 243–244, 257–258
■ CC.7.SP.8b	Represent sample spaces for compound events using methods such as organized lists, tables and tree diagrams. For an event described in everyday language (e.g., "rolling double sixes"), identify the outcomes in the sample space which compose the event.	SE: 215–218, 240–242	SE: 219–220, 227–228, 243–244
■ CC.7.SP.8c	Design and use a simulation to generate frequencies for compound events.	SE: 217–218, 251–254	SE: 220, 255–256, 257–258

■ MAJOR CLUSTERS   ■ SUPPORTING CLUSTERS   ■ ADDITIONAL CLUSTERS

Standard	Descriptor	Taught	Reinforced
8.NS THE NUMBER SYSTEM			
Know that there are numbers that are not rational, and approximate them by rational numbers.			
■ **CC.8.NS.1**	Know that numbers that are not rational are called irrational. Understand informally that every number has a decimal expansion; for rational numbers show that the decimal expansion repeats eventually, and convert a decimal expansion which repeats eventually into a rational number.	SE: 271–273, 276, 279–281, 282	SE: 277–278, 283–284
■ **CC.8.NS.2**	Use rational approximations of irrational numbers to compare the size of irrational numbers, locate them approximately on a number line diagram, and estimate the value of expressions (e.g., π^2).	SE: 274–276, 285–287, 288	SE: 278, 289–290, 290A–290B
8.EE EXPRESSIONS AND EQUATIONS			
Work with radicals and integer exponents.			
■ **CC.8.EE.1**	Know and apply the properties of integer exponents to generate equivalent numerical expressions.	SE: 297–299, 300	SE: 301–302, 302A–302B
■ **CC.8.EE.2**	Use square root and cube root symbols to represent solutions to equations of the form $x^2 = p$ and $x^3 = p$, where p is a positive rational number. Evaluate square roots of small perfect squares and cube roots of small perfect cubes. Know that $\sqrt{2}$ is irrational.	SE: 273–275, 276	SE: 277–278
■ **CC.8.EE.3**	Use numbers expressed in the form of a single digit times an integer power of 10 to estimate very large or very small quantities, and to express how many times as much one is than the other.	SE: 303–305, 306, 308A–308B	SE: 307–308, 313–314
■ **CC.8.EE.4**	Perform operations with numbers expressed in scientific notation, including problems where both decimal and scientific notation are used. Use scientific notation and choose units of appropriate size for measurements of very large or very small quantities (e.g., use millimeters per year for seafloor spreading). Interpret scientific notation that has been generated by technology.	SE: 315–317, 318	SE: 319–320
Understand the connections between proportional relationships, lines, and linear equations.			
■ **CC.8.EE.5**	Graph proportional relationships, interpreting the unit rate as the slope of the graph. Compare two different proportional relationships represented in different ways.	SE: 347–349, 350, 432, 434	SE: 351–352, 435–436

Standard	Descriptor	Taught	Reinforced
■ CC.8.EE.6	Use similar triangles to explain why the slope m is the same between any two distinct points on a non-vertical line in the coordinate plane; derive the equation $y = mx$ for a line through the origin and the equation $y = mx + b$ for a line intercepting the vertical axis at b.	SE: 335–337, 338, 346A–346B, 365, 367, 368, 628–629, 632A–632B	SE: 339–340, 370, 632

Analyze and solve linear equations and pairs of simultaneous linear equations.

Standard	Descriptor	Taught	Reinforced
■ CC.8.EE.7	Solve linear equations in one variable.	SE: 461–463, 464, 467–469, 470, 619, 622, 627–628, 630; *See also below.*	SE: 465–466, 471–472, 623–624, 631–632; *See also below.*
■ CC.8.EE.7a	Give examples of linear equations in one variable with one solution, infinitely many solutions, or no solutions. Show which of these possibilities is the case by successively transforming the given equation into simpler forms, until an equivalent equation of the form $x = a$, $a = a$, or $a = b$ results (where a and b are different numbers).	SE: 479–481, 482	SE: 483–484
■ CC.8.EE.7b	Solve linear equations with rational number coefficients, including equations whose solutions require expanding expressions using the distributive property and collecting like terms.	SE: 461–463, 464, 467–469, 470, 473–475, 476, 621, 622	SE: 465–466, 471–472, 477–478, 484A–484B, 623–624
■ CC.8.EE.8	Analyze and solve pairs of simultaneous linear equations.	SE: 492–495, 496; *See also below.*	SE: 497–498; *See also below.*
■ CC.8.EE.8a	Understand that solutions to a system of two linear equations in two variables correspond to points of intersection of their graphs, because points of intersection satisfy both equations simultaneously.	SE: 491, 496	SE: 497–498
■ CC.8.EE.8b	Solve systems of two linear equations in two variables algebraically, and estimate solutions by graphing the equations. Solve simple cases by inspection.	SE: 499–502, 504, 507–510, 512, 515–518, 520, 523–525, 526	SE: 505–506, 513–514, 521–522, 527–528
■ CC.8.EE.8c	Solve real-world and mathematical problems leading to two linear equations in two variables.	SE: 494–495, 496, 502–503, 504, 510–511, 512, 518–519, 520	SE: 497–498, 505–506, 513–514, 521–522, 528

8.F FUNCTIONS

Define, evaluate, and compare functions.

Standard	Descriptor	Taught	Reinforced
■ CC.8.F.1	Understand that a function is a rule that assigns to each input exactly one output. The graph of a function is the set of ordered pairs consisting of an input and the corresponding output.	SE: 417–421, 422, 425	SE: 423–424, 429–430, 430C–430D

■ MAJOR CLUSTERS   ■ SUPPORTING CLUSTERS   ■ ADDITIONAL CLUSTERS

Standard	Descriptor	Taught	Reinforced
CC.8.F.2	Compare properties of two functions each represented in a different way (algebraically, graphically, numerically in tables, or by verbal descriptions).	SE: 349, 350, 380–382, 431–433, 434	SE: 351–352, 384, 435–436
CC.8.F.3	Interpret the equation $y = mx + b$ as defining a linear function, whose graph is a straight line; give examples of functions that are not linear.	SE: 359–361, 362, 371–372, 374, 377, 381, 426–427, 428, 430A–430B	SE: 363–364, 375–376, 383, 429–430

Use functions to model relationships between quantities.

Standard	Descriptor	Taught	Reinforced
CC.8.F.4	Construct a function to model a linear relationship between two quantities. Determine the rate of change and initial value of the function from a description of a relationship or from two (x, y) values, including reading these from a table or from a graph. Interpret the rate of change and initial value of a linear function in terms of the situation it models, and in terms of its graph or a table of values.	SE: 341–343, 344, 347, 350, 366, 368, 378–379, 381–382, 391–393, 394, 397–399, 400, 431–432, 433, 434, 436A–436B	SE: 340, 345–346, 351, 369–370, 375–376, 383–384, 395–396, 401–402, 435–436
CC.8.F.5	Describe qualitatively the functional relationship between two quantities by analyzing a graph (e.g., where the function is increasing or decreasing, linear or nonlinear). Sketch a graph that exhibits the qualitative features of a function that has been described verbally.	SE: 437–439, 440	SE: 441–442

8.G GEOMETRY

Understand congruence and similarity using physical models, transparencies, or geometry software.

Standard	Descriptor	Taught	Reinforced
CC.8.G.1a	Verify experimentally the properties of rotations, reflections, and translations: Lines are taken to lines, and line segments to line segments of the same length.	SE: 543–545, 546, 549–551, 552, 555–557, 558	SE: 547–548, 553–554, 559–560
CC.8.G.1b	Verify experimentally the properties of rotations, reflections, and translations: Angles are taken to angles of the same measure.	SE: 543–545, 546, 549–551, 552, 555–557, 558	SE: 547–548, 553–554, 559–560
CC.8.G.1c	Verify experimentally the properties of rotations, reflections, and translations: Parallel lines are taken to parallel lines.	SE: 543–545, 546, 549–551, 552, 555–557, 558	SE: 547–548, 553–554, 559–560
CC.8.G.2	Understand that a two-dimensional figure is congruent to another if the second can be obtained from the first by a sequence of rotations, reflections, and translations; given two congruent figures, describe a sequence that exhibits the congruence between them.	SE: 569–571, 572	SE: 573–574

Standard	Descriptor	Taught	Reinforced
■ **CC.8.G.3**	Describe the effect of dilations, translations, rotations, and reflections on two-dimensional figures using coordinates.	SE: 545–546, 551–552, 557–558, 561–564, 580–581, 582, 585–587, 588	SE: 547–548, 553–554, 559–560, 565–566, 583–584, 589–590
■ **CC.8.G.4**	Understand that a two-dimensional figure is similar to another if the second can be obtained from the first by a sequence of rotations, reflections, translations, and dilations; given two similar two-dimensional figures, describe a sequence that exhibits the similarity between them.	SE: 579–580, 581–582, 591–593, 594	SE: 583–584, 595–596, 596A–596B
■ **CC.8.G.5**	Use informal arguments to establish facts about the angle sum and exterior angle of triangles, about the angles created when parallel lines are cut by a transversal, and the angle-angle criterion for similarity of triangles.	SE: 611–614, 617–619, 620, 622, 625–626	SE: 615–616, 623–624, 631–632

Understand and apply the Pythagorean Theorem.

Standard	Descriptor	Taught	Reinforced
■ **CC.8.G.6**	Explain a proof of the Pythagorean Theorem and its converse.	SE: 639–640, 645–647, 648	SE: 644, 649–650
■ **CC.8.G.7**	Apply the Pythagorean Theorem to determine unknown side lengths in right triangles in real-world and mathematical problems in two and three dimensions.	SE: 640–642	SE: 643–644, 650A–650B
■ **CC.8.G.8**	Apply the Pythagorean Theorem to find the distance between two points in a coordinate system.	SE: 651–654	SE: 655–656

Solve real-world and mathematical problems involving volume of cylinders, cones, and spheres.

Standard	Descriptor	Taught	Reinforced
■ **CC.8.G.9**	Know the formulas for the volumes of cones, cylinders, and spheres and use them to solve real-world and mathematical problems.	SE: 663–665, 666, 669–671, 672, 675–677, 678	SE: 667–668, 673–674, 679–670

8.SP STATISTICS AND PROBABILITY

Investigate patterns of association in bivariate data.

Standard	Descriptor	Taught	Reinforced
■ **CC.8.SP.1**	Construct and interpret scatter plots for bivariate measurement data to investigate patterns of association between two quantities. Describe patterns such as clustering, outliers, positive or negative association, linear association, and nonlinear association.	SE: 406–407, 408	SE: 409–410

■ MAJOR CLUSTERS ■ SUPPORTING CLUSTERS ■ ADDITIONAL CLUSTERS

Standard	Descriptor	Taught	Reinforced
CC.8.SP.2	Know that straight lines are widely used to model relationships between two quantitative variables. For scatter plots that suggest a linear association, informally fit a straight line, and informally assess the model fit by judging the closeness of the data points to the line.	SE: 403–404	SE: 409–410
CC.8.SP.3	Use the equation of a linear model to solve problems in the context of bivariate measurement data, interpreting the slope and intercept.	SE: 404–405, 408	SE: 409–410

Standard	Descriptor	Citations
MP MATHEMATICAL PRACTICES STANDARDS		*The mathematical practices standards are integrated throughout the book. See, for example, the citations below.*
CC.MP.1	**Make sense of problems and persevere in solving them.** Mathematically proficient students start by explaining to themselves the meaning of a problem and looking for entry points to its solution. They analyze givens, constraints, relationships, and goals. They make conjectures about the form and meaning of the solution and plan a solution pathway rather than simply jumping into a solution attempt. They consider analogous problems, and try special cases and simpler forms of the original problem in order to gain insight into its solution. They monitor and evaluate their progress and change course if necessary. Older students might, depending on the context of the problem, transform algebraic expressions or change the viewing window on their graphing calculator to get the information they need. Mathematically proficient students can explain correspondences between equations, verbal descriptions, tables, and graphs or draw diagrams of important features and relationships, graph data, and search for regularity or trends. Younger students might rely on using concrete objects or pictures to help conceptualize and solve a problem. Mathematically proficient students check their answers to problems using a different method, and they continually ask themselves, "Does this make sense?" They can understand the approaches of others to solving complex problems and identify correspondences between different approaches.	SE: 56, 116, 158, 223, 278, 384, 442, 466, 475, 483, 506, 518–519, 572, 644, 656, 679
CC.MP.2	**Reason abstractly and quantitatively.** Mathematically proficient students make sense of quantities and their relationships in problem situations. They bring two complementary abilities to bear on problems involving quantitative relationships: the ability to decontextualize—to abstract a given situation and represent it symbolically and manipulate the representing symbols as if they have a life of their own, without necessarily attending to their referents—and the ability to contextualize, to pause as needed during the manipulation process in order to probe into the referents for the symbols involved. Quantitative reasoning entails habits of creating a coherent representation of the problem at hand; considering the units involved; attending to the meaning of quantities, not just how to compute them; and knowing and flexibly using different properties of operations and objects.	SE: 52, 107, 181–182, 226, 278, 302, 346, 352, 367, 375, 417–418, 462–466, 478, 518–519, 618–619, 639–640

Standard	Descriptor	Citations
CC.MP.3	**Construct viable arguments and critique the reasoning of others.** Mathematically proficient students understand and use stated assumptions, definitions, and previously established results in constructing arguments. They make conjectures and build a logical progression of statements to explore the truth of their conjectures. They are able to analyze situations by breaking them into cases, and can recognize and use counterexamples. They justify their conclusions, communicate them to others, and respond to the arguments of others. They reason inductively about data, making plausible arguments that take into account the context from which the data arose. Mathematically proficient students are also able to compare the effectiveness of two plausible arguments, distinguish correct logic or reasoning from that which is flawed, and—if there is a flaw in an argument—explain what it is. Elementary students can construct arguments using concrete referents such as objects, drawings, diagrams, and actions. Such arguments can make sense and be correct, even though they are not generalized or made formal until later grades. Later, students learn to determine domains to which an argument applies. Students at all grades can listen or read the arguments of others, decide whether they make sense, and ask useful questions to clarify or improve the arguments.	SE: 44, 92, 174, 238, 284, 364, 410, 472, 522, 566, 617, 674
CC.MP.4	**Model with mathematics.** Mathematically proficient students can apply the mathematics they know to solve problems arising in everyday life, society, and the workplace. In early grades, this might be as simple as writing an addition equation to describe a situation. In middle grades, a student might apply proportional reasoning to plan a school event or analyze a problem in the community. By high school, a student might use geometry to solve a design problem or use a function to describe how one quantity of interest depends on another. Mathematically proficient students who can apply what they know are comfortable making assumptions and approximations to simplify a complicated situation, realizing that these may need revision later. They are able to identify important quantities in a practical situation and map their relationships using such tools as diagrams, two-way tables, graphs, flowcharts and formulas. They can analyze those relationships mathematically to draw conclusions. They routinely interpret their mathematical results in the context of the situation and reflect on whether the results make sense, possibly improving the model if it has not served its purpose.	SE: 27, 104, 156, 220, 337, 393–394, 468–469, 518–519, 627–628, 677

Standard	Descriptor	Citations
CC.MP.5	**Use appropriate tools strategically.** Mathematically proficient students consider the available tools when solving a mathematical problem. These tools might include pencil and paper, concrete models, a ruler, a protractor, a calculator, a spreadsheet, a computer algebra system, a statistical package, or dynamic geometry software. Proficient students are sufficiently familiar with tools appropriate for their grade or course to make sound decisions about when each of these tools might be helpful, recognizing both the insight to be gained and their limitations. For example, mathematically proficient high school students analyze graphs of functions and solutions generated using a graphing calculator. They detect possible errors by strategically using estimation and other mathematical knowledge. When making mathematical models, they know that technology can enable them to visualize the results of varying assumptions, explore consequences, and compare predictions with data. Mathematically proficient students at various grade levels are able to identify relevant external mathematical resources, such as digital content located on a website, and use them to pose or solve problems. They are able to use technological tools to explore and deepen their understanding of concepts.	SE: 25, 77–80, 157, 256, 286, 317, 461, 491–495, 549, 579, 611–612, 617, 639, 663
CC.MP.6	**Attend to precision.** Mathematically proficient students try to communicate precisely to others. They try to use clear definitions in discussion with others and in their own reasoning. They state the meaning of the symbols they choose, including using the equal sign consistently and appropriately. They are careful about specifying units of measure, and labeling axes to clarify the correspondence with quantities in a problem. They calculate accurately and efficiently, express numerical answers with a degree of precision appropriate for the problem context. In the elementary grades, students give carefully formulated explanations to each other. By the time they reach high school they have learned to examine claims and make explicit use of definitions.	SE: 24, 84, 180, 214, 320, 370, 407, 437–442, 478, 498, 514, 616, 668

Standard	Descriptor	Citations
CC.MP.7	**Look for and make use of structure.** Mathematically proficient students look closely to discern a pattern or structure. Young students, for example, might notice that three and seven more is the same amount as seven and three more, or they may sort a collection of shapes according to how many sides the shapes have. Later, students will see 7×8 equals the well remembered $7 \times 5 + 7 \times 3$, in preparation for learning about the distributive property. In the expression $x^2 + 9x + 14$, older students can see the 14 as 2×7 and the 9 as $2 + 7$. They recognize the significance of an existing line in a geometric figure and can use the strategy of drawing an auxiliary line for solving problems. They also can step back for an overview and shift perspective. They can see complicated things, such as some algebraic expressions, as single objects or as being composed of several objects. For example, they can see $5 - 3(x - y)^2$ as 5 minus a positive number times a square and use that to realize that its value cannot be more than 5 for any real numbers x and y.	SE: 9, 117, 183, 244, 274–275, 297–299, 309, 397–399, 417–418, 472, 561–564, 645
CC.MP.8	**Look for and express regularity in repeated reasoning.** Mathematically proficient students notice if calculations are repeated, and look both for general methods and for shortcuts. Upper elementary students might notice when dividing 25 by 11 that they are repeating the same calculations over and over again, and conclude they have a repeating decimal. By paying attention to the calculation of slope as they repeatedly check whether points are on the line through (1, 2) with slope 3, middle school students might abstract the equation $\frac{(y-2)}{(x-1)} = 3$. Noticing the regularity in the way terms cancel when expanding $(x - 1)(x + 1)$, $(x - 1)(x^2 + x + 1)$, and $(x - 1)(x^3 + x^2 + x + 1)$ might lead them to the general formula for the sum of a geometric series. As they work to solve a problem, mathematically proficient students maintain oversight of the process, while attending to the details. They continually evaluate the reasonableness of their intermediate results.	SE: 37–38, 99, 124, 241, 272, 297–299, 309, 371, 461, 499, 507, 515, 561–564, 652

Succeeding with HMH Go Math

Actively participate in your learning with your write-in Student Edition. Explore concepts, take notes, answer questions, and complete your homework right in your textbook!

Explore Activities help you develop a deeper understanding of math concepts.

Essential Questions ensure that you know exactly what you are learning.

Scan QR codes with your smart phone or device to watch **Math On the Spot** tutorial videos for every example in the book!

Your Turn exercises check your understanding of new concepts.

Play strategy **Games and Activities** with classmates to practice using the concepts you have learned.

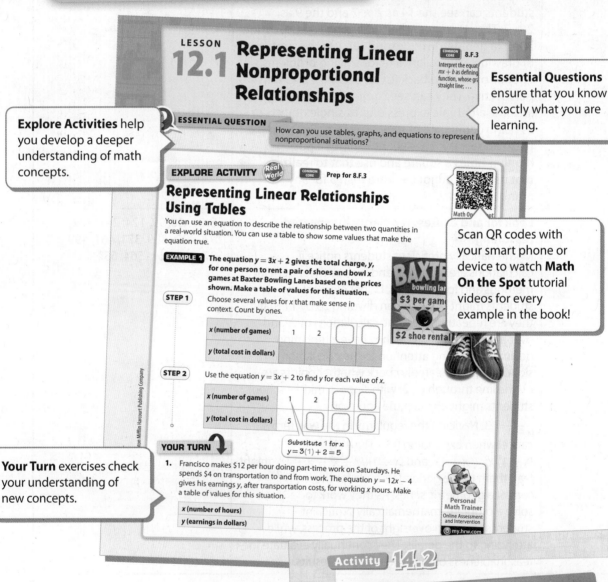

LESSON 12.1 Representing Linear Nonproportional Relationships

COMMON CORE 8.F.3

Interpret the equation $mx + b$ as defining function, whose graph straight line; …

ESSENTIAL QUESTION

How can you use tables, graphs, and equations to represent li nonproportional situations?

EXPLORE ACTIVITY Real World | COMMON CORE Prep for 8.F.3

Representing Linear Relationships Using Tables

You can use an equation to describe the relationship between two quantities in a real-world situation. You can use a table to show some values that make the equation true.

EXAMPLE 1 The equation $y = 3x + 2$ gives the total charge, y, for one person to rent a pair of shoes and bowl x games at Baxter Bowling Lanes based on the prices shown. Make a table of values for this situation.

STEP 1 Choose several values for x that make sense in context. Count by ones.

x (number of games)	1	2		
y (total cost in dollars)				

BAXTE
bowling lan
$3 per game
$2 shoe rental

STEP 2 Use the equation $y = 3x + 2$ to find y for each value of x.

x (number of games)	1	2		
y (total cost in dollars)	5			

Substitute 1 for x:
$y = 3(1) + 2 = 5$

YOUR TURN

1. Francisco makes $12 per hour doing part-time work on Saturdays. He spends $4 on transportation to and from work. The equation $y = 12x - 4$ gives his earnings y, after transportation costs, for working x hours. Make a table of values for this situation.

x (number of hours)				
y (earnings in dollars)				

Personal Math Trainer
Online Assessment and Intervention
my.hrw.com

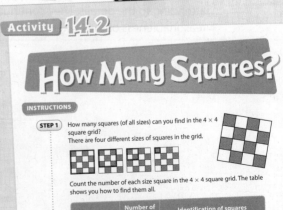

Activity 14.2

How Many Squares?

INSTRUCTIONS

STEP 1 How many squares (of all sizes) can you find in the 4 × 4 square grid? There are four different sizes of squares in the grid.

Count the number of each size square in the 4 × 4 square grid. The table shows you how to find them all.

Size of square	Number of squares	Identification of squares
4 × 4	1	
3 × 3	4	

Houghton Mifflin Harcourt Publishing Company

Are YOU Ready?

Complete these exercises to review skills you will need for this module.

Personal Math Trainer
Online Assessment and Intervention
my.hrw.com

Evaluate Expressions

EXAMPLE	Evaluate $3x - 5$ for $x = -2$.	
	$3x - 5 = 3(-2) - 5$	Substitute the given value of x for x.
	$= -6 - 5$	Multiply.
	$= -11$	Subtract.

Evaluate each expression for the given value of x.

1. $2x + 3$ for $x = 3$ _____
2. $-4x + 7$ for $x = -1$ _____
3. $1.5x - 2.5$ for $x = 3$ _____
4. $0.4x + 6.1$ for $x = -5$ _____
5. $\frac{2}{3}x - 12$ for $x = 18$ _____
6. $-\frac{5}{8}x + 10$ for $x = -8$ _____

Connect Words and Equations

EXAMPLE	Erik's earnings equal 9 dollars per hour.	Define the variables used in the situation.
	e = earnings; h = hours	Identify the operation involved. "Per" indicates multiplication.
	multiplication	
	$e = 9 \times h$	Write the equation.

Define the variables for each situation. Then write an equation.

7. Jana's age plus 5 equals her sister's age.

8. Andrew's class has 3 more students than Lauren's class.

9. The bank is 50 feet shorter than the firehouse.

10. The pencils were divided into 6 groups of 2.

414 Unit 6

Reading Start-Up

Visualize Vocabulary

Use the ✔ words to complete the graphic organizer. You will put one word in each oval.

Types of Quadrilaterals

A quadrilateral in which all sides are congruent and opposite sides are parallel.

A quadrilateral in which opposite sides are parallel and congruent.

A quadrilateral in which at least two sides are parallel.

Vocabulary

Review Words
coordinate plane (plano cartesiano)
✔ parallelogram (paralelogramo)
quadrilateral (cuadrilátero)
✔ rhombus (rombo)
✔ trapezoid (trapecio)

Preview Words
center of rotation (centro de rotación)
congruent (congruente)
image (imagen)
line of reflection (línea de reflexión)
preimage (imagen original)
reflection (reflexión)
rotation (rotación)
transformation (transformación)
translation (traslación)

Understand Vocabulary

Match the term on the left to the correct expression on the right.

1. transformation — A. A function that describes a change in the position, size, or shape of a figure.

2. reflection — B. A function that slides a figure along a straight line.

3. translation — C. A transformation that flips a figure across a line.

Active Reading

Booklet Before beginning the module, create a booklet to help you learn the concepts in this module. Write the main idea of each lesson on each page of the booklet. As you study each lesson, write important details that support the main idea, such as vocabulary and formulas. Refer to your finished booklet as you work on assignments and study for tests.

MODULE QUIZ

Ready to Go On?

Personal Math Trainer
Online Assessment and Intervention
my.hrw.com

14.1 Identifying and Representing Functions

Determine whether each relationship is a function.

1.

x	y
2	0
5	1
8	2
	3

2.
Input, x	Output, y
-1	6
3	5
6	5

3. $(2, 5), (7, 2), (-3, 4),$ $(2, 9), (1, 1)$

14.2 Describing Functions

Determine whether each situation is linear or nonlinear, and proportional or nonproportional.

4. Joanna is paid $14 per hour.

5. Alberto started out bench pressing 50 pounds. He then added 5 pounds every week.

14.3 Comparing Functions

6. Which function is changing more quickly? Explain.

Function 1

Function 2
Input, x	Output, y
2	11
3	6.5
4	2

14.4 Analyzing Graphs

7. Describe a graph that shows Sam running at a constant rate.

? ESSENTIAL QUESTION

8. How can you use functions to solve real-world problems?

Module 14 443

Unit 9 Performance Tasks

1. **CAREERS IN MATH** | **Hydrologist** A hydrologist needs to estimate the mass of water in an underground aquifer, which is roughly cylindrical in shape. The diameter of the aquifer is 65 meters, and its depth is 8 meters. One cubic meter of water has a mass of about 1000 kilograms.

   a. The aquifer is completely filled with water. What is the total mass of the water in the aquifer? Explain how you found your answer. Use 3.14 for π and round your answer to the nearest kilogram.

   b. Another cylindrical aquifer has a diameter of 70 meters and a depth of 9 meters. The mass of the water in it is 27×10^7 kilograms. Is the aquifer totally filled with water? Explain your reasoning.

2. From his home, Myles walked his dog north 5 blocks, east 2 blocks, and then stopped at a drinking fountain. He then walked north 3 more blocks and east 4 more blocks. It started to rain so he cut through a field and walked straight home.

   a. Draw a diagram of his path.

   b. How many blocks did Myles walk in all? How much longer was his walk before it started to rain than his walk home?

Enhance Your Learning!

Interactive Student Editions provide additional multimedia resources to enhance your learning. You can enter in answers, watch videos, explore concepts with virtual manipulatives, and get homework help!

 Real-World Videos show you how specific math topics can be used in all kinds of situations.

 Math On the Spot video tutorials provide step-by-step instruction of the math concepts covered in each example.

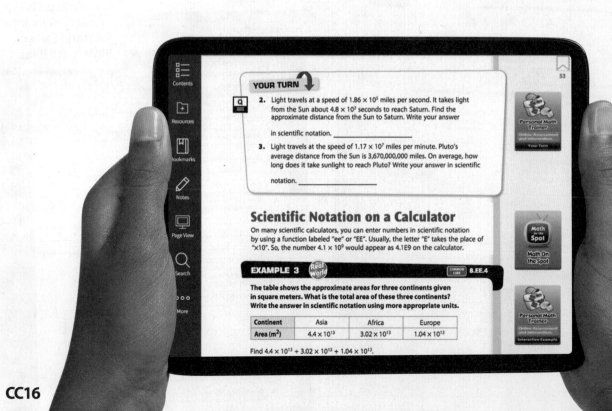

YOUR TURN

2. Light travels at a speed of 1.86×10^5 miles per second. It takes light from the Sun about 4.8×10^3 seconds to reach Saturn. Find the approximate distance from the Sun to Saturn. Write your answer in scientific notation. _____

3. Light travels at the speed of 1.17×10^7 miles per minute. Pluto's average distance from the Sun is 3,670,000,000 miles. On average, how long does it take sunlight to reach Pluto? Write your answer in scientific notation. _____

Scientific Notation on a Calculator

On many scientific calculators, you can enter numbers in scientific notation by using a function labeled "ee" or "EE". Usually, the letter "E" takes the place of "×10". So, the number 4.1×10^9 would appear as 4.1E9 on the calculator.

EXAMPLE 3 | COMMON CORE **8.EE.4**

The table shows the approximate areas for three continents given in square meters. What is the total area of these three continents? Write the answer in scientific notation using more appropriate units.

Continent	Asia	Africa	Europe
Area (m²)	4.4×10^{13}	3.02×10^{13}	1.04×10^{13}

Find $4.4 \times 10^{13} + 3.02 \times 10^{13} + 1.04 \times 10^{13}$.

Personal Math Trainer
Online Assessment and Intervention
Your Turn

Math On the Spot

Personal Math Trainer
Online Assessment and Intervention
Interactive Example

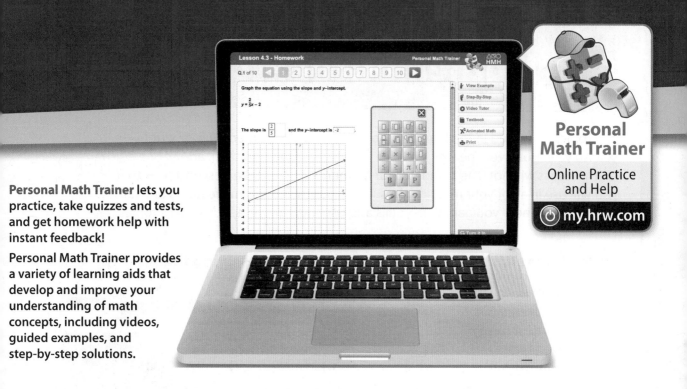

Personal Math Trainer lets you practice, take quizzes and tests, and get homework help with instant feedback!

Personal Math Trainer provides a variety of learning aids that develop and improve your understanding of math concepts, including videos, guided examples, and step-by-step solutions.

Personal Math Trainer

Online Practice and Help

⏻ my.hrw.com

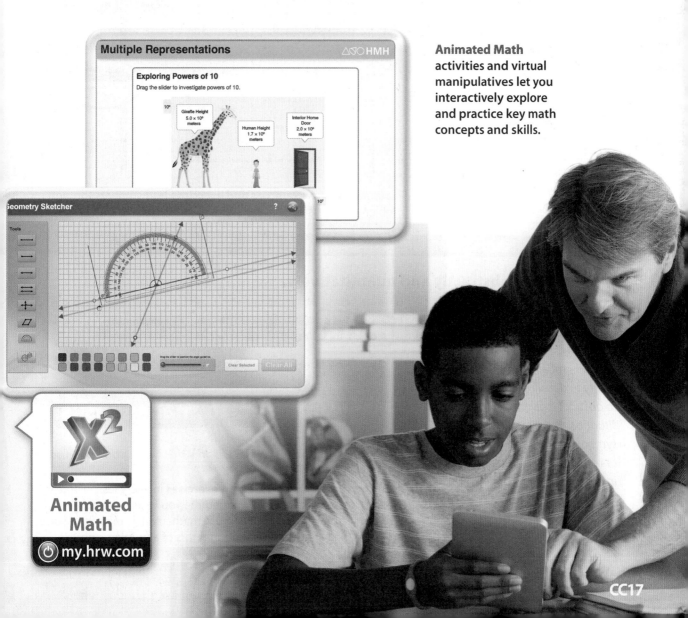

Animated Math activities and virtual manipulatives let you interactively explore and practice key math concepts and skills.

Animated Math

⏻ my.hrw.com

CC17

Standards for Mathematical Practice

The topics described in the Standards for Mathematical Content will vary from year to year. However, the *way* in which you learn, study, and think about mathematics will not. The Standards for Mathematical Practice describe skills that you will use in all of your math courses. These pages show some features of your book that will help you gain these skills and use them to master this year's topics.

MP.1 Make sense of problems and persevere in solving them.

Mathematically proficient students start by explaining to themselves the meaning of a problem... They analyze givens, constraints, relationships, and goals. They make conjectures about the form... of the solution and plan a solution pathway...

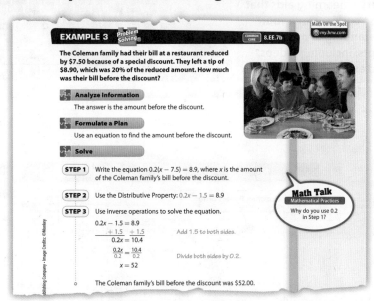

Problem-solving examples and exercises lead students through problem solving steps.

MP.2 Reason abstractly and quantitatively.

Mathematically proficient students... bring two complementary abilities to bear on problems...: the ability to decontextualize— to abstract a given situation and represent it symbolically... and the ability to contextualize, to pause... in order to probe into the referents for the symbols involved.

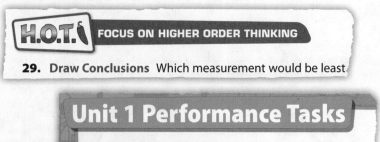

Focus on Higher Order Thinking exercises in every lesson and **Performance Tasks** in every unit require you to use logical reasoning, represent situations symbolically, use mathematical models to solve problems, and state your answers in terms of a problem context.

MP.3 Construct viable arguments and critique the reasoning of others.

Mathematically proficient students... justify their conclusions, [and]... distinguish correct... reasoning from that which is flawed.

Reflect

2. **Make a Conjecture** Use your results from parts **E**, **H**, and a conjecture about translations.

? ESSENTIAL QUESTION CHECK-IN

Essential Question Check-in and **Reflect** in every lesson ask you to evaluate statements, explain relationships, apply mathematical principles, make conjectures, construct arguments, and justify your reasoning.

MP.4 Model with mathematics.

Mathematically proficient students can apply... mathematics... to... problems... in everyday life, society, and the workplace.

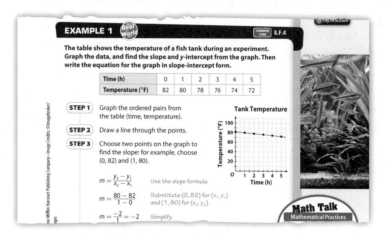

Real-world examples and **mathematical modeling** apply mathematics to other disciplines and real-world contexts such as science and business.

MP.5 Use appropriate tools strategically.

Mathematically proficient students consider the available tools when solving a... problem... [and] are... able to use technological tools to explore and deepen their understanding...

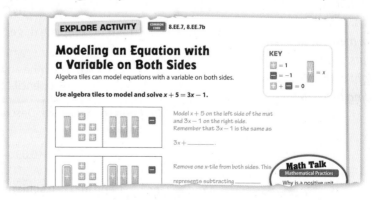

Exploration Activities in lessons use concrete and technological tools, such as manipulatives or graphing calculators, to explore mathematical concepts.

MP.6   Attend to precision.

Mathematically proficient students... communicate precisely... with others and in their own reasoning... [They] give carefully formulated explanations...

19. **Communicate Mathematical Ideas** Explain how you can fi[n] height of a cylinder if you know the diameter and the volum[e] an example with your explana[tion]

> **Key Vocabulary**
>
> **slope** *(pendiente)*
> A measure of the steepness of a line on a graph; the rise divided by the run.

Precision refers not only to the correctness of calculations but also to the proper use of mathematical language and symbols. **Communicate Mathematical Ideas** exercises and **Key Vocabulary** highlighted for each module and unit help you learn and use the language of math to communicate mathematics precisely.

MP.7   Look for and make use of structure.

Mathematically proficient students... look closely to discern a pattern or structure... They can also step back for an overview and shift perspectives.

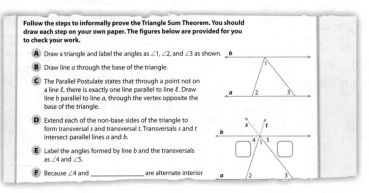

Follow the steps to informally prove the Triangle Sum Theorem. You should draw each step on your own paper. The figures below are provided for you to check your work.

A Draw a triangle and label the angles as ∠1, ∠2, and ∠3 as shown.

B Draw line *a* through the base of the triangle.

C The Parallel Postulate states that through a point not on a line ℓ, there is exactly one line parallel to line ℓ. Draw line *b* parallel to line *a*, through the vertex opposite the base of the triangle.

D Extend each of the non-base sides of the triangle to form transversal *s* and transversal *t*. Transversals *s* and *t* intersect parallel lines *a* and *b*.

E Label the angles formed by line *b* and the transversals as ∠4 and ∠5.

F Because ∠4 and _____ are alternate interior

Throughout the lessons, you will observe regularity in mathematical structures in order to make generalizations and make connections between related problems. For example, you can apply your knowledge of geometric theorems to determine when an auxiliary line would be helpful.

MP.8   Look for and express regularity in repeated reasoning.

Mathematically proficient students... look both for general methods and for shortcuts... [and] maintain oversight of the process, while attending to the details.

Use your pattern to complete this equation: $(7^2)^4 = 7^{\boxed{}}$.

B Describe any patterns you see. Use your pattern to of 1 pencil.

20. **Look for a Pattern** Describe the pattern in the equation. The[n] equation.

$$0.3x + 0.03x + 0.003x + 0.0003x + ... = 3$$

You will look for repeated calculations and mathematical patterns in examples and exercises. Recognizing patterns can help you make generalizations and obtain a better understanding of the underlying mathematics.

GRADE 6 PART 1

Review Test

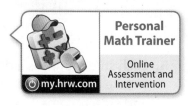

Personal
Math Trainer

my.hrw.com

Online
Assessment and
Intervention

Selected Response

1. Suppose you have developed a scale that indicates the brightness of sunlight. Each category in the table is 5 times brighter than the category above it. For example, a day that is dazzling is 5 times brighter than a day that is radiant. How many times brighter is a dazzling day than a dim day?

Sunlight Intensity	
Category	**Brightness**
Dim	2
Illuminated	3
Radiant	4
Dazzling	5

Ⓐ 125 times brighter

Ⓑ 625 times brighter

Ⓒ 3 times brighter

Ⓓ 25 times brighter

2. Patricia paid $584 for 8 nights at a hotel. Find the unit rate.

Ⓐ $\frac{\$146}{1 \text{ night}}$

Ⓒ $\frac{\$37}{1 \text{ night}}$

Ⓑ $\frac{\$584}{1 \text{ night}}$

Ⓓ $\frac{\$73}{1 \text{ night}}$

3. Valerie sold 6 tickets to the school play and Mark sold 16 tickets. What is the ratio of the number of tickets Valerie sold to the number of tickets Mark sold?

Ⓐ 16 to 6

Ⓒ 2 to 8

Ⓑ 2 to 3

Ⓓ 3 to 8

4. Grant and Pedro are comparing their stocks for the week. On Monday, their results were opposites. Explain how you would graph their results for Monday if Grant lost $4.

Ⓐ Grant's point is 4 units to the right of 0 on a number line, and Pedro's point is 4 units to the left of 0.

Ⓑ Grant's point is 4 units to the right of 0 on a number line, and Pedro's point is the same point.

Ⓒ Grant's loss is a point 4 units to the left of 0 on a number line, and Pedro's point is 4 units to the right of 0.

Ⓓ Grant's loss is a point 4 units to the left of 0 on a number line, and Pedro's point is the same point because it's already negative.

5. The fuel for a chain saw is a mix of oil and gasoline. The label says to mix 5 ounces of oil with 15 gallons of gasoline. How much oil would you use if you had 45 gallons of gasoline?

Ⓐ 21 ounces

Ⓒ 15 ounces

Ⓑ 1.67 ounces

Ⓓ 135 ounces

6. A stack of blocks is 12.3 inches tall. If there are 10 blocks stacked one on top of the other, how tall is each block?

Ⓐ 1.33 inches

Ⓒ 2.3 inches

Ⓑ 1.13 inches

Ⓓ 1.23 inches

7. Which temperature is warmest?

Ⓐ 16 °F

Ⓒ −21 °F

Ⓑ −16 °F

Ⓓ 21 °F

8. Each student needs a pencil and an eraser to take a test. If pencils come 8 in a box and erasers come 12 in a bag, what is the least number of boxes and bags needed for 24 students to each have a pencil and an eraser?

   Ⓐ 3 boxes of pencils, 2 bags of erasers

   Ⓑ 1 box of pencils, 1 bag of erasers

   Ⓒ 8 boxes of pencils, 12 bags of erasers

   Ⓓ 2 boxes of pencils, 3 bags of erasers

9. Find the quotient $7\frac{1}{6} \div \frac{5}{9}$.

   Ⓐ 12   Ⓒ $12\frac{9}{10}$

   Ⓑ $13\frac{1}{2}$ Ⓓ $1\frac{13}{30}$

10. Find the product 4.7×4.75.

   Ⓐ 223.25   Ⓒ 22.325

   Ⓑ 9.45   Ⓓ 2.2325

11. Carla is building a table out of boards that are 4.25 inches wide. She wants the table to be at least 36 inches wide. What is the least number of boards she can use?

   Ⓐ 8   Ⓒ 9.5

   Ⓑ 9   Ⓓ 153

12. How many centimeters are there in 740.2 millimeters?

   Ⓐ 7402 cm   Ⓒ 7.402 cm

   Ⓑ 74.02 cm   Ⓓ 0.7402 cm

Mini-Tasks

13. Jada is making lasagna and pizzas for a large party. Her lasagna recipe calls for $1\frac{1}{4}$ cups of tomato paste, and her pizza recipe uses $\frac{1}{2}$ cup of tomato paste per pizza. She will double her lasagna recipe and make 5 pizzas. Write and evaluate an expression for how many $\frac{3}{4}$-cup cans of tomato paste she will need in all.

_____

14. Explain how you can use multiplication to find the quotient $\frac{3}{5} \div \frac{3}{15}$. Then evaluate the expression.

_____

_____

15. You are working as an assistant to a chef. The chef has 8 cups of berries and will use $\frac{2}{3}$ cup of berries for each dessert he makes. How many desserts can he make?

_____

_____

Performance Task

16. School A has 216 students and 12 classrooms. School B has 104 students and 4 classrooms.

   Part A: What is the ratio of students to classrooms at School A?

   Part B: What is the ratio of students to classrooms at School B?

   Part C: How many students would have to transfer from School B to School A for the ratios of students to classrooms at both schools to be the same? Explain your reasoning.

_____

_____

_____

_____

_____

_____

_____

_____

_____

COMMON CORE

GRADE 6 PART 2

Review Test

Personal
Math Trainer

my.hrw.com

Online
Assessment and
Intervention

Selected Response

1. Kahlil is recording a beat for a song that he is working on. He wants the length of the beat to be more than 17 seconds long. His friend tells him the beat needs to be 9 seconds longer than that to match the lyrics he has written.

Write an inequality to represent the beat's length. Give three possible beat lengths that satisfy the inequality.

Ⓐ $t < 17$
   8, 6, 5

Ⓒ $t > 8$
   27, 35, 33

Ⓑ $t > 26$
   27, 35, 33

Ⓓ $t < 26$
   8, 6, 5

2. Write an expression for the missing value in the table.

Tom's Age	Kim's Age
11	14
12	15
13	16
a	?

Ⓐ $a + 16$

Ⓒ $a + 1$

Ⓑ $a + 11$

Ⓓ $a + 3$

3. A plant's height is 1.6 times its age. Write an equation for the situation. Tell what each variable you use represents.

Ⓐ h = plant's height; y = plant's age;
   $1.6 = hy$

Ⓑ h = plant's height; y = plant's age;
   $y = 1.6h$

Ⓒ h = plant's age; y = plant's height;
   $h = 1.6y$

Ⓓ h = plant's height; y = plant's age;
   $h = 1.6y$

4. A driveway is 162 feet long, 6 feet wide, and 4 inches deep. How many cubic feet of concrete will be required for the driveway?

Ⓐ 355 ft³

Ⓒ 3,888 ft³

Ⓑ 324 ft³

Ⓓ 254 ft³

5. Write the phrase as an algebraic expression.

6 less than a number times 11

Ⓐ $6y - 11y$

Ⓒ $11y - 6$

Ⓑ $11 \div y$

Ⓓ $11 + y$

6. Wilson bought gift cards for some lawyers and their assistants. Each lawyer got a gift card worth $\$\ell$. Each assistant got a gift card worth $\$a$. There are 14 lawyers. Each lawyer has three assistants. The expression for total cost of the gift cards is $14\ell + 42a$. Write an expression that is equivalent to the given expression.

Ⓐ $14(\ell + 2a)$

Ⓒ $14(\ell + 42a)$

Ⓑ $14(\ell + 3a)$

Ⓓ $42(\ell + 3a)$

7. At the beginning of the year, Jason had $80 in his savings account. Each month, he added $15 to his account. Write an expression for the amount of money in Jason's savings account each month. Then use the expression to find the amount of money in his account at the end of the year.

Month	January	February	March	m
Amount	$95	$110	$125	$?

Ⓐ $95 + 15m$; $275

Ⓑ $95 + m$; $107

Ⓒ $80 + 12m$; $224

Ⓓ $15m + 80$; $260

8. In a fish tank, $\frac{6}{7}$ of the fish have a red stripe on them. If 18 of the fish have red stripes, how many total fish are in the tank?

Ⓐ 26 fish   Ⓒ 23 fish

Ⓑ 21 fish   Ⓓ 25 fish

9. Solve the equation $s + 2.8 = 6.59$.

Ⓐ $s = 4.13$ Ⓒ $s = 9.39$

Ⓑ $s = 3.79$ Ⓓ $s = 3$

10. Which question is a statistical question?

Ⓐ How long is lunch period at your school?

Ⓑ How old is the oldest student in your class?

Ⓒ How many classrooms are there in your school?

Ⓓ What are the ages of all the people in your class?

11. In a box-and-whisker plot, the *interquartile range* is a measure of the spread of the middle half of the data. Find the interquartile range for the data set: 10, 3, 7, 6, 9, 12, 13.

Ⓐ 12   Ⓒ 6

Ⓑ 7   Ⓓ 8

12. Mike was in charge of collecting contributions for the Food Bank. He received contributions of $50, $80, $60, $50, and $90. Find the mean and median of the contributions.

Ⓐ mean: $66   Ⓒ mean: $50
      median: $60   median: $60

Ⓑ mean: $50   Ⓓ mean: $60
      median: $66   median: $66

13. Which expression is NOT equivalent to the expression $11y + 5$?

Ⓐ $0.5(22y + 10)$

Ⓑ $5y + 11 + 6y - 6$

Ⓒ $5(2y + 1) + y$

Ⓓ $6y + 3 + 5y - 2$

Mini-Tasks

14. It costs $9 to go to Pete's Pottery Place to make your own bowls for $3 per bowl. Natalie goes to Pete's Pottery Place and makes *b* bowls. She decides to make bowls 5 days this month so she can sell them at a crafts fair.

Part A: Write an expression that will represent Natalie's total cost for this month.

Part B: If she makes 4 bowls each time she goes to Pete's Pottery Place, what will her total cost be?

_____

_____

15. To find the mileage, or how many miles per gallon a car can travel, you can use the expression $\frac{m}{g}$, where *m* is the distance in miles and *g* is the number of gallons of gas used. Find the mileage for a car that travels 576 miles on 18 gallons of gas.

_____

Performance Task

16. **Part A:** Is $x = 6$ a solution of the equation $8x + 8 = 56$? Explain.

Part B: Suppose the solution $x = 6$ increases to $x = 9$, and the left side of the equation stays the same. How would the right side need to change if the solution is now $x = 9$?

_____

_____

_____

_____

_____

_____

_____

_____

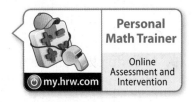
Selected Response

1. What are the actual dimensions of the Check-out Area?

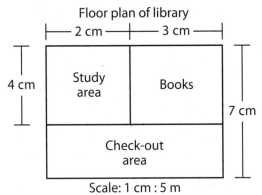

Floor plan of library

Study area

Books

Check-out area

2 cm | 3 cm

4 cm

7 cm

Scale: 1 cm : 5 m

- Ⓐ 25 m × 15 m
- Ⓒ 15 m × 35 m
- Ⓑ 15 m × 20 m
- Ⓓ 2 m × 4 m

2. For a history fair, a school is building a circular wooden stage that will stand 2 feet off the ground. Find the area of the stage if the radius of the stage is 19 feet. Use 3.14 for π.

- Ⓐ 1,133.54 ft²
- Ⓒ 2,267.08 ft²
- Ⓑ 119.32 ft²
- Ⓓ 4534.16 ft²

3. Find the area of the circle to the nearest tenth. Use 3.14 for π.

4.4 mm

- Ⓐ 47.7 mm²
- Ⓒ 60.8 mm²
- Ⓑ 15.2 mm²
- Ⓓ 13.8 mm²

4. What is the solution of the inequality $-0.4x - 1.2 > 0.8$?

- Ⓐ $x < -5$
- Ⓒ $x < -0.8$
- Ⓑ $x < -1$
- Ⓓ $x > 5$

5. Find m∠LMN.

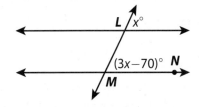

L $x°$

$(3x-70)°$ N

M

- Ⓐ m∠LMN = 40°
- Ⓒ m∠LMN = 35°
- Ⓑ m∠LMN = 45°
- Ⓓ m∠LMN = 50°

6. Ralph is an electrician. He charges an initial fee of $32, plus $33 per hour. If Ralph earned $197 on a job, how long did the job take?

- Ⓐ 5.1 hours
- Ⓒ 5 hours
- Ⓑ 132 hours
- Ⓓ 4 hours

7. Find the volume of the cylinder. Use 3.14 for π. Round your answer to the nearest tenth.

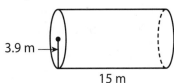

3.9 m

15 m

- Ⓐ 183.7 m³
- Ⓒ 2,865.6 m³
- Ⓑ 716.4 m³
- Ⓓ 2,755.4 m³

8. Which is the least valid way to simulate how many boys and girls are in a random sample of 20 students from a school population that is half boys and half girls?

- Ⓐ Flip a coin 20 times, assigning one outcome to boys and the other to girls.
- Ⓑ Drop 20 coins at once and count the number of each outcome.
- Ⓒ Count how many boys and girls are in your math class and use a proportion.
- Ⓓ Have a calculator generate 20 random integers and count the number of even and odd integers.

9. Roberto plays on the school baseball team. In the last 9 games, Roberto was at bat 32 times and got 11 hits. What is the experimental probability that Roberto will get a hit during his next time at bat? Express your answer as a fraction in simplest form.

(A) $\frac{32}{11}$ (C) $\frac{21}{32}$

(B) $\frac{11}{32}$ (D) $\frac{11}{21}$

10. A coin-operated machine sells plastic rings. It contains 14 pink rings, 10 green rings, 9 purple rings, and 13 black rings. Sarah puts a coin into the machine. Find the theoretical probability she gets a pink ring. Express your answer as a decimal. If necessary, round your answer to the nearest thousandth.

(A) 3.286   (C) 4.6

(B) 0.304   (D) 0.217

11. A manufacturer inspects a sample of 400 personal video players and finds that 399 of them have no defects. The manufacturer sent a shipment of 2000 video players to a distributor. Predict the number of players in the shipment that are likely to have no defects.

(A) 5   (C) 399

(B) 1995   (D) 1950

12. An experiment consists of rolling two fair number cubes. What is the probability that the sum of the two numbers will be 8? Express your answer as a fraction in simplest form.

(A) $\frac{5}{36}$ (C) $\frac{36}{5}$

(B) $\frac{1}{9}$ (D) $\frac{31}{36}$

Mini-Tasks

13. A map of Australia has a scale of 1 cm : 110 km. If the distance between Darwin and Alice Springs is 1444 kilometers, how far apart are they on the map, to the nearest tenth of a centimeter?

_____

14. The student council president wants to find out the opinion of the students on the issue of school lunch options. The president sends out a survey to a random sample of students in the school. What type of sample is this? Explain.

_____

_____

_____

_____

15. Using the following data, state the errors in the box-and-whisker plot.

33, 27, 6, 34, 31, 59, 26, 1, 30

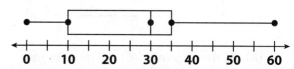

_____

_____

Performance Task

16. The number of goals scored by a hockey team in each of its first 10 games is 2, 4, 0, 3, 4, 1, 3, 1, 1, and 5.

a. Find the mean number of goals scored.

_____

b. Find the mean absolute deviation (MAD) of the number of goals scored.

_____

c. A second team in the same division scores a mean of 4.5 goals in its first 10 games, with the same MAD as the team above. Compare the difference in the teams' mean number of goals with the MAD in the number of goals scored.

_____

_____

Selected Response

1. Multiply. Write the product as one power.
$a^8 \cdot a^5$

Ⓐ a^{13} Ⓒ a^{40}

Ⓑ a^3 Ⓓ Cannot combine

2. Simplify $(6^{-4})^6$.

Ⓐ -24^6 Ⓒ 6^2

Ⓑ $\frac{1}{6^{24}}$ Ⓓ $\frac{1}{6^{10}}$

3. A square mosaic is made of small glass squares. If there are 196 small squares in the mosaic, how many are along an edge?

Ⓐ 98 squares   Ⓒ 14 squares

Ⓑ 49 squares   Ⓓ 16 squares

4. Simplify $2\sqrt{-19 + 44}$.

Ⓐ 13.3   Ⓒ 10

Ⓑ 44   Ⓓ 27

5. A passenger plane travels at about 7.97×10^2 feet per second. The plane takes 1.11×10^4 seconds to reach its destination.

About how far must the plane travel to reach its destination? Write your answer in scientific notation.

Ⓐ 8.85×10^8 feet   Ⓒ 8.85×10^6 feet

Ⓑ 9.08×10^6 feet   Ⓓ 9.08×10^8 feet

6. Approximate $\sqrt{158}$ to the nearest hundredth.

Ⓐ 12.57   Ⓒ 16.57

Ⓑ 16.62   Ⓓ 8.52

7. Write a rule for the linear function.

x	y
−3	12
−2	10
3	0
5	−4

Ⓐ $y = -2x - 6$ Ⓒ $y = \frac{1}{2}x + 6$

Ⓑ $y = -2x + 6$ Ⓓ $y = \frac{1}{2}x - 6$

8. A remote-control airplane descends at a rate of 2 feet per second. After 3 seconds it is 67 feet above the ground. Write the equation in point-slope form that models the situation. Then, find the height of the plane after 8 seconds.

Ⓐ $y - 67 = -2(x - 3)$; 57 feet

Ⓑ $y - 67 = -3(x - 2)$; 49 feet

Ⓒ $y - 3 = -2(x - 67)$; 121 feet

Ⓓ $y - 2 = 67(x - 3)$; 337 feet

9. A bicyclist heads east at 19 km/h. After she has traveled 24.2 kilometers, another cyclist sets out in the same direction going 30 km/h. About how long will it take the second cyclist to catch up to the first cyclist?

Ⓐ It will take the second cyclist 3.2 hours to catch up to the first cyclist.

Ⓑ It will take the second cyclist 3.7 hours to catch up to the first cyclist.

Ⓒ It will take the second cyclist 2.2 hours to catch up to the first cyclist.

Ⓓ It will take the second cyclist 1.7 hours to catch up to the first cyclist.

10. What is the equation of the graph in slope-intercept form?

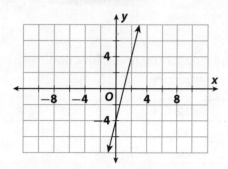

   Ⓐ $y = -4x - 4$ Ⓒ $y = -5x - 4$

   Ⓑ $y = 4x - 4$ Ⓓ $y = 5x - 4$

11. Solve $-2z + 3 + 7z = -12$.

   Ⓐ $z = -3$ Ⓒ $z = 1$

   Ⓑ $z = -15$ Ⓓ $z = -1.8$

12. Which equation has only one solution?

   Ⓐ $c + 2 = c + 2$ Ⓒ $c + 2 = c - 2$

   Ⓑ $c = -c + 2$ Ⓓ $c - c = 2$

13. Which ordered pair is a solution of the system of equations?
$y = 3x + 1$
$y = 5x - 1$

   Ⓐ (2, 3)   Ⓒ (1, 2)

   Ⓑ (0, 1)   Ⓓ (1, 4)

14. Which of these functions is *not* linear?

   Ⓐ $y = x^2 - x$ Ⓒ $y = \frac{x}{3}$

   Ⓑ $y = 1 - x$ Ⓓ $y = \frac{2}{3}x - 2x$

15. Which function has the greatest rate of change?

   Ⓐ $y = -5x$

   Ⓑ {(−1, −2), (1, 2), (3, 6), (5, 10), (7, 14)}

   Ⓒ A fitness club charges a $200 membership fee plus monthly fees of $25.

   Ⓓ $y = 3x - 16$

Mini-Tasks

16. The graph below shows an airplane's speed over a period of time. Describe the events.

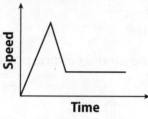

_____

_____

_____

_____

17. Identify $\sqrt{\frac{169}{64}}$ as *rational* or *irrational*. Explain your reasoning.

_____

Performance Task

18. Ashley reads 2 pages/minute for 10 minutes, takes a 10 minute break, and then reads at the same rate for 10 more minutes. Adam reads at the same rate the entire time. The equation for the number of pages he reads is $y = 1.2x$. How are these functions similar? How are they different?

_____

_____

_____

_____

_____

_____

_____

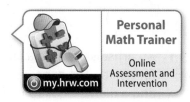
Selected Response

1. In the gift shop of the History of Flight museum, Elisa bought a kit to make a model of a jet airplane. The actual plane is 21 feet long with a wingspan of 17.5 feet. If the finished model will be 12 inches long, what will the wingspan be?

Ⓐ 30.6 in.   Ⓒ 14.4 in.

Ⓑ 10 in.   Ⓓ 5 in.

2. Find the angle measures in the isosceles triangle.

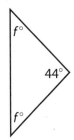

Ⓐ $f = 18°$ Ⓒ $f = 68°$

Ⓑ $f = 118°$ Ⓓ $f = 11.7°$

3. Which ordered pair is a solution of the system of equations?
$y = 3x - 1$
$y = 5x + 1$

Ⓐ $(4, 1)$ Ⓒ $(-4, -1)$

Ⓑ $(1, 4)$ Ⓓ $(-1, -4)$

4. Melanie is making a piece of jewelry that is in the shape of a right triangle. The two shorter sides of the piece of jewelry are 9 mm and 12 mm. Find the perimeter of the piece of jewelry.

Ⓐ 32 mm   Ⓒ 30 mm

Ⓑ 36 mm   Ⓓ 34 mm

5. Find the distance, to the nearest tenth, from $T(4, -2)$ to $U(-2, 3)$.

Ⓐ -1.0 units   Ⓒ 0.0 units

Ⓑ 3.4 units   Ⓓ 7.8 units

6. Which of the following is *not* a congruence transformation?

Ⓐ A reflection over the *x*-axis.

Ⓑ A dilation with scale factor 0.5.

Ⓒ A translation 1 unit left.

Ⓓ A dilation with scale factor 1.

7. Harry and Selma start driving from the same location. Harry drives 42 miles north while Selma drives 144 miles east. How far apart are Harry and Selma when they stop?

Ⓐ 1,764 miles   Ⓒ 22,500 miles

Ⓑ 150 miles   Ⓓ 20,736 miles

8. Which triangle with side lengths given below is a right triangle?

Ⓐ 10, 15, 20   Ⓒ 9, 40, 41

Ⓑ 10, 24, 25   Ⓓ 16, 20, 25

9. Angles *B* and *F* are corresponding angles formed by a transversal intersecting two parallel lines. Angle *B* has a measure of 44°. What is the measure of Angle *F*?

Ⓐ 44°   Ⓒ 90°

Ⓑ 46°   Ⓓ 136°

10. Which transformation below preserves similarity between the preimage and image, but does not preserve congruence?

Ⓐ reflections   Ⓒ translations

Ⓑ rotations   Ⓓ dilations

11. An artist is creating a large conical sculpture for a park. The cone has a height of 16 m and a diameter of 25 m. Find the volume of the sculpture to the nearest hundredth.

    Ⓐ 833.33 m³   Ⓒ 2,616.67 m³

    Ⓑ 7,850 m³   Ⓓ 209.33 m³

12. A cylindrical barrel has a radius of 7.6 ft and a height of 10.8 ft. Tripling which dimension(s) will triple the volume of the barrel?

    Ⓐ height

    Ⓑ radius

    Ⓒ both height and radius

    Ⓓ neither height nor radius

13. A square mosaic is made of small glass squares. If there are 196 small squares in the mosaic, how many are along an edge?

_____

Mini-Tasks

14. On Monday, a work group eats at Ava's café, where a lunch special is $8 and a dessert is $2. The total is $108. On Friday, the group eats at Bo's café, where a lunch special is $6 and a dessert is $3. The total is $90. Each time, the group orders the same number of lunches and the same number of desserts. How many lunches and desserts are ordered?

_____

15. Dilate the figure by a scale factor of 0.5 with the origin as the center of dilation.

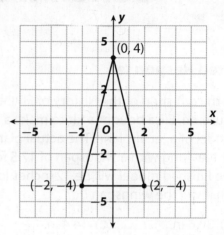

Performance Task

16. A company makes a paperweight in the shape of a hemisphere. The paperweight is made of an alloy of different metals. The area of the flat base is 28.26 square centimeters.

    a. What is the volume of the paperweight in cubic centimeters? Use 3.14 for π. Explain how you arrive at your answer.

    _____

    _____

    _____

    _____

    b. The paperweight weighs about 14 ounces. What is the density of the alloy used to make the paperweight in ounces per cubic centimeter?

    _____

    c. How many cubic centimeters of the alloy would weigh exactly 1 ounce?

    _____

Expressions, Equations, and Inequalities

MODULE 1

Expressions and Equations

COMMON CORE 7.EE.1, 7.EE.2, 7.EE.4, 7.EE.4a

MODULE 2

Inequalities

COMMON CORE 7.EE.4, 7.EE.4b

CAREERS IN MATH

Mechanical Engineer A mechanical engineer designs, develops, and manufactures mechanical devices and technological systems. Mechanical engineers use math to solve diverse problems, from calculating the strength of materials to determining energy consumption of a device.

If you are interested in a career in mechanical engineering, you should study these mathematical subjects:
- Algebra
- Geometry
- Trigonometry
- Statistics
- Calculus

Research other careers that require the daily use of mathematics to solve problems.

Unit 1 Performance Task

At the end of the unit, check out how **mechanical engineers** use math.

Vocabulary Preview

Use the puzzle to preview key vocabulary from this unit. Unscramble the circled letters to answer the riddle at the bottom of the page.

An expression that contains at least one variable. (Lesson 1.1)

__ __ __ (O) __ __ __ __ __ __

__ __ __ __ __ __ (O) __ __ __

An equation with more than one operation. (Lesson 1.3)

__ __ __ __ __ __ __ __ (O) __ __ __ __ (O)

A variable whose value is less than zero. (Lesson 1.3)

__ (O) __ __ __ __ __ __ __ __ __ __ __ __ __ (O)

A variable whose value is greater than zero. (Lesson 1.3)

__ (O) __ __ (O) __ __ __ __ __ __ (O) __ __ __ __

A mathematical sentence that shows the relationship between quantities that are not equivalent. (Lesson 2.1)

__ (O) __ __ __ __ __ (O) __ __

Q: Why does the sum of −4 and 3 complain more than the sum of −3 and 5?

A: It's the __ __ __ __ __ __ __ __ __ __ __ __ __ __ __!

Expressions and Equations

ESSENTIAL QUESTION

How can you use algebraic expressions and equations to solve real-world problems?

Real-World Video

When you take a taxi, you will be charged an initial fee plus a charge per mile. To describe situations like this, you can write a two-step equation.

ⓟ my.hrw.com

GO DIGITAL
my.hrw.com

my.hrw.com

Go digital with your write-in student edition, accessible on any device.

Math On the Spot

Scan with your smart phone to jump directly to the online edition, video tutor, and more.

Animated Math

Interactively explore key concepts to see how math works.

Personal Math Trainer

Get immediate feedback and help as you work through practice sets.

Are YOU Ready?

Complete these exercises to review skills you will need for this chapter.

Personal Math Trainer

Online Assessment and Intervention

⏻ my.hrw.com

Words for Operations

EXAMPLE   the difference of 2 and b *Difference means subtraction.*
            $2 - b$

            the product of -8 and a number   *Product means multiplication.*
            $(-8)x$ or $-8x$ *Let x represent the unknown number.*

Write an algebraic expression for each word expression.

1. the sum of 5 and a number x _____   **2.** 11 decreased by n _____

3. the quotient of -9 and y _____   **4.** twice a number, minus 13 _____

Evaluate Expressions

EXAMPLE   Evaluate $3x - 5$ for $x = -2$.
            $3x - 5 = 3(-2) - 5$ *Substitute the given value of x for x.*
            $\quad\quad\quad = -6 - 5$ *Multiply.*
            $\quad\quad\quad = -11$ *Subtract.*

Evaluate each expression for the given value of x.

5. $2x + 3$ for $x = 3$ _____   **6.** $-4x + 7$ for $x = -1$ ___   **7.** $1.5x - 2.5$ for $x = 3$ ____

8. $0.4x + 6.1$ for $x = -5$ ___   **9.** $\frac{2}{3}x - 12$ for $x = 18$ ____   **10.** $-\frac{5}{8}x + 10$ for $x = -8$ ____

Operations with Fractions

EXAMPLE $\frac{2}{5} \div \frac{7}{10}$ $\frac{2}{5} \div \frac{7}{10} = \frac{2}{5} \times \frac{10}{7}$ *Multiply by the reciprocal of the divisor.*

                    $= \frac{2}{{}_1\cancel{5}} \times \frac{\cancel{10}^2}{7}$ *Divide by the common factors.*

                    $= \frac{4}{7}$ *Simplify.*

Divide.

11. $\frac{1}{2} \div \frac{1}{4}$ _____   **12.** $\frac{3}{8} \div \frac{13}{16}$ _____   **13.** $\frac{2}{5} \div \frac{14}{15}$ _____   **14.** $\frac{4}{9} \div \frac{16}{27}$ _____

Reading Start-Up

Visualize Vocabulary

Use the ✔ words to complete the graphic.

Identify the operation performed on the variable in the equation.

↓

Apply the inverse _____ to both sides of the _____.

↓

The _____ in the equation is alone, and set equal to the _____.

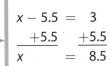

$$x - 5.5 = 3$$
$$\underline{+5.5 \quad +5.5}$$
$$x \quad = 8.5$$

Add 5.5 to both sides.
The solution is $x = 8.5$.

Vocabulary

Review Words

algebraic expression
(*expresión algebraica*)
Distributive Property
(*Propiedad distributiva*)
✔ equation (*ecuación*)
factor (*factor*)
✔ operation (*operación*)
✔ solution (*solución*)
✔ variable (*variable*)

Understand Vocabulary

Complete the sentences using the review words.

1. A(n) _____ contains at least one variable.

2. A mathematical sentence that shows that two expressions are equivalent

   is called a(n) _____.

Active Reading

Tri-Fold Before beginning the module, create a tri-fold to help you learn the concepts and vocabulary in this module. Fold the paper into three sections. Label the columns "What I Know," "What I Need to Know," and "What I Learned." Complete the first two columns before you read. After studying the module, complete the third column.

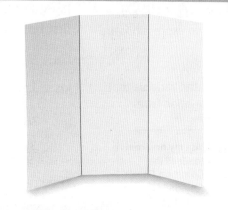

Unpacking the Standards

Understanding the standards and the vocabulary terms in the standards will help you know exactly what you are expected to learn in this module.

COMMON CORE **7.EE.1**

Apply properties of operations as strategies to add, subtract, factor, and expand linear expressions with rational coefficients.

Key Vocabulary

coefficient *(coeficiente)*
The number that is multiplied by the variable in an algebraic expression.

rational number *(número racional)* Any number that can be expressed as a ratio of two integers.

What It Means to You

You will use your knowledge of properties of operations to write equivalent expressions.

UNPACKING EXAMPLE 7.EE.1

Expand the expression $2(a + 7)$ using the distributive property.

$2(a + 7) = 2 \cdot a + 2 \cdot 7$ Multiply each term in parentheses by 2.

$ = 2a + 14$

COMMON CORE **7.EE.4a**

Solve word problems leading to equations of the form $px + q = r$ and $p(x + q) = r$, where p, q, and r are specific rational numbers. Solve equations of these forms fluently.

Key Vocabulary

equation *(ecuación)*
A mathematical sentence that shows that two expressions are equivalent.

solution *(solución)*
The value for the variable that makes the equation true.

What It Means to You

You will write and solve real-world equations that require two steps.

UNPACKING EXAMPLE 7.EE.4a

Jai and Lúpe plan to rent a kayak. The rental is $12 for the first hour and $9 for each hour after that. If they have $50, for how long can they rent the kayak?

Rental Charge $= 12 + 9x$, where x is the number of hours after the first hour.

$50 = 12 + 9x$

$50 - 12 = 12 - 12 + 9x$ Subtract 12 from both sides.

$38 = 9x$

$\frac{38}{9} = x$, or $x \approx 4.2$ Divide both sides by 9.

They can rent the kayak for 4 hours.

Visit **my.hrw.com** to see all the **Common Core Standards** unpacked.

my.hrw.com

1.1 Algebraic Expressions

COMMON CORE **7.EE.1**

Apply properties of operations as strategies to add, subtract, factor, and expand linear expressions with rational coefficients. *Also 7.EE.2*

ESSENTIAL QUESTION

How do you add, subtract, factor, and multiply algebraic expressions?

EXPLORE ACTIVITY COMMON CORE **7.EE.1, 7.EE.2**

Simplifying Algebraic Expressions

When you simplify expressions using properties, you can combine like terms due to the Distributive Property: $a(b + c) = ab + ac$ and $a(b - c) = ab - ac$.

Math On the Spot
my.hrw.com

EXAMPLE 1 Jill and Kyle get paid per project. Jill is paid a project fee of $25 plus $10.50 per hour. Kyle is paid a project fee of $18 plus $14.25 per hour. Write an expression to represent how much a company will pay to hire both to work the same number of hours on a project.

 STEP 1 Write expressions for how much the company will pay each person. Let h represent the number of hours they will work on the project.

Jill: $25 + \$_____h$ Kyle: $18 + \$_____h$

 STEP 2 Add the expressions, and simplify by combining like terms to represent the amount the company will pay to hire both.

Combine their pay.	$25 + 10.50h + 18 + 14.25h$
Associative and Commutative Properties of Addition	$= (25 + _____) + (10.50h + _____)$
Combine like terms.	$= _____ + _____h$

The company will pay _____ dollars to hire both Jill and Kyle.

Reflect

1. **Critical Thinking** What can you read directly from $43 + 24.75h$ that you cannot read directly from $25 + 10.50h + 18 + 14.25h$?

_____

YOUR TURN

Personal Math Trainer

Online Assessment and Intervention

my.hrw.com

Simplify each expression.

2. $\left(3x + \dfrac{1}{2}\right) + \left(7x - 4\dfrac{1}{2}\right)$

3. $(-0.25x + 3) + (1.5x + 1.4)$

_____   _____

Simplifying More Complex Expressions

You can use the Distributive Property to remove parentheses when simplifying, or *expanding*, an algebraic expression, but be careful with negative signs and subtraction. Consider $-(x + 5)$. You can rewrite the expression as shown.

$$-(x + 5) = (-1)(x + 5) = (-1)(x) + (-1)(5) = -x + (-5) = -x - 5$$

Notice that you can get $-x - 5$ from $-(x + 5)$ by removing the parentheses and reversing the sign of each term. This process is called *distributing the negative*. It also applies when you distribute over subtraction, as shown.

$$-(x - 5) = (-1)(x - 5) = (-1)(x) - (-1)(5) = -x - (-5) = -x + 5$$

EXAMPLE 2

COMMON CORE 7.EE.1, 7.EE.2

Simplify each expression.

A $5 - 3(7x + 8)$

$5 - 21x - 24$	Use the Distributive Property to distribute -3.
$5 + (-21x) + (-24)$	Rewrite subtraction as adding the opposite.
$5 + (-24) + (-21x)$	Use the Commutative Property of Addition.
$-19 + (-21x)$	Combine like terms.
$-19 - 21x$	Simplify.

Math Talk

Mathematical Practices

In Part A, why is it helpful to write subtraction as adding the opposite?

B $-9a - \frac{1}{3}\left(-\frac{3}{4} - \frac{2}{3}a + 12\right)$

$-9a + \frac{1}{4} + \frac{2}{9}a - 4$	Use the Distributive Property to distribute $-\frac{1}{3}$.
$-9a + \frac{1}{4} + \frac{2}{9}a + (-4)$	Rewrite subtraction as adding the opposite.
$-9a + \frac{2}{9}a + \frac{1}{4} + (-4)$	Use the Commutative Property of Addition.
$-8\frac{7}{9}a - 3\frac{3}{4}$	Use the Associative Property of Addition and combine like terms.

Reflect

4. Why is the Associative Property of Addition applied in Part B?

_____

YOUR TURN

Simplify each expression.

5. $0.2(3b - 15c)$

6. $5x - 3(x - 2) - x$

7. $8.3 + 3.4y - 0.5(12y - 7)$

_____ _____ _____

Factoring Expressions

A factor is a number that is multiplied by another number to get a product. To **factor** is to write a number or an algebraic expression as a product.

Factor 4x + 8.

A Model the expression with algebra tiles.

Use _____ positive x-tiles and _____ +1-tiles.

B Arrange the tiles to form a rectangle. The total area represents 4x + 8.

C Since the length multiplied by the width equals the area, the length and the width of the rectangle are the factors of 4x + 8. Find the length and width.

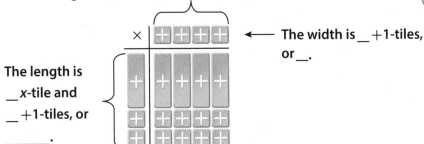

The length is __ x-tile and __ +1-tiles, or _____.

The width is __ +1-tiles, or __.

D Use the expressions for the length and width of the rectangle

to write the area of the rectangle, 4x + 8, in factored form. _____

Reflect

8. **Communicate Mathematical Ideas** How could you use the Distributive Property to check your factoring?

_____

YOUR TURN

Factor each expression.

9. 2x + 2   **10.** 3x + 9   **11.** 5x + 15   **12.** 4x + 16

_____   _____   _____   _____

1. The manager of a summer camp has 14 baseballs and 23 tennis balls. The manager buys some boxes of baseballs with 12 baseballs to a box and an equal number of boxes of tennis balls with 16 tennis balls to a box. Write an expression to represent the total number of balls. (Explore Activity Example 1)

STEP 1 Write expressions for the total number of baseballs and tennis balls. Let n represent the number of boxes of each type.

baseballs: _____ + (_____)n tennis balls: _____ + (_____)n

STEP 2 Find an expression for the total number of balls.

_____ + _____ + _____ + _____   *Combine the two expressions.*

_____ + _____ + _____ + _____   *Use the Commutative Property.*

_____ + _____   *Combine like terms.*

So, the total number of baseballs and tennis balls is _____ + _____.

2. Use the expression you found above to find the total number of baseballs and tennis balls if the manager bought 9 boxes of each type. (Explore Activity Example 1) _____

Simplify each expression. (Example 2)

3. $0.5(12m - 22n)$

$0.5(12m - 22n) = 0.5(\underline{\hspace{1cm}}) - 0.5(\underline{\hspace{1cm}})$ *Use the Distributive Property.*

$= \underline{\hspace{1cm}} - \underline{\hspace{1cm}}$ *Multiply.*

4. $2(x - 3) - (6x - 4)$

_____ $- 6 -$ _____ $+ 4 =$ _____ $+$ _____ $+ (-6) + 4 =$ _____ $-$ _____

Factor each expression. (Explore Activity 2)

5. $2x + 12$

6. $12x + 24$

7. $7x + 35$

_____   _____   _____

? ESSENTIAL QUESTION CHECK-IN

8. What is the relationship between multiplying and factoring?

_____

_____

_____

1.1 Independent Practice

COMMON CORE 7.EE.1, 7.EE.2

Personal Math Trainer

Online Assessment and Intervention

my.hrw.com

Write and simplify an expression for each situation.

9. A company rents out 15 food booths and 20 game booths at the county fair. The fee for a food booth is $100 plus $5 per day. The fee for a game booth is $50 plus $7 per day. The fair lasts for d days, and all the booths are rented for the entire time. Write and simplify an expression for the amount in dollars that the company is paid.

_____

10. A rug maker is using a pattern that is a rectangle with a length of 96 inches and a width of 60 inches. The rug maker wants to increase each dimension by a different amount. Let ℓ and w be the increases in inches of the length and width. Write and simplify an expression for the perimeter of the new pattern.

_____

In 11–12, identify the two factors that were multiplied together to form the array of tiles. Then identify the product of the two factors.

11.   _____

12.  _____

13. Explain how the figure illustrates that $6(9) = 6(5) + 6(4)$.

_____

_____

_____

_____

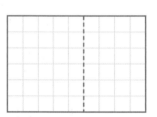

In 14–15, the perimeter of the figure is given. Find the length of the indicated side.

14.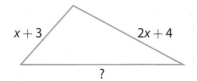

$x + 3$ $2x + 4$

?

Perimeter = $6x$ _____

15.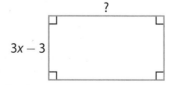

?

$3x - 3$

Perimeter = $10x + 6$ _____

16. Persevere in Problem Solving The figures show the dimensions of a tennis court and a basketball court given in terms of the width, x (in feet), of the tennis court.

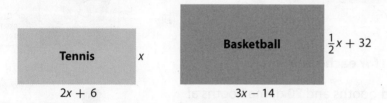

Tennis x

$2x + 6$

Basketball $\frac{1}{2}x + 32$

$3x - 14$

a. Write an expression for the perimeter of each court. _____

b. Write an expression that describes how much greater the perimeter of the basketball court is than the perimeter of the tennis court. _____

c. Suppose the tennis court is 36 feet wide. Find all dimensions of the two courts. _____

 FOCUS ON HIGHER ORDER THINKING

Work Area

17. Draw Conclusions Use the figure to find the product $(x + 3)(x + 2)$. (*Hint:* Find the area of each small square or rectangle, then add.)

$(x + 3)(x + 2) =$ _____

18. Explain the Error Andy and Sylvie each incorrectly simplified the expression $-3 - 4(2x - 3)$. Andy wrote $-14x + 21$ and Sylvie wrote $-8x - 6$. Explain their errors and give the correct answer.

_____

_____

_____

_____

_____

19. Justify Reasoning Describe two different ways that you could find the product 8×997 using mental math. Find the product and explain why your methods work.

_____

_____

_____

_____

Applying Properties to Algebraic Expressions

COMMON CORE **7.EE.1**

Apply properties of operations as strategies to add, subtract, factor, and expand linear expressions with rational coefficients. *Also 7.EE.2*

ESSENTIAL QUESTION

How can using the properties of operations to justify your work help you simplify algebraic expressions?

EXPLORE ACTIVITY   COMMON CORE 7.EE.1, 7.EE.2

Applying Properties to Simplify

Using properties of operations can help you avoid errors when simplifying.

Justify each step in simplifying the expression $4x - 3(2x - 5) - (x + 4)$.

$4x - 3(2x - 5) - (x + 4)$

$4x - 6x + 15 - x - 4$ _____

$4x + (-6x) + 15 + (-x) + (-4)$ Rewrite subtraction as _____ the opposite.

$[4x + (-6x) + (-x)] + [15 + (-4)]$ Commutative and _____ Properties of Addition

$-3x + 11$ Combine like terms.

Reflect

1. What is the coefficient of $-x$? _____

Applying Properties to Factor

You can use the Distributive Property to factor a linear expression like $30x - 42$. To factor it completely, use the greatest common factor of the coefficient of the variable and the constant as one of the factors.

EXAMPLE   COMMON CORE 7.EE.1

Factor the expression $30x - 42$ completely.

STEP 1 Find the greatest common factor of 30 and 42.

Factors of 30: 1, 2, 3, 5, ⑥ 10, 15, 30   The GCF of 30 and 42 is 6.
Factors of 42: 1, 2, 3, ⑥ 7, 14, 21, 42

STEP 2 Factor out the greatest common factor.

$30x - 42 = 6(5x) - 6(7)$ Factor each term using the GCF.

$= 6(5x - 7)$ Distributive Property

The expression $30x - 42$ factored completely is $6(5x - 7)$.

1. Hoon simplified the expression below using the steps shown. Justify each step in his simplification. There may be more than one property for a step.

$8\frac{1}{2} - \frac{1}{2}(17 - 6x) + 2\left(\frac{1}{2} - x\right)$

$8\frac{1}{2} - 8\frac{1}{2} + 3x + 1 - 2x$ _____

$8\frac{1}{2} + \left(-8\frac{1}{2}\right) + 3x + 1 + (-2x)$ _____

$0 + 3x + 1 + (-2x)$ _____

$3x + 1 + (-2x)$ _____

$1 + 3x + (-2x)$ _____

$1 + [3x + (-2x)]$ _____

$1 + x$ _____

Find and correct the error in the student's work.

2. Carole wrote $100 - 10(4 + 2f) = 100 - 40 + 20f$.

_____

_____

3. Adiba wrote $12 - 4(3x - 2) = 12 - 4(2 - 3x)$.

_____

_____

4. **Critical Thinking** The perimeter of the rectangle is $3x + 2 + x + 3x + 2 + x$. Alix expressed the perimeter as $2(3x + 2) + 2x$. Babat expressed it as $8x + 4$. Describe in words how each expression represents the perimeter in terms of the length $3x + 2$, the width x, or both. Then identify one benefit of each form of the expression.

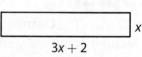

$3x + 2$

_____

_____

_____

Factor each expression completely.

5. $4x - 16$

6. $52x + 13$

7. $8x + 14$

_____   _____   _____

8. $16x - 24$

9. $-12x - 20$

10. $-20x + 50$

_____   _____   _____

One-Step Equations with Rational Coefficients

COMMON CORE 7.EE.4

Use variables to represent quantities in a real-world or mathematical problem, and construct simple equations … to solve problems by reasoning about the quantities.

ESSENTIAL QUESTION

How do you use one-step equations with rational coefficients to solve problems?

EXPLORE ACTIVITY **7.EE.4**

One-Step Equations

You have written and solved one-step equations involving whole numbers. Now you will learn to work with equations containing negative numbers.

Math On the Spot
my.hrw.com

EXAMPLE 1 Use inverse operations to solve each equation.

A Begin with the equation $x + 3.2 = -8.5$.

$x + 3.2 = -8.5$

Subtract 3.2 from both sides.

$$-\boxed{} \quad -\boxed{}$$

$$x = \boxed{}$$

$-7.5 = -1.5n$

B Begin with the equation $-\frac{2}{3} + y = 8$.

$-\frac{2}{3} + y = 8$

Add $\frac{2}{3}$ to both sides.

$$+\boxed{} \quad = +\boxed{}$$

$$y = \boxed{}$$

C Begin with the equation $30 = -0.5a$.

$$\frac{30}{\boxed{}} = \frac{-0.5a}{\boxed{}}$$

Divide both sides by -0.5.

$$\boxed{} = a$$

D Begin with the equation $-\frac{q}{3.5} = 9.2$.

$-\frac{q}{3.5} = 9.2$

Multiply both sides by -3.5.

$$-\frac{q}{3.5}\left(\boxed{}\right) = 9.2\left(\boxed{}\right)$$

$$q = \boxed{}$$

YOUR TURN

Use inverse operations to solve each equation.

1. $4.9 + z = -9$

2. $r - 17.1 = -4.8$

3. $-3c = 36$

_____   _____   _____

Personal Math Trainer

Online Assessment and Intervention

my.hrw.com

Writing and Solving One-Step Addition and Subtraction Equations

Negative numbers often appear in real-world situations. For example, elevations below sea level are represented by negative numbers. When you increase your elevation, you are moving in a positive direction. When you decrease your elevation, you are moving in a negative direction.

EXAMPLE 2

COMMON CORE 7.EE.4

A scuba diver is exploring at an elevation of −12.2 meters. As the diver rises to the surface, she plans to stop and rest briefly at a reef that has an elevation of −4.55 meters. Find the vertical distance that the diver will travel.

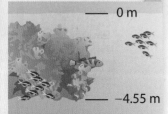

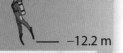

STEP 1 Write an equation. Let x represent the vertical distance between her initial elevation and the elevation of the reef.

$$-12.2 + x = -4.55$$

STEP 2 Solve the equation using an inverse operation.

$$
\begin{array}{rl}
-12.2 + x &= -4.55 \\
\underline{+12.2 \qquad} & \underline{+12.2} \qquad \text{Add 12.2 to both sides.}\\
x &= 7.65
\end{array}
$$

The diver will travel a vertical distance of 7.65 meters.

Reflect

4. **Make a Prediction** Explain how you know whether the diver is moving in a positive or a negative direction before you solve the equation.

_____

_____

_____

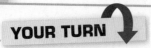

5. An airplane descends 1.5 miles to an elevation of 5.25 miles. Find the elevation of the plane before its descent.

_____

_____

Writing and Solving One-Step Multiplication and Division Problems

Temperatures can be both positive and negative, and they can increase or decrease during a given period of time. A decrease in temperature is represented by a negative number. An increase in temperature is represented by a positive number.

EXAMPLE 3   COMMON CORE 7.EE.4

Between the hours of 10 P.M. and 6 A.M., the temperature decreases an average of $\frac{3}{4}$ of a degree per hour. How many minutes will it take for the temperature to decrease by 5 °F?

STEP 1 Write an equation. Let x represent the number of hours it takes for the temperature to decrease by 5 °F.

$$-\frac{3}{4}x = -5$$

STEP 2 Solve the equation using an inverse operation.

$$-\frac{3}{4}x = -5$$

$$-\frac{4}{3}\left(-\frac{3}{4}x\right) = -\frac{4}{3}(-5) \qquad \text{Multiply both sides by } -\frac{4}{3}.$$

$$x = \frac{20}{3}$$

STEP 3 Convert the number of hours to minutes.

$$\frac{20}{3} \text{ hours} \times \frac{60 \text{ minutes}}{1 \text{ hour}} = 400 \text{ minutes}$$

It takes 400 minutes for the temperature to decrease by 5 °F.

> **Math Talk**
> **Mathematical Practices**
>
> Why is multiplying by $-\frac{4}{3}$ the inverse of multiplying by $-\frac{3}{4}$?

YOUR TURN

6. The value of a share of stock decreases in value at a rate of $1.20 per hour during the first 3.5 hours of trading. Write and solve an equation to find the decrease in the value of the share of stock during that time.

_____

7. After a power failure, the temperature in a freezer increased at an average rate of 2.5 °F per hour. The total increase was 7.5 °F. Write and solve an equation to find the number of hours until the power was restored.

_____

Personal Math Trainer

Online Assessment and Intervention

⊙ my.hrw.com

The table shows the average temperature in Barrow, Alaska, for three months during one year.

Month	Average Temperature (°F)
January	−13.4
June	34.0
November	−1.7

1. How many degrees warmer is the average temperature in November than in January?
(Explore Activity Example 1 and Example 2)

STEP 1 Write an equation. Let x represent _____

_____.

$x +$ _____ $=$ _____ , or $x -$ _____ $=$ _____

STEP 2 Solve the equation. Show your work.

The average temperature in November

is _____ warmer.

2. Suppose that during one period of extreme cold, the average daily temperature decreased $1\frac{1}{2}$ °F each day. How many days did it take for the temperature to decrease by 9 °F?
(Explore Activity Example 1 and Example 3)

STEP 1 Write an equation. Let x represent _____

_____.

_____ $x =$ _____

STEP 2 Solve the equation. Show your work.

It took _____ days for the temperature to decrease by 9 °F.

Use inverse operations to solve each equation. (Explore Activity Example 1)

3. $-2x = 34$

4. $y - 3.5 = -2.1$

5. $\frac{2}{3}z = -6$

_____

_____

_____

? ESSENTIAL QUESTION CHECK-IN

6. How does writing an equation help you solve a problem?

_____

_____

1.2 Independent Practice

 7.EE.4

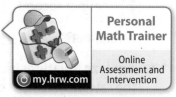

Personal Math Trainer

Online Assessment and Intervention

my.hrw.com

The table shows the elevation in feet at the peaks of several mountains. Use the table for 7–9.

Mountain	Elevation (feet)
Mt. McKinley	20,321.5
K2	28,251.31
Tupungato	22,309.71
Dom	14,911.42

7. Mt. Everest is 8,707.37 feet higher than Mt. McKinley. What is the elevation of Mt. Everest?

_____

8. Liam descended from the summit of K2 to an elevation of 23,201.06 feet. How many feet did Liam descend? What was his change in elevation?

_____

9. K2 is 11,194.21 feet higher than Mt. Kenya. Write and solve an equation to find the elevation of Mt. Kenya.

_____

_____

10. A hot air balloon begins its descent at a rate of $22\frac{1}{2}$ feet per minute. How long will it take for the balloon's elevation to change by −315 feet?

_____

11. During another part of its flight, the balloon in Exercise 10 had a change in elevation of −901 feet in 34 minutes. What was its rate of descent?

_____

The table shows the average temperatures in several states from January through March. Use the table for 12–14.

State	Average Temperature (°C)
Florida	18.1
Minnesota	−2.5
Montana	−0.7
Texas	12.5

12. Write and solve an equation to find how much warmer Montana's average 3-month temperature is than Minnesota's.

_____

13. How much warmer is Florida's average 3-month temperature than Montana's?

_____

14. How would the average temperature in Texas have to change to match the average temperature in Florida?

_____

15. A football team has a net yardage of $-26\frac{1}{3}$ yards on a series of plays. The team needs a net yardage of 10 yards to get a first down. How many yards do they have to get on their next play to get a first down?

_____

16. A diver begins at sea level and descends vertically at a rate of $2\frac{1}{2}$ feet per second. How long does the diver take to reach

−15.6 feet? _____

17. Analyze Relationships In Exercise 16, what is the relationship between the rate at which the diver descends, the elevation he reaches, and the time it takes to reach that elevation?

_____

18. Check for Reasonableness Jane withdrew money from her savings account in each of 5 months. The average amount she withdrew per month was $45.50. How much did she withdraw in all during the 5 months? Show that your answer is reasonable.

_____

_____

H.O.T. **FOCUS ON HIGHER ORDER THINKING**

Work Area

19. Justify Reasoning Consider the two problems below. Which values in the problems are represented by negative numbers? Explain why.

(1) A diver below sea level ascends 25 feet to a reef at −35.5 feet. What was the elevation of the diver before she ascended to the reef?

(2) A plane descends 1.5 miles to an elevation of 3.75 miles. What was the elevation of the plane before its descent?

_____

_____

_____

20. Analyze Relationships How is solving $-4x = -4.8$ different from solving $-\frac{1}{4}x = -4.8$? How are the solutions related?

_____

_____

21. Communicate Mathematical Ideas Flynn opens a savings account. In one 3-month period, he makes deposits of $75.50 and $55.25. He makes withdrawals of $25.15 and $18.65. His balance at the end of the 3-month period is $210.85. Explain how you can find his initial deposit amount.

_____

_____

_____

Writing Two-Step Equations

COMMON CORE 7.EE.4

Use variables to represent quantities in a real-world or mathematical problem, and construct simple equations... to solve problems by reasoning about the quantities.

🔍 **ESSENTIAL QUESTION**

How do you write a two-step equation?

EXPLORE ACTIVITY COMMON CORE Prep for 7.EE.4

Modeling Two-Step Equations

You can use algebra tiles to model two-step equations.

KEY

+ = positive variable

− = negative variable

+ = 1   − = −1

Use algebra tiles to model $3x - 4 = 5$.

A How can you model the left side of the equation?

_____

B How can you model the right side of the equation?

_____

C Use algebra tiles or draw them to model the equation on the mat.

Math Talk

Mathematical Practices

Why is the mat divided into two equal halves with a line?

Reflect

1. What If? How would you change the algebra tile model in the Explore Activity to model $-3x + 4 = 5$?

_____

_____

_____

Writing Two-Step Equations

You can write two-step equations to represent real-world problems by translating the words of the problems into numbers, variables, and operations.

EXAMPLE 1 **Real World**   COMMON CORE 7.EE.4

A one-year membership to Metro Gym costs $460. There is a fee of $40 when you join, and the rest is paid monthly. Write an equation to represent the situation that can help members find how much they pay per month.

STEP 1   Identify what you are trying to find. This will be the variable in the equation.

Let *m* represent the amount of money members pay per month.

STEP 2   Identify important information in the problem that can be used to help write an equation.

one-time joining fee: **$40**
fee charged for 1 year: **12 · m**
total cost for the year: **$460**

> Convert 1 year into 12 months to find how much members pay per month.

STEP 3   Use words in the problem to tie the information together and write an equation.

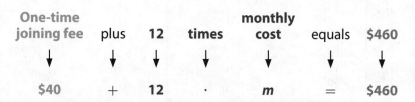

One-time joining fee	plus	12	times	monthly cost	equals	$460
↓	↓	↓	↓	↓	↓	↓
$40	+	12	·	m	=	$460

The equation $40 + 12m = 460$ can help members find out their monthly fee.

Reflect

2. **Multiple Representations** Why would this equation for finding the monthly fee be difficult to model with algebra tiles?

_____

3. Can you rewrite the equation in the form $52m = 460$? Explain.

_____

_____

4. Billy has a gift card with a $150 balance. He buys several video games that cost $35 each. After the purchases, his gift card balance is $45. Write an equation to help find out how many video games Billy bought.

_____

Writing a Verbal Description of a Two-Step Equation

You can also write a verbal description to fit a two-step equation.

EXAMPLE 2

COMMON CORE **7.EE.4**

Write a corresponding real-world problem to represent $5x + 50 = 120$.

STEP 1 Analyze what each part of the equation means mathematically.

x is the solution of the problem, the quantity you are looking for.

$5x$ means that, for a reason given in the problem, the quantity you are looking for is multiplied by 5.

$+ 50$ means that, for a reason given in the problem, 50 is added to $5x$.

$= 120$ means that after multiplying the solution x by 5 and adding 50 to it, the result is 120.

STEP 2 Think of some different situations in which a quantity x might be multiplied by 5.

You have x number of books, each weighing 5 pounds, and you want to know their total weight.	You save $5 each week for x weeks and want to know the total amount you have saved.

STEP 3 Build on the situation and adjust it to create a verbal description that takes all of the information of the equation into account.

• A publisher ships a package of x number of books each weighing 5 pounds, plus a second package weighing 50 pounds. The total weight of both packages is 120 pounds. How many books are being shipped?

• Leon receives a birthday gift of $50 from his parents and decides to save it. Each week he adds $5 to his savings. How many weeks will it take for him to save $120?

My Notes

YOUR TURN

5. Write a real-world problem that can be represented by $10x + 40 = 100$.

_____

_____

Guided Practice

Draw algebra tiles to model the given two-step equation. (Explore Activity)

1. $2x + 5 = 7$

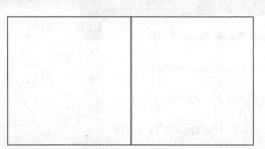

2. $-3 = 5 - 4x$

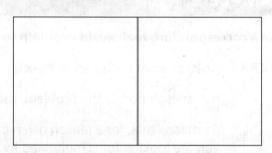

3. A group of adults plus one child attend a movie at Cineplex 15. Tickets cost $9 for adults and $6 for children. The total cost for the movie is $78. Write an equation to find the number of adults in the group. (Example 1) _____

4. Break down the equation $2x + 10 = 16$ to analyze each part. (Example 2)

x is _____ of the problem.

$2x$ is the quantity you are looking for _____.

$+ 10$ means 10 is _____. $= 16$ means the _____ is 16.

5. Write a corresponding real-world problem to represent $2x - 125 = 400$.

(Example 2) _____

_____

? ESSENTIAL QUESTION CHECK-IN

6. Describe the steps you would follow to write a two-step equation you can use to solve a real-world problem.

_____

_____

_____

1.3 Independent Practice

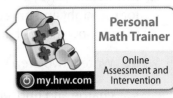
COMMON CORE 7.EE.4

7. Describe how to model $-3x + 7 = 28$ with algebra tiles.

_____

_____

_____

8. Val rented a bicycle while she was on vacation. She paid a flat rental fee of $55.00, plus $8.50 each day. The total cost was $123. Write an equation you can use to find the number of days she rented the bicycle.

_____

9. A restaurant sells a coffee refill mug for $6.75. Each refill costs $1.25. Last month Keith spent $31.75 on a mug and refills. Write an equation you can use to find the number of refills that Keith bought.

_____

10. A gym holds one 60-minute exercise class on Saturdays and several 45-minute classes during the week. Last week all of the classes lasted a total of 285 minutes. Write an equation you can use to find the number of weekday classes.

_____

11. **Multiple Representations** There are 172 South American animals in the Springdale Zoo. That is 45 more than half the number of African animals in the zoo. Write an equation you could use to find n, the number of African animals in the zoo.

_____

12. A school bought $548 in basketball equipment and uniforms costing $29.50 each. The total cost was $2,023. Write an equation you can use to find the number of uniforms the school purchased.

_____

13. **Financial Literacy** Heather has $500 in her savings account. She withdraws $20 per week for gas. Write an equation Heather can use to see how many weeks it will take her to have a balance of $220.

_____

14. **Critique Reasoning** For $9x + 25 = 88$, Deena wrote the situation "I bought some shirts at the store for $9 each and received a $25 discount. My total bill was $88. How many shirts did I buy?"

a. What mistake did Deena make?

_____

_____

_____

b. Rewrite the equation to match Deena's situation.

_____

c. How could you rewrite the situation to make it fit the equation?

_____

_____

_____

_____

15. **Multistep** Sandy charges each family that she babysits a flat fee of $10 for the night and an extra $5 per child. Kimmi charges $25 per night, no matter how many children a family has.

Work Area

a. Write a two-step equation that would compare what the two girls

charge and find when their fees are the same. _____

b. How many children must a family have for Sandy and Kimmi to

charge the same amount? _____

c. The Sanderson family has five children. Which babysitter should they choose if they wish to save some money on babysitting, and why?

_____

_____

H.O.T. FOCUS ON HIGHER ORDER THINKING

16. **Analyze Relationships** Each student wrote a two-step equation. Peter wrote the equation $4x - 2 = 10$, and Andres wrote the equation $16x - 8 = 40$. The teacher looked at their equations and asked them to compare them. Describe one way in which the equations are similar.

_____

_____

_____

_____

17. **What's the Error?** Damon has 5 dimes and some nickels in his pocket, worth a total of $1.20. To find the number of nickels Damon has, a student wrote the equation $5n + 50 = 1.20$. Find the error in the student's equation.

_____

_____

_____

18. **Represent Real-World Problems** Write a real-world problem you could answer by solving the equation $-8x + 60 = 28$.

_____

_____

_____

_____

Solving Two-Step Equations

COMMON CORE 7.EE.4a

Solve word problems leading to equations of the form $px + q = r$ and $p(x + q) = r$ ... Compare an algebraic solution to an arithmetic solution ... Also 7.EE.4

ESSENTIAL QUESTION

How do you solve a two-step equation?

EXPLORE ACTIVITY   COMMON CORE 7.EE.4

Modeling and Solving Two-Step Equations

You can solve two-step equations using algebra tiles.

Math On the Spot
my.hrw.com

EXAMPLE 1 Use algebra tiles to model and solve $3n + 2 = 11$.

STEP 1   Model the equation.

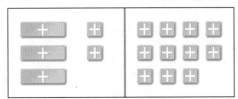

STEP 2   Remove, or subtract, an equal number of +1-tiles from both sides of the mat to help isolate the variable.

Remove _____ +1-tiles from each side of the mat.

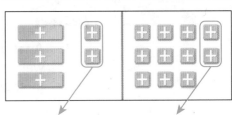

STEP 3   Divide each side into _____ equal groups.

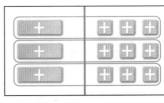

STEP 4   The solution is $n =$ _____.

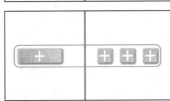

YOUR TURN

Use algebra tiles to model and solve each equation.

1. $2x + 5 = 11$ _____

2. $3n - 1 = 8$ _____

3. $2a - 3 = -5$ _____

4. $-4y + 2 = -2$ _____

Personal Math Trainer

Online Assessment and Intervention

my.hrw.com

Solving Two-Step Equations

You can use inverse operations to solve equations with more than one operation.

EXAMPLE 2

COMMON CORE   7.EE.4a

A dog sled driver added more gear to the sled, doubling its weight. This felt too heavy, so the driver removed 20 pounds to reach the final weight of 180 pounds. Write and solve an equation to find the sled's original weight.

STEP 1　Write an equation. Let w represent the original weight of the sled.

$$2w - 20 = 180.$$

STEP 2　Solve the equation.

$$2w - 20 = 180$$
$$\underline{+\,20 \quad +\,20} \qquad \text{Add 20 to both sides.}$$
$$2w \qquad = 200$$
$$\frac{2w}{2} = \frac{200}{2} \qquad \text{Divide both sides by 2.}$$
$$w = 100$$

The sled's original weight was 100 pounds.

Reflect

5. Analyze Relationships Describe how you could find the original weight of the sled using only arithmetic. Compare this method with the method shown in Example 2.

_____

_____

_____

_____

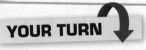

Solve each problem by writing and solving an equation.

6. The Wilsons have triplets and another child who is ten years old. The sum of the ages of their children is 37. How old are the triplets?

_____

7. Five less than the quotient of a number and 4 is 15. What is the number?

_____

Two-Step Equations with Negative Numbers

Many real-world quantities such as altitude or temperature involve negative numbers. You solve equations with negative numbers just as you did equations with positive numbers.

Math On the Spot
my.hrw.com

EXAMPLE 3

COMMON CORE   7.EE.4a

A To convert a temperature from degrees Fahrenheit to degrees Celsius, first subtract 32. Then multiply the result by $\frac{5}{9}$. An outdoor thermometer showed a temperature of $-10\ °C$. What was the temperature in degrees Fahrenheit?

STEP 1 Write an equation. Let x represent the temperature in degrees Fahrenheit.

$$-10 = \frac{5}{9}(x - 32)$$

STEP 2 Solve the equation.

$$\frac{9}{5}(-10) = \frac{9}{5}\left(\frac{5}{9}(x-32)\right) \quad \text{Multiply both sides by } \frac{9}{5}.$$

$$-18 = x - 32$$

$$\underline{+\ 32 \qquad +\ 32} \qquad \text{Add 32 to both sides.}$$

$$14 = x$$

The temperature was 14 degrees Fahrenheit.

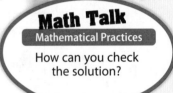

Math Talk
Mathematical Practices

How can you check the solution?

B An airplane flies at an altitude of 38,000 feet. As it nears the airport, the plane begins to descend at a rate of 600 feet per minute. At this rate, how many minutes will the plane take to descend to 18,800 feet?

STEP 1 Write an equation. Let m represent the number of minutes.

$$38,000 - 600m = 18,800$$

STEP 2 Solve the equation. Start by isolating the term that contains the variable.

$$38,000 - 600m = 18,800$$

$$\underline{-\ 38,000 \qquad\qquad -\ 38,000} \qquad \begin{array}{l}\text{Subtract 38,000 from} \\ \text{both sides.}\end{array}$$

$$-600m = -19,200$$

$$\frac{-600m}{-600} = \frac{-19,200}{-600} \qquad \text{Divide both sides by } -600.$$

$$m = 32$$

The plane will take 32 minutes to descend to 18,800 feet.

Animated Math
my.hrw.com

YOUR TURN

Solve each problem by writing and solving an equation.

8. What is the temperature in degrees Fahrenheit of a freezer kept at $-20\,°C$?

_____

9. Jenny earned 92 of a possible 120 points on a test. She lost 4 points for each incorrect answer. How many incorrect answers did she have?

_____

Guided Practice

The equation $2x + 1 = 9$ is modeled below. (Explore Activity Example 1)

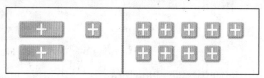

1. To solve the equation with algebra tiles, first remove _____ .

Then divide each side into _____ .

2. The solution is $x =$ _____ .

Solve each problem by writing and solving an equation.

3. A rectangular picture frame has a perimeter of 58 inches. The height of the frame is 18 inches. What is the width of the frame? (Example 2)

_____

4. A school store has 1200 pencils in stock, and sells an average of 25 pencils per day. The manager reorders when the number of pencils in stock is 500. In how many days will the manager have to reorder? (Example 3)

_____

? ESSENTIAL QUESTION CHECK-IN

5. How can you decide which operations to use to solve a two-step equation?

_____

_____

_____

1.4 Independent Practice

COMMON CORE   7.EE.4, 7.EE.4a

Personal Math Trainer

Online Assessment and Intervention

my.hrw.com

Solve.

6. $9s + 3 = 57$

_____

7. $4d + 6 = 42$

_____

8. $-3y + 12 = -48$

_____

9. $\frac{k}{2} + 9 = 30$

_____

10. $\frac{g}{3} - 7 = 15$

_____

11. $\frac{z}{5} + 3 = -35$

_____

12. $-9h - 15 = 93$

_____

13. $-3(n + 5) = 12$

_____

14. $-17 + \frac{b}{8} = 13$

_____

15. $7(c - 12) = -21$

_____

16. $-3 + \frac{p}{7} = -5$

_____

17. $46 = -6t - 8$

_____

18. After making a deposit, Puja had $264 in her savings account. She noticed that if she added $26 to the amount originally in the account and doubled the sum, she would get the new amount. How much did she originally have in the account?

_____

19. The current temperature in Smalltown is 20 °F. This is 6 degrees less than twice the temperature that it was six hours ago. What was the temperature in Smalltown six hours ago?

_____

20. One reading at an Arctic research station showed that the temperature was −35 °C. What is this temperature in degrees Fahrenheit?

_____

21. Artaud noticed that if he takes the opposite of his age and adds 40, he gets the number 28. How old is Artaud?

_____

22. Sven has 11 more than twice as many customers as when he started selling newspapers. He now has 73 customers. How many did he have when he started?

_____

23. Paula bought a ski jacket on sale for $6 less than half its original price. She paid $88 for the jacket. What was the original price?

_____

24. The McIntosh family went apple picking. They picked a total of 115 apples. The family ate a total of 8 apples each day. After how many days did they have 19 apples left?

_____

Use a calculator to solve each equation.

25. $-5.5x + 0.56 = -1.64$

_____

26. $-4.2x + 31.5 = -65.1$

_____

27. $\frac{k}{5.2} + 81.9 = 47.2$

_____

28. Write a two-step equation that involves multiplication and subtraction, includes a negative coefficient, and has a solution of $x = 7$.

_____

29. Write a two-step equation involving division and addition that has a solution of $x = -25$

_____

30. **Explain the Error** A student's solution to the equation $3x + 2 = 15$ is shown. Describe and correct the error that the student made.

$$3x + 2 = 15 \qquad \text{Divide both sides by 3.}$$

$$x + 2 = 5 \qquad \text{Subtract 2 from both sides.}$$

$$x = 3$$

_____

_____

31. **Multiple Representations** Explain how you could use the work backward problem-solving strategy to solve the equation $\frac{x}{4} - 6 = 2$. Compare that method to an algebraic method.

_____

_____

_____

_____

_____

 **FOCUS ON HIGHER ORDER THINKING**

32. **Reason Abstractly** The formula $F = 1.8C + 32$ allows you to find the Fahrenheit (F) temperature for a given Celsius (C) temperature. Solve the equation for C to produce a formula for finding the Celsius temperature for a given Fahrenheit temperature.

_____

33. **Reason Abstractly** The equation $P = 2(\ell + w)$ can be used to find the perimeter P of a rectangle with length ℓ and width w. Solve the equation for w to produce a formula for finding the width of a rectangle given its perimeter and length.

_____

34. **Reason Abstractly** Solve the equation $ax + b = c$ for x.

_____

Arithmetic and Algebraic Solutions

COMMON CORE **7.EE.4a**

...Compare an algebraic solution to an arithmetic solution, identifying the sequence of the operations used in each approach.

ESSENTIAL QUESTION

What are the similarities and differences of arithmetic and algebraic solutions?

EXPLORE ACTIVITY COMMON CORE **7.EE.4a**

Comparing Solution Methods

Chris has a coupon for $1.50 off the price of each T-shirt purchased. He uses the coupon and pays $47.50 for five T-shirts. Complete Parts A and B to find the original price of a T-shirt without the coupon by two methods.

A Work backward using arithmetic to find the original price of a T-shirt.

$47.50 ÷ ☐ = ☐

Divide $47.50 by _____ to find the purchase price of each T-shirt with a coupon.

☐ + ☐ = ☐

Add _____ to find the original price of each T-shirt without the coupon.

The original price of a T-shirt without the coupon is _____.

B Use algebra to find the original price of a T-shirt.

$$5(p - 1.50) = 47.50$$ Write an equation in which p is the original price.

$$\frac{5(p - 1.50)}{☐} = \frac{47.50}{☐}$$ Divide both sides by _____.

$$p - 1.50 = 9.50$$

$$+ ☐ \quad + ☐$$ Add _____ to both sides.

$$p = ☐$$

The original price of a T-shirt without the coupon is _____.

Reflect

1. What was the sequence of operations you performed in Part A? How did this sequence compare to the sequence in Part B?

_____

_____

_____

1. Layla buys a turkey and 3 cans of soup at the grocery store for a total of $20.75. The turkey costs $15.50. What is the cost of each can of soup?

   a. Show how to find the cost of each can of soup using arithmetic.

   _____

   b. Show how to find the cost s of each can of soup using algebra.

   _____

   _____

   c. Compare the solution methods in Parts **a** and **b**.

   _____

   _____

2. Carlos pays for dinner with a friend. He uses a coupon for $5 off the price of dinner, before taxes are applied. The tax rate is 8%. The total cost for dinner after the coupon and taxes is $30.78. What is the original price of dinner before the coupon and taxes?

   a. What operation would you do first to solve this problem using arithmetic? Why?

   _____

   _____

   b. Write an equation relating the original price of dinner d and the total cost after the coupon and taxes. Identify the first step you would use to solve the equation and the meaning of the result of that step.

   _____

   _____

   c. Show how to find the original price of dinner using any method.

   _____

3. Toby's bucket has a leak. The bucket starts with 5 gallons of water. After 7.5 minutes, there are only 2.5 gallons of water in the bucket. The equation $5 + 7.5r = 2.5$ represents this situation, where r is the rate of change of water in the bucket. Suppose you use arithmetic to find the rate of change. How can the equation help guide your steps? What are the steps and what does the result of each step represent?

   _____

   _____

   _____

   _____

   _____

Equality Property Sort

INSTRUCTIONS

STEP 1 At the top of the next page record the number of blue circles that appear in the top corner of each card in your set of activity cards.

STEP 2 Shuffle your activity cards. Working together, sort the activity cards to show the correct solutions of four different two-step equations and the properties that justify each step. An example is shown.

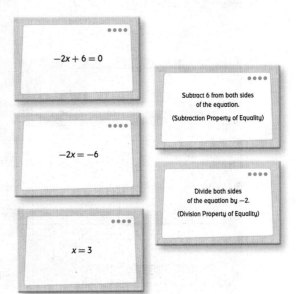

STEP 3 Check that the steps of each solution and the properties are in the correct order. Then record the steps and properties in the flow charts on the next page.

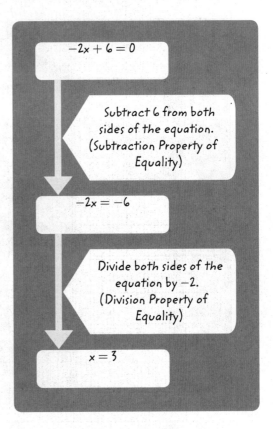

Number of blue circles _____

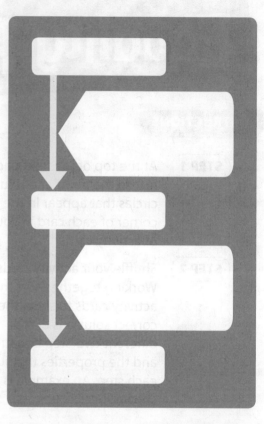

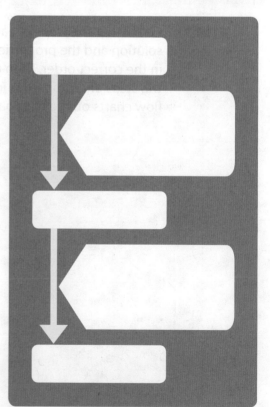

Ready to Go On?

1.1 Algebraic Expressions

1. The Science Club went on a two-day field trip. The first day the members paid $60 for transportation plus $15 per ticket to the planetarium. The second day they paid $95 for transportation plus $12 per ticket to the geology museum. Write an expression to represent the total cost for two days

   for the n members of the club. _____

1.2 One-Step Equations with Rational Coefficients

Solve.

2. $h + 9.7 = -9.7$ _____

3. $-\frac{3}{4} + p = \frac{1}{2}$ _____

4. $-15 = -0.2k$ _____

5. $\frac{y}{-3} = \frac{1}{6}$ _____

6. $-\frac{2}{3}m = -12$ _____

7. $2.4 = -\frac{t}{4.5}$ _____

1.3 Writing Two-Step Equations

8. Jerry started doing sit-ups every day. The first day he did 15 sit-ups. Every day after that he did 2 more sit-ups than he had done the previous day. Today Jerry did 33 sit-ups. Write an equation that could be solved to find the number of days Jerry has been doing sit-ups, not counting the first day.

   _____

1.4 Solving Two-Step Equations

Solve.

9. $5n + 8 = 43$ _____

10. $\frac{y}{6} - 7 = 4$ _____

11. $8w - 15 = 57$ _____

12. $\frac{g}{3} + 11 = 25$ _____

13. $\frac{f}{5} - 22 = -25$ _____

14. $-4p + 19 = 11$ _____

? ESSENTIAL QUESTION

15. How can you use two-step equations to represent and solve real-world problems?

   _____

   _____

MODULE 1 MIXED REVIEW

COMMON CORE

Assessment Readiness

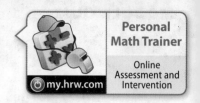

Personal Math Trainer

Online Assessment and Intervention

⏱ my.hrw.com

Selected Response

1. A taxi cab costs $1.50 for the first mile and $0.75 for each additional mile. Which equation could be solved to find how many miles you can travel in a taxi for $10, given that x is the number of additional miles?

   Ⓐ $1.5x + 0.75 = 10$

   Ⓑ $0.75x + 1.5 = 10$

   Ⓒ $1.5x - 0.75 = 10$

   Ⓓ $0.75x - 1.5 = 10$

2. Which is the solution of $\frac{t}{2.5} = -5.2$?

   Ⓐ $t = -13$

   Ⓑ $t = -2.08$

   Ⓒ $t = 2.08$

   Ⓓ $t = 13$

3. Which expression is equivalent to $5x - 30$?

   Ⓐ $5(x - 30)$

   Ⓑ $5(x - 6)$

   Ⓒ $5x(x - 6)$

   Ⓓ $x(5 - 30)$

4. In a science experiment, the temperature of a substance is changed from 42 °F to −54 °F at an average rate of −12 degrees per hour. Over how many hours does the change take place?

   Ⓐ −8 hours

   Ⓑ $\frac{1}{8}$ hour

   Ⓒ 1 hour

   Ⓓ 8 hours

5. Which statement best represents the distance on a number line between −14 and −5?

   Ⓐ $-14 - (-5)$

   Ⓑ $-14 + (-5)$

   Ⓒ $-5 - (-14)$

   Ⓓ $-5 + (-14)$

6. Which cereal costs the most per ounce?

   Ⓐ $4.92 for 12 ounces

   Ⓑ $4.25 for 10 ounces

   Ⓒ $5.04 for 14 ounces

   Ⓓ $3.92 for 8 ounces

Mini-Task

7. Casey bought 9 tickets to a concert. The total charge was $104, including a $5 service charge.

   a. Write an equation you can solve to find c, the cost of one ticket.

   _____

   b. Explain how you could estimate the solution of your equation.

   _____

   _____

   _____

   _____

   c. Solve the equation. How much did each ticket cost?

   _____

Inequalities

 ESSENTIAL QUESTION

How can you use inequalities to solve real-world problems?

Real-World Video

Many school groups and other organizations hold events to raise money. Members can write and solve inequalities to represent the financial goals they are trying to achieve.

my.hrw.com

 GO DIGITAL

my.hrw.com

my.hrw.com

Go digital with your write-in student edition, accessible on any device.

Math On the Spot

Scan with your smart phone to jump directly to the online edition, video tutor, and more.

Animated Math

Interactively explore key concepts to see how math works.

Personal Math Trainer

Get immediate feedback and help as you work through practice sets.

Are YOU Ready?

Complete these exercises to review skills you will need for this module.

Inverse Operations

> **EXAMPLE**
>
> $3x = 24$ x is multiplied by 3.
>
> $\dfrac{3x}{3} = \dfrac{24}{3}$ Use the inverse operation, division.
>   Divide both sides by 3.
>
> $x = 8$
>
> $z + 6 = 4$ 6 is added to z.
> $\underline{-6 = -6}$ Use the inverse operation, subtraction.
> $z = -2$ Subtract 6 from both sides.

Solve each equation, using inverse operations.

1. $9w = -54$ _____

2. $b - 12 = 3$ _____

3. $\dfrac{n}{4} = -11$ _____

Locate Points on a Number Line

> **EXAMPLE**
>
>
>
> Graph $+2$ by starting at 0 and counting 2 units to the *right*.
>
> Graph -4 by starting at 0 and counting 4 units to the *left*.

Graph each number on the number line.

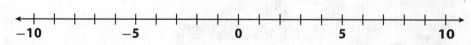

4. 3   **5.** -9 **6.** 7   **7.** -3

Integer Operations

> **EXAMPLE**
>
> $-7 - (-4) = -7 + 4$ To subtract an integer, add its opposite.
>
> $= |-7| - |4|$ The signs are different, so find the difference of the absolute values.
>
> $= 7 - 4$, or 3
>
> $= -3$ Use the sign of the number with the greater absolute value.

8. $3 - (-5)$ _____

9. $-4 - 5$ _____

10. $6 - 10$ _____

11. $-5 - (-3)$ _____

12. $8 - (-8)$ _____

13. $9 - 5$ _____

14. $-3 - 9$ _____

15. $0 - (-6)$ _____

Reading Start-Up

Visualize Vocabulary

Use the ✔ words to complete the graphic. You may put more than one word in each box.

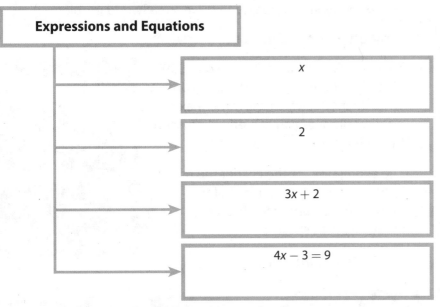

Expressions and Equations

x

2

$3x + 2$

$4x - 3 = 9$

Understand Vocabulary

Complete each sentence, using the review words.

1. A value of the variable that makes the equation true is a _____.

2. The set of all whole numbers and their opposites are _____.

3. An _____ is an expression that contains at least one variable.

Active Reading

Layered Book Before beginning the module, create a layered book to help you learn the concepts in this module. At the top of the first flap, write the title of the module, "Inequalities." Then label each flap with one of the lesson titles in this module. As you study each lesson, write important ideas, such as vocabulary and processes, under the appropriate flap.

Unpacking the Standards

Understanding the standards and the vocabulary terms in the standards will help you know exactly what you are expected to learn in this module.

COMMON CORE 7.EE.4

Use variables to represent quantities in a real-world or mathematical problem, and construct simple equations and inequalities to solve problems by reasoning about the quantities.

Key Vocabulary

inequality *(desigualdad)*
A mathematical sentence that shows that two quantities are not equal.

What It Means to You

You will write an inequality to solve a real-world problem.

UNPACKING EXAMPLE 7.EE.4

To rent a certain car for a day costs $39 plus $0.29 for every mile the car is driven. Write an inequality to show the maximum number of miles you can drive and keep the rental cost under $100.

The expression for the cost of the rental is $39 + 0.29m$. The total cost of the rental must be under $100. So the inequality is as shown.

$$39 + 0.29m < 100$$

COMMON CORE 7.EE.4b

Solve word problems leading to inequalities of the form $px + q > r$ or $px + q < r$, where p, q, and r are specific rational numbers. Graph the solution set of the inequality and interpret it in the context of the problem.

Key Vocabulary

solution *(solución)*
The value(s) for the variable that makes the inequality true.

What It Means to You

You will solve inequalities that involve two steps and interpret the solutions.

UNPACKING EXAMPLE 7.EE.4b

Solve and graph the solution of $-3x + 7 > -8$.

$-3x + 7 > -8$

$\quad -3x > -7 - 8$ Subtract 7 from both sides.

$\quad -3x > -15$ Simplify.

$\quad\quad x < 5$ Divide both sided by -5, and reverse the inequality.

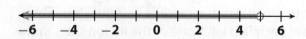

All numbers less than 5 are solutions for this inequality.

Writing and Solving One-Step Inequalities

COMMON CORE 7.EE.4b

Solve word problems leading to inequalities.... Graph the solution set of the inequality and interpret it in the context of the problem.

ESSENTIAL QUESTION

How do you write and solve one-step inequalities?

EXPLORE ACTIVITY COMMON CORE Prep. for 7.EE.4b

Investigating Inequalities

You know that when you perform any of the four basic operations on both sides of an equation, the resulting equation is still true. What effect does performing these operations on both sides of an *inequality* have?

A **Complete the table.**

Inequality	Add to both sides:	New Inequality	Is new inequality true or false?
$2 \geq -3$	3		
$-1 \leq 6$	-1		
$-8 > -10$	-8		

Reflect

1. **Make a Conjecture** When you add the same number to both sides of an inequality, is the inequality still true? Explain how you know that your conjecture holds for *subtracting* the same number.

_____

B **Complete the table.**

Inequality	Divide both sides by:	New Inequality	Is new inequality true or false?
$4 < 8$	4		
$12 \geq -15$	3		
$-16 \leq 12$	-4		
$15 > 5$	-5		

What do you notice when you divide both sides of an inequality by the same negative number?

_____

Reflect

2. **Make a Conjecture** What could you do to make the inequalities that are not true into true statements?

_____

3. **Communicate Mathematical Ideas** Explain how you know that your conjecture holds for multiplying both sides of an inequality by a negative number.

_____

Math On the Spot

ⓞ my.hrw.com

Solving Inequalities Involving Addition and Subtraction

You can use properties of inequality to solve inequalities involving addition and subtraction with rational numbers.

Addition and Subtraction Properties of Inequality

Addition Property of Inequality	Subtraction Property of Inequality
You can add the same number to both sides of an inequality and the inequality will remain true.	You can subtract the same number from both sides of an inequality and the inequality will remain true.

EXAMPLE 1

COMMON CORE 7.EE.4b

Solve each inequality. Graph and check the solution.

A $x + 5 < -12$

STEP 1 Solve the inequality.

$x + 5 < -12$ Use the Subtraction Property of Inequality.

$\underline{-5 \qquad -5}$ Subtract 5 from both sides.

$x \qquad < -17$

STEP 2 Graph the solution.

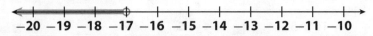

$-20 \ -19 \ -18 \ -17 \ -16 \ -15 \ -14 \ -13 \ -12 \ -11 \ -10$

STEP 3 Check the solution. Substitute a solution from the shaded part of your number line into the original inequality.

$-18 + 5 \overset{?}{<} -12$ Substitute -18 for x into $x + 5 < -12$.

$-13 < -12$ The inequality is true.

B $8 \leq y - 3$

STEP 1 Solve the inequality.

$\quad\quad 8 \leq y - 3 \quad\quad$ Use the Addition Property of Inequality.
$\quad\quad \underline{+\,3 \quad\quad +\,3} \quad\quad$ Add 3 to both sides.
$\quad\quad 11 \leq y \quad\quad\quad$ You can rewrite $11 \leq y$ as $y \geq 11$.

STEP 2 Graph the solution.

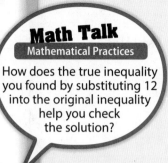

5 6 7 8 9 10 11 12 13 14 15

STEP 3 Check the solution. Substitute a solution from the shaded part of your number line into the original inequality.

$\quad\quad 8 \overset{?}{\leq} 12 - 3 \quad\quad$ Substitute 12 for y in $8 \leq y - 3$.

$\quad\quad 8 \leq 9 \quad\quad\quad$ The inequality is true.

Math Talk

Mathematical Practices

How does the true inequality you found by substituting 12 into the original inequality help you check the solution?

YOUR TURN

Solve each inequality. Graph and check the solution.

4. $y - 5 \geq -7$

_____

−5 −4 −3 −2 −1 0 1 2 3 4 5

5. $21 > 12 + x$

_____

0 1 2 3 4 5 6 7 8 9 10

Personal Math Trainer

Online Assessment and Intervention

my.hrw.com

Solving Inequalities Involving Multiplication and Division

You can use properties of inequality to solve inequalities involving multiplication and division with rational numbers.

Math On the Spot

my.hrw.com

Multiplication and Division Properties of Inequality

- You can multiply or divide both sides of an inequality by the same positive number and the inequality will remain true.

- If you multiply or divide both sides of an inequality by the same negative number, you must reverse the inequality symbol for the statement to still be true.

EXAMPLE 2

COMMON CORE 7.EE.4b

My Notes

Solve each inequality. Graph and check the solution.

A $\frac{y}{3} \geq 5$

STEP 1 Solve the inequality.

$3\left(\frac{y}{3}\right) \geq 3(5)$ Multiply both sides by 3.

$y \geq 15$

Use a closed circle to show that 15 is a solution.

STEP 2 Graph the solution.

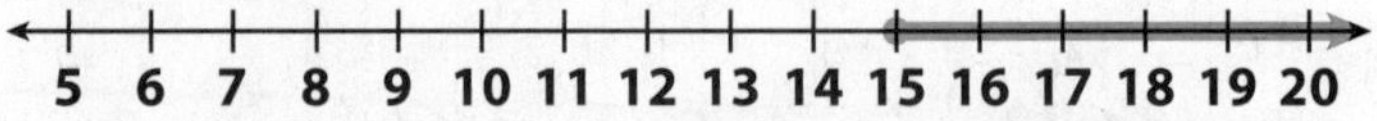

STEP 3 Check the solution by substituting a solution from the shaded part of the graph into the original inequality. For convenience, choose a multiple of 3.

$\frac{18}{3} \overset{?}{\geq} 5$ Substitute 18 for *x* in the original inequality.

$6 \geq 5$ The inequality is true.

B $-4x > 52$

STEP 1 Solve the inequality.

$-4x > 52$

$\frac{-4x}{-4} < \frac{52}{-4}$ Divide both sides by −4. Reverse the inequality symbol.

$x < -13$

STEP 2 Graph the solution.

STEP 3 Check your answer using substitution.

$-4(-15) \overset{?}{>} 52$ Substitute −15 for *x* in $-4x > 52$.

$60 > 52$ The statement is true.

Personal Math Trainer
Online Assessment and Intervention
my.hrw.com

YOUR TURN

Solve each inequality. Graph and check the solution.

6. $-10y < 60$ ________

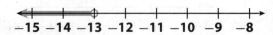

7. $7 \geq -\frac{t}{6}$ ________

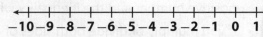

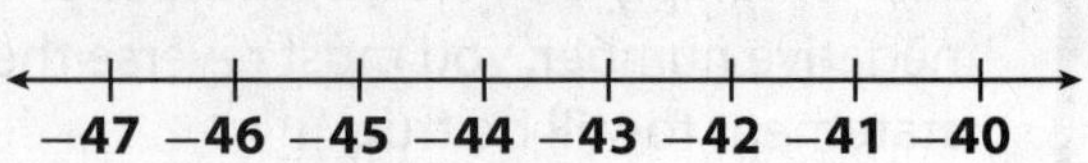

Solving a Real-World Problem

Although elevations below sea level are represented by negative numbers, we often use absolute values to describe these elevations. For example, −50 feet relative to sea level might be described as 50 feet below sea level.

Math On the Spot
⊙ my.hrw.com

EXAMPLE 3   Problem Solving   7.EE.4b

A marine submersible descends more than 40 feet below sea level. As it descends from sea level, the change in elevation is −5 feet per second. For how many seconds does it descend?

 Analyze Information

Rewrite the question as a statement.

- Find the number of seconds that the submersible descends below sea level.

List the important information:

- Final elevation > 40 feet below sea level or final elevation < −40 feet
- Rate of descent = −5 feet per second

 Formulate a Plan

Write and solve an inequality. Use this fact:

Rate of change in elevation × Time in seconds = Final elevation

 Solve

$$-5t < -40 \qquad \text{Rate of change} \times \text{Time} < \text{Final elevation}$$

$$\frac{-5t}{-5} > \frac{-40}{-5} \qquad \text{Divide both sides by } -5. \text{ Reverse the inequality symbol.}$$

$$t > 8$$

The submersible descends for more than 8 seconds.

Animated Math
⊙ my.hrw.com

 Justify and Evaluate

Check your answer by substituting a value greater than 8 seconds in the original inequality.

$$-5(9) \overset{?}{<} -40 \qquad \text{Substitute 9 for } t \text{ in the inequality } -5t < -40.$$

$$-45 < -40 \qquad \text{The statement is true.}$$

YOUR TURN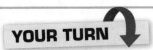

8. Every month, $35 is withdrawn from Tony's savings account to pay for his gym membership. He has enough savings to withdraw no more than $315. For how many months can Tony pay for his gym membership?

_____

_____

Personal Math Trainer
Online Assessment and Intervention
⊙ my.hrw.com

Write the resulting inequality. (Explore Activity)

1. $-5 \leq -2$; Add 7 to both sides _____

2. $-6 < -3$; Divide both sides by -3 _____

3. $7 > -4$; Subtract 7 from both sides _____

4. $-1 \geq -8$; Multiply both sides by -2 _____

Solve each inequality. Graph and check the solution. (Examples 1 and 2)

5. $n - 5 \geq -2$ _____

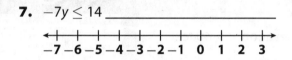

6. $3 + x < 7$ _____

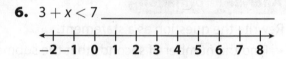

7. $-7y \leq 14$ _____

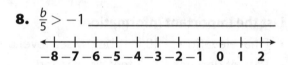

8. $\frac{b}{5} > -1$ _____

9. For a scientific experiment, a physicist must make sure that the temperature of a metal at 0 °C gets no colder than −80 °C. The physicist changes the metal's temperature at a steady rate of −4 °C per hour. For how long can the physicist change the temperature? (Example 3)

   a. Let t represent temperature in degrees Celsius. Write an inequality. Use the fact that the rate of change in temperature times the number of hours equals the final temperature.

   _____

   b. Solve the inequality in part **a**. How long can the physicist change the temperature of the metal?

   _____

   c. The physicist has to repeat the experiment if the metal gets cooler than −80 °C. How many hours would the physicist have to cool the metal for this to happen?

   _____

? ESSENTIAL QUESTION CHECK-IN

10. Suppose you are solving an inequality. Under what circumstances do you reverse the inequality symbol?

   _____

2.1 Independent Practice

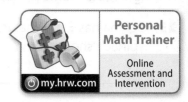

COMMON CORE 7.EE.4b

In 11–16, solve each inequality. Graph and check the solution.

11. $x - 35 > 15$ _____

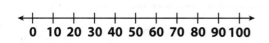
0 10 20 30 40 50 60 70 80 90 100

12. $193 + y \geq 201$ _____

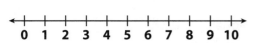
0 1 2 3 4 5 6 7 8 9 10

13. $-\dfrac{q}{7} \geq -1$ _____

0 1 2 3 4 5 6 7 8 9 10

14. $-12x < 60$ _____

−10 −9 −8 −7 −6 −5 −4 −3 −2 −1 0

15. $5 > z - 3$ _____

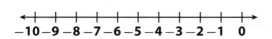
0 1 2 3 4 5 6 7 8 9 10

16. $0.5 \leq \dfrac{y}{8}$ _____

0 1 2 3 4 5 6 7 8 9 10

17. The vet says that Lena's puppy will grow to be at most 28 inches tall. Lena's puppy is currently 1 foot tall. How many more inches will the puppy grow?

_____

18. In a litter of 7 kittens, each kitten weighs less than 3.5 ounces. Find all the possible values of the combined weights of the kittens.

_____

19. **Geometry** The sides of the hexagon shown are equal in length. The perimeter of the hexagon is at most 42 inches. Find the possible side lengths of the hexagon.

_____

20. To get a free meal at his favorite restaurant, Tom needs to spend $50 or more at the restaurant. He has already spent $30.25. How much more does Tom need to spend to get his free meal?

_____

21. To cover a rectangular region of her yard, Penny needs at least 170.5 square feet of sod. The length of the region is 15.5 feet. What are the possible widths of the region?

_____

22. **Draw Conclusions** A submarine descends from sea level to the entrance of an underwater cave. The elevation of the entrance is −120 feet. The rate of change in the submarine's elevation is less than −12 feet per second. Can the submarine reach the entrance to the cave in less than 10 seconds? Explain.

_____

_____

_____

The sign shows some prices at a produce stand.

Produce	Price per Pound
Onions	$1.25
Yellow Squash	$0.99
Spinach	$3.00
Potatoes	$0.50

23. Selena has $10. What is the greatest amount of spinach she can buy?

_____

24. Gary has enough money to buy at most 5.5 pounds of potatoes. How much money does Gary have?

_____

25. Florence wants to spend no more than $3 on onions. Will she be able to buy 2.5 pounds of onions? Explain.

_____

_____

 **FOCUS ON HIGHER ORDER THINKING**

Work Area

26. **Counterexamples** John says that if one side of an inequality is 0, you don't have to reverse the inequality symbol when you multiply or divide both sides by a negative number. Find an inequality that you can use to disprove John's statement. Explain your thinking.

_____

_____

_____

_____

27. **Look for a Pattern** Solve $x + 1 > 10$, $x + 11 > 20$, and $x + 21 > 30$. Describe a pattern. Then use the pattern to predict the solution of $x + 9{,}991 > 10{,}000$.

_____

_____

_____

28. **Persevere in Problem Solving** The base of a rectangular prism has a length of 13 inches and a width of $\frac{1}{2}$ inch. The volume of the prism is less than 65 cubic inches. Find all possible heights of the prism. Show your work.

_____

_____

_____

A Shared Solution

INSTRUCTIONS

STEP 1 Get an activity card from your teacher. Each card has a one-step inequality printed on it. Find the solution of the inequality.

STEP 2 Find and form a group with all other students whose inequalities have the same solution as your inequality.

$x - 6 < -1$

Solution
$x < 5$

$2.5x < 12.5$

$x + 4.5 < 9.5$

$-\frac{x}{5} > -1$

STEP 3 Using one of the diagrams on the next page, work with the members of your group to write each one-step inequality in the rectangle labeled with the property used to solve it. Group members should fill in their own diagrams each round.

STEP 4 Complete the diagram by writing the common solution in the center rectangle.

	ROUND 1	
$2.5x < 12.5$		$x - 6 < -1$
Division Property of Inequality	$x < 5$	**Addition Property of Inequality**
Multiplication Property of Inequality		**Subtraction Property of Inequality**
$-\frac{x}{5} > -1$		$x + 4.5 < 9.5$

STEP 5 If you cannot form a complete group of four students, write your own one-step inequalities with the shared solution in any empty boxes. Highlight any inequalities that you write yourself.

STEP 6 Turn in the inequality cards to the teacher.

STEP 7 Repeat Steps 1–6 for each round.

ROUND 1

Division Property of Inequality

Multiplication Property of Inequality

Addition Property of Inequality

Subtraction Property of Inequality

ROUND 2

Division Property of Inequality

Multiplication Property of Inequality

Addition Property of Inequality

Subtraction Property of Inequality

ROUND 3

Division Property of Inequality

Multiplication Property of Inequality

Addition Property of Inequality

Subtraction Property of Inequality

ROUND 4

Division Property of Inequality

Multiplication Property of Inequality

Addition Property of Inequality

Subtraction Property of Inequality

ROUND 5

Division Property of Inequality

Multiplication Property of Inequality

Addition Property of Inequality

Subtraction Property of Inequality

Writing Two-Step Inequalities

COMMON CORE 7.EE.4

Use variables to represent quantities in a real-world or mathematical problem, and construct simple... inequalities...

ESSENTIAL QUESTION

How do you write a two-step inequality?

EXPLORE ACTIVITY   **COMMON CORE**   Prep for 7.EE.4

Modeling Two-Step Inequalities

You can use algebra tiles to model two-step inequalities.

Use algebra tiles to model $2k + 5 \geq -3$.

A Using the line on the mat, draw in the inequality symbol shown in the inequality.

B How can you model the left side of the inequality?

_____

C How can you model the right side of the inequality?

_____

D Use algebra tiles or draw them to model the inequality on the mat.

Reflect

1. **Multiple Representations** How does your model differ from the one you would draw to model the equation $2k + 5 = -3$?

_____

_____

_____

2. Why might you need to change the inequality sign when you solve an inequality using algebra tiles?

_____

_____

_____

Writing Two-Step Inequalities

You can write two-step inequalities to represent real-world problems by translating the words of the problems into numbers, variables, and operations.

EXAMPLE 1

COMMON CORE 7.EE.4

A mountain climbing team is camped at an altitude of 18,460 feet on Mount Everest. The team wants to reach the 29,029-foot summit within 6 days. Write an inequality to find the average number of feet per day the team must climb to accomplish its objective.

STEP 1 Identify what you are trying to find. This will be the variable in the inequality.

Let d represent the average altitude the team must gain each day.

STEP 2 Identify important information in the problem that you can use to write an inequality.

starting altitude: **18,460 ft**   target altitude: **29,029 ft**
number of days times altitude gained to reach target altitude: $6 \cdot d$

STEP 3 Use words in the problem to tie the information together and write an inequality.

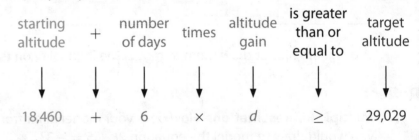

starting altitude	+	number of days	times	altitude gain	is greater than or equal to	target altitude
↓	↓	↓	↓	↓	↓	↓
18,460	+	6	×	d	≥	29,029

$$18,460 + 6d \geq 29,029$$

Math Talk

Mathematical Practices

Why is the inequality sign ≥ used, rather than an equal sign?

YOUR TURN

3. The 45 members of the glee club are trying to raise $6,000 so they can compete in the state championship. They already have $1,240. What inequality can you write to find the amount each member must raise, on

average, to meet the goal? _____

4. Ella has $40 to spend at the State Fair. Admission is $6 and each ride costs $3. Write an inequality to find the greatest number of rides she can go on.

_____

Writing a Verbal Description of a Two-Step Inequality

You can also write a verbal description to fit a two-step inequality.

Math On the Spot
⏱ my.hrw.com

EXAMPLE 2 Real World

COMMON CORE 7.EE.4

Write a corresponding real-world problem to represent $2x + 20 \leq 50$.

STEP 1 Analyze what each part of the inequality means mathematically.

x is the solution of the problem, the quantity you are looking for.

$2x$ means that, for a reason given in the problem, the quantity you are looking for is multiplied by 2.

$+20$ means that, for a reason given in the problem, 20 is added to $2x$.

≤ 50 means that after multiplying the solution x by 2 and adding 20 to it, the result can be no greater than 50.

STEP 2 Think of some different situations in which a quantity x is multiplied by 2.

You run x miles per day for 2 days. So, $2x$ is the total distance run.	You buy 2 items each costing x dollars. So, $2x$ is the total cost.

STEP 3 Build on the situation and adjust it to create a verbal description that takes all of the information into account.

- Tomas has run 20 miles so far this week. If he intends to run 50 miles or less, how many miles on average should he run on each of the 2 days remaining in the week?

- Manny buys 2 work shirts that are each the same price. After using a $20 gift card, he can spend no more than $50. What is the maximum amount he can spend on each shirt?

YOUR TURN

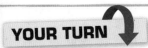

Write a real-world problem for each inequality.

5. $3x + 10 > 30$

6. $5x - 50 \leq 100$

_____

_____

_____

_____

Personal Math Trainer

Online Assessment and Intervention

⏱ my.hrw.com

Draw algebra tiles to model each two-step inequality. (Explore Activity)

1. $4x - 5 < 7$

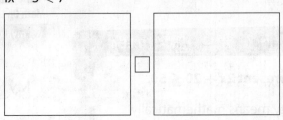

2. $-3x + 6 > 9$

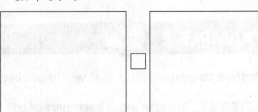

3. The booster club needs to raise at least $7,000 for new football uniforms. So far, they have raised $1,250. Write an inequality to find the average amounts each of the 92 members can raise to meet the club's objective. (Example 1)

Let a represent the amount each member must raise.

amount to be raised: _____ amount already raised: _____ number of members: _____

Use clues in the problem to write an equation.

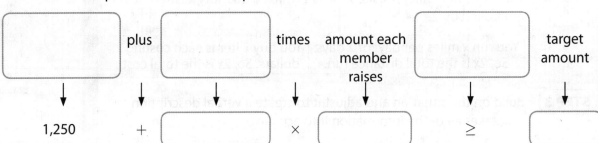

The inequality that represents the situation is _____.

4. Analyze what each part of $7x - 18 \leq 32$ means mathematically. (Example 2)

x is _____. 　　　$7x$ is _____.

-18 means that _____.

≤ 32 means that _____.

5. Write a real-world problem to represent $7x - 18 \leq 32$.

_____

_____

? ESSENTIAL QUESTION CHECK-IN

6. Describe the steps you would follow to write a two-step inequality you can use to solve a real-world problem.

_____

_____

2.2 Independent Practice

Personal Math Trainer

Online Assessment and Intervention

my.hrw.com

7. Three friends earned more than $200 washing cars. They paid their parents $28 for supplies and divided the rest of money equally. Write an inequality to find possible amounts each friend earned. Identify what your variable represents.

_____

_____

8. Nick has $7.00. Bagels cost $0.75 each, and a small container of cream cheese costs $1.29. Write an inequality to find the numbers of bagels Nick can buy. Identify what your variable represents.

_____

_____

9. Chet needs to buy 4 work shirts, all costing the same amount. After he uses a $25 gift certificate, he can spend no more than $75. Write an inequality to find the possible costs for a shirt. Identify what your variable represents.

_____

_____

10. Due to fire laws, no more than 720 people may attend a performance at Metro Auditorium. The balcony holds 120 people. There are 32 rows on the ground floor, each with the same number of seats. Write an inequality to find the numbers of people that can sit in a ground-floor row if the balcony is full. Identify what your variable represents.

_____

_____

11. Liz earns a salary of $2,100 per month, plus a commission of 5% of her sales. She wants to earn at least $2,400 this month. Write an inequality to find amounts of sales that will meet her goal. Identify what your variable represents.

_____

_____

12. Lincoln Middle School plans to collect more than 2,000 cans of food in a food drive. So far, 668 cans have been collected. Write an inequality to find numbers of cans the school can collect on each of the final 7 days of the drive to meet this goal. Identify what your variable represents.

_____

_____

13. Joanna joins a CD club. She pays $7 per month plus $10 for each CD that she orders. Write an inequality to find how many CDs she can purchase in a month if she spends no more than $100. Identify what your variable represents.

_____

_____

14. Lionel wants to buy a belt that costs $22. He also wants to buy some shirts that are on sale for $17 each. He has $80. What inequality can you write to find the number of shirts he can buy? Identify what your variable represents.

_____

_____

15. Write a situation for $15x - 20 \leq 130$ and solve.

_____

_____

_____

Analyze Relationships Write $>$, $<$, $\geq$, or $\leq$ in the blank to express the given relationship.

16. m is at least 25 m _____ 25

17. k is no greater than 9 k _____ 9

18. p is less than 48 p _____ 48

19. b is no more than -5 b _____ -5

20. h is at most 56 h _____ 56

21. w is no less than 0 w _____ 0

22. Critical Thinking Marie scored 95, 86, and 89 on three science tests. She wants her average score for 6 tests to be at least 90. What inequality can you write to find the average scores that she can get on her next three tests to meet this goal? Use s to represent the lowest average score.

_____

_____

H.O.T.   **FOCUS ON HIGHER ORDER THINKING**

Work Area

23. Communicate Mathematical Ideas Write an inequality that expresses the reason the lengths 5 feet, 10 feet, and 20 feet could not be used to make a triangle. Explain how the inequality demonstrates that fact.

_____

_____

_____

_____

24. Analyze Relationships The number m satisfies the relationship $m < 0$. Write an inequality expressing the relationship between $-m$ and 0. Explain your reasoning.

_____

_____

25. Analyze Relationships The number n satisfies the relationship $n > 0$. Write three inequalities to express the relationship between n and $\frac{1}{n}$.

_____

Solving Two-Step Inequalities

COMMON CORE **7.EE.4b**

Solve...inequalities of the form $px + q > r$ or $px + q < r$, where p, q, and r are specific rational numbers. Graph the solution set...and interpret it in the context of the problem.

ESSENTIAL QUESTION

How do you solve a two-step inequality?

EXPLORE ACTIVITY COMMON CORE Prep for 7.EE.4b

Modeling and Solving Two-Step Inequalities

You can solve two-step inequalities using algebra tiles. The method is similar to the one you used to solve two-step equations.

Math On the Spot
my.hrw.com

EXAMPLE 1 **Use algebra tiles to model and solve $4d - 3 \geq 9$.**

STEP 1 Model the inequality. On the left side of the mat, place _____ positive variable tiles and _____ −1-tiles. On the right side, place _____ +1-tiles. Use a "$\geq$" symbol between the sides.

STEP 2 Add _____ +1-tiles to both sides of the mat to produce zero pairs with the three −1-tiles.

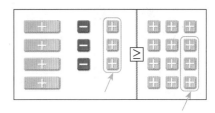

STEP 3 Remove _____ zero pairs from the left side of the mat.

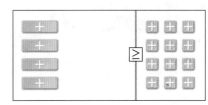

STEP 4 Divide each side into _____ equal groups.

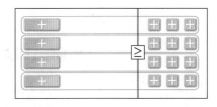

STEP 5 The solution is _____.

YOUR TURN

Use algebra tiles to model and solve each inequality.

1. $2x + 7 > 11$ _____

2. $5h - 4 \geq 11$ _____

Math On the Spot

⏻ my.hrw.com

Solving and Interpreting Solutions

You can apply what you know about solving two-step equations and one-step inequalities to solving two-step inequalities.

EXAMPLE 2

Serena wants to complete the first 3 miles of a 10-mile run in 45 minutes or less running at a steady pace. The inequality $10 - 0.75p \leq 7$ can be used to find p, the pace, in miles per hour, she can run to reach her goal. Solve the inequality. Then graph and interpret the solution.

STEP 1   Use inverse operations to solve the inequality.

$$10 - 0.75p \leq 7$$

$$\underline{-10} \qquad \underline{-10} \qquad \text{Subtract 10 from both sides.}$$

$$-0.75p \leq -3$$

$$\frac{-0.75p}{-0.75} \geq \frac{-3}{-0.75} \qquad \text{Divide both sides by } -0.75.$$
$$\qquad\qquad\qquad\qquad \text{Reverse the inequality symbol.}$$

$$p \geq 4$$

STEP 2   Graph the inequality and interpret the circle and the arrow.

Math Talk
Mathematical Practices

In Example 2, how will the graph change if Serena's maximum pace is 12 miles per hour?

Serena can meet her goal by running at a pace of 4 miles per hour.

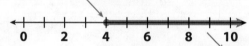

Serena can run at paces faster than 4 miles per hour and reach her goal.

Serena has to run at a steady pace of at least 4 miles per hour.

YOUR TURN

Personal Math Trainer

Online Assessment and Intervention

⏻ my.hrw.com

3. Joshua wants to complete the first mile of a 5-mile run in 10 minutes or less running at a steady pace. The inequality $5 - \frac{p}{6} \leq 4$ can be used to find p, the pace, in miles per hour, he can run to reach his goal. Solve the inequality. Then graph and interpret the solution.

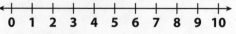

Determining if a Given Value Makes the Inequality True

You can use substitution to decide whether a given value is the solution of an inequality.

EXAMPLE 3 Real World

COMMON CORE 7.EE.4b

At Gas 'n' Wash, gasoline sells for $4.00 a gallon and a car wash costs $12. Harika wants to have her car washed and keep her total purchase under $60. The inequality $4g + 12 < 60$ can be used to find g, the number of gallons of gas she can buy. Determine which, if any, of these values is a solution: $g = 10$; $g = 11$; $g = 12$.

CAR WASH

My Notes

STEP 1 Substitute each value for g in the inequality $4g + 12 < 60$.

$g = 10$	$g = 11$	$g = 12$
$4(10) + 12 < 60$	$4(11) + 12 < 60$	$4(12) + 12 < 60$

STEP 2 Evaluate each expression to see if a true inequality results.

$4(10) + 12 \overset{?}{<} 60$	$4(11) + 12 \overset{?}{<} 60$	$4(12) + 12 \overset{?}{<} 60$
$40 + 12 \overset{?}{<} 60$	$44 + 12 \overset{?}{<} 60$	$48 + 12 \overset{?}{<} 60$
$52 \overset{?}{<} 60$	$56 \overset{?}{<} 60$	$60 \overset{?}{<} 60$
true ✓	true ✓	*not* true ✗

So, Harika can buy 10 or 11 gallons of gas but not 12 gallons.

Check: Solve and graph the inequality.

$4g + 12 < 60$

$\quad 4g < 48$

$\qquad g < 12$

```
←+—+—+—+—+—+—○—+—+—+—+→
  0   2   4   6   8  10  12  14  16  18  20
```

The closed circle at zero represents the minimum amount she can buy, zero gallons. She cannot buy a negative number of gallons. The open circle at 12 means that she can buy any amount up to but not including 12 gallons.

Personal Math Trainer

Online Assessment and Intervention

my.hrw.com

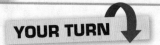

YOUR TURN

Circle any given values that make the inequality true.

4. $3v - 8 > 22$

$v = 9; v = 10; v = 11$

5. $5h + 12 \leq -3$

$h = -3; h = -4; h = -5$

Guided Practice

1. Describe how to solve the inequality $3x + 4 < 13$ using algebra tiles. (Explore Activity Example 1)

_____

_____

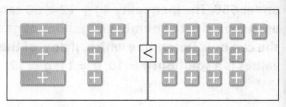

Solve each inequality. Graph and check the solution. (Example 2)

2. $5d - 13 < 32$ _____

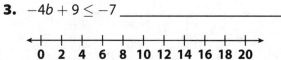

3. $-4b + 9 \leq -7$ _____

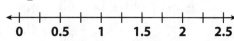

Circle any given values that make the inequality true. (Example 3)

4. $2m + 18 > -4$

$m = -12; m = -11; m = -10$

5. $-6y + 3 \geq 0$

$y = 1; \ y = \frac{1}{2}; y = 0$

6. Lizzy has 6.5 hours to tutor 4 students and spend 1.5 hours in a lab. She plans to tutor each student the same amount of time. The inequality $6.5 - 4t \geq 1.5$ can be used to find t, the amount of time in hours Lizzy could spend with each student. Solve the inequality. Graph and interpret the solution. Can Lizzy tutor each student for 1.5 hours? Explain. (Examples 2 and 3)

_____

_____

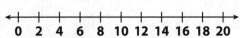

? ESSENTIAL QUESTION CHECK-IN

7. How do you solve a two-step inequality?

_____

_____

_____

Name_____ Class_____ Date_____

2.3 Independent Practice

Personal Math Trainer
Online Assessment and Intervention
my.hrw.com

Solve each inequality. Graph and check the solution.

8. $2s + 5 \geq 49$ _____

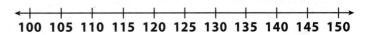
10 12 14 16 18 20 22 24 26 28 30

9. $-3t + 9 \geq -21$ _____

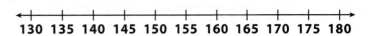
−10 −8 −6 −4 −2 0 2 4 6 8 10

10. $55 > -7v + 6$ _____

−10 −9 −8 −7 −6 −5 −4 −3 −2 −1 0

11. $41 > 6m - 7$ _____

0 1 2 3 4 5 6 7 8 9 10

12. $\dfrac{a}{-8} + 15 > 23$ _____

−70 −69 −68 −67 −66 −65 −64 −63 −62 −61 −60

13. $\dfrac{f}{2} - 22 < 48$ _____

100 105 110 115 120 125 130 135 140 145 150

14. $-25 + \dfrac{t}{2} \geq 50$ _____

130 135 140 145 150 155 160 165 170 175 180

15. $10 + \dfrac{g}{-9} > 12$ _____

−20 −19 −18 −17 −16 −15 −14 −13 −12 −11 −10

16. $25.2 \leq -1.5y + 1.2$ _____

−20 −19 −18 −17 −16 −15 −14 −13 −12 −11 −10

17. $-3.6 \geq -0.3a + 1.2$ _____

10 11 12 13 14 15 16 17 18 19 20

18. What If? The perimeter of a rectangle is at most 80 inches. The length of the rectangle is 25 inches. The inequality $80 - 2w \geq 50$ can be used to find w, the width of the rectangle in inches. Solve the inequality. Graph and interpret the solution. How will the solution change if the width must be at least 10 inches and a whole number?

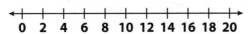
0 2 4 6 8 10 12 14 16 18 20

_____

_____

_____

19. Interpret the Answer Grace earns $7 for each car she washes. She always saves $25 of her weekly earnings. This week, she wants to have at least $65 in spending money. How many cars must she wash? Write and solve an inequality to represent this situation. Interpret the solution in context.

_____

_____

H.O.T. **FOCUS ON HIGHER ORDER THINKING**

Work Area

20. Critical Thinking Is there any value of x with the property that $x < x - 1$? Explain your reasoning.

_____

_____

_____

21. Analyze Relationships A *compound inequality* consists of two simple equalities joined by the word "*and*" or "*or*." Graph the solution sets of each of these compound inequalities.

a. $x > 2$ and $x < 7$

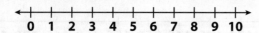

b. $x < 2$ or $x > 7$

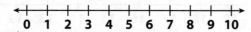

c. Describe the solution set of the compound inequality $x < 2$ and $x > 7$.

_____

d. Describe the solution set of the compound inequality $x > 2$ or $x < 7$.

_____

22. Communicate Mathematical Ideas Joseph used the problem-solving strategy Work Backward to solve the inequality $2n + 5 < 13$. Shawnee solved the inequality using the algebraic method you used in this lesson. Compare the two methods.

_____

_____

_____

_____

_____

Inequalitrio

STEP 1 The teacher will hand three students in your group a stack of Inequalitrio cards.

- If you are given cards with inequalities or graphs, first shuffle the cards. Then deal one card at a time face-down to each student in your group until all the cards are distributed.

- If you are given cards with real-world problems, wait until the other cards are dealt, then deal one card face-up to each student. Set aside any extras.

Savings

Maisey is saving money for a bike. She has already saved $110. How much must she save per week if she wants to have a total of at least $300 saved in 10 weeks?

STEP 2 Examine your real-world problem and record the title of the problem on a piece of paper. Then write and solve an inequality that matches your problem situation. Let the variable be x.

Savings

$$110 + 10x \geq 300$$
$$\underline{-110} \qquad \underline{-110}$$
$$10x \geq 190$$
$$\frac{10x}{10} \geq \frac{190}{10}$$
$$x \geq 19$$

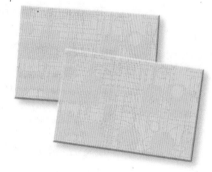

Savings

Maisey is saving money for a bike. She has already saved $110. How much must she save per week if she wants to have a total of at least $300 saved in 10 weeks?

STEP 3 Turn your inequality and graph cards face-up.

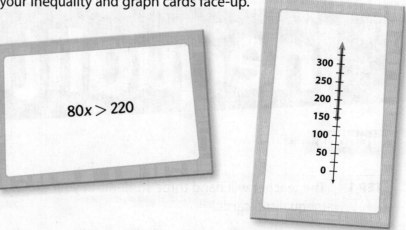

$$80x > 220$$

STEP 4 Keep your real-world problem card, and, using your group members' papers to guide you, take turns distributing your inequality and graph cards to the group members with the matching problem situations. Set aside any inequality and graph cards that don't match any situation.

Continue until you each have a trio of cards—real-world problem, inequality, and graph—that all represent the same situation.

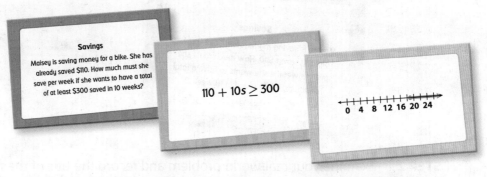

Savings

Maisey is saving money for a bike. She has already saved $110. How much must she save per week if she wants to have a total of at least $300 saved in 10 weeks?

$$110 + 10s \geq 300$$

STEP 5 When you have completed your trios, work with another student in your group to verify that the cards in each of your trios match. If not, identify and correct any mistakes you made on your paper, or exchange cards as needed.

(Note: The inequality on your paper and on the card may not match exactly, but they must be equivalent.)

STEP 6 Once all group members are satisfied that the matches are correct, let your teacher know that you all agree. If instructed, repeat the activity using all of the inequality and graph cards, but only the unused real-world problem cards that you set aside in Step 1.

Ready to Go On?

Personal Math Trainer

Online Assessment and Intervention

⏱ my.hrw.com

2.1 Writing and Solving One-Step Inequalities

Solve each inequality.

1. $n + 7 < -3$ _____

2. $5p \geq -30$ _____

3. $14 < k + 11$ _____

4. $\frac{d}{-3} \leq -6$ _____

5. $c - 2.5 \leq 2.5$ _____

6. $12 \geq -3b$ _____

7. Jose has scored 562 points on his math tests so far this semester. To get an A for the semester, he must score at least 650 points. Write and solve an inequality to find the minimum number of points he must score on the remaining tests in order to get an A.

_____

2.2 Writing Two-Step Inequalities

8. During a scuba dive, Lainey descended to a point 20 feet below the ocean surface. She continued her descent at a rate of 20 feet per minute. Write an inequality you could solve to find the number of minutes she can continue to descend if she does not want to reach a point more than 100 feet below the ocean surface.

_____

2.3 Solving Two-Step Inequalities

Solve.

9. $2s + 3 > 15$ _____

10. $-\frac{d}{12} - 6 < 1$ _____

11. $-6w - 18 \geq 36$ _____

12. $\frac{z}{4} + 22 \leq 38$ _____

13. $\frac{b}{9} - 34 < -36$ _____

14. $-2p + 12 > 8$ _____

? ESSENTIAL QUESTION

15. How can you recognize whether a real-world situation should be represented by an equation or an inequality?

_____

_____

MODULE 2 MIXED REVIEW

Assessment Readiness

COMMON CORE

Personal Math Trainer

Online Assessment and Intervention

my.hrw.com

Selected Response

1. Which graph models the solution of the inequality $-6 \leq -3x$?

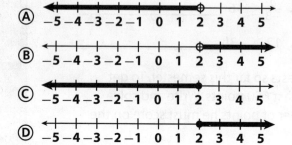

Ⓐ
Ⓑ
Ⓒ
Ⓓ

2. A taxi cab costs $1.75 for the first mile and $0.75 for each additional mile. You have $20 to spend on your ride. Which inequality could be solved to find how many miles you can travel, if n is the number of additional miles?

Ⓐ $1.75n + 0.75 \geq 20$

Ⓑ $1.75n + 0.75 \leq 20$

Ⓒ $0.75n + 1.75 \geq 20$

Ⓓ $0.75n + 1.75 \leq 20$

3. The inequality $\frac{9}{5}C + 32 < -40$ can be used to find Celsius temperatures that are less than $-40°$ Fahrenheit. What is the solution of the inequality?

Ⓐ $C < 40$

Ⓒ $C < -40$

Ⓑ $C < -\frac{40}{9}$

Ⓓ $C < -\frac{72}{5}$

4. The 30 members of a choir are trying to raise at least $1,500 to cover travel costs to a singing camp. They have already raised $600. Which inequality could you solve to find the average amounts each member can raise that will at least meet the goal?

Ⓐ $30x + 600 > 1,500$

Ⓑ $30x + 600 \geq 1,500$

Ⓒ $30x + 600 < 1,500$

Ⓓ $30x + 600 \leq 1,500$

5. Which represents the solution for the inequality $3x - 7 > 5$?

Ⓐ $x < 4$

Ⓒ $x > 4$

Ⓑ $x \leq 4$

Ⓓ $x \geq 4$

6. Which inequality has the following graphed solution?

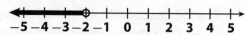

Ⓐ $3x + 8 \leq 2$

Ⓒ $2x + 5 \leq 1$

Ⓑ $4x + 12 < 4$

Ⓓ $3x + 6 < 3$

7. Divide: $-36 \div 6$.

Ⓐ 30

Ⓒ -6

Ⓑ 6

Ⓓ -30

8. Eleni bought 2 pounds of grapes at a cost of $3.49 per pound. She paid with a $10 bill. How much change did she get back?

Ⓐ $3.02

Ⓒ $6.51

Ⓑ $4.51

Ⓓ $6.98

Mini-Task

9. In golf, the lower your score, the better. Negative scores are best of all. Teri scored $+1$ on each of the first three holes at a nine-hole miniature golf course. Her goal is a total score of -9 or better after she has completed the final six holes.

a. Let h represent the score Teri must average on each of the last six holes in order to meet her goal. Write a two-step inequality you can solve to find h.

_____

b. Solve the inequality.

_____

Key Vocabulary
algebraic expression
   (expresión algebraica)
equation *(ecuación)*

? **ESSENTIAL QUESTION**

How can you use equations to solve real-world problems?

EXAMPLE 1

Huang and Belita both repair computers. Huang makes $50 a day plus $25 per repair. Belita makes $20 a day plus $35 per repair. Write an expression for Huang and Belita's total daily earnings if they make the same number of repairs *r*.

Huang: $50 + $25r

Belita: $20 + $35r

Together: $(50 + 25r) + (20 + 35r) = 50 + 20 + 25r + 35r$

$$= 70 + 60r$$

Huang and Belita earn $70 + $60r together.

EXAMPLE 2

A skydiver's parachute opens at a height of 2,790 feet. He then falls at a rate of $-15\frac{1}{2}$ feet per second. How long will it take the skydiver to reach the ground?

Let *x* represent the number of seconds it takes to reach the ground.

$$-15\frac{1}{2}x = -2{,}790$$

$$-\frac{31}{2}x = -2{,}790 \qquad \text{Write as a fraction.}$$

$$\left(-\frac{2}{31}\right)\left(-\frac{31}{2}x\right) = \left(-\frac{2}{31}\right)(-2{,}790) \qquad \text{Multiply both sides by the reciprocal.}$$

$$x = 180$$

It takes 180 seconds for the skydiver to reach the ground.

EXAMPLE 3

A clothing store sells clothing for 2 times the wholesale cost plus \$10. The store sells a pair of pants for \$48. How much did the store pay for the pants? Represent the solution on a number line.

Let w represent the wholesale cost of the pants, or the price paid by the store.

$2w + 10 = 48$

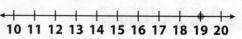

$2w = 38$ Subtract 10 from both sides.

$w = 19$ Divide both sides by 2.

The store paid \$19 for the pants.

EXERCISES

Simplify each expression. (Lesson 1.1)

1. $(2x + 3\frac{2}{5}) + (5x - \frac{4}{5})$ _____

2. $(-0.5x - 4) - (1.5x + 2.3)$ _____

3. $9(3t + 4b)$ _____

4. $0.7(5a - 13p)$ _____

Factor each expression. (Lesson 1.1)

5. $8x + 56$ _____

6. $3x + 57$ _____

Use inverse operations to solve each equation. (Lesson 1.2)

7. $1.6 + y = -7.3$ _____

8. $-\frac{2}{3}n = 12$ _____

9. The cost of a ticket to an amusement park is \$42 per person. For groups of up to 8 people, the cost per ticket decreases by \$3 for each person in the group. Marcos's ticket cost \$30. Write and solve an equation to find the number of people in Marcos's group. (Lesson 1.3, 1.4)

_____

Solve each equation. Graph the solution on a number line. (Lesson 1.4)

10. $8x - 28 = 44$

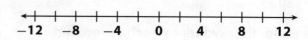

_____

11. $-5z + 4 = 34$

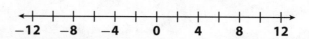

_____

MODULE 2 — Inequalities

? ESSENTIAL QUESTION

How can you use inequalities to solve real-world problems?

EXAMPLE 1

Amy is having her birthday party at a roller skating rink. The rink charges a fee of $50 plus $8 per person. If Amy wants to spend at most $170 for the party at the rink, how many people can she invite to her party?

Let p represent the number of people skating at the party.

$50 + 8p \leq 170$

$\qquad 8p \leq 120 \qquad$ Subtract 50 from both sides.

$\qquad \dfrac{8p}{8} \leq \dfrac{120}{8} \qquad$ Divide both sides by 8.

$\qquad p \leq 15$

Up to 15 people can skate, so Amy can invite up to 14 people to her party.

EXAMPLE 2

Determine which, if any, of these values makes the inequality
$-7x + 42 \leq 28$ **true:** $x = -1, x = 2, x = 5.$

$-7(-1) + 42 \leq 28 \qquad -7(2) + 42 \leq 28 \qquad -7(5) + 42 \leq 28$

$x = 2$ and $x = 5$

Substitute each value for x in the inequality and evaluate the expression to see if a true inequality results.

EXERCISES

1. Prudie needs $90 or more to be able to take her family out to dinner. She has already saved $30 and wants to take her family out to eat in 4 days. (Lesson 2.2)

    a. Suppose that Prudie earns the same each day. Write an inequality to find how much she needs to earn each day.

    _____

    b. Suppose that Prudie earns $18 each day. Will she have enough money to take her family to dinner in 4 days? Explain.

    _____

Solve each inequality. Graph and check the solution. (Lesson 2.3)

2. $11 - 5y < -19$

3. $7x - 2 \leq 61$

_____

_____

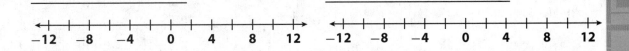

Unit 1 Performance Tasks

1. **CAREERS IN MATH** | **Mechanical Engineer** A mechanical engineer is testing the amount of force needed to make a spring stretch by a given amount. The force y is measured in units called *Newtons*, abbreviated N. The stretch x is measured in centimeters. Her results are shown in the graph.

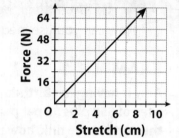

Spring Stretch

a. Write an equation for the line. Explain, using the graph and then using the equation, why the relationship is proportional.

_____

_____

b. Identify the rate of change and the constant of proportionality.

_____

c. What is the meaning of the constant of proportionality in the context of the problem?

_____

d. The engineer applies a force of 41.6 Newtons to the spring. Write and solve an equation to find the corresponding stretch in the spring.

_____

2. A math tutor charges $30 for a consultation, and then $25 per hour. An online tutoring service charges $30 per hour.

a. Does either service represent a proportional relationship? Explain.

_____

_____

_____

b. Write an equation for the cost c of h hours of tutoring for either service. Which service charges less for 4 hours of tutoring? Show your work.

_____

_____

_____

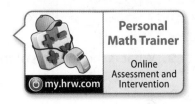
Selected Response

1. Which expression is equivalent to $(9x - 3\frac{1}{8}) - (7x + 1\frac{3}{8})$?

Ⓐ $2x - 4\frac{1}{2}$ Ⓒ $2x - 1\frac{3}{4}$

Ⓑ $16x - 4\frac{1}{2}$ Ⓓ $16x - 1\frac{3}{4}$

2. Timothy began the week with $35. He bought lunch at school, paying $2.25 for each meal. Let x be the number of meals he bought at school and y be the amount of money he had left at the end of the week. Which equation represents the relationship in the situation?

Ⓐ $y = 2.25x + 35$

Ⓑ $y = 35 - 2.25x$

Ⓒ $x = 35 - 2.25y$

Ⓓ $y = 2.25x - 35$

3. Which expression factors to $8(x + 2)$?

Ⓐ $8x + 2$ Ⓒ $16x$

Ⓑ $8x + 10$ Ⓓ $8x + 16$

4. Ramón's toll pass account has a value of $32. Each time he uses the toll road, $1.25 is deducted from the account. When the value drops below $10, he must add value to the toll pass. Which inequality represents how many times Ramón can use the toll road without having to add value to the toll pass?

Ⓐ $10 - 1.25t \geq 0$

Ⓑ $-1.25t + 32 < 10$

Ⓒ $32 - 1.25t \geq 10$

Ⓓ $32 - 10t \geq 1.25$

5. A taxi costs $1.65 for the first mile and $0.85 for each additional mile. Which equation could be solved to find the number x of additional miles traveled in a taxi given that the total cost of the trip is $20?

Ⓐ $1.65x + 0.85 = 20$

Ⓑ $0.85x + 1.65 = 20$

Ⓒ $1.65x - 0.85 = 20$

Ⓓ $0.85x - 1.65 = 20$

6. A sales tax of 6% is added to the price of an item. If Marisa buys an item, which expression indicates how much she will pay in all?

Ⓐ $n + 0.06$ Ⓒ $n + 0.06n$

Ⓑ $0.06n$ Ⓓ $0.06 + 0.06n$

7. Which equation has the solution $x = 12$?

Ⓐ $4x + 3 = 45$

Ⓑ $3x + 6 = 42$

Ⓒ $2x - 5 = 29$

Ⓓ $5x - 8 = 68$

8. The 23 members of the school jazz band are trying to raise at least $1,800 to cover the cost of traveling to a competition. The members have already raised $750. Which inequality could you solve to find the amount that each member should raise to meet the goal?

Ⓐ $23x + 750 > 1,800$

Ⓑ $23x + 750 \geq 1,800$

Ⓒ $23x + 750 < 1,800$

Ⓓ $23x + 750 \leq 1,800$

9. What is the solution of the inequality $2x - 9 < 7$?

(A) $x < 8$

(B) $x \leq 8$

(C) $x > 8$

(D) $x \geq 8$

10. Which inequality has the solution $n < 5$?

(A) $4n + 11 > -9$

(B) $4n + 11 < -9$

(C) $-4n + 11 < -9$

(D) $-4n + 11 > -9$

11. Which inequality has the solution shown?

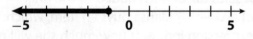

(A) $3x + 5 < 2$

(B) $4x + 12 < 4$

(C) $2x + 5 \leq 1$

(D) $3x + 6 \leq 3$

12. On a $4\frac{1}{2}$ hour trip, Leslie drove $\frac{2}{3}$ of the time. For how many hours did Leslie drive?

(A) 3 hours

(B) $3\frac{1}{2}$ hours

(C) $3\frac{2}{3}$ hours

(D) $3\frac{5}{6}$ hours

13. During a sale, the price of a sweater was changed from $20 to $16. What was the percent of decrease in the price of the sweater?

(A) 4%

(B) 20%

(C) 25%

(D) 40%

Mini-Task

14. Max wants to buy some shorts that are priced at $8 each. He decided to buy a pair of sneakers for $39, but the total cost of the shorts and the sneakers must be less than $75.

a. Write an inequality to find out how many pairs of shorts Max can buy.

_____

_____

_____

_____

b. Suppose that Max wants to buy 6 pairs of shorts. Will he have enough money? Explain.

_____

_____

_____

_____

_____

c. Solve the inequality to find the greatest number of pairs of shorts that Max can buy. Show your work.

_____

_____

_____

_____

_____

Geometry

CAREERS IN MATH

Product Design Engineer A product design engineer works to design and develop manufactured products and equipment. A product design engineer uses math to design and modify models, and to calculate costs in producing their designs.

If you are interested in a career in product design engineering, you should study these mathematical subjects:
- Algebra
- Geometry
- Trigonometry
- Statistics
- Calculus

Research other careers that require the use of mathematics to design and modify products.

Unit 2 Performance Task

At the end of the unit, check out how **product design engineers** use math.

UNIT 2
Vocabulary Preview

Use the puzzle to preview key vocabulary from this unit. Unscramble the circled letters to answer the riddle at the bottom of the page.

1. NEONGTURC LANSEG

2. LEOTECRAYMPMN SEGLAN

3. RIMEUCEEFNRCC

4. LEARATL ERAA

5. PIECOTMOS GUISEFR

1. Angles that have the same measure. (Lesson 3.4)
2. Two angles whose measures have a sum of 90 degrees. (Lesson 3.4)
3. The distance around a circle. (Lesson 3.1)
4. The sum of the areas of the lateral faces of a prism. (Lesson 3.4)
5. A two-dimensional figure made from two or more geometric figures. (Lesson 3.3)

Q: What do you say when you see an empty parrot cage?

A: __ __ __ __ __ __ __ __ __ __ !

Modeling Geometric Figures

ESSENTIAL QUESTION

How can you use proportions to solve real-world geometry problems?

Real-World Video

Architects make blueprints and models of their designs to show clients and contractors. These scale drawings and scale models have measurements in proportion to those of the project when built.

my.hrw.com

GO DIGITAL
my.hrw.com

my.hrw.com

Go digital with your write-in student edition, accessible on any device.

Math On the Spot

Scan with your smart phone to jump directly to the online edition, video tutor, and more.

Animated Math

Interactively explore key concepts to see how math works.

Personal Math Trainer

Get immediate feedback and help as you work through practice sets.

Are YOU Ready?

Complete these exercises to review skills you will need for this module.

Personal Math Trainer

Online Practice and Help

my.hrw.com

Solve Two-Step Equations

EXAMPLE

$5x + 3 = -7$

$5x + 3 - 3 = -7 - 3$ Subtract 3 from both sides.

$5x = -10$ Simplify.

$\frac{5x}{5} = \frac{-10}{5}$ Divide both sides by 5.

$x = -2$

Solve.

1. $3x + 4 = 10$ _____

2. $5x - 11 = 34$ _____

3. $-2x + 5 = -9$ _____

4. $-11 = 8x + 13$ _____

5. $4x - 7 = -27$ _____

6. $\frac{1}{2}x + 16 = 39$ _____

7. $12 = 2x - 16$ _____

8. $5x - 15 = -65$ _____

Solve Proportions

EXAMPLE

$\frac{a}{4} = \frac{27}{18}$

What do you multiply 27 by to get a? $18 \times \frac{2}{9} = 4$.

So multiply 27 by $\frac{2}{9}$.

$a = 27 \times \frac{2}{9} = 6$

Solve for x.

9. $\frac{x}{5} = \frac{18}{30}$ _____

10. $\frac{x}{12} = \frac{24}{36}$ _____

11. $\frac{3}{9} = \frac{x}{3}$ _____

12. $\frac{14}{15} = \frac{x}{75}$ _____

13. $\frac{8}{x} = \frac{14}{7}$ _____

14. $\frac{14}{x} = \frac{2}{5}$ _____

15. $\frac{5}{6} = \frac{x}{15}$ _____

16. $\frac{81}{33} = \frac{x}{5.5}$ _____

Reading Start-Up

Vocabulary

Review Words
- ✔ angle *(ángulo)*
- ✔ degree *(grado)*
- dimension *(dimensión)*
- ✔ length *(longitud)*
- proportion *(proporción)*
- ✔ polygon *(polígono)*
- ratio *(razón)*
- ✔ width *(ancho)*

Preview Words
- adjacent angles *(ángulos adyacentes)*
- complementary angles *(ángulos complementarios)*
- congruent angles *(ángulos congruentes)*
- cross section *(sección transversal)*
- intersection *(intersección)*
- scale *(escala)*
- scale drawing *(dibujo a escala)*
- supplementary angles *(ángulos suplementarios)*
- vertical angles *(ángulos verticales)*

Visualize Vocabulary

Use the ✔ words to complete the graphic. You may put more than one word on each line.

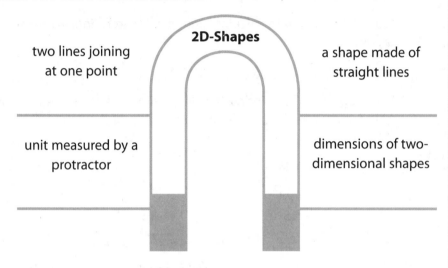

2D-Shapes

two lines joining at one point

a shape made of straight lines

unit measured by a protractor

dimensions of two-dimensional shapes

Understand Vocabulary

Complete each sentence using a preview word.

1. What is a proportional two-dimensional drawing of an object?

   _____

2. _____ are angles that have the same measure.

3. _____ are angles whose measures have a

   sum of 90°.

Active Reading

Key-Term Fold Before beginning the module, create a key-term fold to help you learn the vocabulary in this module. Write each highlighted vocabulary word on one side of a flap. Write the definition for each word on the other side of the flap. Use the key-term fold to quiz yourself on the definitions in this module.

Unpacking the Standards

Understanding the standards and the vocabulary terms in the standards will help you know exactly what you are expected to learn in this module.

COMMON CORE **7.G.1**

Solve problems involving scale drawings of geometric figures, including computing actual lengths and areas from a scale drawing and reproducing a scale drawing at a different scale.

Key Vocabulary

scale *(escala)*
The ratio between two sets of measurements.

What It Means to You

You will learn how to calculate actual measurements from a scale drawing.

UNPACKING EXAMPLE 7.G.1

A photograph of a painting has dimensions 5.4 cm and 4 cm. The scale factor is $\frac{1}{15}$. Find the length and width of the actual painting.

$$\frac{1}{15} = \frac{5.4}{\ell} \qquad\qquad \frac{1}{15} = \frac{4}{w}$$

$$\frac{1 \times 5.4}{15 \times 5.4} = \frac{5.4}{\ell} \qquad \frac{1 \times 4}{15 \times 4} = \frac{4}{w}$$

$$15 \times 5.4 = \ell \qquad\qquad 15 \times 4 = w$$

$$81 = \ell \qquad\qquad\qquad 60 = w$$

The painting is 81 cm long and 60 cm wide.

COMMON CORE **7.G.5**

Use facts about supplementary, complementary, vertical, and adjacent angles in a multi-step problem to write and solve simple equations for an unknown angle in a figure.

Key Vocabulary

supplementary angles
(ángulos suplementarios)
Two angles whose measures have a sum of 180°.

What It Means to You

You will learn about supplementary, complementary, vertical, and adjacent angles. You will solve simple equations to find the measure of an unknown angle in a figure.

UNPACKING EXAMPLE 7.G.5

Suppose $m\angle 1 = 55°$.

Adjacent angles formed by two intersecting lines are supplementary.

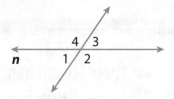

$$m\angle 1 + m\angle 2 = 180°$$

$$55° + m\angle 2 = 180° \qquad \text{Substitute.}$$

$$m\angle 2 = 180° - 55°$$

$$= 125°$$

Visit **my.hrw.com** to see all the **Common Core Standards** unpacked.

⊙ my.hrw.com

Similar Shapes and Scale Drawings

COMMON CORE 7.G.1

Solve problems involving scale drawings of geometric figures, including computing actual lengths and areas from a scale drawing and reproducing a scale drawing at a different scale. *Also 7.RP.2, 7.RP.3*

💬 **ESSENTIAL QUESTION**

How can you use scale drawings to solve problems?

EXPLORE ACTIVITY 1

COMMON CORE **7.G.1, 7.RP.2, 7.RP.3**

Scale Drawings and Proportional Reasoning

A blueprint is a technical drawing that usually displays architectural plans. Pete's blueprint shows a layout of a house. The table shows how the actual lengths in the house are related to the lengths in Pete's blueprint.

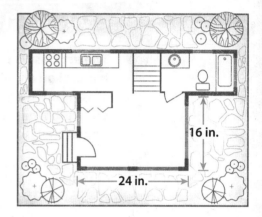

16 in.

24 in.

Blueprint length (in.)	4	8	12	16	20	24
Actual length (ft)	3	6	9	12	15	18

A Use the rates of actual length to blueprint length in the table to explain why the relationship between the two is proportional.

_____

B Show how to use proportional reasoning to find the unit rate.

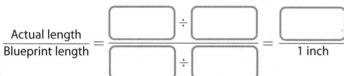

$$\frac{\text{Actual length}}{\text{Blueprint length}} = \frac{\boxed{} \div \boxed{}}{\boxed{} \div \boxed{}} = \frac{\boxed{}}{1 \text{ inch}}$$

C Write an equation for the relationship, where *x* is blueprint length, in inches, and *y* is actual length, in feet. Use the equation to find the actual length for a blueprint length of 21 inches and the blueprint length for an actual length of 7 feet.

_____

Reflect

1. **Check for Reasonableness** Show that your answers to **C** are reasonable.

_____

_____

_____

Finding Length, Width, and Area

A **scale drawing** is a proportional two-dimensional drawing of an object. Scale drawings can represent objects that are smaller or larger than the drawing.

A **scale** is a ratio between two sets of measurements. It shows how a dimension in a scale drawing is related to the actual object. Scales are usually shown as two numbers separated by a colon, such as 1:20 or 1 cm:1 m. Scales can be shown in the same unit or in different units.

You can solve scale-drawing problems by using proportional reasoning.

EXAMPLE 1 | COMMON CORE 7.G.1, 7.RP.3

The art class is planning to paint a mural on an outside wall. This figure is a scale drawing of the wall. What is the area of the actual wall?

28 in.

11 in.

2 in.:3 ft

STEP 1 Find the number of feet represented by 1 inch in the drawing.

$$\frac{2 \text{ in.} \div 2}{3 \text{ ft} \div 2} = \frac{1 \text{ in.}}{1.5 \text{ ft}}$$

1 inch in this drawing equals 1.5 feet on the actual wall.

STEP 2 Find the height of the actual wall labeled 11 inches in the drawing.

$$\frac{1 \text{ in.} \times 11}{1.5 \text{ ft} \times 11} = \frac{11 \text{ in.}}{16.5 \text{ ft}}$$

The height of the actual wall labeled 11 in. is 16.5 ft.

STEP 3 Find the length of the actual wall labeled 28 inches in the drawing.

$$\frac{1 \text{ in.} \times 28}{1.5 \text{ ft} \times 28} = \frac{28 \text{ in.}}{42 \text{ ft}}$$

The length of the actual wall is 42 ft.

STEP 4 Since area is length times width, the area of the actual wall is 16.5 ft × 42 ft = 693 ft².

Math Talk

Mathematical Practices

What are two proportions you could use to find the actual length *L* and width *W*?

Reflect

2. **Analyze Relationships** Write the scale in Example 1 as a unit rate. Show that this unit rate is equal to the ratio of the height of the drawing to the actual height.

_____

3. **Analyze Relationships** Write the ratio of the area of the drawing to the area of the actual wall. Write your answer as a unit rate. Show that this unit rate is equal to the square of the unit rate in Exercise 2.

_____

Personal
Math Trainer

Online Assessment
and Intervention

⏻ my.hrw.com

4. Find the length and width of the actual room, shown in the scale drawing. Then find the area of the actual room. Round your answers to the nearest tenth.

6.5 in.

5 in.

3 in.:8 ft

_____

_____

5. The drawing plan for an art studio shows a rectangle that is 13.2 inches by 6 inches. The scale in the plan is 3 in.:5 ft. Find the length and width of the actual studio. Then find the area of the actual studio.

_____

EXPLORE ACTIVITY 2 *Real World* **COMMON CORE** 7.G.1

Drawing in Different Scales

A A scale drawing of a meeting hall is drawn on centimeter grid paper as shown. The scale is 1 cm:3 m.

Suppose you redraw the rectangle on centimeter grid paper using a scale of 1 cm:6 m. In the new scale, 1 cm

represents [**more/less**] than 1 cm in the old scale.

B Write and simplify the ratio of the new scale to the original scale.

$$\frac{\text{New scale}}{\text{Original scale}} = \frac{\boxed{}}{\frac{1\ \text{cm}}{3\ \text{m}}} = \frac{\boxed{}}{\boxed{}}$$

C The measurement of each side of the new drawing will

be [**twice/half**] as long as the measurement of the original drawing.

D Draw the rectangle for the new scale 1 cm:6 m.

Reflect

6. Show how to find the actual length of each side of the hall using the original drawing and scale. Repeat using your new drawing and the new scale.

_____

_____

1. The table compares actual lengths in a room to lengths in a blueprint of the room. (Explore Activity 1)

Blueprint length (in.)	3	6	9	12	15	18
Actual length (ft)	5	10	15	20	25	30

   a. Write an equation for the relationship, where *y* is the actual length in feet. _____

   b. The length of a wall on the blueprint is 10 inches. Find the actual length of the wall. _____

   c. A window in the room has an actual width of 2.5 feet. Find the width of the window in the blueprint. _____

2. The scale in the drawing is 2 in. : 4 ft. What are the length, width, and area of the actual room? (Example 1)

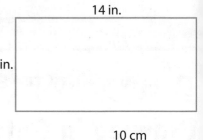

14 in.

7 in.

Length = _____ feet, because 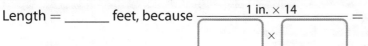 $\dfrac{1 \text{ in.} \times 14}{\boxed{} \times \boxed{}} = \dfrac{14 \text{ in.}}{\boxed{}}$, width = _____ feet, and area = _____ square feet.

3. The scale in the drawing is 2 cm : 5 m. What are the length, width, and area of the actual room? (Example 1)

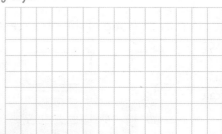

10 cm

6 cm

_____

4. A scale drawing of a cafeteria is drawn on centimeter grid paper as shown. The scale is 1 cm : 4 m. (Explore Activity 2)

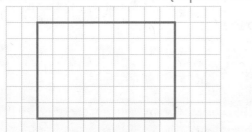

   a. Redraw the rectangle on centimeter grid paper using a scale of 1 cm:6 m.

   b. What are the actual length and width of the cafeteria using the original scale? What are the actual dimensions of the cafeteria using the new scale?

_____

? ESSENTIAL QUESTION CHECK-IN

5. If you have an accurate, complete scale drawing and the scale, which measurements of the object of the drawing can you find?

_____

_____

3.1 Independent Practice

COMMON CORE 7.RP.3, 7.G.1

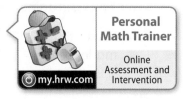

6. Art Marie has a small copy of Rene Magritte's famous painting, *The Schoolmaster*. Her copy has dimensions 2 inches by 1.5 inches. The scale of the copy is 1 in.:40 cm.

   a. Find the dimensions of the original painting.

   _____

   b. Find the area of the original painting.

   _____

   c. Since 1 inch is 2.54 centimeters, find the dimensions of the original painting in inches.

   _____

   d. Find the area of the original painting in square inches.

   _____

7. A game room has a floor that is 120 feet by 75 feet. A scale drawing of the floor on grid paper uses a scale of 1 unit:5 feet. What are the dimensions of the scale drawing?

   _____

8. Multiple Representations The length of a table is 6 feet. On a scale drawing, the length is 2 inches. Write three possible scales for the drawing.

   _____

9. Analyze Relationships A scale for a scale drawing is 10 cm:1 mm. Which is larger, the actual object or the scale drawing? Explain.

   _____

   _____

10. Architecture The scale model of a building is 5.4 feet tall.

   a. If the original building is 810 meters tall, what was the scale used to make the model?

   _____

   b. If the model is made out of tiny bricks each measuring 0.4 inch in height, how many bricks tall is the model?

   _____

11. You have been asked to build a scale model of your school out of toothpicks. Imagine your school is 30 feet tall. Your scale is 1 ft:1.26 cm.

    a. If a toothpick is 6.3 cm tall, how many toothpicks tall will your model be?

    _____

    b. Your mother is out of toothpicks, and suggests you use cotton swabs instead. You measure them, and they are 7.6 cm tall. How many cotton swabs tall will your model be?

    _____

 **FOCUS ON HIGHER ORDER THINKING**

12. Draw Conclusions The area of a square floor on a scale drawing is 100 square centimeters, and the scale of the drawing is 1 cm : 2 ft. What is the area of the actual floor? What is the ratio of the area in the drawing to the actual area?

_____

13. Multiple Representations Describe how to redraw a scale drawing with a new scale.

_____

_____

_____

_____

_____

14. The scale drawing of a room is drawn on a grid that represents quarter-inch grid paper. The scale is $\frac{1}{4}$ in. : 4 ft. Redraw the scale drawing of the same room using a different scale. What scale did you use? What are the length and width of the actual room? What is the area of the actual room?

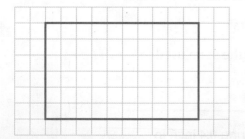 

_____

Scale Drawings and Area

COMMON CORE **7.G.1**

Solve problems involving scale drawings of geometric figures, including computing actual lengths and areas from a scale drawing.... *Also 7.RP.2, 7.RP.3*

ESSENTIAL QUESTION

How can you use the area of a figure on a scale drawing to find the corresponding area on the actual object?

EXPLORE ACTIVITY COMMON CORE 7.G.1, 7.RP.2, 7.RP.3

Using a Scale to Compute Area

The scale drawing is of a banner designed for Elmwood School's awards ceremony.

A The unit rate for the proportional relationship between dimensions x on the scale drawing and dimensions y on the banner is $\dfrac{\boxed{}\ \text{ft}}{0.5\ \text{in.}} = \dfrac{\boxed{}\ \text{ft}}{1\ \text{in.}}$ or _____ feet per inch. So an equation for the relationship is $y =$ _____.

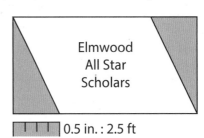

Elmwood All Star Scholars

0.5 in. : 2.5 ft

B Measure the base and height of the white parallelogram on the scale drawing to the nearest half inch. Find the area of the parallelogram.

base = _____ in.   height = _____ in.   area = _____ in²

C Use the equation from Part A and the base and height you found in Part B to find the base and height of the parallelogram on the banner. Then find the area of the parallelogram on the banner.

base = 5 × _____ = _____ ft   height = 5 × _____ = _____ ft   area = _____ ft²

D The ratio of the area of the parallelogram on the banner to the area on the scale drawing is $\dfrac{\boxed{}\ \text{ft}^2}{\boxed{}\ \text{in}^2} = \dfrac{\boxed{}\ \text{ft}^2}{1\ \text{in}^2} = \dfrac{\boxed{}\ \text{ft}^2}{1\ \text{in}^2}$.

E Show how to calculate the area of each triangle on the banner using the relationship described in Part D.

_____

_____

Reflect

1. **Focus on Modeling** Suppose the relationship between a length on a scale drawing d and the actual length a is $a = kd$. Write an equation of the relationship between an area x on the scale drawing and the corresponding actual area y. _____

For Exercises 1 and 2, use the scale drawing of a garden showing regions for different vegetables. Measure dimensions on the scale drawing to the nearest quarter of an inch.

1. Use the scale to find the unit rate for the proportional relationship between dimensions on the scale drawing and dimensions in the garden in yards per inch.

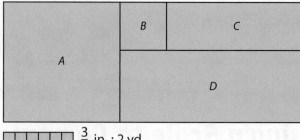

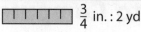

$\frac{3}{4}$ in. : 2 yd

2. Let x represent the area of a region on the scale drawing and y represent the corresponding area in the garden.

   a. Write an equation for the relationship between x and y.

   b. Find the area of regions A, B, C, and D in the garden.

3. Write an equation for the relationship between areas on the blueprint x and the actual areas in the room y. Use the equation to find the area of the actual living room. Then find the cost of carpeting the living room with carpeting that costs $6.52 for each square foot.

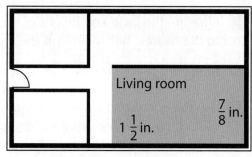

1 in. : 16 ft

4. **Estimation** The map shows a roughly parallelogram-shaped region formed by connecting the dots representing four cities. The map scale is shown as a bar representing distances.

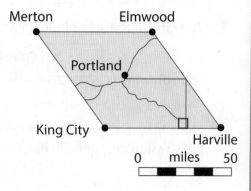

   a. Use the scale to estimate the base and height of the region in miles. Then estimate the area of the region.

   b. The signal of one Portland radio station can reach about 30 miles. Which of the four cities are likely to be able to receive the signal?

Scale a Comic

INSTRUCTIONS

STEP 1 Choose a single frame from the comic strip below or from another comic strip of your own. The comic strip below has three frames.

STEP 2 Carefully draw a 1 cm grid on the comic, starting at the bottom left corner of the frame.

  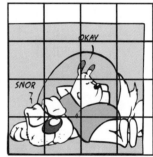

STEP 3 Choose a scale that will enlarge the comic, but will allow the drawing to fit on an $8\frac{1}{2}$ in. × 11 in. sheet of quarter-inch graph paper. An example of a scale is 1 cm : 1.25 in. Record the scale below.

Scale _____

Visual Element	Original Measurement	Predicted Measurement	Scale Drawing Measurement

STEP 4 Measure four visual elements of your original comic and record the measurements in the table in Step 3.

STEP 5 Use your scale to predict corresponding measurements for the four visual elements on the scale drawing. Record the predicted measurements in the table.

STEP 6 Use your chosen scale and the grid lines to help you draw the scaled-up comic *square by square* on an $8\frac{1}{2}$ in. x 11 in. sheet of quarter-inch graph paper. Depending on the size of your comic, the scale you use, and the shape of the comic, the scaled-up comic may not fill the page.

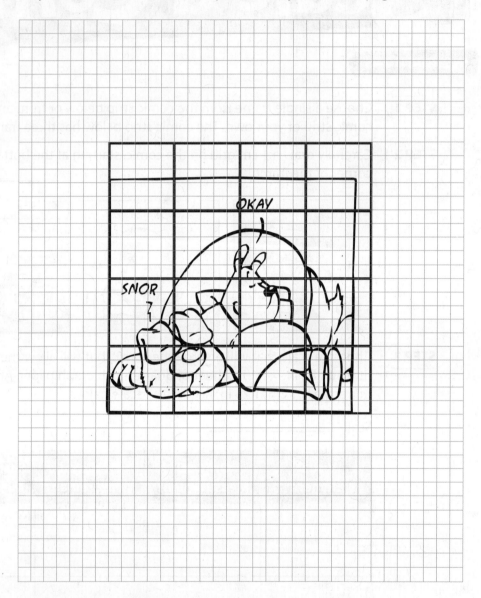

STEP 7 Measure corresponding lengths on the scaled-up drawing for the visual elements previously measured. Record the measurements in the last column of the table.

STEP 8 Compare your predicted measurements to the scale drawing measurements.

LESSON

3.2 Geometric Drawings

COMMON CORE 7.G.2

Draw... geometric shapes with given conditions. Focus on constructing triangles...

ESSENTIAL QUESTION

How can you draw shapes that satisfy given conditions?

EXPLORE ACTIVITY 1   COMMON CORE   7.G.2

Drawing Three Sides

Use geometry software to draw a triangle whose sides have the following lengths: 2 units, 3 units, and 4 units.

A Draw the segments.

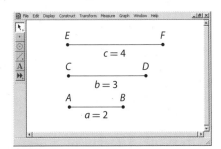

B Let $\overline{AB}$ be the base of the triangle. Place point C on top of point B and point E on top of point A.

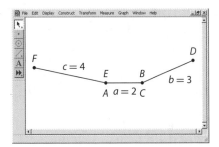

C Using the points C and E as fixed vertices, rotate points F and D to see if they will meet in a single point.

Note that the line segments form a triangle.

D Repeat **A** and **B**, but use a different segment as the base. Do the segments form a triangle? If so, is it the same as the original triangle?

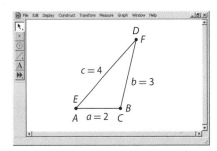

_____

E Use geometry software to draw a triangle with sides of length 2, 3, and 6 units, and one with sides of length 2, 3, and 5 units. Do the line segments form triangles? How does the sum of the lengths of the two shorter sides of each triangle compare to the length of the third side?

_____

Animated Math

my.hrw.com

Reflect

1. Conjecture Do two segments of lengths a and b units and a longer segment of length c units form one triangle, more than one, or none?

_____

Two Angles and Their Included Side

Use a ruler and a protractor to draw each triangle.

Triangle 1	Triangle 2
Angles: 30° and 80°	Angles: 55° and 50°
Length of included side: 2 inches	Length of included side: 1 inch

A Draw Triangle 1.

STEP 1 Use a ruler to draw a line that is 2 inches long. This will be the included side.

STEP 2 Place the center of the protractor on the left end of the 2-in. line. Then make a 30°-angle mark.

STEP 3 Draw a line connecting the left side of the 2-in. line and the 30°-angle mark. This will be the 30° angle.

30°
2 in.

STEP 4 Repeat Step 2 on the right side of the triangle to construct the 80° angle.

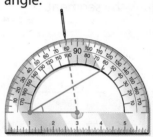

STEP 5 The side of the 80° angle and the side of the 30° angle will intersect. This is Triangle 1 with angles of 30° and 80° and an included side of 2 inches.

B Use the steps in A to draw Triangle 2.

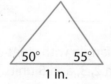

50°   55°
1 in.

Reflect

2. **Conjecture** When you are given two angle measures and the length of the included side, do you get a unique triangle?

_____

_____

Name_____ Class_____ Date_____

Guided Practice

Tell whether each figure creates the conditions to form a unique triangle, more than one triangle, or no triangle. (Explore Activities 1 and 2)

1.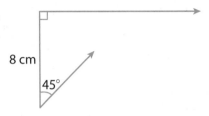

8 cm

45°

_____

2.

4 cm   3 cm

11 cm

_____

3.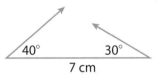

40°   30°

7 cm

_____

4. 6 cm

12 cm

7 cm

_____

? ESSENTIAL QUESTION CHECK-IN

5. Describe lengths of three segments that could **not** be used to form a triangle.

_____

3.2 Independent Practice

COMMON CORE 7.G.2

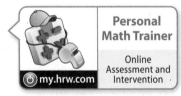

Personal Math Trainer

Online Assessment and Intervention

my.hrw.com

6. On a separate piece of paper, try to draw a triangle with side lengths of 3 centimeters and 6 centimeters, and an included angle of 120°. Determine whether the given segments and angle produce a unique triangle, more than one triangle, or no triangle.

_____

7. A landscape architect submitted a design for a triangle-shaped flower garden with side lengths of 21 feet, 37 feet, and 15 feet to a customer. Explain why the architect was not hired to create the flower garden.

_____

_____

8. **Make a Conjecture** The angles in an actual triangle-shaped traffic sign all have measures of 60°. The angles in a scale drawing of the sign all have measures of 60°. Explain how you can use this information to decide whether three given angle measures can be used to form a unique triangle or more than one triangle.

YIELD

_____

_____

   **FOCUS ON HIGHER ORDER THINKING**

Work Area

9. **Communicate Mathematical Ideas** The figure on the left shows a line segment 2 inches long forming a 45° angle with a dashed line whose length is not given. The figure on the right shows a compass set at a width of $1\frac{1}{2}$ inches with its point on the top end of the 2-inch segment. An arc is drawn intersecting the dashed line twice.

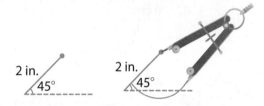

2 in. 45°   2 in. 45°

Explain how you can use this figure to decide whether two sides and an angle **not** included between them can be used to form a unique triangle, more than one triangle, or no triangle.

_____

_____

_____

_____

_____

10. **Critical Thinking** Two sides of an isosceles triangle have lengths of 6 inches and 15 inches, respectively. Find the length of the third side. Explain your reasoning.

_____

_____

_____

_____

Draw a Triangle

INSTRUCTIONS

Part A: Two Angles Specified

STEP 1   Each member of your group should choose a different row of the table below. You will use the table to draw △ABC with two angles specified.

Triangle Number	Angle A	Angle B	Angle C	Sum of Angle Measures
1	45°	50°		
2	30°	90°		
3	25°	100°		

STEP 2   Using a ruler and protractor, draw and label angle A with your assigned angle measure on a sheet of paper or tracing paper. A sample is shown below.

STEP 3   Mark a separate point B on one side of angle A. Using a protractor, draw and label angle B with your assigned angle measure so that angles A and B form two angles of one triangle.

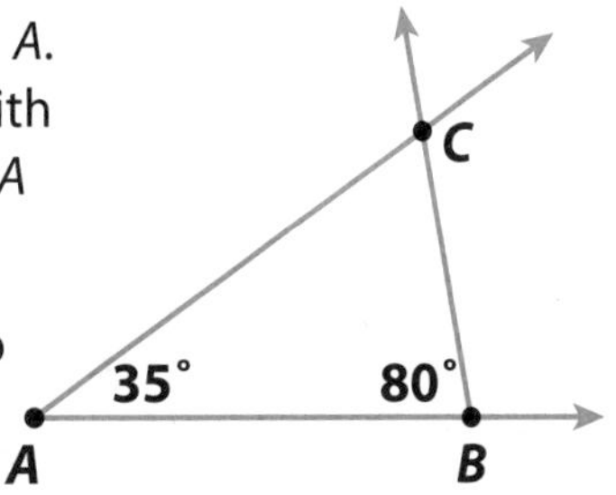

STEP 4   Extend the sides of your angles as needed to complete the triangle at point C. Label the point.

STEP 5   Measure angle C inside the triangle to the nearest degree, and work with your group to complete the remaining columns in your tables. What appears to be true about the sum of the angle measures for each triangle?

STEP 6   Compare the triangles drawn by your group with the triangles drawn by other groups. Does specifying two angles of a triangle determine a unique triangle? Explain.

Part B: Two Angles and a Side Length Specified

STEP 1 Your teacher will assign your group a new △*ABC* and give you two of its angle measures. Record the information below.

Triangle Number	Angle *A*	Angle *B*	Side Length
			5 cm

STEP 2 Each of you will draw a triangle with these angle measures and one side that is 5 cm long. Make sure that $\overline{AB}$ is 5 cm long in one triangle, $\overline{AC}$ is 5 cm long in another, and $\overline{BC}$ is 5 cm long in the third.

STEP 3 Use a protractor and ruler to draw and label your △*ABC* on paper or tracing paper using the assigned angle measures and ensuring that the appropriate side is 5 cm in length. It might help to draw a copy of angle *B* on a separate piece of tracing paper to help guide you, as shown in blue in the example below, where $\overline{AC}$ is 5 cm long.

1) Draw angle *A*.
2) Draw point *C*.
3) Overlay a copy of angle *B* aligned with angle *A* and passing through point *C* as shown to locate point *B*.

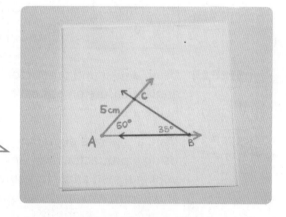

STEP 4 Compare your group's triangles. What do you observe? Did the measures you were given produce a unique triangle?

STEP 5 Find another group that was assigned the same triangle number as your group. Compare your triangles. Did your groups draw six unique triangles? Explain.

STEP 6 Discuss your results as a class. If you are given the measures of two specific angles of a triangle and the length of one specific side, does this determine a unique triangle? Explain.

LESSON
3.3 Cross Sections

COMMON CORE 7.G.3

Describe the two-dimensional figures that result from slicing three-dimensional figures ...

ESSENTIAL QUESTION

How can you identify cross sections of three-dimensional figures?

EXPLORE ACTIVITY 1 | COMMON CORE 7.G.3

Cross Sections of a Right Rectangular Prism

An **intersection** is a point or set of points common to two or more geometric figures. A **cross section** is the intersection of a three-dimensional figure and a plane. Imagine a plane slicing through the pyramid shown, or through a cone or a prism.

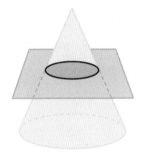

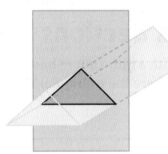

This figure shows the intersection of the cone and a plane. The cross section is a circle.

This figure shows the intersection of a triangular prism and a plane. The cross section is a triangle.

A three-dimensional figure can have several different cross sections depending on the position and the direction of the slice. For example, if the intersection of the plane and cone were vertical, the cross section would form a triangle.

Describe each cross section of the right rectangular prism with the name of its shape. (In a *right* prism, all the sides connecting the bases are rectangles at right angles with the base.)

 A

B

_____   _____

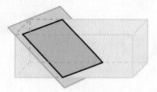

C

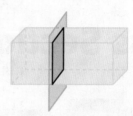

D

_____   _____

Reflect

1. **Conjecture** Is it possible to have a circular cross section in a right rectangular prism?

_____

EXPLORE ACTIVITY 2 COMMON CORE 7.G.3

Describing Cross Sections

A right rectangular pyramid with a non-square base is shown. (In a *right* pyramid, the point where the triangular sides meet is centered over the base.)

A The shape of the base is a _____

The shape of each side is a _____

B Is it possible for a cross section of the pyramid to have each shape?

square   rectangle   triangle   circle   trapezoid

_____   _____   _____   _____   _____

C Sketch the cross sections of the right rectangular pyramid below.

Reflect

2. **What If?** Suppose the figure in **B** had a square base. Would your answers in **B** be the same? Explain.

_____

_____

Math Talk
Mathematical Practices

Describe and compare the cross sections created when two horizontal planes intersect a right rectangular pyramid.

Guided Practice

Describe each cross section.

1.

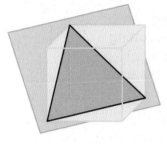

(Explore Activity 1)

_____

2.

(Explore Activity 2)

_____

3.

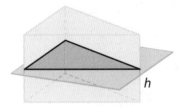

(Explore Activity 2)

_____

4.

(Explore Activity 2)

_____

? ESSENTIAL QUESTION CHECK-IN

5. What is the first step in describing what figure results when a given plane intersects a given three-dimensional figure?

_____

3.3 Independent Practice

Personal Math Trainer

Online Assessment and Intervention

my.hrw.com

COMMON CORE 7.G.3

6. Describe different ways in which a plane might intersect the cylinder, and the cross section that results.

_____

_____

_____

7. Make a Conjecture What cross sections might you see when a plane intersects a cone that you would **not** see when a plane intersects a

pyramid or a prism? _____

Work Area

8. Critical Thinking The two figures on the left below show that you can form a cross section of a cube that is a pentagon. Think of a plane cutting the cube at an angle in such a way as to slice through five of the cube's six faces. Draw dotted lines on the third cube to show how to form a cross section that is a hexagon.

9. Analyze Relationships A sphere has a radius of 12 inches. A horizontal plane passes through the center of the sphere.

a. Describe the cross section formed by the plane and the sphere.

_____

b. Describe the cross sections formed as the plane intersects the interior of the sphere but moves away from the center.

_____

_____

_____

10. Communicate Mathematical Ideas A right rectangular prism is intersected by a horizontal plane and a vertical plane. The cross section formed by the horizontal plane and the prism is a rectangle with dimensions 8 in. and 12 in. The cross section formed by the vertical plane and the prism is a rectangle with dimensions 5 in. and 8 in. Describe the faces of the prism, including their dimensions. Then find its volume.

_____

_____

11. Represent Real-World Problems Describe a real-world situation that could be represented by planes slicing a three-dimensional figure to form cross sections.

_____

_____

_____

3.4 Angle Relationships

COMMON CORE 7.G.5

Use facts about supplementary, complementary, vertical, and adjacent angles in a multi-step problem to write and solve simple equations for an unknown angle in a figure.
Also 7.EE.4a

ESSENTIAL QUESTION

How can you use angle relationships to solve problems?

EXPLORE ACTIVITY　COMMON CORE　Prep. for 7.G.5

Measuring Angles

It is useful to work with pairs of angles and to understand how pairs of angles relate to each other. **Congruent angles** are angles that have the same measure.

STEP 1 Using a ruler, draw a pair of intersecting lines. Label each angle from 1 to 4.

STEP 2 Use a protractor to help you complete the chart.

Angle	Measure of Angle
m∠1	
m∠2	
m∠3	
m∠4	
m∠1 + m∠2	
m∠2 + m∠3	
m∠3 + m∠4	
m∠4 + m∠1	

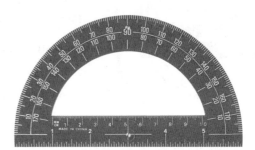

Reflect

1. **Make a Conjecture** Share your results with other students. Make a conjecture about pairs of angles that are opposite each other.

   _____

   _____

2. **Make a Conjecture** When two lines intersect to form four angles, what conjecture can you make about the pairs of angles that are next to each other?

   _____

   _____

Angle Pairs and One-Step Equations

Vertical angles are the opposite angles formed by two intersecting lines. Vertical angles are congruent because the angles have the same measure.

Adjacent angles are pairs of angles that share a *vertex* and one side but do not overlap. The **vertex** of an angle is the point where the sides meet.

Complementary angles are two angles whose measures have a sum of 90°.

Supplementary angles are two angles whose measures have a sum of 180°. You discovered in the Explore Activity that adjacent angles formed by two intersecting lines are supplementary.

EXAMPLE 1

COMMON CORE 7.G.5

Use the diagram.

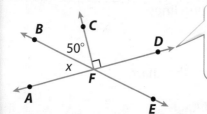

Recall that when multiple angles share a vertex, the angle is named by the vertex and one point on each side of the angle to avoid confusion. So the 50°-angle may be called ∠BFC or ∠CFB.

A **Name a pair of vertical angles.**

Vertical angles are opposite angles formed by intersecting lines.

∠AFB and ∠DFE are vertical angles.

Math Talk
Mathematical Practices

Are ∠BFD and ∠AFE vertical angles? Why or why not?

B **Name a pair of adjacent angles.**

Adjacent angles share a vertex and a side but do not overlap.

∠AFB and ∠BFD are adjacent angles.

C **Name a pair of supplementary angles.**

Adjacent angles formed by intersecting lines are supplementary.

∠AFB and ∠BFD are supplementary angles.

D **Name two pairs of supplementary angles that include ∠DFE.**

Any angle that forms a line with ∠DFE is a supplementary angle to ∠DFE.

∠DFE and ∠EFA are supplementary angles, as are ∠DFE and ∠DFB.

D **Find the measure of ∠AFB.**

Use the fact that ∠AFB and ∠BFD in the diagram are supplementary angles to find m∠AFB.

m∠AFB + m∠BFD = 180°   *They are supplementary angles.*

$\qquad$ x + 140° = 180°   *m∠BFD = 50° + 90° = 140°*

$\qquad$ −140° −140°   *Subtract 140 from both sides.*

$\qquad\qquad$ x = 40°

The measure of ∠AFB is 40°.

Reflect

3. **Analyze Relationships** What is the relationship between ∠AFB and ∠BFC? Explain.

_____

_____

4. **Draw Conclusions** Are ∠AFC and ∠BFC adjacent angles? Why or why not?

_____

_____

YOUR TURN

Use the diagram.

5. Name a pair of supplementary angles.

_____

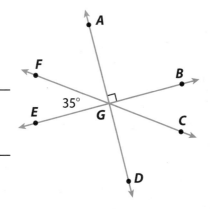

6. Name a pair of vertical angles.

_____

7. Name a pair of adjacent angles.

_____

8. Name a pair of complementary angles.

_____

9. Find the measure of ∠CGD. _____

Personal Math Trainer

Online Assessment and Intervention

⏻ my.hrw.com

Angle Pairs and Two-Step Equations

Sometimes solving an equation is only the first step in using an angle relationship to solve a problem.

My Notes

EXAMPLE 2

COMMON CORE 7.G.5, 7.EE.4a

A Find the measure of ∠EHF.

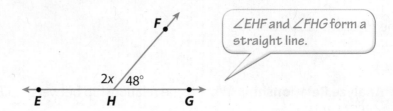

∠EHF and ∠FHG form a straight line.

STEP 1 Identify the relationship between ∠EHF and ∠FHG.

Since angles ∠EHF and ∠FHG form a straight line, the sum of the measures of the angles is 180°.

∠EHF and ∠FHG are supplementary angles.

STEP 2 Write and solve an equation to find x.

$$m\angle EHF + m\angle FHG = 180°$$ The sum of the measures of supplementary angles is 180°.

$$2x + 48° = 180°$$

$$\underline{-48°\quad -48°}$$ Subtract 48 from both sides.

$$2x\qquad = 132°$$ Divide both sides by 2.

$$x = \ 66°$$

STEP 3 Find the measure of ∠EHF.

$$m\angle EHF = 2x$$

$$= 2(66°)$$ Substitute 66° for x.

$$= 132°$$ Multiply.

The measure of ∠EHF is 132°.

Check Confirm that ∠EHF and ∠FHG are supplementary.

$$m\angle EHF + m\angle FHG \stackrel{?}{=} 180°$$

$$132° \ + \ \ \ 48° \stackrel{?}{=} 180°$$

$$180° = 180°$$

B **Find the measure of ∠ZXY.**

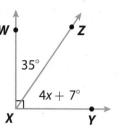

STEP 1 Identify the relationship between ∠WXZ and ∠ZXY.

∠WXZ and ∠ZXY are complementary angles.

STEP 2 Write and solve an equation to find x.

$m\angle WXZ + m\angle ZXY = 90°$ The sum of the measures of complementary angles is 90°.

$4x + 7° + 35° = 90°$ Substitute the values.

$4x + 42° = 90°$ Combine like terms.

$\underline{-42°\quad -42°}$ Subtract 42 from both sides.

$4x \quad\quad = 48°$ Divide both sides by 4.

$x = 12°$

STEP 3 Find the measure of ∠ZXY.

$m\angle ZXY = 4x + 7°$

$= 4(12°) + 7°$ Substitute 12° for x.

$= 55°$ Use the Order of Operations.

The measure of ∠ZXY is 55°.

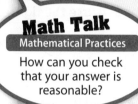

Math Talk

Mathematical Practices

How can you check that your answer is reasonable?

YOUR TURN

10. Write and solve an equation to find the measure of ∠JML.

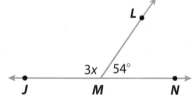

11. Critique Reasoning Cory says that to find m∠JML above, you can stop when you get to the solution step $3x = 126°$. Explain why this works.

_____

_____

_____

For 1–2, use the figure. (Example 1)

1. **Vocabulary** The sum of the measures of ∠UWV and ∠UWZ is 90°, so ∠UWV and ∠UWZ are

   _____ angles.

2. **Vocabulary** ∠UWV and ∠VWX share a vertex and one side. They do not overlap, so ∠UWV and ∠VWX are

   _____ angles.

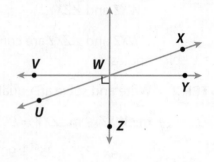

For 3–4, use the figure.

3. ∠AGB and ∠DGE are _____ angles,

   so m∠DGE = _____. (Example 1)

4. Find the measure of ∠EGF. (Example 2)

   m∠CGD + m∠DGE + m∠EGF = 180°

   _____ + _____ + _____ = 180°

   _____ + 2x = 180°

   2x = _____

   m∠EGF = 2x = _____

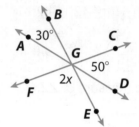

5. Find the value of x and the measure of ∠MNQ. (Example 2)

   m∠MNQ + m∠QNP = 90°

   _____ + _____ = 90°, so 3x + _____ = 90°.

   Then 3x = _____, and x = _____.

   m∠MNQ = 3x − 13° = 3(_____) − 13°

   = _____ − 13°

   = _____

 ESSENTIAL QUESTION CHECK-IN

6. Suppose that you know that ∠T and ∠S are supplementary, and that m∠T = 3(m∠S). How can you find m∠T?

   _____

   _____

3.4 Independent Practice

COMMON CORE 7.G.5

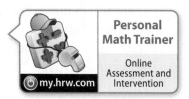

Personal Math Trainer

my.hrw.com — Online Assessment and Intervention

For 7–11, use the figure.

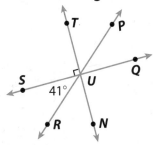

7. Name a pair of adjacent angles. Explain why they are adjacent.

_____

_____

_____

8. Name a pair of acute vertical angles.

_____

9. Name a pair of supplementary angles.

_____

10. Justify Reasoning Find m∠QUR. Justify your answer.

_____

_____

_____

_____

_____

11. Draw Conclusions Which is greater, m∠TUR or m∠RUQ? Explain.

_____

_____

_____

_____

For 12–13, use the figure. A bike path crosses a road as shown. Solve for each indicated angle measure or variable.

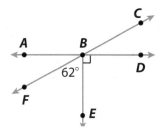

12. x _____

13. m∠KMH _____

For 14–16, use the figure. Solve for each indicated angle measure.

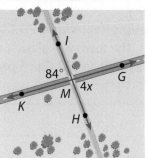

14. m∠CBE _____

15. m∠ABF _____

16. m∠CBA _____

17. The measure of ∠A is 4° greater than the measure of ∠B. The two angles are complementary. Find the measure of each angle.

_____

18. The measure of ∠D is 5 times the measure of ∠E. The two angles are supplementary. Find the measure of each angle.

_____

19. Astronomy Astronomers sometimes use angle measures divided into degrees, minutes, and seconds. One degree is equal to 60 minutes, and one minute is equal to 60 seconds. Suppose that $\angle J$ and $\angle K$ are complementary, and that the measure of $\angle J$ is 48 degrees, 26 minutes, 8 seconds. What is the measure of $\angle K$?

_____

FOCUS ON HIGHER ORDER THINKING

20. Represent Real-World Problems The railroad tracks meet the road as shown. The town will allow a parking lot at angle K if the measure of angle K is greater than 38°. Can a parking lot be built at angle K? Why or why not?

_____

_____

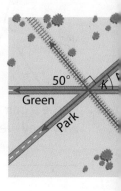

21. Justify Reasoning Kendra says that she can draw $\angle A$ and $\angle B$ so that $m\angle A$ is 119° and $\angle A$ and $\angle B$ are complementary angles. Do you agree or disagree? Explain your reasoning.

_____

_____

_____

_____

Work Area

22. Draw Conclusions If two angles are complementary, each angle is called a *complement* of the other. If two angles are supplementary, each angle is called a *supplement* of the other.

a. Suppose $m\angle A = 77°$. What is the measure of a complement of a complement of $\angle A$? Explain.

_____

_____

_____

b. What conclusion can you draw about a complement of a complement of an angle? Explain.

_____

_____

_____

_____

Ready to Go On?

Personal
Math Trainer

Online Assessment
and Intervention

my.hrw.com

3.1 Similar Shapes and Scale Drawings

1. A house blueprint has a scale of 1 in. : 4 ft. The length and width of each room in the actual house are shown in the table. Complete the table by finding the length and width of each room on the blueprint.

	Living room	Kitchen	Office	Bedroom	Bedroom	Bathroom
Actual $\ell \times w$ (ft)	16×20	12×12	8×12	20×12	12×12	6×8
Blueprint $\ell \times w$ (in.)						

3.2 Geometric Drawings

2. Can a triangle be formed with the side lengths of 8 cm, 4 cm, and 12 cm? _____

3. A triangle has side lengths of 11 cm and 9 cm. Which could be the value of the third side, 20 cm or 15 cm? _____

3.3 Cross Sections

4. Name one possible cross section of a sphere. _____

5. Name at least two shapes that are cross sections of a cylinder.

_____

3.4 Angle Relationships

6. ∠BGC and ∠FGE are _____ angles, so m∠FGE = _____

7. Suppose you know that ∠S and ∠Y are complementary, and

that m∠S = 2(m∠Y) − 30°. Find m∠Y. _____

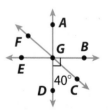

? ESSENTIAL QUESTION

8. How can you model geometry figures to solve real-world problems?

_____

_____

MODULE 3 MIXED REVIEW

COMMON CORE

Assessment Readiness

Personal
Math Trainer

Online
Assessment and
Intervention

my.hrw.com

Selected Response

1. Which number can you add to 15 to get a sum of 0?

Ⓐ −10   Ⓒ 0

Ⓑ −15   Ⓓ 15

2. Students are painting the backdrop for the school play. The backdrop is 15 feet wide and 10 feet high. Every 16 inches on the scale drawing represents 5 feet on the backdrop. What is the area of the scale drawing?

Ⓐ 150 in²   Ⓒ 3,096

Ⓑ 6 in²   Ⓓ 1,536 in²

3. Two sides of a triangle measure 8 cm and 12 cm. Which of the following CANNOT be the measure of the third side?

Ⓐ 4   Ⓒ 8

Ⓑ 12   Ⓓ 16

4. A cross section is the intersection of a three-dimensional figure and a _____.

Ⓐ point   Ⓒ line

Ⓑ plane   Ⓓ set

For 5–6, use the diagram.

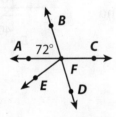

5. What is the measure of ∠BFC?

Ⓐ 18°   Ⓒ 72°

Ⓑ 108°   Ⓓ 144°

6. Which describes the relationship between ∠BFA and ∠CFD?

Ⓐ adjacent angles

Ⓑ complementary angles

Ⓒ supplementary angles

Ⓓ vertical angles

7. All clothing is being marked down 15%. Which expression represents the new retail price?

Ⓐ $0.85x$ Ⓒ $1.85x$

Ⓑ $1.15x$ Ⓓ $0.15x$

Mini-Tasks

8. Ira built a model of the Great Pyramid in Egypt for a school project. The Great Pyramid has a square base with sides of length 756 feet. The height of the Great Pyramid is 481 feet. Ira made his model pyramid using a scale of 1 inch : 20 feet.

a. What is the length of each side of the base of Ira's pyramid?

_____

b. What is the area of the base of Ira's pyramid?

_____

c. What is the height of Ira's pyramid?

_____

d. Ira built his model using cross sections that were cut parallel to the base. What shape was each cross section?

_____

Circumference, Area, and Volume

ESSENTIAL QUESTION

How can you apply geometry concepts to solve real-world problems?

Real-World Video

A 16-inch pizza has a diameter of 16 inches. You can use the diameter to find circumference and area of the pizza. You can also determine how much pizza in one slice of different sizes of pizzas.

my.hrw.com

GO DIGITAL

my.hrw.com

my.hrw.com
Go digital with your write-in student edition, accessible on any device.

Math On the Spot
Scan with your smart phone to jump directly to the online edition, video tutor, and more.

Animated Math
Interactively explore key concepts to see how math works.

Personal Math Trainer
Get immediate feedback and help as you work through practice sets.

Are YOU Ready?

Complete these exercises to review skills you will need for this module.

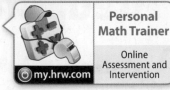
Multiply with Fractions and Decimals

EXAMPLE	
7.3	Multiply as you would with whole numbers.
× 2.4	Count the total number of decimal places in the two factors.
2 9 2	
+1 4 6	Place the decimal point in the product so that there are the
1 7.5 2	same number of digits after the decimal point.

Multiply.

1.   4.16
      × 13

2.   6.47
      × 0.4

3.   7.05
      × 9.4

4.   25.6
      × 0.49

Area of Squares, Rectangles, and Triangles

EXAMPLE

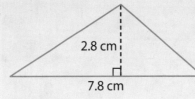

2.8 cm

7.8 cm

$A = \frac{1}{2}bh$ Use the formula for area of a triangle.

$= \frac{1}{2}(7.8)(2.8)$ Substitute for each variable.

$= 10.92 \text{ cm}^2$ Multiply.

Find the area of each figure.

5. triangle with base 14 in. and height 10 in. _____

6. square with sides of 3.5 ft _____

7. rectangle with length $8\frac{1}{2}$ in. and width 6 in. _____

8. triangle with base 12.5 m and height 2.4 m _____

Reading Start-Up

Visualize Vocabulary

Use the ✔ words to complete the graphic. You will put one word in each oval. Then write examples of formulas in each rectangle.

Measuring Geometric Figures

Distance around a two-dimensional figure

Square units covered by a two-dimensional figure

Capacity of a three-dimensional figure

Distance around a _____ is

$P = 2l + 2w$.

Square units covered by a

_____ is

$A = \frac{1}{2} bh$.

Space taken up by a rectangular prism is

$V = lwh$.

Vocabulary

Review Words

✔ area (*área*)

parallelogram (*paralelogramo*)

✔ perimeter (*perímetro*)

prism (*prisma*)

rectangle (*rectángulo*)

square (*cuadrado*)

trapezoid (*trapecio*)

triangle (*triángulo*)

✔ volume (*volumen*)

Preview Words

circumference (*circunferencia*)

composite figure (*figura compuesta*)

diameter (*diámetro*)

radius (*radio*)

Understand Vocabulary

Match the term on the left to the correct expression on the right.

1. _____ circumference

2. _____ diameter

3. _____ radius

A. A line segment that passes through the center of a circle and has endpoints on the circle, or the length of that segment.

B. A line segment with one endpoint at the center of the circle and the other on the circle, or the length of that segment.

C. The distance around a circle.

Active Reading

Four-Corner Fold Before beginning the module, create a four-corner fold to help you organize what you learn. As you study this module, note important ideas, such as vocabulary, properties, and formulas, on the flaps. Use one flap each for circumference, area, surface area, and volume. You can use your FoldNote later to study for tests and complete assignments.

Unpacking the Standards

Understanding the standards and the vocabulary terms in the standards will help you know exactly what you are expected to learn in this module.

COMMON CORE **7.G.6**

Know the formulas for the area and circumference of a circle and use them to solve problems; give an informal derivation of the relationship between the circumference and area of a circle.

Key Vocabulary

circumference *(circunferencia)*
The distance around a circle.

What It Means to You

You will use formulas to solve problems involving the area and circumference of circles.

UNPACKING EXAMPLE 7.G.6

Lily is drawing plans for a circular fountain. The diameter of the fountain is 20 feet. What is the approximate circumference?

$$C = \pi d$$

$$C \approx 3.14 \cdot 20 \quad \text{Substitute.}$$

$$C \approx 62.8$$

The circumference of the fountain is about 62.8 feet.

COMMON CORE **7.G.4**

Solve real-world and mathematical problems involving area, volume and surface area of two- and three-dimensional objects composed of triangles, quadrilaterals, polygons, cubes, and right prisms.

Key Vocabulary

volume *(volumen)*
The number of cubic units inside a three-dimensional solid.

surface area *(área total)*
The sum of the areas of all the surfaces of a three-dimensional solid.

What It Means to You

You will find area, volume and surface area of real-world objects.

UNPACKING EXAMPLE 7.G.4

Find the volume and the surface area of a tissue box before the hole is cut in the top.

The tissue box is a right rectangular prism. The base is $4\frac{3}{8}$ in. by $4\frac{3}{8}$ in. and the height is 5 in.

Use the volume and surface area formulas:

B is the area of the base, h is the height of the box, and P is the perimeter of the base.

$$V = Bh \qquad\qquad\qquad S = 2B + Ph$$
$$= \left(4\frac{3}{8} \cdot 4\frac{3}{8}\right)5 \qquad\qquad = 2\left(4\frac{3}{8} \cdot 4\frac{3}{8}\right) + \left(4 \cdot 4\frac{3}{8}\right)5$$
$$= 95\frac{45}{64} \text{ in}^3 \qquad\qquad = 125\frac{25}{32} \text{ in}^2$$

The volume is $95\frac{45}{64}$ in³ and the surface area is $125\frac{25}{32}$ in².

LESSON
4.1 Circumference

COMMON CORE 7.G.4

Know the formulas for the area and circumference of a circle and use them to solve problems . . . *Also 7.RP.2a*

ESSENTIAL QUESTION

How do you find and use the circumference of a circle?

EXPLORE ACTIVITY COMMON CORE **7.G.4, 7.RP.2a**

Exploring Circumference

A circle is a set of points in a plane that are a fixed distance from the center.

A **radius** is a line segment with one endpoint at the center of the circle and the other endpoint on the circle. The length of a radius is called the radius of the circle.

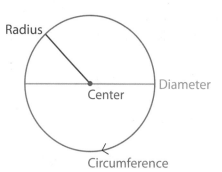

A **diameter** of a circle is a line segment that passes through the center of the circle and whose endpoints lie on the circle. The length of the diameter is twice the length of the radius. The length of a diameter is called the diameter of the circle.

The **circumference** of a circle is the distance around the circle.

A **Use a measuring tape to find the circumference of five circular objects. Then measure the distance across each item to find its diameter. Record the measurements of each object in the table.**

Object	Circumference C	Diameter d	$\frac{C}{d}$

B **Divide the circumference of each object by its diameter. Record your answer, rounded to the nearest hundredth, in the table above.**

Reflect

1. **Make a Conjecture** Describe what you notice about the ratio $\frac{C}{d}$ in your table. Does the relationship between the circumference and diameter of a circle appear to be proportional? Explain.

_____

_____

Finding Circumference

The ratio of the circumference to the diameter $\frac{C}{d}$ is the same for all circles. This ratio is called π or *pi*, and you can approximate it as 3.14 or as $\frac{22}{7}$. You can use π to find a formula for circumference.

For any circle, $\frac{C}{d} = \pi$. Solve the equation for C to give an equation for the circumference of a circle in terms of the diameter.

$$\frac{C}{d} = \pi \qquad \text{The ratio of the circumference to the diameter is } \pi.$$

$$\frac{C}{d} \times d = \pi \times d \qquad \text{Multiply both sides by } d.$$

$$C = \pi d \qquad \text{Simplify.}$$

The diameter of a circle is twice the radius. You can use the equation $C = \pi d$ to find a formula for the circumference C in terms of the radius r.

$$C = \pi d = \pi(2r) = 2\pi r$$

The two equivalent formulas for circumference are $C = \pi d$ and $C = 2\pi r$. These are proportional relationships. The constants of proportionality are π and 2π.

EXAMPLE 1

COMMON CORE 7.G.4

An irrigation sprinkler waters a circular region with a radius of 14 feet. Find the circumference of the region watered by the sprinkler. Use $\frac{22}{7}$ for π.

Use the formula.

$C = 2\pi r$ ⟵ The radius is 14 feet.

$C = 2\pi(14)$ Substitute 14 for r.

$C \approx 2\left(\frac{22}{7}\right)(14)$ Substitute $\frac{22}{7}$ for π.

$C \approx 88$ Multiply.

14 ft

The circumference of the region watered by the sprinkler is about 88 feet.

Reflect

2. **Analyze Relationships** When is it logical to use $\frac{22}{7}$ instead of 3.14 for π?

_____

 **YOUR TURN**

3. Find the circumference of the circle to the nearest hundredth.

_____

11 cm

Using Circumference

Given the circumference of a circle, you can use the appropriate circumference formula to find the radius or the diameter of the circle. You can use that information to solve problems.

Math On the Spot
my.hrw.com

EXAMPLE 2   COMMON CORE 7.G.4

A circular pond has a circumference of 628 feet. A model boat is moving directly across the pond, along a radius, at a rate of 5 feet per second. How long does it take the boat to get from the edge of the pond to the center?

My Notes

STEP 1 Find the radius of the pond.

$C = 2\pi r$	Use the circumference formula.
$628 \approx 2(3.14)r$	Substitute for the circumference and for π.
$\dfrac{628}{6.28} \approx \dfrac{6.28r}{6.28}$	Divide both sides by 6.28.
$100 \approx r$	Simplify.

C = 628 ft

$r = ?$ ft

The radius is about 100 feet.

STEP 2 Find the time it takes the boat to get from the edge of the pond to the center along the radius. Divide the radius of the pond by the speed of the model boat.

$$100 \div 5 = 20$$

It takes the boat about 20 seconds to get to the center of the pond.

Reflect

4. **Analyze Relationships** Dante checks the answer to Step 1 by multiplying it by 6 and comparing it with the given circumference. Explain why Dante's estimation method works. Use it to check Step 1.

_____

5. **What If?** Suppose the model boat were traveling at a rate of 4 feet per second. How long would it take the model boat to

get from the edge of the pond to the center? _____

Math Talk
Mathematical Practices

Would it be reasonable to solve Your Turn 6 using $\frac{22}{7}$ for π? Explain.

6. A circular garden has a circumference of 44 yards. Lars is digging a straight line along a diameter of the garden at a rate of 7 yards per hour. How many hours will it take him to dig across the garden?

_____

Personal Math Trainer

Online Assessment and Intervention

my.hrw.com

Find the circumference of each circle. (Example 1)

1. $C = \pi d$

9 in.

$C \approx$ _____

$C \approx$ _____ inches

2. $C = 2\pi r$

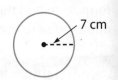
7 cm

$C \approx 2\left(\frac{22}{7}\right)$ (_____)

$C \approx$ _____ cm

Find the circumference of each circle. Use 3.14 or $\frac{22}{7}$ for π. Round to the nearest hundredth, if necessary. (Example 1)

3.

25 m

_____

4.

4.8 yd

_____

5.

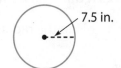
7.5 in.

_____

6. A round swimming pool has a circumference of 66 feet. Carlos wants to buy a rope to put across the diameter of the pool. The rope costs $0.45 per foot, and Carlos needs 4 feet more than the diameter of the pool. How much will Carlos pay for the rope? (Example 2)

Find the diameter.

$C = \pi d$

_____ $\approx 3.14d$

$\dfrac{\boxed{}}{3.14} \approx \dfrac{3.14d}{3.14}$

_____ $\approx d$

Find the cost.

Carlos needs _____ feet of rope.

_____ $\times \$0.45 =$ _____

Carlos will pay _____ for the rope.

Find each missing measurement to the nearest hundredth. Use 3.14 for π. (Examples 1 and 2)

7. $r =$ _____

$d =$ _____

$C = \pi$ yd

8. $r \approx$ _____

$d \approx$ _____

$C = 78.8$ ft

9. $r \approx$ _____

$d \approx 3.4$ in.

$C =$ _____

? ESSENTIAL QUESTION CHECK-IN

10. Norah knows that the diameter of a circle is 13 meters. How would you tell her to find the circumference?

_____

_____

4.1 Independent Practice

COMMON CORE 7.G.4

Personal Math Trainer

Online Assessment and Intervention

my.hrw.com

For 11–13, find the circumference of each circle. Use 3.14 or $\frac{22}{7}$ for π. Round to the nearest hundredth, if necessary.

11.

5.9 ft

_____

12.

56 cm

_____

13.

35 in.

_____

14. In Exercises 11–13, for which problems did you use $\frac{22}{7}$ for π? Explain your choice.

_____

_____

_____

15. A circular fountain has a radius of 9.4 feet. Find its diameter and circumference to the nearest tenth.

_____

16. Find the radius and circumference of a CD with a diameter of 4.75 inches.

_____

17. A dartboard has a diameter of 18 inches. What are its radius and circumference?

_____

18. **Multistep** Randy's circular garden has a radius of 1.5 feet. He wants to enclose the garden with edging that costs $0.75 per foot. About how much will the edging cost? Explain.

_____

_____

19. **Represent Real-World Problems** The Ferris wheel shown makes 12 revolutions per ride. How far would someone travel during one ride?

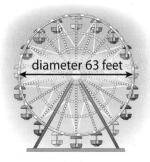

diameter 63 feet

_____

20. The diameter of a bicycle wheel is 2 feet. About how many revolutions does the wheel make to travel 2 kilometers? Explain. Hint: 1 km ≈ 3,280 ft

_____

_____

_____

21. **Multistep** A map of a public park shows a circular pond. There is a bridge along a diameter of the pond that is 0.25 mi long. You walk across the bridge, while your friend walks halfway around the pond to meet you at the other side of the bridge. How much farther does your friend walk?

_____

22. Architecture The Capitol Rotunda connects the House and the Senate sides of the U.S. Capitol. Complete the table. Round your answers to the nearest foot.

Capitol Rotunda Dimensions	
Height	180 ft
Circumference	301.5 ft
Radius	
Diameter	

 FOCUS ON HIGHER ORDER THINKING

Work Area

23. Multistep A museum groundskeeper is creating a semicircular statuary garden with a diameter of 30 feet. There will be a fence around the garden. The fencing costs $9.25 per linear foot. About how much will the fencing cost altogether?

_____

24. Critical Thinking Sam is placing rope lights around the edge of a circular patio with a diameter of 18 feet. The lights come in lengths of 54 inches. How many strands of lights does he need to surround the patio edge?

_____

25. Represent Real-World Problems A circular path 2 feet wide has an inner diameter of 150 feet. How much farther is it around the outer edge of the path than around the inner edge?

_____

26. Critique Reasoning Two gears on a bicycle have the shape of circles. Gear 1 has a diameter of 4 inches, and gear 2 has a diameter of 2 inches. Justin says that the circumference of gear 1 is 2 inches more than the circumference of gear 2. Do you agree? Explain your answer using proportional reasoning.

_____

_____

_____

_____

27. Persevere in Problem Solving Consider two circular swimming pools. Pool A has a radius of 12 feet, and Pool B has a diameter of 7.5 meters. Which pool has a greater circumference? How much greater? Justify your answers. (Use 1 foot ≈ 0.305 meter.)

_____

_____

_____

_____

4.2 Area of Circles

COMMON CORE 7.G.4

Know the formulas for the area and circumference of a circle and use them to solve problems; give an informal derivation of the relationship between the circumference and area of a circle. *Also 7.EE.2*

ESSENTIAL QUESTION

How do you find the area of a circle?

EXPLORE ACTIVITY 1 7.G.4

Exploring Area of Circles

You can use what you know about circles and π to help find the formula for the area of a circle.

STEP 1 Use a compass to draw a circle and cut it out.

STEP 2 Fold the circle three times as shown to get equal wedges.

STEP 3 Unfold and shade one-half of the circle.

STEP 4 Cut out the wedges, and fit the pieces together to form a figure that looks like a parallelogram.

The base and height of the parallelogram relate to the parts of the circle.

base $b = \dfrac{\square}{\square}$ the circumference of the circle, or _____

Radius

Half the circumference

height $h =$ the _____ of the circle, or _____

Recall that the area A of a parallelogram is given by the formula $A = bh$. To find the area of the circle, substitute for b and h in the area formula.

$A = bh$

$A = \boxed{}\, h$ *Substitute for b.*

$A = \pi r \boxed{}$ *Substitute for h.*

$A = \pi \boxed{}$ *Write using an exponent.*

Reflect

1. How can you make the wedges look more like a parallelogram?

_____

_____

Math On the Spot

my.hrw.com

Finding the Area of a Circle

Area of a Circle

The area of a circle is equal to π times the radius squared.

$$A = \pi r^2$$

Remember that area is given in square units.

EXAMPLE 1

COMMON CORE 7.G.4

A biscuit recipe calls for the dough to be rolled out and circles to be cut from the dough. The biscuit cutter has a radius of 4 cm. Find the area of the top of the biscuit once it is cut. Use 3.14 for π.

$A = \pi r^2$	Use the formula.
$A = \pi(4)^2$	Substitute. Use 4 for r.
$A \approx 3.14 \times 4^2$	Substitute. Use 3.14 for π.
$A \approx 3.14 \times 16$	Evaluate the power.
$A \approx 50.24$	Multiply.

Math Talk

Mathematical Practices

If the radius increases by 1 centimeter, how does the area of the top of the biscuit change?

The area of the biscuit is about 50.24 cm².

Reflect

2. Compare finding the area of a circle when given the radius with finding the area when given the diameter.

_____

_____

_____

3. Why do you evaluate the power in the equation before multiplying by π?

_____

_____

Personal Math Trainer

Online Assessment and Intervention

my.hrw.com

YOUR TURN

4. A circular pool has a radius of 10 feet. What is the area of the *surface* of the water in the pool? Use 3.14 for π. _____

COMMON CORE 7.G.4, 7.EE.2

Finding the Relationship between Circumference and Area

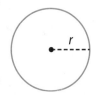

You can use what you know about circumference and area of circles to find a relationship between them.

Find the relationship between the circumference and area of a circle.

Start with a circle that has radius r.

Solve the equation $C = 2\pi r$ for r.

$$r = \dfrac{\boxed{}}{\boxed{}}$$

Substitute your expression for r in the formula for area of a circle.

$$A = \pi\left(\dfrac{\boxed{}}{\boxed{}}\right)^2$$

> Remember: Because the exponent is outside the parentheses, you must apply it to the numerator and to each factor of the denominator.

Square the term in the parentheses.

$$A = \pi\left(\dfrac{\boxed{}^2}{\boxed{}^2 \cdot \boxed{}^2}\right)$$

Evaluate the power.

$$A = \dfrac{\boxed{} \cdot \boxed{}^2}{\boxed{} \cdot \boxed{}^2}$$

Simplify.

$$A = \dfrac{\boxed{}^2}{\boxed{} \cdot \boxed{}}$$

Solve for C^2.

$$C^2 = 4\,\boxed{}\,\boxed{}$$

The circumference of the circle squared is equal to

_____.

Reflect

5. Does this formula work for a circle with a radius of 3 inches? Show your work.

Guided Practice

Find the area of each circle. Round to the nearest tenth if necessary. Use 3.14 for π.
(Explore Activity 1)

1.

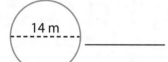

14 m _____

2.

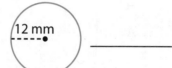

12 mm _____

3.

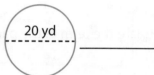

20 yd _____

Solve. Use 3.14 for π. (Example 1)

4. A clock face has a radius of 8 inches. What is the area of the clock face? Round your answer to the nearest hundredth. _____

5. A DVD has a diameter of 12 centimeters. What is the area of the DVD? Round your answer to the nearest hundredth. _____

6. A company makes steel lids that have a diameter of 13 inches. What is the area of each lid? Round your answer to the nearest hundredth. _____

Find the area of each circle. Give your answers in terms of π.
(Explore Activity 2)

7. $C = 4\pi$

$A =$ _____

8. $C = 12\pi$

$A =$ _____

9. $C = \dfrac{\pi}{2}$

$A =$ _____

10. A circular pen has an area of 64π square yards. What is the circumference of the pen? Give your answer in terms of π.
(Explore Activity 2) _____

 ESSENTIAL QUESTION CHECK-IN

11. What is the formula for the area A of a circle in terms of the radius r? _____

4.2 Independent Practice

COMMON CORE 7.G.4

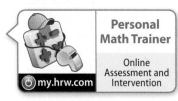

Personal Math Trainer

my.hrw.com

Online Assessment and Intervention

12. The most popular pizza at Pavone's Pizza is the 10-inch personal pizza with one topping. What is the area of a pizza with a diameter of 10 inches? Round your answer to the nearest hundredth.

_____

13. A hubcap has a radius of 16 centimeters. What is the area of the hubcap? Round your answer to the nearest hundredth.

16 cm

_____

14. A stained glass window is shaped like a semicircle. The bottom edge of the window is 36 inches long. What is the area of the stained glass window? Round your answer to the nearest hundredth.

_____

15. **Analyze Relationships** The point (3, 0) lies on a circle with the center at the origin. What is the area of the circle to the nearest hundredth?

_____

16. **Multistep** A radio station broadcasts a signal over an area with a radius of 50 miles. The station can relay the signal and broadcast over an area with a radius of 75 miles. How much greater is the area of the broadcast region when the signal is relayed? Round your answer to the nearest square mile.

_____

17. **Multistep** The sides of a square field are 12 meters. A sprinkler in the center of the field sprays a circular area with a diameter that corresponds to a side of the field. How much of the field is **not** reached by the sprinkler? Round your answer to the nearest hundredth.

_____

18. **Justify Reasoning** A small silver dollar pancake served at a restaurant has a circumference of 2π inches. A regular pancake has a circumference of 4π inches. Is the area of the regular pancake twice the area of the silver dollar pancake? Explain.

_____

_____

_____

_____

_____

_____

19. **Analyze Relationships** A bakery offers a small circular cake with a diameter of 8 inches. It also offers a large circular cake with a diameter of 24 inches. Does the top of the large cake have three times the area of that of the small cake? If not, how much greater is its area? Explain.

_____

_____

_____

_____

_____

20. Communicate Mathematical Ideas You can use the formula $A = \frac{C^2}{4\pi}$ to find the area of a circle given the circumference. Describe another way to find the area of a circle when given the circumference.

_____

_____

_____

21. Draw Conclusions Mark wants to order a pizza. Which is the better deal? Explain.

Donnie's Pizza Palace		
Diameter (in.)	12	18
Cost ($)	10	20

_____

_____

_____

22. Multistep A bear was seen near a campground. Searchers were dispatched to the region to find the bear.

a. Assume the bear can walk in any direction at a rate of 2 miles per hour. Suppose the bear was last seen 4 hours ago. How large an area must the searchers cover? Use 3.14 for π. Round your answer to the

nearest square mile. _____

b. What If? How much additional area would the searchers have to

cover if the bear were last seen 5 hours ago? _____

H.O.T. FOCUS ON HIGHER ORDER THINKING

Work Area

23. Analyze Relationships Two circles have the same radius. Is the combined area of the two circles the same as the area of a circle with twice the radius? Explain.

_____

_____

24. Look for a Pattern How does the area of a circle change if the radius is multiplied by a factor of n, where n is a whole number? Explain.

_____

_____

25. Represent Real World Problems The bull's-eye on a target has a diameter of 3 inches. The whole target has a diameter of 15 inches. What part of the whole target is the bull's-eye? Explain.

_____

LESSON 4.3 Area of Composite Figures

COMMON CORE 7.G.6

Solve real-world and mathematical problems involving area, ... of ... objects composed of triangles, quadrilaterals, polygons, ...

ESSENTIAL QUESTION

How do you find the area of composite figures?

EXPLORE ACTIVITY **COMMON CORE** 7.G.6

Exploring Areas of Composite Figures

Aaron was plotting the shape of his garden on grid paper. While it was an irregular shape, it was perfect for his yard. Each square on the grid represents 1 square meter.

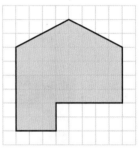

A Describe one way you can find the area of this garden.

_____

_____

_____

B The area of the garden is _____ square meters.

C Compare your results with other students. What other methods were used to find the area?

_____

_____

_____

D How does the area you found compare with the area found using different methods?

_____

Reflect

1. Use dotted lines to show two different ways Aaron's garden could be divided up into simple geometric figures.

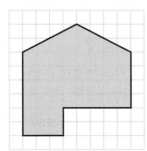
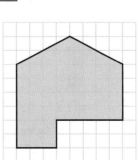

Lesson 4.3 **111**

Finding the Area of a Composite Figure

A composite figure is made up of simple geometric shapes. To find the area of a composite figure or other irregular-shaped figure, divide it into simple, nonoverlapping figures. Find the area of each simpler figure, and then add the areas together to find the total area of the composite figure.

Use the chart below to review some common area formulas.

Shape	Area Formula
triangle	$A = \frac{1}{2}bh$
square	$A = s^2$
rectangle	$A = \ell w$
parallelogram	$A = bh$
trapezoid	$A = \frac{1}{2}h(b_1 + b_2)$

EXAMPLE 1

COMMON CORE 7.G.6

Find the area of the figure.

STEP 1 Separate the figure into smaller, familiar figures: a parallelogram and a trapezoid.

10 cm
3 cm 1.5 cm
4 cm 1.5 cm 2 cm
7 cm

STEP 2 Find the area of each shape.

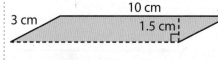

Area of the Parallelogram

10 cm
3 cm 1.5 cm

base = 10 cm

height = 1.5 cm

Use the formula.

$A = bh$

$A = 10 \cdot 1.5$

$A = 15$

The area of the parallelogram is 15 cm².

Area of the Trapezoid

4 cm 1.5 cm 2 cm
7 cm

base₁ = 7 cm   base₂ = 10 cm

$\text{base}_1 = 7 \text{ cm}$ $\text{base}_2 = 10 \text{ cm}$

height 1.5 cm

Use the formula.

$A = \frac{1}{2}h(b_1 + b_2)$

$A = \frac{1}{2}(1.5)(7 + 10)$

$A = \frac{1}{2}(1.5)(17) = 12.75$

The area of the trapezoid is 12.75 cm².

> The top base of the trapezoid is 10 cm since it is the same length as the base o the parallelogram.

STEP 3 Add the areas to find the total area.

$A = 15 + 12.75 = 27.75 \text{ cm}^2$

The area of the figure is 27.75 cm².

YOUR TURN

Find the area of each figure. Use 3.14 for π.

2.

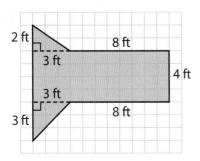

2 ft
8 ft
3 ft
4 ft
3 ft
8 ft
3 ft

3.

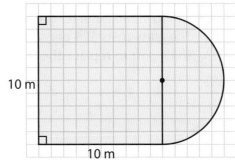

10 m
10 m

_____

_____

Personal Math Trainer

Online Assessment and Intervention

⏻ my.hrw.com

Using Area to Solve Problems

EXAMPLE 2 Real World

COMMON CORE 7.G.6

Math On the Spot

⏻ my.hrw.com

A banquet room is being carpeted. A floor plan of the room is shown at right. Each unit represents 1 yard. The carpet costs $23.50 per square yard. How much will it cost to carpet the room?

STEP 1 Separate the composite figure into simpler shapes as shown by the dashed lines: a parallelogram, a rectangle, and a triangle.

STEP 2 Find the area of the simpler figures. Count units to find the dimensions.

Parallelogram	Rectangle	Triangle
$A = bh$	$A = \ell w$	$A = \frac{1}{2}bh$
$A = 4 \cdot 2$	$A = 6 \cdot 4$	$A = \frac{1}{2}(1)(2)$
$A = 8 \text{ yd}^2$	$A = 24 \text{ yd}^2$	$A = 1 \text{ yd}^2$

Math Talk
Mathematical Practices

Describe how you can estimate the cost to carpet the room.

STEP 3 Find the area of the composite figure.

$A = 8 + 24 + 1 = 33$ square yards

STEP 4 Calculate the cost to carpet the room.

Area · Cost per yard = Total cost

33 · $23.50 = $775.50

The cost to carpet the banquet room is $775.50.

4. A window is being replaced with tinted glass. The plan at the right shows the design of the window. Each unit length represents 1 foot. The glass costs $28 per square foot. How much will it cost to replace the glass? Use 3.14 for π.

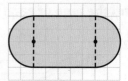

_____

Guided Practice

1. A tile installer plots an irregular shape on grid paper. Each square on the grid represents 1 square centimeter. What is the area of the irregular shape? (Explore Activity, Example 2)

   STEP 1 Separate the figure into a triangle, a _____, and a parallelogram.

   STEP 2 Find the area of each figure.

   triangle: ____ cm²; rectangle: ____ cm²; parallelogram: ____ cm²

   STEP 3 Find the area of the composite figure: ____ + ____ + ____ = ____ cm²

   The area of the irregular shape is ____ cm².

2. Show two different ways to divide the composite figure. Find the area both ways. Show your work below. (Example 1)

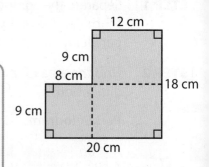

3. Sal is tiling his entryway. The floor plan is drawn on a unit grid. Each unit length represents 1 foot. Tile costs $2.25 per square foot. How much will Sal pay to tile his entryway? (Example 2)

   _____

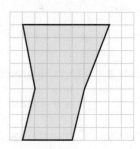

❓ ESSENTIAL QUESTION CHECK-IN

4. What is the first step in finding the area of a composite figure?

   _____

4.3 Independent Practice

COMMON CORE 7.G.6

Personal Math Trainer

Online Assessment and Intervention

my.hrw.com

5. A banner is made of a square and a semicircle. The square has side lengths of 26 inches. One side of the square is also the diameter of the semicircle. What is the total area of the banner? Use 3.14 for π.

_____

6. Multistep Erin wants to carpet the floor of her closet. A floor plan of the closet is shown.

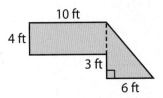

10 ft

4 ft

3 ft

6 ft

a. How much carpet does Erin need?

_____

b. The carpet Erin has chosen costs $2.50 per square foot. How much will it cost her to carpet the floor?

_____

7. Multiple Representations Hexagon ABCDEF has vertices $A(-2, 4)$, $B(0, 4)$, $C(2, 1)$, $D(5, 1)$, $E(5, -2)$, and $F(-2, -2)$. Sketch the figure on a coordinate plane. What is the area of the hexagon?

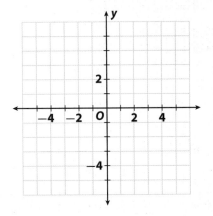

8. A field is shaped like the figure shown. What is the area of the field? Use 3.14 for π.

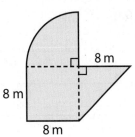

8 m

8 m

8 m

_____

9. A bookmark is shaped like a rectangle with a semicircle attached at both ends. The rectangle is 12 cm long and 4 cm wide. The diameter of each semicircle is the width of the rectangle. What is the area of the bookmark? Use 3.14 for π.

_____

10. Multistep Alex is making 12 pennants for the school fair. The pattern he is using to make the pennants is shown in the figure. The fabric for the pennants costs $1.25 per square foot. How much will it cost Alex to make 12 pennants?

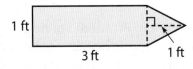

1 ft

3 ft

1 ft

_____

11. Reasoning A composite figure is formed by combining a square and a triangle. Its total area is 32.5 ft². The area of the triangle is 7.5 ft². What is the length of each side of the square? Explain.

_____

_____

_____

_____

12. Represent Real-World Problems Christina plotted the shape of her garden on graph paper. She estimates that she will get about 15 carrots from each square unit. She plans to use the entire garden for carrots. About how many carrots can she expect to grow? Explain.

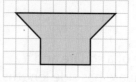

_____

_____

_____

13. Analyze Relationships The figure shown is made up of a triangle and a square. The perimeter of the figure is 56 inches. What is the area of the figure? Explain.

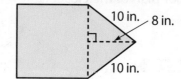

10 in. 8 in.

10 in.

_____

_____

_____

_____

14. Critical Thinking The pattern for a scarf is shown at right. What is the area of the scarf? Use 3.14 for π.

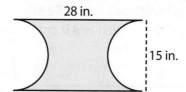

28 in.

15 in.

_____

15. Persevere in Problem Solving The design for the palladium window shown includes a semicircular shape at the top. The bottom is formed by squares of equal size. A shade for the window will extend 4 inches beyond the perimeter of the window, shown by the dashed line around the window. Each square in the window has an area of 100 in².

a. What is the area of the window? Use 3.14 for π.

_____

b. What is the area of the shade? Round your answer to the nearest whole number.

_____

Solving Surface Area Problems

COMMON CORE   7.G.6

Solve real-world and mathematical problems involving ... surface area of ... three-dimensional objects composed of ... cubes, and right prisms. *Also 7.EE.2*

ESSENTIAL QUESTION

How can you find the surface area of a figure made up of cubes and prisms?

EXPLORE ACTIVITY   **COMMON CORE**   7.G.6, 7.EE.2

Modeling Surface Area of a Prism

The surface area of a three-dimensional figure is the sum of the areas of all its surfaces. You know how to use the net of a figure to find its surface area. Now you will discover a formula that you can use.

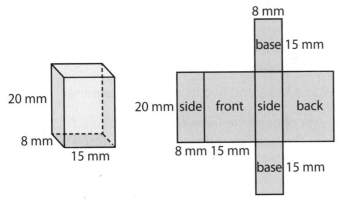

A The lateral area *L* of a prism is the area of all faces except the bases.

$L = 2(\underline{\hspace{2cm}}) + 2(\underline{\hspace{2cm}}) = \underline{\hspace{2cm}}$.

B The area *B* of each base is \underline{\hspace{3cm}}.

C The surface area *S* of the prism is the sum of the lateral area *L* and the

total area of the bases, or \underline{\hspace{3cm}}.

Reflect

1. **Analyze Relationships** Use the net above.

   a. How does the product of the perimeter *P* of the base of the prism and the height *h* of the prism compare to the lateral area *L*?   \underline{\hspace{3cm}}

   b. How can you express the surface area *S* of the prism in terms of *P*, *h*, and *B*?   \underline{\hspace{3cm}}

2. A cube is a rectangular prism with six identical square faces. Rewrite your equation from **1b** for a cube with edge length *e*. Write the expression for the surface area in simplified form.   \underline{\hspace{3cm}}

Finding the Surface Area of a Prism

Given a prism's dimensions, you can use a formula to find the surface area.

Surface Area of a Prism

The surface area S of a prism with base perimeter P, height h, and base area B is $S = Ph + 2B$.

EXAMPLE 1 Real World

COMMON CORE 7.G.6

Erin is making a jewelry box of wood in the shape of a rectangular prism. The jewelry box will have the dimensions shown. She plans to spray paint the exterior of the box. How many square inches will she have to paint?

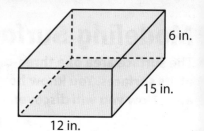

6 in.

15 in.

12 in.

STEP 1 Make a sketch of the box. Drawing a diagram helps you understand and solve the problem.

STEP 2 Identify a base, and find its area and perimeter.

Any pair of opposite faces can be the bases. For example, you can choose the bottom and top of the box as the bases.

$B = \ell \times w$ 　　　　　　　$P = 2(12) + 2(15)$

　$= 12 \times 15$ 　　　　　　　$= 24 + 30$

　$= 180$ square inches 　　　$= 54$ inches

STEP 3 Identify the height, and find the surface area.

The height h of the prism is 6 inches. Use the formula to find the surface area.

$S = Ph + 2B$

$S = 54(6) + 2(180) = 684$ square inches

Erin will have to spray paint 684 square inches of wood.

Math Talk
Mathematical Practices

How can you express the formula for the surface area S of a rectangular prism in terms of its dimensions ℓ, w, and h?

YOUR TURN

3. A brand of uncooked spaghetti comes in a box that is a rectangular prism with a length of 9 inches, a width of 2 inches, and a height of $1\frac{1}{2}$ inches.

What is the surface area of the box? _____

Finding the Surface Area of a Composite Solid

A composite solid is made up of two or more solid figures. To find the surface area of a composite solid, find the surface area of each figure. Subtract any area not on the surface.

Math On the Spot
my.hrw.com

EXAMPLE 2 *Problem Solving* COMMON CORE 7.G.6

Daniel built the birdhouse shown. What was the surface area of the birdhouse before the hole was drilled?

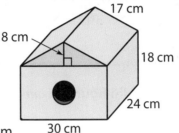

Analyze Information

Identify the important information.

- The top is a triangular prism with $h = 24$ cm. The base is a triangle with height 8 cm and base 30 cm.
- The bottom is a rectangular prism with $h = 18$ cm. The base is a 30 cm by 24 cm rectangle.
- One face of each prism is not on the surface of the figure.

Formulate a Plan

Find the surface area of each prism.

Add the surface areas. Subtract the areas of the parts not on the surface.

Solve

Find the surface area of the triangular prism.

Perimeter $= 17 + 17 + 30 = 64$ cm; Base area $= \frac{1}{2}(30)(8) = 120$ cm²

Surface area $= Ph + 2B$

$= 64(24) + 2(120) = 1{,}776$ cm²

Find the surface area of the rectangular prism.

Perimeter $= 2(30) + 2(24) = 108$ cm; Base area $= 30(24) = 720$ cm²

Surface area $= Ph + 2B$

$= 108(18) + 2(720) = 3{,}384$ cm²

Add. Then subtract the areas of the parts not on the surface.

Surface area $= 1{,}776 + 3{,}384 - 2(720) = 3{,}720$ cm²

The surface area before the hole was drilled was 3,720 cm².

Math Talk
Mathematical Practices

How could you find the surface area by letting the front and back of the prism be the bases?

Justify and Evaluate

You can check your work by using a net to find the surface areas.

YOUR TURN

4. Dara is building a plant stand. She wants to stain the plant stand, except for the bottom of the larger prism. Find the surface area of the part of the plant stand she will stain. _____

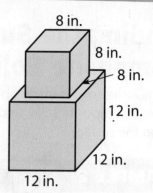

8 in.
8 in.
8 in.
12 in.
12 in.
12 in.

Guided Practice

Find the surface area of each solid figure. (Examples 1 and 2)

1.

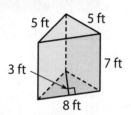

5 ft   5 ft
3 ft   7 ft
8 ft

Perimeter of base = _____

Height = _____

Base area = _____

Surface area:

S = (_____)(_____) + 2(_____)

= _____

2.

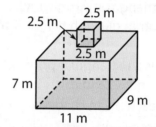

2.5 m   2.5 m
2.5 m
7 m
9 m
11 m

Surface area of cube:

S = _____

Surface area of rectangular prism:

S = _____

Overlapping area: A = _____

Surface area of composite figure:

= _____ + _____ − 2 (_____) =

_____ m²

? ESSENTIAL QUESTION CHECK-IN

3. How can you find the surface area of a composite solid made up of prisms?

_____

_____

_____

4.4 Independent Practice

 COMMON CORE 7.G.6

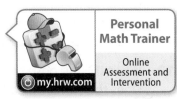

Personal Math Trainer

Online Assessment and Intervention

my.hrw.com

4. Carla is wrapping a present in the box shown. How much wrapping paper does she need, not including overlap?

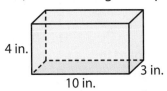

4 in.
10 in.
3 in.

_____

5. Dmitri wants to cover the top and sides of the box shown with glass tiles that are 5 mm square. How many tiles does he need?

9 cm
20 cm
15 cm

_____

6. Shera is building a cabinet. She is making wooden braces for the corners of the cabinet. Find the surface area of each brace.

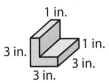

1 in.
3 in.
1 in.
3 in.
3 in.

_____

7. The doghouse shown has a floor, but no windows. Find the total surface area of the doghouse, including the door.

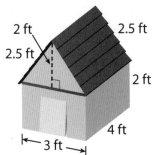

2 ft
2.5 ft
2.5 ft
2 ft
4 ft
3 ft

_____

Eddie built the ramp shown to train his puppy to do tricks. Use the figure for 8–9.

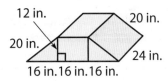

12 in.
20 in.
20 in.
24 in.
16 in. 16 in. 16 in.

8. **Analyze Relationships** Describe two ways to find the surface area of the ramp.

_____

_____

_____

_____

9. What is the surface area of the ramp?

_____

Marco and Elaine are building a stand like the one shown to display trophies. Use the figure for 10–11.

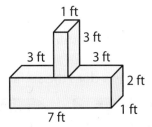

1 ft
3 ft
3 ft
3 ft
2 ft
7 ft
1 ft

10. What is the surface area of the stand?

_____

11. **Critique Reasoning** Marco and Elaine want to paint the entire stand silver. A can of paint covers 25 square feet and costs $6.79. They set aside $15 for paint. Is that enough? Explain.

_____

_____

12. Henry wants to cover the box shown with paper without any overlap. How many square centimeters will be covered with paper?

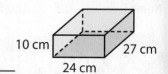

10 cm   27 cm   24 cm

_____

13. **What If?** Suppose the length and width of the box in Exercise 12 double. Does the surface area S double? Explain.

_____

 **FOCUS ON HIGHER ORDER THINKING**

14. **Persevere in Problem Solving** Enya is building a storage cupboard in the shape of a rectangular prism. The rectangular prism has a square base with side lengths of 2.5 feet and a height of 3.5 feet. Compare the amount of paint she would use to paint all but the bottom surface of the prism to the amount she would use to paint the entire prism.

_____

_____

_____

15. **Interpret the Answer** The oatmeal box shown is shaped like a cylinder. Use a net to find the surface area S of the oatmeal box to the nearest tenth. Then find the number of square feet of cardboard needed for 1,500 oatmeal boxes. Round your answer to the nearest whole number.

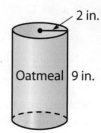

2 in.

Oatmeal   9 in.

_____

_____

16. **Analyze Relationships** A prism is made of centimeter cubes. How can you find the surface area of the prism in Figure 1 without using a net or a formula? How does the surface area change in Figures 2, 3, and 4? Explain.

Figure 1   Figure 2   Figure 3   Figure 4

_____

_____

_____

_____

LESSON 4.5

Solving Volume Problems

COMMON CORE 7.G.6

Solve real-world and mathematical problems involving ... volume of ... three-dimensional objects composed of ... cubes, and right prisms.

ESSENTIAL QUESTION

How do you find the volume of a figure made of cubes and prisms?

EXPLORE ACTIVITY COMMON CORE 7.G.6

Volume of a Triangular Prism

The formula for the volume of a rectangular prism can be used for *any* prism.

Math On the Spot

⏻ my.hrw.com

Volume of a Prism

The volume *V* of a prism is the area of its base *B* times its height *h*.

$$V = Bh$$

EXAMPLE 1 Bradley's tent is in the shape of a triangular prism. How many cubic feet of space are in his tent?

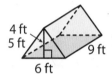
4 ft
5 ft
9 ft
6 ft

STEP 1 Find the base area *B* of the triangular prism.

Area of a triangle (*b* = base length, *h* = height) $B = \frac{1}{2}bh$

Substitute 6 for *b* and 4 for *h*. $= \frac{1}{2}\left(\right)\left(\right)$

Multiply to find the base area *B*. $= \boxed{}$ ft²

STEP 2 Find the volume of the prism.

Volume of a prism (*B* = base area, *h* = height) $V = Bh$

Substitute 12 for *B* and 9 for *h*. $= \left(\right)\left(\right)$

Multiply to find the volume. $= \boxed{}$ ft³

The volume of Bradley's tent is _____ ft³.

Reflect

1. **Analyze Relationships** For a prism that is **not** a rectangular prism, how do you determine which sides are the bases?

_____

Personal Math Trainer

Online Assessment and Intervention

2. Find the volume of the prism. _____

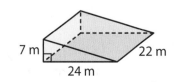
7 m
22 m
24 m

⏻ my.hrw.com

Volume of a Trapezoidal Prism

Prisms are named for the polygons that form their bases. In this lesson, you will focus on prisms whose bases are either triangles or quadrilaterals other than squares and rectangles.

EXAMPLE 2

COMMON CORE 7.G.6

Cherise is setting up her tent. Her tent is in the shape of a trapezoidal prism. How many cubic feet of space are in her tent?

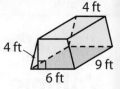

4 ft
4 ft
9 ft
6 ft

STEP 1 Find the base area B of the trapezoidal prism.

$B = \frac{1}{2}(b_1 + b_2)h$ Area of a trapezoid with bases of lengths b_1 and b_2 and height h

$= \frac{1}{2}(6 + 4)4$ Substitute 6 for b_1, 4 for b_2, and 4 for h.

$= \frac{1}{2}(10)4 = 20$ ft^2

STEP 2 Find the volume of the prism.

$V = Bh$ Volume of a prism with base area B and height h

$= (20)(9)$ Substitute 20 for B and 9 for h.

$= 180$ ft^3

The volume of Cherise's tent is 180 ft^3.

Math Talk
Mathematical Practices

Without calculating the volumes, how can you know whether Bradley's or Cherise's tent has a greater volume?

Reflect

3. **Look for a Pattern** How could you double the volume of the tent by doubling just one of its dimensions?

_____

_____

4. **What If?** How would doubling *all* the dimensions of the prism affect the volume of the tent?

_____

YOUR TURN

5. Find the volume of the prism.

_____

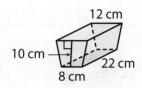

12 cm
10 cm
22 cm
8 cm

Volume of a Composite Solid

You can use the formula for the volume of a prism to find the volume of a composite figure that is made up of prisms.

EXAMPLE 3 **Real World**   COMMON CORE   7.G.6

Math On the Spot
my.hrw.com

Allie has two aquariums connected by a small square prism. Find the volume of the double aquarium.

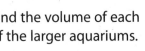

STEP 1 Find the volume of each of the larger aquariums.

$V = Bh$ Volume of a prism

$= (12)(3)$ Substitute $3 \times 4 = 12$ for B and 3 for h.

$= 36 \text{ ft}^3$

STEP 2 Find the volume of the connecting prism.

$V = Bh$ Volume of a prism

$= (1)(2)$ Substitute $1 \times 1 = 1$ for B and 2 for h.

$= 2 \text{ ft}^3$

STEP 3 Add the volumes of the three parts of the aquarium.

$V = 36 + 36 + 2 = 74 \text{ ft}^3$

The volume of the aquarium is 74 ft³.

Reflect

6. **What If?** Find the volume of one of the large aquariums on either end using another pair of opposite sides as the bases. Do you still get the same volume? Explain.

_____

_____

My Notes

YOUR TURN

7. The figure is composed of a rectangular prism and a triangular prism. Find the volume of the figure.

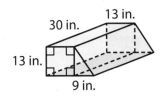

_____

Personal
Math Trainer

Online Assessment
and Intervention

my.hrw.com

1. Find the volume of the triangular prism.
   (Explore Activity Example 1)

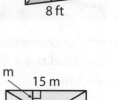

$B = \frac{1}{2}bh = \frac{1}{2}(8)(3) = 12 \text{ ft}^{\boxed{}}$

$V = Bh = \left(\boxed{} \times \boxed{}\right) \text{ ft}^{\boxed{}} = \boxed{} \text{ ft}^3$

2. Find the volume of the trapezoidal prism. (Example 2)

$B = \frac{1}{2}(b_1 + b_2)h = \frac{1}{2}(15 + 5)(3) = 30 \text{ m}^{\boxed{}}$

$V = Bh = \left(\boxed{} \times \boxed{}\right) \text{ m}^{\boxed{}} = \boxed{} \text{ m}^3$

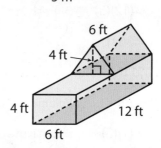

3. Find the volume of the composite figure. (Example 3)

   Volume of rectangular prism = _____

   Volume of triangular prism = _____

   Volume of composite figure = _____

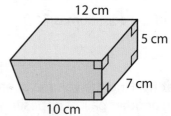

Find the volume of each figure. (Examples 2 and 3)

4. The figure shows a barn that Mr. Fowler is building for his farm.

   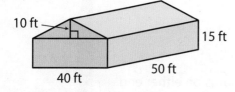

   _____

5. The figure shows a container, in the shape of a trapezoidal prism, that Pete filled with sand.

   12 cm
   5 cm
   7 cm
   10 cm

   _____

? ESSENTIAL QUESTION CHECK-IN

6. How do you find the volume of a composite solid formed by two or more prisms?

   _____

   _____

4.5 Independent Practice

COMMON CORE 7.G.6

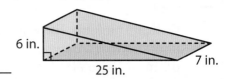
Personal Math Trainer

Online Assessment and Intervention

my.hrw.com

7. A trap for insects is in the shape of a triangular prism. The area of the base is 3.5 in² and the height of the prism is 5 in. What is the volume of this trap?

_____

8. Arletta built a cardboard ramp for her little brothers' toy cars. Identify the shape of the ramp. Then find its volume.

_____

6 in.

25 in.

7 in.

9. Alex made a sketch for a homemade soccer goal he plans to build. The goal will be in the shape of a triangular prism. The legs of the right triangles at the sides of his goal measure 4 ft and 8 ft, and the opening along the front is 24 ft. How much space is contained within this goal?

_____

10. A gift box is in the shape of a trapezoidal prism with base lengths of 7 inches and 5 inches and a height of 4 inches. The height of the gift box is 8 inches. What is the volume of the gift box?

_____

11. Explain the Error A student wrote this statement: "A triangular prism has a height of 15 inches and a base area of 20 square inches. The volume of the prism is 300 square inches." Identify and correct the error.

_____

Find the volume of each figure. Round to the nearest hundredth if necessary.

12. B ≈ 23.4 in²

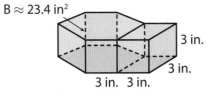

3 in.

3 in.

3 in. 3 in.

13.

7.5 m

7.5 m

3.75 m

3.75 m

15 m

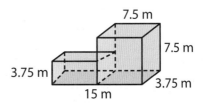

_____   _____

14. Multi-Step Josie has 260 cubic centimeters of candle wax. She wants to make a hexagonal prism candle with a base area of 21 square centimeters and a height of 8 centimeters. She also wants to make a triangular prism candle with a height of 14 centimeters. Can the base area of the triangular prism candle be 7 square centimeters? Explain.

_____

15. A movie theater offers popcorn in two different containers for the same price. One container is a trapezoidal prism with a base area of 36 square inches and a height of 5 inches. The other container is a triangular prism with a base area of 32 square inches and a height of 6 inches. Which container is the better deal? Explain.

_____

_____

16. Critical Thinking The wading pool shown is a trapezoidal prism with a total volume of 286 cubic feet. What is the missing dimension?

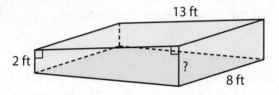

_____

17. Persevere in Problem Solving Lynette has a metal doorstop with the dimensions shown. Each cubic centimeter of the metal in the doorstop has a mass of about 8.6 grams. Find the volume of the metal in the doorstop. Then find the mass of the doorstop.

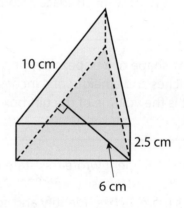

_____

_____

18. Analyze Relationships What effect would tripling all the dimensions of a triangular prism have on the volume of the prism? Explain your reasoning.

_____

_____

_____

_____

19. Persevere in Problem Solving Each of two trapezoidal prisms has a volume of 120 cubic centimeters. The prisms have no dimensions in common. Give possible dimensions for each prism.

_____

_____

_____

Ready to Go On?

4.1, 4.2 Circumference and Area of Circles

Find the circumference and area of each circle. Use 3.14 for π. Round to the nearest hundredth if necessary.

1.
7 m

_____

2.
12 ft

_____

4.3 Area of Composite Figures

Find the area of each figure. Use 3.14 for π.

3.
10 m
16 m

_____

4.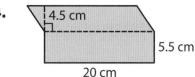
4.5 cm
5.5 cm
20 cm

_____

4.4, 4.5 Solving Surface Area and Volume Problems

Find the surface area and volume of each figure.

5.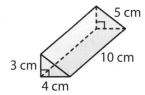
5 cm
3 cm
10 cm
4 cm

_____

6.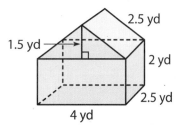
2.5 yd
1.5 yd
2 yd
2.5 yd
4 yd

_____

? ESSENTIAL QUESTION

7. How can you use geometry figures to solve real-world problems?

_____

_____

Personal
Math Trainer

Online
Assessment and
Intervention

my.hrw.com

Selected Response

1. What is the circumference of the circle?

11 m

Ⓐ 34.54 m

Ⓑ 69.08 m

Ⓒ 379.94 m

Ⓓ 1,519.76 m

2. What is the area of the circle?

15 m

Ⓐ 23.55 m² Ⓒ 176.625 m²

Ⓑ 47.1 m² Ⓓ 706.5 m²

3. What is the area of the figure?

6 m

6 m

Ⓐ 28.26 m² Ⓒ 64.26 m²

Ⓑ 36 m² Ⓓ 92.52 m²

4. A one-year membership to a health club costs $480. This includes a $150 fee for new members that is paid when joining. Which equation represents the monthly cost x in dollars for a new member?

Ⓐ $12x + 150 = 480$

Ⓑ $\frac{x}{12} + 150 = 480$

Ⓒ $12x + 480 = 150$

Ⓓ $\frac{x}{12} + 480 = 150$

5. What is the volume of the prism?

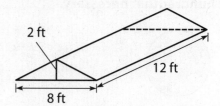

2 ft

12 ft

8 ft

Ⓐ 192 ft³ Ⓒ 69 ft³

Ⓑ 48 ft³ Ⓓ 96 ft³

6. A school snack bar sells a mix of granola and raisins. The mix includes 2 pounds of granola for every 3 pounds of raisins. How many pounds of granola are needed for a mix that includes 24 pounds of raisins?

Ⓐ 16 pounds Ⓒ 48 pounds

Ⓑ 36 pounds Ⓓ 120 pounds

7. Find the percent change from $20 to $25.

Ⓐ 25% decrease Ⓒ 20% decrease

Ⓑ 25% increase Ⓓ 20% increase

Mini-Task

8. Each dimension of the smaller prism is half the corresponding dimension of the larger prism.

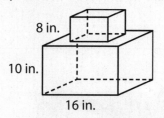

8 in.

10 in.

16 in.

a. What is the surface area of the figure?

_____

b. What is the volume of the figure?

_____

MODULE 3 **Modeling Geometric Figures**

Key Vocabulary

adjacent angles *(ángulos adyacentes)*

complementary angles *(ángulos complementarios)*

congruent angles *(ángulos congruentes)*

cross section *(sección transversal)*

intersection *(intersección)*

scale *(escala)*

scale drawing *(dibujo a escala)*

supplementary angles *(ángulos suplementarios)*

vertical angles *(ángulos opuestos por el vértice)*

? ESSENTIAL QUESTION

How can you apply geometry concepts to solve real-world problems?

EXAMPLE 1

Use the scale drawing to find the perimeter of Tim's yard.

15 cm

4 cm

2 cm : 14 ft

$\dfrac{2\ cm}{14\ ft} = \dfrac{1\ cm}{7\ ft}$ 1 cm in the drawing equals 7 feet in the actual yard.

$\dfrac{1\ cm \times 15}{7\ ft \times 15} = \dfrac{15\ cm}{105\ ft}$ 15 cm in the drawing equals 105 feet in the actual yard. Tim's yard is 105 feet long.

$\dfrac{1\ cm \times 4}{7\ ft \times 4} = \dfrac{4\ cm}{28\ ft}$ 4 cm in the drawing equals 7 feet in the actual yard. Tim's yard is 28 feet wide.

Perimeter is twice the sum of the length and the width. So the perimeter of Tim's yard is 2(105 + 28) = 2(133), or 266 feet.

EXAMPLE 2

Find (a) the value of *x* and (b) the measure of ∠*APY*.

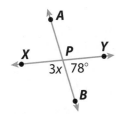

a. ∠*XPB* and ∠*YPB* are supplementary.

$3x + 78° = 180°$

$3x = 102°$

$x = 34°$

b. ∠*APY* and ∠*XPB* are vertical angles.

m∠*APY* = m∠*XPB* = 3*x* = 102°

EXERCISES

1. In the scale drawing of a park, the scale is 1 cm: 10 m. Find the area of the actual park.

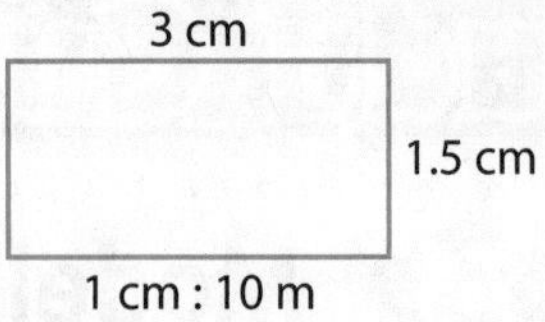

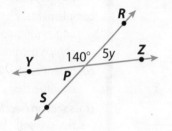

3 cm

1.5 cm

1 cm : 10 m

(Lesson 3.1) _____

2. Find the value of y and the measure of ∠YPS (Lesson 3.4)

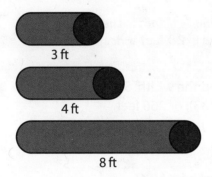

140° 5y

y = _____

m ∠YPS = _____

3. Kanye wants to make a triangular flower bed using logs with the lengths shown below to form the border. Can Kanye form a triangle with the logs without cutting any of them? Explain. (Lesson 3.2)

3 ft

4 ft

8 ft

_____

_____

_____

4. In shop class, Adriana makes a pyramid with a 4-inch square base and a height of 6 inches. She then cuts the pyramid vertically in half as shown. What is the area of each cut surface? (Lesson 3.3)

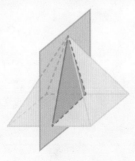

_____

 **Circumference, Area, and Volume**

Key Vocabulary
circumference
  (*circunferencia*)
composite figure (*figura compuesta*)
diameter (*diámetro*)
radius (*radio*)

? **ESSENTIAL QUESTION**

How can you use geometry concepts to solve real-world problems?

EXAMPLE 1

Find the area of the composite figure. It consists of a semicircle and a rectangle.

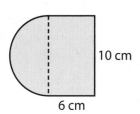

10 cm

6 cm

Area of semicircle $= 0.5(\pi r^2)$

$\approx 0.5(3.14)25$

$\approx 39.25 \text{ cm}^2$

Area of rectangle $= \ell w$

$= 10(6)$

$= 60 \text{ cm}^2$

The area of the composite figure is approximately 99.25 square centimeters.

EXAMPLE 2

Find the volume and surface area of the regular hexagonal prism hat box shown. Each side of the hexagonal base is 20 inches.

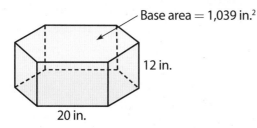

Base area $= 1,039$ in.²

12 in.

20 in.

Use the formulas for volume and surface area of a prism.

$V = Bh$

$= 1,039(12)$

$= 12,468 \text{ in}^3$

$S = Ph + 2B$

$= 120(12) + 2(1,039)$

$= 1,440 + 2,078$

$= 3,518 \text{ in}^2$

Perimeter $= 6(20) = 120$ in.

Find the circumference and area of each circle. Round to the nearest hundredth. (Lessons 4.1, 4.2)

1.

   22 in.

   _____

2.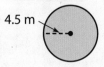

   4.5 m

   _____

Find the area of each composite figure. Round to the nearest hundredth if necessary. (Lesson 4.3)

3.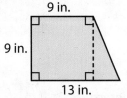

   9 in.

   9 in.

   13 in.

   Area _____

4.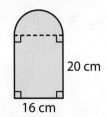

   20 cm

   16 cm

   Area _____

Find the volume of the figure. (Lesson 4.5)

5.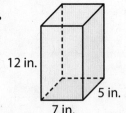

   12 in.

   5 in.

   7 in.

   _____

6. The volume of a triangular prism is 264 cubic feet. The area of a base of the prism is 48 square feet. Find the height of the prism.

   (Lesson 4.5) _____

EXERCISES

A glass paperweight has a composite shape: a square pyramid fitting exactly on top of an 8 centimeter cube. The pyramid has a height of 3 cm. Each triangular face has a height of 5 centimeters. (Lessons 4.4, 4.5)

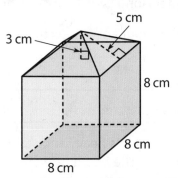

7. What is the volume of the paperweight? _____

8. What is the total surface area of the paperweight? _____

Unit 2 Performance Tasks

1. **CAREERS IN MATH** Product Design Engineer Miranda is a product design engineer working for a sporting goods company. She designs a tent in the shape of a triangular prism. The approximate dimensions of the tent are shown in the diagram.

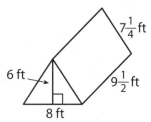

a. How many square feet of material does Miranda need to make the tent (including the floor)? Show your work.

_____

_____

b. What is the volume of the tent? Show your work.

_____

c. Suppose Miranda wants to increase the volume of the tent by 10%. The specifications for the height (6 feet) and the width (8 feet) must stay the same. How can Miranda meet this new requirement? Explain.

_____

_____

2. Li is making a stand to display a sculpture made in art class. The stand will be 45 centimeters wide, 25 centimeters long, and 1.2 meters high.

   a. What is the volume of the stand? Write your answer in cubic centimeters.

   _____

   _____

   b. Li needs to fill the stand with sand so that it is heavy and stable. Each piece of wood is 1 centimeter thick. The boards are put together as shown in the figure, which is not drawn to scale. How many cubic centimeters of sand does she need to fill the stand? Explain how you found your answer.

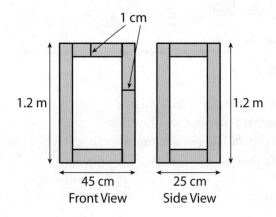

   45 cm
   Front View   25 cm
                 Side View

   _____

   _____

   _____

   _____

COMMON CORE

UNIT 2 MIXED REVIEW

Assessment Readiness

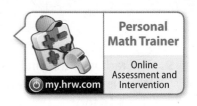

Personal Math Trainer

my.hrw.com

Online Assessment and Intervention

Selected Response

1. What is the value of x?

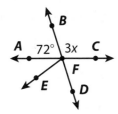

Ⓐ 108°

Ⓑ 72°

Ⓒ 36°

Ⓓ 18°

2. On a map with a scale of 2 cm = 1 km, the distance from Beau's house to the beach is 4.6 centimeters. What is the actual distance?

Ⓐ 2.3 km

Ⓑ 4.6 km

Ⓒ 6.5 km

Ⓓ 9.2 km

3. Lalasa and Yasmin are designing a triangular banner to hang in the school gymnasium. They first draw the design on paper. The triangle has a base of 5 inches and a height of 7 inches. If 1 inch on the drawing is equivalent to 1.5 feet on the actual banner, what will the area of the actual banner be?

Ⓐ 17.5 ft²

Ⓑ 52.5 ft²

Ⓒ 39.375 ft²

Ⓓ 78.75 ft²

4. Sonya has four straws of different lengths: 2 cm, 8 cm, 14 cm, and 16 cm. How many triangles can she make using the straws?

Ⓐ no triangle

Ⓑ one triangle

Ⓒ two triangles

Ⓓ more than two triangles

5. A one-topping pizza costs $15.00. Each additional topping costs $1.25. Let x be the number of additional toppings. You have $20 to spend. Which equation can you solve to find the number of additional toppings you can get on your pizza?

Ⓐ $15x + 1.25 = 20$

Ⓑ $1.25x + 15 = 20$

Ⓒ $15x - 1.25 = 20$

Ⓓ $1.25x - 15 = 20$

6. A bank offers a home improvement loan with simple interest at an annual rate of 12%. J.T. borrows $14,000 over a period of 3 years. How much will he pay back altogether?

Ⓐ $15,680

Ⓑ $17,360

Ⓒ $19,040

Ⓓ $20,720

7. What is the volume of a triangular prism that is 75 centimeters long and that has a base with an area of 30 square centimeters?

Ⓐ 2.5 cubic centimeters

Ⓑ 750 cubic centimeters

Ⓒ 1,125 cubic centimeters

Ⓓ 2,250 cubic centimeters

8. Consider the right circular cone shown.

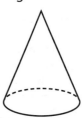

If a vertical plane slices through the cone to create two identical half cones, what is the shape of the cross section?

Ⓐ a rectangle

Ⓒ a triangle

Ⓑ a square

Ⓓ a circle

9. The radius of the circle is given in meters. What is the circumference of the circle? Use 3.14 for π.

Ⓐ 25.12 meters

Ⓑ 50.24 meters

Ⓒ 200.96 meters

Ⓓ 803.84 meters

10. The dimensions of the figure are given in millimeters. What is the area of the two-dimensional figure?

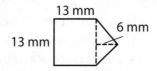

Ⓐ 39 square millimeters

Ⓑ 169 square millimeters

Ⓒ 208 square millimeters

Ⓓ 247 square millimeters

11. A forest ranger wants to determine the radius of the trunk of a tree. She measures the circumference to be 8.6 feet. What is the trunk's radius to the nearest tenth of a foot?

Ⓐ 1.4 ft   Ⓑ 4.3 ft

Ⓒ 2.7 ft   Ⓓ 17.2 ft

It is helpful to draw or redraw a figure. Answers to geometry problems may become clearer as you redraw the figure.

12. What is the measure in degrees of an angle that is supplementary to a 74° angle?

Ⓐ 16°

Ⓑ 74°

Ⓒ 90°

Ⓓ 106°

13. What is the volume in cubic centimeters of a rectangular prism that has a length of 6.2 centimeters, a width of 3.5 centimeters, and a height of 10 centimeters?

Ⓐ 19.7 cm³   Ⓒ 217.0 cm³

Ⓑ 108.5 cm³   Ⓓ 237.4 cm³

14. A patio is the shape of a circle with diameter shown.

What is the area of the patio? Use 3.14 for π.

Ⓐ 9.00 m²

Ⓑ 28.26 m²

Ⓒ 254.34 m²

Ⓓ 1,017.36 m²

Mini-Tasks

15. Petra fills a small cardboard box with sand. The dimensions of the box are 3 inches by 4 inches by 2 inches.

a. What is the volume of the box?

_____

b. Petra decides to cover the box by gluing on wrapping paper. How much wrapping paper does she need to cover all six sides of the box?

_____

c. Petra has a second, larger box that is 6 inches by 8 inches by 4 inches. How many times larger is the volume of this second box? The surface area?

_____

_____

Statistics

MODULE **5**

Random Samples and Populations

COMMON CORE 7.RP.2c, 7.SP.1, 7.SP.2

MODULE **6**

Analyzing and Comparing Data

COMMON CORE 7.SP.3, 7.SP.4

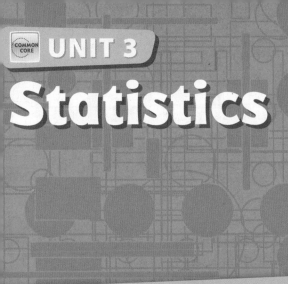

CAREERS IN MATH

Entomologist An entomologist is a biologist who studies insects. These scientists analyze data and use mathematical models to understand and predict the behavior of insect populations.

If you are interested in a career in entomology, you should study these mathematical subjects:
- Algebra
- Trigonometry
- Probability and Statistics
- Calculus

Research other careers that require the analysis of data and use of mathematical models.

Unit 3 Performance Task

At the end of the unit, check out how **entomologists** use math.

Vocabulary Preview

Use the puzzle to preview key vocabulary from this unit. Unscramble the circled letters to answer the riddle at the bottom of the page.

Across

2. A sample in which every person, object, or event has an equal chance of being selected (2 words). (Lesson 5.1)

4. Part of a population chosen to represent the entire group. (Lesson 5.1)

5. A display in which each piece of data is represented by a dot above a number line (2 words). (Lesson 6.2)

6. An integer generated by chance, such as by rolling a number cube or using a graphing calculator. (Lesson 5.1)

Down

1. The entire group of objects, individuals, or events in a set of data. (Lesson 5.1)

3. A display that shows how the values in a data set are distributed (2 words). (Lesson 6.3)

Q: Where do cowboys who love statistics live?

A: on the ___ ___ ___ ___ ___!

Random Samples and Populations

MODULE

COMMON CORE

ESSENTIAL QUESTION

How can you use random samples and populations to solve real-world problems?

Real-World Video

Scientists study animals like dart frogs to learn more about characteristics such as behavior, diet, and communication.

my.hrw.com

GO DIGITAL

my.hrw.com

my.hrw.com

Go digital with your write-in student edition, accessible on any device.

Math On the Spot

Scan with your smart phone to jump directly to the online edition, video tutor, and more.

Animated Math

Interactively explore key concepts to see how math works.

Personal Math Trainer

Get immediate feedback and help as you work through practice sets.

Are YOU Ready?

Complete these exercises to review skills you will need for this module.

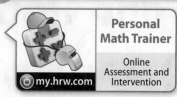
Solve Proportions

EXAMPLE

$$\frac{a}{1} = \frac{30}{1.5}$$

$a \times 1.5 = 1 \times 30$ Write the cross products.

$1.5a = 30$ Simplify.

$\frac{1.5a}{1.5} = \frac{30}{1.5}$ Divide both sides by 1.5.

$a = 20$

Solve for x.

1. $\frac{x}{16} = \frac{45}{40}$ _____

2. $\frac{x}{5} = \frac{1}{4}$ _____

3. $\frac{2.5}{10} = \frac{x}{50}$ _____

4. $\frac{x}{6} = \frac{2}{9}$ _____

Find the Range

EXAMPLE

29, 26, 21, 30, 32, 19   Order the data from least to greatest.
19, 21, 26, 29, 30, 32

range $= 32 - 19$ The range is the difference between the
$= 13$ greatest and the least data items.

Find the range of the data.

5. 52, 48, 57, 47, 49, 60, 59, 51 _____

6. 5, 9, 13, 6, 4, 5, 8, 12, 12, 6 _____

7. 97, 106, 99, 97, 115, 95, 108, 100 _____

8. 27, 13, 35, 19, 71, 12, 66, 47, 39 _____

Find the Mean

EXAMPLE

21, 15, 26, 19, 25, 14

mean $= \frac{21 + 15 + 26 + 19 + 25 + 14}{6}$ The mean is the sum of the data items divided by the number of items.

$= \frac{120}{6}$

$= 20$

Find the mean of each set of data.

9. 3, 5, 7, 3, 6, 4, 8, 6, 9, 5 _____

10. 8.1, 9.4, 11.3, 6.7, 6.2, 7.5 _____

Reading Start-Up

Visualize Vocabulary

Use the ✔ words to complete the right column of the chart.

Box Plots to Display Data	
Definition	**Review Word**
A display that uses values from a data set to show how the values are spread out.	
The middle value of a data set.	
The median of the lower half of the data.	
The median of the upper half of the data.	

Understand Vocabulary

Complete each sentence, using the preview words.

1. An entire group of objects, individuals, or events is a

   _____.

2. A _____ is part of the population chosen to represent the entire group.

3. A sample that does not accurately represent the population is a

   _____.

Active Reading

Tri-Fold Before beginning the module, create a tri-fold to help you learn the concepts and vocabulary in this module. Fold the paper into three sections. Label the columns "What I Know," "What I Need to Know," and "What I Learned." Complete the first two columns before you read. After studying the module, complete the third column.

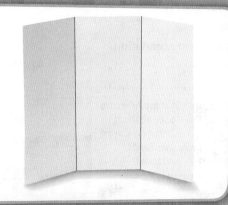

Unpacking the Standards

Understanding the standards and the vocabulary terms in the standards will help you know exactly what you are expected to learn in this module.

COMMON CORE 7.SP.1

Understand that statistics can be used to gain information about a population by examining a sample of the population; generalizations about a population from a sample are valid only if the sample is representative of that population. Understand that random sampling tends to produce representative samples and support valid inferences.

What It Means to You

You will learn how a random sample can be representative of a population.

UNPACKING EXAMPLE 7.SP.1

Avery wants to survey residents who live in an apartment building. She writes down all of the apartment numbers on slips of paper, and draws slips from a box without looking to decide who to survey. Will this produce a random sample?

The population is all of the residents or people who live in the apartment building. The sample is a valid random sample because every apartment number has the same chance of being selected.

COMMON CORE 7.SP.2

Use data from a random sample to draw inferences about a population with an unknown characteristic of interest. Generate multiple samples (or simulated samples) of the same size to gauge the variation in estimates or predictions.

Key Vocabulary

population (*población*)
  The entire group of objects or individuals considered for a survey.

sample (*muestra*)
  A part of the population.

What It Means to You

You will use data collected from a random sample to make inferences about a population.

UNPACKING EXAMPLE 7.SP.2

Alexi surveys a random sample of 80 students at his school and finds that 22 of them usually walk to school. There are 1,760 students at the school. Predict the number of students who usually walk to school.

$$\frac{\text{number in sample who walk}}{\text{size of sample}} = \frac{\text{number in population who walk}}{\text{size of population}}$$

$$\frac{22}{80} = \frac{x}{1,760}$$

$$x = \frac{22}{80} \cdot 1,760$$

$$x = \frac{38,720}{80} = 484$$

Approximately 484 students usually walk to school.

Visit **my.hrw.com** to see all the **Common Core Standards** unpacked.

⏱ my.hrw.com

LESSON 5.1 Populations and Samples

COMMON CORE 7.SP.1
... Understand that random sampling tends to produce representative samples and support valid inferences.

ESSENTIAL QUESTION

How can you use a sample to gain information about a population?

EXPLORE ACTIVITY   COMMON CORE 7.SP.1

Random and Non-Random Sampling

When information is being gathered about a group, the entire group of objects, individuals, or events is called the **population**. A **sample** is part of the population that is chosen to represent the entire group.

A vegetable garden has 36 tomato plants arranged in a 6-by-6 array as shown. The number in a given cell tells how many tomatoes are on that plant.

The gardener decides to find the average number of tomatoes on the plants based on a randomly chosen sample, because counting the number of tomatoes on all of the plants is too time-consuming.

To simulate a random selection: roll two number cubes a number of times. Let the first number cube represent the row, and the second represent the column. Record the number in each randomly selected cell. Do not count any cell more than once.

						Row
8	9	13	18	24	15	**1**
34	42	46	20	13	41	**2**
29	21	14	45	27	43	**3**
22	45	46	41	22	33	**4**
12	42	44	17	42	11	**5**
18	26	43	32	33	26	**6**
Column	**1**	**2**	**3**	**4**	**5**	**6**

A Find the average number of tomatoes on 6 randomly selected plants. _____

B Find the average number of tomatoes on the plants in the first row. _____

C Find the average number of tomatoes on 12 randomly selected plants. _____

D A *representative* sample has the same characteristics as the population.

In which part, **A** or **B**, is the sample more likely representative? Explain.

_____

_____

E The samples in Parts **A** and **C** were both chosen randomly, but one is more likely to be representative. Which one is it? Explain.

_____

_____

Reflect

1. How do the averages you got with each sampling method compare to the average for the entire population, which is 28.25?

   _____

   _____

2. Why might selecting only the plants in the first row not give a close average?

   _____

   _____

Math On the Spot

my.hrw.com

Random Samples and Biased Samples

A sample in which every person, object, or event has an equal chance of being selected is called a **random sample**. A random sample is more likely to be representative of a population than a sample not chosen randomly. When a sample does not accurately represent the population, it is called a **biased sample**.

EXAMPLE 1

COMMON CORE 7.SP.1

Identify the population. Determine whether each sample is a random sample or a biased sample. Explain your reasoning.

A Roberto wants to know the favorite sport of adults in his hometown. He surveys 50 adults at a baseball game.

The population is adults in Roberto's hometown.

The sample is biased.

Think: People who don't like baseball will not be represented in this sample.

Math Talk

Mathematical Practices

Why do you think samples are used? Why not survey each member of the population?

B Paula wants to know the favorite type of music for students in her class. She puts the names of all students in a hat, draws 8 names, and surveys those students.

The population is students in Paula's class.

The sample is random.

Think: Each student has an equal chance of being selected.

Reflect

3. **What if?** Suppose Paula draws 14 names for her random sample in Part **B** . Predict how this will affect the likelihood that the sample is representative.

   _____

   _____

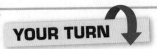

4. For a survey, a company manager assigned a number to each of the company's 500 employees, and put the numbers in a bag. The manager chose 20 numbers and surveyed the employees with those numbers. Did the manager choose a random sample?

_____

_____

Personal Math Trainer
Online Assessment and Intervention
⏻ my.hrw.com

Bias in Survey Questions

Once you have selected a representative sample of the population, be sure that the data is gathered without bias. Make sure that the survey questions themselves do not sway people to respond a certain way.

Math On the Spot
⏻ my.hrw.com

EXAMPLE 2 COMMON CORE 7.SP.1

In Madison County, residents were surveyed about a new skateboard park. Determine whether each survey question may be biased. Explain.

A Would you like to waste the taxpayers' money to build a frivolous skateboard park?

This question is biased. It discourages residents from saying yes to a new skateboard park by implying it is a waste of money.

B Do you favor a new skateboard park?

This question is not biased. It does not include an opinion on the skateboard park.

C Studies have shown that having a safe place to go keeps kids out of trouble. Would you like to invest taxpayers' money to build a skateboard park?

This question is biased. It leads people to say yes because it mentions having a safe place for kids to go and to stay out of trouble.

YOUR TURN

Determine whether each question may be biased. Explain.

5. When it comes to pets, do you prefer cats?

_____

6. What is your favorite season?

_____

_____

Personal Math Trainer
Online Assessment and Intervention
⏻ my.hrw.com

1. Follow each method described below to collect data to estimate the average shoe size of seventh grade boys. (Explore Activity)

Method 1

A Randomly select 6 seventh grade boys and ask each his shoe size. Record your results in a table like the one shown.

_____

Random Sample of Seventh Grade Male Students	
Student	Shoe Size

B Find the mean of this data. Mean:

_____

Method 2

A Find the 6 boys in your math class with the largest shoes and ask their shoe size. Record your results in a table like the one shown in Method 1.

_____

B Find the mean of this data. Mean: _____

2. Method 1 produces results that are | **more / less** | representative of the entire student population because it is a | **random / biased** | sample. (Example 1)

3. Method 2 produces results that are | **more / less** | representative of the entire student population because it is a | **random / biased** | sample. (Example 1)

4. Heidi decides to use a random sample to determine her classmates' favorite color. She asks, "Is green your favorite color?" Is Heidi's question biased? If so, give an example of an unbiased question that would serve Heidi better. (Example 2)

_____

? **ESSENTIAL QUESTION CHECK-IN**

5. How can you select a sample so that the information gained represents the entire population?

_____

_____

5.1 Independent Practice

  7.SP.1

6. A school cafeteria is considering new menu options. The manager puts a comment box in the cafeteria where students can anonymously submit their choices. Is this a representative sample? Explain why or why not.

_____

_____

_____

7. Nancy hears a report that the average price of gasoline is $2.82. She averages the prices of stations near her home. She finds the average price of gas to be $3.03. Why are the averages different?

_____

_____

_____

For 8–10, determine whether each sample is a random sample or a biased sample. Explain.

8. Carol wants to find out the favorite foods of students at her middle school. She asks the boys' basketball team about their favorite foods.

_____

_____

9. Dallas wants to know what elective subjects the students at his school like best. He surveys students who are leaving band class.

_____

_____

_____

10. To choose a sample for a survey of seventh graders, the student council puts pieces of paper with the names of all the seventh graders in a bag, and selects 20 names.

_____

_____

_____

11. Members of a polling organization survey 700 of the 7,453 registered voters in a town by randomly choosing names from a list of all registered voters. Is their sample likely to be representative?

_____

_____

_____

For 12–13, determine whether each question may be biased. Explain.

12. Joey wants to find out what sport seventh grade girls like most. He asks girls, "Is basketball your favorite sport?"

_____

_____

_____

13. Jae wants to find out what type of art her fellow students enjoy most. She asks her classmates, "What is your favorite type of art?"

_____

_____

_____

Work Area

14. Draw Conclusions Determine which sampling method will better represent the entire population. Justify your answer.

Student Attendance at Football Games	
Sampling Method	**Results of Survey**
Collin surveys 78 students by randomly choosing names from the school directory.	63% attend football games.
Karl surveys 25 students that were sitting near him during lunch.	84% attend football games.

_____

_____

_____

_____

_____

15. Multistep Barbara surveyed students in her school by looking at an alphabetical list of the 600 student names, dividing them into groups of 10, and randomly choosing one from each group.

a. How many students did she survey? What type of sample is this?

_____

b. Barbara found that 35 of the survey participants had pets. About what percent of the students she surveyed had pets? Is it safe to believe that about the same percent of students in the school have pets? Explain your thinking.

_____

_____

_____

16. Communicating Mathematical Ideas Carlo is shown the results of two surveys about the preferred practice day of all players in a soccer league. The surveys are based on two different samples, and the results are very different. What information about the samples and surveys might help Carlo decide which result is likely to be more accurate?

_____

_____

_____

Applying Proportional Reasoning

COMMON CORE 7.RP.3

Use proportional relationships to solve multistep ratio and percent problems.
Also 7.RP.2

ESSENTIAL QUESTION

How can you use proportional reasoning to solve multistep ratio problems?

EXPLORE ACTIVITY **COMMON CORE** 7.RP.2, 7.RP.3

Proportional Reasoning in Recipes

Melinda uses 3 cups of salt for every 5 cups of flour to make modeling clay. How much flour will she use when she uses 30 cups of salt?

A Explain how you know that the dependent variable in the proportional relationship should represent the number of cups of salt.

_____

_____

B The unit rate for the relationship is ☐ cup of salt to 1 cup of flour.

C The graph helps you visualize the relationship. The triangles represent the fact that for each 1 cup increase in the amount of flour, the amount of salt increases

by ☐ cup. For each triangle, the ratio of the

height to the base is ☐, the constant of proportionality.

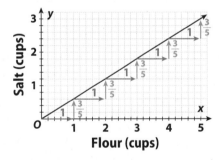

D An equation for the relationship is _____. When $y = 30$, $x =$ _____.

When Melinda uses 30 cups of salt, she uses _____ cups of flour.

Reflect

1. Melinda models the situation with the proportion $\frac{3}{5} = \frac{x}{30}$. Explain her error. Then show how to use the correct proportion to solve the problem.

_____

_____

1. Celine mixes raisins and peanuts to make a snack. She uses 0.75 cup of raisins for every 0.5 cup of peanuts. Write a proportion and use it to find the number of cups of raisins she uses if she uses 4.25 cups of peanuts.

   _____

2. Corey's salsa recipe calls for $2\frac{1}{2}$ cups of onions for every 4 pounds of tomatoes. Corey plans to use 10 pounds of tomatoes and wonders how many cups of onion he needs.

   a. Identify the quantities represented by the dependent and independent variables in the proportional relationship.

   _____

   b. **Explain the Error** Corey writes the equation $y = \frac{8}{5}x$ and finds that he needs 16 cups of onions. Describe and correct his error.

   _____

   _____

   _____

   c. **Focus on Reasoning** Explain why Corey should have known without calculating that the correct answer could not be 16 cups.

   _____

   _____

3. Neal makes a cleaning solution by mixing water and vinegar. He uses 7 cups of water for every 3 cups of vinegar. Write and use an equation to find how many more cups of vinegar he needs when he uses $7\frac{1}{2}$ cups of water than when he uses $4\frac{1}{2}$ cups of water. Define the variables.

   _____

   _____

4. **Explain the Error** In one middle school, there are 8 girls for every 7 boys. The total number of students is 330. Mischa wrote the proportion $\frac{8}{7} = \frac{x}{330}$ to find the number of girls in the school. Describe and correct her error.

   _____

   _____

   _____

LESSON 5.2

Making Inferences from a Random Sample

COMMON CORE 7.SP.2

Use data from a random sample to draw inferences about a population with an unknown characteristic of interest ... *Also 7.RP.2c, 7.SP.1*

ESSENTIAL QUESTION

How can you use a random sample to make inferences about a population?

EXPLORE ACTIVITY 1 COMMON CORE 7.SP.2, 7.SP.1

Using Dot Plots to Make Inferences

After obtaining a random sample of a population, you can make inferences about the population. Random samples are usually representative and support valid inferences.

Rosee asked students on the lunch line how many books they had in their backpacks. She recorded the data as a list: 2, 6, 1, 0, 4, 1, 4, 2, 2. Make a dot plot for the books carried by this sample of students.

STEP 1 Order the data from least to greatest. Find the least and greatest values in the data set.

STEP 2 Draw a number line from 0 to 6. Place a dot above each number on the number line for each time it appears in the data set.

> Notice that the dot plot puts the data values in order.

> **Math Talk**
> **Mathematical Practices**
> No students in Rosee's sample carry 3 books. Do you think this is true of all the students at the school? Explain.

Reflect

1. **Critical Thinking** How are the number of dots you plotted related to the number of data values?

   _____

2. **Draw Conclusions** Complete each qualitative inference about the population.

   Most students have _____ 1 book in their backpacks.

   Most students have fewer than _____ books in their backpacks.

   Most students have between _____ books in their backpacks.

3. **Analyze Relationships** What could Rosee do to improve the quality of her data?

   _____

Using Box Plots to Make Inferences

You can also analyze box plots to make inferences about a population.

The number of pets owned by a random sample of students at Park Middle school is shown below. Use the data to make a box plot.

9, 2, 0, 4, 6, 3, 3, 2, 5

STEP 1 Order the data from least to greatest. Then find the least and greatest values, the median, and the lower and upper quartiles.

STEP 2 The lower and upper quartiles can be calculated by finding the medians of each "half" of the number line that includes all the data.

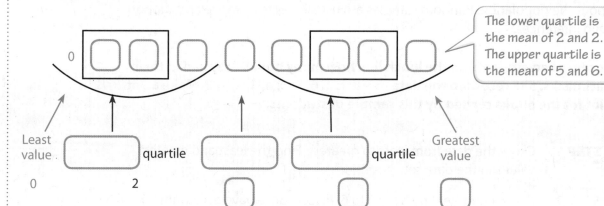

The lower quartile is the mean of 2 and 2. The upper quartile is the mean of 5 and 6.

Least value _____ quartile _____ _____ quartile Greatest value

0   2

Draw a number line that includes all the data values.

Plot a point for each of the values found in Step 1.

STEP 3 Draw a box from the lower to upper quartile. Inside the box, draw a vertical line through the median. Finally, draw the whiskers by connecting the least and greatest values to the box.

Math Talk
Mathematical Practices

What can you see from a box plot that is not readily apparent in a dot plot?

Reflect

4. **Draw Conclusions** Complete each qualitative inference about the population.

A good measure for the most likely number of pets is _____.

50% of the students have between _____ and 3 pets.

Almost every student in Parkview has at least _____ pet.

Using Proportions to Make Inferences

If a sample is representative of the population, then the number of objects in the population with a given characteristic is proportional to the number of objects in the sample with that characteristic.

You can use data based on a random sample, along with proportional reasoning, to make inferences or predictions about the population.

Math On the Spot
my.hrw.com

EXAMPLE 1

COMMON CORE   7.SP.2, 7.RP.2c

A shipment to a warehouse consists of 3,500 MP3 players. The manager chooses a random sample of 50 MP3 players and finds that 3 are defective. How many MP3 players in the shipment are likely to be defective?

It is reasonable to make a prediction about the population because this sample is random.

STEP 1 Set up a proportion.

$$\frac{\text{defective MP3s in sample}}{\text{size of sample}} = \frac{\text{defective MP3s in population}}{\text{size of population}}$$

STEP 2 Substitute values into the proportion.

$$\frac{3}{50} = \frac{x}{3,500}$$

Substitute known values. Let x be the number of defective MP3 players in the population.

$$\frac{3 \cdot 70}{50 \cdot 70} = \frac{x}{3,500}$$

$50 \cdot 70 = 3,500$, so multiply the numerator and denominator by 70.

$$\frac{210}{3,500} = \frac{x}{3,500}$$

$$210 = x$$

Based on the sample, you can predict that 210 MP3 players in the shipment would be defective.

Animated Math
my.hrw.com

YOUR TURN

5. **What If?** How many MP3 players in the shipment would you predict to be damaged if 6 MP3s in the sample had been damaged?

_____

Reflect

6. **Check for Reasonableness** How could you use estimation to check if your answer is reasonable?

_____

_____

Personal Math Trainer
Online Assessment and Intervention
my.hrw.com

Patrons in the children's section of a local branch library were randomly selected and asked their ages. The librarian wants to use the data to infer the ages of all patrons of the children's section so he can select age appropriate activities. In 3–5, complete each inference. (Explore Activities 1 and 2)

7, 4, 7, 5, 4, 10, 11, 6, 7, 4

1. Make a dot plot of the sample population data.

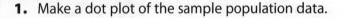

2. Make a box plot of the sample population data.

3. The most common ages of children that use the library are _____ and _____.

4. The range of ages of children that use the library is from _____ to _____.

5. The median age of children that use the library is _____.

6. A manufacturer fills an order for 4,200 smart phones. The quality inspector selects a random sample of 60 phones and finds that 4 are defective. How many smart phones in the order are likely to be defective? (Example 1)

   About _____ smart phones in the order are likely to be defective.

7. Part of the population of 4,500 elk at a wildlife preserve is infected with a parasite. A random sample of 50 elk shows that 8 of them are infected. How many elk are likely to be infected? (Example 1)

   _____

? ESSENTIAL QUESTION CHECK-IN

8. How can you use a random sample of a population to make predictions?

   _____

   _____

   _____

   _____

   _____

5.2 Independent Practice

COMMON CORE 7.RP.2c, 7.SP.1, 7.SP.2

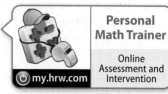

Personal Math Trainer

Online Assessment and Intervention

my.hrw.com

9. A manager samples the receipts of every fifth person who goes through the line. Out of 50 people, 4 had a mispriced item. If 600 people go to this store each day, how many people would you expect to have a mispriced item?

_____

10. Jerry randomly selects 20 boxes of crayons from the shelf and finds 2 boxes with at least one broken crayon. If the shelf holds 130 boxes, how many would you expect to have at least one broken crayon?

_____

11. A random sample of dogs at different animal shelters in a city shows that 12 of the 60 dogs are puppies. The city's animal shelters collectively house 1,200 dogs each year. About how many dogs in all of the city's animal shelters are puppies?

_____

12. Part of the population of 10,800 hawks at a national park are building a nest. A random sample of 72 hawks shows that 12 of them are building a nest. Estimate the number of hawks building a nest in the population.

_____

13. In a wildlife preserve, a random sample of the population of 150 raccoons was caught and weighed. The results, given in pounds, were 17, 19, 20, 21, 23, 27, 28, 28, 28 and 32. Jean made the qualitative statement, "The average weight of the raccoon population is 25 pounds." Is her statement reasonable? Explain.

_____

_____

_____

14. Greta collects the number of miles run each week from a random sample of female marathon runners. Her data are shown below. She made the qualitative statement, "25% of female marathoners run 13 or more miles a week." Is her statement reasonable? Explain. Data: 13, 14, 18, 13, 12, 17, 15, 12, 13, 19, 11, 14, 14, 18, 22, 12

_____

_____

_____

15. A random sample of 20 of the 200 students at Garland Elementary is asked how many siblings each has. The data are ordered as shown. Make a dot plot of the data. Then make a qualitative statement about the population. Data: 0, 1, 1, 1, 1, 1, 1, 2, 2, 2, 2, 2, 3, 3, 3, 3, 4, 4, 4, 6

_____

_____

16. Linda collects a random sample of 12 of the 98 Wilderness Club members' ages. She makes an inference that most wilderness club members are between 20 and 40 years old. Describe what a box plot that would confirm Linda's inference should look like.

_____

_____

_____

17. What's the Error? Kudrey was making a box plot. He first plotted the least and greatest data values. He then divided the distance into half, and then did this again for each half. What did Kudrey do wrong and what did his box plot look like?

_____

_____

_____

_____

H.O.T. **FOCUS ON HIGHER ORDER THINKING**

18. Communicating Mathematical Ideas A dot plot includes all of the actual data values. Does a box plot include any of the actual data values?

_____

_____

_____

19. Make a Conjecture Sammy counted the peanuts in several packages of roasted peanuts. He found that the bags had 102, 114, 97, 85, 106, 120, 107, and 111 peanuts. Should he make a box plot or dot plot to represent the data? Explain your reasoning.

_____

_____

_____

_____

_____

20. Represent Real-World Problems The salaries for the eight employees at a small company are $20,000, $20,000, $22,000, $24,000, $24,000, $29,000, $34,000 and $79,000. Make a qualitative inference about a typical salary at this company. Would an advertisement that stated that the average salary earned at the company is $31,500 be misleading? Explain.

_____

_____

_____

Generating Random Samples

COMMON CORE   7.SP.2

Use data from a random sample ... Generate multiple samples (or simulated samples) of the same size to gauge the variation in estimates or predictions.

ESSENTIAL QUESTION

How can you generate and use random samples to represent a population?

EXPLORE ACTIVITY 1

COMMON CORE   7.SP.2

Generating a Random Sample Using Technology

In an earlier lesson, you generated random samples by rolling number cubes. You can also generate random samples by using technology. In Explore Activity 1, you will generate samples using a graphing calculator.

Each of the 200 students in a school will have a chance to vote on one of two names, Tigers or Bears, for the school's athletic teams. A group of students decides to select a random sample of 20 students and ask them for which name they intend to vote. How can the group choose a random sample to represent the entire population of 200 students?

A One way to identify a random sample is to use a graphing calculator to generate random integers.

To simulate choosing 20 students at random from among 200 students:

- Press **MATH**, scroll right and select **PRB**, then select **5: randInt(**.

- Enter the least value, comma, greatest possible value.

randInt (1, 200)
43
93
75
178

In this specific case, the students will enter **randInt**

because there are _____ students in school.

- Hit **ENTER** _____ times to generate _____ random numbers.

The group gets a list of all the students in the school and assigns a number to each one. The group surveys the students with the given numbers.

Of the 20 students surveyed, 9 chose Tigers. The percent choosing

Tigers was _____. What might the group infer?

_____

_____

B You can simulate multiple random samples to see how much statistical measures vary for different samples of size 20.

Assume that the 200 students are evenly divided among those voting for Tigers and those voting for Bears. You can generate random numbers and let each number represent a vote. Let numbers from 1 to 100 represent votes for Tigers, and numbers from 101 to 200 represent votes for Bears. For each simulated sample, use randInt(1, 200) and generate 20 numbers.

Perform the simulation 10 times and record how many numbers from 1 to 100 are generated. How many of the samples indicated that there were 9 or fewer votes for Tigers?

_____

Combine your results with those of your classmates. Make a dot plot showing the number of numbers from 1 to 100 generated in each simulation.

_____

Reflect

1. **Communicate Mathematical Reasoning** Assume that it was accurate to say that the 200 students are evenly divided among those voting for Tigers and those voting for Bears. Based on your results, does it seem likely that in a sample of size 20, there would be 9 or fewer votes for Tigers?

_____

2. **Make a Prediction** Based on your answers, do you think it is likely that Tigers will win? Explain.

_____

3. **Multiple Representations** Suppose you wanted to simulate a random sample for the situation in Explore Activity 1 without using technology. One way would be to use marbles of two different colors to represent students choosing the different names. Describe how you could perform a simulation.

_____

_____

_____

_____

_____

Generating a Random Sample without Technology

A tree farm has a 100 acre square field arranged in a 10-by-10 array. The farmer wants to know the average number of trees per acre. Each cell in the table represents an acre. The number in each cell represents the number of trees on that acre.

22	24	27	29	31	24	27	29	30	25
37	22	60	53	62	42	64	53	41	62
61	54	57	34	44	66	39	60	65	40
45	33	64	36	33	51	62	66	42	42
37	34	57	33	47	43	66	33	61	66
66	45	46	67	60	59	51	46	67	48
53	46	35	35	55	56	61	46	38	64
55	51	54	62	55	58	51	45	41	53
61	38	48	48	43	59	64	48	49	47
41	53	53	59	58	48	62	53	45	59

The farmer decides to choose a random sample of 10 of the acres.

A To simulate the random selection, number the table columns 1–10 from left to right, and the rows 1–10 from top to bottom. Write the numbers 1–10 on identical pieces of paper. Place the pieces into a bag. Draw one at random, replace it, and draw another. Let the first number represent a table column, and the second represent a row. For instance, a draw of 2 and then 3 represents the cell in the second column and third row of the table, an acre containing 54 trees. Repeat this process 9 more times.

B Based on your sample, predict the average number of trees per acre. How does your answer compare with the actual mean number, 48.4?

_____

_____

C Compare your answer to **B** with several of your classmates' answers. Do they vary a lot? Is it likely that you can make a valid prediction about the average number of trees per acre? Explain.

_____

Reflect

4. **Communicate Mathematical Ideas** Suppose that you use the method in **A** to collect a random sample of 25 acres. Do you think any resulting prediction would be more or less reliable than your original one? Explain.

_____

_____

5. **Multiple Representations** How could you use technology to select the acres for your sample?

_____

_____

Guided Practice

A manufacturer gets a shipment of 600 batteries of which 50 are defective. The store manager wants to be able to test random samples in future shipments. She tests a random sample of 20 batteries in this shipment to see whether a sample of that size produces a reasonable inference about the entire shipment. (Explore Activities 1 and 2)

1. The manager selects a random sample using the formula

   randInt $\left(\boxed{} , \boxed{} \right)$ to generate _____ random numbers.

2. She lets numbers from 1 to _____ represent defective batteries, and

   _____ to _____ represent working batteries. She generates this list: 120, 413, 472, 564, 38, 266, 344, 476, 486, 177, 26, 331, 358, 131, 352, 227, 31, 253, 31, 277.

3. Does the sample produce a reasonable inference?

   _____

   _____

? ESSENTIAL QUESTION CHECK-IN

4. What can happen if a sample is too small or is not random?

   _____

   _____

5.3 Independent Practice

COMMON
CORE   7.SP.2

Personal
Math Trainer

Online
Assessment and
Intervention

my.hrw.com

Maureen owns three bagel shops. Each shop sells 500 bagels per day. Maureen asks her store managers to use a random sample to see how many whole-wheat bagels are sold at each store each day. The results are shown in the table. Use the table for 5–7.

	Total bagels in sample	Whole-wheat bagels
Shop A	50	10
Shop B	100	23
Shop C	25	7

5. If you assume the samples are representative, how many whole-wheat bagels might you infer are sold at each store?

_____

6. Rank the samples for the shops in terms of how representative they are likely to be. Explain your rankings.

_____

_____

7. Which sample or samples should Maureen use to tell her managers how many whole-wheat bagels to make each day? Explain.

_____

_____

_____

8. In a shipment of 1,000 T-shirts, 75 do not meet quality standards. The table below simulates a manager's random sample of 20 T-shirts to inspect. For the simulation, the integers 1 to 75 represent the below-standard shirts.

124	876	76	79	12	878	86	912	435	91
340	213	45	678	544	271	714	777	812	80

In the sample, how many of the shirts are below quality standards? _____

If someone used the sample to predict the number of below standard shirts in the shipment, how far off would the prediction be?

_____

_____

9. **Multistep** A 64-acre coconut farm is arranged in an 8-by-8 array. Mika wants to know the average number of coconut palms on each acre. Each cell in the table represents an acre of land. The number in each cell tells how many coconut palms grow on that particular acre.

56	54	40	34	44	66	43	65
66	33	42	36	33	51	62	63
33	34	66	33	47	43	66	61
46	35	48	67	60	59	52	67
46	32	64	35	55	47	61	38
45	51	53	62	55	58	51	41
48	38	47	48	43	59	64	54
53	67	59	59	58	48	62	45

a. The numbers in green represent Mika's random sample of 10 acres. What is the average number of coconut palms on the randomly selected acres?

_____

b. Project the number of palms on the entire farm.

_____

 **FOCUS ON HIGHER ORDER THINKING**

Work Area

10. **Draw Conclusions** A random sample of 15 of the 78 competitors at a middle school gymnastics competition are asked their height. The data set lists the heights in inches: 55, 57, 57, 58, 59, 59, 59, 59, 59, 61, 62, 62, 63, 64, 66. What is the mean height of the sample? Do you think this is a reasonable prediction of the mean height of all competitors? Explain.

_____

_____

11. **Critical Thinking** The six-by-six grid contains the ages of actors in a youth Shakespeare festival. Describe a method for randomly selecting 8 cells by using number cubes. Then calculate the average of the 8 values you found.

12	15	16	9	21	11
9	10	14	10	13	12
16	21	14	12	8	14
16	20	9	16	19	18
17	14	12	15	10	15
12	20	14	10	12	9

_____

_____

_____

_____

12. **Communicating Mathematical Ideas** Describe how the size of a random sample affects how well it represents a population as a whole.

_____

_____

Ready to Go On?

**Personal
Math Trainer**

Online Assessment
and Intervention

my.hrw.com

5.1 Populations and Samples

1. A company uses a computer to identify their 600 most loyal customers from its database and then surveys those customers to find out how they like their service. Identify the population and determine whether the sample is random or biased.

_____

_____

5.2 Making Inferences from a Random Sample

2. A university has 30,330 students. In a random sample of 270 students, 18 speak three or more languages. Predict the number of students at the university who speak three or more languages.

_____

5.3 Generating Random Samples

A store receives a shipment of 5,000 MP3 players. In a previous shipment of 5,000 MP3 players, 300 were defective. A store clerk generates random numbers to simulate a random sample of this shipment. The clerk lets the numbers 1 through 300 represent defective MP3 players, and the numbers 301 through 5,000 represent working MP3 players. The results are given.

13   2,195   3,873   525   900   167   1,094   1,472   709   5,000

3. Based on the sample, how many of the MP3 players might the clerk predict would be defective?

_____

4. Can the manufacturer assume the prediction is valid? Explain.

_____

? ESSENTIAL QUESTION

5. How can you use random samples to solve real-world problems?

_____

_____

COMMON CORE
Assessment Readiness

Personal
Math Trainer

Online
Assessment and
Intervention

my.hrw.com

Selected Response

1. A farmer is using a random sample to predict the number of broken eggs in a shipment of 3,000 eggs. Using a calculator, the farmer generates the following random numbers. The numbers 1–250 represent broken eggs.

| 477 | 2,116 | 1,044 | 81 | 619 | 755 |
| 2,704 | 900 | 238 | 1,672 | 187 | 1,509 |

Based on this sample, how many broken eggs might the farmer expect?

(A) 250 broken eggs

(B) 375 broken eggs

(C) 750 broken eggs

(D) 900 broken eggs

2. A middle school has 490 students. Mae surveys a random sample of 60 students and finds that 24 of them have pet dogs. How many students are likely to have pet dogs?

(A) 98

(B) 196

(C) 245

(D) 294

3. A pair of shoes that normally costs $75 is on sale for $55. What is the percent decrease in the price, to the nearest whole percent?

(A) 20%

(B) 27%

(C) 36%

(D) 73%

4. Which of the following is a random sample?

(A) A radio DJ asks the first 10 listeners who call in if they liked the last song.

(B) 20 customers at a chicken restaurant are surveyed on their favorite food.

(C) A polling organization numbers all registered voters, then generates 800 random integers. The polling organization interviews the 800 voters assigned those numbers.

(D) Rebecca used an email poll to survey 100 students about how often they use the internet.

Mini-Task

5. Each cell in the table represents the number of people who work in one 25-square-block section of the town of Middleton. The mayor uses a random sample to estimate the average number of workers per block.

47	61	56	48	56
60	39	63	60	46
51	58	49	63	45
55	58	50	43	48
62	53	44	66	55

a. The circled numbers represent the mayor's random sample. What is the mean number of workers in this sample?

_____

b. Predict the number of workers in the entire 25-block section of Middleton.

_____

Analyzing and Comparing Data

ESSENTIAL QUESTION

How can you solve real-world problems by analyzing and comparing data?

Real-World Video

Scientists place radio frequency tags on some animals within a population of that species. Then they track data, such as migration patterns, about the animals.

my.hrw.com

GO DIGITAL
my.hrw.com

my.hrw.com

Go digital with your write-in student edition, accessible on any device.

Math On the Spot

Scan with your smart phone to jump directly to the online edition, video tutor, and more.

Animated Math

Interactively explore key concepts to see how math works.

Personal Math Trainer

Get immediate feedback and help as you work through practice sets.

Are YOU Ready?

Complete these exercises to review skills you will need for this module.

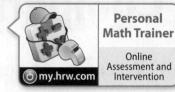

Personal Math Trainer

Online Assessment and Intervention

my.hrw.com

Fractions, Decimals, and Percents

EXAMPLE   Write $\frac{13}{20}$ as a decimal and a percent.

$$\begin{array}{r} 0.65 \\ 20\overline{)13.00} \\ -12\,0 \\ \hline 1\,00 \\ -1\,00 \\ \hline 0 \end{array}$$

$0.65 = 65\%$

Write the fraction as a division problem.
Write a decimal point and zeros in the dividend.
Place a decimal point in the quotient.

Write the decimal as a percent.

Write each fraction as a decimal and a percent.

1. $\frac{7}{8}$ _____   2. $\frac{4}{5}$ _____   3. $\frac{1}{4}$ _____   4. $\frac{3}{10}$ _____

5. $\frac{19}{20}$ _____   6. $\frac{7}{25}$ _____   7. $\frac{37}{50}$ _____   8. $\frac{29}{100}$ _____

Find the Median and Mode

EXAMPLE   17, 14, 13, 16, 13, 11
11, 13, 13, 14, 16, 17

$\text{median} = \dfrac{13 + 14}{2} = 13.5$

$\text{mode} = 13$

Order the data from least to greatest.

The median is the middle item or the average of the two middle items.

The mode is the item that appears most frequently in the data.

Find the median and the mode of the data.

9.   11, 17, 7, 6, 7, 4, 15, 9 _____   10.   43, 37, 49, 51, 56, 40, 44, 50, 36 _____

Find the Mean

EXAMPLE   17, 14, 13, 16, 13, 11

$\text{mean} = \dfrac{17 + 14 + 13 + 16 + 13 + 11}{6}$

$= \dfrac{84}{6}$

$= 14$

The mean is the sum of the data items divided by the number of items.

Find the mean of the data.

11.   9, 16, 13, 14, 10, 16, 17, 9 _____   12.   108, 95, 104, 96, 97, 106, 94 _____

Reading Start-Up

Visualize Vocabulary

Use the ✔ words to complete the right column of the chart.

Statistical Data		
Definition	**Example**	**Review Word**
A group of facts.	Grades on history exams: 85, 85, 90, 92, 94	
The middle value of a data set.	85, 85, 90, 92, 94	
A value that summarizes a set of values, found through addition and division.	Results of the survey show that students typically spend 5 hours a week studying.	

Understand Vocabulary

Complete each sentence using the preview words.

1. A display that uses values from a data set to show how the

   values are spread out is a _____.

2. A _____ uses a number line to display data.

Vocabulary

Review Words
- ✔ data (datos)
- interquartile range (rango entre cuartiles)
- ✔ mean (media)
- measure of center (medida central)
- measure of spread (medida de dispersión)
- ✔ median (mediana)
- survey (encuesta)

Preview Words
- box plot (diagrama de caja)
- dot plot (diagrama de puntos)
- mean absolute deviation (MAD) (desviación absoluta media, (DAM))

Active Reading

Layered Book Before beginning the module, create a layered book to help you learn the concepts in this module. Label the first flap with the module title. Label the remaining flaps with the lesson titles. As you study each lesson, write important ideas, such as vocabulary and formulas, under the appropriate flap. Refer to your finished layered book as you work on exercises from this module.

Unpacking the Standards

Understanding the standards and the vocabulary terms in the standards will help you know exactly what you are expected to learn in this module.

COMMON CORE 7.SP.3

Informally assess the degree of visual overlap of two numerical data distributions with similar variabilities, measuring the difference between the centers by expressing it as a multiple of a measure of variability.

Key Vocabulary

measure of center *(medida de centro)*
A measure used to describe the middle of a data set; the mean and median are measures of center.

What It Means to You

You will compare two populations based on random samples.

UNPACKING EXAMPLE 7.SP.3

Melinda surveys a random sample of 16 students from two college dorms to find the average number of hours of sleep they get. Use the results shown in the dot plots to compare the two populations.

Average Daily Hours of Sleep

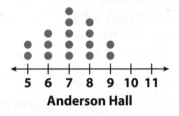
Anderson Hall

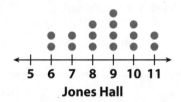
Jones Hall

Students in Jones Hall tend to sleep more than students in Anderson Hall, but the variation in the data sets is similar.

COMMON CORE 7.SP.3

Informally assess… distributions with similar variabilities, measuring the difference between the centers by expressing it as a multiple of a measure of variability.

Key Vocabulary

measure of spread *(medida de la dispersión)*
A measure used to describe how much a data set varies; the range, IQR, and mean absolute deviation are measures of spread.

What It Means to You

You will compare two groups of data by comparing the difference in the means to the variability.

UNPACKING EXAMPLE 7.SP.3

The tables show the number of items that students in a class answered correctly on two different math tests. How does the difference in the means of the data sets compare to the variability?

Items Correct on Test 1
20, 13, 18, 19, 15, 18, 20, 20, 15, 15, 19, 18

Mean: 17.5; Mean absolute deviation: 2

Items Correct on Test 2
8, 12, 12, 8, 15, 16, 14, 12, 13, 9, 14, 11

Mean: 12; Mean absolute deviation: 2

The means of the two data sets differ by $\frac{17.5-12}{2}=2.75$ times the variability of the data sets.

Comparing Data Displayed in Dot Plots

COMMON CORE 7.SP.4

Use measures of center and measures of variability . . . to draw informal comparative inferences about two populations. *Also 7.SP.3*

ESSENTIAL QUESTION

How do you compare two sets of data displayed in dot plots?

EXPLORE ACTIVITY Real World   COMMON CORE 7.SP.4

Analyzing Dot Plots

You can use dot plots to analyze a data set, especially with respect to its center and spread.

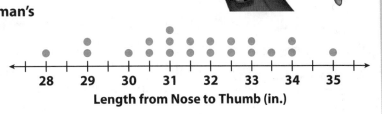

People once used body parts for measurements. For example, an inch was the width of a man's thumb. In the 12th century, King Henry I of England stated that a yard was the distance from his nose to his outstretched arm's thumb. The dot plot shows the different lengths, in inches, of the "yards" for students in a 7th grade class.

Length from Nose to Thumb (in.)

A Describe the shape of the dot plot. Are the dots evenly distributed or grouped on one side?

_____

B Describe the center of the dot plot. What single dot would best represent the data?

_____

_____

C Describe the spread of the dot plot. Are there any outliers?

_____

_____

Reflect

1. Calculate the mean, median, and range of the data in the dot plot.

_____

Comparing Dot Plots Visually

You can compare dot plots visually using various characteristics, such as center, spread, and shape.

EXAMPLE 1 Real World

COMMON CORE 7.SP.3

The dot plots show the heights of 15 high school basketball players and the heights of 15 high school softball players.

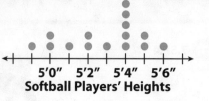

A Visually compare the shapes of the dot plots.

Softball: All the data is 5'6" or less.
Basketball: Most of the data is 5'8" or greater.
As a group, the softball players are shorter than the basketball players.

B Visually compare the centers of the dot plots.

Softball: The data is centered around 5'4".
Basketball: The data is centered around 5'8".
This means that the most common height for the softball players is 5 feet 4 inches, and for the basketball players 5 feet 8 inches.

C Visually compare the spreads of the dot plots.

Softball: The spread is from 4'11" to 5'6".
Basketball: The spread is from 5'2" to 6'0".
There is a greater spread in heights for the basketball players.

Math Talk
Mathematical Practices

How do the heights of field hockey players compare with the heights of softball and basketball players?

YOUR TURN

2. Visually compare the dot plot of heights of field hockey players to the dot plots for softball and basketball players.

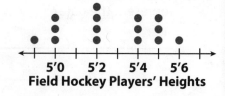
Field Hockey Players' Heights

Shape: _____

_____

Center: _____

_____

Spread: _____

_____

Comparing Dot Plots Numerically

You can also compare the shape, center, and spread of two dot plots numerically by calculating values related to the center and spread. Remember that outliers can affect your calculations.

Math On the Spot
⊙ my.hrw.com

EXAMPLE 2 (Real World)   COMMON CORE 7.SP.4

Numerically compare the dot plots of the number of hours a class of students exercises each week to the number of hours they play video games each week.

Exercise (h)

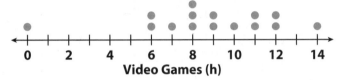
Video Games (h)

A Compare the shapes of the dot plots.

Exercise: Most of the data is less than 4 hours.
Video games: Most of the data is 6 hours or greater.

B Compare the centers of the dot plots by finding the medians.

Median for exercise: 2.5 hours. Even though there are outliers at 12 hours, most of the data is close to the median.
Median for video games: 9 hours. Even though there is an outlier at 0 hours, these values do not seem to affect the median.

C Compare the spreads of the dot plots by calculating the range.

Exercise range with outlier: $12 - 0 = 12$ hours
Exercise range without outlier: $7 - 0 = 7$ hours
Video games range with outlier: $14 - 0 = 14$ hours
Video games range without outlier: $14 - 6 = 8$ hours

Animated Math
⊙ my.hrw.com

Math Talk
Mathematical Practices

How do outliers affect the results of this data?

YOUR TURN

3. Calculate the median and range of the data in the dot plot. Then compare the results to the dot plot for Exercise in Example 2.

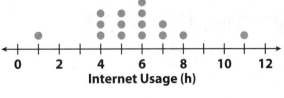
Internet Usage (h)

_____

_____

_____

Personal Math Trainer
Online Assessment and Intervention
⊙ my.hrw.com

The dot plots show the number of miles run per week for two different classes. For 1–5, use the dot plots shown.

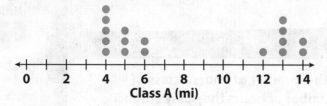

Class A (mi)

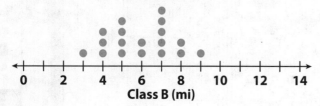

Class B (mi)

1. Compare the shapes of the dot plots.

   _____

   _____

2. Compare the centers of the dot plots.

   _____

   _____

3. Compare the spreads of the dot plots.

   _____

   _____

4. Calculate the medians of the dot plots.

   _____

5. Calculate the ranges of the dot plots.

   _____

? **ESSENTIAL QUESTION CHECK-IN**

6. What do the medians and ranges of two dot plots tell you about the data?

   _____

   _____

   _____

Name _____ **Class** _____ **Date** _____

6.1 Independent Practice

 7.SP.3, 7.SP.4

Personal
Math Trainer

Online
Assessment and
Intervention

The dot plot shows the number of letters in the spellings of the 12 months. Use the dot plot for 7–10.

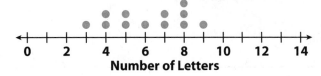

Number of Letters

7. Describe the shape of the dot plot.

_____

8. Describe the center of the dot plot.

_____

9. Describe the spread of the dot plot.

_____

10. Calculate the mean, median, and range of the data in the dot plot.

_____

The dot plots show the mean number of days with rain per month for two cities.

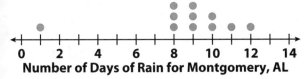

Number of Days of Rain for Montgomery, AL

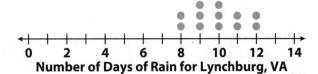

Number of Days of Rain for Lynchburg, VA

11. Compare the shapes of the dot plots.

_____

_____

12. Compare the centers of the dot plots.

_____

_____

13. Compare the spreads of the dot plots.

_____

_____

14. What do the dot plots tell you about the two cities with respect to their average monthly rainfall?

_____

_____

The dot plots show the shoe sizes of two different groups of people.

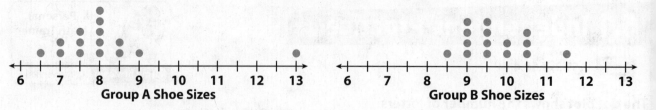

Group A Shoe Sizes

Group B Shoe Sizes

15. Compare the shapes of the dot plots.

_____

_____

16. Compare the medians of the dot plots.

_____

17. Compare the ranges of the dot plots (with and without the outliers).

_____

_____

18. Make A Conjecture Provide a possible explanation for the results of the dot plots.

_____

_____

H.O.T. FOCUS ON HIGHER ORDER THINKING

Work Area

19. Analyze Relationships Can two dot plots have the same median and range but have completely different shapes? Justify your answer using examples.

_____

_____

_____

_____

20. Draw Conclusions What value is most affected by an outlier, the median or the range? Explain. Can you see these effects in a dot plot?

_____

_____

_____

Comparing Data Displayed in Box Plots

COMMON CORE **7.SP.3**
Informally assess the degree of visual overlap of two numerical data distributions with similar variabilities, ...
Also 7.SP.4

ESSENTIAL QUESTION

How do you compare two sets of data displayed in box plots?

 EXPLORE ACTIVITY COMMON CORE **7.SP.4**

Analyzing Box Plots

Box plots show five key values to represent a set of data, the least and greatest values, the lower and upper quartile, and the median. To create a box plot, arrange the data in order, and divide them into four equal-size parts or quarters. Then draw the box and the whiskers as shown.

The number of points a high school basketball player scored during the games he played this season are organized in the box plot shown.

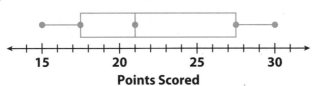

Points Scored

A Find the least and greatest values.

Least value: _____   Greatest value: _____

B Find the median and describe what it means for the data.

_____

_____

_____

C Find and describe the lower and upper quartiles.

_____

_____

_____

Math Talk
Mathematical Practices

How do the lengths of the whiskers compare? Explain what this means.

D The interquartile range is the difference between the upper and lower quartiles, which is represented by the length of the box. Find the interquartile range.

$Q_3 - Q_1 =$ _____ $-$ _____ $=$ _____

Reflect

1. Why is one-half of the box wider than the other half of the box?

_____

_____

Box Plots with Similar Variability

You can compare two box plots numerically according to their centers, or medians, and their spreads, or variability. Range and interquartile range (IQR) are both measures of spread. Box plots with similar variability should have similar boxes and whiskers.

My Notes

EXAMPLE 1   COMMON CORE 7.SP.3

The box plots show the distribution of times spent shopping by two different groups.

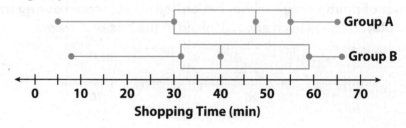

Shopping Time (min)

A Compare the shapes of the box plots.

The positions and lengths of the boxes and whiskers appear to be very similar. In both plots, the right whisker is shorter than the left whisker.

B Compare the centers of the box plots.

Group A's median, 47.5, is greater than Group B's, 40. This means that the median shopping time for Group A is 7.5 minutes more.

C Compare the spreads of the box plots.

The box shows the interquartile range. The boxes are similar.

Group A: $55 - 30 = 25$ min   Group B: About $59 - 32 = 27$ min

The whiskers have similar lengths, with Group A's slightly shorter than Group B's.

Math Talk

Mathematical Practices

Which store has the shopper who shops longest? Explain how you know.

Reflect

2. Which group has the greater variability in the bottom 50% of shopping times? The top 50% of shopping times? Explain how you know.

_____

_____

3. The box plots show the distribution of weights in pounds of two different groups of football players. Compare the shapes, centers, and spreads of the box plots.

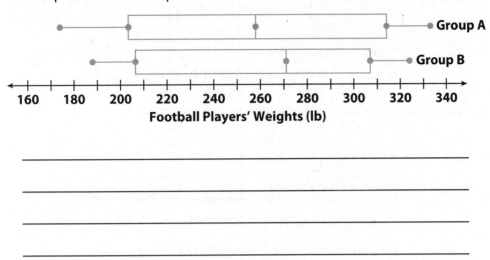

Football Players' Weights (lb)

_____

_____

_____

_____

_____

Box Plots with Different Variability

You can compare box plots with greater variability, where there is less overlap of the median and interquartile range.

EXAMPLE 2 Real World

COMMON CORE 7.SP.4

Math On the Spot

ⓞ my.hrw.com

The box plots show the distribution of the number of team wristbands sold daily by two different stores over the same time period.

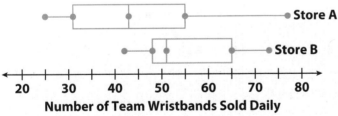

Number of Team Wristbands Sold Daily

A Compare the shapes of the box plots.

Store A's box and right whisker are longer than Store B's.

B Compare the centers of the box plots.

Store A's median is about 43, and Store B's is about 51. Store A's median is close to Store B's minimum value, so about 50% of Store A's daily sales were less than sales on Store B's worst day.

C Compare the spreads of the box plots.

Store A has a greater spread. Its range and interquartile range are both greater. Four of Store B's key values are greater than Store A's corresponding value. Store B had a greater number of sales overall.

YOUR TURN

4. Compare the shape, center, and spread of the data in the box plot with the data for Stores A and B in the two box plots in Example 2.

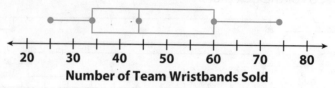

Number of Team Wristbands Sold

_____

_____

_____

Guided Practice

For 1–3, use the box plot Terrence created for his math test scores. Find each value. (Explore Activity)

1. Minimum = _____ Maximum = _____

2. Median = _____

3. Range = _____ IQR = _____

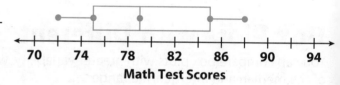

Math Test Scores

For 4–7, use the box plots showing the distribution of the heights of hockey and volleyball players. (Examples 1 and 2)

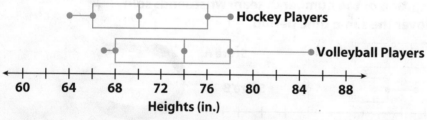

Hockey Players

Volleyball Players

Heights (in.)

4. Which group has a greater median height? _____

5. Which group has the shortest player? _____

6. Which group has an interquartile range of about 10? _____

 ESSENTIAL QUESTION CHECK-IN

7. What information can you use to compare two box plots?

_____

_____

6.2 Independent Practice

 COMMON CORE 7.SP.3, 7.SP.4

For 8–11, use the box plots of the distances traveled by two toy cars that were jumped from a ramp.

8. Compare the minimum, maximum, and median of the box plots.

_____

_____

_____

_____

_____

9. Compare the ranges and interquartile ranges of the data in box plots.

_____

_____

_____

10. What do the box plots tell you about the jump distances of two cars?

_____

_____

_____

_____

_____

11. Critical Thinking What do the whiskers tell you about the two data sets?

_____

_____

_____

_____

_____

For 12–14, use the box plots to compare the costs of leasing cars in two different cities.

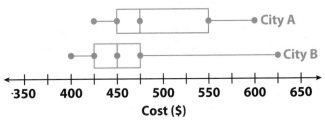

12. In which city could you spend the least amount of money to lease a car? The greatest?

_____

_____

_____

13. Which city has a higher median price? How much higher is it?

_____

14. Make a Conjecture In which city is it more likely to choose a car at random that leases for less than $450? Why?

_____

_____

_____

15. Summarize Look back at the box plots for 12–14 on the previous page. What do the box plots tell you about the costs of leasing cars in those two cities?

_____

_____

_____

_____

H.O.T. FOCUS ON HIGHER ORDER THINKING

Work Area

16. Draw Conclusions Two box plots have the same median and equally long whiskers. If one box plot has a longer box than the other box plot, what does this tell you about the difference between the data sets?

_____

_____

17. Communicate Mathematical Ideas What you can learn about a data set from a box plot? How is this information different from a dot plot?

_____

_____

_____

_____

_____

_____

_____

_____

_____

18. Analyze Relationships In mathematics, _central tendency_ is the tendency of data values to cluster around some central value. What does a measure of variability tell you about the central tendency of a set of data? Explain.

_____

_____

_____

Using Statistical Measures to Compare Populations

COMMON CORE 7.SP.3

Informally assess ... two numerical data distributions ... measuring the difference between the centers by expressing it as a multiple of a measure of variability. *Also 7.SP.4*

ESSENTIAL QUESTION

How can you use statistical measures to compare populations?

EXPLORE ACTIVITY COMMON CORE 7.SP.3

Math On the Spot
my.hrw.com

Comparing Differences in Centers to Variability

Recall that the mean and the mean absolute deviation (MAD) of a data set are measures of center and variability respectively. To find the MAD, first find the mean of the data. Next, take the absolute value of the difference between the mean and each data point. Finally, find the mean of those absolute values.

EXAMPLE 1 The tables show the number of minutes per day students in a class spend exercising and playing video games. What is the difference of the means as a multiple of the mean absolute deviations?

Minutes Per Day Exercising
0, 7, 7, 18, 20, 38, 33, 24, 22, 18, 11, 6

Minutes Per Day Playing Video Games
13, 18, 19, 30, 32, 46, 50, 34, 36, 30, 23, 19

STEP 1 Calculate the mean number of minutes per day exercising.

• Add: $0 + 7 + 7 + 18 + 20 + 38 + 33 + 24 + 22 + 18 + 11 + 6 = \boxed{}$

• Divide the sum by the number of students: $\boxed{} \div 12 = \boxed{}$

STEP 2 Calculate the absolute deviations for the exercise data. Then find their mean.

$|0-17| = 17 \qquad |7-17| = 10 \qquad |7-17| = 10 \qquad |18-17| = 1$

$|20-17| = 3 \qquad |38-17| = 21 \qquad |33-17| = 16 \qquad |24-17| = 7$

$|22-17| = \boxed{} \qquad |18-17| = \boxed{} \qquad |11-\boxed{}| = \boxed{} \qquad |6-\boxed{}| = \boxed{}$

Find the mean absolute deviation.

• Find the sum: $17 + 10 + 10 + 1 + 3 + 21 + 16 + 7 + \boxed{} + \boxed{} + \boxed{} + \boxed{} = \boxed{}$

• Divide the sum by the number of students: $\boxed{} \div 12 = \boxed{}$

STEP 3   Calculate the mean number of minutes per day playing video games. Round to the nearest tenth.

- Add: $13 + 18 + 19 + 30 + 32 + 46 + 50 + 34 + 36 + 30 + 23 + 19 =$ ☐

- Divide the sum by the number of students: ☐ $\div$ ☐ $\approx$ ☐

STEP 4   Calculate the absolute deviations for the video game data. Then find their mean.

$|13 - 29.2| = 16.2$ $|18 - 29.2| = 11.2$ $|19 - 29.2| = 10.2$

$|30 - 29.2| = 0.8$ $|32 - 29.2| = 2.8$ $|46 - 29.2| = 16.8$

$|50 - 29.2| = 20.8$ $|34 - 29.2| = 4.8$ $|36 - 29.2| = 6.8$

$|$☐$-29.2| =$ ☐ $|$☐$-29.2| =$ ☐ $|$☐$-29.2| =$ ☐

Find the mean absolute deviation. Round to the nearest tenth.

- Add: $16.2 + 11.2 + 10.2 + 0.8 + 2.8 + 16.8 +$

  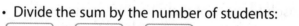 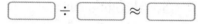 $=$ ☐

- Divide the sum by the number of students:

  ☐ $\div$ ☐ $\approx$ ☐

STEP 5   Find the difference in the means.

- Subtract the lesser mean from the greater mean:

  ☐ $-$ ☐ $\approx$ ☐

STEP 6   Write the difference of the means as a multiple of the mean absolute deviations, which are similar but not identical. Round to the nearest tenth.

- Divide the difference of the means by the MAD:

  ☐ $\div$ ☐ $\approx$ ☐

The means of the two data sets differ by about _____ times the variability of the two data sets.

YOUR TURN

1. The high jumps in inches of the students on two intramural track and field teams are shown below. What is the difference of the means as a multiple of the mean absolute deviations?

High Jumps for Students on Team 1 (in.)
44, 47, 67, 89, 55, 76, 85, 80, 87, 69, 47, 58

High Jumps for Students on Team 2 (in.)
40, 32, 52, 75, 65, 70, 72, 61, 54, 43, 29, 32

Personal Math Trainer

Online Assessment and Intervention

my.hrw.com

Using Multiple Samples to Compare Populations

Many different random samples are possible for any given population, and their measures of center can vary. Using multiple samples can give us an idea of how reliable any inferences or predictions we make are.

Math On the Spot
my.hrw.com

EXAMPLE 2 COMMON CORE 7.SP.4

A group of about 250 students in grade 7 and about 250 students in grade 11 were asked, "How many hours per month do you volunteer?" Responses from one random sample of 10 students in grade 7 and one random sample of 10 students in grade 11 are summarized in the box plots.

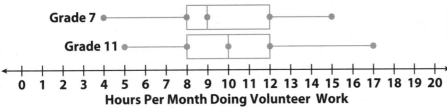

Two Random Samples of Size 10

Hours Per Month Doing Volunteer Work

How can we tell if the grade 11 students do more volunteer work than the grade 7 students?

STEP 1 The median is higher for the students in grade 11. But there is a great deal of variation. To make an inference for the entire population, it is helpful to consider how the medians vary among multiple samples.

STEP 2 The box plots below show how the medians from 10 different random samples for each group vary.

> **Math Talk**
> **Mathematical Practices**
>
> Why doesn't the first box plot establish that students in grade 11 volunteer more than students in grade 7?

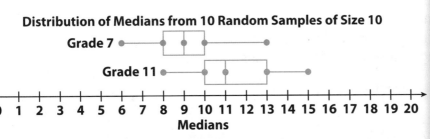

Distribution of Medians from 10 Random Samples of Size 10

Medians

The medians vary less than the actual data. Half of the grade 7 medians are within 1 hour of 9. Half of the grade 11 medians are within 1 or 2 hours of 11. Although the distributions overlap, the middle halves of the data barely overlap. This is fairly convincing evidence that the grade 11 students volunteer more than the grade 7 students.

YOUR TURN

2. The box plots show the variation in the means for 10 different random samples for the groups in the example. Why do these data give less convincing evidence that the grade 11 students volunteer more?

Distribution of Means from 10 Random Samples of Size 10

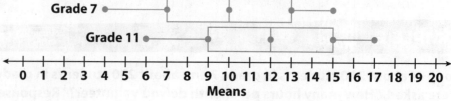

_____

Guided Practice

**The tables show the numbers of miles run by the students in two classes.
Use the tables in 1–2.** (Explore Activity Example 1)

Miles Run by Class 1 Students
12, 1, 6, 10, 1, 2, 3, 10, 3, 8, 3, 9, 8, 6, 8

Miles Run by Class 2 Students
11, 14, 11, 13, 6, 7, 8, 6, 8, 13, 8, 15, 13, 17, 15

1. For each class, what is the mean? What is the mean absolute deviation?

_____

2. The difference of the means is about _____ times the mean absolute deviations.

3. Mark took 10 random samples of 10 students from two schools. He asked how many minutes they spend per day going to and from school. The tables show the medians and the means of the samples. Compare the travel times using distributions of the medians and means. (Example 2)

School A
Medians: 28, 22, 25, 10, 40, 36, 30, 14, 20, 25
Means: 27, 24, 27, 15, 42, 36, 32, 18, 22, 29

School B
Medians: 22, 25, 20, 14, 20, 18, 21, 18, 26, 19
Means: 24, 30, 22, 15, 20, 17, 22, 15, 36, 27

_____

_____

 ESSENTIAL QUESTION CHECK-IN

4. Why is it a good idea to use multiple random samples when making comparative inferences about two populations?

_____

6.3 Independent Practice

 COMMON CORE 7.SP.3, 7.SP.4

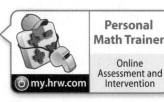

Josie recorded the average monthly temperatures for two cities in the state where she lives. Use the data for 5–7.

Average Monthly Temperatures for City 1 (°F)
23, 38, 39, 48, 55, 56, 71, 86, 57, 53, 43, 31

Average Monthly Temperatures for City 2 (°F)
8, 23, 24, 33, 40, 41, 56, 71, 42, 38, 28, 16

5. For City 1, what is the mean of the average monthly temperatures? What is the mean absolute deviation of the average monthly temperatures?

_____

6. What is the difference between each average monthly temperature for

City 1 and the corresponding temperature for City 2? _____

7. Draw Conclusions Based on your answers to Exercises 5 and 6, what do you think the mean of the average monthly temperatures for City 2 is? What do you think the mean absolute deviation of the average monthly temperatures for City 2 is? Give your answers without actually calculating the mean and the mean absolute deviation. Explain your reasoning.

_____

_____

8. What is the difference in the means as a multiple of the mean absolute

deviations? _____

9. Make a Conjecture The box plots show the distributions of mean weights of 10 samples of 10 football players from each of two leagues, A and B. What can you say about any comparison of the weights of the two populations? Explain.

Distribution of Means from 10 Random Samples of Size 10

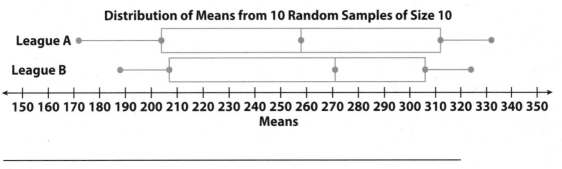

_____

_____

10. Justify Reasoning Statistical measures are shown for the ages of middle school and high school teachers in two states.

State A: Mean age of middle school teachers = 38, mean age of high school teachers = 48, mean absolute deviation for both = 6

State B: Mean age of middle school teachers = 42, mean age of high school teachers = 50, mean absolute deviation for both = 4

In which state is the difference in ages between members of the two groups more significant? Support your answer.

_____

_____

11. Analyze Relationships The tables show the heights in inches of all the adult grandchildren of two sets of grandparents, the Smiths and the Thompsons. What is the difference in the medians as a multiple of the ranges?

Heights of the Smiths' Adult Grandchildren (in.)	Heights of the Thompsons' Adult Grandchildren (in.)
64, 65, 68, 66, 65, 68, 69, 66, 70, 67	75, 80, 78, 77, 79, 76, 75, 79, 77, 74

 **FOCUS ON HIGHER ORDER THINKING**

Work Area

12. Critical Thinking Jill took many samples of 10 tosses of a standard number cube. What might she reasonably expect the median of the medians of the samples to be? Why?

_____

_____

13. Analyze Relationships Elly and Ramon are both conducting surveys to compare the average numbers of hours per month that men and women spend shopping. Elly plans to take many samples of size 10 from both populations and compare the distributions of both the medians and the means. Ramon will do the same, but will use a sample size of 100. Whose results will probably produce more reliable inferences? Explain.

_____

_____

14. Counterexamples Seth believes that it is always possible to compare two populations of numerical values by finding the difference in the means of the populations as a multiple of the mean absolute deviations. Describe a situation that explains why Seth is incorrect.

_____

Ready to Go On?

Personal Math Trainer

Online Assessment and Intervention

ⓞ my.hrw.com

6.1 Comparing Data Displayed in Dot Plots

The two dot plots show the number of miles run by 14 students at the start and at the end of the school year. Compare each measure for the two dot plots. Use the data for 1–3.

Start of School Year

End of School Year

Miles Run   Miles Run

1. means _____

2. medians _____   3. ranges _____

6.2 Comparing Data Displayed in Box Plots

The box plots show lengths of flights in inches flown by two model airplanes. Use the data for 4–5.

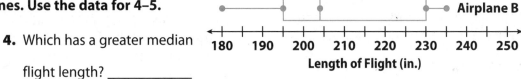

Airplane A

Airplane B

Length of Flight (in.)

4. Which has a greater median flight length? _____

5. Which has a greater interquartile range? _____

6.3 Using Statistical Measures to Compare Populations

6. Roberta grows pea plants, some in shade and some in sun. She picks 8 plants of each type at random and records the heights.

Shade plant heights (in.)	7	11	11	12	9	12	8	10
Sun plant heights (in.)	21	24	19	19	22	23	24	24

Express the difference in the means as a multiple of their ranges.

_____

? ESSENTIAL QUESTION

7. How can you use and compare data to solve real-world problems?

_____

COMMON CORE

MODULE 6 MIXED REVIEW

Assessment Readiness

Personal Math Trainer

Online Assessment and Intervention

my.hrw.com

Selected Response

1. Which statement about the data is true?

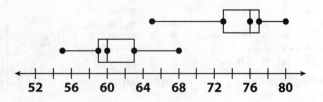

- Ⓐ The difference between the medians is about 4 times the range.
- Ⓑ The difference between the medians is about 4 times the IQR.
- Ⓒ The difference between the medians is about 2 times the range.
- Ⓓ The difference between the medians is about 2 times the IQR.

2. Which is a true statement based on the box plots below?

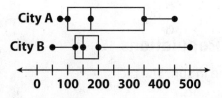

- Ⓐ The data for City A has the greater range.
- Ⓑ The data for City B is more symmetric.
- Ⓒ The data for City A has the greater interquartile range.
- Ⓓ The data for City B has the greater median.

3. What is $-3\frac{1}{2}$ written as a decimal?

- Ⓐ -3.5
- Ⓑ -3.05
- Ⓒ -0.35
- Ⓓ -0.035

4. Which is a true statement based on the dot plots below?

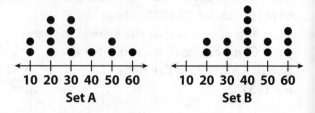

- Ⓐ Set A has the lesser range.
- Ⓑ Set B has the greater median.
- Ⓒ Set A has the greater mean.
- Ⓓ Set B is less symmetric than Set A.

Mini-Task

5. The dot plots show the lengths of a random sample of words in a fourth-grade book and a seventh-grade book.

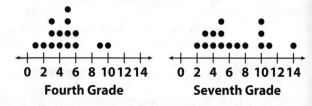

a. Compare the shapes of the plots.

_____

_____

_____

b. Compare the ranges of the plots. Explain what your answer means in terms of the situation.

_____

_____

_____

_____

Study Guide Review

Random Samples and Populations

Key Vocabulary

biased sample *(muestra sesgada)*

population *(población)*

random sample *(muestra aleatoria)*

sample *(muestra)*

? ESSENTIAL QUESTION

How can you use random samples and populations to solve real-world problems?

EXAMPLE 1

An engineer at a lightbulb factory chooses a random sample of 100 lightbulbs from a shipment of 2,500 and finds that 2 of them are defective. How many lightbulbs in the shipment are likely to be defective?

$$\frac{\text{defective lightbulbs}}{\text{size of sample}} = \frac{\text{defective lightbulbs in population}}{\text{size of population}}$$

$$\frac{2}{100} = \frac{x}{2,500}$$

$$\frac{2 \cdot 25}{100 \cdot 25} = \frac{x}{2,500}$$

$$x = 50$$

In a shipment of 2,500 lightbulbs, 50 are likely to be defective.

EXAMPLE 2

The 300 students in a school are about to vote for student body president. There are two candidates, Jay and Serena, and each candidate has about the same amount of support. Use a simulation to generate a random sample. Interpret the results.

Step 1: Write the digits 0 through 9 on 10 index cards, one digit per card. Draw and replace a card three times to form a 3-digit number. For example, if you draw 0-4-9, the number is 49. If you draw 1-0-8, the number is 108. Repeat this process until you have a sample of 30 3-digit numbers.

Step 2: Let the numbers from 1 to 150 represent votes for Jay and the numbers from 151 to 300 represent votes for Serena. For example:

Jay: 83, 37, 16, 4, 127, 93, 9, 62, 91, 75, 13, 35, 94, 26, 60, 120, 36, 73

Serena: 217, 292, 252, 186, 296, 218, 284, 278, 209, 296, 190, 300

Step 3: Notice that 18 of the 30 numbers represent votes for Jay. The results suggest that Jay will receive $\frac{18}{30} = 60\%$ of the 300 votes, or 180 votes.

Step 4: Based on this one sample, Jay will win the election. The results of samples can vary. Repeating the simulation many times and looking at the pattern across the different samples will produce more reliable results.

EXERCISES

1. Molly uses the school directory to select, at random, 25 students from her school for a survey on which sports people like to watch on television. She calls the students and asks them, "Do you think basketball is the best sport to watch on television?" (Lesson 5.1)

   a. Did Molly survey a random sample or a biased sample of the students at her school?

   _____

   b. Was the question she asked an unbiased question? Explain your answer.

   _____

   _____

2. There are 2,300 licensed dogs in Clarkson. A random sample of 50 of the dogs in Clarkson shows that 8 have ID microchips implanted. How many dogs in Clarkson are likely to have ID microchips implanted? (Lesson 5.2)

   _____

3. A store gets a shipment of 500 MP3 players. Twenty-five of the players are defective, and the rest are working. A graphing calculator is used to generate 20 random numbers to simulate a random sample of the players. (Lesson 5.3)

   A list of 20 randomly generated numbers representing MP3 players is:

474	77	101	156	378	188	116	458	230	333
78	19	67	5	191	124	226	496	481	161

   a. Let numbers 1 to 25 represent players that are _____.

   b. Let numbers 21 to 500 represent players that are _____.

   c. How many players in this sample are expected to be defective? _____

   d. If 300 players are chosen at random from the shipment, how many are expected to be defective based on the sample? Does the sample provide a reasonable inference? Explain.

   _____

   _____

   _____

Analyzing and Comparing Data

Key Vocabulary
mean absolute deviation (MAD) *(desviación absoluta media, (DAM))*

? ESSENTIAL QUESTION

How can you solve real-world problems by analyzing and comparing data?

EXAMPLE

The box plots show amounts donated to two charities at a fundraising drive. Compare the shapes, centers and spreads of the box plots.

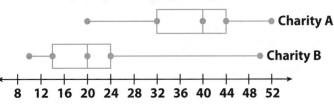

Shapes: The lengths of the boxes and overall plot lengths are fairly similar, but while the whiskers for Charity A are similar in length, Charity B has a very short whisker and a very long whisker.

Centers: The median for Charity A is $40, and for Charity B is $20.

Spreads: The interquartile range for Charity A is $44 - 32 = 12$. The interquartile range for Charity B is slightly less, $24 - 14 = 10$.

The donations varied more for Charity B and were lower overall.

EXERCISES

The dot plots show the number of hours a group of students spends online each week, and how many hours they spend reading. Compare the dot plots visually. *(Lesson 6.1)*

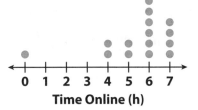

1. Compare the shapes, centers, and spreads of the dot plots.

Shape: _____

_____

Center: _____

_____

Spread: _____

_____

2. Calculate the medians of the dot plots. _____

3. Calculate the ranges of the dot plots. _____

4. The average times (in minutes) a group of students spends studying and watching TV per school day are given. (Lesson 6.3)

    Studying: 25, 30, 35, 45, 60, 60, 70, 75
    Watching TV: 0, 35, 35, 45, 50, 50, 70, 75

a. Find the mean times for studying and for watching TV.

_____

b. Find the mean absolute deviations (MADs) for each data set.

_____

c. Find the difference of the means as a multiple of the MAD, to two decimal places.

_____

Unit 3 Performance Tasks

1. **CAREERS IN MATH**   Entomologist   An entomologist is studying how two different types of flowers appeal to butterflies. The box-and-whisker plots show the number of butterflies that visited one of two different types of flowers in a field. The data were collected over a two-week period, for one hour each day.

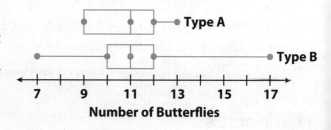

a. Find the median, range, and interquartile range for each data set.

_____

_____

b. Which measure makes it appear that flower type A had a more consistent number of butterfly visits? Which measure makes it appear that flower type B did? If you had to choose one flower as having the more consistent visits, which would you choose? Explain your reasoning.

_____

_____

_____

_____

UNIT 3 MIXED REVIEW

Assessment Readiness

COMMON CORE

Personal Math Trainer

Online Assessment and Intervention

my.hrw.com

Selected Response

1. Which is a true statement based on the dot plots below?

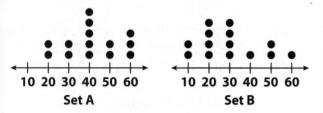

Ⓐ Set B has the greater range.

Ⓑ Set B has the greater median.

Ⓒ Set B has the greater mean.

Ⓓ Set A is less symmetric than Set B.

2. Which is a solution to the equation $7g - 2 = 47$?

Ⓐ $g = 5$

Ⓑ $g = 6$

Ⓒ $g = 7$

Ⓓ $g = 8$

3. Which is a true statement based on the box plots below?

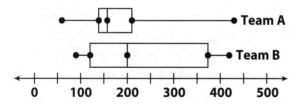

Ⓐ The data for Team B have the greater range.

Ⓑ The data for Team A are more symmetric.

Ⓒ The data for Team B have the greater interquartile range.

Ⓓ The data for Team A have the greater median.

4. Which is the best way to choose a random sample of people from a sold-out movie audience for a survey?

Ⓐ Survey all audience members who visit the restroom during the movie.

Ⓑ Assign each seat a number, write each number on a slip of paper, and then draw several slips from a hat. Survey the people in those seats.

Ⓒ Survey all of the audience members who sit in the first or last row of seats in the movie theater.

Ⓓ Before the movie begins, ask for volunteers to participate in a survey. Survey the first twenty people who volunteer.

5. Find the percent change from 84 to 63.

Ⓐ 30% decrease Ⓒ 25% decrease

Ⓑ 30% increase Ⓓ 25% increase

6. A survey asked 100 students in a school to name the temperature at which they feel most comfortable. The box plot below shows the results for temperatures in degrees Fahrenheit. Which could you infer based on the box plot below?

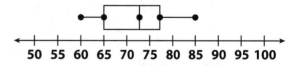

Ⓐ Most students prefer a temperature less than 65 degrees.

Ⓑ Most students prefer a temperature of at least 70 degrees.

Ⓒ Almost no students prefer a temperature of less than 75 degrees.

Ⓓ Almost no students prefer a temperature of more than 65 degrees.

7. The box plots below show data from a survey of students under 14 years old. They were asked on how many days in a month they read and draw. Based on the box plots, which is a true statement about students?

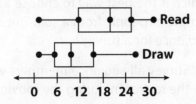

Ⓐ Most students draw at least 12 days a month.

Ⓑ Most students read less than 12 days a month.

Ⓒ Most students read more often than they draw.

Ⓓ Most students draw more often than they read.

Use logic to eliminate answer choices that are incorrect. This will help you to make an educated guess if you are having trouble with the question.

8. Which describes the relationship between ∠NOM and ∠JOK in the diagram?

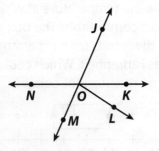

Ⓐ adjacent angles

Ⓑ complementary angles

Ⓒ supplementary angles

Ⓓ vertical angles

Mini-Task

9. The tables show the typical number of minutes spent exercising each week for a group of fourth-grade students and a group of seventh-grade students.

Weekly Exercising (minutes), 4ᵗʰ Grade
120, 75, 30, 30, 240, 90, 100, 180, 125, 300

Weekly Exercising (minutes), 7ᵗʰ Grade
410, 145, 240, 250, 125, 95, 210, 190, 245, 300

a. What is the mean number of minutes spent exercising for fourth graders? For seventh graders?

_____

b. What is the mean absolute deviation of each data set?

_____

c. Compare the two data sets with respect to their measures of center and their measures of variability.

_____

_____

_____

_____

d. How many times the MADs is the difference between the means, to the nearest tenth?

_____

_____

_____

Probability

MODULE 7

Experimental Probability

COMMON CORE 7.RP.2c, 7.RP.3, 7.NS.3, 7.SP.5, 7.SP.6, 7.SP.7a, 7.SP.7b, 7.SP.8, 7.SP.8a, 7.SP.8b, 7.SP.8c

MODULE 8

Theoretical Probability and Simulations

COMMON CORE 7.RP.3, 7.SP.6, 7.SP.7, 7.SP.7a, 7.SP.8, 7.SP.8a, 7.SP.8b, 7.SP.8c

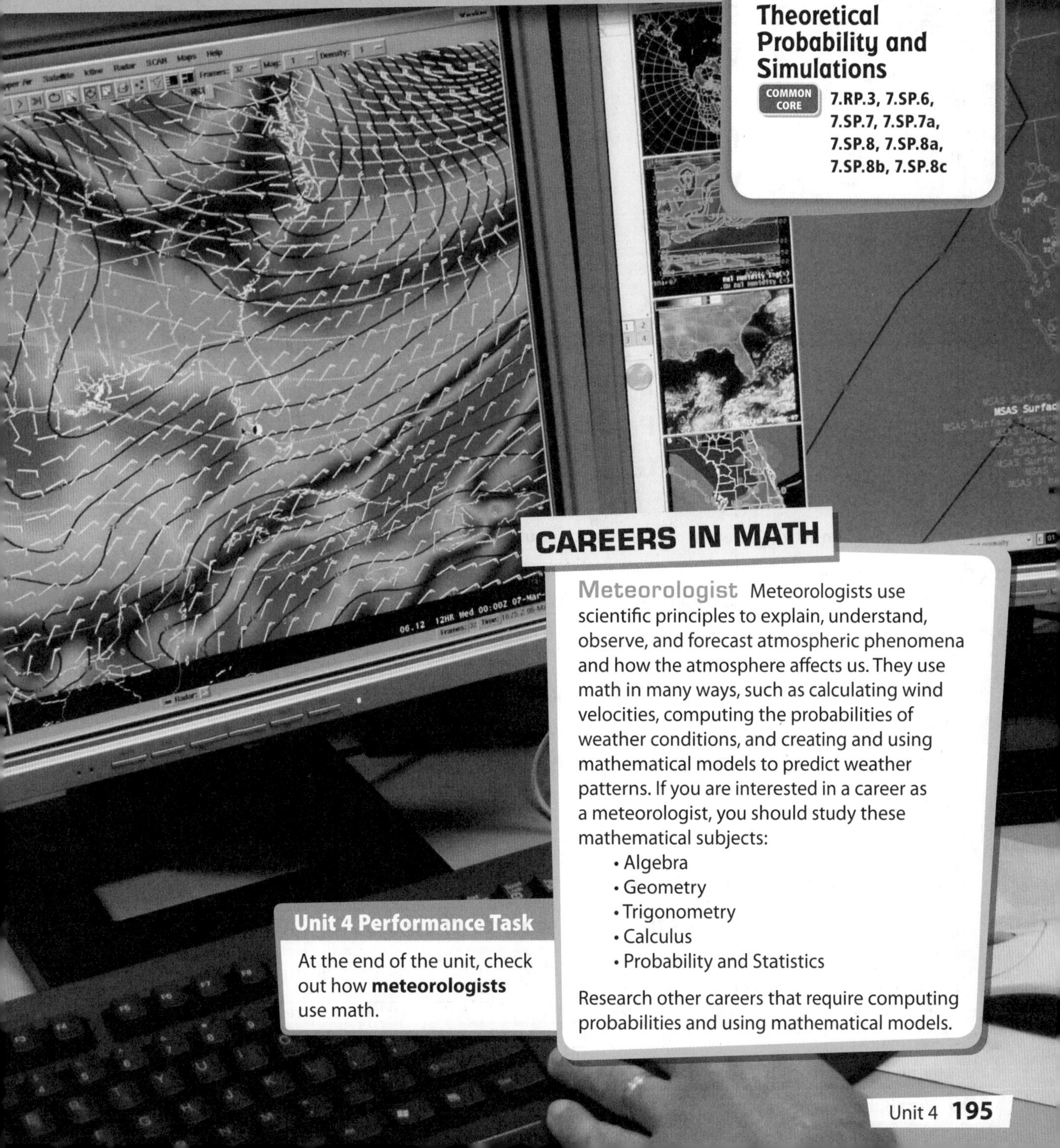

CAREERS IN MATH

Meteorologist Meteorologists use scientific principles to explain, understand, observe, and forecast atmospheric phenomena and how the atmosphere affects us. They use math in many ways, such as calculating wind velocities, computing the probabilities of weather conditions, and creating and using mathematical models to predict weather patterns. If you are interested in a career as a meteorologist, you should study these mathematical subjects:

- Algebra
- Geometry
- Trigonometry
- Calculus
- Probability and Statistics

Research other careers that require computing probabilities and using mathematical models.

Unit 4 Performance Task

At the end of the unit, check out how **meteorologists** use math.

Vocabulary Preview

Use the puzzle to preview key vocabulary from this unit. Unscramble the circled letters within found words to answer the riddle at the bottom of the page.

```
Y R F S P D A U L B S T Y C P
T N U E A G V V X I Y R C A R
N N B A H M C P M F U I Y H O
R E E X C K P P L O O A A X B
K V H M H O L L D G H L T O A
Q L R B I E W V E Z I W S B
L F E B E R X E X S I F Y I I
Q V I V T N E M E L P M O C L
Q O E S H J R P S R K A L E I
A N H C J D D O X H P F C X T
T P Z K V Z V F N E P F U E Y
U V K S I M U L A T I O N P J
K X O L P M O M S U Z J W A P
R O C P T U N D N V E R T U A
U W O G L B U H K E S F A P B
```

- An activity based on chance in which results are observed. (Lesson 7.1)
- The set of all outcomes that are not included in the event. (Lesson 7.1)
- Each observation of an experiment. (Lesson 7.1)
- A model of an experiment that would be difficult or too time-consuming to perform. (Lesson 7.2)
- Measures the likelihood that the event will occur. (Lesson 7.1)
- An event with only one outcome (2 words). (Lesson 7.2)
- A set of all possible outcomes for an event (2 words). (Lesson 7.1)

Q: Why was there little chance of success for the clumsy thieves?

A: Because they had low ___ ___ ___ – ___ ___ ___ ___ ___ ___ ___ ___!

Experimental Probability

ESSENTIAL QUESTION

How can you use experimental probability to solve real-world problems?

Real-World Video

Meteorologists use sophisticated equipment to gather data about the weather. Then they use experimental probability to forecast, or predict, what the weather conditions will be.

my.hrw.com

GO DIGITAL

my.hrw.com

my.hrw.com

Go digital with your write-in student edition, accessible on any device.

Math On the Spot

Scan with your smart phone to jump directly to the online edition, video tutor, and more.

Animated Math

Interactively explore key concepts to see how math works.

Personal Math Trainer

Get immediate feedback and help as you work through practice sets.

Are YOU Ready?

Complete these exercises to review skills you will need for this module.

Simplify Fractions

EXAMPLE   Simplify $\frac{12}{21}$.

12: 1, 2, ③ 4, 6, 12   List all the factors of the numerator and denominator.
21: 1, ③ 7, 21   Circle the greatest common factor (GCF).

$\frac{12 \div 3}{21 \div 3} = \frac{4}{7}$ Divide the numerator and denominator by the GCF.

Write each fraction in simplest form.

1. $\frac{6}{10}$ _____

2. $\frac{9}{15}$ _____

3. $\frac{16}{24}$ _____

4. $\frac{9}{36}$ _____

5. $\frac{45}{54}$ _____

6. $\frac{30}{42}$ _____

7. $\frac{36}{60}$ _____

8. $\frac{14}{42}$ _____

Write Fractions as Decimals

EXAMPLE $\frac{13}{25} \rightarrow$ $\begin{array}{r} 0.52 \\ 25\overline{)13.00} \\ -12.5 \\ \hline 50 \\ -50 \\ \hline 0 \end{array}$ Write the fraction as a division problem.
Write a decimal point and a zero in the dividend.
Place a decimal point in the quotient.
Write more zeros in the dividend if necessary.

Write each fraction as a decimal.

9. $\frac{3}{4}$ _____

10. $\frac{7}{8}$ _____

11. $\frac{3}{20}$ _____

12. $\frac{19}{50}$ _____

Percents and Decimals

EXAMPLE $109\% = 100\% + 9\%$ Write the percent as the sum of 1 whole and a percent remainder.
$= \frac{100}{100} + \frac{9}{100}$ Write the percents as fractions.
$= 1 + 0.09$ Write the fractions as decimals.
$= 1.09$ Simplify.

Write each percent as a decimal.

13. 67% _____

14. 31% _____

15. 7% _____

16. 146% _____

Write each decimal as a percent.

17. 0.13 _____

18. 0.55 _____

19. 0.08 _____

20. 1.16 _____

Reading Start-Up

Visualize Vocabulary

Use the ✔ words to complete the graphic. You can put more than one word in each box.

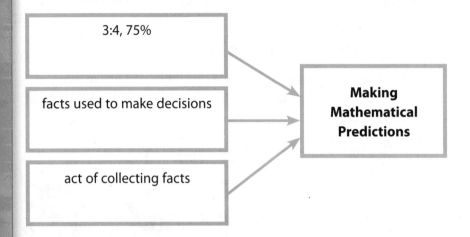

3:4, 75%

facts used to make decisions

act of collecting facts

→ **Making Mathematical Predictions**

Vocabulary

Review Words
- ✔ data *(datos)*
- ✔ observation *(observación)*
- ✔ percent *(porcentaje)*
- ✔ ratio *(razón)*

Preview Words
- complement *(complemento)*
- compound event *(suceso compuesto)*
- event *(suceso)*
- experiment *(experimento)*
- experimental probability *(probabilidad experimental)*
- outcome *(resultado)*
- probability *(probabilidad)*
- simple event *(suceso simple)*
- simulation *(simulación)*
- trial *(prueba)*

Understand Vocabulary

Match the term on the left to the definition on the right.

1. probability   **A.** Measures the likelihood that the event will occur.

2. trial   **B.** A set of one or more outcomes.

3. event   **C.** Each observation of an experiment.

Active Reading

Pyramid Before beginning the module, create a rectangular pyramid to help you organize what you learn. Label each side with one of the lesson titles from this module. As you study each lesson, write important ideas, such as vocabulary, properties, and formulas, on the appropriate side.

COMMON CORE
Unpacking the Standards

Understanding the standards and the vocabulary terms in the standards will help you know exactly what you are expected to learn in this module.

COMMON CORE 7.SP.6

Approximate the probability of a chance event by collecting data on the chance process that produces it and observing its long-run relative frequency, and predict the approximate relative frequency given the probability.

Key Vocabulary

simple event *(suceso simple)*
An event consisting of only one outcome.

experimental probability *(probabilidad experimental)*
The ratio of the number of times an event occurs to the total number of trials, or times that the activity is performed.

What It Means to You

You will use experimental probabilities to make predictions and solve problems.

UNPACKING EXAMPLE 7.SP.6

Caitlyn finds that the experimental probability of her making a goal in hockey is 30%. Out of 500 attempts to make a goal, about how many could she predict she would make?

$$\frac{3}{10} \cdot 500 = x$$

$$150 = x$$

Caitlyn can predict that she will make about 150 of the 500 goals that she attempts.

COMMON CORE 7.SP.7b

Develop a probability model (which may not be uniform) by observing frequencies in data generated from a chance process.

Key Vocabulary

sample space *(espacio muestral)*
All possible outcomes of an experiment.

What It Means to You

You will use data to determine experimental probabilities.

UNPACKING EXAMPLE 7.SP.7b

Anders buys a novelty coin that is weighted more heavily on one side. He flips the coin 60 times and a head comes up 36 times. Based on his results, what is the experimental probability of flipping a head?

$$\text{experimental probability} = \frac{\text{number of times event occurs}}{\text{total number of trials}}$$

$$= \frac{36}{60} = \frac{3}{5}$$

The experimental probability of flipping a head is $\frac{3}{5}$.

Visit **my.hrw.com** to see all the **Common Core Standards** unpacked.

my.hrw.com

LESSON 7.1 Probability

COMMON CORE 7.SP.5

Understand that the probability of a chance event is a number between 0 and 1 that expresses the likelihood of the event occurring. Larger numbers indicate greater likelihood.... *Also 7.SP.7a*

ESSENTIAL QUESTION

How can you describe the likelihood of an event?

EXPLORE ACTIVITY 7.SP.5

Finding the Likelihood of an Event

Each time you roll a number cube, a number from 1 to 6 lands face up. This is called an *event*.

Work with a partner to decide how many of the six possible results of rolling a number cube match the described event.

Then order the events from least likely (1) to most likely (9) by writing a number in each box to the right.

Rolling a number less than 7 _____ ☐

Rolling an 8 _____ ☐

Rolling a number greater than 4 _____ ☐

Rolling a 5 _____ ☐

Rolling a number other than 6 _____ ☐

Rolling an even number _____ ☐

Rolling a number less than 5 _____ ☐

Rolling an odd number _____ ☐

Rolling a number divisible by 3 _____ ☐

Reflect

1. Are any of the events impossible? _____

_____

Describing Events

An **experiment** is an activity involving chance in which results are observed. Each observation of an experiment is a **trial**, and each result is an **outcome**. A set of one or more outcomes is an **event**.

The **probability** of an event, written *P*(event), measures the likelihood that the event will occur. Probability is a measure between 0 and 1 as shown on the number line, and can be written as a fraction, a decimal, or a percent.

If the event is not likely to occur, the probability of the event is close to 0. If an event is likely to occur, the event's probability is closer to 1.

Impossible	Unlikely	As likely as not	Likely	Certain
0		$\frac{1}{2}$		1
0		0.5		1.0
0%		50%		100%

EXAMPLE 1

COMMON CORE 7.SP.5

Tell whether each event is impossible, unlikely, as likely as not, likely, or certain. Then, tell whether the probability is 0, close to 0, $\frac{1}{2}$, close to 1, or 1.

A You roll a six-sided number cube and the number is 1 or greater.

> Because you can roll the numbers 1, 2, 3, 4, 5, and 6 on a number cube, there are 6 possible outcomes.

This event is certain to happen. Its probability is 1.

B You roll two number cubes and the sum of the numbers is 3.

This event is unlikely to happen. Its probability is close to 0.

C A bowl contains disks marked with the numbers 1 through 10. You close your eyes and select a disk at random. You pick an odd number.

This event is as likely as not. The probability is $\frac{1}{2}$.

D A spinner has 8 equal sections marked 0 through 7. You spin and land on a prime number.

> Remember that a prime number is a whole number greater than 1 and has exactly 2 divisors, 1 and itself.

This event is as likely as not. The probability is $\frac{1}{2}$.

Math Talk

Mathematical Practices

Is an event that is *not* certain an impossible event? Explain.

Reflect

2. The probability of event *A* is $\frac{1}{3}$. The probability of event *B* is $\frac{1}{4}$. What can you conclude about the two events?

_____

_____

3. A hat contains pieces of paper marked with the numbers 1 through 16. Tell whether picking an even number is impossible, unlikely, as likely as not, likely, or certain. Tell whether the probability is 0, close to 0, $\frac{1}{2}$, close to 1, or 1.

_____

Personal Math Trainer

Online Assessment and Intervention

⊙ my.hrw.com

Finding Probability

A **sample space** is the set of all possible outcomes for an experiment. A sample space can be small, such as the 2 outcomes when a coin is flipped. Or a sample space can be large, such as the possible number of Texas Classic automobile license plates. Identifying the sample space can help you calculate the probability of an event.

Math On the Spot

⊙ my.hrw.com

Probability of An Event

$$P(\text{event}) = \frac{\text{number of outcomes in the event}}{\text{number of outcomes in the sample space}}$$

EXAMPLE 2 Real World

COMMON CORE 7.SP.7a

What is the probability of rolling an even number on a standard number cube?

STEP 1 Find the sample space for a standard number cube.

{1, 2, 3, 4, 5, 6} *There are 6 possible outcomes.*

STEP 2 Find the number of ways to roll an even number.

2, 4, 6 *The event can occur 3 ways.*

STEP 3 Find the probability of rolling an even number.

$$P(\text{even}) = \frac{\text{number of ways to roll an even number}}{\text{number of faces on a number cube}}$$

$$= \frac{3}{6} = \frac{1}{2}$$ *Substitute values and simplify.*

The probability of rolling an even number is $\frac{1}{2}$.

YOUR TURN

Find each probability. Write your answer in simplest form.

4. Picking a purple marble from a jar with 10 green and 10 purple marbles. _____

5. Rolling a number greater than 4 on a standard number cube.

_____

Using the Complement of an Event

The **complement** of an event is the set of all outcomes in the sample space that are *not* included in the event. For example, in the event of rolling a 3 on a number cube, the complement is rolling any number other than 3, which means the complement is rolling a 1, 2, 4, 5, or 6.

> ### An Event and Its Complement
>
> The sum of the probabilities of an event and its complement equals 1.
> $$P(\text{event}) + P(\text{complement}) = 1$$

You can apply probabilities to situations involving random selection, such as drawing a card out of a shuffled deck or pulling a marble out of a closed bag.

EXAMPLE 3

COMMON CORE 7.SP.7a

There are 2 red jacks in a standard deck of 52 cards. What is the probability of not getting a red jack if you select one card at random?

$P(\text{event}) + P(\text{complement}) = 1$

$P(\text{red jack}) + P(\text{not a red jack}) = 1$ *The probability of getting a red jack is $\frac{2}{52}$.*

$\frac{2}{52} + P(\text{not a red jack}) = 1$ *Substitute $\frac{2}{52}$ for $P(\text{red jack})$.*

$\frac{2}{52} + P(\text{not a red jack}) = \frac{52}{52}$ *Subtract $\frac{2}{52}$ from both sides.*

$\underline{-\frac{2}{52} \qquad\qquad\qquad\qquad -\frac{2}{52}}$

$P(\text{not a red jack}) = \frac{50}{52}$

$P(\text{not a red jack}) = \frac{25}{26}$ *Simplify.*

The probability that you will not draw a red jack is $\frac{25}{26}$. It is likely that you will not select a red jack.

Reflect

6. Why do the probability of an event and the probability of its complement add up to 1?

_____

_____

_____

_____

_____

7. A jar contains 8 marbles marked with the numbers 1 through 8. You pick a marble at random. What is the probability of not picking the

marble marked with the number 5? _____

8. You roll a standard number cube. Use the probability of rolling an even

number to find the probability of rolling an odd number. _____

Personal Math Trainer

Online Assessment and Intervention

⏻ my.hrw.com

Guided Practice

1. In a hat, you have index cards with the numbers 1 through 10 written on them. Order the events from least likely to happen (1) to most likely to happen (8) when you pick one card at random. In the boxes, write a number from 1 to 8 to order the eight different events. (Explore Activity)

You pick a number greater than 0.

You pick an even number.

You pick a number that is at least 2.

You pick a number that is at most 0.

You pick a number divisible by 3.

You pick a number divisible by 5.

You pick a prime number.

You pick a number less than the greatest prime number.

Guided Practice

Determine whether each event is impossible, unlikely, as likely as not, likely, or certain. Then, tell whether the probability is 0, close to 0, $\frac{1}{2}$, close to 1, or 1. (Example 1)

2. randomly picking a green card from a standard deck of playing cards

_____

3. randomly picking a red card from a standard deck of playing cards

_____

4. picking a number less than 15 from a jar with papers labeled from 1 to 12

_____

5. picking a number that is divisible by 5 from a jar with papers labeled from 1 to 12

_____

Find each probability. Write your answer in simplest form. (Example 2)

6. spinning a spinner that has 5 equal sections marked 1 through 5 and landing on an even number

_____

7. picking a diamond from a standard deck of playing cards which has 13 cards in each of four suits: spades, hearts, diamonds and clubs

_____

Use the complement to find each probability. (Example 3)

8. What is the probability of not rolling a 5 on a standard number cube?

_____

9. A spinner has 3 equal sections that are red, white, and blue. What is the probability of not landing on blue?

_____

10. A spinner has 5 equal sections marked 1 through 5. What is the probability of not landing on 4?

_____

11. There are 4 queens in a standard deck of 52 cards. You pick one card at random. What is the probability of not picking a queen?

_____

? **ESSENTIAL QUESTION CHECK-IN**

12. Describe an event that has a probability of 0% and an event that has a probability of 100%.

_____

_____

_____

7.1 Independent Practice

Personal
Math Trainer

Online
Assessment and
Intervention

my.hrw.com

13. There are 4 aces and 4 kings in a standard deck of 52 cards. You pick one card at random. What is the probability of selecting an ace or a king? Explain your reasoning.

_____

_____

14. There are 12 pieces of fruit in a bowl. Seven of the pieces are apples and two are peaches. What is the probability that a randomly selected piece of fruit will not be an apple or a peach? Justify your answer.

_____

_____

15. Critique Reasoning For breakfast, Clarissa can choose from oatmeal, cereal, French toast, or scrambled eggs. She thinks that if she selects a breakfast at random, it is likely that it will be oatmeal. Is she correct? Explain your reasoning.

_____

_____

_____

16. Draw Conclusions A researcher's garden contains 90 sweet pea plants, which have either white or purple flowers. About 70 of the plants have purple flowers, and about 20 have white flowers. Would you expect that one plant randomly selected from the garden will have purple or white flowers? Explain.

_____

_____

_____

17. The power goes out as Sandra is trying to get dressed. If she has 4 white T-shirts and 10 colored T-shirts in her drawer, is it likely that she will pick a colored T-shirt in the dark? What is the probability she will pick a colored T-shirt? Explain your answers.

_____

_____

18. James counts the hair colors of the 22 people in his class, including himself. He finds that there are 4 people with blonde hair, 8 people with brown hair, and 10 people with black hair. What is the probability that a randomly chosen student in the class does not have red hair? Explain.

_____

_____

19. Persevere in Problem Solving A bag contains 8 blue coins and 6 red coins. A coin is removed at random and replaced by three of the other color.

a. What is the probability that the removed coin is blue?

_____

b. If the coin removed is blue, what is the probability of drawing a red coin after three red coins are put in the bag to replace the blue one?

_____

c. If the coin removed is red, what is the probability of drawing a red coin after three blue coins are put in the bag to replace the red one?

_____

H.O.T. FOCUS ON HIGHER ORDER THINKING

Work Area

20. Draw Conclusions Give an example of an event in which all of the outcomes are not equally likely. Explain.

_____

_____

_____

21. Critique Reasoning A box contains 150 black pens and 50 red pens. Jose said the sum of the probability that a randomly selected pen will not be black and the probability that the pen will not be red is 1. Explain whether you agree.

_____

_____

_____

22. Communicate Mathematical Ideas A spinner has 7 identical sections. Two sections are blue, 1 is red, and 4 of the sections are green. Suppose the probability of an event happening is $\frac{2}{7}$. What does each number in the ratio represent? What outcome matches this probability?

_____

_____

Experimental Probability of Simple Events

COMMON CORE 7.SP.6

Approximate the probability of a chance event by collecting data on the chance process that produces it and observing its long-run relative frequency ... *Also 7.SP.7b*

ESSENTIAL QUESTION

How do you find the experimental probability of a simple event?

EXPLORE ACTIVITY 7.SP.6, 7.SP.7b

Finding Experimental Probability

You can toss a paper cup to demonstrate *experimental probability*.

A Consider tossing a paper cup. Fill in the Outcome column of the table with the three different ways the cup could land.

B Toss a paper cup twenty times. Record your observations in the table.

Outcome	Number of Times

Reflect

1. Do the outcomes appear to be equally likely? _____

2. Describe the three outcomes using the words *likely* and *unlikely*.

_____

_____

3. Use the number of times each event occurred to approximate the probability of each event.

4. **Make a Prediction** What do you think would happen if you performed more trials?

_____

_____

_____

5. What is the sum of the probabilities in 3?

_____

Outcome	Experimental Probability
Open-end up	$\dfrac{\text{open-end up}}{20} = \dfrac{\boxed{}}{20}$
Open-end down	$\dfrac{\text{open-end down}}{20} = \dfrac{\boxed{}}{20}$
On its side	$\dfrac{\text{on its side}}{20} = \dfrac{\boxed{}}{20}$

Calculating Experimental Probability

You can use *experimental probability* to approximate the probability of an event. An **experimental probability** of an event is found by comparing the number of times the event occurs to the total number of trials. When there is only one outcome for an event, it is called a **simple event**.

Experimental Probability

For a given experiment:

Experimental probability = $\dfrac{\text{number of times the event occurs}}{\text{total number of trials}}$

EXAMPLE 1

COMMON CORE 7.SP.7b

Martin has a bag of marbles. He removed one marble at random, recorded the color and then placed it back in the bag. He repeated this process several times and recorded his results in the table. Find the experimental probability of drawing each color.

Color	Frequency
Red	12
Blue	10
Green	15
Yellow	13

STEP 1 Identify the number of trials: $12 + 10 + 15 + 13 = 50$

STEP 2 Complete the table of experimental probabilities. Write each answer as a fraction in simplest form.

Color	Experimental Probability
Red	$\dfrac{\text{frequency of the event}}{\text{total number of trials}} = \dfrac{12}{50} = \dfrac{6}{25}$
Blue	$\dfrac{\text{frequency of the event}}{\text{total number of trials}} = \dfrac{10}{50} = \dfrac{1}{5}$
Green	$\dfrac{\text{frequency of the event}}{\text{total number of trials}} = \dfrac{15}{50} = \dfrac{3}{10}$
Yellow	$\dfrac{\text{frequency of the event}}{\text{total number of trials}} = \dfrac{13}{50}$

> Substitute the results recorded in the table. You can also write each probability as a decimal or as a percent.

Reflect

6. Communicate Mathematical Ideas What are two different ways you could find the experimental probability of the event that Martin does **not** draw a red marble?

_____

_____

_____

_____

Math Talk
Mathematical Practices

Will everyone who does this experiment get the same results?

7. A spinner has three unequal sections: red, yellow, and blue. The table shows the results of Nolan's spins. Find the experimental probability of landing on each color. Write your answers in simplest form.

Color	Frequency
Red	10
Yellow	14
Blue	6

_____

Making Predictions with Experimental Probability

A **simulation** is a model of an experiment that would be difficult or inconvenient to actually perform. You can use a simulation to find an experimental probability and make a prediction.

Math On the Spot
my.hrw.com

EXAMPLE 2   COMMON CORE 7.SP.6

My Notes

A baseball team has a batting average of 0.250 so far this season. This means that the team's players get hits in 25% of their chances at bat. Use a simulation to predict the number of hits the team's players will have in their next 34 chances at bat.

STEP 1 Choose a model.

Batting average $= 0.250 = \frac{250}{1,000} = \frac{1}{4}$

A standard deck of cards has four suits, hearts, diamonds, spades, and clubs. Since $\frac{1}{4}$ of the cards are hearts, you can let hearts represent a "hit." Diamonds, clubs, and spades then represent "no hit."

STEP 2 Perform the simulation.

Draw a card at random from the deck, record the result, and put the card back into the deck. Continue until you have drawn and replaced 34 cards in all.

Since the team has 34 chances at bat, you must draw a card 34 times.

(H = heart, D = diamond, C = club, S = spade)

H D D S H C H S D H C D C C D H H
S D D H C C H C H H D S S S C H D

STEP 3 Make a prediction.

Count the number of hearts in the simulation.

Since there are 11 hearts, you can predict that the team will have 11 hits in its next 34 chances at bat.

YOUR TURN

8. A toy machine has equal numbers of red, white, and blue foam balls which it releases at random. Ross wonders which color ball will be released next. Describe how you could use a standard number cube to predict the answer.

_____

_____

_____

_____

_____

Guided Practice

1. A spinner has four sections lettered A, B, C, and D. The table shows the results of several spins. Find the experimental probability of spinning each letter as a fraction in simplest form, a decimal, and a percent.
   (Explore Activity and Example 1)

Letter	A	B	C	D
Frequency	14	7	11	8

A: _____   B: _____

C: _____   D: _____

2. Rachel's free-throw average for basketball is 60%. She wants to predict how many times in the next 50 tries she will make a free throw. Describe how she could use 10 index cards to predict the answer. (Example 2)

_____

_____

_____

❓ ESSENTIAL QUESTION CHECK-IN

3. **Essential Question Follow Up** How do you find an experimental probability of a simple event?

_____

_____

7.2 Independent Practice

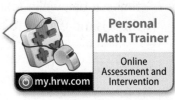

COMMON CORE **7.SP.6, 7.SP.7b**

4. Dree rolls a strike in 6 out of the 10 frames of bowling. What is the experimental probability that Dree will roll a strike in the first frame of the next game? Explain why a number cube would not be a good way to simulate this situation.

_____

_____

_____

5. To play a game, you spin a spinner like the one shown. You win if the arrow lands in one of the areas marked "WIN". Lee played this game many times and recorded her results. She won 8 times and lost 40 times. Use Lee's data to explain how to find the experimental probability of winning this game.

_____

_____

6. The names of the students in Mr. Hayes' math class are written on the board. Mr. Hayes writes each name on an index card and shuffles the cards. Each day he randomly draws a card, and the chosen student explains a math problem at the board. What is the probability that Ryan is chosen today? What is the probability that Ryan is **not** chosen today?

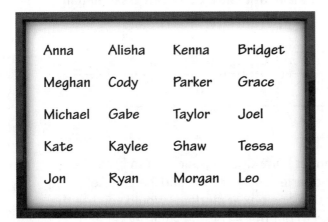

Anna	Alisha	Kenna	Bridget
Meghan	Cody	Parker	Grace
Michael	Gabe	Taylor	Joel
Kate	Kaylee	Shaw	Tessa
Jon	Ryan	Morgan	Leo

_____

7. Critique Reasoning A meteorologist reports an 80% chance of precipitation. Is this an example of experimental probability, written as a percent? Explain your reasoning.

_____

8. Mica and Joan are on the same softball team. Mica got 8 hits out of 48 times at bat, while Joan got 12 hits out of 40 times at bat. Who do you think is more likely to get a hit her next time at bat? Explain.

_____

_____

9. **Make a Prediction** In tennis, Gabby serves an ace, a ball that can't be returned, 4 out of the 10 times she serves. What is the experimental probability that Gabby will serve an ace in the first match of the next game? Make a prediction about how many aces Gabby will have for the next 40 serves. Justify your reasoning.

_____

10. **Represent Real-World Problems** Patricia finds that the experimental probability that her dog will want to go outside between 4 P.M. and 5 P.M. is $\frac{7}{12}$. About what percent of the time does her dog **not** want to go out between 4 P.M. and 5 P.M.?

_____

H.O.T. **FOCUS ON HIGHER ORDER THINKING**

Work Area

11. **Explain the Error** Talia tossed a penny many times. She got 40 heads and 60 tails. She said the experimental probability of getting heads was $\frac{40}{60}$. Explain and correct her error.

_____

12. **Communicate Mathematical Ideas** A high school has 438 students, with about the same number of males as females. Describe a simulation to predict how many of the first 50 students who leave school at the end of the day are female.

_____

_____

_____

13. **Critical Thinking** For a scavenger hunt, Chessa put one coin in each of 10 small boxes. Four coins are quarters, 4 are dimes, and 2 are nickels. How could you simulate choosing one box at random? Would you use the same simulation if you planned to put these coins in your pocket and choose one? Explain your reasoning.

_____

_____

_____

Experimental Probability of Compound Events

COMMON CORE 7.SP.8
Find probabilities of compound events using... tables, ..., and simulation. *Also 7.SP.8a, 7.SP.8b, 7.SP.8c*

ESSENTIAL QUESTION How do you find the experimental probability of a compound event?

EXPLORE ACTIVITY COMMON CORE **7.SP.8a, 7.SP.8b**

Exploring Compound Probability

A **compound event** is an event that includes two or more simple events, such as flipping a coin *and* rolling a number cube. A compound event can include events that depend on each other or are independent. Events are independent if the occurrence of one event does not affect the probability of the other event, such as flipping a coin and rolling a number cube.

A What are the possible outcomes of flipping a coin once? _____

B What are the possible outcomes of rolling a standard number cube once? _____

C Complete the list for all possible outcomes for flipping a coin *and* rolling a number cube.

H1, H2, _____, _____, _____, _____, T1, _____, _____, _____, _____, _____

There are _____ possible outcomes for this compound event.

D Flip a coin and roll a number cube 50 times. Use tally marks to record your results in the table.

> H1 would mean the coin landed on heads, and the number cube showed a 1.

	1	2	3	4	5	6
H						
T						

E Based on your data, which compound event had the greatest experimental probability and what was it? The least experimental

probability? _____

F **Draw Conclusions** Did you expect to have the same probability for each possible combination of flips and rolls? Why or why not?

_____

_____

Calculating Experimental Probability of Compound Events

The experimental probability of a compound event can be found using recorded data.

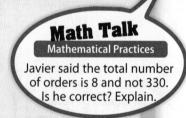

EXAMPLE 1

COMMON CORE   7.SP.8, 7.SP.8a

A food trailer serves chicken and records the order size and sides on their orders, as shown in the table. What is the experimental probability that the next order is for 3-pieces with cole slaw?

	Green Salad	Macaroni & Cheese	French Fries	Cole Slaw
2 pieces	33	22	52	35
3 pieces	13	55	65	55

STEP 1 Find the total number of trials, or orders.

$$33 + 22 + 52 + 35 + 13 + 55 + 65 + 55 = 330$$

STEP 2 Find the number of orders that are for 3 pieces with cole slaw: 55.

STEP 3 Find the experimental probability.

$$P(\text{3 piece} + \text{slaw}) = \frac{\text{number of 3 piece} + \text{slaw}}{\text{total number of orders}}$$

$$= \frac{55}{330} \quad \text{Substitute the values.}$$

$$= \frac{1}{6} \quad \text{Simplify.}$$

The experimental probability that the next order is for 3 pieces of chicken with cole slaw is $\frac{1}{6}$.

Math Talk

Mathematical Practices

Javier said the total number of orders is 8 and not 330. Is he correct? Explain.

YOUR TURN

1. Drink sales for an afternoon at the school carnival were recorded in the table. What is the experimental probability that the next drink is a small cocoa?

	Soda	Water	Cocoa
Small	77	98	60
Large	68	45	52

_____

Using a Simulation to Make a Prediction

You can use a simulation or model of an experiment to find the experimental probability of compound events.

Math On the Spot
my.hrw.com

EXAMPLE 2   7.SP.8c

At a street intersection, a vehicle is classified either as a *car* or a *truck*, and it can turn *left*, *right*, or go *straight*. About an equal number of cars and trucks go through the intersection and turn in each direction. Use a simulation to find the experimental probability that the next vehicle will be a car that turns right.

STEP 1 Choose a model.
Use a coin toss to model the two vehicle types.
Let Heads = Car and Tails = Truck

Use a spinner divided into 3 equal sectors to represent the *three* directions as shown.

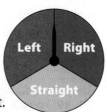

STEP 2 Find the sample space for the compound event.

There are 6 possible outcomes: CL, CR, CS, TL, TR, TS

STEP 3 Perform the simulation.

A coin was tossed and a spinner spun 50 times.
The results are shown in the table.

	Car	Truck
Left	8	9
Right	6	11
Straight	9	7

STEP 4 Find the experimental probability that a car turns right.

$$P(\text{Car turns right}) = \frac{\text{frequency of compound event}}{\text{total number of trials}}$$

$$= \frac{6}{50} \quad \text{Substitute the values.}$$

$$= \frac{3}{25} \quad \text{Simplify.}$$

Based on the simulation, the experimental probability is $\frac{3}{25}$ that the next vehicle will be a car that turns right.

Reflect

2. **Make a Prediction** Predict the number of cars that turn right out of 100 vehicles that enter the intersection. Explain your reasoning.

_____

_____

My Notes

YOUR TURN

3. A jeweler sells necklaces made in three sizes and two different metals. Use the data from a simulation to find the experimental probability that the next necklace sold is a 20-inch gold necklace.

	Silver	Gold
12 in.	12	22
16 in.	16	8
20 in.	5	12

_____

Guided Practice

1. A dentist has 400 male and female patients that range in ages from 10 years old to 50 years old and up as shown in the table. What is the experimental probability that the next patient will be female and in the age range 22–39? (Explore Activity and Example 1)

	Range: 10–21	Range: 22–39	Range: 40–50	Range: 50+
Male	44	66	32	53
Female	36	50	45	74

_____

2. At a car wash, customers can choose the type of wash and whether to use the interior vacuum. Customers are equally likely to choose each type of wash and whether to use the vacuum. Use a simulation to find the experimental probability that the next customer purchases a deluxe wash and no interior vacuum. Describe your simulation. (Example 2)

_____

_____

_____

CAR WASH

Standard

Deluxe

Superior

Vacuum   yes   no

? ESSENTIAL QUESTION CHECK-IN

3. How do you find the experimental probability of a compound event?

_____

_____

7.3 Independent Practice

 7.SP.8, 7.SP.8a, 7.SP.8b, 7.SP.8c

Personal
Math Trainer

Online
Assessment and
Intervention

my.hrw.com

4. Represent Real-World Problems For the same food trailer mentioned in Example 1, explain how to find the experimental probability that the next order is two pieces of chicken with a green salad.

_____

_____

The school store sells spiral notebooks in four colors and three different sizes. The table shows the sales by size and color for 400 notebooks.

	Red	Green	Blue	Yellow
100 Pages	55	37	26	12
150 Pages	60	44	57	27
200 Pages	23	19	21	19

5. What is the experimental probability that the next customer buys a red notebook with 150 pages?

_____

6. What is the experimental probability that the next customer buys any red notebooks?

_____

7. Analyze Relationships How many possible combined page count and color choices are possible? How does this number relate to the number of page size choices and to the number of color choices?

_____

_____

A middle school English teacher polled random students about how many pages of a book they read per week.

	6th	7th	8th
75 Pages	24	18	22
100 Pages	22	32	24
150 Pages	30	53	25

8. Critique Reasoning Jennie says the experimental probability that a 7th grade student reads at least 100 pages per week is $\frac{16}{125}$. What is her error and the correct experimental probability?

_____

9. Analyze Relationships Based on the data, which group(s) of students should be encouraged to read more? Explain your reasoning.

_____

_____

10. Make a Conjecture Would you expect the probability for the simple event "rolling a 6" to be greater than or less than the probability of the compound event "rolling a 6 and getting heads on a coin"? Explain.

_____

_____

11. Critique Reasoning Donald says he uses a standard number cube for simulations that involve 2, 3, or 6 equal outcomes. Explain how Donald can do this.

_____

_____

_____

12. Draw Conclusions Data collected in a mall recorded the shoe styles worn by 150 male and for 150 female customers. What is the probability that the next customer is male and has an open-toe shoe (such as a sandal)? What is the probability that the next male customer has an open-toe shoe? Are the two probabilities the same? Explain.

	Male	Female
Open toe	11	92
Closed toe	139	58

_____

_____

_____

13. What If? Suppose you wanted to perform a simulation to model the shoe style data shown in the table. Could you use two coins? Explain.

_____

_____

14. Represent Real-World Problems A middle school is made up of grades 6, 7, and 8, and has about the same number of male and female students in each grade. Explain how to use a simulation to find the experimental probability that the first 50 students who arrive at school are male and 7th graders.

_____

_____

_____

_____

Making Predictions with Experimental Probability

COMMON CORE   7.SP.6

Approximate the probability of a chance event by collecting data on the chance process that produces it…, and predict the approximate relative frequency given the probability. *Also 7.RP.2c, 7.RP.3, 7.NS.3*

ESSENTIAL QUESTION

How do you make predictions using experimental probability?

EXPLORE ACTIVITY COMMON CORE 7.SP.6

Math On the Spot
my.hrw.com

Using Experimental Probability to Make a Prediction

Scientists study data to make predictions. You can use probabilities to make predictions in your daily life.

EXAMPLE 1 Danae found that the experimental probability of her making a bull's-eye when throwing darts is $\frac{2}{10}$, or 20%. Out of 75 throws, about how many bull's-eyes could she predict she would make?

Method 1: Use a proportion.

Write a proportion. 2 out of 10 is how many out of 75?

$$\frac{2}{10} = \frac{x}{75}$$

Since 10 times _____ is 75, multiply

2 times _____ to find the value of *x*.

$$\frac{\boxed{}}{10} = \frac{\boxed{}}{75}$$

$$x = \boxed{}$$

Method 2: Use a percent equation.

Write an equation to find 20% of 75. $\boxed{} \times 75 = x$ *You can write probabilities as ratios, decimals, or percents.*

Multiply. $15 = x$

Danae can predict that she will make about 15 bull's-eye throws out of 75.

Personal Math Trainer
Online Assessment and Intervention
my.hrw.com

1. A car rental company sells accident insurance to 24% of its customers. Out of 550 customers, about how many customers are predicted to

purchase insurance? _____

Using Experimental Probability to Make a Qualitative Prediction

A prediction is something you reasonably expect to happen in the future. A qualitative prediction helps you decide which situation is more likely in general.

EXAMPLE 2

COMMON CORE 7.SP.6

A doctor's office records data and concludes that, on average, 11% of patients call to reschedule their appointments per week. The office manager predicts that 23 appointments will be rescheduled out of the 240 total appointments during next week. Explain whether the prediction is reasonable.

Method 1: Use a proportion.

$$\frac{11}{100} = \frac{x}{240}$$

Write a proportion. 11 out of 100 is how many out of 240?

$$\frac{11}{100} = \frac{x}{240}$$
$\times 2.4$

$\times 2.4$
$$\frac{11}{100} = \frac{26.4}{240}$$
$\times 2.4$

Since 100 times 2.4 is 240, multiply 11 times 2.4 to find the value of x.

$$x = 26.4$$

> 26.4 is the average number of patients that would call to reschedule.

Method 2: Use a percent equation.

$$0.11 \cdot 240 = x$$ Find 11% of 240.

$$26.4 = x$$ Solve for x.

The prediction of 23 is reasonable but a little low, because 23 is a little less than 26.4.

Reflect

2. Does 26.4 make sense for the number of patients?

_____

_____

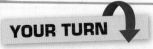
YOUR TURN

3. In emails to monthly readers of a newsletter 3% of the emails come back undelivered. The editor predicts that if he sends out 12,372 emails, he will receive 437 notices for undelivered email. Do you agree with his prediction?

Explain. _____

_____

Making a Quantitative Prediction

You can use proportional reasoning to make quantitative predictions and compare options in real-world situations.

EXAMPLE 3 · Problem Solving

COMMON CORE | 7.SP.6

An online poll for a movie site shows its polling results for a new movie. If a newspaper surveys 150 people leaving the movie, how many people can it predict will like the movie based on the online poll? Is the movie site's claim accurate if the newspaper has 104 people say they like the movie?

My Notes

Analyze Information

The **answer** is a prediction for how many people out of 150 will like the movie based on the online poll. Also tell whether the 104 people that say they like the movie is enough to support the movie site's claim.

List the important information:
• The online poll says 72% of movie goers like the new movie.
• A newspaper surveys 150 people.

Formulate a Plan

Use a proportion to calculate 72% of the 150 people surveyed.

Solve

$$\frac{72}{100} = \frac{x}{150}$$

Set up a proportion. 72 out of 100 is how many out of 150?

$$\frac{72}{100} = \frac{x}{150}$$
×1.5

×1.5
$$\frac{72}{100} = \frac{108}{150}$$
×1.5

Since 100 times 1.5 is 150, multiply 72 times 1.5 to find the value of x.

$$x = 108$$

The newspaper can predict that 108 out of 150 people will say they like the movie, based on the online poll.

Justify and Evaluate

Since 108 is close to 104, the newspaper survey and the online poll show that about same percent of people like the movie.

Personal
Math Trainer

Online Assessment
and Intervention

⏻ my.hrw.com

YOUR TURN

4. On average, 24% of customers who buy shoes in a particular store buy two or more pairs. One weekend, 350 customers purchased shoes. How many can be predicted to buy two or more pairs? If 107 customers buy more than two pairs, did more customers than normal buy two or more pairs?

_____

_____

Guided Practice

1. A baseball player reaches first base 30% of the times he is at bat. Out of 50 times at bat, about how many times will the player reach first base?
(Explore Activity Example 1)

_____

2. The experimental probability that it will rain on any given day in Houston, Texas, is about 15%. Out of 365 days, about how many days can residents predict rain?
(Explore Activity Example 1)

_____

3. A catalog store has 6% of its orders returned for a refund. The owner predicts that a new candle will have 812 returns out of the 16,824 sold. Do you agree with this prediction? Explain. (Example 2)

_____

_____

4. On a toy assembly line, 3% of the toys are found to be defective. The quality control officer predicts that 872 toys will be found defective out of 24,850 toys made. Do you agree with this prediction? Explain. (Example 2)

_____

_____

5. A light-rail service claims to be on time 98% of the time. Jeanette takes the light-rail 40 times one month, how many times can she predict she will be on time? Is the light-rail's claim accurate if she is late 6 times? (Example 3)

_____

_____

6. On average, a college claims to accept 18% of its applicants. If the college has 5,000 applicants, predict how many will be accepted. If 885 applicants are accepted, is the college's claim accurate? (Example 3)

_____

_____

? ESSENTIAL QUESTION CHECK-IN

7. How do you make predictions using experimental probability?

_____

_____

_____

7.4 Independent Practice

COMMON CORE 7.SP.6

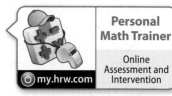

Personal Math Trainer

Online Assessment and Intervention

my.hrw.com

The table shows the number of students in a middle school at the beginning of the year and the percentage that can be expected to move out of the area by the end of the year.

	6th	7th	8th
Number of Students	250	200	150
% Moves	2%	4%	8%

8. How many 7th grade students are expected to move by the end of the year? If 12 students actually moved, did more or fewer 7th grade students move than expected? Justify your answer.

_____

_____

9. Critique Reasoning The middle school will lose some of its funding if 50 or more students move away in any year. The principal claims he only loses about 30 students a year. Do the values in the table support his claim? Explain.

_____

_____

_____

10. Represent Real-World Problems An airline knows that, on average, the probability that a passenger will not show up for a flight is 6%. If an airplane is fully booked and holds 300 passengers, how many seats are expected to be empty? If the airline overbooked the flight by 10 passengers, about how many passengers are expected to show up for the flight? Justify your answer.

_____

_____

_____

_____

11. Draw Conclusions In a doctor's office, an average of 94% of the clients pay on the day of the appointment. If the office has 600 clients per month, how many are expected not to pay on the day of the appointment? If 40 clients do not pay on the day of their appointment in a month, did more or fewer than the average not pay?

_____

12. Counterexamples The soccer coach claimed that, on average, only 80% of the team come to practice each day. The table shows the number of students that came to practice for 8 days. If the team has 20 members, how many team members should come to practice to uphold the coach's claim? Was the coach's claim accurate? Explain your reasoning.

	1	2	3	4	5	6	7	8
Number of Students	18	15	18	17	17	19	20	20

_____

_____

13. What's the Error? Ronnie misses the school bus 1 out of every 30 school days. He sets up the proportion $\frac{1}{30} = \frac{180}{x}$ to predict how many days he will miss the bus in the 180-day school year. What is Ronnie's error?

_____

 **FOCUS ON HIGHER ORDER THINKING**

Work Area

14. Persevere in Problem Solving A gas pump machine rejects 12% of credit card transactions. If this is twice the normal rejection rate for a normal gas pump, how many out of 500 credit cards transactions would a

normal gas pump machine reject? _____

15. Make Predictions An airline's weekly flight data showed a 98% probability of being on time. If this airline has 15,000 flights in a year, how many flights would you predict to arrive on time? Explain whether you can use the data to predict whether a specific flight with this airline will be on time.

_____

_____

_____

_____

16. Draw Conclusions An average response rate for a marketing letter is 4%, meaning that 4% of the people who receive the letter respond to it. A company writes a new type of marketing letter, sends out 2,400 of them, and gets 65 responses. Explain whether the new type of letter would be considered to be a success.

_____

_____

_____

Ready to Go On?

7.1 Probability

1. Josue tosses a coin and spins the spinner at the right. What are all the possible outcomes?

_____

7.2 Experimental Probability of Simple Events

2. While bowling with friends, Brandy rolls a strike in 6 out of 10 frames. What is the experimental probability that Brandy will roll a strike in the first frame of the next game?

_____

3. Ben is greeting customers at a music store. Of the first 20 people he sees enter the store, 13 are wearing jackets and 7 are not. What is the experimental probability that the next person to enter the store will be wearing a jacket?

_____

7.3 Experimental Probability of Compound Events

4. Auden rolled two number cubes and recorded the results.

Roll #1	Roll #2	Roll #3	Roll #4	Roll #5	Roll #6	Roll #7
2, 1	4, 5	3, 2	2, 2	1, 3	6, 2	5, 3

What is the experimental probability that the sum of the next two numbers rolled is greater than 5?

_____

7.4 Making Predictions with Experimental Probability

5. A player on a school baseball team reaches first base $\frac{3}{10}$ of the time he is at bat. Out of 80 times at bat, about how many times would you predict he will reach first base?

_____

? ESSENTIAL QUESTION

6. How is experimental probability used to make predictions?

_____

_____

_____

MODULE 7 MIXED REVIEW

Assessment Readiness

COMMON CORE

Personal Math Trainer

Online Assessment and Intervention

my.hrw.com

Selected Response

1. A frozen yogurt shop offers scoops in cake cones, waffle cones, or cups. You can get vanilla, chocolate, strawberry, pistachio, or coffee flavored frozen yogurt. If you order a single scoop, how many outcomes are in the sample space?

Ⓐ 3

Ⓒ 8

Ⓑ 5

Ⓓ 15

2. A bag contains 7 purple beads, 4 blue beads, and 4 pink beads. What is the probability of **not** drawing a pink bead?

Ⓐ $\frac{4}{15}$

Ⓒ $\frac{8}{15}$

Ⓑ $\frac{7}{15}$

Ⓓ $\frac{11}{15}$

3. During the month of June, Ava kept track of the number of days she saw birds in her garden. She saw birds on 18 days of the month. What is the experimental probability that she will see birds in her garden on July 1?

Ⓐ $\frac{1}{18}$

Ⓒ $\frac{1}{2}$

Ⓑ $\frac{2}{5}$

Ⓓ $\frac{3}{5}$

4. A rectangle has a width of 4 inches and a length of 6 inches. A similar rectangle has a width of 12 inches. What is the length of the similar rectangle?

Ⓐ 8 inches

Ⓒ 14 inches

Ⓑ 12 inches

Ⓓ 18 inches

5. The experimental probability of hearing thunder on any given day in Ohio is 30%. Out of 600 days, on about how many days can Ohioans expect to hear thunder?

Ⓐ 90 days

Ⓒ 210 days

Ⓑ 180 days

Ⓓ 420 days

6. Isidro tossed two coins several times and then recorded the results in the table below.

Toss 1	Toss 2	Toss 3	Toss 4	Toss 5
H; T	T; T	T; H	H; T	H; H

What is the experimental probability that both coins will land on the same side on Isidro's next toss?

Ⓐ $\frac{1}{5}$

Ⓒ $\frac{3}{5}$

Ⓑ $\frac{2}{5}$

Ⓓ $\frac{4}{5}$

Mini-Task

7. Magdalena had a spinner that was evenly divided into sections of red, blue, and green. She spun the spinner and tossed a coin several times. The table below shows the results.

Trial 1	Trial 2	Trial 3	Trial 4	Trial 5
blue; T	green; T	green; H	red; T	blue; H

a. What are all the possible outcomes?

_____

_____

b. What experimental probability did Magdalena find for spinning blue? Give your answer as a fraction in simplest form, as a decimal, and as a percent.

_____

c. Out of 90 trials, how many times should Magdalena predict she will spin green while tossing tails?

_____

Theoretical Probability and Simulations

ESSENTIAL QUESTION

How can you use theoretical probability to solve real-world problems?

Real-World Video

Many carnival games rely on theoretical probability to set the chance of winning fairly low. Understanding how the game is set up might help you be more likely to win.

Ⓞ my.hrw.com

GO DIGITAL

my.hrw.com

my.hrw.com

Go digital with your write-in student edition, accessible on any device.

Math On the Spot

Scan with your smart phone to jump directly to the online edition, video tutor, and more.

Animated Math

Interactively explore key concepts to see how math works.

Personal Math Trainer

Get immediate feedback and help as you work through practice sets.

Are YOU Ready?

Complete these exercises to review skills you will need for this module.

my.hrw.com

Personal Math Trainer

Online Assessment and Intervention

Fractions, Decimals, and Percents

EXAMPLE   Write $\frac{3}{8}$ as a decimal and a percent.

$$\begin{array}{r} 0.375 \\ 8{\overline{)3.000}} \\ -2\,4 \\ \hline 60 \\ -56 \\ \hline 40 \\ -40 \\ \hline 0 \end{array}$$

Write the fraction as a division problem. Write a decimal point and zeros in the dividend.
Place a decimal point in the quotient.
Divide as with whole numbers.

$0.375 = 37.5\%.$ Write the decimal as a percent.

Write each fraction as a decimal and a percent.

1. $\frac{3}{4}$ _____

2. $\frac{2}{5}$ _____

3. $\frac{9}{10}$ _____

4. $\frac{7}{20}$ _____

5. $\frac{7}{8}$ _____

6. $\frac{1}{20}$ _____

7. $\frac{19}{25}$ _____

8. $\frac{23}{50}$ _____

Operations with Fractions

EXAMPLE
$$1 - \frac{7}{12} = \frac{12}{12} - \frac{7}{12}$$
$$= \frac{12 - 7}{12}$$
$$= \frac{5}{12}$$

Use the denominator of the fraction to write 1 as a fraction.
Subtract the numerators.

Simplify.

Find each difference.

9. $1 - \frac{1}{5}$ _____

10. $1 - \frac{2}{9}$ _____

11. $1 - \frac{8}{13}$ _____

12. $1 - \frac{3}{20}$ _____

Multiply Fractions

EXAMPLE
$$\frac{4}{15} \times \frac{5}{6} = \frac{\overset{2}{\cancel{4}}}{\cancel{15}_3} \times \frac{\cancel{5}^1}{\cancel{6}_3}$$
$$= \frac{2}{9}$$

Divide by the common factors.

Simplify.

Multiply. Write each product in simplest form.

13. $\frac{8}{15} \times \frac{5}{8}$ _____

14. $\frac{2}{9} \times \frac{3}{4}$ _____

15. $\frac{9}{16} \times \frac{12}{13}$ _____

16. $\frac{7}{10} \times \frac{5}{28}$ _____

Reading Start-Up

Visualize Vocabulary

Use the ✔ words to complete the graphic.

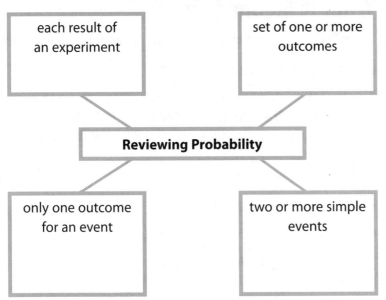

each result of
an experiment

set of one or more
outcomes

Reviewing Probability

only one outcome
for an event

two or more simple
events

Vocabulary

Review Words
- complement
  (complemento)
- ✔ compound event *(suceso compuesto)*
- ✔ event *(suceso)*
- experiment *(experimento)*
- ✔ outcome *(resultado)*
- ✔ simple event *(suceso simple)*
- probability *(probabilidad)*

Preview Words
- theoretical probability *(probabilidad teórica)*

Understand Vocabulary

Match the term on the left to the correct expression on the right.

1. compound event
2. theoretical probability
3. complement

A. The set of all outcomes that are not the desired event.

B. An event made of two or more simple events.

C. The ratio of the number of equally likely outcomes in an event to the total number of possible outcomes.

Active Reading

Two-Panel Flip Chart Create a two-panel flip chart, to help you understand the concepts in this module. Label one flap "Simple Events" and the other flap "Compound Events." As you study each lesson, write important ideas under the appropriate flap. Include information that will help you remember the concepts later when you look back at your notes.

Unpacking the Standards

Understanding the standards and the vocabulary terms in the standards will help you know exactly what you are expected to learn in this module.

COMMON CORE **7.SP.7a**

Develop a uniform probability model by assigning equal probability to all outcomes, and use the model to determine probabilities of events.

What It Means to You

You will find the probabilities of a simple event and its complement.

UNPACKING EXAMPLE 7.SP.7A

Tara has a bag that contains 8 white marbles, 10 green marbles, and 7 red marbles. She selects a marble at random. Find the probability that the marble is red, and the probability that it is **not** red.

$$P(\text{red}) = \frac{\text{number of red marbles}}{\text{total number of marbles}}$$

$$= \frac{7}{25}$$

$$P(\text{not red}) = 1 - P(\text{red}) = 1 - \frac{7}{25} = \frac{25}{25} - \frac{7}{25} = \frac{18}{25}$$

The probability that the marble is red is $\frac{7}{25}$, and the probability that it is not red is $\frac{18}{25}$.

COMMON CORE **7.SP.8b**

Represent sample spaces for compound events using methods such as organized lists, tables and tree diagrams. For an event described in everyday language (e.g., "rolling double sixes"), identify the outcomes in the sample space which compose the event.

Key Vocabulary

compound event *(suceso compuesto)*
An event made of two or more simple events.

What It Means to You

You will identify the outcomes in the sample space of a compound event.

UNPACKING EXAMPLE 7.SP.8B

Identify the sample space for flipping a coin and rolling a number cube.

Make a table to organize the information.

		Number Cube Outcomes					
		1	2	3	4	5	6
C O I N	H	H1	H2	H3	H4	H5	H6
	T	T1	T2	T3	T4	T5	T6

The sample space includes 12 possible outcomes: H1, H2, H3, H4, H5, H6, T1, T2, T3, T4, T5, and T6.

Visit **my.hrw.com** to see all the **Common Core Standards** unpacked.

my.hrw.com

COMMON CORE 7.SP.7a

Develop a uniform probability model by assigning equal probability to all outcomes, and use the model to determine probabilities of events. *Also 7.SP.6, 7.SP.7*

LESSON 8.1 Theoretical Probability of Simple Events

How can you find the theoretical probability of a simple event?

EXPLORE ACTIVITY 1 COMMON CORE 7.SP.7a

Finding Theoretical Probability

In previous lessons, you found probabilities based on observing data, or experimental probabilities. In this lesson, you will find *theoretical probabilities*.

At a school fair, you have a choice of spinning Spinner A or Spinner B. You win an MP3 player if the spinner lands on a section with a star in it. Which spinner should you choose if you want a better chance of winning?

A Complete the table.

	Spinner A	Spinner B
Total number of outcomes		
Number of sections with stars		
P(winning MP3) $= \dfrac{\text{number of sections with stars}}{\text{total number of outcomes}}$		

Spinner A

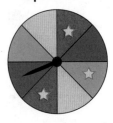

Spinner B

B Compare the ratios for Spinner A and Spinner B.

The ratio for Spinner _____ is greater than the ratio for Spinner _____.

I should choose _____ for a better chance of winning.

Math Talk
Mathematical Practices

Describe a way to change Spinner B to make your chances of winning equal to your chances of not winning. Explain.

Reflect

1. *Theoretical probability* is a way to describe how you found the chance of winning an MP3 player in the scenario above. Using the spinner example to help you, explain in your own words how to find the theoretical probability of an event.

_____

_____

_____

Calculating Theoretical Probability of Simple Events

Theoretical probability is the probability that an event occurs when all of the outcomes of the experiment are equally likely.

> ## Theoretical Probability
>
> $$P(\text{event}) = \frac{\text{number of ways the event can occur}}{\text{total number of equally likely outcomes}}$$

Probability can be written as a fraction, a decimal, or a percent. For example, the probability you win with Spinner B is $\frac{5}{16}$. You can also write that as 0.3125 or as 31.25%.

EXAMPLE 1

COMMON CORE 7.SP.7a

A bag contains 6 red marbles and 12 blue ones. You select one marble at random from the bag. What is the probability that you select a red marble? Write your answer in simplest form.

STEP 1 Find the number of ways the event can occur, that is, the number of red marbles: 6

STEP 2 Add to find the total number of equally likely outcomes.

number of red marbles	+	number of blue marbles	=	total number of marbles
6	+	12	=	**18**

There are 18 possible outcomes in the sample space.

STEP 3 Find the probability of selecting a red marble.

$$P(\text{red marble}) = \frac{\text{number of red marbles}}{\text{total number of marbles}} = \frac{6}{\textbf{18}}$$

The probability that you select a red marble is $\frac{6}{18}$, or $\frac{1}{3}$.

Math Talk
Mathematical Practices

Describe a situation that has a theoretical probability of $\frac{1}{4}$.

YOUR TURN

2. You roll a number cube one time. What is the probability that you roll a 3 or 4? Write your answer in simplest form.

$$P(\text{rolling a 3 or 4}) = \frac{}{} = \frac{\square}{\square} = \frac{\square}{\square}$$

3. How is the sample space for an event related to the formula for theoretical probability? _____

_____

Comparing Theoretical and Experimental Probability

Now that you have calculated theoretical probabilities, you may wonder how theoretical and experimental probabilities compare.

Six students are performing in a talent contest. You roll a number cube to determine the order of the performances.

STEP 1 You roll the number cube once. Complete the table of theoretical probabilities for the different outcomes.

Number	1	2	3	4	5	6
Theoretical probability						

STEP 2 Predict the number of times each number will be rolled out of 30 total rolls.

1: ☐ times   3: ☐ times   5: ☐ times

2: ☐ times   4: ☐ times   6: ☐ times

STEP 3 Roll a number cube 30 times. Complete the table for the frequency of each number and then find its experimental probability.

Number	1	2	3	4	5	6
Frequency						
Experimental probability						

STEP 4 Look at the tables you completed. How do the experimental probabilities compare with the theoretical probabilities?

_____

_____

STEP 5 **Conjecture** By performing more trials, you tend to get experimental results that are closer to the theoretical probabilities. Combine your table from **Step 3** with those of your classmates to make one table for the class. How do the class experimental probabilities compare with the theoretical probabilities?

_____

_____

Reflect

4. Could the experimental probabilities ever be exactly equal to the theoretical probability? If so, how likely is it? If not, why not?

_____

_____

Guided Practice

At a school fair, you have a choice of randomly picking a ball from Basket A or Basket B. Basket A has 5 green balls, 3 red balls, and 8 yellow balls. Basket B has 7 green balls, 4 red balls, and 9 yellow balls. You can win a digital book reader if you pick a red ball. (Explore Activity 1)

	Basket A	Basket B
Total number of outcomes		
Number of red balls		
$P(\text{win}) = \dfrac{\text{number of red balls}}{\text{total number of outcomes}}$		

1. Complete the chart. Write each answer in simplest form.

2. Which basket should you choose if you want the better chance of winning? _____

A spinner has 11 equal-sized sections marked 1 through 11. Find each probability. (Example 1)

3. You spin once and land on an odd number.

$P(\text{odd}) = \dfrac{\text{number of } \qquad \text{sections}}{\text{total number of}} = \dfrac{\Box}{\Box}$

4. You spin once and land on an even number.

$P(\text{even}) = \dfrac{\text{number of } \qquad \text{sections}}{\text{total number of}} = \dfrac{\Box}{\Box}$

You roll a number cube once.

5. What is the theoretical probability that you roll a 3 or 4? (Example 1) _____

6. Suppose you rolled the number cube 199 more times. Would you expect the experimental probability of rolling a 3 or 4 to be the same as your answer to Exercise 5? (Explore Activity 2)

_____

_____

? ESSENTIAL QUESTION CHECK-IN

7. How can you find the probability of a simple event if the total number of equally likely outcomes is 20?

_____

_____

Name_____ Class_____ Date_____

8.1 Independent Practice

 COMMON CORE 7.SP.7, 7.SP.7a

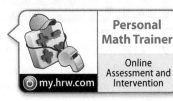

Find the probability of each event. Write each answer as a fraction in simplest form, as a decimal to the nearest hundredth, and as a percent to the nearest whole number.

8. You spin the spinner shown. The spinner lands on yellow.

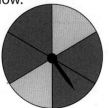

_____

9. You spin the spinner shown. The spinner lands on blue or green.

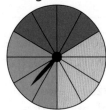

_____

10. A jar contains 4 cherry cough drops and 10 honey cough drops. You choose one cough drop without looking. The cough drop is cherry. _____

11. You pick one card at random from a standard deck of 52 playing cards. You pick a black card. _____

12. There are 12 pieces of fruit in a bowl. Five are lemons and the rest are limes. You choose a piece of fruit without looking. The piece of fruit is a lime. _____

13. You choose a movie disc at random from a case containing 8 comedy discs, 5 science fiction discs, and 7 adventure discs. The disc is **not** a comedy. _____

14. You roll a number cube. You roll a number that is greater than 2 and less than 5. _____

15. Communicate Mathematical Ideas The theoretical probability of a given event is $\frac{9}{13}$. Explain what each number represents.

_____

_____

_____

16. Leona has 4 nickels, 6 pennies, 4 dimes, and 2 quarters in a change purse. Leona lets her little sister Daisy pick a coin at random. If Daisy is equally likely to pick each type of coin, what is the probability that her coin is worth more than five cents? Explain.

_____

_____

17. Critique Reasoning A bowl of flower seeds contains 5 petunia seeds and 15 begonia seeds. Riley calculated the probability that a randomly selected seed is a petunia seed as $\frac{1}{3}$. Describe and correct Riley's error.

_____

_____

_____

_____

18. There are 20 seventh graders and 15 eighth graders in a club. A club president will be chosen at random.

a. Analyze Relationships Compare the probabilities of choosing a seventh grader or an eighth grader.

_____

_____

b. Critical Thinking If a student from one grade is more likely to be chosen than a student from the other, is the method unfair? Explain.

_____

_____

A jar contains 8 red marbles, 10 blue ones, and 2 yellow ones. One marble is chosen at random. The color is recorded in the table, and then it is returned to the jar. This is repeated 40 times.

Red	Blue	Yellow
14	16	10

19. Communicate Mathematical Ideas Use proportional reasoning to explain how you know that for each color, the theoretical and experimental probabilities are not the same.

_____

_____

_____

_____

20. Persevere in Problem Solving For which color marble is the experimental probability closest to the theoretical probability? Explain.

_____

_____

Theoretical Probability of Compound Events

COMMON CORE 7.SP.8

Find probabilities of compound events using organized lists, tables, tree diagrams, ... *7.SP.8a*, *7.SP.8b*

ESSENTIAL QUESTION

How do you find the probability of a compound event?

EXPLORE ACTIVITY COMMON CORE 7.SP.8, 7.SP.8a, 7.SP.8b

Finding Probability Using a Table

Recall that a compound event consists of two or more simple events. To find the probability of a compound event, you write a ratio of the number of ways the compound event can happen to the total number of equally likely possible outcomes.

Jacob rolls two fair number cubes. Find the probability that the sum of the numbers he rolls is 8.

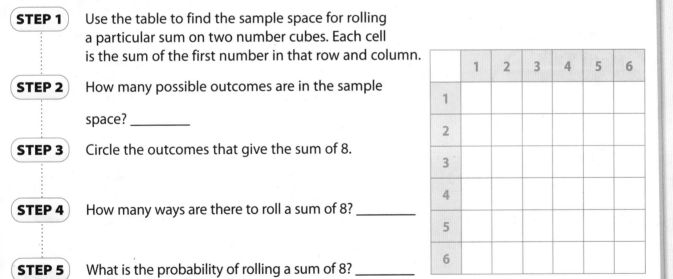

STEP 1 Use the table to find the sample space for rolling a particular sum on two number cubes. Each cell is the sum of the first number in that row and column.

STEP 2 How many possible outcomes are in the sample space? _____

STEP 3 Circle the outcomes that give the sum of 8.

STEP 4 How many ways are there to roll a sum of 8? _____

STEP 5 What is the probability of rolling a sum of 8? _____

	1	2	3	4	5	6
1						
2						
3						
4						
5						
6						

Reflect

1. Give an example of an event that is more likely than rolling a sum of 8.

_____

2. Give an example of an event that is less likely than rolling a sum of 8.

_____

Finding Probability Using a Tree Diagram

You can also use a tree diagram to calculate theoretical probabilities of compound events.

EXAMPLE 1 ⟨Real World⟩

COMMON CORE 7.SP.8, 7.SP.8b

A deli prepares sandwiches with one type of bread (white or wheat), one type of meat (ham, turkey, or chicken), and one type of cheese (cheddar or Swiss). Each combination is equally likely. Find the probability of choosing a sandwich at random and getting turkey and Swiss on wheat bread.

STEP 1 Make a tree diagram to find the sample space for the compound event.

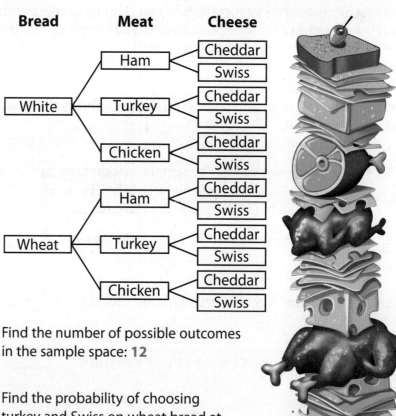

Math Talk
Mathematical Practices

How many sandwich combinations are possible if one of the meat options is unavailable?

STEP 2 Find the number of possible outcomes in the sample space: **12**

STEP 3 Find the probability of choosing turkey and Swiss on wheat bread at random: $\frac{1}{12}$

Personal Math Trainer

Online Assessment and Intervention

⊙ my.hrw.com

YOUR TURN

Use the diagram from Example 1 to find the given probabilities.

3. ham sandwich _____

4. sandwich containing Swiss cheese _____

Finding Probability Using a List

One way to provide security for a locker or personal account is to assign it an access code number known only to the owner.

EXAMPLE 2

COMMON CORE 7.SP.8, 7.SP.8b

The combination for Khiem's locker is a 3-digit code that uses the numbers 1, 2, and 3. Any of these numbers may be repeated. Find the probability that Khiem's randomly-assigned number is 222.

My Notes

Make an organized list to find the sample space.

STEP 1 List all the codes that start with 1 and have 1 as a second digit.

1	1	1
1	1	2
1	1	3

STEP 2 List all the codes that start with 1 and have 2 as a second digit.

1	2	1
1	2	2
1	2	3

STEP 3 List all the codes that start with 1 and have 3 as a second digit.

1	3	1
1	3	2
1	3	3

STEP 4 You have now listed all the codes that start with 1. Repeat Steps 1–3 for codes that start with 2, and then for codes that start with 3.

2	1	1
2	1	2
2	1	3

2	2	1
2	2	2
2	2	3

2	3	1
2	3	2
2	3	3

3	1	1
3	1	2
3	1	3

3	2	1
3	2	2
3	2	3

3	3	1
3	3	2
3	3	3

> Notice that there are 3 possible first numbers, 3 possible second numbers, and 3 possible third numbers, or $3 \times 3 \times 3 = 27$ numbers in all.

STEP 5 Find the number of outcomes in the sample space by counting all the possible codes. There are **27** such codes.

STEP 6 Find the probability that Khiem's locker code is 222.

$$P(\text{Code } 222) = \frac{\text{number of favorable outcomes}}{\text{total number of possible outcomes}} = \frac{1}{27}$$

Math Talk
Mathematical Practices

How could you find the probability that Khiem's locker code includes exactly two 1s?

YOUR TURN

5. Martha types a 4-digit code into a keypad to unlock her car doors. The code uses the numbers 1 and 0. If the digits are selected at random, what is the probability of getting a code with exactly two 0s? _____

Personal Math Trainer

Online Assessment and Intervention

my.hrw.com

Guided Practice

Drake rolls two fair number cubes. (Explore Activity)

1. Complete the table to find the sample space for rolling a particular product on two number cubes.

2. What is the probability that the product of the two numbers Drake rolls is a multiple of 4? _____

3. What is the probability that the product of the two numbers Drake rolls is less than 13? _____

	1	2	3	4	5	6
1						
2						
3						
4						
5						
6						

You flip three coins and want to explore probabilities of certain events. (Examples 1 and 2)

4. Complete the tree diagram and make a list to find the sample space.

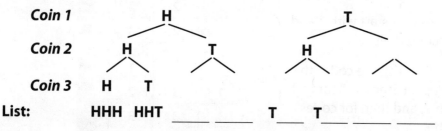

List: HHH   HHT   ____ ____   T___ T___ ____ ____

5. How many outcomes are in the sample space? _____

6. List all the ways to get three tails. _____

7. Complete the expression to find the probability of getting three tails.

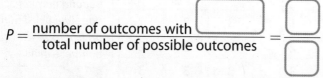

$$P = \frac{\text{number of outcomes with } \boxed{}}{\text{total number of possible outcomes}} = \frac{\boxed{}}{\boxed{}}$$

The probability of getting three tails when three coins are flipped is _____.

8. What is the probability of getting exactly two heads?

There are _____ way(s) to obtain exactly two heads: HHT, _____

$$P = \frac{\text{number of outcomes with } \boxed{}}{\text{total number of possible outcomes}} = \frac{\boxed{}}{\boxed{}}$$

? ESSENTIAL QUESTION CHECK-IN

9. There are 6 ways a given compound event can occur. What else do you need to know to find the theoretical probability of the event?

_____

8.2 Independent Practice

7.SP.8, 7.SP.8a, 7.SP.8b

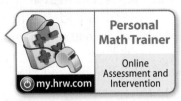

Personal Math Trainer

Online Assessment and Intervention

In Exercises 10–12, use the following information. Mattias gets dressed in the dark one morning and chooses his clothes at random. He chooses a shirt (green, red, or yellow), a pair of pants (black or blue), and a pair of shoes (checkered or red).

10. Use the space below to make a tree diagram to find the sample space.

11. What is the probability that Mattias picks an outfit at random that includes

red shoes? _____

12. What is the probability that no part of

Mattias's outfit is red? _____

13. Rhee and Pamela are two of the five members of a band. Every week, the band picks two members at random to play on their own for five minutes. What is the probability that Rhee and Pamela are

chosen this week? _____

14. Ben rolls two number cubes. What is the probability that the sum of the numbers he

rolls is less than 6? _____

15. Nhan is getting dressed. He considers two different shirts, three pairs of pants, and three pairs of shoes. He chooses one of each of the articles at random. What is the probability that he will wear his jeans but not his sneakers?

Shirt	Pants	Shoes
collared	khakis	sneakers
T-shirt	jeans	flip-flops
	shorts	sandals

_____

16. **Communicate Mathematical Ideas** A ski resort has 3 chair lifts, each with access to 6 ski trails. Explain how you can find the number of possible outcomes when choosing a chair lift and a ski trail without making a list, a tree diagram, or table.

_____

_____

_____

_____

17. **Explain the Error** For breakfast, Sarah can choose eggs, granola or oatmeal as a main course, and orange juice or milk for a drink. Sarah says that the sample space for choosing one of each contains $3^2 = 9$ outcomes. What is her error? Explain.

_____

_____

_____

_____

18. **Represent Real-World Problems** A new shoe comes in two colors, black or red, and in sizes from 5 to 12, including half sizes. If a pair of the shoes is chosen at random for a store display, what is the probability it will be

    red and size 9 or larger? _____

H.O.T. FOCUS ON HIGHER ORDER THINKING

19. **Analyze Relationships** At a diner, Sondra tells the server, "Give me one item from each column." Gretchen says, "Give me one main dish and a vegetable." Who has a greater probability of getting a meal that includes salmon? Explain.

Main Dish	Vegetable	Side
Pasta	Carrots	Tomato soup
Salmon	Peas	Tossed salad
Beef	Asparagus	
Pork	Sweet potato	

_____

_____

20. The digits 1 through 5 are used for a set of locker codes.

    a. **Look for a Pattern** Suppose the digits cannot repeat. Find the number of possible two-digit codes and three-digit codes. Describe any pattern and use it to predict the number of possible five-digit codes.

    _____

    _____

    _____

    b. **Look for a Pattern** Repeat part **a**, but allow digits to repeat.

    _____

    _____

    _____

    c. **Justify Reasoning** Suppose that a gym plans to issue numbered locker codes by choosing the digits at random. Should the gym use codes in which the digits can repeat or not? Justify your reasoning.

    _____

    _____

    _____

Making Predictions with Theoretical Probability

COMMON CORE 7.SP.6

... predict the approximate relative frequency given the probability. *Also 7.RP.3, 7.SP.7a*

ESSENTIAL QUESTION

How do you make predictions using theoretical probability?

EXPLORE ACTIVITY COMMON CORE 7.SP.6

Using Theoretical Probability to Make a Quantitative Prediction

You can make quantitative predictions based on theoretical probability just as you did with experimental probability earlier.

Math On the Spot
my.hrw.com

EXAMPLE 1 Use proportional reasoning to solve each problem.

A You roll a standard number cube 150 times. Predict how many times you will roll a 3 or a 4.

The probability of rolling a 3 or a 4 is $\frac{2}{6} = \frac{1}{3}$.

Method 1: Set up a proportion.

Write a proportion. The ratio 1 out of 3 is how many out of 150?

$$\frac{\square}{3} = \frac{\square}{150}$$

Since 3 times _____ is 150, multiply 1 by _____ to find the value of x.

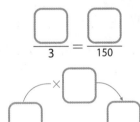

$$x = \underline{\qquad}$$

Method 2: Set up an equation and solve.

p(rolling a 3 or 4) · Number of events = Prediction

Multiply the probability by the total number of rolls.

$$\frac{\square}{\square} \cdot \square = x$$

Solve for x.

$$\underline{\qquad} = x$$

You can expect to roll a 3 or a 4 about _____ times out of 150.

B Celia volunteers at her local animal shelter. She has an equally likely chance to be assigned to the dog, cat, bird, or reptile section. If she volunteers 24 times, about how many times should she expect to be assigned to the dog section?

The probability of being assigned to the dog section is $\dfrac{\square}{\square}$.

Write a proportion. The ratio 1 out of 4 is how many out of 24?

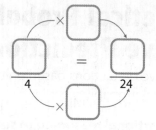

$$\frac{\square}{4} = \frac{\square}{24}$$

Since 4 times _____ is 24, multiply 1 by _____ to find the value of x.

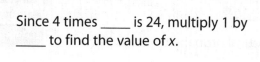

Celia can expect to be assigned to the dog section about _____ times out of 24.

**YOUR TURN**

1. Predict how many times you will roll a number less than 5 if you roll a standard number cube 250 times.

   _____

2. You flip a fair coin 18 times. About how many times would you expect heads to appear?

   _____

Personal Math Trainer

Online Assessment and Intervention

⏻ my.hrw.com

Math On the Spot
⏻ my.hrw.com

Using Theoretical Probability to Make a Qualitative Prediction

Earlier, you learned how to make predictions using experimental probability. You can use theoretical probabilities in the same way to help you predict or compare how likely events are.

EXAMPLE 2 Real World

COMMON CORE 7.SP.6, 7.SP.7a

A Herschel pulls a sock out of his drawer without looking and puts it on. The sock is black. There are 7 black socks, 8 white socks, and 5 striped socks left in the drawer. He pulls out a second sock without looking. Is it likely that he will be wearing matching socks to school?

Find the theoretical probability that Herschel picks a matching sock and the probability that he picks one that does not match.

$P(\text{matching}) = \frac{7}{20}$ $P(\text{not matching}) = 1 - \frac{7}{20} = \frac{13}{20}$

> $P(\text{not matching}) = 1 - P(\text{matching})$

The probability that Herschel picks a matching sock is about half the probability that he picks one that does not match. It is likely that he will **not** be wearing matching socks to school.

B All 2,000 customers at a gym are randomly assigned a 3-digit security code that they use to access their online accounts. The codes are made up of the digits 0 through 4, and the digits can be repeated. Is it likely that fewer than 10 of the customers are issued the code 103?

Set up a proportion. The probability of the code 103 is $\frac{1}{125}$.

$\frac{1}{125} = \frac{x}{2,000}$ Write a proportion. 1 out of 125 is how many out of 2,000?

$\overset{\times 16}{\underset{\times 16}{\frac{1}{125} = \frac{16}{2,000}}}$ Since 125 times 16 is 2,000, multiply 1 times 16 to find the value of x.

> There are 5 possible first numbers, 5 possible second numbers, and 5 possible third numbers. So, the probability of any one code is $\frac{1}{5} \cdot \frac{1}{5} \cdot \frac{1}{5} = \frac{1}{125}$.

It is **not** likely that fewer than 10 of the customers get the same code. It is more likely that 16 members get the code 103.

YOUR TURN

3. A bag of marbles contains 8 red marbles, 4 blue marbles, and 5 white marbles. Tom picks a marble at random. Is it more likely that he picks a red marble or a marble of another color?

_____

4. At a fundraiser, a school group charges $6 for tickets for a "grab bag." You choose one bill at random from a bag that contains 40 $1 bills, 20 $5 bills, 5 $10 bills, 5 $20 bills, and 1 $100 bill. Is it likely that you will win enough to pay for your ticket? Justify your answer.

_____

_____

_____

Personal Math Trainer

Online Assessment and Intervention

⊙ my.hrw.com

1. Bob works at a construction company. He has an equally likely chance to be assigned to work different crews every day. He can be assigned to work on crews building apartments, condominiums, or houses. If he works 18 days a month, about how many times should he expect to be assigned to the house crew? (Explore Activity Example 1)

   STEP 1 Find the probabilities of being assigned to each crew.

   Apartment ☐   Condo ☐   House ☐

   The probability of being assigned to the house crew is _____

   STEP 2 Set up and solve a proportion.

   $$\frac{\Box}{\Box} = \frac{x}{\Box} \quad x = \text{_____}$$

   Bob can expect to be assigned to the house crew about

   _____ times out of 18.

2. During a raffle drawing, half of the ticket holders will receive a prize. The winners are equally likely to win one of three prizes: a book, a gift certificate to a restaurant, or a movie ticket. If there are 300 ticket holders, predict the number of people who will win a movie ticket.

   (Explore Activity Example 1) _____

3. In Mr. Jawarani's first period math class, there are 9 students with hazel eyes, 10 students with brown eyes, 7 students with blue eyes, and 2 students with green eyes. Mr. Jawarani picks a student at random. Which color eyes is the student most likely to have? Explain. (Example 2)

   _____

   _____

ESSENTIAL QUESTION CHECK-IN

4. How do you make predictions using theoretical probability?

   _____

   _____

   _____

8.3 Independent Practice

COMMON CORE 7.SP.6, 7.SP.7a

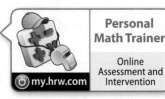

Personal Math Trainer

Online Assessment and Intervention

my.hrw.com

5. A bag contains 6 red marbles, 2 white marbles, and 1 gray marble. You randomly pick out a marble, record its color, and put it back in the bag. You repeat this process 45 times. How many white or gray marbles do you expect to get?

_____

6. Using the blank circle below, draw a spinner with 8 equal sections and 3 colors—red, green, and yellow. The spinner should be such that you are equally likely to land on green or yellow, but more likely to land on red than either on green or yellow.

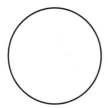

Use the following for Exercises 7–9.
In a standard 52-card deck, half of the cards are red and half are black. The 52 cards are divided evenly into 4 suits: spades, hearts, diamonds, and clubs. Each suit has three face cards (jack, queen, king), and an ace. Each suit also has 9 cards numbered from 2 to 10.

7. Dawn draws 1 card, replaces it, and draws another card. Is it more likely that she draws 2 red cards or 2 face cards?

_____

_____

8. Luis draws 1 card from a deck, 39 times. Predict how many times he draws an ace.

_____

9. Suppose a solitaire player has played 1,000 games. Predict how many times the player turned over a red card as the first card.

_____

10. John and O'Neal are playing a board game in which they roll two number cubes. John needs to get a sum of 8 on the number cubes to win. O'Neal needs a sum of 11. If they take turns rolling the number cube, who is more likely to win? Explain.

_____

_____

_____

11. Every day, Navya's teacher randomly picks a number from 1 to 20 to be the number of the day. The number of the day can be repeated. There are 180 days in the school year. Predict how many days the number of

the day will be greater than 15. _____

12. Eben rolls two standard number cubes 36 times. Predict how many times he will

roll a sum of 4. _____

13. Communicate Mathematical Ideas Can you always show that a prediction based on theoretical probability is true by performing the event often enough? If so, explain why. If not, describe a situation that justifies your response.

_____

_____

_____

_____

14. Represent Real-World Problems Give a real-world example of an experiment in which all of the outcomes are not equally likely. Can you make a prediction for this experiment, using theoretical probability?

_____

_____

_____

_____

H.O.T. **FOCUS ON HIGHER ORDER THINKING**

Work Area

15. Critical Thinking Pierre asks Sherry a question involving the theoretical probability of a compound event in which you flip a coin and draw a marble from a bag of marbles. The bag of marbles contains 3 white marbles, 8 green marbles, and 9 black marbles. Sherry's answer, which is correct, is $\frac{12}{40}$. What was Pierre's question?

_____

_____

_____

16. Make a Prediction Horace is going to roll a standard number cube and flip a coin. He wonders if it is more likely that he rolls a 5 **and** the coin lands on heads, or that he rolls a 5 **or** the coin lands on heads. Which event do you think is more likely to happen? Find the probability of both events to justify or reject your initial prediction.

_____

_____

_____

_____

17. Communicate Mathematical Ideas Cecil solved a theoretical prediction problem and got this answer: "The spinner will land on the red section 4.5 times." Is it possible to have a prediction that is not a whole number? If so, give an example.

_____

_____

_____

_____

Using Technology to Conduct a Simulation

COMMON CORE 7.SP.8c

Design and use a simulation to generate frequencies for compound events. *Also* 7.SP.8

ESSENTIAL QUESTION

How can you use technology simulations to estimate probabilities?

EXPLORE ACTIVITY COMMON CORE 7.SP.8c

Designing and Conducting a Simulation for a Simple Event

You can use a graphing calculator or computer to generate random numbers and conduct a simulation.

Math On the Spot
my.hrw.com

EXAMPLE 1 **A cereal company is having a contest. There are codes for winning prizes in 30% of its cereal boxes. Find an experimental probability that you have to buy *exactly* 3 boxes of cereal before you find a winning code.**

STEP 1 Choose a model to simulate the event.

The probability of finding a winning code is $30\% = \dfrac{}{10}$.

Let 3 out of 10 numbers represent buying a box with a winning code. Use whole numbers from 1 to 10.

Winning: 1, 2, 3   Nonwinning: _____

STEP 2 Generate random numbers from 1 to 10 until you get one that represents a box with a winning code. Record how many boxes you bought before finding a winning code.

Sample Trial 1: 9, 6, 7, 8, 1

For Trial 1, you got the winning code ____ after buying ____ boxes.

STEP 3 Perform multiple trials by repeating Step ____.

STEP 4 Find the experimental probability of the event.

Circle the trial(s) where you bought exactly ____ boxes of cereal before finding a winning code.
In ____ of 10 trials, you bought exactly 3 boxes of cereal before finding a winning code.

The experimental probability is $\dfrac{}{10}$ or ____ %.

Trial	Numbers generated	Boxes bought
1	9, 6, 7, 8, 1	5
2	2	1
3	10, 4, 8, 1	4
4	4, 10, 7, 1	4
5	2	1
6	4, 3	2
7	3	1
8	7, 5, 2	3
9	8, 5, 4, 8, 10, 3	6
10	9, 1	2

Animated Math
my.hrw.com

YOUR TURN

1. An elephant has a 50% chance of giving birth to a male or a female calf. Use a simulation to find an experimental probability that the elephant gives birth to 3 male calves before having a female calf. (*Hint:* Use 0s and 1s. Let 0 represent a male calf, and 1 represent a female calf. Generate random numbers until you get a 1.)

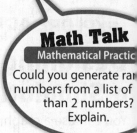

Personal Math Trainer

Online Assessment and Intervention

⏱ my.hrw.com

Trial	Numbers generated	3 Males first	Trial	Numbers generated	3 Males first
1			6		
2			7		
3			8		
4			9		
5			10		

Math Talk

Mathematical Practic

Could you generate ra numbers from a list of than 2 numbers? Explain.

Math On the Spot

⏱ my.hrw.com

Designing and Conducting a Simulation for a Compound Event

You can use random numbers to simulate compound events as well as simple events.

EXAMPLE 2

COMMON CORE 7.SP.8c, 7.SP.3.8

Suppose that there is a 20% chance that a particular volcano will erupt in any given decade. Find an experimental probability that the volcano will erupt in at least 1 of the next 5 decades.

STEP 1 Choose a model.

The probability of an eruption is $20\% = \frac{1}{5}$.
Use whole numbers from 1 to 5.

Let 1 represent a decade with an eruption.

Let 2, 3, 4, and 5 represent a decade without an eruption.

STEP 2 Generate 5 random numbers from 1 to 5. Record the number of decades with an eruption.

5 numbers generated: 3, 1, 3, 4, 2   Eruption decades: 1

STEP 3 Perform multiple trials by repeating Step 2. Calculate the percent of trials in which there was an eruption in at least 1 of the 5 decades.

Trial	Numbers generated	Eruption decades
1	3, 1, 3, 4, 2	1
2	3, 2, 2, 4, 5	0
3	1, 3, 3, 2, 5	1
4	5, 3, 4, 5, 4	0
5	5, 5, 3, 2, 4	0

Trial	Numbers generated	Eruption decades
6	2, 3, 3, 4, 2	0
7	1, 2, 4, 1, 4	2
8	1, 3, 2, 1, 5	2
9	1, 2, 4, 2, 5	1
10	5, 5, 3, 2, 4	0

In 5 out of the 10 trials, there was an eruption in at least 1 of the 5 decades. The experimental probability of an eruption in at least 1 of the next 5 decades is $\frac{5}{10} = 50\%$.

YOUR TURN

2. Matt guesses the answers on a quiz with 5 true-false questions. The probability of guessing a correct answer on each question is 50%. Use a simulation to find an experimental probability that he gets at least 2 questions right. (*Hint:* Use 0s and 1s. Let 0s represent incorrect answers, and 1s represent correct answers. Perform 10 trials, generating 5 random numbers in each, and count the number of 1s.)

Trial	Numbers generated	Correct answers
1		
2		
3		
4		
5		

Trial	Numbers generated	Correct answers
6		
7		
8		
9		
10		

Personal Math Trainer

Online Assessment and Intervention

my.hrw.com

There is a 30% chance that T'Shana's county will have a drought during any given year. She performs a simulation to find the experimental probability of a drought in at least 1 of the next 4 years.
(Explore Activity Example 1 and Example 2)

1. T'Shana's model involves the whole numbers from 1 to 10. Complete the description of her model.

   Let the numbers 1 to 3 represent [   ]

   and the numbers 4 to 10 represent [   ]

   Perform multiple trials, generating [   ] random numbers each time.

2. Suppose T'Shana used the model described in Exercise 1 and got the results shown in the table. Complete the table.

Trial	Numbers generated	Drought years
1	10, 3, 5, 1	
2	10, 4, 6, 5	
3	3, 2, 10, 3	
4	2, 10, 4, 4	
5	7, 3, 6, 3	

Trial	Numbers generated	Drought years
6	8, 4, 8, 5	
7	6, 2, 2, 8	
8	6, 5, 2, 4	
9	2, 2, 3, 2	
10	6, 3, 1, 5	

3. According to the simulation, what is the experimental probability that there will be a drought in the county in at least 1 of the next 4 years? _____

? ESSENTIAL QUESTION CHECK-IN

4. You want to generate random numbers to simulate an event with a 75% chance of occurring. Describe a model you could use.

   _____

   _____

   _____

   _____

8.4 Independent Practice

 COMMON CORE 7.SP.8, 7.SP.8c

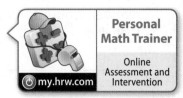

Personal
Math Trainer

Online
Assessment and
Intervention

Every contestant on a game show has a 40% chance of winning. In the
simulation below, the numbers 1–4 represent a winner, and the numbers
5–10 represent a nonwinner. Numbers were generated until one that
represented a winner was produced.

Trial	Numbers generated
1	7, 4
2	6, 5, 2
3	1
4	9, 1
5	3

Trial	Numbers generated
6	8, 8, 6, 2
7	2
8	5, 9, 4
9	10, 3
10	1

5. In how many of the trials did it take exactly 4 contestants to get a winner? _____

6. Based on the simulation, what is the experimental probability that it will
take exactly 4 contestants to get a winner? _____

Over a 100-year period, the probability that a hurricane struck Rob's city
in any given year was 20%. Rob performed a simulation to find an
experimental probability that a hurricane would strike the city in at least
4 of the next 10 years. In Rob's simulation, 1 represents a year with a
hurricane.

Trial	Numbers generated
1	2, 5, 3, 2, 5, 5, 1, 4, 5, 2
2	1, 1, 5, 2, 2, 1, 3, 1, 1, 5
3	4, 5, 4, 5, 5, 4, 3, 5, 1, 1
4	1, 5, 5, 5, 1, 2, 2, 3, 5, 3
5	5, 1, 5, 3, 5, 3, 4, 5, 3, 2

Trial	Numbers generated
6	1, 1, 5, 5, 1, 4, 2, 2, 3, 4
7	2, 1, 5, 3, 1, 5, 1, 2, 1, 4
8	2, 4, 3, 2, 4, 4, 2, 1, 3, 1
9	3, 2, 1, 4, 5, 3, 5, 5, 1, 2
10	3, 4, 2, 4, 3, 5, 2, 3, 5, 1

7. According to Rob's simulation, what was the experimental probability
that a hurricane would strike the city in at least 4 of the next 10 years? _____

8. Analyze Relationships Suppose that over the 10 years following Rob's
simulation, there was actually 1 year in which a hurricane struck. How did
this compare to the results of Rob's simulation?

_____

_____

9. **Communicate Mathematical Ideas** You generate three random whole numbers from 1 to 10. Do you think that it is unlikely or even impossible that all of the numbers could be 10? Explain?

_____

_____

_____

_____

_____

10. Erika collects baseball cards, and 60% of the packs contain a player from her favorite team. Use a simulation to find an experimental probability that she has to buy exactly 2 packs before she gets a player from her favorite team.

_____

_____

H.O.T. FOCUS ON HIGHER ORDER THINKING

11. **Represent Real-World Problems** When Kate plays basketball, she usually makes 37.5% of her shots. Design and conduct a simulation to find the experimental probability that she makes at least 3 of her next 10 shots. Justify the model for your simulation.

_____

_____

_____

_____

_____

_____

12. **Justify Reasoning** George and Susannah used a simulation to simulate the flipping of 8 coins 50 times. In all of the trials, at least 5 heads came up. What can you say about their simulation? Explain.

_____

_____

_____

_____

Ready to Go On?

Personal
Math Trainer

Online Assessment
and Intervention

my.hrw.com

8.1, 8.2 Theoretical Probability of Simple and Compound Events

Find the probability of each event. Write your answer as a fraction, as a decimal, and as a percent.

1. You choose a marble at random from a bag containing 12 red, 12 blue, 15 green, 9 yellow, and 12 black marbles. The marble is red. _____

2. You draw a card at random from a shuffled deck of 52 cards. The deck has four 13-card suits (diamonds, hearts, clubs, spades). The card is a diamond or a spade. _____

8.3 Making Predictions with Theoretical Probability

3. A bag contains 23 red marbles, 25 green marbles, and 18 blue marbles. You choose a marble at random from the bag. What color marble will you most likely choose? _____

8.4 Using Technology to Conduct a Simulation

4. Bay City has a 25% chance of having a flood in any given decade. The table shows the results of a simulation using random numbers to find the experimental probability that there will be a flood in Bay City in at least 1 of the next 5 decades. In the table, the number 1 represents a decade with a flood. The numbers 2 through 5 represent a decade without a flood.

Trial	Numbers generated	Trial	Numbers generated
1	2, 2, 5, 5, 5	6	4, 2, 2, 5, 4
2	3, 2, 3, 5, 4	7	1, 3, 2, 4, 4
3	5, 5, 5, 4, 3	8	3, 5, 5, 2, 1
4	5, 1, 3, 3, 5	9	4, 3, 3, 2, 5
5	4, 5, 5, 3, 2	10	5, 4, 1, 2, 1

According to the simulation, what is the experimental probability of a flood in Bay City in at least 1 of the next 5 decades? _____

? ESSENTIAL QUESTION

5. How can you use theoretical probability to make predictions in real-world situations?

_____

_____

Selected Response

1. What is the probability of flipping two fair coins and having both show tails?

- (A) $\frac{1}{8}$
- (C) $\frac{1}{3}$
- (B) $\frac{1}{4}$
- (D) $\frac{1}{2}$

2. A bag contains 8 white marbles and 2 black marbles. You pick out a marble, record its color, and put the marble back in the bag. If you repeat this process 45 times, how many times would you expect to remove a white marble from the bag?

- (A) 9
- (C) 36
- (B) 32
- (D) 40

3. Philip rolls a standard number cube 24 times. Which is the best prediction for the number of times he will roll a number that is even and less than 4?

- (A) 2
- (C) 4
- (B) 3
- (D) 6

4. A set of cards includes 24 yellow cards, 18 green cards, and 18 blue cards. What is the probability that a card chosen at random is **not** green?

- (A) $\frac{3}{10}$
- (C) $\frac{3}{5}$
- (B) $\frac{4}{10}$
- (D) $\frac{7}{10}$

5. A rectangle made of square tiles measures 10 tiles long and 8 tiles wide. What is the width of a similar rectangle whose length is 15 tiles?

- (A) 3 tiles
- (C) 13 tiles
- (B) 12 tiles
- (D) 18.75 tiles

6. The Fernandez family drove 273 miles in 5.25 hours. How far would they have driven at that rate in 4 hours?

- (A) 208 miles
- (C) 280 miles
- (B) 220 miles
- (D) 358 miles

7. There are 20 tennis balls in a bag. Five are orange, 7 are white, 2 are yellow, and 6 are green. You choose one at random. Which color ball are you **least** likely to choose?

- (A) green
- (C) white
- (B) orange
- (D) yellow

Mini-Task

8. Center County has had a 1 in 6 (or about 16.7%) chance of a tornado in any given decade. In a simulation to consider the probability of tornadoes in the next 5 decades, Ava rolled a number cube. She let a 1 represent a decade with a tornado, and 2–6 represent decades without tornadoes. What experimental probability did Ava find for each event?

Trial	Numbers Generated	Trial	Numbers Generated
1	2, 2, 3, 1, 5	6	4, 5, 2, 2, 4
2	3, 5, 6, 4, 5	7	5, 1, 6, 3, 1
3	1, 3, 3, 2, 2	8	1, 2, 1, 2, 4
4	6, 3, 3, 5, 4	9	1, 4, 4, 1, 4
5	4, 1, 4, 4, 4	10	3, 6, 5, 3, 6

a. That Center County has a tornado in at least one of the next five decades.

_____

b. That Center County has a tornado in exactly one of the next five decades.

_____

Study Guide Review

Key Vocabulary

complement *(complemento)*
compound event *(suceso compuesto)*
event *(suceso)*
experiment *(experimento)*
experimental probability *(probabilidad experimental)*
outcome *(resultado)*
probability *(probabilidad)*
sample space *(espacio muestral)*
simple event *(suceso simple)*
simulation *(simulación)*
trial *(prueba)*

? ESSENTIAL QUESTION

How can you use experimental probability to solve real-world problems?

EXAMPLE 1

What is the probability of picking a red marble from a jar with 5 green marbles and 2 red marbles?

$$P(\text{picking a red marble}) = \frac{\text{number of red marbles}}{\text{number of total marbles}}$$

$$= \frac{2}{7} \qquad \text{There are 2 red marbles.}$$
$$\text{The total number of marbles is } 2 + 5 = 7.$$

EXAMPLE 2

For one month, a doctor recorded information about new patients as shown in the table.

	Senior	Adult	Young adult	Child
Female	5	8	2	14
Male	3	10	1	17

What is the experimental probability that his next new patient is a female adult?

$$P\left(\begin{array}{c}\text{new patient is a}\\\text{female adult}\end{array}\right) = \frac{\text{number of female adults}}{\text{total number of patients}}$$

$$P = \frac{8}{60} = \frac{2}{15}$$

What is the experimental probability that his next new patient is a child?

$$P\left(\begin{array}{c}\text{new patient is}\\\text{a child}\end{array}\right) = \frac{\text{number of children}}{\text{total number of patients}}$$

$$P = \frac{31}{60}$$

EXERCISES

Find the probability of each event. (Lesson 7.1)

1. Rolling a 5 on a fair number cube.

2. Picking a 7 from a standard deck of 52 cards. A standard deck includes 4 cards of each number from 2 to 10.

3. Picking a blue marble from a bag of 4 red marbles, 6 blue marbles, and 1 white marble.

4. Rolling a number greater than 7 on a 12-sided number cube.

5. Christopher picked coins randomly from his piggy bank and got the numbers of coins shown in the table. Find each experimental probability. (Lessons 7.2, 7.3)

Penny	Nickel	Dime	Quarter
7	2	8	6

   a. The next coin that Christopher picks is a quarter. _____

   b. The next coin that Christopher picks is not a quarter. _____

   c. The next coin that Christopher picks is a penny or a nickel. _____

6. A grocery store manager found that 54% of customers usually bring their own bags. In one afternoon, 82 out of 124 customers brought their own grocery bags. Did a greater or lesser number of people than usual bring their own bags? (Lesson 7.4)

_____

MODULE **8** # Theoretical Probability

Key Vocabulary
theoretical probability
(probabilidad teórica)

? ESSENTIAL QUESTION

How can you use theoretical probability to solve real-world problems?

EXAMPLE 1

A. Lola rolls two fair number cubes. What is the probability that the two numbers Lola rolls include at least one 4 and have a product of at least 16?

There are 5 pairs of numbers that include a 4 and have a product of at least 16:

$(4, 4), (4, 5), (4, 6), (5, 4), (6, 4)$

Find the probability.

$$P = \frac{\text{number of possible ways}}{\text{total number of possible outcomes}} = \frac{5}{36}$$

	1	2	3	4	5	6
1	1	2	3	4	5	6
2	2	4	6	8	10	12
3	3	6	9	12	15	18
4	4	8	12	16	20	24
5	5	10	15	20	25	30
6	6	12	18	24	30	36

B. Suppose Lola rolls the two number cubes 180 times. Predict how many times she will roll two numbers that include a pair of numbers like the ones described above.

One way to answer is to write and solve an equation.

$\frac{5}{36} \times 180 = x$ *Multiply the probability by the total number of rolls.*

$\quad\quad 25 = x$ *Solve for x.*

Lola can expect to roll two numbers that include at least one 4 and have a product of 16 or more about 25 times.

EXAMPLE 2

A store has a sale bin of soup cans. There are 6 cans of chicken noodle soup, 8 cans of split pea soup, 8 cans of minestrone, and 13 cans of vegetable soup. Find the probability of picking each type of soup at random. Then predict what kind of soup a customer is most likely to pick.

$P(\text{chicken noodle}) = \frac{6}{35}$ $\qquad\qquad$ $P(\text{split pea}) = \frac{8}{35}$

$P(\text{minestrone}) = \frac{8}{35}$ $\qquad\qquad$ $P(\text{vegetable}) = \frac{13}{35}$

The customer is most likely to pick vegetable soup. That is the event that has the greatest probability.

EXERCISES

Find the probability of each event. (Lessons 8.1, 8.2)

1. Graciela picks a white mouse at random from a bin of 8 white mice, 2 gray mice, and 2 brown mice.

2. Theo spins a spinner that has 12 equal sections marked 1 through 12. It does **not** land on 1.

3. Tania flips a coin three times. The coin lands on heads twice and on tails once, not necessarily in that order.

4. Students are randomly assigned two-digit codes. Each digit is either 1, 2, 3, or 4. Guy is given the number 11.

5. Patty tosses a coin and rolls a number cube. (Lesson 8.3)

   a. Find the probability that the coin lands on heads and the cube lands on an even number.

   b. Patty tosses the coin and rolls the number cube 60 times. Predict how many times the coin will land on heads and the cube will land on an even number.

6. Rajan's school is having a raffle. The school sold raffle tickets with 3-digit numbers. Each digit is either 1, 2, or 3. The school also sold 2 tickets with the number 000. Which number is more likely to be picked, 123 or 000? (Lesson 8.3)

7. Suppose you know that over the last 10 years, the probability that your town would have at least one major storm was 40%. Describe a simulation that you could use to find the experimental probability that your town will have at least one major storm in at least 3 of the next 5 years. (Lesson 8.4)

_____

_____

_____

_____

Unit 4 Performance Tasks

1. **CAREERS IN MATH** Meteorologist A meteorologist predicts a 20% chance of rain for the next two nights, and a 75% chance of rain on the third night.

a. On which night is it most likely to rain? On that night, is it *likely* to rain or *unlikely* to rain?

_____

_____

b. Tara would like to go camping for the next 3 nights, but will not go if it is likely to rain on all 3 nights. Should she go? Use probability to justify your answer.

_____

_____

2. Sinead tossed 4 coins at the same time. She did this 50 times, and 6 of those times, all 4 coins showed the same result (heads or tails).

a. Find the experimental probability that all 4 coins show the same result when tossed.

_____

b. Can you determine the experimental probability that **no** coin shows heads? Explain.

_____

c. Suppose Sinead tosses the coins 125 more times. Use experimental probability to predict the number of times that all 4 coins will show heads or tails. Show your work.

_____

COMMON CORE

UNIT 4 MIXED REVIEW

Assessment Readiness

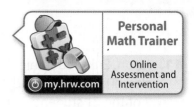

Personal
Math Trainer

Online
Assessment and
Intervention

my.hrw.com

Selected Response

1. A pizza parlor offers thin, thick, and traditional style pizza crusts. You can get pepperoni, beef, mushrooms, olives, or peppers for toppings. You order a one-topping pizza. How many outcomes are in the sample space?

  Ⓐ 3   Ⓒ 8

  Ⓑ 5   Ⓓ 15

2. A bag contains 9 purple marbles, 2 blue marbles, and 4 pink marbles. The probability of randomly drawing a blue marble is $\frac{2}{15}$. What is the probability of **not** drawing a blue marble?

  Ⓐ $\frac{2}{15}$ Ⓒ $\frac{11}{15}$

  Ⓑ $\frac{4}{15}$ Ⓓ $\frac{13}{15}$

3. During the month of April, Dora kept track of the bugs she saw in her garden. She saw a ladybug on 23 days of the month. What is the experimental probability that she will see a ladybug on May 1?

  Ⓐ $\frac{1}{23}$ Ⓒ $\frac{1}{2}$

  Ⓑ $\frac{7}{30}$ Ⓓ $\frac{23}{30}$

4. Ryan flips a coin 8 times and gets tails all 8 times. What is the experimental probability that Ryan will get heads the next time he flips the coin?

  Ⓐ 1   Ⓒ $\frac{1}{8}$

  Ⓑ $\frac{1}{2}$ Ⓓ 0

5. A used guitar is on sale for $280. Derek offers the seller $\frac{3}{4}$ of the advertised price. How much does Derek offer for the guitar?

  Ⓐ $180   Ⓒ $240

  Ⓑ $210   Ⓓ $270

6. Jay tossed two coins several times and then recorded the results in the table below.

Coin Toss Results				
Toss 1	Toss 2	Toss 3	Toss 4	Toss 5
H; H	H; T	T; H	T; T	T; H

What is the experimental probability that the coins will land on different sides on his next toss?

  Ⓐ $\frac{1}{5}$ Ⓒ $\frac{3}{5}$

  Ⓑ $\frac{2}{5}$ Ⓓ $\frac{4}{5}$

7. What is the probability of tossing two fair coins and having exactly one land tails side up?

  Ⓐ $\frac{1}{8}$ Ⓒ $\frac{1}{3}$

  Ⓑ $\frac{1}{4}$ Ⓓ $\frac{1}{2}$

8. Find the percent change from 60 to 96.

  Ⓐ 37.5% decrease

  Ⓑ 37.5% increase

  Ⓒ 60% decrease

  Ⓓ 60% increase

9. A bag contains 6 white beads and 4 black beads. You pick out a bead, record its color, and put the bead back in the bag. You repeat this process 35 times. Which is the best prediction of how many times you would expect to remove a white bead from the bag?

  Ⓐ 6   Ⓒ 18

  Ⓑ 10   Ⓓ 21

10. A set of cards includes 20 yellow cards, 16 green cards, and 24 blue cards. What is the probability that a blue card is chosen at random?

  Ⓐ 0.04   Ⓒ 0.4

  Ⓑ 0.24   Ⓓ 0.66

11. Jason, Erik, and Jamie are friends in art class. The teacher randomly chooses 2 of the 21 students in the class to work together on a project. What is the probability that two of these three friends will be chosen?

Ⓐ $\frac{1}{105}$

Ⓑ $\frac{1}{70}$

Ⓒ $\frac{34}{140}$

Ⓓ $\frac{4}{50}$

12. Philip rolls a number cube 12 times. Which is the best prediction for the number of times that he will roll a number that is odd and less than 5?

Ⓐ 2   Ⓒ 4

Ⓑ 3   Ⓓ 6

Hot Tip!

Estimate your answer before solving the problem. Use your estimate to check the reasonableness of your answer.

13. A survey reveals that one airline's flights have a 92% probability of being on time. Based on this, out of 4000 flights in a year, how many flights would you predict will arrive on time?

Ⓐ 368   Ⓒ 3,680

Ⓑ 386   Ⓓ 3,860

14. Matt's house number is a two-digit number. Neither of the digits is 0 and the house number is even. What is the probability that Matt's house number is 18?

Ⓐ $\frac{1}{45}$ Ⓒ $\frac{1}{18}$

Ⓑ $\frac{1}{36}$ Ⓓ $\frac{1}{16}$

Mini-Tasks

15. Laura picked a crayon randomly from a box, recorded the color, and then placed it back in the box. She repeated the process and recorded the results in the table.

Red	Blue	Yellow	Green
5	6	7	2

Find each experimental probability. Write your answers in simplest form.

a. The next crayon Laura picks is red.

_____

b. The next crayon Laura picks is **not** red.

_____

16. For breakfast, Trevor has a choice of 3 types of bagels (plain, sesame, or multigrain), 2 types of eggs (scrambled or poached), and 2 juices (orange or apple).

a. Use the space below to make a tree diagram to find the sample space.

b. If he chooses at random, what is the probability that Trevor eats a breakfast that has orange juice?

_____

Real Numbers, Exponents, and Scientific Notation

MODULE 9

Real Numbers

COMMON CORE 8.NS.1, 8.NS.2, 8.EE.2

MODULE 10

Exponents and Scientific Notation

COMMON CORE 8.EE.1, 8.EE.3, 8.EE.4

CAREERS IN MATH

Astronomer An astronomer is a scientist who studies and tries to interpret the universe beyond Earth. Astronomers use math to calculate distances to celestial objects and to create mathematical models to help them understand the dynamics of systems from stars and planets to black holes. If you are interested in a career as an astronomer, you should study the following mathematical subjects:

- Algebra
- Geometry
- Trigonometry
- Calculus

Research other careers that require creating mathematical models to understand physical phenomena.

Unit 5 Performance Task

At the end of the unit, check out how **astronomers** use math.

Vocabulary Preview

Use the puzzle to preview key vocabulary from this unit. Unscramble the circled letters to answer the riddle at the bottom of the page.

1. **TCREEFP SEAQUR**

2. **NOLRATAI RUNMEB**

3. **PERTIANEG MALCEDI**

4. **LAER SEBMNUR**

5. **NIISICFTCE OITANTON**

1. Has integers as its square roots. (Lesson 9.1)
2. Any number that can be written as a ratio of two integers. (Lesson 9.1)
3. A decimal in which one or more digits repeat infinitely. (Lesson 9.1)
4. The set of rational and irrational numbers. (Lesson 9.2)
5. A method of writing very large or very small numbers by using powers of 10. (Lesson 10.2)

Q: What keeps a square from moving?

A: _ _ _ _ _ _ _ _ _ _ _ _ _ _ _ _!

Real Numbers

COMMON CORE

? ESSENTIAL QUESTION

How can you use real numbers to solve real-world problems?

Real-World Video

Living creatures can be classified into groups. The sea otter belongs to the kingdom Animalia and class Mammalia. Numbers can also be classified into groups such as rational numbers and integers.

 my.hrw.com

GO DIGITAL
my.hrw.com

my.hrw.com

Go digital with your write-in student edition, accessible on any device.

Math On the Spot

Scan with your smart phone to jump directly to the online edition, video tutor, and more.

Animated Math

Interactively explore key concepts to see how math works.

Personal Math Trainer

Get immediate feedback and help as you work through practice sets.

Are YOU Ready?

Complete these exercises to review skills you will need for this module.

Find the Square of a Number

EXAMPLE Find the square of $\frac{2}{3}$.

$\frac{2}{3} \times \frac{2}{3} = \frac{2 \times 2}{3 \times 3}$ Multiply the number by itself.

$= \frac{4}{9}$ Simplify.

Find the square of each number.

1. 7 _____   **2.** 21 _____   **3.** -3 _____   **4.** $\frac{4}{5}$ _____

5. 2.7 _____   **6.** $-\frac{1}{4}$ _____   **7.** -5.7 _____   **8.** $1\frac{2}{5}$ _____

Exponents

EXAMPLE $5^3 = 5 \times 5 \times 5$ Use the base, 5, as a factor 3 times.

$= 25 \times 5$ Multiply from left to right.

$= 125$

Simplify each exponential expression.

9. 9^2 _____   **10.** 2^4 _____   **11.** $\left(\frac{1}{3}\right)^2$ _____   **12.** $(-7)^2$ _____

13. 4^3 _____   **14.** $(-1)^5$ _____   **15.** 4.5^2 _____   **16.** 10^5 _____

Write a Mixed Number as an Improper Fraction

EXAMPLE $2\frac{2}{5} = 2 + \frac{2}{5}$ Write the mixed number as a sum of a whole number and a fraction.

$= \frac{10}{5} + \frac{2}{5}$ Write the whole number as an equivalent fraction with the same denominator as the fraction in the mixed number.

$= \frac{12}{5}$ Add the numerators.

Write each mixed number as an improper fraction.

17. $3\frac{1}{3}$ _____   **18.** $1\frac{5}{8}$ _____   **19.** $2\frac{3}{7}$ _____   **20.** $5\frac{5}{6}$ _____

Reading Start-Up

Vocabulary

Review Words
integers *(enteros)*
✔ negative numbers *(números negativos)*
✔ positive numbers *(números positivos)*
✔ whole number *(número entero)*

Preview Words
cube root *(raíz cúbica)*
irrational numbers *(número irracional)*
perfect cube *(cubo perfecto)*
perfect square *(cuadrado perfecto)*
principal square root *(raíz cuadrada principal)*
rational number *(número racional)*
real numbers *(número real)*
repeating decimal *(decimal periódico)*
square root *(raíz cuadrada)*
terminating decimal *(decimal finito)*

Visualize Vocabulary

Use the ✔ words to complete the graphic. You can put more than one word in each section of the triangle.

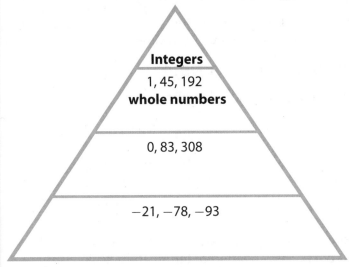

Integers
1, 45, 192
whole numbers

0, 83, 308

−21, −78, −93

Understand Vocabulary

Complete the sentences using the preview words.

1. One of the two equal factors of a number is a _____.

2. A _____ has integers as its square roots.

3. The _____ is the nonnegative square root of a number.

Active Reading

Layered Book Before beginning the lessons in this module, create a layered book to help you learn the concepts in this module. Label the flaps "Rational Numbers," "Irrational Numbers," "Square Roots," and "Real Numbers." As you study each lesson, write important ideas such as vocabulary, models, and sample problems under the appropriate flap.

Unpacking the Standards

Understanding the standards and the vocabulary terms in the standards will help you know exactly what you are expected to learn in this module.

COMMON CORE 8.NS.1

Know that numbers that are not rational are called irrational. Understand informally that every number has a decimal expansion; for rational numbers show that the decimal expansion repeats eventually, and convert a decimal expansion which repeats eventually into a rational number.

Key Vocabulary

rational number *(número racional)*
A number that can be expressed as a ratio of two integers.

irrational number *(número irracional)*
A number that cannot be expressed as a ratio of two integers or as a repeating or terminating decimal.

What It Means to You

You will recognize a number as rational or irrational by looking at its fraction or decimal form.

UNPACKING EXAMPLE 8.NS.1

Classify each number as rational or irrational.

$$0.\overline{3} = \frac{1}{3} \qquad\qquad 0.25 = \frac{1}{4}$$

These numbers are rational because they can be written as ratios of integers or as repeating or terminating decimals.

$$\pi \approx 3.141592654\ldots \qquad\qquad \sqrt{5} \approx 2.236067977\ldots$$

These numbers are irrational because they cannot be written as ratios of integers or as repeating or terminating decimals.

COMMON CORE 8.NS.2

Use rational approximations of irrational numbers to compare the size of irrational numbers, locate them approximately on a number line diagram, and estimate the value of expressions (e.g., π^2).

Visit **my.hrw.com** to see all the **Common Core Standards** unpacked.

my.hrw.com

What It Means to You

You will learn to estimate the values of irrational numbers.

UNPACKING EXAMPLE 8.NS.2

Estimate the value of $\sqrt{8}$.

8 is not a perfect square. Find the two perfect squares closest to 8.

8 is between the perfect squares 4 and 9.
So $\sqrt{8}$ is between $\sqrt{4}$ and $\sqrt{9}$.
    $\sqrt{8}$ is between 2 and 3.

8 is close to 9, so $\sqrt{8}$ is close to 3.
$2.8^2 = 7.84 \qquad 2.85^2 = 8.1225 \qquad 2.9^2 = 8.41$
$\sqrt{8}$ is between 2.8 and 2.9, but closer to 2.8.
A good estimate for $\sqrt{8}$ is 2.8.

Rational and Irrational Numbers

COMMON CORE 8.NS.1

Know that numbers that are not rational are called irrational. Understand informally that every number has a decimal expansion; ...
Also 8.NS.2, 8.EE.2

ESSENTIAL QUESTION

How do you rewrite rational numbers and decimals, take square roots and cube roots, and approximate irrational numbers?

EXPLORE ACTIVITY COMMON CORE 8.NS.1

Math On the Spot
⏻ my.hrw.com

Expressing Rational Numbers as Decimals

A **rational number** is any number that can be written as a ratio in the form $\frac{a}{b}$, where a and b are integers and b is not 0. Examples of rational numbers are 6 and 0.5.

$$6 \text{ can be written as } \frac{6}{1}. \qquad 0.5 \text{ can be written as } \frac{1}{2}.$$

Every rational number can be written as a terminating decimal or a repeating decimal. A **terminating decimal**, such as 0.5, has a finite number of digits. A **repeating decimal** has a block of one or more digits that repeats indefinitely.

EXAMPLE 1 Write each fraction as a decimal.

A $\frac{1}{4}$

The fraction bar is a division symbol.
Divide the numerator by the denominator: $1 \div 4$.

Divide until the remainder is zero, adding zeros after the decimal point in the dividend as needed.

The rational number $\frac{1}{4}$ can be written as a terminating decimal.

$$\frac{1}{4} = \boxed{}$$

$$
\begin{array}{r}
\boxed{} \\
4\overline{)1.00} \\
-\boxed{} \\
\hline
20 \\
-\boxed{} \\
\hline
0
\end{array}
$$

B $\frac{1}{3}$

Divide the numerator by the denominator: $1 \div 3$.

Divide until the remainder is zero or until the digits in the quotient begin to repeat.

Add zeros after the decimal point in the dividend as needed.

The rational number $\frac{1}{3}$ can be written as a repeating decimal, with a bar over the repeating digit(s).

$$\frac{1}{3} = \boxed{}$$

$$
\begin{array}{r}
\boxed{} \\
3\overline{)1.000} \\
-\boxed{} \\
\hline
10 \\
-\boxed{} \\
\hline
10 \\
-\boxed{} \\
\hline
1
\end{array}
$$

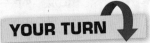

YOUR TURN

Write each fraction as a decimal.

1. $\frac{5}{11}$ _____

2. $\frac{1}{8}$ _____

3. $2\frac{1}{3}$ _____

Personal Math Trainer

Online Assessment and Intervention

<svg>⏻</svg> my.hrw.com

Math On the Spot

<svg>⏻</svg> my.hrw.com

Expressing Decimals as Rational Numbers

You can express terminating and repeating decimals as rational numbers.

EXAMPLE 2

COMMON CORE **8.NS.1**

Write each decimal as a fraction in simplest form.

My Notes

(A) 0.825

The decimal 0.825 means "825 thousandths." Write this as a fraction.

$\frac{825}{1000}$ To write "825 thousandths", put 825 over 1000.

Then simplify the fraction.

$\frac{825 \div 25}{1000 \div 25} = \frac{33}{40}$ Divide both the numerator and the denominator by 25.

$0.825 = \frac{33}{40}$

(B) $0.\overline{37}$

Let $x = 0.\overline{37}$. The number $0.\overline{37}$ has 2 repeating digits, so multiply each side of the equation $x = 0.\overline{37}$ by 10^2, or 100.

$x = 0.\overline{37}$

$(100)x = 100(0.\overline{37})$

$100x = 37.\overline{37}$ 100 times $0.\overline{37}$ is $37.\overline{37}$.

Because $x = 0.\overline{37}$, you can subtract x from one side and $0.\overline{37}$ from the other.

$100x = 37.\overline{37}$

$\underline{-x \quad\quad -0.\overline{37}}$

$99x = 37$ $37.\overline{37}$ minus $0.\overline{37}$ is 37.

Now solve the equation for x. Simplify if necessary.

$\frac{99x}{99} = \frac{37}{99}$ Divide both sides of the equation by 99.

$x = \frac{37}{99}$

Write each decimal as a fraction in simplest form.

4. 0.12 _____   **5.** 0.$\overline{57}$ _____   **6.** 1.4 _____

Finding Square Roots and Cube Roots

The **square root** of a positive number p is x if $x^2 = p$. There are two square roots for every positive number. For example, the square roots of 36 are 6 and -6 because $6^2 = 36$ and $(-6)^2 = 36$. The square roots of $\frac{1}{25}$ are $\frac{1}{5}$ and $-\frac{1}{5}$. You can write the square roots of $\frac{1}{25}$ as $\pm\frac{1}{5}$. The symbol $\sqrt{}$ indicates the positive, or **principal square root**.

A number that is a **perfect square** has square roots that are integers. The number 81 is a perfect square because its square roots are 9 and -9.

The **cube root** of a positive number p is x if $x^3 = p$. There is one cube root for every positive number. For example, the cube root of 8 is 2 because $2^3 = 8$. The cube root of $\frac{1}{27}$ is $\frac{1}{3}$ because $\left(\frac{1}{3}\right)^3 = \frac{1}{27}$. The symbol $\sqrt[3]{}$ indicates the cube root.

A number that is a **perfect cube** has a cube root that is an integer. The number 125 is a perfect cube because its cube root is 5.

EXAMPLE 3

Solve each equation for x.

A $x^2 = 121$

$x^2 = 121$ *Solve for x by taking the square root of both sides.*

$x = \pm\sqrt{121}$ *Apply the definition of square root.*

$x = \pm 11$ *Think: What numbers squared equal 121?*

The solutions are 11 and -11.

B $x^2 = \frac{16}{169}$

$x^2 = \frac{16}{169}$ *Solve for x by taking the square root of both sides.*

$x = \pm\sqrt{\frac{16}{169}}$ *Apply the definition of square root.*

$x = \pm\frac{4}{13}$ *Think: What numbers squared equal $\frac{16}{169}$?*

The solutions are $\frac{4}{13}$ and $-\frac{4}{13}$.

> ### Math Talk
> **Mathematical Practices**
>
> Can you square an integer and get a negative number? What does this indicate about whether negative numbers have square roots?

C $729 = x^3$

$\sqrt[3]{729} = \sqrt[3]{x^3}$ Solve for x by taking the cube root of both sides.

$\sqrt[3]{729} = x$ Apply the definition of cube root.

$9 = x$ Think: What number cubed equals 729?

The solution is 9.

D $x^3 = \frac{8}{125}$

$\sqrt[3]{x^3} = \sqrt[3]{\frac{8}{125}}$ Solve for x by taking the cube root of both sides.

$x = \sqrt[3]{\frac{8}{125}}$ Apply the definition of cube root.

$x = \frac{2}{5}$ Think: What number cubed equals $\frac{8}{125}$?

The solution is $\frac{2}{5}$.

Personal Math Trainer

Online Assessment and Intervention

⊙ my.hrw.com

 YOUR TURN

Solve each equation for x.

7. $x^2 = 196$ _____

8. $x^2 = \frac{9}{256}$ _____

9. $x^3 = 512$ _____

10. $x^3 = \frac{64}{343}$ _____

EXPLORE ACTIVITY 2   COMMON CORE   8.NS.2, 8.EE.2

Estimating Irrational Numbers

Irrational numbers are numbers that are not rational. In other words, they cannot be written in the form $\frac{a}{b}$, where a and b are integers and b is not 0. Square roots of perfect squares are rational numbers. Square roots of numbers that are not perfect squares are irrational. The number $\sqrt{3}$ is irrational because 3 is not a perfect square of any rational number.

Estimate the value of $\sqrt{2}$.

A Since 2 is not a perfect square, $\sqrt{2}$ is irrational.

B To estimate $\sqrt{2}$, first find two consecutive perfect squares that 2 is between. Complete the inequality by writing these perfect squares in the boxes.

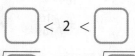

C Now take the square root of each number.

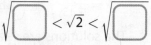

D Simplify the square roots of perfect squares.

$\sqrt{2}$ is between _____ and _____.

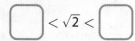

E Estimate that $\sqrt{2} \approx 1.5$.

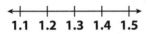

$\sqrt{2} \approx 1.5$

F To find a better estimate, first choose some numbers between 1 and 2 and square them. For example, choose 1.3, 1.4, and 1.5.

$1.3^2 = $ _____ $1.4^2 = $ _____ $1.5^2 = $ _____

Is $\sqrt{2}$ between 1.3 and 1.4? How do you know?

_____

_____

Is $\sqrt{2}$ between 1.4 and 1.5? How do you know?

_____

_____

$\sqrt{2}$ is between _____ and _____, so $\sqrt{2} \approx$ _____.

G Locate and label this value on the number line.

1.1   1.2   1.3   1.4   1.5

Reflect

11. How could you find an even better estimate of $\sqrt{2}$?

_____

_____

12. Find a better estimate of $\sqrt{2}$. Draw a number line and locate and label your estimate.

$\sqrt{2}$ is between _____ and _____, so $\sqrt{2} \approx$ _____.

13. Estimate the value of $\sqrt{7}$ to two decimal places. Draw a number line and locate and label your estimate.

$\sqrt{7}$ is between _____ and _____, so $\sqrt{7} \approx$ _____.

Guided Practice

Write each fraction or mixed number as a decimal. (Explore Activity Example 1)

1. $\frac{2}{5}$ _____

2. $\frac{8}{9}$ _____

3. $3\frac{3}{4}$ _____

4. $\frac{7}{10}$ _____

5. $2\frac{3}{8}$ _____

6. $\frac{5}{6}$ _____

Write each decimal as a fraction or mixed number in simplest form. (Example 2)

7. 0.675 _____

8. 5.6 _____

9. 0.44 _____

10. $0.\overline{4}$

$10x = \boxed{}$

$-x \quad -\boxed{}$

$\overline{\boxed{} x = \boxed{}}$

$x =$ _____

11. $0.\overline{26}$

$100x = \boxed{}$

$-x \quad -\boxed{}$

$\overline{\boxed{} x = \boxed{}}$

$x =$ _____

12. $0.3\overline{25}$

$1000x = \boxed{}$

$-x \quad -\boxed{}$

$\overline{\boxed{} x = \boxed{}}$

$x =$ _____

Solve each equation for x. (Example 3)

13. $x^2 = 144$

$x = \pm\sqrt{\boxed{}} = \pm\boxed{}$

14. $x^2 = \frac{25}{289}$

$x = \pm\sqrt{\dfrac{\boxed{}}{\boxed{}}} = \pm\dfrac{\boxed{}}{\boxed{}}$

15. $x^3 = 216$

$x = \sqrt[3]{\boxed{}} = \boxed{}$

Approximate each irrational number to two decimal places without a calculator. (Explore Activity 2)

16. $\sqrt{5} \approx \boxed{}$

17. $\sqrt{3} \approx \boxed{}$

18. $\sqrt{10} \approx \boxed{}$

? ESSENTIAL QUESTION CHECK-IN

19. What is the difference between rational and irrational numbers?

_____

_____

9.1 Independent Practice

COMMON CORE 8.NS.1, 8.NS.2, 8.EE.2

Personal Math Trainer

Online Assessment and Intervention

my.hrw.com

20. A $\frac{7}{16}$-inch-long bolt is used in a machine. What is the length of the bolt written as a decimal?

_____

21. The weight of an object on the moon is $\frac{1}{6}$ its weight on Earth. Write $\frac{1}{6}$ as a decimal.

_____

22. The distance to the nearest gas station is $2\frac{4}{5}$ kilometers. What is this distance written as a decimal?

_____

23. A baseball pitcher has pitched $98\frac{2}{3}$ innings. What is the number of innings written as a decimal?

_____

24. A heartbeat takes 0.8 second. How many seconds is this written as a fraction?

_____

25. There are 26.2 miles in a marathon. Write the number of miles using a fraction.

_____

26. The average score on a biology test was $72.\overline{1}$. Write the average score using a fraction.

_____

27. The metal in a penny is worth about 0.505 cent. How many cents is this written as a fraction?

_____

28. Multistep An artist wants to frame a square painting with an area of 400 square inches. She wants to know the length of the wood trim that is needed to go around the painting.

a. If x is the length of one side of the painting, what equation can you set up to find the length of a side? _____

b. Solve the equation you wrote in part a. How many solutions does the equation have?

_____

_____

c. Do all of the solutions that you found in part b make sense in the context of the problem? Explain.

_____

_____

_____

d. What is the length of the wood trim needed to go around the painting?

_____

29. Analyze Relationships To find $\sqrt{15}$, Beau found $3^2 = 9$ and $4^2 = 16$. He said that since 15 is between 9 and 16, $\sqrt{15}$ must be between 3 and 4. He thinks a good estimate for $\sqrt{15}$ is $\frac{3+4}{2} = 3.5$. Is Beau's estimate high, low, or correct? Explain.

_____

_____

_____

30. Justify Reasoning What is a good estimate for the solution to the equation $x^3 = 95$? How did you come up with your estimate?

_____

_____

_____

31. The volume of a sphere is 36π ft³. What is the radius of the sphere? Use the formula $V = \frac{4}{3}\pi r^3$ to find your answer.

_____

 **FOCUS ON HIGHER ORDER THINKING**

Work Area

32. Draw Conclusions Can you find the cube root of a negative number? If so, is it positive or negative? Explain your reasoning.

_____

_____

_____

33. Make a Conjecture Evaluate and compare the following expressions.

$$\sqrt{\frac{4}{25}} \text{ and } \frac{\sqrt{4}}{\sqrt{25}} \qquad \sqrt{\frac{16}{81}} \text{ and } \frac{\sqrt{16}}{\sqrt{81}} \qquad \sqrt{\frac{36}{49}} \text{ and } \frac{\sqrt{36}}{\sqrt{49}}$$

Use your results to make a conjecture about a division rule for square roots. Since division is multiplication by the reciprocal, make a conjecture about a multiplication rule for square roots.

_____

_____

34. Persevere in Problem Solving The difference between the solutions to the equation $x^2 = a$ is 30. What is a? Show that your answer is correct.

_____

_____

9.2 Sets of Real Numbers

COMMON CORE 8.NS.1

Know that numbers that are not rational are called irrational. . . .

ESSENTIAL QUESTION

How can you describe relationships between sets of real numbers?

EXPLORE ACTIVITY COMMON CORE 8.NS.1

Classifying Real Numbers

Biologists classify animals based on shared characteristics. A cardinal is an animal, a vertebrate, a bird, and a passerine.

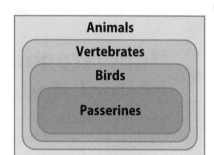

Animals
Vertebrates
Birds
Passerines

Math On the Spot
my.hrw.com

You know that the set of rational numbers consists of whole numbers, integers, decimals, and fractions. The set of **real numbers** consists of the set of rational numbers and the set of irrational numbers.

Real Numbers		
Rational Numbers		**Irrational Numbers**

$\frac{27}{4}$ $0.\overline{3}$ $-\frac{6}{7}$

Integers
-3

Whole Numbers
-2

-1 0

1 3
$\sqrt{4}$

4.5

$\sqrt{17}$

$-\sqrt{11}$

$\sqrt{2}$

π

Passerines, such as the cardinal, are also called "perching birds."

EXAMPLE 1 Write all the names that apply to each number.

A $\sqrt{5}$
The number 5 under the square root symbol is a whole number that is not a perfect square.

_____
_____

Animated Math
my.hrw.com

B -17.84
-17.84 is a terminating decimal.

_____
_____

C $\frac{\sqrt{81}}{9}$

$\frac{\sqrt{81}}{9} = \frac{9}{9} = 1$

_____
_____
_____
_____

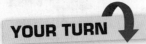

YOUR TURN

Write all names that apply to each number.

1. A baseball pitcher has pitched $12\frac{2}{3}$ innings.

_____

2. The length of the side of a square that has an

area of 10 square yards. _____

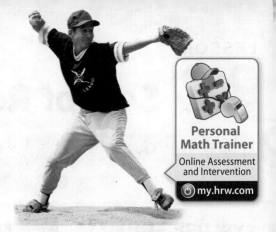

Personal Math Trainer

Online Assessment and Intervention

⊙ my.hrw.com

Math On the Spot

⊙ my.hrw.com

Understanding Sets and Subsets of Real Numbers

By understanding which sets are subsets of types of numbers, you can verify whether statements about the relationships between sets are true or false.

EXAMPLE 2

COMMON CORE **8.NS.1**

Tell whether the given statement is true or false. Explain your choice.

A All irrational numbers are real numbers.

True. Every irrational number is included in the set of real numbers. Irrational numbers are a subset of real numbers.

B No rational numbers are whole numbers.

False. A whole number can be written as a fraction with a denominator of 1, so every whole number is included in the set of rational numbers. Whole numbers are a subset of rational numbers.

Math Talk
Mathematical Practices

Give an example of a rational number that is a whole number. Show that the number is both whole and rational.

YOUR TURN

Tell whether the given statement is true or false. Explain your choice.

3. All rational numbers are integers.

_____

_____

_____

4. Some irrational numbers are integers.

_____

_____

Personal Math Trainer

Online Assessment and Intervention

⊙ my.hrw.com

Identifying Sets for Real-World Situations

Real numbers can be used to represent real-world quantities. Highways have posted speed limit signs that are represented by natural numbers such as 55 mph. Integers appear on thermometers. Rational numbers are used in many daily activities, including cooking. For example, ingredients in a recipe are often given in fractional amounts such as $\frac{2}{3}$ cup flour.

EXAMPLE 3   **8.NS.1**

Identify the set of numbers that best describes each situation. Explain your choice.

A   the number of people wearing glasses in a room

The set of whole numbers best describes the situation. The number of people wearing glasses may be 0 or a counting number.

B   the circumference of a flying disk has a diameter of 8, 9, 10, 11, or 14 inches

The set of irrational numbers best describes the situation. Each circumference would be a product of π and the diameter, and any multiple of π is irrational.

My Notes

YOUR TURN

Identify the set of numbers that best describes the situation. Explain your choice.

5. the amount of water in a glass as it evaporates

_____

_____

_____

6. the number of seconds remaining when a song is playing, displayed as a negative number

_____

_____

_____

Personal Math Trainer

Online Assessment and Intervention

my.hrw.com

Write all names that apply to each number. (Explore Activity Example 1)

1. $\frac{7}{8}$

_____

2. $\sqrt{36}$

_____

3. $\sqrt{24}$

_____

4. 0.75

_____

5. 0

_____

6. $-\sqrt{100}$

_____

7. $5.\overline{45}$

_____

8. $-\frac{18}{6}$

_____

Tell whether the given statement is true or false. Explain your choice.
(Example 2)

9. All whole numbers are rational numbers.

_____

_____

10. No irrational numbers are whole numbers.

_____

Identify the set of numbers that best describes each situation. Explain your choice. (Example 3)

11. the change in the value of an account when given to the nearest dollar

_____

_____

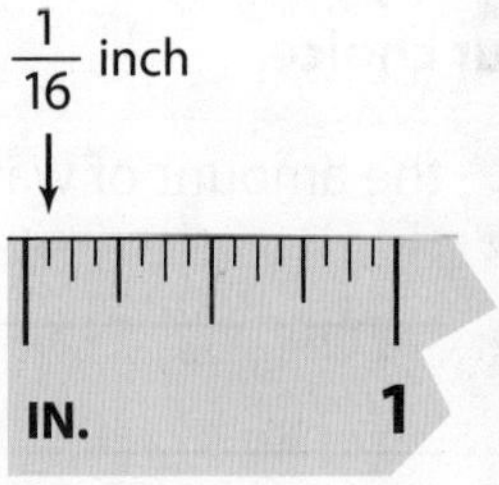

12. the markings on a standard ruler

_____

$\frac{1}{16}$ inch

IN.   1

ESSENTIAL QUESTION CHECK-IN

13. What are some ways to describe the relationships between sets of numbers?

_____

_____

Name_____ Class_____ Date_____

9.2 Independent Practice

 8.NS.1

Personal Math Trainer

Online Assessment and Intervention

my.hrw.com

Write all names that apply to each number. Then place the numbers in the correct location on the Venn diagram.

14. $\sqrt{9}$ _____

15. 257 _____

16. $\sqrt{50}$ _____

17. $8\frac{1}{2}$ _____

18. 16.6 _____

19. $\sqrt{16}$ _____

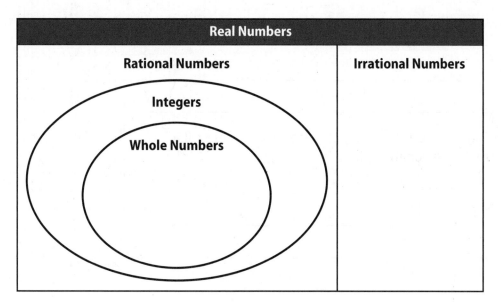

Identify the set of numbers that best describes each situation. Explain your choice.

20. the height of an airplane as it descends to an airport runway

_____

21. the score with respect to par of several golfers: 2, −3, 5, 0, −1

_____

_____

22. **Critique Reasoning** Ronald states that the number $\frac{1}{11}$ is not rational because, when converted into a decimal, it does not terminate. Nathaniel says it is rational because it is a fraction. Which boy is correct? Explain.

_____

_____

23. Critique Reasoning The circumference of a circular region is shown. What type of number best describes the diameter of the circle? Explain your answer. _____

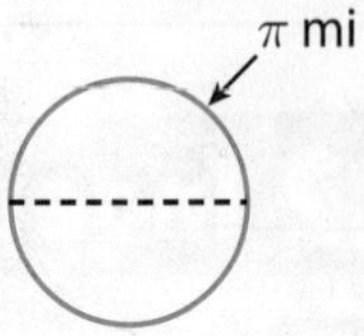

π mi

24. Critical Thinking A number is not an integer. What type of number can it be?

_____

25. A grocery store has a shelf with half-gallon containers of milk. What type of number best represents the total number of gallons?

_____

H.O.T. FOCUS ON HIGHER ORDER THINKING

Work Area

26. Explain the Error Katie said, "Negative numbers are integers." What was her error?

_____

_____

27. Justify Reasoning Can you ever use a calculator to determine if a number is rational or irrational? Explain.

_____

_____

_____

_____

_____

_____

_____

28. Draw Conclusions The decimal $0.\overline{3}$ represents $\frac{1}{3}$. What type of number best describes $0.\overline{9}$, which is $3 \cdot 0.\overline{3}$? Explain.

_____

29. Communicate Mathematical Ideas Irrational numbers can never be precisely represented in decimal form. Why is this?

_____

_____

_____

Ordering Real Numbers

COMMON CORE 8.NS.2

Use rational approximations of irrational numbers to compare the size of irrational numbers, locate them approximately on a number line diagram, and estimate the value of expressions (e.g., π^2).

ESSENTIAL QUESTION

How do you order a set of real numbers?

EXPLORE ACTIVITY
COMMON CORE 8.NS.2

Comparing Irrational Numbers

Between any two real numbers is another real number. To compare and order real numbers, you can approximate irrational numbers as decimals.

Math On the Spot
my.hrw.com

EXAMPLE 1 Compare $\sqrt{3} + 5$ $\bigcirc$ $3 + \sqrt{5}$. Write $<$, $>$, or $=$.

STEP 1 Use perfect squares to estimate square roots.

Approximate $\sqrt{3}$. $\sqrt{3}$ is between $\sqrt{1}$ and $\sqrt{4}$, or between ____ and ____.

Approximate $\sqrt{5}$. $\sqrt{5}$ is between $\sqrt{4}$ and $\sqrt{9}$, or between ____ and ____.

STEP 2 Use your estimations to simplify the expressions.

$\sqrt{3} + 5$ is between $\boxed{} + 5$ and $\boxed{} + 5$, or between ____ and ____.

$3 + \sqrt{5}$ is between $3 + \boxed{}$ and $3 + \boxed{}$, or between ____ and ____.

So, $\sqrt{3} + 5$ $\bigcirc$ $3 + \sqrt{5}$.

Reflect

1. If $7 + \sqrt{5}$ is equal to $\sqrt{5}$ plus a number, what do you know about the number? Why?

   _____

2. What are the closest two integers that $\sqrt{300}$ is between?

   _____

YOUR TURN

Personal Math Trainer
Online Assessment and Intervention
my.hrw.com

Compare. Write $<$, $>$, or $=$.

3. $\sqrt{2} + 4$ $\bigcirc$ $2 + \sqrt{4}$

4. $\sqrt{12} + 6$ $\bigcirc$ $12 + \sqrt{6}$

Ordering Real Numbers

You can compare and order real numbers and list them from least to greatest.

My Notes

EXAMPLE 2

Order $\sqrt{22}$, $\pi + 1$, and $4\frac{1}{2}$ from least to greatest.

STEP 1 First approximate $\sqrt{22}$.

$\sqrt{22}$ is between 4 and 5. Since you don't know where it falls between 4 and 5, you need to find a better estimate for $\sqrt{22}$ so you can compare it to $4\frac{1}{2}$.

Since 22 is closer to 25 than 16, use squares of numbers between 4.5 and 5 to find a better estimate of $\sqrt{22}$.

$4.5^2 = 20.25$ $4.6^2 = 21.16$ $4.7^2 = 22.09$ $4.8^2 = 23.04$

Since $4.7^2 = 22.09$, an approximate value for $\sqrt{22}$ is 4.7.

An approximate value of π is 3.14. So an approximate value of $\pi + 1$ is 4.14.

STEP 2 Plot $\sqrt{22}$, $\pi + 1$, and $4\frac{1}{2}$ on a number line.

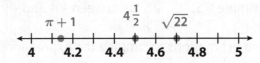

Read the numbers from left to right to place them in order from least to greatest.

From least to greatest, the numbers are $\pi + 1$, $4\frac{1}{2}$, and $\sqrt{22}$.

YOUR TURN

Order the numbers from least to greatest. Then graph them on the number line.

5. $\sqrt{5}$, 2.5, $\sqrt{3}$ _____

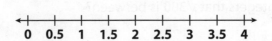

6. π^2, 10, $\sqrt{75}$ _____

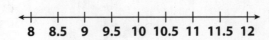

Math Talk
Mathematical Practices

If real numbers *a*, *b*, and *c* are in order from least to greatest, what is the order of their opposites from least to greatest? Explain.

Ordering Real Numbers in a Real-World Context

Calculations and estimations in the real world may differ. It can be important to know not only which are the most accurate but which give the greatest or least values, depending upon the context.

Math On the Spot

⏻ my.hrw.com

EXAMPLE 3

COMMON CORE **8.NS.2**

Four people have found the distance in kilometers across a canyon using different methods. Their results are given in the table. Order the distances from greatest to least.

Distance Across Quarry Canyon (km)			
Juana	**Lee Ann**	**Ryne**	**Jackson**
$\sqrt{28}$	$\frac{23}{4}$	$5.\overline{5}$	$5\frac{1}{2}$

STEP 1 Write each value as a decimal.

$\sqrt{28}$ is between 5.2 and 5.3. Since $5.3^2 = 28.09$, an approximate value for $\sqrt{28}$ is 5.3.

$\frac{23}{4} = 5.75$

$5.\overline{5}$ is 5.555…, so $5.\overline{5}$ to the nearest hundredth is 5.56.

$5\frac{1}{2} = 5.5$

STEP 2 Plot $\sqrt{28}$, $\frac{23}{4}$, $5.\overline{5}$, and $5\frac{1}{2}$ on a number line.

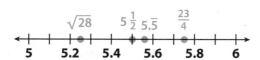

From greatest to least, the distances are:

$\frac{23}{4}$ km, $5.\overline{5}$ km, $5\frac{1}{2}$ km, $\sqrt{28}$ km.

YOUR TURN

7. Four people have found the distance in miles across a crater using different methods. Their results are given below.

Jonathan: $\frac{10}{3}$, Elaine: $3.\overline{45}$, José: $3\frac{1}{2}$, Lashonda: $\sqrt{10}$

Order the distances from greatest to least.

_____

Personal Math Trainer

Online Assessment and Intervention

⏻ my.hrw.com

Compare. Write <, >, or =. (Explore Activity Example 1)

1. $\sqrt{3} + 2$ ◯ $\sqrt{3} + 3$

2. $\sqrt{11} + 15$ ◯ $\sqrt{8} + 15$

3. $\sqrt{6} + 5$ ◯ $6 + \sqrt{5}$

4. $\sqrt{9} + 3$ ◯ $9 + \sqrt{3}$

5. $\sqrt{17} - 3$ ◯ $-2 + \sqrt{5}$

6. $10 - \sqrt{8}$ ◯ $12 - \sqrt{2}$

7. $\sqrt{7} + 2$ ◯ $\sqrt{10} - 1$

8. $\sqrt{17} + 3$ ◯ $3 + \sqrt{11}$

9. Order $\sqrt{3}$, 2π, and 1.5 from least to greatest. Then graph them on the number line. (Example 2)

$\sqrt{3}$ is between _____ and _____, so $\sqrt{3} \approx$ _____.

$\pi \approx 3.14$, so $2\pi \approx$ _____.

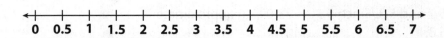

0 0.5 1 1.5 2 2.5 3 3.5 4 4.5 5 5.5 6 6.5 7

From least to greatest, the numbers are _____, _____,

_____.

10. Four people have found the perimeter of a forest using different methods. Their results are given in the table. Order their calculations from greatest to least. (Example 3)

Forest Perimeter (km)			
Leon	Mika	Jason	Ashley
$\sqrt{17} - 2$	$1 + \dfrac{\pi}{2}$	$\dfrac{12}{5}$	2.5

_____

_____

? ESSENTIAL QUESTION CHECK-IN

11. Explain how to order a set of real numbers.

_____

_____

_____

_____

9.3 Independent Practice

COMMON CORE 8.NS.2

Personal Math Trainer

Online Assessment and Intervention

my.hrw.com

Order the numbers from least to greatest.

12. $\sqrt{7}, 2, \dfrac{\sqrt{8}}{2}$

_____

13. $\sqrt{10}, \pi, 3.5$

_____

14. $\sqrt{220}, -10, \sqrt{100}, 11.5$

_____

15. $\sqrt{8}, -3.75, 3, \dfrac{9}{4}$

_____

16. Your sister is considering two different shapes for her garden. One is a square with side lengths of 3.5 meters, and the other is a circle with a diameter of 4 meters.

a. Find the area of the square. _____

b. Find the area of the circle. _____

c. Compare your answers from parts **a** and **b**. Which garden would give your sister the most space to plant?

_____

_____

17. Winnie measured the length of her father's ranch four times and got four different distances. Her measurements are shown in the table.

Distance Across Father's Ranch (km)			
1	**2**	**3**	**4**
$\sqrt{60}$	$\dfrac{58}{8}$	$7.\overline{3}$	$7\dfrac{3}{5}$

a. To estimate the actual length, Winnie first approximated each distance to the nearest hundredth. Then she averaged the four numbers. Using a calculator, find Winnie's estimate.

_____

_____

b. Winnie's father estimated the distance across his ranch to be $\sqrt{56}$ km. How does this distance compare to Winnie's estimate?

_____

Give an example of each type of number.

18. a real number between $\sqrt{13}$ and $\sqrt{14}$ _____

19. an irrational number between 5 and 7 _____

20. A teacher asks his students to write the numbers shown in order from least to greatest. Paul thinks the numbers are already in order. Sandra thinks the order should be reversed. Who is right?

$$\sqrt{115}, \frac{115}{11}, \text{ and } 10.5624$$

_____

_____

_____

21. Math History There is a famous irrational number called Euler's number, symbolized with an *e*. Like π, its decimal form never ends or repeats. The first few digits of *e* are 2.7182818284.

   a. Between which two square roots of integers could you find this number?

   _____

   b. Between which two square roots of integers can you find π?

   _____

H.O.T.   **FOCUS ON HIGHER ORDER THINKING**

Work Area

22. Analyze Relationships There are several approximations used for π, including 3.14 and $\frac{22}{7}$. π is approximately 3.14159265358979…

   a. Label π and the two approximations on the number line.

        3.140   3.141   3.142   3.143

   b. Which of the two approximations is a better estimate for π? Explain.

   _____

   c. Find a whole number x so that the ratio $\frac{x}{113}$ is a better estimate for π than the two given approximations. _____

23. Communicate Mathematical Ideas What is the fewest number of distinct points that must be graphed on a number line, in order to represent natural numbers, whole numbers, integers, rational numbers, irrational numbers, and real numbers? Explain.

_____

_____

_____

24. Critique Reasoning Jill says that $12.\overline{6}$ is less than 12.63. Explain her error.

_____

Root-O!

INSTRUCTIONS

Playing the Game

STEP 1 Choose one person to be the caller. The caller can be a teacher, or students can take turns being caller. The caller gets a set of caller cards. All the other players get a game card and some counters. The center is a free space. Players should cover the center square before play begins.

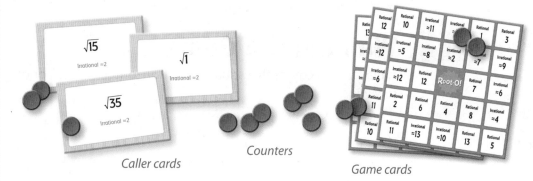

Caller cards

Counters

Game cards

STEP 2 The caller randomly draws a caller card and reads aloud the square-root expression to the players.

STEP 3 Players write down the expression on a piece of scratch paper and determine the classification (rational or irrational) and the equivalent or approximate integer value. If the same classification and value appear on a square of his/her game card, the player covers that square with a counter.

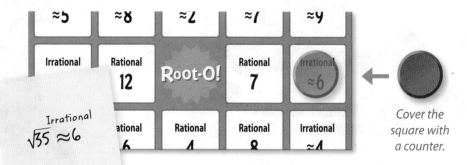

Cover the square with a counter.

STEP 4 Caller will then draw another caller card to continue the game.

STEP 5 Continue the game in this way until a player covers five squares in a row horizontally, vertically, or diagonally, and calls out "Root-O!"

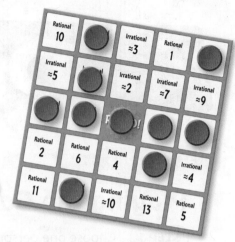

STEP 6 The prospective winning player will then check with the caller to verify that the squares covered on his/her game card correspond to cards that have been called. If there is a discrepancy, the player's game card is corrected and the game continues.

Winning the Game

A player who covers five squares in a horizontal, vertical, or diagonal row wins.

Ready to Go On?

Personal Math Trainer

Online Assessment and Intervention

(○) my.hrw.com

9.1 Rational and Irrational Numbers

Write each fraction as a decimal or each decimal as a fraction.

1. $\frac{7}{20}$ _____

2. $1.\overline{27}$ _____

3. $1\frac{7}{8}$ _____

Solve each equation for x.

4. $x^2 = 81$ _____

5. $x^3 = 343$ _____

6. $x^2 = \frac{1}{100}$ _____

7. A square patio has an area of 200 square feet. How long is each side

of the patio to the nearest 0.05? _____

9.2 Sets of Real Numbers

Write all names that apply to each number.

8. $\frac{121}{\sqrt{121}}$ _____

9. $\frac{\pi}{2}$ _____

10. Tell whether the statement "All integers are rational numbers" is true or false. Explain your choice.

_____

_____

9.3 Ordering Real Numbers

Compare. Write $<$, $>$, or $=$.

11. $\sqrt{8} + 3$ ◯ $8 + \sqrt{3}$

12. $\sqrt{5} + 11$ ◯ $5 + \sqrt{11}$

Order the numbers from least to greatest.

13. $\sqrt{99}, \pi^2, 9.\overline{8}$ _____

14. $\sqrt{\frac{1}{25}}, \frac{1}{4}, 0.\overline{2}$ _____

? **ESSENTIAL QUESTION**

15. How are real numbers used to describe real-world situations?

_____

_____

MODULE 9 MIXED REVIEW

Assessment Readiness

COMMON CORE

Personal Math Trainer

Online Assessment and Intervention

my.hrw.com

Selected Response

1. The square root of a number is 9. What is the other square root?

Ⓐ −9

Ⓒ 3

Ⓑ −3

Ⓓ 81

2. A square acre of land is 4,840 square yards. Between which two integers is the length of one side?

Ⓐ between 24 and 25 yards

Ⓑ between 69 and 70 yards

Ⓒ between 242 and 243 yards

Ⓓ between 695 and 696 yards

3. Which of the following is an integer but not a whole number?

Ⓐ −9.6

Ⓒ 0

Ⓑ −4

Ⓓ 3.7

4. Which statement is false?

Ⓐ No integers are irrational numbers.

Ⓑ All whole numbers are integers.

Ⓒ No real numbers are irrational numbers.

Ⓓ All integers greater than 0 are whole numbers.

5. Which set of numbers best describes the displayed weights on a digital scale that shows each weight to the nearest half pound?

Ⓐ whole numbers

Ⓑ rational numbers

Ⓒ real numbers

Ⓓ integers

6. Which of the following is not true?

Ⓐ $\pi^2 < 2\pi + 4$

Ⓒ $\sqrt{27} + 3 > \frac{17}{2}$

Ⓑ $3\pi > 9$

Ⓓ $5 - \sqrt{24} < 1$

7. Which number is between $\sqrt{21}$ and $\frac{3\pi}{2}$?

Ⓐ $\frac{14}{3}$

Ⓒ 5

Ⓑ $2\sqrt{6}$

Ⓓ $\pi + 1$

8. What number is shown on the graph?

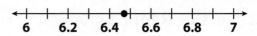

Ⓐ $\pi + 3$

Ⓒ $\sqrt{20} + 2$

Ⓑ $\sqrt{4} + 2.5$

Ⓓ $6.\overline{14}$

9. Which is in order from least to greatest?

Ⓐ $3.3, \frac{10}{3}, \pi, \frac{11}{4}$

Ⓒ $\pi, \frac{10}{3}, \frac{11}{4}, 3.3$

Ⓑ $\frac{10}{3}, 3.3, \frac{11}{4}, \pi$

Ⓓ $\frac{11}{4}, \pi, 3.3, \frac{10}{3}$

Mini-Task

10. The volume of a cube is given by $V = x^3$, where x is the length of an edge of the cube. The area of a square is given by $A = x^2$, where x is the length of a side of the square. A given cube has a volume of 1728 cubic inches.

a. Find the length of an edge.

_____

b. Find the area of one side of the cube.

_____

c. Find the surface area of the cube.

_____

d. What is the surface area in square feet?

_____

Exponents and Scientific Notation

ESSENTIAL QUESTION

How can you use scientific notation to solve real-world problems?

Real-World Video

The distance from Earth to other planets, moons, and stars is a very great number of kilometers. To make it easier to write very large and very small numbers, we use scientific notation.

my.hrw.com

GO DIGITAL
my.hrw.com

my.hrw.com

Go digital with your write-in student edition, accessible on any device.

Math On the Spot

Scan with your smart phone to jump directly to the online edition, video tutor, and more.

Animated Math

Interactively explore key concepts to see how math works.

Personal Math Trainer

Get immediate feedback and help as you work through practice sets.

Are YOU Ready?

Complete these exercises to review skills you will need for this module.

Exponents

> **EXAMPLE** $10^4 = 10 \times 10 \times 10 \times 10$
>
> $= 10,000$
>
> Write the exponential expression as a product.
> Simplify.

Write each exponential expression as a decimal.

1. 10^2 _____   **2.** 10^3 _____   **3.** 10^5 _____   **4.** 10^7 _____

Multiply and Divide by Powers of 10

> **EXAMPLE** $0.0478 \times 10^5 = 0.0478 \times 100,000$
>
> $= 4,780$
>
> Identify the number of zeros in the power of 10.
> When multiplying, move the decimal point to the *right* the same number of places as the number of zeros.
>
> $37.9 \div 10^4 = 37.9 \div 10,000$
>
> $= 0.00379$
>
> Identify the number of zeros in the power of 10.
> When dividing, move the decimal point to the *left* the same number of places as the number of zeros.

Find each product or quotient.

5. 45.3×10^3 **6.** $7.08 \div 10^2$ **7.** 0.00235×10^6 **8.** $3,600 \div 10^4$

_____   _____   _____   _____

9. 0.5×10^2 **10.** $67.7 \div 10^5$ **11.** 0.0057×10^4 **12.** $195 \div 10^6$

_____   _____   _____   _____

Reading Start-Up

Visualize Vocabulary

Use the ✔ words to complete the Venn diagram. You can put more than one word in each section of the diagram.

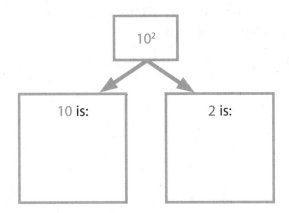

10 is:

2 is:

Understand Vocabulary

Complete the sentences using the preview words.

1. A number produced by raising a base to an exponent

   is a _____.

2. _____ is a method of writing very large or
   very small numbers by using powers of 10.

3. A _____ is any number that can be expressed
   as a ratio of two integers.

Vocabulary

Review Words

✔ base *(base)*

✔ exponent *(exponente)*

   integers *(enteros)*

✔ positive number *(número positivo)*

   standard notation *(notación estándar)*

Preview Words

   power *(potencia)*

   rational number *(número racional)*

   real numbers *(número real)*

   scientific notation *(notación científica)*

   whole number *(número entero)*

Active Reading

Two-Panel Flip Chart Create a two-panel flip chart to help you understand the concepts in this module. Label one flap "Positive Powers of 10" and the other flap "Negative Powers of 10." As you study each lesson, write important ideas under the appropriate flap. Include sample problems that will help you remember the concepts later when you look back at your notes.

COMMON CORE

Unpacking the Standards

Understanding the standards and the vocabulary terms in the standards will help you know exactly what you are expected to learn in this module.

COMMON CORE 8.EE.1

Know and apply the properties of integer exponents to generate equivalent numerical expressions.

Key Vocabulary

integer *(entero)*
The set of whole numbers and their opposites

exponent *(exponente)*
The number that indicates how many times the base is used as a factor.

What It Means to You

You will use the properties of integer exponents to find equivalent expressions.

UNPACKING EXAMPLE 8.EE.1

Evaluate two different ways.

$$\frac{8^3}{8^5}$$

$$\frac{8^3}{8^5} = \frac{8 \cdot 8 \cdot 8}{8 \cdot 8 \cdot 8 \cdot 8 \cdot 8} = \frac{1}{8 \cdot 8} = \frac{1}{64}$$

$$\frac{8^3}{8^5} = 8^{(3-5)} = 8^{-2} = \frac{1}{8^2} = \frac{1}{8 \cdot 8} = \frac{1}{64}$$

$$(3^2)^4$$

$$(3^2)^4 = (3^2)(3^2)(3^2)(3^2) = 3^{2+2+2+2} = 3^8 = 6{,}561$$

$$(3^2)^4 = 3^{(2 \cdot 4)} = 3^8 = 6{,}561$$

COMMON CORE 8.EE.3

Use numbers expressed in the form of a single digit times an integer power of 10 to estimate very large or very small quantities, and to express how many times as much one is than the other.

Key Vocabulary

scientific notation *(notación científica)*
A method of writing very large or very small numbers by using powers of 10.

What It Means to You

You will convert very large numbers to scientific notation.

UNPACKING EXAMPLE 8.EE.3

There are about 55,000,000,000 cells in an average-sized adult. Write this number in scientific notation.

Move the decimal point to the left until you have a number that is greater than or equal to 1 and less than 10.

5.5 0 0 0 0 0 0 0 0 0   *Move the decimal point 10 places to the left.*

5.5   *Remove the extra zeros.*

You would have to multiply 5.5 by 10^{10} to get 55,000,000,000.

$$55{,}000{,}000{,}000 = 5.5 \times 10^{10}$$

Visit **my.hrw.com** to see all the **Common Core Standards** unpacked.

my.hrw.com

10.1 Integer Exponents

COMMON CORE 8.EE.1

Know and apply the properties of integer exponents to generate equivalent numerical expressions.

ESSENTIAL QUESTION

How can you develop and use the properties of integer exponents?

EXPLORE ACTIVITY 1 8.EE.1

Using Patterns of Integer Exponents

The table below shows powers of 5, 4, and 3.

$5^4 = 625$	$5^3 = 125$	$5^2 = 25$	$5^1 = 5$	$5^0 = \boxed{}$	$5^{-1} = \boxed{}$	$5^{-2} = \boxed{}$
$4^4 = 256$	$4^3 = 64$	$4^2 = 16$	$4^1 = 4$	$4^0 = \boxed{}$	$4^{-1} = \boxed{}$	$4^{-2} = \boxed{}$
$3^4 = 81$	$3^3 = 27$	$3^2 = 9$	$3^1 = 3$	$3^0 = \boxed{}$	$3^{-1} = \boxed{}$	$3^{-2} = \boxed{}$

A What pattern do you see in the powers of 5?

_____

_____

B What pattern do you see in the powers of 4?

_____

_____

C What pattern do you see in the powers of 3?

_____

_____

D Complete the table for the values of $5^0, 5^{-1}, 5^{-2}$.

E Complete the table for the values of $4^0, 4^{-1}, 4^{-2}$.

F Complete the table for the values of $3^0, 3^{-1}, 3^{-2}$.

Reflect

1. **Make a Conjecture** Write a general rule for the value of a^0. _____

2. **Make a Conjecture** Write a general rule for the value of a^{-n}. _____

Exploring Properties of Integer Exponents

A Complete the following equations.

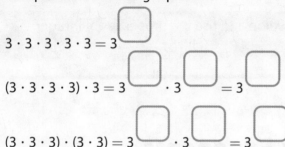

$3 \cdot 3 \cdot 3 \cdot 3 \cdot 3 = 3^{\boxed{}}$

$(3 \cdot 3 \cdot 3 \cdot 3) \cdot 3 = 3^{\boxed{}} \cdot 3^{\boxed{}} = 3^{\boxed{}}$

$(3 \cdot 3 \cdot 3) \cdot (3 \cdot 3) = 3^{\boxed{}} \cdot 3^{\boxed{}} = 3^{\boxed{}}$

What pattern do you see when multiplying two powers with the same base?

_____

_____

Use your pattern to complete this equation: $5^2 \cdot 5^5 = 5^{\boxed{}}$.

B Complete the following equation:

$\dfrac{4^5}{4^3} = \dfrac{4 \cdot 4 \cdot 4 \cdot 4 \cdot 4}{4 \cdot 4 \cdot 4} = \dfrac{\overset{1}{\cancel{4}} \cdot \overset{1}{\cancel{4}} \cdot \overset{1}{\cancel{4}} \cdot 4 \cdot 4}{\underset{1}{\cancel{4}} \cdot \underset{1}{\cancel{4}} \cdot \underset{1}{\cancel{4}}} = 4 \cdot 4 = 4^{\boxed{}}$

What pattern do you see when dividing two powers with the same base?

_____

_____

_____

Use your pattern to complete this equation: $\dfrac{6^8}{6^3} = 6^{\boxed{}}$.

C Complete the following equations:

$(5^3)^2 = (5 \cdot 5 \cdot 5)^{\boxed{}} = (5 \cdot 5 \cdot 5) \cdot (5 \cdot 5 \cdot 5) = 5^{\boxed{}}$

What pattern do you see when raising a power to a power?

_____

_____

Use your pattern to complete this equation: $(7^2)^4 = 7^{\boxed{}}$.

> ## Math Talk
> **Mathematical Practices**
>
> Do the patterns you found in parts A–C apply if the exponents are negative? If so, give an example of each.

Reflect

Let *m* and *n* be integers.

3. **Make a Conjecture** Write a general rule for the value of $a^m \cdot a^n$. _____

4. **Make a Conjecture** Write a general rule for the value of $\frac{a^m}{a^n}$, $a \neq 0$. _____

5. **Make a Conjecture** Write a general rule for the value of $(a^m)^n$. _____

Applying Properties of Integer Exponents

You can use the general rules you found in the Explore Activities to simplify more complicated expressions.

Math On the Spot
my.hrw.com

EXAMPLE 1

COMMON CORE 8.EE.1

Simplify each expression.

A $(5 - 2)^5 \cdot 3^{-8} + (5 + 2)^0$

$(3)^5 \cdot 3^{-8} + (7)^0$ — Simplify within parentheses.

$3^{5 + (-8)} + 1$ — Use properties of exponents.

$3^{-3} + 1$ — Simplify.

$\frac{1}{27} + 1 = 1\frac{1}{27}$ — Apply the rule for negative exponents and add.

B $\dfrac{\left[(3 + 1)^2\right]^3}{(7 - 3)^2}$

$\dfrac{(4^2)^3}{4^2}$ — Simplify within parentheses.

$\dfrac{4^6}{4^2}$ — Use properties of exponents.

4^{6-2} — Use properties of exponents.

$4^4 = 256$ — Simplify.

My Notes

YOUR TURN

Simplify each expression.

6. $\dfrac{\left[(6 - 1)^2\right]^2}{(3 + 2)^3}$

7. $(2^2)^3 - (10 - 6)^3 \cdot 4^{-5}$

_____   _____

Personal Math Trainer

Online Assessment and Intervention

my.hrw.com

Guided Practice

Find the value of each power. (Explore Activity 1)

1. $8^{-1} =$ _____

2. $6^{-2} =$ _____

3. $256^0 =$ _____

4. $10^2 =$ _____

5. $5^4 =$ _____

6. $2^{-5} =$ _____

7. $4^{-5} =$ _____

8. $89^0 =$ _____

9. $11^{-3} =$ _____

Use properties of exponents to write an equivalent expression. (Explore Activity 2)

10. $4 \cdot 4 \cdot 4 = 4^{\boxed{}}$

11. $(2 \cdot 2) \cdot (2 \cdot 2 \cdot 2) = 2^{\boxed{}} \cdot 2^{\boxed{}} = 2^{\boxed{}}$

12. $\dfrac{6^7}{6^5} = \dfrac{6 \cdot 6 \cdot 6 \cdot 6 \cdot 6 \cdot 6 \cdot 6}{6 \cdot 6 \cdot 6 \cdot 6 \cdot 6} = \boxed{}^{\boxed{}}$

13. $\dfrac{8^{12}}{8^9} = 8^{\boxed{} - \boxed{}} = \boxed{}^{\boxed{}}$

14. $5^{10} \cdot 5 \cdot 5 = 5^{\boxed{}}$

15. $7^8 \cdot 7^5 = \boxed{}^{\boxed{}}$

16. $(6^2)^4 = (6 \cdot 6)^{\boxed{}}$

$= (6 \cdot 6) \cdot (6 \cdot 6) \cdot \left(\boxed{} \cdot \boxed{} \right) \cdot \underline{}$

$= \boxed{}^{\boxed{}}$

17. $(3^3)^3 = (3 \cdot 3 \cdot 3)^3$

$= (3 \cdot 3 \cdot 3) \cdot \left(\boxed{} \cdot \boxed{} \cdot \boxed{} \right) \underline{}$

$= \boxed{}^{\boxed{}}$

Simplify each expression. (Example 1)

18. $(10 - 6)^3 \cdot 4^2 + (10 + 2)^2$ _____

19. $\dfrac{(12 - 5)^7}{\left[(3 + 4)^2 \right]^2}$ _____

? **ESSENTIAL QUESTION CHECK-IN**

20. Summarize the rules for multiplying powers with the same base, dividing powers with the same base, and raising a power to a power.

_____

_____

_____

_____

10.1 Independent Practice

COMMON CORE 8.EE.1

21. Explain why the exponents cannot be added in the product $12^3 \cdot 11^3$.

_____

22. List three ways to express 3^5 as a product of powers.

_____

23. **Astronomy** The distance from Earth to the moon is about 22^4 miles. The distance from Earth to Neptune is about 22^7 miles. Which distance is the greater distance and about how many times greater is it?

_____

24. **Critique Reasoning** A student claims that $8^3 \cdot 8^{-5}$ is greater than 1. Explain whether the student is correct or not.

_____

_____

Find the missing exponent.

25. $\left(b^2\right)^{\boxed{}} = b^{-6}$

26. $x^{\boxed{}} \cdot x^6 = x^9$

27. $\dfrac{y^{25}}{y^{\boxed{}}} = y^6$

28. **Communicate Mathematical Ideas** Why do you subtract exponents when dividing powers with the same base?

_____

_____

_____

29. **Astronomy** The mass of the Sun is about 2×10^{27} metric tons, or 2×10^{30} kilograms. How many kilograms are in one metric ton?

_____

30. **Represent Real-World Problems** In computer technology, a kilobyte is 2^{10} bytes in size. A gigabyte is 2^{30} bytes in size. The size of a terabyte is the product of the size of a kilobyte and the size of a gigabyte. What is the size of a terabyte?

_____

31. Write equivalent expressions for $x^7 \cdot x^{-2}$ and $\frac{x^7}{x^2}$. What do you notice? Explain how your results relate to the properties of integer exponents.

_____

_____

_____

_____

A toy store is creating a large window display of different colored cubes stacked in a triangle shape. The table shows the number of cubes in each row of the triangle, starting with the top row.

Row	1	2	3	4
Number of cubes in each row	3	3^2	3^3	3^4

32. Look for a Pattern Describe any pattern you see in the table.

_____

33. Using exponents, how many cubes will be in Row 6? How many times as many cubes will be in Row 6 than in Row 3?

_____

34. Justify Reasoning If there are 6 rows in the triangle, what is the total number of cubes in the triangle? Explain how you found your answer.

_____

_____

 **FOCUS ON HIGHER ORDER THINKING**

Work Area

35. Critique Reasoning A student simplified the expression $\frac{6^2}{36^2}$ as $\frac{1}{3}$. Do you agree with this student? Explain why or why not.

_____

36. Draw Conclusions Evaluate $-a^n$ when $a = 3$ and $n = 2, 3, 4,$ and 5. Now evaluate $(-a)^n$ when $a = 3$ and $n = 2, 3, 4,$ and 5. Based on this sample, does it appear that $-a^n = (-a)^n$? If not, state the relationships, if any, between $-a^n$ and $(-a)^n$.

_____

_____

_____

_____

37. Persevere in Problem Solving A number to the 12th power divided by the same number to the 9th power equals 125. What is the number?

_____

Zero and Negative Exponents

COMMON CORE 8.EE.1

Know and apply the properties of integer exponents to generate equivalent numerical expressions.

ESSENTIAL QUESTION

How can you derive the definition of a zero exponent and the definition of a negative exponent?

EXPLORE ACTIVITY 1   **COMMON CORE** 8.EE.1

Definition of Zero Exponent

You can use the properties of exponents and the properties of division with x^a to show that $x^0 = 1$.

A Complete the statement: $\dfrac{x^a}{x^a} = x^{\boxed{} - \boxed{}} = x^{\boxed{}}$

B Anything divided by itself is _____, so $\dfrac{x^a}{x^a} =$ _____.

C If $\dfrac{x^a}{x^a} = x^{\boxed{}}$ from Part A and $\dfrac{x^a}{x^a} =$ _____ from Part B, then $x^0 =$ _____.

Reflect

1. **Justify Reasoning** What property did you use to complete Part A?

_____

EXPLORE ACTIVITY 2   **COMMON CORE** 8.EE.1

Definition of Negative Exponent

You can use the definition and properties of exponents with $\dfrac{x^3}{x^5}$ to show that $x^{-2} = \dfrac{1}{x^2}$.

A Complete the statement: $\dfrac{x^3}{x^5} = x^{\boxed{} - \boxed{}} = x^{\boxed{}}$

B Complete the statement: $\dfrac{x^3}{x^5} = \dfrac{x \cdot \boxed{} \cdot \boxed{}}{x \cdot x \cdot \boxed{} \cdot \boxed{} \cdot \boxed{}} = \dfrac{1}{\boxed{} \cdot \boxed{}} = \dfrac{1}{\boxed{}_x}$

C If $\dfrac{x^3}{x^5} = x^{\boxed{}}$ from Part A and $\dfrac{x^3}{x^5} = \dfrac{1}{\boxed{}_x}$ from Part B, then $x^{-2} = \dfrac{1}{\boxed{}_x}$.

Reflect

2. Critique Reasoning As you saw in Steps A–C, it can be shown that $x^{-n} = \frac{1}{x^n}$ for any n by using $\frac{x^a}{x^b}$, where $b > a$. Why is it necessary that $b > a$?

_____

_____

_____

Practice

1. Use x^4 to show that $x^0 = 1$.

_____

2. Use $\frac{x^4}{x^7}$ to show that $x^{-3} = \frac{1}{x^3}$.

_____

3. Use x^6 to show that $x^0 = 1$.

_____

4. Use x^7 to show that $x^0 = 1$.

_____

5. Use $\frac{x^3}{x^9}$ to show that $x^{-6} = \frac{1}{x^6}$.

_____

6. Use $\frac{x^2}{x^5}$ to show that $x^{-3} = \frac{1}{x^3}$.

_____

LESSON
10.2

COMMON CORE 8.EE.3

Use numbers expressed in the form of a single digit times an integer power of 10 to estimate very large or very small quantities, ...

Scientific Notation with Positive Powers of 10

ESSENTIAL QUESTION

How can you use scientific notation to express very large quantities?

EXPLORE ACTIVITY COMMON CORE 8.EE.3

Using Scientific Notation

Scientific notation is a method of expressing very large and very small numbers as a product of a number greater than or equal to 1 and less than 10, and a power of 10.

The weights of various sea creatures are shown in the table. Write the weight of the blue whale in scientific notation.

Sea Creature	Blue whale	Gray whale	Whale shark
Weight (lb)	250,000	68,000	41,200

A Move the decimal point in 250,000 to the left as many places as necessary to find a number that is greater than or equal to 1 and less than 10.

What number did you find? _____

B Divide 250,000 by your answer to **A**. Write your answer as a power of 10.

_____

C Combine your answers to **A** and **B** to represent 250,000.

$250{,}000 = \boxed{} \times 10^{\boxed{}}$

Repeat steps **A** through **C** to write the weight of the whale shark in scientific notation.

$41{,}200 = \boxed{} \times 10^{\boxed{}}$

Reflect

1. How many places to the left did you move the decimal point to write

41,200 in scientific notation? _____

2. What is the exponent on 10 when you write 41,200 in scientific notation?

_____

Writing a Number in Scientific Notation

To translate between standard notation and scientific notation, you can count the number of places the decimal point moves.

Writing Large Quantities in Scientific Notation

When the number is greater than or equal to 10, use a positive exponent.	$8\,4{,}000 = 8.4 \times 10^4$	*The decimal point moves 4 places to the left.*

EXAMPLE 1

COMMON CORE 8.EE.3

The distance from Earth to the Sun is about 93,000,000 miles. Write this distance in scientific notation.

STEP 1 Move the decimal point in 93,000,000 to the left until you have a number that is greater than or equal to 1 and less than 10.

$9.3\,0\,0\,0\,0\,0\,0.$ *Move the decimal point 7 places to the left.*

9.3 *Remove extra zeros.*

STEP 2 Divide the original number by the result from Step 1.

$10{,}000{,}000$ *Divide 93,000,000 by 9.3.*

10^7 *Write your answer as a power of 10.*

STEP 3 Write the product of the results from Steps 1 and 2.

$93{,}000{,}000 = 9.3 \times 10^7$ miles   *Write a product to represent 93,000,000 in scientific notation.*

> ### Math Talk
> Mathematical Practices
>
> Is 12×10^7 written in scientific notation? Explain.

YOUR TURN

Write each number in scientific notation.

3. 6,400

4. 570,000,000,000

5. A light-year is the distance that light travels in a year and is equivalent to 9,461,000,000,000 km. Write this distance in scientific notation.

Writing a Number in Standard Notation

To translate between scientific notation and standard notation, move the decimal point the number of places indicated by the exponent in the power of 10. When the exponent is positive, move the decimal point to the right and add placeholder zeros as needed.

Math On the Spot
my.hrw.com

EXAMPLE 2

COMMON CORE 8.EE.3

Write 3.5×10^6 in standard notation.

STEP 1 Use the exponent of the power of 10 to see how many places to move the decimal point.

6 places

STEP 2 Place the decimal point. Since you are going to write a number greater than 3.5, move the decimal point to the *right*. Add placeholder zeros if necessary.

3 5 0 0 0 0 0.

The number 3.5×10^6 written in standard notation is 3,500,000.

My Notes

Reflect

6. Explain why the exponent in 3.5×10^6 is 6, while there are only 5 zeros in 3,500,000.

_____

_____

_____

7. What is the exponent on 10 when you write 5.3 in scientific notation?

_____

YOUR TURN

Write each number in standard notation.

8. 7.034×10^9

9. 2.36×10^5

_____   _____

10. The mass of one roosting colony of Monarch butterflies in Mexico was estimated at 5×10^6 grams. Write this mass in standard notation.

_____

Personal Math Trainer
Online Assessment and Intervention
my.hrw.com

Write each number in scientific notation. (Explore Activity and Example 1)

1. 58,927
Hint: Move the decimal left 4 places.

_____

2. 1,304,000,000
Hint: Move the decimal left 9 places.

_____

3. 6,730,000

_____

4. 13,300

_____

5. An ordinary quarter contains about 97,700,000,000,000,000,000,000 atoms.

_____

6. The distance from Earth to the Moon is about 384,000 kilometers.

_____

Write each number in standard notation. (Example 2)

7. 4×10^5
Hint: Move the decimal right 5 places.

_____

8. 1.8499×10^9
Hint: Move the decimal right 9 places.

_____

9. 6.41×10^3

_____

10. 8.456×10^7

_____

11. 8×10^5

_____

12. 9×10^{10}

_____

13. Diana calculated that she spent about 5.4×10^4 seconds doing her math homework during October. Write this time in standard notation. (Example 2)

_____

14. The town recycled 7.6×10^6 cans this year. Write the number of cans in standard notation. (Example 2)

_____

? **ESSENTIAL QUESTION CHECK-IN**

15. Describe how to write 3,482,000,000 in scientific notation.

_____

_____

_____

10.2 Independent Practice

COMMON CORE 8.EE.3

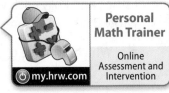

Personal Math Trainer

Online Assessment and Intervention

my.hrw.com

Paleontology Use the table for problems 16–21. Write the estimated weight of each dinosaur in scientific notation.

Estimated Weight of Dinosaurs	
Name	**Pounds**
Argentinosaurus	220,000
Brachiosaurus	100,000
Apatosaurus	66,000
Diplodocus	50,000
Camarasaurus	40,000
Cetiosauriscus	19,850

16. Apatosaurus _____

17. Argentinosaurus _____

18. Brachiosaurus _____

19. Camarasaurus _____

20. Cetiosauriscus _____

21. Diplodocus _____

22. A single little brown bat can eat up to 1,000 mosquitoes in a single hour. Express in scientific notation how many mosquitoes a little brown bat might eat in 10.5 hours.

_____

23. **Multistep** Samuel can type nearly 40 words per minute. Use this information to find the number of hours it would take him to type 2.6×10^5 words.

_____

_____

24. **Entomology** A tropical species of mite named *Archegozetes longisetosus* is the record holder for the strongest insect in the world. It can lift up to 1.182×10^3 times its own weight.

a. If you were as strong as this insect, explain how you could find how many pounds you could lift.

_____

_____

_____

b. Complete the calculation to find how much you could lift, in pounds, if you were as strong as an *Archegozetes longisetosus* mite. Express your answer in both scientific notation and standard notation.

_____

_____

25. During a discussion in science class, Sharon learns that at birth an elephant weighs around 230 pounds. In four herds of elephants tracked by conservationists, about 20 calves were born during the summer. In scientific notation, express approximately how much the calves weighed all together.

_____

26. **Classifying Numbers** Which of the following numbers are written in scientific notation?

0.641×10^3 9.999×10^4

2×10^1 4.38×5^{10}

27. Explain the Error Polly's parents' car weighs about 3500 pounds. Samantha, Esther, and Polly each wrote the weight of the car in scientific notation. Polly wrote 35.0×10^2, Samantha wrote 0.35×10^4, and Esther wrote 3.5×10^4.

Work Area

a. Which of these girls, if any, is correct?

_____

b. Explain the mistakes of those who got the question wrong.

_____

_____

_____

28. Justify Reasoning If you were a biologist counting very large numbers of cells as part of your research, give several reasons why you might prefer to record your cell counts in scientific notation instead of standard notation.

_____

_____

_____

H.O.T. FOCUS ON HIGHER ORDER THINKING

29. Draw Conclusions Which measurement would be least likely to be written in scientific notation: number of stars in a galaxy, number of grains of sand on a beach, speed of a car, or population of a country? Explain your reasoning.

_____

_____

30. Analyze Relationships Compare the two numbers to find which is greater. Explain how you can compare them without writing them in standard notation first.

$$4.5 \times 10^6 \qquad 2.1 \times 10^8$$

_____

_____

31. Communicate Mathematical Ideas To determine whether a number is written in scientific notation, what test can you apply to the first factor, and what test can you apply to the second factor?

_____

_____

Comparing Very Large Numbers

COMMON CORE 8.EE.3

Use numbers expressed in the form of a single digit times an integer power of 10 to... express how many times as much one is than the other.

ESSENTIAL QUESTION

How can you compare very large numbers in scientific notation?

EXPLORE ACTIVITY 8.EE.3

Comparing Very Large Numbers

A Compare 8,000 and 200 using standard notation.

$\dfrac{8,000}{200} = \boxed{}$, so 8,000 is _____ times greater than 200.

B Compare 8,000 and 200 using scientific notation.

$8,000 = 8 \times 10^{\boxed{}}$ and $200 = 2 \times 10^{\boxed{}}$

First compare the powers of 10 in a ratio of greater to lesser:

$$\frac{10^3}{10^2} = 10^{\boxed{}} = \boxed{}$$

Then compare the corresponding multipliers: $\dfrac{\boxed{}}{2} = $ _____

So 8×10^3 is $10 \cdot$ _____ = _____ times greater than 2×10^2.

Reflect

1. When comparing two numbers in scientific notation, why would you compare the powers of 10 first to find which number is greater?

_____

_____

2. When comparing two numbers in scientific notation, if the powers of 10 are equal, how can you tell which number is greater?

_____

_____

Comparing Very Large Numbers in the Real World

Using scientific notation can help you compare very large numbers.

EXAMPLE

COMMON CORE 8.EE.3

The average mass of a human is about 6×10^1 kilograms, and the average mass of an African elephant is about 6×10^3 kilograms. About how many times greater is the mass of an African elephant than the mass of a human?

$$\frac{10^3}{10^1} = 10^2 \qquad \text{Compare the powers of 10.}$$

$$\frac{6}{6} = 1 \qquad \text{Compare the multipliers.}$$

So, the mass of an African elephant is about 1×10^2, or 100 times greater than the mass of a human.

Practice

1. Complete the statements to express how many times greater 6×10^7 is than 3×10^7.

   $\dfrac{\boxed{}}{10^7} = 10^{\boxed{}} =$ _____ , and $\dfrac{\boxed{}}{3} =$ _____

   So, 6×10^7 is $1 \cdot$ _____ = _____ times greater than 3×10^7.

2. The average mouse has a mass of about 2×10^4 milligrams, and the average housefly has a mass of about 1×10^1 milligrams. About how many times greater is the mass of a mouse than the mass of a housefly? Explain.

   _____

   _____

Determine which quantity is greater, and determine about how many times greater.

3. Chile: about 2×10^7 people

   Argentina: about 4×10^7 people

   _____

4. African elephant mass: 6×10^3 kg

   Asian elephant mass: 5×10^3 kg

   _____

Scientific Notation with Negative Powers of 10

COMMON CORE 8.EE.3

Use numbers expressed in the form of a single digit times an integer power of 10 to estimate very large or very small quantities, ...

ESSENTIAL QUESTION

How can you use scientific notation to express very small quantities?

EXPLORE ACTIVITY

COMMON CORE 8.EE.3

Animated Math

my.hrw.com

Negative Powers of 10

You can use what you know about writing very large numbers in scientific notation to write very small numbers in scientific notation.

A typical human hair has a diameter of 0.000025 meter. Write this number in scientific notation.

A Notice how the decimal point moves in the list below. Complete the list.

$2.345 \times 10^0 \quad = 2.3\,4\,5$ It moves one place to the right with each increasing power of 10.

$2.345 \times 10^1 \quad = 2\,3.4\,5$

$2.345 \times 10^2 \quad = 2\,3\,4.5$

$2.345 \times 10^{\boxed{}} \quad = 2\,3\,4\,5.$

$2.345 \times 10^0 \quad = \quad 2.3\,4\,5$ It moves one place to the left with each decreasing power of 10.

$2.345 \times 10^{-1} \quad = \quad 0.2\,3\,4\,5$

$2.345 \times 10^{-2} \quad = \quad 0.0\,2\,3\,4\,5$

$2.345 \times 10^{\boxed{}} \quad = 0.0\,0\,2\,3\,4\,5$

B Move the decimal point in 0.000025 to the right as many places as necessary to find a number that is greater than or equal to 1 and less than 10. What number did you find? _____

C Divide 0.000025 by your answer to **B**. _____

Write your answer as a power of 10. _____

D Combine your answers to **B** and **C** to represent 0.000025 in scientific notation. _____

Reflect

1. When you move the decimal point, how can you know whether you are increasing or decreasing the number?

_____

2. Explain how the two steps of moving the decimal and multiplying by a power of 10 leave the value of the original number unchanged.

_____

Writing a Number in Scientific Notation

To write a number less than 1 in scientific notation, move the decimal point right and use a negative exponent.

Writing Small Quantities in Scientific Notation		
When the number is between 0 and 1, use a negative exponent.	$0.0783 = 7.83 \times 10^{-2}$	*The decimal point moves 2 places to the right.*

EXAMPLE 1

COMMON CORE 8.EE.3

The average size of an atom is about 0.00000003 centimeter across. Write the average size of an atom in scientific notation.

Move the decimal point as many places as necessary to find a number that is greater than or equal to 1 and less than 10.

STEP 1 Place the decimal point. 3.0

STEP 2 Count the number of places you moved the decimal point. 8

STEP 3 Multiply 3.0 times a power of 10. 3.0×10^{-8}

Since 0.00000003 is less than 1, you moved the decimal point to the right and the exponent on 10 is negative.

The average size of an atom in scientific notation is 3.0×10^{-8}.

Reflect

3. **Critical Thinking** When you write a number that is less than 1 in scientific notation, how does the power of 10 differ from when you write a number greater than 1 in scientific notation?

_____

Write each number in scientific notation.

4. 0.0000829

_____

5. 0.000000302

_____

6. A typical red blood cell in human blood has a diameter of approximately 0.000007 meter. Write this diameter

in scientific notation. _____

Writing a Number in Standard Notation

To translate between scientific notation and standard notation with very small numbers, you can move the decimal point the number of places indicated by the exponent on the power of 10. When the exponent is negative, move the decimal point to the left.

Math On the Spot
my.hrw.com

EXAMPLE 2

COMMON CORE 8.EE.3

Platelets are one component of human blood. A typical platelet has a diameter of approximately 2.33×10^{-6} meter. Write 2.33×10^{-6} in standard notation.

STEP 1 Use the exponent of the power of 10 to see how many places to move the decimal point.

6 places

STEP 2 Place the decimal point. Since you are going to write a number less than 2.33, move the decimal point to the *left*. Add placeholder zeros if necessary.

0.00000233

The number 2.33×10^{-6} in standard notation is 0.00000233.

> **Math Talk**
> Mathematical Practices
>
> Describe the two factors that multiply together to form a number written in scientific notation.

Reflect

7. **Justify Reasoning** Explain whether 0.9×10^{-5} is written in scientific notation. If not, write the number correctly in scientific notation.

_____

_____

_____

8. Which number is larger, 2×10^{-3} or 3×10^{-2}? Explain.

_____

Write each number in standard notation.

9. 1.045×10^{-6}

10. 9.9×10^{-5}

_____   _____

11. Jeremy measured the length of an ant as 1×10^{-2} meter. Write this length in standard notation.

_____

Personal Math Trainer

Online Assessment and Intervention

my.hrw.com

Write each number in scientific notation. (Explore Activity and Example 1)

1. 0.000487
Hint: Move the decimal right 4 places.

2. 0.000028
Hint: Move the decimal right 5 places.

3. 0.000059

4. 0.0417

5. Picoplankton can be as small as 0.00002 centimeter.

6. The average mass of a grain of sand on a beach is about 0.000015 gram.

Write each number in standard notation. (Example 2)

7. 2×10^{-5}
Hint: Move the decimal left 5 places.

8. 3.582×10^{-6}
Hint: Move the decimal left 6 places.

9. 8.3×10^{-4}

10. 2.97×10^{-2}

11. 9.06×10^{-5}

12. 4×10^{-5}

13. The average length of a dust mite is approximately 0.0001 meter. Write this number in scientific notation. (Example 1)

14. The mass of a proton is about 1.7×10^{-24} gram. Write this number in standard notation. (Example 2)

? ESSENTIAL QUESTION CHECK-IN

15. Describe how to write 0.0000672 in scientific notation.

10.3 Independent Practice

 8.EE.3

Personal Math Trainer

Online Assessment and Intervention

my.hrw.com

Use the table for problems 16–21. Write the diameter of the fibers in scientific notation.

Average Diameter of Natural Fibers	
Animal	Fiber Diameter (cm)
Vicuña	0.0008
Angora rabbit	0.0013
Alpaca	0.00277
Angora goat	0.0045
Llama	0.0035
Orb web spider	0.015

16. Alpaca

_____

17. Angora rabbit

_____

18. Llama

_____

19. Angora goat

_____

20. Orb web spider

_____

21. Vicuña

_____

22. Make a Conjecture Which measurement would be least likely to be written in scientific notation: the thickness of a dog hair, the radius of a period on this page, the ounces in a cup of milk? Explain your reasoning.

_____

_____

23. Multiple Representations Convert the length 7 centimeters to meters. Compare the numerical values when both numbers are written in scientific notation.

_____

_____

_____

_____

24. Draw Conclusions A graphing calculator displays 1.89×10^{12} as 1.89E12. How do you think it would display 1.89×10^{-12}? What does the E stand for?

_____

_____

25. Communicate Mathematical Ideas When a number is written in scientific notation, how can you tell right away whether or not it is greater than or equal to 1?

_____

_____

_____

26. The volume of a drop of a certain liquid is 0.000047 liter. Write the volume of the drop of liquid in scientific notation.

_____

27. Justify Reasoning If you were asked to express the weight in ounces of a ladybug in scientific notation, would the exponent of the 10 be positive or negative? Justify your response.

_____

_____

Physical Science The table shows the length of the radii of several very small or very large items. Complete the table.

	Item	Radius in Meters (Standard Notation)	Radius in Meters (Scientific Notation)
28.	The Moon	1,740,000	
29.	Atom of silver		1.25×10^{-10}
30.	Atlantic wolfish egg	0.0028	
31.	Jupiter		7.149×10^7
32.	Atom of aluminum	0.000000000182	
33.	Mars		3.397×10^6

34. List the items in the table in order from the smallest to the largest.

_____

_____

 **FOCUS ON HIGHER ORDER THINKING**

Work Area

35. Analyze Relationships Write the following diameters from least to greatest.
1.5×10^{-2} m 1.2×10^2 m 5.85×10^{-3} m 2.3×10^{-2} m 9.6×10^{-1} m

_____

_____

36. Critique Reasoning Jerod's friend Al had the following homework problem:

Express 5.6×10^{-7} in standard form.

Al wrote 56,000,000. How can Jerod explain Al's error and how to correct it?

_____

_____

_____

37. Make a Conjecture Two numbers are written in scientific notation. The number with a positive exponent is divided by the number with a negative exponent. Describe the result. Explain your answer.

_____

_____

_____

Comparing Very Small Numbers

COMMON CORE **8.EE.3**

Use numbers expressed in the form of a single digit times an integer power of 10 to... express how many times as much one is than the other.

ESSENTIAL QUESTION

How can you compare very small numbers in scientific notation?

EXPLORE ACTIVITY COMMON CORE 8.EE.3

Comparing Very Small Numbers

A Compare 0.0000003 and 0.00009 using standard notation.

Multiply the fraction by a ratio equal to 1, and simplify.

$$\frac{0.00009}{0.0000003} = \frac{0.00009}{0.0000003} \cdot \frac{10^{\boxed{}}}{10^7} = \frac{\boxed{}}{3} = \boxed{}$$

So, 0.00009 is _____ times greater than 0.0000003.

B Compare 0.0000003 and 0.00009 using scientific notation.

$$0.0000003 = 3 \times 10^{\boxed{}} \quad \text{and} \quad 0.00009 = 9 \times 10^{\boxed{}}$$

First compare the powers of 10 in a ratio of greater to lesser:

$$\frac{10^{-5}}{10^{-7}} = 10^{\boxed{}} = \boxed{}$$

Then compare the corresponding multipliers: $\dfrac{\boxed{}}{3} = $ _____

So, 9×10^{-5} is $100 \cdot$ _____ $= $ _____ times greater than 3×10^{-7}.

Reflect

1. Explain why 9×10^{-5} is greater than 3×10^{-7}.

_____

_____

2. Use both standard notation and scientific notation to explain why 1×10^{-1} is less than 1×10^0.

_____

_____

_____

Comparing Very Small Numbers in the Real World

Using scientific notation can help you compare very small numbers.

EXAMPLE

COMMON CORE 8.EE.3

The thickness of a piece of paper is about 8×10^{-5} meter. The thickness of a human hair is about 2×10^{-5} meter. About how many times thicker is a piece of paper than a human hair?

$$\frac{10^{-5}}{10^{-5}} = 10^0 = 1 \qquad \textit{Compare the powers of 10.}$$

$$\frac{8}{2} = 4 \qquad \textit{Compare the multipliers.}$$

So, a piece of paper is about $1 \cdot 4 = 4$ times thicker than a human hair.

Practice

1. Complete the statements to express how many times greater 4×10^{-2} is than 2×10^{-4}.

$$\frac{\boxed{}}{10^{-4}} = 10^{\boxed{}} = \underline{\hspace{2cm}}, \text{ and } \frac{\boxed{}}{2} = \underline{\hspace{2cm}}$$

So, 4×10^{-2} is $100 \cdot \boxed{} = \boxed{}$ times greater than 2×10^{-4}.

2. The diameter of a human red blood cell is about 7×10^{-3} mm, and the diameter of a grain of salt is about 3×10^{-1} mm. Which is larger? About how many times larger? Explain.

_____

_____

3. The average mass of a golden hamster is about 100 grams. The average mass of an African elephant is about 6×10^3 kilograms. About how many times greater is the mass of the elephant than the mass of the hamster? Use scientific notation to explain.

_____

_____

4. The diameter of a cold virus cell is about 3×10^{-9} meter, and the diameter of a streptococcus bacterium cell is about 9×10^{-7} meter. Which is greater and about how many times greater?

_____

_____

Operations with Scientific Notation

COMMON CORE 8.EE.4

Perform operations ... in scientific notation. ... choose units of appropriate size for measurements .... Interpret scientific notation ... generated by technology.

ESSENTIAL QUESTION

How do you add, subtract, multiply, and divide using scientific notation?

EXPLORE ACTIVITY COMMON CORE 8.EE.4

Adding and Subtracting with Scientific Notation

Numbers in scientific notation can be added and subtracted, either directly or by rewriting them in standard form.

Math On the Spot

⏱ my.hrw.com

EXAMPLE 1 The table below shows the population of the three largest countries in North America in 2011. Find the total population of these countries.

Country	United States	Canada	Mexico
Population	3.1×10^8	3.38×10^7	1.1×10^8

Method 1:

STEP 1 Write each population with the same power of 10.

United States: _____ $\times 10^8$

Canada: _____ $\times 10^8$

Mexico: _____ $\times 10^8$

STEP 2 Add the multipliers for each population.

$3.1 + \boxed{} + \boxed{} = \boxed{}$

STEP 3 Write the final answer in scientific notation: _____ $\times 10^8$.

Method 2:

STEP 1 Write each number in standard notation.

United States: _____

Canada: _____

Mexico: _____

STEP 2 Find the sum of the numbers in standard notation.

$310{,}000{,}000 + \boxed{} + \boxed{} = \boxed{}$

STEP 3 Write the final answer in scientific notation: _____ $\times 10^8$.

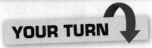

YOUR TURN

1. Using the population table above, how many more people live in Mexico than in Canada? Write your answer in scientific notation.

Math On the Spot

my.hrw.com

Multiplying and Dividing with Scientific Notation

Numbers in scientific notation can be multiplied and divided directly by using properties of exponents.

EXAMPLE 2 Problem Solving   COMMON CORE **8.EE.4**

When the Sun makes an orbit around the center of the Milky Way, it travels 2.025×10^{14} kilometers. The orbit takes 225 million years. At what rate does the Sun travel? Write your answer in scientific notation.

 Analyze Information

The answer is the number of kilometers per year that the Sun travels around the Milky Way.

 Formulate a Plan

Set up a division problem using Rate $= \frac{\text{Distance}}{\text{Time}}$ to represent the situation.

 Solve

STEP 1 Substitute the values from the problem into the Rate formula.

$$\text{Rate} = \frac{2.025 \times 10^{14} \text{ kilometers}}{225,000,000 \text{ years}}$$

STEP 2 Write the expression for rate with years in scientific notation.

$$\text{Rate} = \frac{2.025 \times 10^{14} \text{ kilometers}}{2.25 \times 10^8 \text{ years}} \qquad 225 \text{ million} = 2.25 \times 10^8$$

STEP 3 Find the quotient by dividing the decimals and using the laws of exponents.

$2.025 \div 2.25 = 0.9$ *Divide the multipliers.*

$\dfrac{10^{14}}{10^8} = 10^{14-8} = 10^6$ *Divide the powers of 10.*

STEP 4 Combine the answers to write the rate in scientific notation.

Rate $= 0.9 \times 10^6 = 9.0 \times 10^5$ km per year

Math Talk

Mathematical Practices

Could you write 2.025×10^{14} in standard notation to do the division? Would this be a good way to solve the problem?

 Justify and Evaluate

Check your answer using multiplication.

$900,000 \times 225,000,000 = 202,500,000,000,000$, or 2.025×10^{14}. The answer is correct.

YOUR TURN

2. Light travels at a speed of 1.86×10^5 miles per second. It takes light from the Sun about 4.8×10^3 seconds to reach Saturn. Find the approximate distance from the Sun to Saturn. Write your answer

   in scientific notation. _____

3. Light travels at the speed of 1.17×10^7 miles per minute. Pluto's average distance from the Sun is 3,670,000,000 miles. On average, how long does it take sunlight to reach Pluto? Write your answer in scientific

   notation. _____

Scientific Notation on a Calculator

On many scientific calculators, you can enter numbers in scientific notation by using a function labeled "ee" or "EE". Usually, the letter "E" takes the place of "×10". So, the number 4.1×10^9 would appear as 4.1E9 on the calculator.

EXAMPLE 3 

COMMON CORE 8.EE.4

The table shows the approximate areas for three continents given in square meters. What is the total area of these three continents? Write the answer in scientific notation using more appropriate units.

Continent	Asia	Africa	Europe
Area (m²)	4.4×10^{13}	3.02×10^{13}	1.04×10^{13}

Find $4.4 \times 10^{13} + 3.02 \times 10^{13} + 1.04 \times 10^{13}$.

Enter 4.4E13 + 3.02E13 + 1.04E13 on your calculator.

Write the results from your calculator: 8.46E13.

Write this number in scientific notation: 8.46×10^{13} m².

Square kilometers is more appropriate: 8.46×10^7 km².

> Because 1 km = 1,000 m, $1\ km^2 = 1,000^2\ m^2$, or $10^6\ m^2$. Divide by 10^6.

YOUR TURN

Write each number using calculator notation.

4. 7.5×10^5

5. 3×10^{-7}

6. 2.7×10^{13}

_____ _____ _____

Write each number using scientific notation.

7. 4.5E−1

8. 5.6E12

9. 6.98E−8

_____ _____ _____

Add or subtract. Write your answer in scientific notation. (Explore Activity Example 1)

1. $4.2 \times 10^6 + 2.25 \times 10^5 + 2.8 \times 10^6$

$4.2 \times 10^6 + \boxed{} \times 10^{\boxed{}} + 2.8 \times 10^6$

$4.2 + \boxed{} + \boxed{}$

$\boxed{} \times 10^{\boxed{}}$

2. $8.5 \times 10^3 - 5.3 \times 10^3 - 1.0 \times 10^2$

$8.5 \times 10^3 - 5.3 \times 10^3 - \boxed{} \times 10^{\boxed{}}$

$\boxed{} - \boxed{} - \boxed{}$

$\boxed{} \times 10^{\boxed{}}$

3. $1.25 \times 10^2 + 0.50 \times 10^2 + 3.25 \times 10^2$

_____

4. $6.2 \times 10^5 - 2.6 \times 10^4 - 1.9 \times 10^2$

_____

Multiply or divide. Write your answer in scientific notation. (Example 2)

5. $\left(1.8 \times 10^9\right)\left(6.7 \times 10^{12}\right)$ _____

6. $\dfrac{3.46 \times 10^{17}}{2 \times 10^9}$ _____

7. $\left(5 \times 10^{12}\right)\left(3.38 \times 10^6\right)$ _____

8. $\dfrac{8.4 \times 10^{21}}{4.2 \times 10^{14}}$ _____

Write each number using calculator notation. (Example 3)

9. 3.6×10^{11}

_____

10. 7.25×10^{-5}

_____

11. 8×10^{-1}

_____

Write each number using scientific notation. (Example 3)

12. 7.6E−4

_____

13. 1.2E16

_____

14. 9E1

_____

? ESSENTIAL QUESTION CHECK-IN

15. How do you add, subtract, multiply, and divide numbers written in scientific notation?

_____

_____

_____

_____

10.4 Independent Practice

 8.EE.4

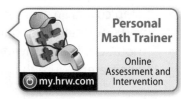

Personal Math Trainer

Online Assessment and Intervention

my.hrw.com

16. An adult blue whale can eat 4.0×10^7 krill in a day. At that rate, how many krill can an adult blue whale eat in 3.65×10^2 days?

_____

17. A newborn baby has about 26,000,000,000 cells. An adult has about 4.94×10^{13} cells. How many times as many cells does an adult have than a newborn? Write your answer in scientific notation.

_____

Represent Real-World Problems The table shows the number of tons of waste generated and recovered (recycled) in 2010.

	Paper	Glass	Plastics
Tons generated	7.131×10^7	1.153×10^7	3.104×10^7
Tons recovered	4.457×10^7	0.313×10^7	0.255×10^7

18. What is the total amount of paper, glass, and plastic waste generated?

_____

_____

19. What is the total amount of paper, glass, and plastic waste recovered?

_____

20. What is the total amount of paper, glass, and plastic waste **not** recovered?

_____

21. Which type of waste has the lowest recovery ratio?

_____

Social Studies **The table shows the approximate populations of three countries.**

Country	China	France	Australia
Population	1.3×10^9	6.48×10^7	2.15×10^7

22. How many more people live in France than in Australia?

_____

23. The area of Australia is 2.95×10^6 square miles. What is the approximate average number of people per square mile in Australia?

_____

_____

24. How many times greater is the population of China than the population of France? Write your answer in standard notation.

_____

_____

25. Mia is 7.01568×10^6 minutes old. Convert her age to more appropriate units using years, months, and days. Assume each month to have 30.5 days.

_____

_____

26. Courtney takes 2.4×10^4 steps during her a long-distance run. Each step covers an average of 810 mm. What total distance (in mm) did Courtney cover during her run? Write your answer in scientific notation. Then convert the distance to the more appropriate unit kilometers. Write that answer in standard form.

_____

27. Social Studies The U.S. public debt as of October 2010 was 9.06×10^{12}. What was the average U.S. public debt per American if the population in 2010 was 3.08×10^8 people?

_____

 FOCUS ON HIGHER ORDER THINKING

28. Communicate Mathematical Ideas How is multiplying and dividing numbers in scientific notation different from adding and subtracting numbers in scientific notation?

_____

_____

_____

_____

_____

29. Explain the Error A student found the product of 8×10^6 and 5×10^9 to be 4×10^{15}. What is the error? What is the correct product?

_____

_____

30. Communicate Mathematical Ideas Describe a procedure that can be used to simplify $\dfrac{\left(4.87 \times 10^{12}\right) - \left(7 \times 10^{10}\right)}{\left(3 \times 10^7\right) + \left(6.1 \times 10^8\right)}$. Write the expression in scientific notation in simplified form.

_____

_____

_____

_____

_____

_____

Ready to Go On?

10.1 Integer Exponents

Find the value of each power.

1. 3^{-4} _____

2. 35^0 _____

3. 4^4 _____

Use the properties of exponents to write an equivalent expression.

4. $8^3 \cdot 8^7$ _____

5. $\frac{12^6}{12^2}$ _____

6. $(10^3)^5$ _____

10.2 Scientific Notation with Positive Powers of 10

Convert each number to scientific notation or standard notation.

7. 2,000 _____

8. 91,007,500 _____

9. 1.0395×10^9 _____

10. 4×10^2 _____

10.3 Scientific Notation with Negative Powers of 10

Convert each number to scientific notation or standard notation.

11. 0.02 _____

12. 0.000701 _____

13. 8.9×10^{-5} _____

14. 4.41×10^{-2} _____

10.4 Operations with Scientific Notation

Perform the operation. Write your answer in scientific notation.

15. $7 \times 10^6 - 5.3 \times 10^6$ _____

16. $3.4 \times 10^4 + 7.1 \times 10^5$ _____

17. $(2 \times 10^4)(5.4 \times 10^6)$ _____

18. $\frac{7.86 \times 10^9}{3 \times 10^4}$ _____

19. Neptune's average distance from the Sun is 4.503×10^9 km. Mercury's average distance from the Sun is 5.791×10^7 km. About how many times farther from the Sun is Neptune than Mercury? Write your answer in scientific notation.

_____

ESSENTIAL QUESTION

20. How is scientific notation used in the real world?

_____

_____

_____

COMMON CORE

MODULE 10 MIXED REVIEW
Assessment Readiness

Personal Math Trainer

Online Assessment and Intervention

my.hrw.com

Selected Response

1. Which of the following is equivalent to 6^{-3}?

Ⓐ 216

Ⓑ $\frac{1}{216}$

Ⓒ $-\frac{1}{216}$

Ⓓ −216

2. About 786,700,000 passengers traveled by plane in the United States in 2010. What is this number written in scientific notation?

Ⓐ $7,867 \times 10^5$ passengers

Ⓑ 7.867×10^2 passengers

Ⓒ 7.867×10^8 passengers

Ⓓ 7.867×10^9 passengers

3. In 2011, the population of Mali was about 1.584×10^7 people. What is this number written in standard notation?

Ⓐ 1.584 people

Ⓑ 1,584 people

Ⓒ 15,840,000 people

Ⓓ 158,400,000 people

4. The square root of a number is between 7 and 8. Which could be the number?

Ⓐ 72

Ⓒ 51

Ⓑ 83

Ⓓ 66

5. Each entry-level account executive in a large company makes an annual salary of 3.48×10^4. If there are 5.2×10^2 account executives in the company, how much do they make in all?

Ⓐ 6.69×10^1

Ⓑ 3.428×10^4

Ⓒ 3.532×10^4

Ⓓ 1.8096×10^7

6. Place the numbers in order from least to greatest.

0.24, 4×10^{-2}, 0.042, 2×10^{-4}, 0.004

Ⓐ 2×10^{-4}, 4×10^{-2}, 0.004, 0.042, 0.24

Ⓑ 0.004, 2×10^{-4}, 0.042, 4×10^{-2}, 0.24

Ⓒ 0.004, 2×10^{-4}, 4×10^{-2}, 0.042, 0.24

Ⓓ 2×10^{-4}, 0.004, 4×10^{-2}, 0.042, 0.24

7. Guillermo is $5\frac{5}{6}$ feet tall. What is this number of feet written as a decimal?

Ⓐ 5.7 feet

Ⓒ 5.83 feet

Ⓑ $5.\overline{7}$ feet

Ⓓ $5.8\overline{3}$ feet

8. A human hair has a width of about 6.5×10^{-5} meter. What is this width written in standard notation?

Ⓐ 0.00000065 meter

Ⓑ 0.0000065 meter

Ⓒ 0.000065 meter

Ⓓ 0.00065 meter

Mini-Task

9. Consider the following numbers: 7000, 700, 70, 0.7, 0.07, 0.007

a. Write the numbers in scientific notation.

_____

_____

b. Look for a pattern in the given list and the list in scientific notation. Which numbers are missing from the lists?

_____

c. Make a conjecture about the missing numbers.

_____

_____

Study Guide Review

MODULE 9 Real Numbers

ESSENTIAL QUESTION

How can you use real numbers to solve real-world problems?

EXAMPLE 1

Write $0.\overline{81}$ as a fraction in simplest form.

$$x = 0.\overline{81}$$
$$100x = 81.\overline{81}$$
$$\underline{-x \quad -0.\overline{81}}$$
$$99x = 81$$
$$x = \frac{81}{99}$$
$$x = \frac{9}{11}$$

EXAMPLE 2

Solve each equation for x.

A $x^2 = 289$

$x = \pm\sqrt{289}$

$x = \pm 17$

The solutions are 17 and -17.

B $x^3 = 1{,}000$

$x = \sqrt[3]{1{,}000}$

$x = 10$

The solution is 10.

EXAMPLE 3

Write all names that apply to each number.

A $5.\overline{4}$
rational, real

$5.\overline{4}$ *is a repeating decimal.*

B $\frac{8}{4}$
whole, integer, rational, real

$\frac{8}{4} = 2$

C $\sqrt{13}$
irrational, real

13 is a whole number that is not a perfect square.

EXAMPLE 4

Order 6, 2π, and $\sqrt{38}$ from least to greatest.

2π is approximately equal to 2×3.14, or 6.28.

$\sqrt{38}$ is approximately 6.15 based on the following reasoning.

$$\sqrt{36} < \sqrt{38} < \sqrt{49} \qquad 6 < \sqrt{38} < 7 \qquad 6.1^2 = 37.21 \qquad 6.2^2 = 38.44$$

From least to greatest, the numbers are 6, $\sqrt{38}$, and 2π.

EXERCISES

Find the two square roots of each number. If the number is not a perfect square, approximate the values to the nearest 0.05.
(Lesson 9.1)

1. 16 _____

2. $\frac{4}{25}$ _____

3. 225 _____

4. $\frac{1}{49}$ _____

5. $\sqrt{10}$ _____

6. $\sqrt{18}$ _____

Write each decimal as a fraction in simplest form. (Lesson 9.1)

7. $0.\overline{5}$ _____

8. $0.\overline{63}$ _____

9. $0.2\overline{14}$ _____

Solve each equation for x. (Lesson 9.1)

10. $x^2 = 361$

11. $x^3 = 1,728$

12. $x^2 = \frac{49}{121}$

_____

_____

_____

Write all names that apply to each number. (Lesson 9.2)

13. $\frac{2}{3}$

14. $-\sqrt{100}$

_____

_____

15. $\frac{15}{5}$

16. $\sqrt{21}$

_____

_____

Compare. Write $<$, $>$, or $=$. (Lesson 9.3)

17. $\sqrt{7} + 5 \bigcirc 7 + \sqrt{5}$

18. $6 + \sqrt{8} \bigcirc \sqrt{6} + 8$

19. $\sqrt{4} - 2 \bigcirc 4 - \sqrt{2}$

Order the numbers from least to greatest. (Lesson 9.3)

20. $\sqrt{81}, \frac{72}{7}, 8.9$ _____

21. $\sqrt{7}, 2.55, \frac{7}{3}$ _____

 MODULE 10

Exponents and Scientific Notation

Key Vocabulary

scientific notation
(notación científica)

? ESSENTIAL QUESTION

How can you use scientific notation to solve real-world problems?

EXAMPLE 1

Write each measurement in scientific notation.

A The diameter of Earth at the equator is approximately 12,700 kilometers.

Move the decimal point in 12,700 four places to the left: 1.2 7 0 0.

$12{,}700 = 1.27 \times 10^4$

B The diameter of a human hair is approximately 0.00254 centimeters.

Move the decimal point in 0.00254 three places to the right: 0.0 0 2.5 4

$0.00254 = 2.54 \times 10^{-3}$

EXAMPLE 2

Find the quotient: $\dfrac{2.4 \times 10^7}{9.6 \times 10^3}$

Divide the multipliers: $2.4 \div 9.6 = 0.25$

Divide the powers of ten: $\dfrac{10^7}{10^3} = 10^{7-3} = 10^4$

Combine the answers and write the product in scientific notation.

$0.25 \times 10^4 = 0.25 \times (10 \times 10^3) = (0.25 \times 10) \times 10^3 = 2.5 \times 10^3$

EXERCISES

Write each number in scientific notation. (Lessons 10.2, 10.3)

1. 25,500,000 _____

2. 0.00734 _____

Write each number in standard notation. (Lessons 10.2, 10.3)

3. 5.23×10^4 _____

4. 1.33×10^{-5} _____

Simplify each expression. (Lessons 10.1, 10.4)

5. $(9 - 7)^3 \cdot 5^0 + (8 + 3)^2$ _____

6. $\dfrac{(4 + 2)^2}{[(9 - 3)^3]^2}$ _____

7. $3.2 \times 10^5 + 1.25 \times 10^4 + 2.9 \times 10^5$

8. $(2{,}600)(3.24 \times 10^4)$

_____ _____

Unit 5 Performance Tasks

1. **CAREERS IN MATH** | Astronomer An astronomer is studying Proxima Centauri, which is the closest star to our Sun. Proxima Centauri is 39,900,000,000,000,000 meters away.

   a. Write this distance in scientific notation.

   _____

   b. Light travels at a speed of 3.0×10^8 m/s (meters per second). How can you use this information to calculate the time in seconds it takes for light from Proxima Centauri to reach Earth? How many seconds does it take? Write your answer in scientific notation.

   _____

   _____

   c. Knowing that 1 year $= 3.1536 \times 10^7$ seconds, how many years does it take for light to travel from Proxima Centauri to Earth? Write your answer in standard notation. Round your answer to two decimal places.

   _____

2. Cory is making a poster of common geometric shapes. He draws a square with a side of length 4^3 cm, an equilateral triangle with a height of $\sqrt{200}$ cm, a circle with a circumference of 8π cm, a rectangle with length $\frac{122}{5}$ cm, and a parallelogram with base 3.14 cm.

   a. Which of these numbers are irrational?

   _____

   b. Write the numbers in this problem in order from least to greatest. Approximate π as 3.14.

   _____

   c. Explain why 3.14 is rational, but π is not.

   _____

   _____

   _____

Selected Response

1. A square on a large calendar has an area of 4,220 square millimeters. Between which two integers is the length of one side of the square?

Ⓐ between 20 and 21 millimeters

Ⓑ between 64 and 65 millimeters

Ⓒ between 204 and 205 millimeters

Ⓓ between 649 and 650 millimeters

2. Which of the following numbers is rational but **not** an integer?

Ⓐ -9 Ⓒ 0

Ⓑ -4.3 Ⓓ 3

3. Which statement is false?

Ⓐ No integers are irrational numbers.

Ⓑ All whole numbers are integers.

Ⓒ All rational numbers are real numbers.

Ⓓ All integers are whole numbers.

4. In 2011, the population of Laos was about 6.586×10^6 people. What is this number written in standard notation?

Ⓐ 6,586 people

Ⓑ 658,600 people

Ⓒ 6,586,000 people

Ⓓ 65,860,000 people

5. Which of the following is **not** true?

Ⓐ $\sqrt{16} + 4 > \sqrt{4} + 5$

Ⓑ $4\pi > 12$

Ⓒ $\sqrt{18} + 2 < \frac{15}{2}$

Ⓓ $6 - \sqrt{35} < 0$

6. Which number is between $\sqrt{50}$ and $\frac{5\pi}{2}$?

Ⓐ $\frac{22}{3}$ Ⓒ 6

Ⓑ $2\sqrt{8}$ Ⓓ $\pi + 3$

7. Which number is indicated on the number line?

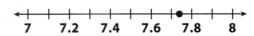

Ⓐ $\pi + 4$

Ⓑ $\frac{152}{20}$

Ⓒ $\sqrt{14} + 4$

Ⓓ $7.\overline{8}$

8. Which of the following is the number 5.03×10^{-5} written in standard form?

Ⓐ 503,000

Ⓑ 50,300,000

Ⓒ 0.00503

Ⓓ 0.0000503

9. In a recent year, about 20,700,000 passengers traveled by train in the United States. What is this number written in scientific notation?

Ⓐ 2.07×10^1 passengers

Ⓑ 2.07×10^4 passengers

Ⓒ 2.07×10^7 passengers

Ⓓ 2.07×10^8 passengers

10. A quarter weighs about 0.025 pounds. What is this weight written in scientific notation?

Ⓐ 2.5×10^{-2} pounds

Ⓑ 2.5×10^1 pounds

Ⓒ 2.5×10^{-1} pounds

Ⓓ 2.5×10^2 pounds

11. Which fraction is equivalent to $0.\overline{45}$?

Ⓐ $\frac{4}{9}$ Ⓒ $\frac{4}{5}$

Ⓑ $\frac{5}{9}$ Ⓓ $\frac{5}{11}$

12. What is the value of x if $x^2 = \frac{36}{81}$?

Ⓐ $\frac{2}{3}$ Ⓒ $\frac{4}{9}$

Ⓑ $\pm\frac{2}{3}$ Ⓓ $\pm\frac{4}{9}$

13. What is $\frac{[(9-2)^2]^4}{(4+3)^5}$ written in simplest form?

Ⓐ 7

Ⓑ 21

Ⓒ 49

Ⓓ 343

14. The total land area on Earth is about 6×10^7 square miles. The land area of Australia is about 3×10^6 square miles. About how many times larger is the land area on Earth than the land area of Australia?

Ⓐ 2

Ⓑ 10

Ⓒ 20

Ⓓ 60

15. What is the value of the expression $8.3 \times 10^4 - 2.5 \times 10^3 - 1.9 \times 10^4$ written in scientific notation?

Ⓐ 3.9×10^3

Ⓑ 3.9×10^4

Ⓒ 6.15×10^3

Ⓓ 6.15×10^4

16. What is the value of the expression $(2.3 \times 10^7)(1.4 \times 10^{-2})$ written in scientific notation?

Ⓐ 3.7×10^{-14}

Ⓑ 3.7×10^5

Ⓒ 0.322×10^6

Ⓓ 3.22×10^5

17. What is the value of $\sqrt[3]{64}$?

Ⓐ 2

Ⓑ 4

Ⓒ 8

Ⓓ 16

Mini-Task

18. Amanda says that a human fingernail has a thickness of about 4.2×10^{-4} meter. Justin says that a human fingernail has a thickness of about 0.42 millimeter.

a. What is the width in meters written in standard notation?

_____

b. Do Justin's and Amanda's measurements agree? Explain.

_____

_____

_____

c. Explain why Justin's estimate of the thickness of a human fingernail is more appropriate than Amanda's estimate.

_____

_____

_____

_____

_____

_____

Proportional and Nonproportional Relationships and Functions

CAREERS IN MATH

Cost Estimator A cost estimator determines the cost of a product or project, which helps businesses decide whether or not to manufacture a product or build a structure. Cost estimators analyze the costs of labor, materials, and use of equipment, among other things. Cost estimators use math when they assemble and analyze data. If you are interested in a career as a cost estimator, you should study these mathematical subjects:
- Algebra
- Trigonometry
- Calculus

Research other careers that require analyzing costs.

Unit 6 Performance Task

At the end of the unit, check out how **cost estimators** use math.

Use the puzzle to preview key vocabulary from this unit. Unscramble the circled letters within the found words to answer the riddle at the bottom of the page.

- The *y*-coordinate of the point where the graph crosses the *y*-axis. (Lesson 12.2)
- A rule that assigns exactly one output to each input. (Lesson 14.1)
- The result after applying the function machine's rule. (Lesson 14.1)
- A rate in which the second quantity in the comparison is one unit. (Lesson 11.3)
- The ratio of change in rise to the corresponding change in run on a graph. (Lesson 11.2)
- A set of data that is made up of two paired variables. (Lesson 13.3)
- An equation whose solutions form a straight line on a coordinate plane. (Lesson 12.1)

Q: How much of the money earned does a professional sports team pay its star athlete?

A: An ___ ___ ___ ___ ___ ___ – ___ ___ ___ ___ ___ ___ ___ ___!

Proportional Relationships

? **ESSENTIAL QUESTION**

How can you use proportional relationships to solve real-world problems?

Real-World Video

Speedboats can travel at fast rates while sailboats travel more slowly. If you graphed distance versus time for both types of boats, you could tell by the steepness of the graph which boat was faster.

⏻ my.hrw.com

GO DIGITAL
my.hrw.com

my.hrw.com

Go digital with your write-in student edition, accessible on any device.

Math On the Spot

Scan with your smart phone to jump directly to the online edition, video tutor, and more.

X²

Animated Math

Interactively explore key concepts to see how math works.

Personal Math Trainer

Get immediate feedback and help as you work through practice sets.

Are YOU Ready?

Complete these exercises to review skills you will need for this module.

Write Fractions as Decimals

EXAMPLE $\dfrac{1.7}{2.5} = ?$

Multiply the numerator and the denominator by a power of 10 so that the denominator is a whole number.

$$\dfrac{1.7 \times 10}{2.5 \times 10} = \dfrac{17}{25}$$

Write the fraction as a division problem.
Write a decimal point and zeros in the dividend.
Place a decimal point in the quotient.
Divide as with whole numbers.

$$\begin{array}{r} 0.68 \\ 25\overline{)17.00} \\ -15\,0 \\ \hline 2\,00 \\ -2\,00 \\ \hline 0 \end{array}$$

Write each fraction as a decimal.

1. $\dfrac{3}{8}$ _____

2. $\dfrac{0.3}{0.4}$ _____

3. $\dfrac{0.13}{0.2}$ _____

4. $\dfrac{0.39}{0.75}$ _____

5. $\dfrac{4}{5}$ _____

6. $\dfrac{0.1}{2}$ _____

7. $\dfrac{3.5}{14}$ _____

8. $\dfrac{7}{14}$ _____

9. $\dfrac{0.3}{10}$ _____

Solve Proportions

EXAMPLE $\dfrac{5}{7} = \dfrac{x}{14}$

$\dfrac{5 \times 2}{7 \times 2} = \dfrac{x}{14}$ $7 \times 2 = 14$, so multiply the numerator and denominator by 2.

$\dfrac{10}{14} = \dfrac{x}{14}$ $5 \times 2 = 10$

$x = 10$

Solve each proportion for x.

10. $\dfrac{20}{18} = \dfrac{10}{x}$ _____

11. $\dfrac{x}{12} = \dfrac{30}{72}$ _____

12. $\dfrac{x}{4} = \dfrac{4}{16}$ _____

13. $\dfrac{11}{x} = \dfrac{132}{120}$ _____

14. $\dfrac{36}{48} = \dfrac{x}{4}$ _____

15. $\dfrac{x}{9} = \dfrac{21}{27}$ _____

16. $\dfrac{24}{16} = \dfrac{x}{2}$ _____

17. $\dfrac{30}{15} = \dfrac{6}{x}$ _____

18. $\dfrac{3}{x} = \dfrac{18}{36}$ _____

Reading Start-Up

Visualize Vocabulary

Use the ✔ words to complete the diagram.

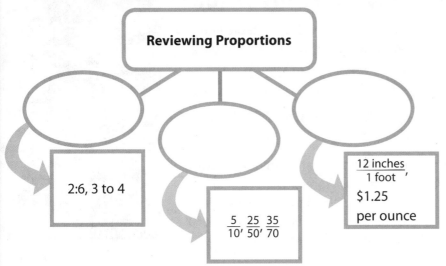

Reviewing Proportions

2:6, 3 to 4

$\frac{5}{10}, \frac{25}{50}, \frac{35}{70}$

$\frac{12 \text{ inches}}{1 \text{ foot}}$,
$1.25
per ounce

Vocabulary

Review Words

constant *(constante)*

✔ equivalent ratios *(razones equivalentes)*

proportion *(proporción)*

rate *(tasa)*

✔ ratios *(razón)*

✔ unit rates *(tasas unitarias)*

Preview Words

constant of proportionality *(constante de proporcionalidad)*

proportional relationship *(relación proporcional)*

rate of change *(tasa de cambio)*

slope *(pendiente)*

Understand Vocabulary

Match the term on the left to the definition on the right.

1. unit rate

2. constant of proportionality

3. proportional relationship

A. A constant ratio of two variables related proportionally.

B. A rate in which the second quantity in the comparison is one unit.

C. A relationship between two quantities in which the ratio of one quantity to the other quantity is constant.

Active Reading

Key-Term Fold Before beginning the module, create a key-term fold to help you learn the vocabulary in this module. Write the highlighted vocabulary words on one side of the flap. Write the definition for each word on the other side of the flap. Use the key-term fold to quiz yourself on the definitions used in this module.

Unpacking the Standards

Understanding the standards and the vocabulary terms in the standards will help you know exactly what you are expected to learn in this module.

Graph proportional relationships, interpreting the unit rate as the slope of the graph. Compare two different proportional relationships represented in different ways.

Key Vocabulary

proportional relationship
(relación proporcional)
A relationship between two quantities in which the ratio of one quantity to the other quantity is constant.

slope *(pendiente)*
A measure of the steepness of a line on a graph; the rise divided by the run.

unit rate *(tasa unitaria)*
A rate in which the second quantity in the comparison is one unit.

What It Means to You

You will use data from a table and a graph to apply your understanding of rates to analyzing real-world situations.

UNPACKING EXAMPLE 8.EE.5

The table shows the volume of water released by Hoover Dam over a certain period of time. Use the data to make a graph. Find the slope of the line and explain what it shows.

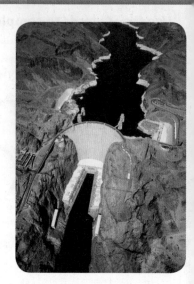

Water Released from Hoover Dam	
Time (s)	Volume of water (ft³)
5	75,000
10	150,000
15	225,000
20	300,000

Water Released from Hoover Dam

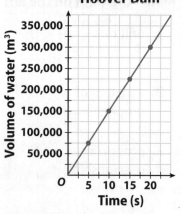

The slope of the line is 15,000. This means that for every second that passed, 15,000 ft³ of water was released from Hoover Dam.

Suppose another dam releases water over the same period of time at a rate of 180,000 ft³ per minute. How do the two rates compare?

180,000 ft³ per minute is equal to 3,000 ft³ per second. This rate is one fifth the rate released by the Hoover Dam over the same time period.

Representing Proportional Relationships

COMMON CORE **8.EE.6**
...derive the equation $y = mx$ for a line through the origin... *Also 8.F.4*

ESSENTIAL QUESTION

How can you use tables, graphs, and equations to represent proportional situations?

EXPLORE ACTIVITY   COMMON CORE **Prep for 8.EE.6**

Representing Proportional Relationships with Tables

In 1870, the French writer Jules Verne published *20,000 Leagues Under the Sea*, one of the most popular science fiction novels ever written. One definition of a *league* is a unit of measure equaling 3 miles.

A Complete the table.

Distance (leagues)	1	2	6		20,000
Distance (miles)	3			36	

B What relationships do you see among the numbers in the table?

_____

_____

C For each column of the table, find the ratio of the distance in miles to the distance in leagues. Write each ratio in simplest form.

$$\frac{3}{1} = \boxed{} \qquad \frac{\boxed{}}{2} = \boxed{} \qquad \frac{\boxed{}}{6} = \boxed{} \qquad \frac{36}{\boxed{}} = \boxed{} \qquad \frac{\boxed{}}{20,000} = \boxed{}$$

D What do you notice about the ratios? _____

Reflect

1. If you know the distance between two points in leagues, how can you

find the distance in miles? _____

2. If you know the distance between two points in miles, how can you find

the distance in leagues? _____

Representing Proportional Relationships with Equations

The ratio of the distance in miles to the distance in leagues is constant. This relationship is said to be *proportional*. A **proportional relationship** is a relationship between two quantities in which the ratio of one quantity to the other quantity is constant.

A proportional relationship can be described by an equation of the form $y = kx$, where k is a number called the **constant of proportionality**.

Sometimes it is useful to use another form of the equation, $k = \frac{y}{x}$.

EXAMPLE 1

Meghan earns $12 an hour at her part-time job. Show that the relationship between the amount she earned and the number of hours she worked is a proportional relationship. Then write an equation for the relationship.

STEP 1 Make a table relating amount earned to number of hours.

> For every hour Meghan works, she earns $12. So, for 8 hours of work, she earns 8 × $12 = $96.

Number of hours	1	2	4	8
Amount earned ($)	12	24	48	96

STEP 2 For each number of hours, write the relationship of the amount earned and the number of hours as a ratio in simplest form.

$\frac{\text{amount earned}}{\text{number of hours}}$ $\qquad \frac{12}{1} = \frac{12}{1} \qquad \frac{24}{2} = \frac{12}{1} \qquad \frac{48}{4} = \frac{12}{1} \qquad \frac{96}{8} = \frac{12}{1}$

Since the ratios for the two quantities are all equal to $\frac{12}{1}$, the relationship is proportional.

STEP 3 Write an equation.

> First tell what the variables represent.

Let x represent the number of hours.
Let y represent the amount earned.

Use the ratio as the constant of proportionality in the equation $y = kx$.

The equation is $y = \frac{12}{1}x$ or $y = 12x$.

Math Talk

Mathematical Practices

Describe two real-world quantities with a proportional relationship that can be described by the equation $y = 25x$.

YOUR TURN

3. Fifteen bicycles are produced each hour at the Speedy Bike Works. Show that the relationship between the number of bikes produced and the number of hours is a proportional relationship. Then write an equation for the relationship. _____

Representing Proportional Relationships with Graphs

You can represent a proportional relationship with a graph. The graph will be a line that passes through the origin (0, 0). The graph shows the relationship between distance measured in miles to distance measured in leagues.

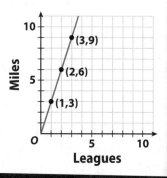

EXAMPLE 2

COMMON CORE 8.EE.6

The graph shows the relationship between the weight of an object on the Moon and its weight on Earth. Write an equation for this relationship.

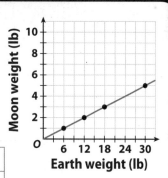

STEP 1 Use the points on the graph to make a table.

Earth weight (lb)	6	12	18	30
Moon weight (lb)	1	2	3	5

STEP 2 Find the constant of proportionality.

$\dfrac{\text{Moon weight}}{\text{Earth weight}}$ $\dfrac{1}{6} = \dfrac{1}{6}$ $\dfrac{2}{12} = \dfrac{1}{6}$ $\dfrac{3}{18} = \dfrac{1}{6}$ $\dfrac{5}{30} = \dfrac{1}{6}$

The constant of proportionality is $\dfrac{1}{6}$.

STEP 3 Write an equation.

Let x represent weight on Earth.

Let y represent weight on the Moon.

The equation is $y = \dfrac{1}{6}x$.   *Replace k with $\dfrac{1}{6}$ in $y = kx$.*

YOUR TURN

The graph shows the relationship between the amount of time that a backpacker hikes and the distance traveled.

4. What does the point (5, 6) represent?

_____

5. What is the equation of the relationship?

_____

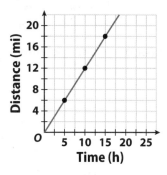

1. **Vocabulary** A proportional relationship is a relationship between two quantities in which the ratio of one quantity to the other quantity

   | is / is not | constant.

2. **Vocabulary** When writing an equation of a proportional relationship in the form $y = kx$, k represents the _____.

3. Write an equation that describes the proportional relationship between the number of days and the number of weeks in a given length of time. (Explore Activity and Example 1)

   a. Complete the table.

Time (weeks)	1	2	4		10
Time (days)	7			56	

   b. Let x represent _____.

   Let y represent _____.

   The equation that describes the relationship is _____.

Each table or graph represents a proportional relationship. Write an equation that describes the relationship. (Example 1 and Example 2)

4. **Physical Science** The relationship between the numbers of oxygen atoms and hydrogen atoms in water is shown below.

Oxygen atoms	2	5		120
Hydrogen atoms	4		34	

   _____

5.

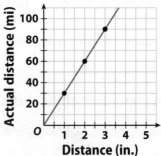

   Map of Iowa

   _____

6. If you know the equation of a proportional relationship, how can you draw the graph of the equation?

   _____

   _____

11.1 Independent Practice

COMMON CORE 8.EE.6, 8.F.4

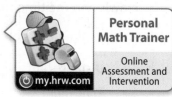

Personal
Math Trainer

Online
Assessment and
Intervention

The table shows the relationship between temperatures measured on the
Celsius and Fahrenheit scales.

Celsius temperature	0	10	20	30	40	50
Fahrenheit temperature	32	50	68	86	104	122

7. Is the relationship between the temperature scales proportional?
Why or why not?

_____

_____

8. Describe the graph of the Celsius-Fahrenheit relationship.

_____

_____

9. Analyze Relationships Ralph opened a savings account with a deposit
of $100. Every month after that, he deposited $20 more.

a. Why is the relationship described not proportional?

_____

_____

b. How could the situation be changed to make the situation
proportional?

_____

_____

10. Represent Real-World Problems Describe a real-world situation that
can be modeled by the equation $y = \frac{1}{20}x$. Be sure to describe what each
variable represents.

_____

_____

Look for a Pattern The variables x and y are related proportionally.

11. When $x = 8$, $y = 20$. Find y when $x = 42$. _____

12. When $x = 12$, $y = 8$. Find x when $y = 12$. _____

13. The graph shows the relationship between the distance that a snail crawls and the time that it crawls.

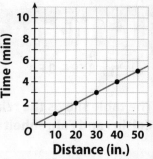

Snail Crawling

a. Use the points on the graph to make a table.

Distance (in.)					
Time (min)					

b. Write the equation for the relationship and tell what each variable represents.

_____

_____

c. How long does it take the snail to crawl 85 inches? _____

H.O.T. **FOCUS ON HIGHER ORDER THINKING**

Work Area

14. **Communicate Mathematical Ideas** Explain why all of the graphs in this lesson show the first quadrant but omit the other three quadrants.

_____

_____

_____

15. **Analyze Relationships** Complete the table.

Length of side of square	1	2	3	4	5
Perimeter of square					
Area of square					

a. Are the length of a side of a square and the perimeter of the square related proportionally? Why or why not?

_____

_____

b. Are the length of a side of a square and the area of the square related proportionally? Why or why not?

_____

_____

16. **Make a Conjecture** A table shows a proportional relationship where k is the constant of proportionality. The rows are then switched. How does the new constant of proportionality relate to the original one?

_____

Rate of Change and Slope

COMMON CORE 8.F.4
...Determine the rate of change...of the function from...two (x, y) values, including reading these from a table or from a graph....

💬 **ESSENTIAL QUESTION**

How do you find a rate of change or a slope?

EXPLORE ACTIVITY COMMON CORE 8.F.4

Investigating Rates of Change

A **rate of change** is a ratio of the amount of change in the dependent variable, or *output*, to the amount of change in the independent variable, or *input*.

Math On the Spot

⏱ my.hrw.com

EXAMPLE 1 Eve keeps a record of the number of lawns she has mowed and the money she has earned. Tell whether the rates of change are constant or variable.

	Day 1	Day 2	Day 3	Day 4
Number of lawns	1	3	6	8
Amount earned ($)	15	45	90	120

STEP 1 Identify the input and output variables.

Input: _____ Output: _____

STEP 2 Find the rates of change.

Day 1 to Day 2: $\dfrac{\text{change in \$}}{\text{change in lawns}} = \dfrac{45 - 15}{3 - 1} = \dfrac{\boxed{}}{\boxed{}} = \boxed{}$

Day 2 to Day 3: $\dfrac{\text{change in \$}}{\text{change in lawns}} = \dfrac{\boxed{} - \boxed{}}{6 - 3} = \dfrac{\boxed{}}{\boxed{}} = \boxed{}$

Day 3 to Day 4: $\dfrac{\text{change in \$}}{\text{change in lawns}} = \dfrac{120 - \boxed{}}{\boxed{} - 6} = \dfrac{\boxed{}}{\boxed{}} = \boxed{}$

The rates of change are constant: $ _____ per lawn.

YOUR TURN

1. The table shows the approximate height of a football after it is kicked. Tell whether the rates of change are constant or variable.

Find the rates of change in ft/s: _____

The rates of change are ⟨ **constant / variable**. ⟩

Time (s)	Height (ft)
0	0
0.5	18
1.5	31
2	26

Personal Math Trainer

Online Assessment and Intervention

⏱ my.hrw.com

Using Graphs to Find Rates of Change

You can also use a graph to find rates of change.

**The graph shows the distance Nathan bicycled over time.
What is Nathan's rate of change?**

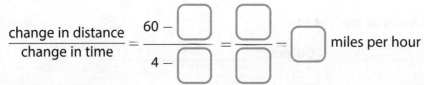

A Find the rate of change from 1 hour to 2 hours.

$$\dfrac{\text{change in distance}}{\text{change in time}} = \dfrac{30 - \boxed{}}{2 - 1} = \dfrac{\boxed{}}{1} = \boxed{} \text{ miles per hour}$$

B Find the rate of change from 1 hour to 4 hours.

$$\dfrac{\text{change in distance}}{\text{change in time}} = \dfrac{60 - \boxed{}}{4 - \boxed{}} = \dfrac{\boxed{}}{\boxed{}} = \boxed{} \text{ miles per hour}$$

C Find the rate of change from 2 hours to 4 hours.

$$\dfrac{\text{change in distance}}{\text{change in time}} = \dfrac{60 - \boxed{}}{4 - \boxed{}} = \dfrac{\boxed{}}{\boxed{}} = \boxed{} \text{ miles per hour}$$

D Recall that the graph of a proportional relationship is a line through the origin. Explain whether the relationship between Nathan's time and distance is a proportional relationship.

_____

_____

Reflect

2. Make a Conjecture Does a proportional relationship have a constant rate of change?

_____

3. Does it matter what interval you use when you find the rate of change of a proportional relationship? Explain.

_____

_____

Calculating Slope *m*

When the rate of change of a relationship is constant, any segment of its graph has the same steepness. The constant rate of change is called the *slope* of the line.

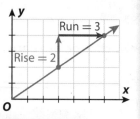

Math On the Spot

my.hrw.com

Slope Formula

The **slope** of a line is the ratio of the change in *y*-values (rise) for a segment of the graph to the corresponding change in *x*-values (run).

$$m = \frac{y_2 - y_1}{x_2 - x_1}$$

EXAMPLE 2

COMMON CORE 8.F.4

Find *m*, the slope of the line.

My Notes

STEP 1 Choose two points on the line.
$P_1(x_1, y_1) = (-3, 2)$ $P_2(x_2, y_2) = (-6, 4)$

STEP 2 Find the change in *y*-values (rise $= y_2 - y_1$) and the change in *x*-values (run $= x_2 - x_1$) as you move from one point to the other.

$$\textbf{rise} = y_2 - y_1 \qquad \textbf{run} = x_2 - x_1$$
$$= 4 - 2 \qquad\qquad = -6 - (-3)$$
$$= 2 \qquad\qquad\quad = -3$$

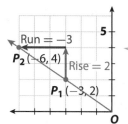

> If you move up or right, the change is positive. If you move down or left, the change is negative.

STEP 3 $m = \dfrac{\textbf{rise}}{\textbf{run}} = \dfrac{y_2 - y_1}{x_2 - x_1}$

$$= \frac{2}{-3}$$

$$= -\frac{2}{3}$$

YOUR TURN

4. The graph shows the rate at which water is leaking from a tank. The slope of the line gives the leaking rate in gallons per minute. Find the slope of the line.

Rise = _____   Run = _____

Slope = _____

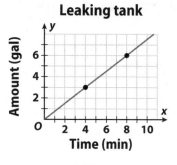

Leaking tank

Personal Math Trainer

Online Assessment and Intervention

my.hrw.com

Tell whether the rates of change are constant or variable. (Explore Activity Example 1)

1. building measurements _____

Feet	3	12	27	75
Yards	1	4	9	25

2. computers sold _____

Week	2	4	9	20
Number Sold	6	12	25	60

3. distance an object falls _____

Distance (ft)	16	64	144	256
Time (s)	1	2	3	4

4. cost of sweaters _____

Number	2	4	7	9
Cost ($)	38	76	133	171

Erica walks to her friend Philip's house. The graph shows Erica's distance from home over time. (Explore Activity 2)

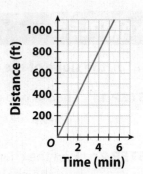

5. Find the rate of change from 1 minute to 2 minutes.

$$\frac{\text{change in distance}}{\text{change in time}} = \frac{400 - \boxed{}}{2 - \boxed{}} = \frac{\boxed{}}{\boxed{}} = \boxed{} \text{ ft per min}$$

6. Find the rate of change from 1 minute to 4 minutes. _____

Find the slope of each line. (Example 2)

7.

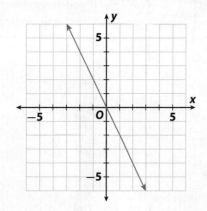

slope = _____

8.

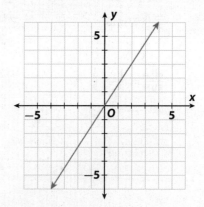

slope = _____

? ESSENTIAL QUESTION CHECK-IN

9. If you know two points on a line, how can you find the rate of change of the variables being graphed?

_____

_____

_____

11.2 Independent Practice

COMMON CORE 8.F.4

Personal Math Trainer

Online Assessment and Intervention

my.hrw.com

10. Rectangle *EFGH* is graphed on a coordinate plane with vertices at $E(-3, 5)$, $F(6, 2)$, $G(4, -4)$, and $H(-5, -1)$.

   a. Find the slopes of each side.

   _____

   b. What do you notice about the slopes of opposite sides?

   _____

   c. What do you notice about the slopes of adjacent sides?

   _____

11. A bicyclist started riding at 8:00 A.M. The diagram below shows the distance the bicyclist had traveled at different times. What was the bicyclist's average rate of speed in miles per hour?

8:00 A.M. ◄— 4.5 miles —► 8:18 A.M. ◄——— 7.5 miles ———► 8:48 A.M.

_____

12. **Multistep** A line passes through $(6, 3)$, $(8, 4)$, and $(n, -2)$. Find the value of n.

_____

13. A large container holds 5 gallons of water. It begins leaking at a constant rate. After 10 minutes, the container has 3 gallons of water left.

   a. At what rate is the water leaking?

   _____

   b. After how many minutes will the container be empty?

   _____

14. **Critique Reasoning** Billy found the slope of the line through the points $(2, 5)$ and $(-2, -5)$ using the equation $\frac{2 - (-2)}{5 - (-5)} = \frac{2}{5}$. What mistake did he make?

_____

_____

15. Multiple Representations Graph parallelogram *ABCD* on a coordinate plane with vertices at *A*(3, 4), *B*(6, 1), *C*(0, −2), and *D*(−3, 1).

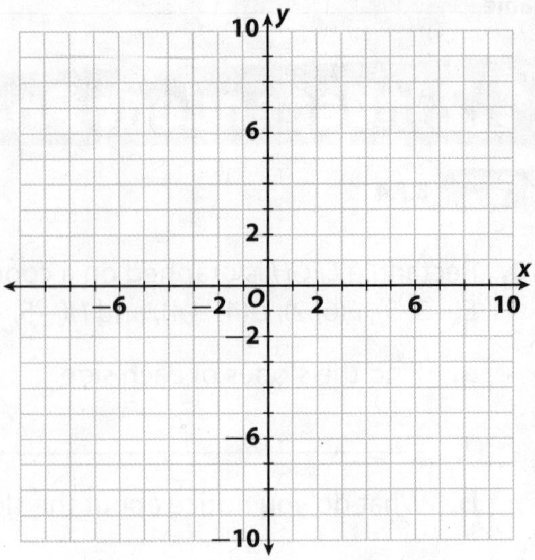

a. Find the slope of each side.

_____

_____

b. What do you notice about the slopes?

_____

_____

c. Draw another parallelogram on the coordinate plane. Do the slopes have the same characteristics?

_____

H.O.T. **FOCUS ON HIGHER ORDER THINKING**

Work Area

16. Communicate Mathematical Ideas Ben and Phoebe are finding the slope of a line. Ben chose two points on the line and used them to find the slope. Phoebe used two different points to find the slope. Did they get the same answer? Explain.

_____

_____

_____

17. Analyze Relationships Two lines pass through the origin. The lines have slopes that are opposites. Compare and contrast the lines.

_____

_____

_____

_____

18. Reason Abstractly What is the slope of the *x*-axis? Explain.

_____

_____

_____

Using Right Triangles to Explore Slope

COMMON CORE 8.EE.6

Use similar triangles to explain why the slope *m* is the same between any two distinct points on a non-vertical line in the coordinate plane; ...

ESSENTIAL QUESTION

How can you show that the slope of a non-vertical line is constant between any two points on a line?

EXPLORE ACTIVITY 8.EE.6

Using Right Triangles to Find Slope

A Plot the points (0, 2) and (8, 6) on the grid. Draw a line through the points.

B Draw and label two different right triangles *A* and *B* with each hypotenuse on the line and a right-angle vertex at the intersection of two gridlines. Make sure that your triangles are the same shape but different sizes.

_____

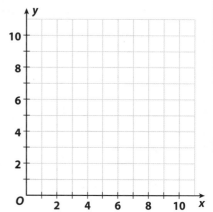

C Use the triangles *A* and *B* that you drew to complete the table.

Triangle	Rise	Run	$\frac{Rise}{Run}$
A			
B			

D Are the ratios of *rise* to *run* of triangles *A* and *B* equivalent? Explain.

_____

_____

E Is the slope of the line constant between the points (0, 2) and (2, 3) and the points (2, 3) and (8, 6)? Explain.

_____

_____

Reflect

1. How does a slope of $\frac{3}{9}$ compare with a slope of $\frac{4}{12}$?

_____

1. Select any two pairs of points on the line graphed, draw corresponding right triangles indicating the rise and run for each pair, and show that the slope is the same between the two pairs of points.

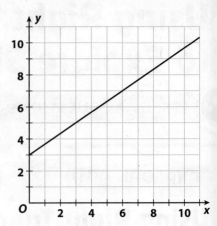

_____

_____

_____

_____

2. The same line is used below to generate different triangles. Verify that the slope ratios are the same for all the triangles generated by points on this line.

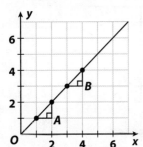 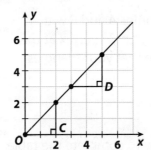 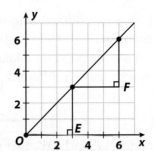

_____

_____

Use slope to determine whether the given points are all on the same line.

3. $(-6, -2), (0, -5), (2, -6)$

_____

_____

4. $(-10, -2), (-5, 0), (10, 6)$

_____

_____

5. A line passes through the point $(0, 0)$ and has a *rise* over *run* ratio of $\frac{4}{3}$. Give two other points that the line passes through.

_____

6. A wheelchair ramp is allowed a maximum of one inch of rise for every foot of run. Give the dimensions of three different wheelchair ramps that would meet this requirement.

_____

_____

LESSON 11.3 Interpreting the Unit Rate as Slope

COMMON CORE 8.EE.5

Graph proportional relationships, interpreting the unit rate as the slope of the graph. Compare two different proportional relationships represented in different ways. *Also 8.F.2, 8.F.4*

ESSENTIAL QUESTION

How do you interpret the unit rate as slope?

EXPLORE ACTIVITY   **COMMON CORE** 8.EE.5, 8.F.4

Relating the Unit Rate to Slope

A rate is a comparison of two quantities that have different units, such as miles and hours. A **unit rate** is a rate in which the second quantity in the comparison is one unit.

A storm is raging on Misty Mountain. The graph shows the constant rate of change of the snow level on the mountain.

Misty Mountain Storm

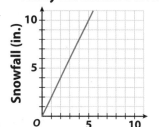

> A Find the slope of the graph using the points (1, 2) and (5, 10). Remember that the slope is the constant rate of change.

> B Find the unit rate of snowfall in inches per hour. Explain your method.

_____

_____

> C Compare the slope of the graph and the unit rate of change in the snow level. What do you notice?

_____

> D Which unique point on this graph gives you the slope of the graph and the unit rate of change in the snow level? Explain how you found the point.

_____

_____

_____

_____

Graphing Proportional Relationships

You can use a table and a graph to find the unit rate and slope that describe a real-world proportional relationship. The constant of proportionality for a proportional relationship is the same as the slope.

EXAMPLE 1

Every 3 seconds, 4 cubic feet of water pass over a dam. Draw a graph of the situation. Find the unit rate of this proportional relationship.

STEP 1 Make a table.

Time (s)	3	6	9	12	15
Volume (ft³)	4	8	12	16	20

STEP 2 Draw a graph.

STEP 3 Find the slope.

$$\text{slope} = \frac{\text{rise}}{\text{run}} = \frac{8}{6}$$

$$= \frac{4}{3}$$

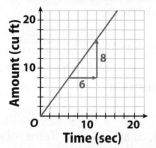

Water Over the Dam

Math Talk
Mathematical Practices

In a proportional relationship, how are the constant of proportionality, the unit rate, and the slope of the graph of the relationship related?

The unit rate of water passing over the dam and the slope of the graph of the relationship are equal, $\frac{4}{3}$ cubic feet per second.

Reflect

1. **What If?** Without referring to the graph, how do you know that the point $\left(1, \frac{4}{3}\right)$ is on the graph?

_____

_____

YOUR TURN

2. Tomas rides his bike at a steady rate of 2 miles every 10 minutes. Graph the situation. Find the unit rate of this proportional relationship.

_____

_____

_____

Tomas's Ride

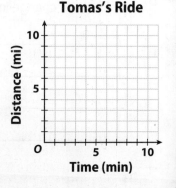

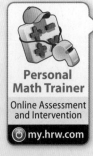

Using Slopes to Compare Unit Rates

You can compare proportional relationships presented in different ways.

EXAMPLE 2

COMMON CORE 8.EE.5, 8.F.2

The equation $y = 2.75x$ represents the rate, in barrels per hour, that oil is pumped from Well A. The graph represents the rate that oil is pumped from Well B. Which well pumped oil at a faster rate?

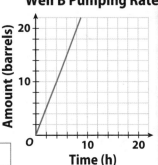

Well B Pumping Rate

STEP 1 Use the equation $y = 2.75x$ to make a table for Well A's pumping rate, in barrels per hour.

Time (h)	1	2	3	4
Quantity (barrels)	2.75	5.5	8.25	11

STEP 2 Use the table to find the slope of the graph of Well A.

$$\text{slope} = \text{unit rate} = \frac{5.5 - 2.75}{2 - 1} = \frac{2.75}{1} = \textbf{2.75 barrels/hour}$$

STEP 3 Use the graph to find the slope of the graph of Well B.

$$\text{slope} = \text{unit rate} = \frac{\text{rise}}{\text{run}} = \frac{10}{4} = \textbf{2.5 barrels/hour}$$

STEP 4 Compare the unit rates.

$2.75 > 2.5$, so Well A's rate, 2.75 barrels/hour, is faster.

Reflect

3. Describe the relationships among the slope of the graph of Well A's rate, the equation representing Well A's rate, and the constant of proportionality.

_____

_____

YOUR TURN

4. The equation $y = 375x$ represents the relationship between x, the time that a plane flies in hours, and y, the distance the plane flies in miles for Plane A. The table represents the relationship for Plane B. Find the slope of the graph for each plane and the plane's rate of speed. Determine which plane is flying at a faster rate of speed.

Time (h)	1	2	3	4
Distance (mi)	425	850	1275	1700

_____

Personal
Math Trainer

Online Assessment
and Intervention

my.hrw.com

Give the slope of the graph and the unit rate. (Explore Activity and Example 1)

1. Jorge: 5 miles every 6 hours

Jorge

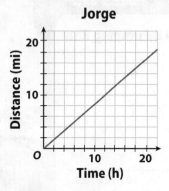

2. Akiko

Time (h)	4	8	12	16
Distance (mi)	5	10	15	20

Akiko

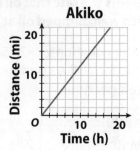

_____   _____

3. The equation $y = 0.5x$ represents the distance Henry hikes, in miles, over time, in hours. The graph represents the rate that Clark hikes. Determine which hiker is faster. Explain. (Example 2)

Clark

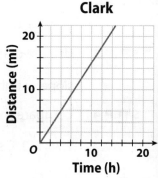

_____

_____

_____

Write an equation relating the variables in each table. (Example 2)

4.

Time (x)	1	2	4	6
Distance (y)	15	30	60	90

5.

Time (x)	16	32	48	64
Distance (y)	6	12	18	24

_____   _____

? ESSENTIAL QUESTION CHECK-IN

6. Describe methods you can use to show a proportional relationship between two variables, x and y. For each method, explain how you can find the unit rate and the slope.

_____

_____

_____

_____

_____

11.3 Independent Practice

COMMON CORE 8.EE.5, 8.F.2, 8.F.4

7. A Canadian goose migrated at a steady rate of 3 miles every 4 minutes.

   a. Fill in the table to describe the relationship.

Time (min)	4	8			20
Distance (mi)			9	12	

   b. Graph the relationship.

   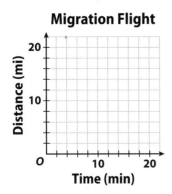

   Migration Flight

   c. Find the slope of the graph and describe what it means in the context of this problem.

   _____

   _____

   _____

   _____

8. **Vocabulary** A unit rate is a rate in which the

   first quantity / second quantity in the comparison is one unit.

9. The table and the graph represent the rate at which two machines are bottling milk in gallons per second.

   Machine 1

Time (s)	1	2	3	4
Amount (gal)	0.6	1.2	1.8	2.4

   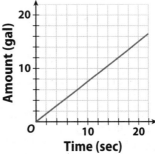

   Machine 2

   a. Determine the slope and unit rate of each machine.

   _____

   _____

   b. Determine which machine is working at a faster rate.

   _____

10. Cycling The equation $y = \frac{1}{9}x$ represents the distance y, in kilometers, that Patrick traveled in x minutes while training for the cycling portion of a triathlon. The table shows the distance y Jennifer traveled in x minutes in her training. Who has the faster training rate?

Time (min)	40	64	80	96
Distance (km)	5	8	10	12

_____

_____

_____

 **FOCUS ON HIGHER ORDER THINKING**

11. Analyze Relationships There is a proportional relationship between minutes and dollars per minute, shown on a graph of printing expenses. The graph passes through the point (1, 4.75). What is the slope of the graph? What is the unit rate? Explain.

_____

_____

_____

12. Draw Conclusions Two cars start at the same time and travel at different constant rates. A graph for Car A passes through the point (0.5, 27.5), and a graph for Car B passes through (4, 240). Both graphs show distance in miles and time in hours. Which car is traveling faster? Explain.

_____

_____

_____

_____

13. Critical Thinking The table shows the rate at which water is being pumped into a swimming pool.

Time (min)	2	5	7	12
Amount (gal)	36	90	126	216

Use the unit rate and the amount of water pumped after 12 minutes to find how much water will have been pumped into the pool after $13\frac{1}{2}$ minutes. Explain your reasoning.

_____

_____

_____

_____

Ready to Go On?

11.1 Representing Proportional Relationships

1. Find the constant of proportionality for the table of values.

x	2	3	4	5
y	3	4.5	6	7.5

_____

2. Phil is riding his bike. He rides 25 miles in 2 hours, 37.5 miles in 3 hours, and 50 miles in 4 hours. Find the constant of proportionality and write an equation to describe the situation.

_____

11.2 Rate of Change and Slope

Find the slope of each line.

3.

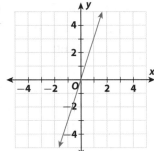

_____

4.

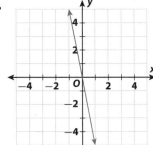

_____

11.3 Interpreting the Unit Rate as Slope

5. The distance Train A travels is represented by $d = 70t$, where d is the distance in kilometers and t is the time in hours. The distance Train B travels at various times is shown in the table. What is the unit rate of each train? Which train is going faster?

Time (hours)	Distance (km)
2	150
4	300
5	375

_____

? ESSENTIAL QUESTION

6. What is the relationship among proportional relationships, lines, rates of change, and slope?

_____

_____

COMMON CORE

Assessment Readiness

Personal
Math Trainer

Online
Assessment and
Intervention

my.hrw.com

Selected Response

1. Which of the following is equivalent to 5^{-1}?

Ⓐ 4

Ⓒ $-\frac{1}{5}$

Ⓑ $\frac{1}{5}$

Ⓓ -5

2. Prasert earns $9 an hour. Which table represents this proportional relationship?

Ⓐ
Hours	4	6	8
Earnings ($)	36	54	72

Ⓑ
Hours	4	6	8
Earnings ($)	36	45	54

Ⓒ
Hours	2	3	4
Earnings ($)	9	18	27

Ⓓ
Hours	2	3	4
Earnings ($)	18	27	54

3. A factory produces widgets at a constant rate. After 4 hours, 3,120 widgets have been produced. At what rate are the widgets being produced?

Ⓐ 630 widgets per hour

Ⓑ 708 widgets per hour

Ⓒ 780 widgets per hour

Ⓓ 1,365 widgets per hour

4. A full lake begins dropping at a constant rate. After 4 weeks it has dropped 3 feet. What is the unit rate of change in the lake's level compared to its full level?

Ⓐ 0.75 feet per week

Ⓑ 1.33 feet per week

Ⓒ −0.75 feet per week

Ⓓ −1.33 feet per week

5. What is the slope of the line below?

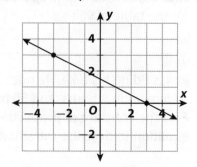

Ⓐ −2

Ⓒ $\frac{1}{2}$

Ⓑ $-\frac{1}{2}$

Ⓓ 2

6. Jim earns $41.25 in 5 hours. Susan earns $30.00 in 4 hours. Pierre's hourly rate is less than Jim's, but more than Susan's. What is his hourly rate?

Ⓐ $6.50

Ⓒ $7.35

Ⓑ $7.75

Ⓓ $8.25

Mini-Task

7. Joelle can read 3 pages in 4 minutes, 4.5 pages in 6 minutes, and 6 pages in 8 minutes.

a. Make a table of the data.

Minutes			
Pages			

b. Use the values in the table to find the unit rate.

_____

c. Graph the relationship between minutes and pages read.

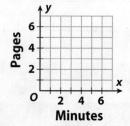

Nonproportional Relationships

? ESSENTIAL QUESTION

How can you use non-proportional relationships to solve real-world problems?

Real-World Video

The distance a car can travel on a tank of gas or a full battery charge in an electric car depends on factors such as fuel capacity and the car's efficiency. This is described by a nonproportional relationship.

my.hrw.com

GO DIGITAL
my.hrw.com

my.hrw.com

Go digital with your write-in student edition, accessible on any device.

Math On the Spot

Scan with your smart phone to jump directly to the online edition, video tutor, and more.

Animated Math

Interactively explore key concepts to see how math works.

Personal Math Trainer

Get immediate feedback and help as you work through practice sets.

Are YOU Ready?

Complete these exercises to review skills you will need for this module.

Integer Operations

> **EXAMPLE**
>
> $-7 - (-4) = -7 + 4$ To subtract an integer, add its opposite.
>
> $|-7| - |4|$ The signs are different, so find the difference
>
> $7 - 4$, or 3 of the absolute values.
>
> $= -3$ Use the sign of the number with the greater absolute value.

Find each difference.

1. $3 - (-5)$ _____

2. $-4 - 5$ _____

3. $6 - 10$ _____

4. $-5 - (-3)$ _____

5. $8 - (-8)$ _____

6. $9 - 5$ _____

7. $-3 - 9$ _____

8. $0 - (-6)$ _____

9. $12 - (-9)$ _____

10. $-6 - (-4)$ _____

11. $-7 - 10$ _____

12. $5 - 14$ _____

Graph Ordered Pairs (First Quadrant)

> **EXAMPLE**
>
>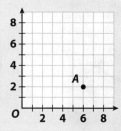
>
> To graph a point at (6, 2), start at the origin.
>
> Move 6 units right.
>
> Then move 2 units up.
>
> Graph point A(6, 2).

Graph each point on the coordinate grid.

13. B (0, 5)

14. C (8, 0)

15. D (5, 7)

16. E (2, 3)

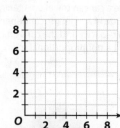

Reading Start-Up

Visualize Vocabulary

Use the ✔ words to complete the diagram. You can put more than one word in each box.

Reviewing Slope

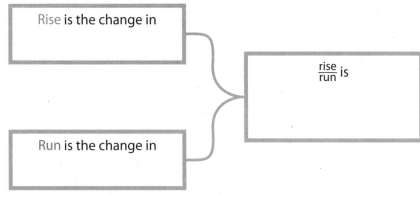

Rise is the change in

Run is the change in

$\frac{rise}{run}$ is

Vocabulary

Review Words

ordered pair *(par ordenado)*

proportional relationship *(relación proporcional)*

✔ rate of change *(tasa de cambio)*

✔ slope *(pendiente)*

✔ *x*-coordinate *(coordenada x)*

✔ *y*-coordinate *(coordenada y)*

Preview Words

linear equation *(ecuación lineal)*

slope-intercept form of an equation *(forma de pendiente-intersección)*

y-intercept *(intersección con el eje y)*

Understand Vocabulary

Complete the sentences using the preview words.

1. The *y*-coordinate of the point where a graph of a line crosses the *y*-axis is the _____.

2. A _____ is an equation whose solutions form a straight line on a coordinate plane.

3. A linear equation written in the form $y = mx + b$ is the _____.

Active Reading

Booklet Before beginning the module, create a booklet to help you learn the concepts. Write the main idea of each lesson on each page of the booklet. As you study each lesson, write important details that support the main idea, such as vocabulary and formulas. Refer to your finished booklet as you work on assignments and study for tests.

COMMON CORE

Unpacking the Standards

Understanding the standards and the vocabulary terms in the standards will help you know exactly what you are expected to learn in this module.

COMMON CORE 8.F.3

Interpret the equation $y = mx + b$ as defining a linear function whose graph is a straight line.

Key Vocabulary

slope *(pendiente)*
A measure of the steepness of a line on a graph; the rise divided by the run.

y-intercept *(intersección con el eje y)*
The y-coordinate of the point where the graph of a line crosses the y-axis.

What It Means to You

You will identify the slope and the y-intercept of a line by looking at its equation and use them to graph the line.

UNPACKING EXAMPLE 8.F.3

Graph $y = 3x - 2$ using the slope and the y-intercept.

$$y = mx + b$$

slope   y-intercept

The slope *m* is 3, and the y-intercept is −2.

Plot the point (0, −2). Use the slope $3 = \frac{3}{1}$ to find another point by moving *up* 3 and to the *right* 1. Draw the line through the points.

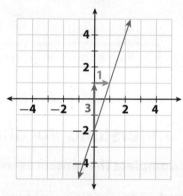

COMMON CORE 8.F.3

Give examples of functions that are not linear.

Key Vocabulary

function *(función)*
An input-output relationship that has exactly one output for each input.

linear function *(función lineal)*
A function whose graph is a straight line.

What It Means to You

You will distinguish linear relationships from nonlinear relationships by looking at graphs.

UNPACKING EXAMPLE 8.F.3

Which relationship is linear and which is nonlinear?

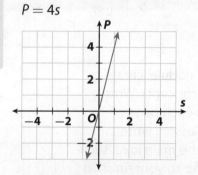

$P = 4s$ is linear because its graph is a line.

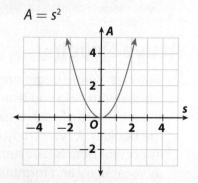

$A = s^2$ is not linear because its graph is not a line.

12.1 Representing Linear Nonproportional Relationships

COMMON CORE 8.F.3

Interpret the equation $y = mx + b$ as defining a linear function, whose graph is a straight line; ...

ESSENTIAL QUESTION

How can you use tables, graphs, and equations to represent linear nonproportional situations?

EXPLORE ACTIVITY   COMMON CORE Prep for 8.F.3

Math On the Spot

⏱ my.hrw.com

Representing Linear Relationships Using Tables

You can use an equation to describe the relationship between two quantities in a real-world situation. You can use a table to show some values that make the equation true.

EXAMPLE 1 The equation $y = 3x + 2$ gives the total charge, y, for one person to rent a pair of shoes and bowl x games at Baxter Bowling Lanes based on the prices shown. Make a table of values for this situation.

STEP 1 Choose several values for x that make sense in context. Count by ones.

x (number of games)	1	2		
y (total cost in dollars)				

STEP 2 Use the equation $y = 3x + 2$ to find y for each value of x.

x (number of games)	1	2		
y (total cost in dollars)	5			

Substitute 1 for x:
$y = 3(1) + 2 = 5$

1. Francisco makes $12 per hour doing part-time work on Saturdays. He spends $4 on transportation to and from work. The equation $y = 12x - 4$ gives his earnings y, after transportation costs, for working x hours. Make a table of values for this situation.

x (number of hours)				
y (earnings in dollars)				

Personal Math Trainer

Online Assessment and Intervention

⏱ my.hrw.com

Examining Linear Relationships

Recall that a proportional relationship is a relationship between two quantities in which the ratio of one quantity to the other quantity is constant. The graph of a proportional relationship is a line through the origin. Relationships can have a constant rate of change but not be proportional.

The entrance fee for Mountain World theme park is $20. Visitors purchase additional $2 tickets for rides, games, and food. The equation $y = 2x + 20$ gives the total cost, y, to visit the park, including purchasing x tickets.

STEP 1 Complete the table.

x (number of tickets)	0	2	4	6	8
y (total cost in dollars)	20				

STEP 2 Plot the ordered pairs from the table. Describe the shape of the graph.

_____

STEP 3 Find the rate of change between each point and the next. Is the rate constant?

_____

STEP 4 Calculate $\frac{y}{x}$ for the values in the table. Explain why the relationship between number of tickets and total cost is not proportional.

_____

_____

_____

Theme Park Costs

Reflect

2. **Analyze Relationships** Would it make sense to add more points to the graph from $x = 0$ to $x = 10$? Would it make sense to connect the points with a line? Explain.

_____

_____

_____

_____

Representing Linear Relationships Using Graphs

A **linear equation** is an equation whose solutions are ordered pairs that form a line when graphed on a coordinate plane. Linear equations can be written in the form $y = mx + b$. When $b \neq 0$, the relationship between x and y is *nonproportional*.

EXAMPLE 2

COMMON CORE 8.F.3

My Notes

The diameter of a Douglas fir tree is currently 10 inches when measured at chest height. Over the next 50 years, the diameter is expected to increase by an average growth rate of $\frac{2}{5}$ inch per year. The equation $y = \frac{2}{5}x + 10$ gives y, the diameter of the tree in inches, after x years. Draw a graph of the equation. Describe the relationship.

STEP 1 Make a table. Choose several values for x that make sense in context. To make calculations easier, choose multiples of 5.

x (years)	0	10	20	30	50
y (diameter in inches)	10	14	18	22	30

STEP 2 Plot the ordered pairs from the table. Then draw a line connecting the points to represent all the possible solutions.

STEP 3 The relationship is linear but nonproportional. The graph is a line but it does not go through the origin.

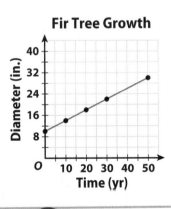

Fir Tree Growth

YOUR TURN

3. Make a table and graph the solutions of the equation $y = -2x + 1$.

x	−1	0	1	2
y				

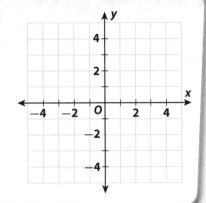

Guided Practice

Make a table of values for each equation. (Explore Activity Example 1)

1. $y = 2x + 5$

x	−2	−1	0	1	2
y					

2. $y = \frac{3}{8}x - 5$

x	−8	0	8
y			

Explain why each relationship is not proportional. (Explore Activity 2)

3.

x	0	2	4	6	8
y	3	7	11	15	19

First calculate $\frac{y}{x}$ for the values in the table.

_____

_____

_____

_____

4.

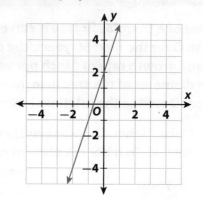

_____

Complete the table for the equation. Then use the table to graph the equation. (Example 2)

5. $y = x - 1$

x	−2	−1	0	1	2
y					

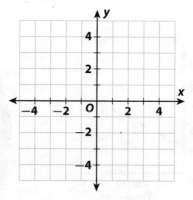

? ESSENTIAL QUESTION CHECK-IN

6. How can you choose values for x when making a table of values representing a real world situation?

_____

_____

_____

12.1 Independent Practice

COMMON CORE 8.F.3

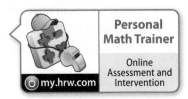

Personal Math Trainer

Online Assessment and Intervention

my.hrw.com

State whether the graph of each linear relationship is a solid line or a set of unconnected points. Explain your reasoning.

7. The relationship between the number of $4 lunches you buy with a $100 school lunch card and the money remaining on the card

_____

_____

_____

_____

8. The relationship between time and the distance remaining on a 3-mile walk for someone walking at a steady rate of 2 miles per hour

_____

_____

_____

_____

9. Analyze Relationships Simone paid $12 for an initial year's subscription to a magazine. The renewal rate is $8 per year. This situation can be represented by the equation $y = 8x + 12$, where x represents the number of years the subscription is renewed and y represents the total cost.

a. Make a table of values for this situation.

b. Draw a graph to represent the situation. Include a title and axis labels.

c. Explain why this relationship is not proportional.

_____

_____

_____

_____

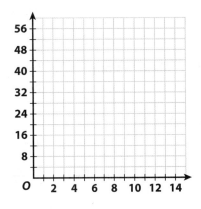

d. Does it make sense to connect the points on the graph with a solid line? Explain.

_____

_____

_____

10. Analyze Relationships A proportional relationship is a linear relationship because the rate of change is constant (and equal to the constant of proportionality). What is required of a proportional relationship that is *not* required of a general linear relationship?

_____

_____

11. Communicate Mathematical Ideas Explain how you can identify a linear non-proportional relationship from a table, a graph, and an equation.

_____

_____

_____

H.O.T. FOCUS ON HIGHER ORDER THINKING

12. Critique Reasoning George observes that for every increase of 1 in the value of *x*, there is an increase of 60 in the corresponding value of *y*. He claims that the relationship represented by the table is proportional. Critique George's reasoning.

x	1	2	3	4	5
y	90	150	210	270	330

_____

_____

_____

_____

_____

13. Make a Conjecture Two parallel lines are graphed on a coordinate plane. How many of the lines could represent proportional relationships? Explain.

_____

_____

_____

_____

_____

_____

Determining Slope and *y*-intercept

COMMON CORE **8.EE.6**
...; derive the equation *y* = *mx* for a line through the origin and the equation *y* = *mx* + *b* for a line intercepting the vertical axis at *b*. *Also 8.F.4*

ESSENTIAL QUESTION

How can you determine the slope and the *y*-intercept of a line?

EXPLORE ACTIVITY 1 8.EE.6

Investigating Slope and *y*-intercept

The graph of every nonvertical line crosses the *y*-axis. The **y-intercept** is the *y*-coordinate of the point where the graph intersects the *y*-axis. The *x*-coordinate of this point is always 0.

The graph represents the linear equation $y = -\frac{2}{3}x + 4$.

STEP 1 Find the slope of the line using the points (0, 4) and (−3, 6).

$$m = \frac{6 - \boxed{}}{\boxed{} - 0} = \frac{\boxed{}}{\boxed{}} = \boxed{}$$

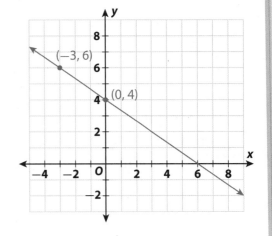

STEP 2 The line also contains the point (6, 0). What is the slope using (0, 4) and (6, 0)? Using (−3, 6) and (6, 0). What do you notice?

_____

STEP 3 Compare your answers in Steps 1 and 2 with the equation of the graphed line.

_____

_____

STEP 4 Find the value of *y* when *x* = 0 using the equation $y = -\frac{2}{3}x + 4$. Describe the point on the graph that corresponds to this solution.

_____

STEP 5 Compare your answer in Step 4 with the equation of the line.

_____

_____

Determining Rate of Change and Initial Value

The linear equation shown is written in the **slope-intercept form of an equation**. Its graph is a line with **slope m** and **y-intercept b**.

$$y = mx + b$$

slope y-intercept

A linear relationship has a constant rate of change. You can find the **rate of change m** and the **initial value b** for a linear situation from a table of values.

EXAMPLE 1

COMMON CORE   8.F.4

A phone salesperson is paid a minimum weekly salary and a commission for each phone sold, as shown in the table. Confirm that the relationship is linear and give the constant rate of change and the initial value.

STEP 1 Confirm that the rate of change is constant.

$$\frac{\text{change in income}}{\text{change in phones sold}} = \frac{630-480}{20-10} = \frac{150}{10} = 15$$

$$\frac{\text{change in income}}{\text{change in phones sold}} = \frac{780-630}{30-20} = \frac{150}{10} = 15$$

$$\frac{\text{change in income}}{\text{change in phones sold}} = \frac{930-780}{40-30} - \frac{150}{10} = 15$$

Number of Phones Sold	Weekly Income ($)
10	$480
20	$630
30	$780
40	$930

The rate of change is a constant, **15**.

The salesperson receives a $15 commission for each phone sold.

STEP 2 Find the initial value when the number of phones sold is 0.

−10 −10

Number of phones sold	0	10	20
Weekly income ($)	330	480	630

Work backward from $x = 10$ to $x = 0$ to find the initial value.

−150 −150

The initial value is $330. The salesperson receives a salary of $330 each week before commissions.

Math Talk
Mathematical Practices

How do you use the rate of change to work backward to find the initial value?

YOUR TURN

Find the slope and y-intercept of the line represented by each table.

1.

x	2	4	6	8
y	22	32	42	52

2.

x	1	2	3	4
y	8	15	22	29

_____   _____

Deriving the Slope-intercept Form of an Equation

In the following Explore Activity, you will derive the slope-intercept form of an equation.

STEP 1   Let L be a line with slope m and y-intercept b. Circle the point that must be on the line. Justify your choice.

   $(b, 0)$ $(0, b)$ $(0, m)$ $(m, 0)$

   _____

   _____

STEP 2   Recall that slope is the ratio of change in y to change in x. Complete the equation for the slope m of the line using the y-intercept $(0, b)$ and another point (x, y) on the line.

$$m = \frac{y - \boxed{}}{\boxed{} - 0}$$

STEP 3   In an equation of a line, we often want y by itself on one side of the equation. Solve the equation from Step 2 for y.

$$m = \frac{y - b}{x}$$ Simplify the denominator.

$$m \cdot \boxed{} = \frac{y - b}{x} \cdot \boxed{}$$ Multiply both sides of the equation by _____.

$$m\boxed{} = y - b$$

$$mx + \boxed{} = y - b + \boxed{}$$ Add _____ to both sides of the equation.

$$mx + \boxed{} = y$$

$$y = mx + \boxed{}$$ Write the equation with y on the left side.

Reflect

3. **Critical Thinking** Write the equation of a line with slope m that passes through the origin. Explain your reasoning.

   _____

   _____

   _____

Find the slope and y-intercept of the line in each graph. (Explore Activity 1)

1.

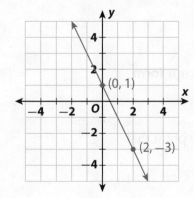

slope m = _____ y-intercept b = _____

2.

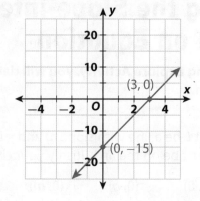

slope m = _____ y-intercept b = _____

3.

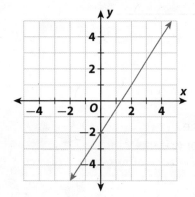

slope m = _____ y-intercept b = _____

4.

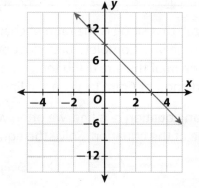

slope m = _____ y-intercept b = _____

Find the slope and y-intercept of the line represented by each table. (Example 1)

5.

x	0	2	4	6	8
y	1	7	13	19	25

slope m = _____ y-intercept b = _____

6.

x	0	5	10	15	20
y	140	120	100	80	60

slope m = _____ y-intercept b = _____

? ESSENTIAL QUESTION CHECK-IN

7. How can you determine the slope and the y-intercept of a line from a graph?

_____

_____

_____

Name _____ Class _____ Date _____

12.2 Independent Practice

COMMON CORE 8.EE.6, 8.F.4

8. Some carpet cleaning costs are shown in the table. The relationship is linear. Find and interpret the rate of change and the initial value for this situation.

Rooms cleaned	1	2	3	4
Cost ($)	125	175	225	275

_____

_____

_____

9. **Make Predictions** The total cost to pay for parking at a state park for the day and rent a paddleboat are shown.

a. Find the cost to park for a day and the hourly rate to rent a paddleboat.

_____

b. What will Lin pay if she rents a paddleboat for 3.5 hours and splits the total cost with a friend? Explain.

_____

_____

Number of Hours	Cost ($)
1	$17
2	$29
3	$41
4	$53

10. **Multi-Step** Raymond's parents will pay for him to take sailboard lessons during the summer. He can take half-hour group lessons or half-hour private lessons. The relationship between cost and number of lessons is linear.

Lessons	1	2	3	4
Group ($)	55	85	115	145
Private ($)	75	125	175	225

a. Find the rate of change and the initial value for the group lessons.

_____

_____

b. Find the rate of change and the initial value for the private lessons.

_____

_____

c. Compare and contrast the rates of change and the initial values.

_____

_____

_____

Vocabulary Explain why each relationship is not linear.

11.

x	1	2	3	4
y	4.5	6.5	8.5	11.5

12.

x	3	5	7	9
y	140	126	110	92

_____

_____

_____

_____

13. Communicate Mathematical Ideas Describe the procedure you performed to derive the slope-intercept form of a linear equation.

_____

_____

_____

 **FOCUS ON HIGHER ORDER THINKING**

Work Area

14. Critique Reasoning Your teacher asked your class to describe a real-world situation in which a *y*-intercept is 100 and the slope is 5. Your partner gave the following description: *My younger brother originally had 100 small building blocks, but he has lost 5 of them every month since.*

a. What mistake did your partner make?

_____

_____

b. Describe a real-world situation that does match the situation.

_____

_____

15. Justify Reasoning John has a job parking cars. He earns a fixed weekly salary of $300 plus a fee of $5 for each car he parks. His potential earnings for a week are shown in the graph. At what point does John begin to earn more from fees than his fixed salary? Justify your answer.

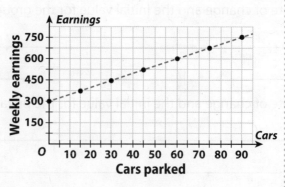

_____

_____

_____

Graphing Linear Nonproportional Relationships Using Slope and *y*-intercept

COMMON CORE 8.F.4

... Interpret the rate of change and initial value of a linear function in terms of the situation it models, and in terms of its graph.... *Also* 8.F.3

ESSENTIAL QUESTION

How can you graph a line using the slope and *y*-intercept?

EXPLORE ACTIVITY

COMMON CORE 8.F.3

Math On the Spot

my.hrw.com

Using Slope-intercept Form to Graph a Line

Recall that $y = mx + b$ is the slope-intercept form of the equation of a line. In this form, it is easy to see the slope *m* and the *y*-intercept *b*. So you can use this form to quickly graph a line by plotting the point $(0, b)$ and using the slope to find a second point.

Animated Math

my.hrw.com

EXAMPLE 1 Graph each equation.

A $y = \frac{2}{3}x - 1$

STEP 1 The *y*-intercept is $b =$ ____.
Plot (0, ____).

STEP 2 Use the slope $m =$ ____ to find a
second point. From (0, ____),
count *up* ____ and *right* ____.
The new point is (3, ____).

STEP 3 Draw a line through the points.

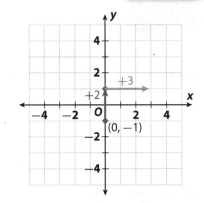

B $y = -\frac{5}{2}x + 3$

STEP 1 The *y*-intercept is $b =$ ____. Plot (0, ____).

STEP 2 Use the slope $m =$ ____ to find a second
point. From (____, ____), count *down* ____
and _____ 2 to the new point (____, ____),
OR from (____, ____), count *up* 5 and
_____ 2 to the new point (____, ____).

STEP 3 Draw a line through the points.

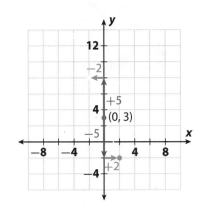

Reflect

1. **Draw Conclusions** How can you use the slope of a line to predict the way the line will be slanted? Explain.

_____

_____

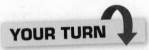

YOUR TURN

Graph each equation.

2. $y = \frac{1}{2}x + 1$

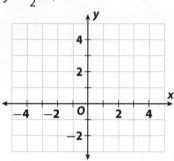

3. $y = -3x + 4$

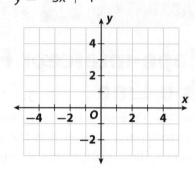

Personal Math Trainer

Online Assessment and Intervention

my.hrw.com

Math On the Spot

my.hrw.com

Analyzing a Graph

Many real-world situations can be represented by linear relationships. You can use graphs of linear relationships to visualize situations and solve problems.

EXAMPLE 2 Real World

COMMON CORE 8.F.4

Ken has a weekly goal of burning 2400 calories by taking brisk walks. The equation $y = -300x + 2400$ represents the number of calories y Ken has left to burn after x hours of walking which burns 300 calories per hour.

A Graph the equation $y = -300x + 2400$.

STEP 1 Write the slope as a fraction.

$$m = \frac{-300}{1} = \frac{-600}{2} = \frac{-900}{3}$$

Using the slope as $\frac{-900}{3}$ helps in drawing a more accurate graph.

STEP 2 Plot the point for the y-intercept: (0, 2400).

STEP 3 Use the slope to locate a second point.

From (0, 2400), count *down* 900 and *right* 3.

The new point is (3, 1500).

STEP 4 Draw a line through the two points.

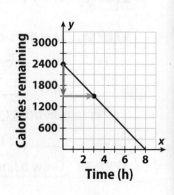

B After how many hours of walking will Ken have 600 calories left to burn? After how many hours will he reach his weekly goal?

STEP 1 Locate 600 calories on the *y*-axis. Read across and down to the *x*-axis.

Ken will have 600 calories left to burn after 6 hours.

STEP 2 Ken will reach his weekly goal when the number of calories left to burn is 0. Because every point on the *x*-axis has a *y*-value of 0, find the point where the line crosses the *x*-axis.

Ken will reach his goal after 8 hours of brisk walking.

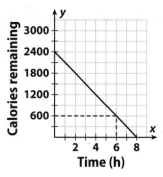

YOUR TURN

What If? Ken decides to modify his exercise plans from Example 2 by slowing the speed at which he walks. The equation for the modified plan is $y = -200x + 2400$.

4. Graph the equation.

5. How does the graph of the new equation compare with the graph in Example 2?

   _____

   _____

   _____

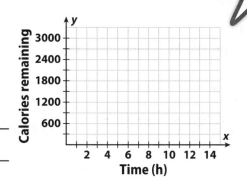

Math Talk
Mathematical Practices

What do the slope and the *y*-intercept of the line represent in this situation?

6. Will Ken have to exercise more or less to meet his goal? Explain.

   _____

   _____

   _____

7. Suppose that Ken decides that instead of walking, he will jog, and that jogging burns 600 calories per hour. How do you think that this would change the graph?

   _____

   _____

   _____

Personal Math Trainer

Online Assessment and Intervention

my.hrw.com

Graph each equation using the slope and the y-intercept. (Explore Activity Example 1)

1. $y = \frac{1}{2}x - 3$

slope = _____   y-intercept = _____

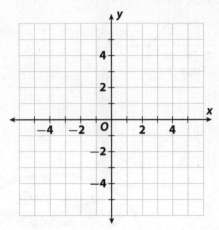

2. $y = -3x + 2$

slope = _____   y-intercept = _____

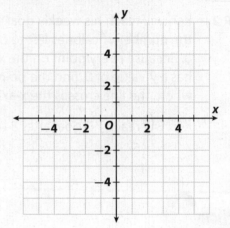

3. A friend gives you two baseball cards for your birthday. Afterward, you begin collecting them. You buy the same number of cards once each week. The equation $y = 4x + 2$ describes the number of cards, y, you have after x weeks. (Example 2)

a. Find and interpret the slope and the y-intercept of the line that represents this situation. Graph $y = 4x + 2$. Include axis labels.

_____

_____

b. Discuss which points on the line do not make sense in this situation. Then plot three more points on the line that do make sense.

_____

_____

_____

? ESSENTIAL QUESTION CHECK-IN

4. Why might someone choose to use the y-intercept and the slope to graph a line?

_____

_____

_____

_____

12.3 Independent Practice

 8.F.3, 8.F.4

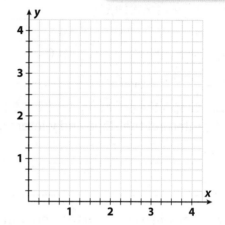

5. **Science** A spring stretches in relation to the weight hanging from it according to the equation $y = 0.75x + 0.25$ where x is the weight in pounds and y is the length of the spring in inches.

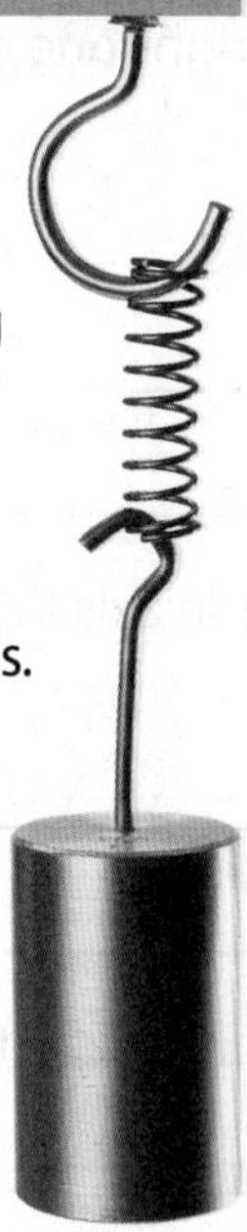

   a. Graph the equation. Include axis labels.

   b. Interpret the slope and the y-intercept of the line.

   _____

   _____

   _____

   _____

   _____

   c. How long will the spring be if a 2-pound weight is hung on it? Will the length double if you double the weight? Explain

   _____

Look for a Pattern **Identify the coordinates of four points on the line with each given slope and y-intercept.**

6. slope = 5, y-intercept = −1

   _____

7. slope = −1, y-intercept = 8

   _____

8. slope = 0.2, y-intercept = 0.3

   _____

9. slope = 1.5, y-intercept = −3

   _____

10. slope = $-\frac{1}{2}$, y-intercept = 4

   _____

11. slope = $\frac{2}{3}$, y-intercept = −5

   _____

12. A music school charges a registration fee in addition to a fee per lesson. Music lessons last 0.5 hour. The equation $y = 40x + 30$ represents the total cost y of x lessons. Find and interpret the slope and y-intercept of the line that represents this situation. Then find four points on the line.

   _____

   _____

13. A public pool charges a membership fee and a fee for each visit. The equation $y = 3x + 50$ represents the cost y for x visits.

   a. After locating the y-intercept on the coordinate plane shown, can you move up three gridlines and right one gridline to find a second point? Explain.

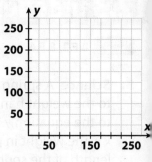

   _____

   _____

   _____

   b. Graph the equation $y = 3x + 50$. Include axis labels. Then interpret the slope and y-intercept.

   _____

   _____

   c. How many visits to the pool can a member get for $200?

   _____

 **FOCUS ON HIGHER ORDER THINKING**

Work Area

14. Explain the Error A student says that the slope of the line for the equation $y = 20 - 15x$ is 20 and the y-intercept is 15. Find and correct the error.

_____

_____

_____

15. Critical Thinking Suppose you know the slope of a linear relationship and a point that its graph passes through. Can you graph the line even if the point provided does *not* represent the y-intercept? Explain.

_____

_____

_____

16. Make a Conjecture Graph the lines $y = 3x$, $y = 3x - 3$, and $y = 3x + 3$. What do you notice about the lines? Make a conjecture based on your observation.

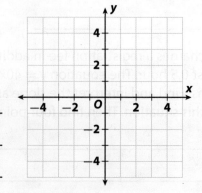

_____

_____

_____

Proportional and Nonproportional Situations

COMMON CORE 8.F.2

Compare properties of two functions each represented in a different way (algebraically, graphically, numerically in tables, or by verbal descriptions). *Also 8.F.3, 8.F.4*

ESSENTIAL QUESTION

How can you distinguish between proportional and nonproportional situations?

EXPLORE ACTIVITY   COMMON CORE 8.F.3

Math On the Spot
my.hrw.com

Distinguish Between Proportional and Nonproportional Situations Using a Graph

If a relationship is nonlinear, it is nonproportional. If it is linear, it may be either proportional or nonproportional. When the graph of the linear relationship contains the origin, the relationship is proportional.

EXAMPLE 1 The graph shows the sales tax charged based on the amount spent at a video game store in a particular city. Does the graph show a linear relationship? Is the relationship proportional or nonproportional?

The graph shows a linear _____ relationship

because it is a _____ that contains the _____ .

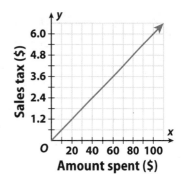

YOUR TURN

Determine if each of the following graphs represents a proportional or nonproportional relationship.

1.

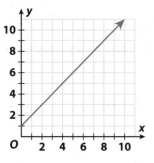

2.

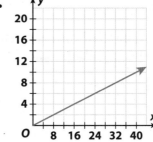

Personal Math Trainer
Online Assessment and Intervention
my.hrw.com

_____   _____

Distinguish Between Proportional and Nonproportional Situations Using an Equation

If an equation is not a linear equation, it represents a nonproportional relationship. A linear equation of the form $y = mx + b$ may represent either a proportional ($b = 0$) or nonproportional ($b \neq 0$) relationship.

EXAMPLE 2

 COMMON CORE 8.F.4

The number of years since Keith graduated from middle school can be represented by the equation $y = a - 14$, where y is the number of years and a is his age. Is the relationship between the number of years since Keith graduated and his age proportional or nonproportional?

$$y = a - 14$$

The equation is in the form $y = mx + b$, with a being used as the variable instead of x. The value of m is 1, and the value of b is -14. Since b is not 0, the relationship between the number of years since Keith graduated and his age is nonproportional.

Reflect

3. **Communicate Mathematical Ideas** In a proportional relationship, the ratio $\frac{y}{x}$ is constant. Show that this ratio is not constant for the equation $y = a - 14$.

_____

_____

4. **What If?** Suppose another equation represents Keith's age in months y given his age in years a. Is this relationship proportional? Explain.

_____

_____

YOUR TURN

Determine if each of the following equations represents a proportional or nonproportional relationship.

5. $d = 65t$

_____

6. $p = 0.1s + 2000$

_____

7. $n = 450 - 3p$

_____

8. $36 = 12d$

_____

Distinguish Between Proportional and Nonproportional Situations Using a Table

Math On the Spot
my.hrw.com

If there is not a constant rate of change in the data displayed in a table, then the table represents a nonlinear nonproportional relationship.

A linear relationship represented by a table is a proportional relationship when the quotient of each pair of numbers is constant. Otherwise, the linear relationship is nonproportional.

EXAMPLE 3

COMMON CORE   8.F.4

The values in the table represent the numbers of U.S. dollars three tourists traded for Mexican pesos. The relationship is linear. Is the relationship proportional or nonproportional?

U.S. Dollars Traded	Mexican Pesos Received
130	1,690
255	3,315
505	6,565

$$\frac{1,690}{130} = \frac{169}{13} = 13$$

$$\frac{3,315}{255} = \frac{221}{17} = 13$$

> Simplify the ratios to compare the pesos received to the dollars traded.

$$\frac{6,565}{505} = \frac{1313}{101} = 13$$

The ratio of pesos received to dollars traded is constant at 13 Mexican pesos per U.S. dollar. This is a proportional relationship.

Animated Math
my.hrw.com

Math Talk
Mathematical Practices

How could you confirm that the values in the table have a linear relationship?

YOUR TURN

Determine if the linear relationship represented by each table is a proportional or nonproportional relationship.

9.

x	y
2	30
8	90
14	150

10.

x	y
5	1
40	8
65	13

Personal Math Trainer

Online Assessment and Intervention

my.hrw.com

Comparing Proportional and Nonproportional Situations

You can use what you have learned about proportional and nonproportional relationships to compare similar real-world situations that are given using different representations.

EXAMPLE 4

COMMON CORE 8.F.2

A A laser tag league has the choice of two arenas for a tournament. In both cases, *x* is the number of hours and *y* is the total charge. Compare and contrast these two situations.

Arena A

$y = 225x$

Arena B

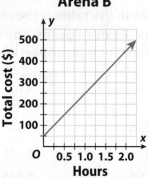

- **Arena A's** equation has the form $y = mx + b$, where $b = 0$. So, Arena A's charges are a proportional relationship. The hourly rate, $225, is greater than Arena B's, but there is no additional fee.

- **Arena B's** graph is a line that does not include the origin. So, Arena B's charges are a nonproportional relationship. Arena B has a $50 initial fee but its hourly rate, $200, is lower.

B Jessika is remodeling and has the choice of two painters. In both cases, *x* is the number of hours and *y* is the total charge. Compare and contrast these two situations.

Painter A

$y = \$45x$

Painter B

x	0	1	2	3
y	20	55	90	125

Painter A's equation has the form $y = mx + b$, where $b = 0$. So, Painter A's charges are proportional. The hourly rate, $45, is greater than Painter B's, but there is no additional fee.

Painter B's table is a nonproportional relationship because the ratio of *y* to *x* is not constant. Because the table contains the ordered pair (0, 20), Painter B charges an initial fee of $20, but the hourly rate, $35, is less than Painter A's.

11. Compare and contrast the following two situations.

Test-Prep Center A	Test-Prep Center B
The cost for Test-Prep Center A is given by $c = 20h$, where c is the cost in dollars and h is the number of hours you attend.	Test-Prep Center B charges $25 per hour to attend, but you have a $100 coupon that you can use to reduce the cost.

_____

_____

_____

_____

Guided Practice

Determine if each relationship is a proportional or nonproportional situation. Explain your reasoning.
(Explore Activity Example 1, Example 2, Example 4)

1.

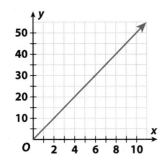

Look at the origin.

_____

_____

2.

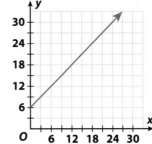

_____

_____

3. $q = 2p + \frac{1}{2}$

Compare the equation with $y = mx + b$.

_____

_____

_____

4. $v = \frac{1}{10} u$

_____

_____

_____

The tables represent linear relationships. Determine if each relationship is a proportional or nonproportional situation. (Example 3, Example 4)

5.

x	y
3	12
9	36
21	84

6.

x	y
22	4
46	8
58	10

Find the quotient of y and x.

_____   _____

_____   _____

_____   _____

7. The values in the table represent the numbers of households that watched three TV shows and the ratings of the shows. The relationship is linear. Describe the relationship in other ways. (Example 4)

Number of Households that Watched TV Show	TV Show Rating
15,000,000	12
20,000,000	16
25,000,000	20

_____

_____

_____

_____

? ESSENTIAL QUESTION CHECK-IN

8. How are using graphs, equations, and tables similar when distinguishing between proportional and nonproportional linear relationships?

_____

_____

_____

12.4 Independent Practice

 8.F.2, 8.F.3, 8.F.4

Personal
Math Trainer

Online
Assessment and
my.hrw.com Intervention

9. The graph shows the weight of a cross-country team's beverage cooler based on how much sports drink it contains.

a. Is the relationship proportional or nonproportional? Explain.

_____

_____

b. Identify and interpret the slope and the *y*-intercept.

_____

_____

In 10–11, tell if the relationship between a rider's height above the first floor and the time since the rider stepped on the elevator or escalator is proportional or nonproportional. Explain your reasoning.

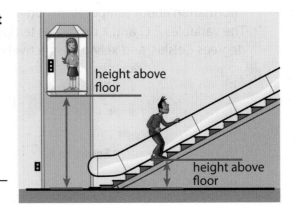

height above floor

height above floor

10. The elevator paused for 10 seconds after you stepped on before beginning to rise at a constant rate of 8 feet per second.

_____

_____

_____

11. Your height, *h*, in feet above the first floor on the escalator is given by $h = 0.75t$, where *t* is the time in seconds.

_____

12. Analyze Relationships Compare and contrast the two graphs.

Graph A

$y = \frac{1}{3}x$

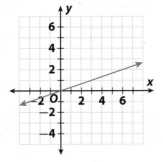

Graph B

$y = \sqrt{x}$

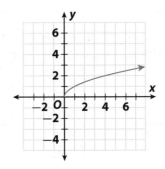

_____

_____

13. Represent Real-World Problems Describe a real-world situation where the relationship is linear and nonproportional.

_____

_____

H.O.T. FOCUS ON HIGHER ORDER THINKING

14. Mathematical Reasoning Suppose you know the slope of a linear relationship and one of the points that its graph passes through. How can you determine if the relationship is proportional or nonproportional?

_____

_____

_____

15. Multiple Representations An entrant at a science fair has included information about temperature conversion in various forms, as shown. The variables F, C, and K represent temperatures in degrees Fahrenheit, degrees Celsius, and kelvin, respectively.

Equation A $F = \frac{9}{5}C + 32$ Equation B $K = C + 273.15$	Table C	
	Degrees Celsius	kelvin
	8	281.15
	15	288.15
	36	309.15

a. Is the relationship between kelvins and degrees Celsius proportional? Justify your answer in two different ways.

_____

_____

_____

_____

b. Is the relationship between degrees Celsius and degrees Fahrenheit proportional? Why or why not?

_____

_____

_____

_____

Ready to Go On?

Personal Math Trainer

Online Assessment and Intervention

🔘 my.hrw.com

12.1 Representing Linear Nonproportional Relationships

1. Complete the table using the equation $y = 3x + 2$.

x	−1	0	1	2	3
y					

12.2 Determining Slope and *y*-intercept

2. Find the slope and *y*-intercept of the line in the graph.

_____

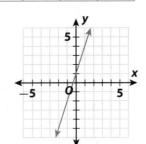

12.3 Graphing Linear Nonproportional Relationships

3. Graph the equation $y = 2x - 3$ using slope and *y*-intercept.

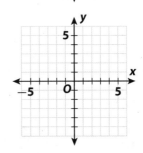

12.4 Proportional and Nonproportional Situations

4. Does the table represent a proportional or a nonproportional linear relationship?

x	1	2	3	4	5
y	4	8	12	16	20

_____

5. Does the graph in Exercise 2 represent a proportional or a nonproportional linear relationship? _____

6. Does the graph in Exercise 3 represent a proportional or a nonproportional relationship? _____

❓ ESSENTIAL QUESTION

7. How can you identify a linear nonproportional relationship from a table, a graph, and an equation?

_____

_____

MODULE 12 MIXED REVIEW

Assessment Readiness

COMMON CORE

Personal Math Trainer

Online Assessment and Intervention

my.hrw.com

Selected Response

1. The table below represents which equation?

x	-1	0	1	2
y	-10	-6	-2	2

(A) $y = -x - 10$ (C) $y = 4x - 6$

(B) $y = -6x$ (D) $y = -4x + 2$

2. The graph of which equation is shown below?

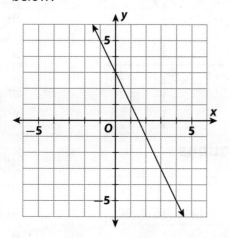

(A) $y = -2x + 3$ (C) $y = 2x + 3$

(B) $y = -2x + 1.5$ (D) $y = 2x + 1.5$

3. The table below represents a linear relationship.

x	2	3	4	5
y	4	7	10	13

What is the y-intercept?

(A) -4 (C) 2

(B) -2 (D) 3

4. Which equation represents a nonproportional relationship?

(A) $y = 3x + 0$ (C) $y = 3x + 5$

(B) $y = -3x$ (D) $y = \frac{1}{3}x$

5. The table shows a proportional relationship. What is the missing y-value?

x	4	10	12
y	6	15	$?$

(A) 16 (C) 18

(B) 20 (D) 24

6. What is 0.00000598 written in scientific notation?

(A) 5.98×10^{-6} (C) 59.8×10^{-6}

(B) 5.98×10^{-5} (D) 59.8×10^{-7}

Mini-Task

7. The graph shows a linear relationship.

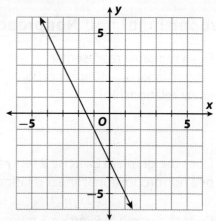

a. Is the relationship proportional or nonproportional?

_____

b. What is the slope of the line?

_____

c. What is the y-intercept of the line?

_____

d. What is the equation of the line?

_____

Writing Linear Equations

? ESSENTIAL QUESTION

How can you use linear equations to solve real-world problems?

Real-World Video

Linear equations can be used to describe many situations related to shopping. If a store advertised four books for $32.00, you could write and solve a linear equation to find the price of each book.

my.hrw.com

G◉ DIGITAL

my.hrw.com

my.hrw.com

Go digital with your write-in student edition, accessible on any device.

Math On the Spot

Scan with your smart phone to jump directly to the online edition, video tutor, and more.

Animated Math

Interactively explore key concepts to see how math works.

Personal Math Trainer

Get immediate feedback and help as you work through practice sets.

Are YOU Ready?

Complete these exercises to review skills you will need for this module.

Write Fractions as Decimals

EXAMPLE $\dfrac{0.5}{0.8} = ?$ Multiply the numerator and the denominator by a power of 10 so that the denominator is a whole number.

$$\dfrac{0.5 \times 10}{0.8 \times 10} = \dfrac{5}{8}$$

Write the fraction as a division problem.
Write a decimal point and zeros in the dividend.
Place a decimal point in the quotient.
Divide as with whole numbers.

$$\begin{array}{r} 0.625 \\ 8)\overline{5.000} \\ -48 \\ \overline{20} \\ -16 \\ \overline{40} \\ -40 \\ \overline{0} \end{array}$$

Write each fraction as a decimal.

1. $\dfrac{3}{8}$ _____

2. $\dfrac{0.3}{0.4}$ _____

3. $\dfrac{0.13}{0.2}$ _____

4. $\dfrac{0.39}{0.75}$ _____

Inverse Operations

EXAMPLE

$$5n = 20$$
$$\dfrac{5n}{5} = \dfrac{20}{5}$$
$$n = 4$$

n is multiplied by 5.
To solve the equation, use the inverse operation, division.

$$k + 7 = 9$$
$$k + 7 - 7 = 9 - 7$$
$$k = 2$$

7 is added to k.
To solve the equation, use the inverse operation, subtraction.

Solve each equation using the inverse operation.

5. $7p = 28$ _____

6. $h - 13 = 5$ _____

7. $\dfrac{y}{3} = -6$ _____

8. $b + 9 = 21$ _____

9. $c - 8 = -8$ _____

10. $3n = -12$ _____

11. $-16 = m + 7$ _____

12. $\dfrac{t}{-5} = -5$ _____

Reading Start-Up

Visualize Vocabulary

Use the ✔ words to complete the diagram. You can put more than one word in each bubble.

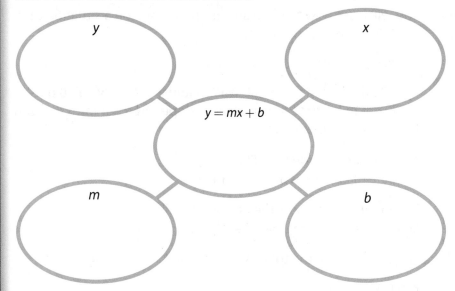

Understand Vocabulary

Complete the sentences using the preview words.

1. A set of data that is made up of two paired variables

   is _____.

2. When the rate of change varies from point to point, the relationship

   is a _____.

Vocabulary

Review Words

✔ linear equation *(ecuación lineal)*

   ordered pair *(par ordenado)*

   proportional relationship *(relación proporcional)*

   rate of change *(tasa de cambio)*

✔ slope *(pendiente)*

✔ slope-intercept form of an equation *(forma de pendiente-intersección)*

✔ x-coordinate *(coordenada x)*

✔ y-coordinate *(coordenada y)*

✔ y-intercept *(intersección con el eje y)*

Preview Words

   bivariate data *(datos bivariados)*

   nonlinear relationship *(relación no lineal)*

Active Reading

Tri-Fold Before beginning the module, create a tri-fold to help you learn the concepts and vocabulary in this module. Fold the paper into three sections. Label the columns "What I Know," "What I Need to Know," and "What I Learned." Complete the first two columns before you read. After studying the module, complete the third column.

Unpacking the Standards

Understanding the standards and the vocabulary terms in the standards will help you know exactly what you are expected to learn in this module.

COMMON CORE **8.F.4**

Construct a function to model a linear relationship between two quantities. Determine the rate of change and initial value of the function from a description of a relationship ... Interpret the rate of change and initial value of a linear function in terms of the situation it models, and in terms of its graph or a table of values.

Key Vocabulary

rate of change *(tasa de cambio)*
A ratio that compares the amount of change in a dependent variable to the amount of change in an independent variable.

What It Means to You

You will learn how to write an equation based on a situation that models a linear relationship.

UNPACKING EXAMPLE 8.F.4

In 2006 the fare for a taxicab was an initial charge of $2.50 plus $0.30 per mile. Write an equation in slope-intercept form that can be used to calculate the total fare.

The constant charge is $2.50.
The rate of change is $0.30 per mile.

The input variable, x, is the number of miles driven.
So $0.3x$ is the cost for the miles driven.

The equation for the total fare, y, is as follows:

$$y = 0.3x + 2.5$$

COMMON CORE **8.SP.3**

Use the equation of a linear model to solve problems in the context of bivariate measurement data, interpreting the slope and intercept.

Key Vocabulary

bivariate data *(datos bivariados)*
A set of data that is made up of two paired variables.

What It Means to You

You will see how to use a linear relationship between sets of data to make predictions.

UNPACKING EXAMPLE 8.SP.3

The graph shows the temperatures in degrees Celsius inside the earth at certain depths in kilometers. Use the graph to write an equation and find the temperature at a depth of 12 km.

The initial temperature is 20°C.
It increases at a rate of 10°C/km.

The equation is $t = 10d + 20$.
At a depth of 12 km, the temperature is 140°C.

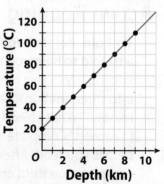

Temperature Inside Earth

Writing Linear Equations from Situations and Graphs

COMMON CORE 8.F.4

Construct a function to model a linear relationship between two quantities. Determine the rate of change and initial value.... Interpret the rate of change and initial value....

ESSENTIAL QUESTION

How do you write an equation to model a linear relationship given a graph or a description?

EXPLORE ACTIVITY   COMMON CORE 8.F.4

Writing an Equation in Slope-Intercept Form

Greta makes clay mugs and bowls as gifts at the Crafty Studio. She pays a membership fee of $15 a month and an equipment fee of $3.00 an hour to use the potter's wheel, table, and kiln. Write an equation in the form $y = mx + b$ that Greta can use to calculate her monthly costs.

A What is the input variable, x, for this situation?

_____

What is the output variable, y, for this situation?

_____

B During April, Greta does not use the equipment at all. What will be her number of hours (x) for April? _____

What will be her cost (y) for April? _____

What will be the y-intercept, b, in the equation? _____

> **Math Talk**
> **Mathematical Practices**
>
> What change could the studio make that would make a difference to the y-intercept of the equation?

C Greta spends 8 hours in May for a cost of $15 + 8(\$3) =$ _____.

In June, she spends 11 hours for a cost of _____.

From May to June, the change in x-values is _____.

From May to June, the change in y-values is _____.

What will be the slope, m, in the equation? _____

D Use the values for m and b to write an equation for Greta's costs in the form $y = mx + b$: _____

Writing an Equation from a Graph

You can use information presented in a graph to write an equation in slope-intercept form.

EXAMPLE 1 Real World

COMMON CORE   8.F.4

A video club charges a one-time membership fee plus a rental fee for each DVD borrowed. Use the graph to write an equation in slope-intercept form to represent the amount spent, y, on x DVD rentals.

Video Club Costs

STEP 1 Choose two points on the graph, (x_1, y_1) and (x_2, y_2), to find the slope.

$m = \dfrac{y_2 - y_1}{x_2 - x_1}$ Find the change in y-values over the change in x-values.

$m = \dfrac{18 - 8}{8 - 0}$ Substitute $(0, 8)$ for (x_1, y_1) and $(8, 18)$ for (x_2, y_2).

$m = \dfrac{10}{8} = 1.25$ Simplify.

STEP 2 Read the y-intercept from the graph.

The y-intercept is 8.

STEP 3 Use your slope and y-intercept values to write an equation in slope-intercept form.

$y = mx + b$ Slope-intercept form

$y = 1.25x + 8$ Substitute 1.25 for m and 8 for y.

Math Talk

Mathematical Practices

If the graph of an equation is a line that goes through the origin, what is the value of the y-intercept?

Reflect

1. What does the value of the slope represent in this context?

   _____

2. Describe the meaning of the y-intercept.

   _____

YOUR TURN

3. The cash register subtracts $2.50 from a $25 Coffee Café gift card for every medium coffee the customer buys. Use the graph to write an equation in slope-intercept form to represent this situation.

   _____

Amount on Gift Card

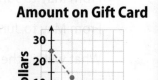

Writing an Equation from a Description

You can use information from a description of a linear relationship to find the slope and *y*-intercept and to write an equation.

EXAMPLE 2 *Real World*

COMMON CORE 8.F.4

The rent charged for space in an office building is a linear relationship related to the size of the space rented. Write an equation in slope-intercept form for the rent at West Main Street Office Rentals.

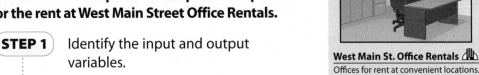

West Main St. Office Rentals 🏢
Offices for rent at convenient locations.

Monthly Rates:
600 square feet for **$750**
900 square feet for **$1150**

My Notes

STEP 1 Identify the input and output variables.

The input variable is the square footage of floor space.

The output variable is the monthly rent.

STEP 2 Write the information given in the problem as ordered pairs.

The rent for 600 square feet of floor space is $750: (600, 750)

The rent for 900 square feet of floor space is $1150: (900, 1150)

STEP 3 Find the slope.

$$m = \frac{y_2 - y_1}{x_2 - x_1} = \frac{1150 - 750}{900 - 600} = \frac{400}{300} = \frac{4}{3}$$

STEP 4 Find the *y*-intercept. Use the slope and one of the ordered pairs.

$y = mx + b$ Slope-intercept form

$750 = \frac{4}{3} \cdot 600 + b$ Substitute for *y*, *m*, and *x*.

$750 = 800 + b$ Multiply.

$-50 = b$ Subtract 800 from both sides.

STEP 5 Substitute the slope and *y*-intercept.

$y = mx + b$ Slope-intercept form

$y = \frac{4}{3}x - 50$ Substitute $\frac{4}{3}$ for *m* and −50 for *b*.

Reflect

4. Without graphing, tell whether the graph of this equation rises or falls from left to right. What does the sign of the slope mean in this context?

_____

_____

_____

YOUR TURN

5. Hari's weekly allowance varies depending on the number of chores he does. He received $16 in allowance the week he did 12 chores, and $14 in allowance the week he did 8 chores. Write an equation for his allowance in slope-intercept form. _____

Guided Practice

1. Li is making beaded necklaces. For each necklace, she uses 27 spacers, plus 5 beads per inch of necklace length. Write an equation to find how many beads Li needs for each necklace. (Explore Activity)

   a. input variable: _____

   b. output variable: _____

   c. equation: _____

2. Kate is planning a trip to the beach. She estimates her average speed to graph her expected progress on the trip. Write an equation in slope-intercept form that represents the situation. (Example 1)

   Choose two points on the graph to find the slope.

   $m = \dfrac{y_2 - y_1}{x_2 - x_1} =$ _____

   Read the y-intercept from the graph: $b =$ _____

   Use your slope and y-intercept values to write an equation in slope-intercept form. _____

   My Beach Trip

   Distance to beach (mi) — 300, 200, 100

   O 1 2 3 4 5 6
   Driving time (h)

3. At 59°F, crickets chirp at a rate of 76 times per minute, and at 65°F, they chirp 100 times per minute. Write an equation in slope-intercept form that represents the situation. (Example 2)

   Input variable: _____   Output variable: _____

   $m = \dfrac{y_2 - y_1}{x_2 - x_1} =$ _____ Use the slope and one of the ordered

   pairs in $y = mx + b$ to find b. _____ = _____ · _____ + b; _____ = b

   Write an equation in slope-intercept form. _____

? ESSENTIAL QUESTION CHECK-IN

4. Explain what m and b in the equation $y = mx + b$ tell you about the graph of the line with that equation.

   _____

   _____

13.1 Independent Practice

 COMMON CORE 8.F.4

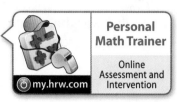
Personal Math Trainer

Online Assessment and Intervention

my.hrw.com

5. A dragonfly can beat its wings 30 times per second. Write an equation in slope-intercept form that shows the relationship between flying time in seconds and the number of times the dragonfly beats its wings.

_____

6. A balloon is released from the top of a platform that is 50 meters tall. The balloon rises at the rate of 4 meters per second. Write an equation in slope-intercept form that tells the height of the balloon above the ground after a given number of seconds.

_____

The graph shows a scuba diver's ascent over time.

7. Use the graph to find the slope of the line. Tell what the slope means in this context.

_____

_____

Scuba Diver's Ascent

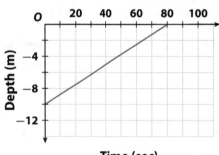

8. Identify the *y*-intercept. Tell what the *y*-intercept means in this context.

_____

9. Write an equation in slope-intercept form that represents the diver's depth over time.

_____

10. The formula for converting Celsius temperatures to Fahrenheit temperatures is a linear equation. Water freezes at 0 °C, or 32 °F, and it boils at 100 °C, or 212 °F. Find the slope and *y*-intercept for a graph that gives degrees Celsius on the horizontal axis and degrees Fahrenheit on the vertical axis. Then write an equation in slope-intercept form that converts degrees Celsius into degrees Fahrenheit.

_____

_____

11. The cost of renting a sailboat at a lake is $20 per hour plus $12 for lifejackets. Write an equation in slope-intercept form that can be used to calculate the total amount you would pay for using this sailboat.

_____

The graph shows the activity in a savings account.

12. What was the amount of the initial deposit that started this savings account?

   _____

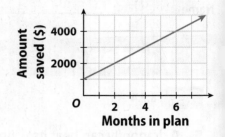

13. Find the slope and *y*-intercept of the graphed line.

   _____

14. Write an equation in slope-intercept form for the activity in this savings account.

   _____

15. Explain the meaning of the slope in this graph.

   _____

   _____

 FOCUS ON HIGHER ORDER THINKING

Work Area

16. **Communicate Mathematical Ideas** Explain how you decide which part of a problem will be represented by the variable *x*, and which part will be represented by the variable *y* in a graph of the situation.

   _____

   _____

   _____

   _____

17. **Represent Real-World Problems** Describe what would be true about the rate of change in a situation that could *not* be represented by a graphed line and an equation in the form $y = mx + b$.

   _____

   _____

   _____

18. **Draw Conclusions** Must *m*, in the equation $y = mx + b$, always be a positive number? Explain.

   _____

   _____

   _____

Writing Linear Equations from a Table

COMMON CORE 8.F.4

Construct a function to model a linear relationship between two quantities. Determine the rate of change and initial value.... Interpret the rate of change and initial value....

ESSENTIAL QUESTION

How do you write an equation to model a linear relationship given a table?

EXPLORE ACTIVITY COMMON CORE 8.F.4

Graphing from a Table to Write an Equation

Math On the Spot
⏻ my.hrw.com

You can use information from a table to draw a graph of a linear relationship and to write an equation for the graphed line.

EXAMPLE 1 The table shows the temperature of a fish tank during an experiment. Graph the data, and find the slope and *y*-intercept from the graph. Then write the equation for the graph in slope-intercept form.

Time (h)	0	1	2	3	4	5
Temperature (°F)	82	80	78	76	74	72

STEP 1 Graph the ordered pairs from the table (time, temperature).

STEP 2 Draw a line through the points.

STEP 3 Choose two points on the graph to find the slope: for example, choose (0, 82) and (1, 80).

$$m = \frac{y_2 - y_1}{x_2 - x_1} = \frac{\boxed{} - \boxed{}}{\boxed{} - \boxed{}} = \underline{}$$

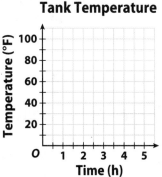

Tank Temperature

STEP 4 Read the *y*-intercept from the graph.

$$b = \underline{}$$

STEP 5 Use these slope and *y*-intercept values to write an equation in slope-intercept form.

$$y = mx + b$$

$$y = \boxed{}x + \boxed{}$$

YOUR TURN

1. The table shows the volume of water released by Hoover Dam over a certain period of time. Graph the data, and find the slope and *y*-intercept from the graph. Then write the equation for the graph in slope-intercept form.

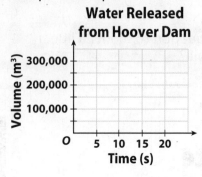

Water Released from Hoover Dam

Time (s)	Volume of water (m³)
5	75,000
10	150,000
15	225,000
20	300,000

Personal Math Trainer

Online Assessment and Intervention

⏱ my.hrw.com

Math On the Spot

⏱ my.hrw.com

Animated Math

⏱ my.hrw.com

Writing an Equation from a Table

The information from a table can also help you to write the equation that represents a given situation without drawing the graph.

EXAMPLE 2

 8.F.4

Elizabeth's cell phone plan lets her choose how many minutes are included each month. The table shows the plan's monthly cost *y* for a given number of included minutes *x*. Write an equation in slope-intercept form to represent the situation.

Minutes included, x	100	200	300	400	500
Cost of plan ($), y	14	20	26	32	38

STEP 1 Notice that the change in cost is the same for each increase of 100 minutes. So, the relationship is linear. Choose any two ordered pairs from the table to find the slope.

$$m = \frac{y_2 - y_1}{x_2 - x_1} = \frac{(20 - 14)}{(200 - 100)} = \frac{6}{100} = 0.06$$

STEP 2 Find the *y*-intercept. Use the slope and any point from the table.

$y = mx + b$	Slope-intercept form
$14 = 0.06 \cdot 100 + b$	Substitute for *y*, *m*, and *x*.
$14 = 6 + b$	Multiply.
$8 = b$	Subtract 6 from both sides.

STEP 3 Substitute the slope and *y*-intercept.

$y = mx + b$	Slope-intercept form
$y = 0.06x + 8$	Substitute 0.06 for *m* and 8 for *b*.

Reflect

2. What is the base price for the cell phone plan, regardless of how many minutes are included? What is the cost per minute? Explain.

_____

_____

_____

_____

_____

3. **What If?** Elizabeth's cell phone company changes the cost of her plan as shown below. Write an equation in slope-intercept form to represent the situation. How did the plan change?

Minutes included, x	100	200	300	400	500
Cost of plan ($), y	30	35	40	45	50

_____

_____

Math Talk

Mathematical Practices

Explain the meaning of the slope and y-intercept of the equation.

YOUR TURN

4. A salesperson receives a weekly salary plus a commission for each computer sold. The table shows the total pay, p, and the number of computers sold, n. Write an equation in slope-intercept form to represent this situation.

Number of computers sold, n	4	6	8	10	12
Total pay ($), p	550	700	850	1000	1150

_____

5. To rent a van, a moving company charges $40.00 plus $0.50 per mile. The table shows the total cost, c, and the number of miles driven, d. Write an equation in slope-intercept form to represent this situation.

Number of miles driven, d	10	20	30	40	50
Total cost ($), c	45	50	55	60	65

_____

Personal Math Trainer

Online Assessment and Intervention

my.hrw.com

1. Jaime purchased a $20 bus pass. Each time he rides the bus, a certain amount is deducted from the pass. The table shows the amount, *y*, left on his pass after *x* rides. Graph the data, and find the slope and *y*-intercept from the graph or from the table. Then write the equation for the graph in slope-intercept form. (Explore Activity Example 1)

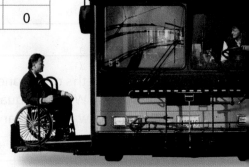

Number of rides, *x*	0	4	8	12	16
Amount left on pass ($), *y*	20	15	10	5	0

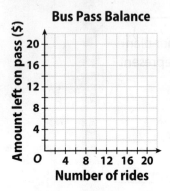

Bus Pass Balance

_____

The table shows the temperature (*y*) at different altitudes (*x*). This is a linear relationship. (Example 2)

Altitude (ft), *x*	0	2,000	4,000	6,000	8,000	10,000	12,000
Temperature (°F), *y*	59	51	43	35	27	19	11

2. Find the slope for this relationship.

_____

3. Find the *y*-intercept for this relationship.

_____

4. Write an equation in slope-intercept form that represents this relationship.

_____

5. Use your equation to determine the temperature at an altitude of 5000 feet.

_____

? ESSENTIAL QUESTION CHECK-IN

6. Describe how you can use the information in a table showing a linear relationship to find the slope and *y*-intercept for the equation.

_____

_____

_____

13.2 Independent Practice

COMMON CORE 8.F.4

Personal Math Trainer

Online Assessment and Intervention

my.hrw.com

7. The table shows the costs of a large cheese pizza with toppings at a local pizzeria. Graph the data, and find the slope and y-intercept from the graph. Then write the equation for the graph in slope-intercept form.

Cost of Large Pizza

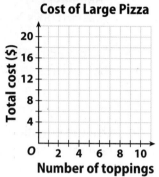

Number of toppings, t	0	1	2	3	4	5
Total cost ($), C	8	10	12	14	16	18

_____

8. The table shows how much an air-conditioning repair company charges for different numbers of hours of work. Graph the data, and find the slope and y-intercept from the graph. Then write the equation for the graph in slope-intercept form.

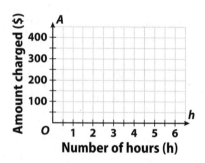

Number of hours (h), t	0	1	2	3	4	5
Amount charged ($), A	50	100	150	200	250	300

_____

9. A friend gave Ms. Morris a gift card for a local car wash. The table shows the linear relationship of how the value left on the card relates to the number of car washes.

Number of car washes, x	0	8	12
Amount left on card ($), y	30	18	12

a. Write an equation that shows the number of dollars left on the card.

_____

b. Explain the meaning of the negative slope in this situation.

_____

_____

c. What is the maximum value of x that makes sense in this context? Explain.

_____

The tables show linear relationships between x and y. Write an equation in slope-intercept form for each relationship.

10.

x	−2	−1	0	2
y	−1	0	1	3

11.

x	−4	1	0	6
y	14	4	6	−6

_____

12. Finance Desiree starts a savings account with $125.00. Every month, she deposits $53.50.

   a. Complete the table to model the situation.

Month, x					
Amount in Savings ($), y					

   b. Write an equation in slope-intercept form that shows how much money Desiree has in her savings account after x months.

   _____

   c. Use the equation to find how much money Desiree will have in savings after 11 months.

   _____

13. Monty documented the amount of rain his farm received on a monthly basis, as shown in the table.

Month, x	1	2	3	4	5
Rainfall (in.), y	5	3	4.5	1	7

   a. Is the relationship linear? Why or why not?

   _____

   _____

   b. Can an equation be written to describe the amount of rain? Explain.

   _____

H.O.T. **FOCUS ON HIGHER ORDER THINKING**

Work Area

14. Analyze Relationships If you have a table that shows a linear relationship, when can you read the value for b, in $y = mx + b$, directly from the table without drawing a graph or doing any calculations? Explain.

   _____

   _____

15. What If? Jaíme graphed linear data given in the form (cost, number). The y-intercept was 0. Jayla graphed the same data given in the form (number, cost). What was the y-intercept of her graph? Explain.

   _____

   _____

   _____

Linear Relationships and Bivariate Data

COMMON CORE 8.SP.1

Construct and interpret scatter plots for bivariate measurement data.... .
Describe patterns such as... linear association, and nonlinear association. *Also 8.SP.2, 8.SP.3*

ESSENTIAL QUESTION

How can you contrast linear and nonlinear sets of bivariate data?

EXPLORE ACTIVITY COMMON CORE **8.SP.2**

Math On the Spot
my.hrw.com

Finding the Equation of a Linear Relationship

You can use the points on a graph of a linear relationship to write an equation for the relationship. The equation of a linear relationship is $y = mx + b$, where m is the rate of change, or slope, and b is the value of y when x is 0.

EXAMPLE 1 **A handrail runs alongside a stairway. As the horizontal distance from the bottom of the stairway changes, the height of the handrail changes. Show that the relationship is linear, and then find the equation for the relationship.**

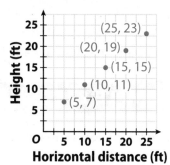

STEP 1 Show that the relationship is linear.

All of the points (5, 7), (10, 11), (15, 15), (20, 19), and (25, 23) lie on the same _____, so the relationship is _____. Draw a line through the points on the graph.

STEP 2 Write the equation of the linear relationship.

Choose two points to find the slope: (5, 7) and (25, 23).

$$m = \frac{23 - \boxed{}}{\boxed{} - 5}$$

$$= \frac{\boxed{}}{\boxed{}}, \text{ or } \underline{}$$

Choose a point and use the slope to substitute values for x, y, and m.

$$y = mx + b$$

$$\boxed{} = \boxed{}(5) + b$$

$$\boxed{} = \boxed{} + b$$

$$\boxed{} = b$$

The equation of the linear relationship is $y = \boxed{}x + \boxed{}$.

YOUR TURN

Find the equation of each linear relationship.

1.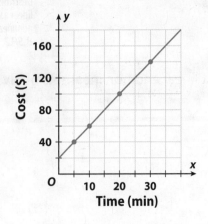
_____

2.

Hours (x)	Number of units (y)
2	480
15	3,600
24	5,760
30	7,200
48	11,520
55	13,200

_____

Personal Math Trainer

Online Assessment and Intervention

🔵 my.hrw.com

Math On the Spot

🔵 my.hrw.com

Making Predictions

You can use an equation of a linear relationship to predict a value between data points that you already know.

EXAMPLE 2 *Real World*

COMMON CORE 8.SP.3

The graph shows the cost for taxi rides of different distances. Predict the cost of a taxi ride that covers a distance of 6.5 miles.

STEP 1 Write the equation of the linear relationship.

(2, 7) and (6, 15) Select two points.

$m = \dfrac{15 - 7}{6 - 2}$ Calculate the rate of change.

$= \dfrac{8}{4}$ Simplify.

$= 2$

$y = mx + b$

$15 = 2(6) + b$ Fill in values for x, y, and m.

$15 = 12 + b$ Simplify.

$3 = b$ Solve for b.

The equation of the linear relationship is $y = 2x + 3$.

You can check your equation using another point on the graph. Try (8, 19). Substituting gives $19 = 2(8) + 3$. The right side simplifies to 19, so $19 = 19$. ✓

STEP 2 Use your equation from Step 1 to predict the cost of a 6.5-mile taxi ride.

$y = 2x + 3$

$y = 2(6.5) + 3$ Substitute $x = 6.5$.

Solve for y.

$y = 16$

A taxi ride that covers a distance of 6.5 miles will cost $16.

Reflect

3. **What If?** Suppose a regulation changes the cost of the taxi ride to $1.80 per mile, plus a fee of $4.30. How does the price of the 6.5 mile ride compare to the original price?

_____

_____

4. How can you use a graph of a linear relationship to predict an unknown value of y for a given value of x within the region of the graph?

_____

_____

_____

5. How can you use a table of linear data to predict a value?

_____

_____

_____

YOUR TURN

Paulina's income from a job that pays her a fixed amount per hour is shown in the graph. Use the graph to find the predicted value.

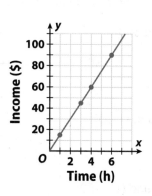

6. Income earned for working 2 hours

_____

7. Income earned for working 3.25 hours

_____

8. Total income earned for working for five 8-hour days all at the standard rate _____

Personal Math Trainer

Online Assessment and Intervention

⏻ my.hrw.com

Contrasting Linear and Nonlinear Data

Bivariate data is a set of data that is made up of two paired variables. If the relationship between the variables is linear, then the rate of change (slope) is constant. If the graph shows a **nonlinear relationship**, then the rate of change varies between pairs of points.

Andrew has two options in which to invest $200. Option A earns simple interest of 5%, while Option B earns interest of 5% compounded annually. The table shows the amount of the investment for both options over 20 years. Graph the data and describe the differences between the two graphs.

Year, x	Option A Total ($)	Option B Total ($)
0	200.00	200.00
5	250.00	255.26
10	300.00	325.78
15	350.00	415.79
20	400.00	530.66

STEP 1 Graph the data from the table for Options A and B on the same coordinate grid.

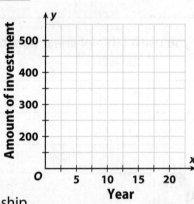

STEP 2 Find the rate of change between pairs of points for Option A and classify the relationship.

Option A	Rate of Change
(0, 200) and (5, 250)	$m = \dfrac{250 - 200}{5 - 0} = $ _____
(5, 250) and (10, 300)	
(10, 300) and (15, 350)	

The rate of change between the data values is _____, so

the graph of Option A shows a _____ relationship.

STEP 3 Find the rate of change between pairs of points for Option B and classify the relationship.

Option B	Rate of Change
(0, 200) and (5, 255.26)	$m = \dfrac{252.26 - 200}{5 - 0} \approx$ _____
(5, 255.26) and (10, 325.78)	
(10, 325.78) and (15, 415.79)	

The rate of change between the data values is _____,

so the graph of Option B shows a _____ relationship.

Reflect

9. Why are the graphs drawn as lines or curves and not discrete points?

_____

_____

_____

_____

10. Can you determine by viewing the graph if the data have a linear or nonlinear relationship? Explain.

_____

_____

_____

_____

11. Draw Conclusions Find the differences in the account balances to the nearest dollar at 5 year intervals for Option B. How does the length of time that money is in an account affect the advantage that compound interest has over simple interest?

_____

_____

_____

Guided Practice

Use the following graphs to find the equation of the linear relationship. (Explore Activity Example 1)

1.

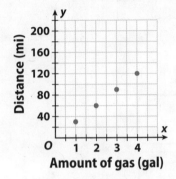

_____

2.

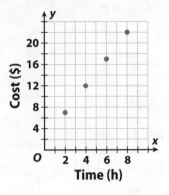

_____

3. The graph shows the relationship between the number of hours a kayak is rented and the total cost of the rental. Write an equation of the relationship. Then use the equation to predict the cost of a rental that lasts 5.5 hours. (Example 2)

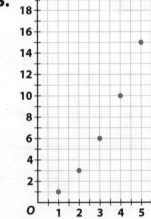

_____

Does each of the following graphs represent a linear relationship? Why or why not? (Explore Activity 2)

4.

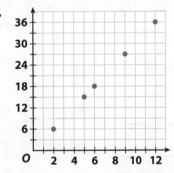

_____

_____

5.

_____

_____

ESSENTIAL QUESTION CHECK-IN

6. How can you tell if a set of bivariate data shows a linear relationship?

_____

_____

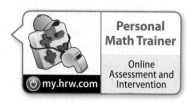

13.3 Independent Practice

COMMON CORE 8.SP.1, 8.SP.2, 8.SP.3

Does each of the following tables represent a linear relationship? Why or why not?

7.

Number of boxes	Weight (kg)
3	15
9	45
21	105

8.

Day	Height (cm)
5	30
8	76.8
14	235.2

_____   _____

_____   _____

Explain whether or not you think each relationship is linear.

9. the cost of equal-priced DVDs and the number purchased

_____

10. the height of a person and the person's age

_____

11. the area of a square quilt and its side length

_____

_____

12. the number of miles to the next service station and the number of kilometers

_____

_____

13. Multistep The Mars Rover travels 0.75 feet in 6 seconds. Add the point to the graph. Then determine whether the relationship between distance and time is linear, and if so, predict the distance that the Mars Rover would travel in 1 minute.

_____

_____

_____

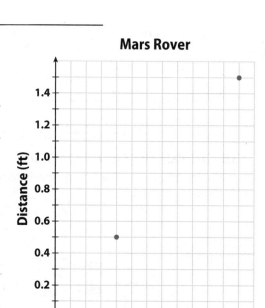

Mars Rover

14. **Make a Conjecture** Zefram analyzed a linear relationship, found that the slope-intercept equation was $y = 3.5x + 16$, and made a prediction for the value of y for a given value of x. He realized that he made an error calculating the y-intercept and that it was actually 12. Can he just subtract 4 from his prediction if he knows that the slope is correct? Explain.

_____

_____

 **FOCUS ON HIGHER ORDER THINKING**

15. **Communicate Mathematical Ideas** The table shows a linear relationship. How can you predict the value of y when $x = 6$ without finding the equation of the relationship?

x	y
4	38
8	76
12	114

_____

_____

_____

16. **Critique Reasoning** Louis says that if the differences between the values of x are constant between all the points on a graph, then the relationship is linear. Do you agree? Explain.

_____

_____

_____

17. **Make a Conjecture** Suppose you know the slope of a linear relationship and one of the points that its graph passes through. How could you predict another point that falls on the graph of the line?

_____

_____

_____

18. **Explain the Error** Thomas used (7, 17.5) and (18, 45) from a graph to find the equation of a linear relationship as shown. What was his mistake?

$$m = \frac{45 - 7}{18 - 17.5} = \frac{38}{0.5} = 79$$

$$y = 79x + b$$

$$45 = 79 \cdot 18 + b$$

$$45 = 1422 + b, \text{ so } b = -1377$$

The equation is $y = 79x - 1377$.

Ready to Go On?

Personal
Math Trainer

Online Assessment
and Intervention

⏻ my.hrw.com

13.1 Writing Linear Equations from Situations and Graphs

Write the equation of each line in slope-intercept form.

1.

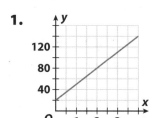

_____

2.

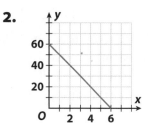

_____

13.2 Writing Linear Equations from a Table

Write the equation of each linear relationship in slope-intercept form.

3.

x	0	100	200	300
y	1.5	36.5	71.5	106.5

_____

4.

x	25	35	45	55
y	94	88	82	76

_____

13.3 Linear Relationships and Bivariate Data

Write the equation of the line that connects each set of data points.

5.

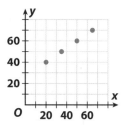

_____

6.

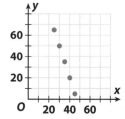

_____

❓ ESSENTIAL QUESTION

7. Write a real-world situation that can be represented by a linear
relationship.

_____

_____

MODULE 13 MIXED REVIEW

COMMON CORE

Assessment Readiness

Personal Math Trainer

Online Assessment and Intervention

my.hrw.com

Selected Response

1. An hourglass is turned over with the top part filled with sand. After 3 minutes, there are 855 mL of sand in the top half. After 10 minutes, there are 750 mL of sand in the top half. Which equation represents this situation?

Ⓐ $y = 285x$

Ⓑ $y = -10.5x + 900$

Ⓒ $y = -15x + 900$

Ⓓ $y = 75x$

2. Which graph shows a linear relationship?

Ⓐ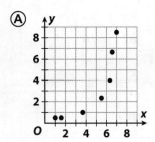

Ⓑ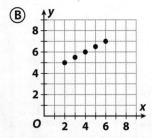

Ⓒ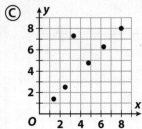

Ⓓ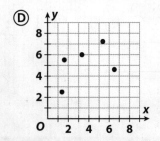

3. What are the slope and y-intercept of the relationship shown in the table?

x	10,000	20,000	30,000
y	2,500	3,000	3,500

Ⓐ slope = 0.05, y-intercept = 1,500

Ⓑ slope = 0.5, y-intercept = 1,500

Ⓒ slope = 0.05, y-intercept = 2,000

Ⓓ slope = 0.5, y-intercept = 2,000

4. Which is the sum of $3.15 \times 10^7 + 9.3 \times 10^6$? Write your answer in scientific notation.

Ⓐ 4.08×10^7

Ⓑ 4.08×10^6

Ⓒ 0.408×10^8

Ⓓ 40.8×10^6

Mini-Task

5. Franklin's faucet was leaking, so he put a bucket underneath to catch the water. After a while, Franklin started keeping track of how much water was in the bucket. His data is in the table below.

Hours	2	3	4	5
Quarts	5	6.5	8	9.5

a. Is the relationship linear or nonlinear?

_____

b. Write the equation for the relationship.

_____

c. Predict how much water will be in the bucket after 14 hours if Franklin doesn't stop the leak.

_____

Functions

? **ESSENTIAL QUESTION**

How can you use functions to solve real-world problems?

Real-World Video

Computerized machines can assist doctors in surgeries such as laser vision correction. Each action the surgeon takes results in one end action by the machine. In math, functions also have a one-in-one-out relationship.

my.hrw.com

 GO DIGITAL
my.hrw.com

my.hrw.com

Go digital with your write-in student edition, accessible on any device.

Math On the Spot

Scan with your smart phone to jump directly to the online edition, video tutor, and more.

Animated Math

Interactively explore key concepts to see how math works.

Personal Math Trainer

Get immediate feedback and help as you work through practice sets.

Are YOU Ready?

Complete these exercises to review skills you will need for this module.

Personal Math Trainer

Online Assessment and Intervention

my.hrw.com

Evaluate Expressions

EXAMPLE Evaluate $3x - 5$ for $x = -2$.

$$3x - 5 = 3(-2) - 5$$ *Substitute the given value of x for x.*

$$= -6 - 5$$ *Multiply.*

$$= -11$$ *Subtract.*

Evaluate each expression for the given value of x.

1. $2x + 3$ for $x = 3$ _____

2. $-4x + 7$ for $x = -1$ _____

3. $1.5x - 2.5$ for $x = 3$ _____

4. $0.4x + 6.1$ for $x = -5$ _____

5. $\frac{2}{3}x - 12$ for $x = 18$ _____

6. $-\frac{5}{8}x + 10$ for $x = -8$ _____

Connect Words and Equations

EXAMPLE Erik's earnings equal 9 dollars per hour.

e = earnings; h = hours

multiplication

$e = 9 \times h$

Define the variables used in the situation.

Identify the operation involved. "Per" indicates multiplication.

Write the equation.

Define the variables for each situation. Then write an equation.

7. Jana's age plus 5 equals her sister's age.

_____

8. Andrew's class has 3 more students than Lauren's class.

_____

9. The bank is 50 feet shorter than the firehouse.

_____

10. The pencils were divided into 6 groups of 2.

_____

Reading Start-Up

Visualize Vocabulary

Use the ✔ words to complete the diagram. You can put more than one word in each section of the diagram.

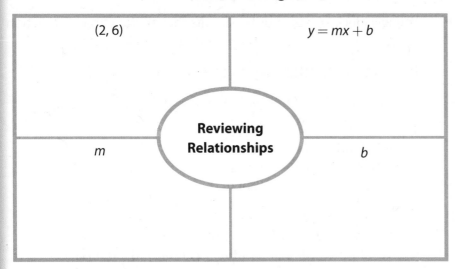

(2, 6)	$y = mx + b$
m	b

Reviewing Relationships

Understand Vocabulary

Complete the sentences using the preview words.

1. A rule that assigns exactly one output to each input

   is a _____.

2. The value that is put into a function is the _____.

3. The result after applying the function machine's rule is

   the _____.

Vocabulary

Review Words

✔ bivariate data (*datos bivariados*)

✔ linear equation (*ecuación lineal*)

  nonlinear relationship (*relación no lineal*)

✔ ordered pair (*par ordenado*)

  proporational relationship (*relación proporcional*)

✔ slope (*pendiente*)

✔ x-coordinate (*coordenada x*)

✔ y-coordinate (*coordenada y*)

✔ y-intercept (*intersección con el eje y*)

Preview Words

  function (*función*)

  input (*valor de entrada*)

  linear function (*función lineal*)

  output (*valor de salida*)

Active Reading

Double-Door Fold Create a double-door fold to help you understand the concepts in this module. Label one flap "Proportional Functions" and the other flap "Non-proportional Functions." As you study each lesson, write important ideas under the appropriate flap. Include any sample problems that will help you remember the concepts when you look back at your notes.

Unpacking the Standards

Understanding the standards and the vocabulary terms in the standards will help you know exactly what you are expected to learn in this module.

COMMON CORE **8.F.1**

Understand that a function is a rule that assigns to each input exactly one output. The graph of a function is the set of ordered pairs consisting of an input and the corresponding output.

Key Vocabulary

function *(función)*
An input-output relationship that has exactly one output for each input.

What It Means to You

You will identify sets of ordered pairs that are functions. A function is a rule that assigns exactly one output to each input.

UNPACKING EXAMPLE 8.F.1

Does the following table of inputs and outputs represent a function?

Yes, it is a function because each number in the input column is assigned to only one number in the output column.

Input	Output
14	110
20	130
22	120
30	110

The graph of the function is the set of ordered pairs (14, 110), (20, 130), (22, 120), and (30, 110).

COMMON CORE **8.F.2**

Compare properties of two functions each represented in a different way (algebraically, graphically, numerically in tables, or by verbal descriptions).

What It Means to You

You will learn to identify and compare functions expressed as equations and tables.

UNPACKING EXAMPLE 8.F.2

A spider descends a 20-foot drainpipe at a rate of 2.5 feet per minute. Another spider descends a drainpipe as shown in the table. Find and compare the rates of change and initial values of the linear functions in terms of the situations they model.

Spider #1: $f(x) = -2.5x + 20$

Spider #2:

Time (min)	0	1	2
Height (ft)	32	29	26

For Spider #1, the rate of change is -2.5, and the initial value is 20. For Spider #2, the rate of change is -3, and the initial value is 32.

Spider #2 started at 32 feet, which is 12 feet higher than Spider #1. Spider #1 is descending at 2.5 feet per minute, which is 0.5 foot per minute slower than Spider #2.

Visit **my.hrw.com** to see all the **Common Core Standards** unpacked.

my.hrw.com

LESSON 14.1 Identifying and Representing Functions

COMMON CORE 8.F.1

Understand that a function is a rule that assigns to each input exactly one output. The graph of a function is the set of ordered pairs consisting of an input and the corresponding output.

ESSENTIAL QUESTION

How can you identify and represent functions?

EXPLORE ACTIVITY **COMMON CORE** 8.F.1

Understanding Relationships

Carlos needs to buy some new pencils from the school supply store at his school. Carlos asks his classmates if they know how much pencils cost. Angela says she bought 2 pencils for $0.50. Paige bought 3 pencils for $0.75, and Spencer bought 4 pencils for $1.00.

Carlos thinks about the rule for the price of a pencil as a machine. When he puts the number of pencils he wants to buy into the machine, the machine applies a rule and tells him the total cost of that number of pencils.

Input  **Output**

	Number of Pencils	Rule	Total Cost
i.	2	?	
ii.	3	?	
iii.	4	?	
iv.	x		
v.	12		

A Use the prices in the problem to fill in total cost in rows **i–iii** of the table.

B Describe any patterns you see. Use your pattern to determine the cost of 1 pencil.

_____

_____

_____

C Use the pattern you identified to write the rule applied by the machine. Write the rule as an algebraic expression and fill in rule column row **iv** of the table.

D Carlos wants to buy 12 pencils. Use your rule to fill in row **v** of the table to show how much Carlos will pay for 12 pencils.

Reflect

1. How did you decide what operation to use in your rule?

_____

_____

2. **What If?** Carlos decides to buy erasers in a package. There are 6 pencil-top erasers in 2 packages of erasers.

a. Write a rule in words for the number of packages Carlos needs to buy to get *x* erasers. Then write the rule as an algebraic expression.

_____

_____

b. How many packages does Carlos need to buy to get 18 erasers?

_____

Math On the Spot
🔵 my.hrw.com

Identifying Functions from Mapping Diagrams

A **function** assigns exactly one output to each input. The value that is put into a function is the **input**. The result is the **output**.

A mapping diagram can be used to represent a relationship between input values and output values. A mapping diagram represents a function if each input value is paired with only one output value.

EXAMPLE 1   COMMON CORE 8.F.1

Determine whether each relationship is a function.

A

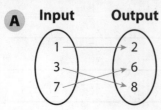

Since each input value is paired with only one output value, the relationship is a function.

Determine whether each relationship is a function.

B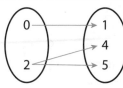

Since 2 is paired with more than one output value (both 4 and 5), the relationship is not a function.

Reflect

3. Is it possible for a function to have more than one input value but only one output value? Provide an illustration to support your answer.

_____

Determine whether each relationship is a function. Explain.

4.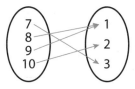

_____

_____

_____

5.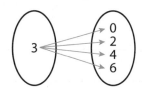

_____

_____

_____

Personal Math Trainer

Online Assessment and Intervention

ⓒ my.hrw.com

Math Talk

Mathematical Practices

What is always true about a mapping diagram that represents a function?

Identifying Functions from Tables

Relationships between input values and output values can also be represented using tables. The values in the first column are the input values. The values in the second column are the output values. The relationship represents a function if each input value is paired with only one output value.

Math On the Spot

ⓒ my.hrw.com

EXAMPLE 2

COMMON CORE 8.F.1

My Notes

Determine whether each relationship is a function.

A

Input	Output
5	7
10	6
15	15
20	2
25	15

Since 15 is a repeated output value, one output value is paired with two input values. If this occurs in a relationship, the relationship can still be a function.

Since each input value is paired with only one output value, the relationship is a function.

Determine whether each relationship is a function.

B

Input	Output
1	10
5	8
4	6
1	4
7	2

> Since 1 is a repeated input value, one input value is paired with two output values. Look back at the rule for functions. Is this relationship a function?

Since the input value 1 is paired with more than one output value (both 10 and 4), the relationship is not a function.

Reflect

6. What is always true about the numbers in the first column of a table that represents a function? Why must this be true?

_____

_____

_____

_____

_____

YOUR TURN

Determine whether each relationship is a function. Explain

7.

Input	Output
53	53
24	24
32	32
17	17
45	45

8.

Input	Output
14	52
8	21
27	16
36	25
8	34

_____   _____

_____   _____

_____   _____

_____   _____

Personal Math Trainer

Online Assessment and Intervention

⏻ my.hrw.com

Identifying Functions from Graphs

Graphs can be used to display relationships between two sets of numbers. Each point on a graph represents an ordered pair. The first coordinate in each ordered pair is the input value. The second coordinate is the output value. The graph represents a function if each input value is paired with only one output value.

Math On the Spot
my.hrw.com

EXAMPLE 3

COMMON CORE 8.F.1

The graph shows the relationship between the number of hours students spent studying for an exam and the exam grades. Is the relationship represented by the graph a function?

The input values are the number of hours spent studying by each student. The output values are the exam grades. The points represent the following ordered pairs:

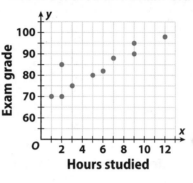

Hours Studied and Exam Grade

| (1, 70) | (2, 70) | (2, 85) | (3, 75) | (5, 80) |
| (6, 82) | (7, 88) | (9, 90) | (9, 95) | (12, 98) |

Notice that 2 is paired with both 70 and 85, and 9 is paired with both 90 and 95. Therefore, since these input values are paired with more than one output value, the relationship is not a function.

Reflect

9. Many real-world relationships are functions. For example, the amount of money made at a car wash is a function of the number of cars washed. Give another example of a real-world function.

_____

_____

YOUR TURN

10. The graph shows the relationship between the heights and weights of the members of a basketball team. Is the relationship represented by the graph a function? Explain.

_____

_____

_____

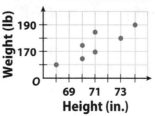

Heights and Weights of Team Members

Personal Math Trainer

Online Assessment and Intervention

my.hrw.com

Complete each table. In the row with *x* as the input, write a rule as an algebraic expression for the output. Then complete the last row of the table using the rule. (Explore Activity)

1.

Input	Output
Tickets	Cost ($)
2	40
5	100
7	140
x	
10	

2.

Input	Output
Minutes	Pages
2	1
10	5
20	10
x	
30	

3.

Input	Output
Muffins	Cost ($)
1	2.25
3	6.75
6	13.50
x	
12	

Determine whether each relationship is a function. (Examples 1 and 2)

4.

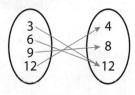

_____

_____

_____

5.

Input	Output
3	20
4	25
5	30
4	35
6	40

_____

_____

_____

6. The graph shows the relationship between the weights of 5 packages and the shipping charge for each package. Is the relationship represented by the graph a function? Explain.

_____

_____

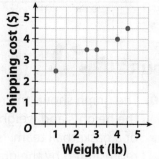

Weights and Shipping Costs

? ESSENTIAL QUESTION CHECK-IN

7. What are four different ways of representing functions? How can you tell if a relationship is a function?

_____

_____

14.1 Independent Practice

 8.F.1

Personal Math Trainer

Online Assessment and Intervention

my.hrw.com

Determine whether each relationship represented by the ordered pairs is a function. Explain.

8. (2, 2), (3, 1), (5, 7), (8, 0), (9, 1)

_____

_____

_____

9. (0, 4), (5, 1), (2, 8), (6, 3), (5, 9)

_____

_____

_____

10. Draw Conclusions Joaquin receives $0.40 per pound for 1 to 99 pounds of aluminum cans he recycles. He receives $0.50 per pound if he recycles more than 100 pounds. Is the amount of money Joaquin receives a function of the weight of the cans he recycles? Explain your reasoning.

_____

_____

_____

11. A biologist tracked the growth of a strain of bacteria, as shown in the graph.

a. Explain why the relationship represented by the graph is a function.

_____

_____

_____

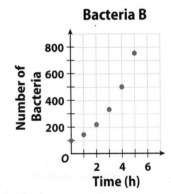

Bacteria B

b. What If? Suppose there was the same number of bacteria for two consecutive hours. Would the graph still represent a function? Explain.

_____

12. Multiple Representations Give an example of a function in everyday life, and represent it as a graph, a table, and a set of ordered pairs. Describe how you know it is a function.

_____

x				
y				

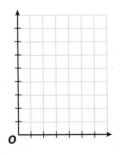

The graph shows the relationship between the weights of six wedges of cheese and the price of each wedge.

Cost of Cheese

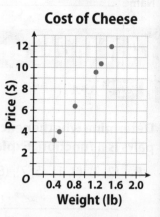

13. Is the relationship represented by the graph a function? Justify your reasoning. Use the words "input" and "output" in your explanation, and connect them to the context represented by the graph.

_____

_____

14. **Analyze Relationships** Suppose the weights and prices of additional wedges of cheese were plotted on the graph. Might that change your answer to question 13? Explain your reasoning.

_____

_____

_____

_____

  FOCUS ON HIGHER ORDER THINKING

Work Area

15. **Justify Reasoning** A mapping diagram represents a relationship that contains three different input values and four different output values. Is the relationship a function? Explain your reasoning.

_____

_____

_____

_____

16. **Communicate Mathematical Ideas** An onion farmer is hiring workers to help harvest the onions. He knows that the number of days it will take to harvest the onions is a function of the number of workers he hires. Explain the use of the word "function" in this context.

_____

_____

_____

_____

_____

_____

LESSON
14.2 Describing Functions

COMMON CORE 8.F.3

Interpret the equation $y = mx + b$ as defining a linear function, whose graph is a straight line; give examples of functions that are not linear.
Also 8.F.1.1

? ESSENTIAL QUESTION

What are some characteristics that you can use to describe functions?

EXPLORE ACTIVITY COMMON CORE 8.F.1

Investigating a Constant Rate of Change

The U.S. Department of Agriculture defines heavy rain as rain that falls at a rate of 1.5 centimeters per hour.

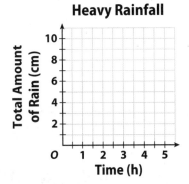

A The table shows the total amount of rain that falls in various amounts of time during a heavy rain. Complete the table.

Time (h)	0	1	2	3	4	5
Total Amount of Rain (cm)	0	1.5				

B Plot the ordered pairs from the table on the coordinate plane at the right.

C How much rain falls in 3.5 hours? _____

D Plot the point corresponding to 3.5 hours of heavy rain.

E What do you notice about all of the points you plotted?

_____

F Is the total amount of rain that falls a function of the number of hours that rain has been falling? Why or why not?

_____

_____

Heavy Rainfall

Total Amount of Rain (cm) vs Time (h)

Reflect

1. Suppose you continued to plot points for times between those in the table, such as 1.2 hours or 4.5 hours. What can you say about the locations of these points?

_____

_____

Graphing Linear Functions

The relationship you investigated in the previous activity can be represented by the equation $y = 1.5x$, where x is the time and y is the total amount of rain. The graph of the relationship is a line, so the equation is a **linear equation**. Since there is exactly one value of y for each value of x, the relationship is a function. It is a **linear function** because its graph is a nonvertical line.

EXAMPLE 1

COMMON CORE 8.F.3

The temperature at dawn was 8 °F and increased steadily 2 °F every hour. The equation $y = 2x + 8$ gives the temperature y after x hours. State whether the relationship between the time and the temperature is proportional or nonproportional. Then graph the function.

Math Talk

Mathematical Practices

Carrie said that for a function to be a linear function, the relationship it represents must be proportional. Do you agree or disagree? Explain.

STEP 1 Compare the equation with the general linear equation $y = mx + b$. $y = 2x + 8$ is in the form $y = mx + b$, with $m = 2$ and $b = 8$. Therefore, the equation is a linear equation. Since $b \neq 0$, the relationship is nonproportional.

STEP 2 Choose several values for the input x. Substitute these values for x in the equation to find the output y.

x	$2x + 8$	y	(x, y)
0	$2(0) + 8$	8	$(0, 8)$
2	$2(2) + 8$	12	$(2, 12)$
4	$2(4) + 8$	16	$(4, 16)$
6	$2(6) + 8$	20	$(6, 20)$

STEP 3 Graph the ordered pairs. Then draw a line through the points to represent the solutions of the function.

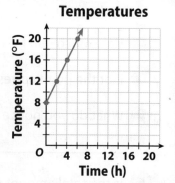

Temperatures

YOUR TURN

2. State whether the relationship between x and y in $y = 0.5x$ is proportional or nonproportional. Then graph the function.

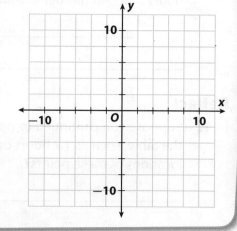

Determining Whether a Function is Linear

The linear equation in Example 1 has the form $y = mx + b$, where m and b are real numbers. Every equation in the form $y = mx + b$ is a linear equation. The linear equations represent linear functions. Equations that cannot be written in this form are not linear equations, and therefore are not linear functions.

Math On the Spot
my.hrw.com

EXAMPLE 2

COMMON CORE 8.F.3

A square tile has a side length of x inches. The equation $y = x^2$ gives the area of the tile in square inches. Determine whether the relationship between x and y is linear and, if so, if it is proportional.

STEP 1 Choose several values for the input x. Substitute these values for x in the equation to find the output y.

STEP 2 Graph the ordered pairs.

x	x^2	y	(x, y)
1	1^2	1	$(1, 1)$
2	2^2	4	$(2, 4)$
3	3^2	9	$(3, 9)$
4	4^2	16	$(4, 16)$

STEP 3 Identify the shape of the graph. The points suggest a curve, not a line. Draw a curve through the points to represent the solutions of the function.

STEP 4 Describe the relationship between x and y.

The graph is not a line so the relationship is not linear.

Only a linear relationship can be proportional, so the relationship is not proportional.

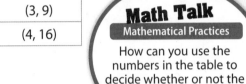

Animated Math
my.hrw.com

Math Talk
Mathematical Practices

How can you use the numbers in the table to decide whether or not the relationship between x and y is linear?

YOUR TURN

3. A soda machine makes $\frac{2}{3}$ gallon of soda every minute. The total amount y that the machine makes in x minutes is given by the equation $y = \frac{2}{3}x$. Determine whether the relationship between x and y is linear and, if so, if it is proportional.

Time (min), x	0	3		9
Amount (gal), y			4	

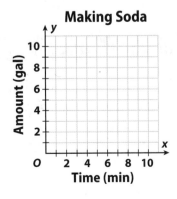

Making Soda

Personal Math Trainer

Online Assessment and Intervention

my.hrw.com

Plot the ordered pairs from the table. Then graph the function represented by the ordered pairs and tell whether the function is linear or nonlinear. (Examples 1 and 2)

1. $y = 5 - 2x$

Input, x	−1	1	3	5
Output, y				

2. $y = 2 - x^2$

Input, x	−2	−1	0	1	2
Output, y					

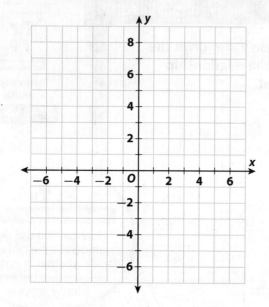

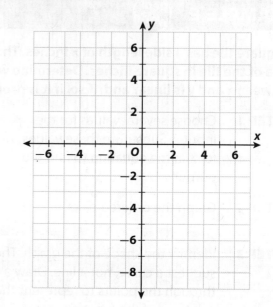

_____

_____

Explain whether each equation is a linear equation. (Example 2)

3. $y = x^2 - 1$

_____
_____
_____
_____

4. $y = 1 - x$

_____
_____
_____
_____

ESSENTIAL QUESTION CHECK-IN

5. Explain how you can use a table of values, an equation, and a graph to determine whether a function represents a proportional relationship.

_____
_____
_____

14.2 Independent Practice

Personal Math Trainer

Online Assessment and Intervention

my.hrw.com

6. State whether the relationship between x and y in $y = 4x - 5$ is proportional or nonproportional. Then graph the function.

_____

7. The Fortaleza telescope in Brazil is a radio telescope. Its shape can be approximated with the equation $y = 0.013x^2$. Is the relationship between x and y linear? Is it proportional? Explain.

_____

_____

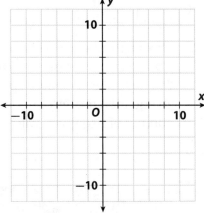

8. Kiley spent $20 on rides and snacks at the state fair. If x is the amount she spent on rides, and y is the amount she spent on snacks, the total amount she spent can be represented by the equation $x + y = 20$. Is the relationship between x and y linear? Is it proportional? Explain.

_____

_____

_____

9. **Represent Real-World Problems** The drill team is buying new uniforms. The table shows y, the total cost in dollars, and x, the number of uniforms purchased.

Number of uniforms, x	1	3	5	9
Total cost ($), y	60	180	300	540

a. Use the data to draw a graph. Is the relationship between x and y linear? Explain.

_____

b. Use your graph to predict the cost of purchasing 12 uniforms.

_____

Drill Team Uniforms

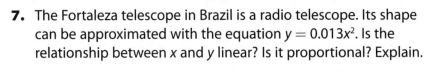

10. Marta, a whale calf in an aquarium, is fed a special milk formula. Her handler uses a graph to track the number of gallons of formula y the calf drinks in x hours. Is the relationship between x and y linear? Is it proportional? Explain.

_____

_____

Marta's Feedings

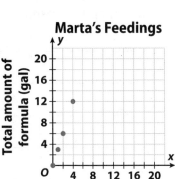

11. **Critique Reasoning** A student claims that the equation $y = 7$ is not a linear equation because it does not have the form $y = mx + b$. Do you agree or disagree? Why?

_____

_____

_____

12. **Make a Prediction** Let x represent the number of hours you read a book and y represent the total number of pages you have read. You have already read 70 pages and can read 30 pages per hour. Write an equation relating x hours and y pages you read. Then predict the total number of pages you will have read after another 3 hours.

_____

_____

H.O.T. **FOCUS ON HIGHER ORDER THINKING**

Work Area

13. **Draw Conclusions** Rebecca draws a graph of a real-world relationship that turns out to be a set of unconnected points. Can the relationship be linear? Can it be proportional? Explain your reasoning.

_____

_____

_____

14. **Communicate Mathematical Ideas** Write a real-world problem involving a proportional relationship. Explain how you know the relationship is proportional.

_____

_____

_____

_____

15. **Justify Reasoning** Show that the equation $y + 3 = 3(2x + 1)$ is linear and that it represents a proportional relationship between x and y.

_____

_____

_____

_____

_____

Creating Nonlinear Functions

COMMON CORE 8.F.3

...give examples of functions that are not linear.

ESSENTIAL QUESTION

How can you create functions that are not linear?

EXPLORE ACTIVITY 8.F.3

Creating Functions That Are Not Linear

A A linear function can be written in the form $y = mx + b$. If a function cannot be written in the form $y = mx + b$, it is not linear. Use this information to write a function that is *not* linear.

_____

B A table of values for a linear function shows a constant difference in corresponding output values when there is a constant difference in the input values. Use this information to create a table of values for a function that is *not* linear.

x				
f(x)				

C A graph of a linear function consists of points that all lie along a line. Use this information to create a graph of a function that is *not* linear.

_____

D The perimeter P of a square with side length x is given by the linear function $P = 4x$. Create a nonlinear function based on a geometry formula that you know. HINT: What do you know about the area A of a square with side length x?

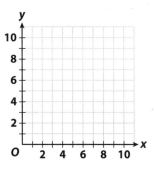

_____

_____

Reflect

1. Explain why the values in your table in Part B are nonlinear. Explain why the graph you created in Part C is not linear.

_____

_____

_____

Marco has read 7 books for a summer reading club. He plans to read 2 books each week for the rest of the summer. The table shows the total number of books he will read over time.

Week, x	0	1	2	3	4
Total books read, $f(x)$	7	9	11	13	15

1. Create a table to show the reading plan for another book club member whose plan is represented with a nonlinear function.

Week, x	0	1	2	3	4
Total books read, $f(x)$					

2. Explain how you know the second book club member's plan is not linear.

_____

_____

For each linear situation described, give an adapted description that is not linear.

3. An art museum charges $6.50 per ticket.

_____

4. A hat collector gets 2 new hats each month.

_____

5. A game club gives members 200 points for beginning membership and 50 points for each game purchased.

_____

_____

Determine whether the graph is linear or nonlinear. Then write a situation for the graph.

6.
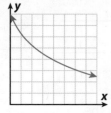

7.
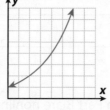

8.
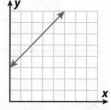

_____   _____   _____

_____   _____   _____

_____   _____   _____

How Many Squares?

INSTRUCTIONS

STEP 1 How many squares (of all sizes) can you find in the 4×4 square grid?

There are four different sizes of squares in the grid.

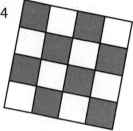

Count the number of each size square in the 4×4 square grid. The table shows you how to find them all.

Size of square	Number of squares	Identification of squares
4×4	1	
3×3	4	
2×2	9	
1×1	16	
Total	30	

The total number of squares in the 4×4 square grid is:

$f(4) = 1 + 4 + 9 + 16 = 30$

Notice the pattern. All the terms in $f(4)$ are perfect squares:

$f(4) = 1^2 + 2^2 + 3^2 + 4^2$

Draw a 5 × 5 square grid. Find the total number of different-sized squares in the grid to complete the table. Look for a pattern.

Size of square	5×5	4×4	3×3	2×2	1×1
Identification of squares					
Number of squares					

The total number of squares in the 5 × 5 square grid is:

$$f(5) = 1 + 4 + \boxed{} + \boxed{} + \boxed{} = \boxed{}$$

STEP 3 Repeat with a 6 × 6 grid and a 7 × 7 grid. Verify the pattern.

$f(6) =$ _____

$f(7) =$ _____

STEP 4 Use the pattern to write a function for the total number $f(n)$ of different-sized squares in an $n \times n$ grid.

$$f(n) = 1^2 + 2^2 + \boxed{}^2 + \cdots + \boxed{}$$

STEP 5 The function for the total number $f(n)$ of different-sized squares in an $n \times n$ grid can also be written $f(n) = \dfrac{n(n+1)(2n+1)}{6}$. Verify that this function works for 5 × 5, 6 × 6, and 7 × 7 square grids.

$$f(5) = \frac{\boxed{}\left(\boxed{} + 1\right)\left(2 \times \boxed{} + 1\right)}{6} = \boxed{}$$

$$f(6) = \frac{\boxed{}\left(\boxed{} + 1\right)\left(2 \times \boxed{} + 1\right)}{6} = \boxed{}$$

$$f(7) = \frac{\boxed{}\left(\boxed{} + 1\right)\left(2 \times \boxed{} + 1\right)}{6} = \boxed{}$$

_____

_____

14.3 Comparing Functions

COMMON CORE 8.F.2

Compare properties of two functions each represented in a different way (algebraically, graphically, numerically in tables, or by verbal descriptions). *Also 8.EE.5, 8.F.4*

ESSENTIAL QUESTION

How can you use tables, graphs, and equations to compare functions?

EXPLORE ACTIVITY   COMMON CORE 8.F.2, 8.F.4

Comparing a Table and an Equation

You can compare functions by writing them both as equations.

EXAMPLE 1 Josh and Maggie buy MP3 files from different music services. The monthly cost, y dollars, for x songs is linear. The cost of Josh's service is $y = 0.50x + 10$. The cost of Maggie's service is shown below.

Monthly Cost of MP3s at Maggie's Music Service					
Songs, x	5	10	15	20	25
Cost ($), y	4.95	9.90	14.85	19.80	24.75

A Write an equation to represent the monthly cost of Maggie's service.

STEP 1 Choose any two ordered pairs from the table to find the slope: for example, (5, 4.95) and (10, 9.90).

$$m = \frac{y_2 - y_1}{x_2 - x_1} = \frac{\boxed{} - 4.95}{10 - \boxed{}} = \frac{\boxed{}}{\boxed{}} = \underline{}$$

STEP 2 Find the y-intercept. Use the slope and any point.

Begin with slope-intercept form. $y = mx + b$

Substitute for y, m, and x. $4.95 = \boxed{} \cdot \boxed{} + b$

$\boxed{} = b$

STEP 3 Write the equation in slope-intercept form.

$y = \boxed{} x + \boxed{}$, or $y = \boxed{} x$

B Which service is cheaper when 30 songs are downloaded?

Josh's service: Maggie's service:

$y = 0.50x + 10$ $y = 0.99x$

$y = 0.50 \cdot \boxed{} + 10 = \boxed{}$ $y = 0.99 \cdot \boxed{} = \boxed{}$

_____ service is cheaper for 30 songs.

Math On the Spot
my.hrw.com

YOUR TURN

1. Quentin is choosing between buying books at the bookstore or buying online versions of the books for his tablet. The cost, y dollars, of ordering books online for x books is $y = 6.95x + 1.50$. The cost of buying the books at the bookstore is shown in the table. Which method of buying books is more expensive if Quentin wants to buy 6 books?

Cost of Books at the Bookstore					
Books, x	1	2	3	4	5
Cost ($), y	7.50	15.00	22.50	30.00	37.50

_____

EXPLORE ACTIVITY 2   COMMON CORE 8.F.2, 8.EE.5

Comparing a Table and a Graph

The table and graph show how many words Morgan and Brian typed correctly on a typing test. For both students, the relationship between words typed correctly and time is linear.

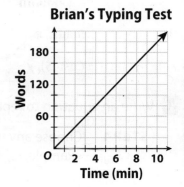

Brian's Typing Test

Morgan's Typing Test					
Time (min)	2	4	6	8	10
Words	30	60	90	120	150

A Find Morgan's unit rate.

_____

B Find Brian's unit rate.

_____

C Which student types more correct words per minute?

_____

Reflect

2. Katie types 17 correct words per minute. Explain how a graph of Katie's test results would compare to Morgan's and Brian's.

_____

_____

Comparing a Graph and a Description

Jamal wants to buy a new game system that costs $200. He does not have enough money to buy it today, so he compares layaway plans at different stores.

The plan at Store A is shown on the graph.

Store B requires an initial payment of $60 and weekly payments of $20 until the balance is paid in full.

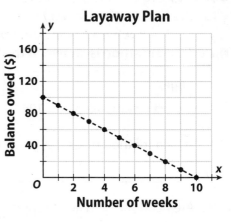

Layaway Plan

A Write an equation in slope-intercept form for Store A's layaway plan. Let x represent number of weeks and y represent balance owed.

_____

B Write an equation in slope-intercept form for Store B's layaway plan. Let x represent number of weeks and y represent balance owed.

_____

C Sketch a graph of the plan at Store B on the same grid as Store A.

D How can you use the graphs to tell which plan requires the greater down payment? How can you use the equations?

_____

_____

_____

E How can you use the graphs to tell which plan requires the greater weekly payment?

_____

_____

_____

F Which plan allows Jamal to pay for the game system faster? Explain.

_____

_____

Doctors have two methods of calculating maximum heart rate.
With the first method, maximum heart rate, y, in beats per minute
is $y = 220 - x$, where x is the person's age. Maximum heart rate with
the second method is shown in the table. (Explore Activity Example 1)

Age, x	20	30	40	50	60
Heart rate (bpm), y	194	187	180	173	166

1. Which method gives the greater maximum heart rate for a 70-year-old?

_____

2. Are heart rate and age proportional or nonproportional for each method?

_____

Aisha runs a tutoring business. With Plan 1, students may choose to
pay $15 per hour. With Plan 2, they may follow the plan shown on
the graph. (Explore Activity 2 and 3)

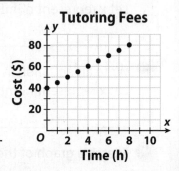

Tutoring Fees

3. Describe the plan shown on the graph.

_____

4. Sketch a graph showing the $15 per hour option.

5. What does the intersection of the two graphs mean?

_____

6. Which plan is cheaper for 10 hours of tutoring?

_____

7. Are cost and time proportional or nonproportional for each plan?

_____

_____

? ESSENTIAL QUESTION CHECK-IN

8. When using tables, graphs, and equations to compare functions, why do
you find the equations for tables and graphs?

_____

_____

14.3 Independent Practice

COMMON CORE 8.EE.5, 8.F.2, 8.F.4

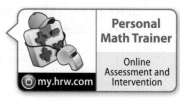

Personal Math Trainer

Online Assessment and Intervention

my.hrw.com

The table and graph show the miles driven and gas used for two scooters.

Scooter A	
Distance (mi), x	Gas used (gal), y
150	2
300	4
450	6
600	8
750	10

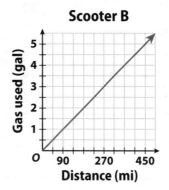

Scooter B

9. Which scooter uses fewer gallons of gas when 1350 miles are driven?

_____

10. Are gas used and miles proportional or nonproportional for each scooter?

_____

A cell phone company offers two texting plans to its customers. The monthly cost, y dollars, of one plan is $y = 0.10x + 5$, where x is the number of texts. The cost of the other plan is shown in the table.

Number of texts, x	100	200	300	400	500
Cost ($), y	20	25	30	35	40

11. Which plan is cheaper for under 200 texts? _____

12. The graph of the first plan does not pass through the origin. What does this indicate?

_____

_____

13. Brianna wants to buy a digital camera for a photography class. One store offers the camera for $50 down and a payment plan of $20 per month. The payment plan for a second store is described by $y = 15x + 80$, where y is the total cost in dollars and x is the number of months. Which camera is cheaper when the camera is paid off in 12 months? Explain.

_____

_____

14. The French club and soccer team are washing cars to earn money. The amount earned, y dollars, for washing x cars is a linear function. Which group makes the most money per car? Explain.

French Club	
Number of cars, x	Amount earned ($), y
2	10
4	20
6	30
8	40
10	50

Soccer Team

_____

_____

_____

 FOCUS ON HIGHER ORDER THINKING

Work Area

15. Draw Conclusions Gym A charges $60 a month plus $5 per visit. The monthly cost at Gym B is represented by $y = 5x + 40$, where x is the number of visits per month. What conclusion can you draw about the monthly costs of the gyms?

_____

_____

_____

16. Justify Reasoning Why will the value of y for the function $y = 5x + 1$ always be greater than that for the function $y = 4x + 2$ when $x > 1$?

_____

_____

_____

17. Analyze Relationships The equations of two functions are $y = -21x + 9$ and $y = -24x + 8$. Which function is changing more quickly? Explain.

_____

_____

_____

_____

Rate of Change and Initial Value

COMMON CORE 8.F.4

... Determine the rate of change and initial value of the function from a description of a relationship or from two (x, y) values, including reading these from a table or from a graph. ...

ESSENTIAL QUESTION

How can you interpret the rate of change and initial value of a linear function in terms of the situation it models?

EXPLORE ACTIVITY COMMON CORE 8.F.4

Determining Rate of Change and Initial Value

A pitcher with a maximum capacity of 4 cups contains 1 cup of apple juice concentrate. A faucet is turned on, filling the pitcher at a rate of $\frac{1}{4}$ cup per second. The amount A of liquid in the pitcher (in cups) is a function $A(t)$ of the time t (in seconds) that the water is running.

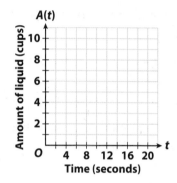

A The y-intercept, _____, is the initial amount in cups in the pitcher at time 0. Plot the point that corresponds to the y-intercept.

B The slope is the rate of change: _____ cup per second, or 1 cup every

_____ seconds. So, the rise is _____ and the run is _____.

C Use the rise and run to move from the first point to a second point on the line, and plot a second point.

_____

D Connect the points and extend the line to the maximum value of the function,

where $A(t) =$ _____ cups.

Reflect

1. How do you know what the maximum value of the function is in Part D?

_____

_____

The increase in pressure P (in pounds per square inch, or psi) is a linear function of the depth d (in feet) to which a scuba diver descends. This function, $P(d) = 0.445d + 14.7$, is graphed.

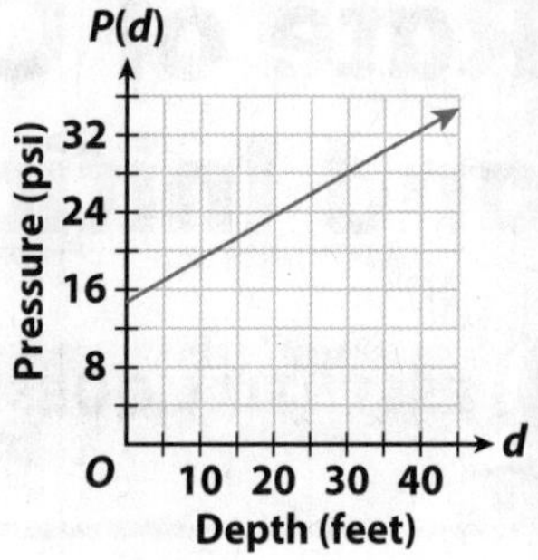

P(d)

Pressure (psi)

32
24
16
8

O   10 20 30 40   d
     Depth (feet)

1. What is the initial value, and what does it represent?

_____

_____

2. What is the rate of change, and what does it represent?

_____

_____

The cost of catering for a scholarship presentation dinner is $300 plus $10 per student. The cost C is a function of the number n of students.

3. Write the linear function $C(n)$.

_____

4. What are the initial value and rate of change, and what do they represent?

_____

_____

_____

_____

The cost for a plumber to make a repair is $50 for the service call plus $75 per hour.

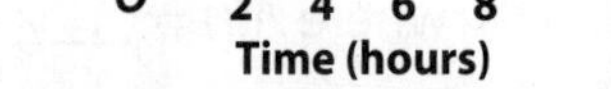

5. Write the linear function $C(t)$.

_____

6. Identify the initial value, the rate of change, and their meanings.

C(t)

Cost (dollars)

400
300
200
100

O   2   4   6   8   t
     Time (hours)

_____

_____

_____

LESSON
14.4 Analyzing Graphs

COMMON CORE 8.F.5

Describe qualitatively the functional relationship between two quantities by analyzing a graph … . Sketch a graph that exhibits the qualitative features of a function that has been described verbally.

ESSENTIAL QUESTION

How can you describe a relationship given a graph and sketch a graph given a description?

EXPLORE ACTIVITY 1 COMMON CORE 8.F.5

Interpreting Graphs

A roller coaster park is open from May to October each year. The graph shows the number of park visitors over its season.

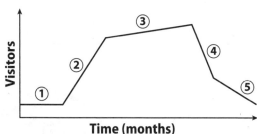

Park Visitors

A Segment 1 shows that attendance during the opening weeks of the park's season stayed constant. Describe what Segment 2 shows.

_____

B Based on the time frame, give a possible explanation for the change in attendance represented by Segment 2.

_____

C Which segments of the graph show decreasing attendance? Give a possible explanation.

_____

_____

Reflect

1. Explain how the slope of each segment of the graph is related to whether attendance increases or decreases.

_____

_____

Matching Graphs to Situations

Grace, Jet, and Mike are studying 100 words for a spelling bee.

- Grace started by learning how to spell many words each day, but then learned fewer and fewer words each day.

- Jet learned how to spell the same number of words each day.

- Mike started by learning how to spell only a few words each day, but then learned a greater number of words each day.

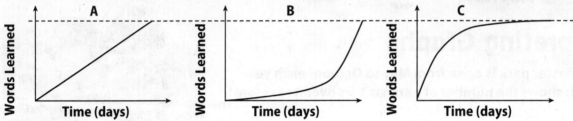

_____   _____   _____

A Describe the progress represented by Graph A.

_____

_____

> **Math Talk**
> **Mathematical Practices**
>
> Tell whether each graph is linear or nonlinear and proportional or nonproportional.

B Describe the progress represented by Graph B.

_____

_____

_____

C Describe the progress represented by Graph C.

_____

_____

_____

D Determine which graph represents each student's study progress and write the students' names under the appropriate graphs.

Reflect

2. What would it mean if one of the graphs slanted downward?

_____

Sketching a Graph for a Situation

Mrs. Sutton provides free math tutoring to her students every day after school. No one comes to tutoring sessions during the first week of school. Over the next two weeks, use of the tutoring service gradually increases.

A Sketch a graph showing the number of students who use the tutoring service over the first three weeks of school.

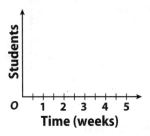

B Mrs. Sutton's students are told that they will have a math test at the end of the fifth week of school. How do you think this will affect the number of students who come to tutoring?

_____

_____

C Considering your answer to **B**, sketch a graph showing the number of students who might use the tutoring service over the first six weeks of school.

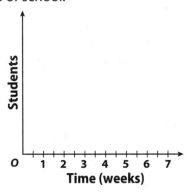

Reflect

3. If Mrs. Sutton offers bonus credit to students who come to tutoring, how might this affect the number of students?

_____

4. How would your answer to Question 3 affect the graph?

_____

_____

In a lab environment, colonies of bacteria follow a predictable pattern of growth. The graph shows this growth over time. (Explore Activity 1)

Bacterial Growth Curve

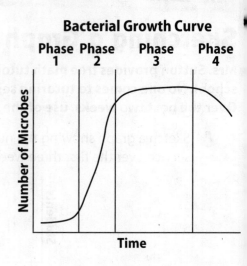

1. What is happening to the population during Phase 2?

   _____

   _____

2. What is happening to the population during Phase 4?

   _____

   _____

The graphs give the speeds of three people who are riding snowmobiles. Tell which graph corresponds to each situation. (Explore Activity 2)

Graph 1

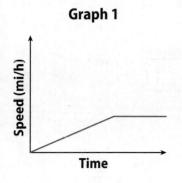

Graph 2

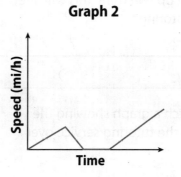

Graph 3

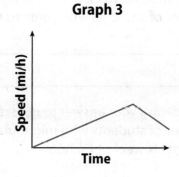

3. Chip begins his ride slowly but then stops to talk with some friends. After a few minutes, he continues his ride, gradually increasing his speed.

   _____

4. Linda steadily increases her speed through most of her ride. Then she slows down as she nears some trees.

   _____

5. Paulo stood at the top of a diving board. He walked to the end of the board, and then dove forward into the water. He plunged down below the surface, then swam straight forward while underwater. Finally, he swam forward and upward to the surface of the water. Draw a graph to represent Paulo's elevation at different distances from the edge of the pool. (Explore Activity 3)

   Paulo's elevation

   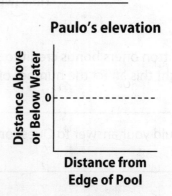

14.4 Independent Practice

COMMON CORE 8.F.5

Personal Math Trainer

Online Assessment and Intervention

my.hrw.com

Tell which graph corresponds to each situation below.

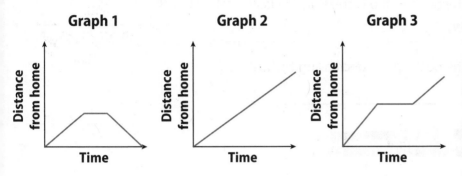

Graph 1   Graph 2   Graph 3

6. Arnold started from home and walked to a friend's house. He stayed with his friend for a while and then walked to another friend's house farther from home.

_____

7. Francisco started from home and walked to the store. After shopping, he walked back home.

_____

8. Celia walks to the library at a steady pace without stopping.

_____

Regina rented a motor scooter. The graph shows how far away she is from the rental site after each half hour of riding.

9. **Represent Real-World Problems** Use the graph to describe Regina's trip. You can start the description like this: "Regina left the rental shop and rode for an hour…"

_____

_____

_____

_____

_____

Distance from Rental Site

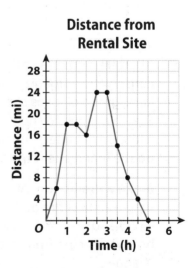

10. **Analyze Relationships** Determine during which half hour Regina covered the greatest distance.

_____

The data in the table shows the speed of a ride at an amusement park at different times one afternoon.

Time	3:20	3:21	3:22	3:23	3:24	3:25
Speed (mi/h)	0	14	41	62	8	0

11. Sketch a graph that shows the speed of the ride over time.

12. Between which times is the ride's speed increasing the fastest?

_____

13. Between which times is the ride's speed decreasing the fastest?

_____

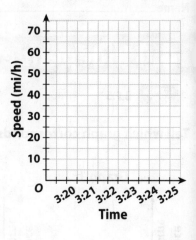

H.O.T.   **FOCUS ON HIGHER ORDER THINKING**

A woodland area on an island contains a population of foxes. The graph describes the changes in the population over time.

Fox Population

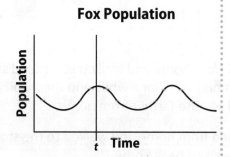

14. Justify Reasoning What is happening to the fox population before time *t*? Explain your reasoning.

_____

_____

_____

_____

_____

15. What If? Suppose at time *t*, a conservation organization moves a large group of foxes to the island. Sketch a graph to show how this action might affect the population on the island after time *t*.

Fox Population

16. Make a Prediction At some point after time *t*, a forest fire destroys part of the woodland area on the island. Describe how your graph from problem 15 might change.

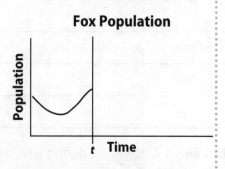

_____

_____

_____

Ready to Go On?

14.1 Identifying and Representing Functions

Determine whether each relationship is a function.

1.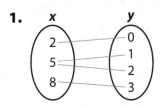

x	y
2	0
5	1
8	2
	3

_____

2.

Input, x	Output, y
−1	6
3	5
6	5

_____

3. (2, 5), (7, 2), (−3, 4), (2, 9), (1, 1)

_____

14.2 Describing Functions

Determine whether each situation is linear or nonlinear, and proportional or nonproportional.

4. Joanna is paid $14 per hour.

_____

5. Alberto started out bench pressing 50 pounds. He then added 5 pounds every week.

_____

14.3 Comparing Functions

6. Which function is changing more quickly? Explain.

_____

_____

_____

Function 1

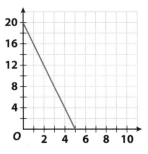

Function 2	
Input, x	Output, y
2	11
3	6.5
4	2

14.4 Analyzing Graphs

7. Describe a graph that shows Sam running at a constant rate.

_____

? ESSENTIAL QUESTION

8. How can you use functions to solve real-world problems?

_____

MODULE 14 MIXED REVIEW

Assessment Readiness

Personal
Math Trainer

Online
Assessment and
Intervention

my.hrw.com

Selected Response

1. Which table shows a proportional function?

(A)
x	0	5	10
y	3	15	30

(B)
x	0	5	10
y	10	20	30

(C)
x	0	5	10
y	0	50	100

(D)
x	0	5	10
y	10	5	0

2. What is the slope and y-intercept of the function shown in the table?

x	1	4	7
y	6	12	18

(A) $m = -2; b = -4$

(B) $m = -2; b = 4$

(C) $m = 2; b = 4$

(D) $m = 4; b = 2$

3. The table below shows some input and output values of a function.

Input	4	5	6	7
Output	14	17.5		24.5

What is the missing output value?

(A) 20

(B) 21

(C) 22

(D) 23

4. Tom walked to school at a steady pace, met his sister, and they walked home at a steady pace. Describe this graph.

(A) V-shaped

(B) upside down V-shaped

(C) Straight line sloping up

(D) Straight line sloping down

Mini-Task

5. Linear functions can be used to find the price of a building based on its floor area. Below are two of these functions.
$y = 40x + 15,000$

Floor Area (ft²)	400	700	1,000
Price ($1,000s)	32	56	80

a. Find and compare the slopes.

_____

_____

_____

b. Find and compare the y-intercepts.

_____

_____

_____

c. Describe each function as proportional or nonproportional.

_____

_____

_____

Study Guide Review

MODULE 11 **Proportional Relationships**

Key Vocabulary

constant of proportionality
(constante de proporcionalidad)
proportional relationship
(relación proporcional)
slope *(pendiente)*

? ESSENTIAL QUESTION

How can you use proportional relationships to solve real-world problems?

EXAMPLE 1

Write an equation that represents the proportional relationship shown in the graph.

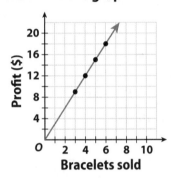

Use the points on the graph to make a table.

Bracelets sold	3	4	5	6
Profit ($)	9	12	15	18

Let x represent the number of bracelets sold.

Let y represent the profit.

The equation is $y = 3x$.

EXAMPLE 2

Find the slope of the line.

$\text{slope} = \frac{\text{rise}}{\text{run}}$

$= \frac{3}{-4}$

$= -\frac{3}{4}$

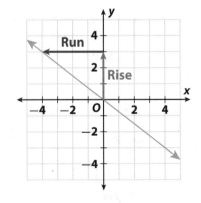

EXERCISES

1. The table represents a proportional relationship. Write an equation that describes the relationship. Then graph the relationship represented by the data. (Lessons 11.1, 11.3, 11.4)

Time (x)	6	8	10	12
Distance (y)	3	4	5	6

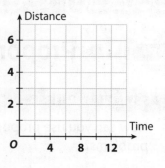

_____

Find the slope and the unit rate represented on each graph. (Lesson 11.2)

2.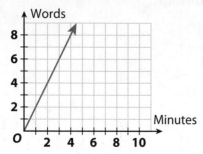

_____

3.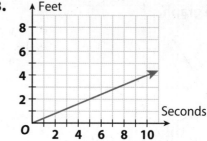

_____

 MODULE 12 ·

Nonproportional Relationships

? ESSENTIAL QUESTION

How can you use nonproportional relationships to solve real-world problems?

EXAMPLE 1

Jai is saving to buy his mother a birthday gift. Each week, he saves $5. He started with $25. The equation $y = 5x + 25$ gives the total Jai has saved, y, after x weeks. Draw a graph of the equation. Then describe the relationship.

Use the equation to make a table. Then, graph the ordered pairs from the table, and draw a line through the points.

x (weeks)	0	1	2	3	4
y (savings in dollars)	25	30	35	40	45

The relationship is linear but nonproportional.

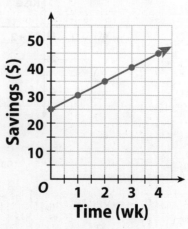

EXAMPLE 2

Graph $y = -\frac{1}{2}x - 2$.

The slope is $\frac{-1}{2}$, or $-\frac{1}{2}$.

The y-intercept is –2.

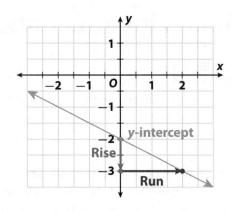

EXERCISES

Complete each table. Explain whether the relationship between x and y is proportional or nonproportional and whether it is linear. (Lesson 12.1)

1. $y = 10x - 4$

x	0	2		6
y	–4		36	

2. $y = -\frac{3}{2}x$

x	0		2	
y		–1.5		–4.5

_____

_____

3. Find the slope and y-intercept for the linear relationship shown in the table. Graph the line. Is the relationship proportional or nonproportional? (Lessons 12.2, 12.4)

x	–4	–1	0	1
y	–4	2	4	6

slope _____

y-intercept _____

The relationship is _____.

4. Tom's Taxis charges a fixed rate of $4 per ride plus $0.50 per mile. Carla's Cabs does not charge a fixed rate but charges $1.00 per mile. (Lesson 12.3)

a. Write an equation that represents the cost of Tom's Taxis. _____

b. Write an equation that represents the cost of Carla's cabs. _____

c. Steve calculated that for the distance he needs to travel, Tom's Taxis will charge the same amount as Carla's Cabs. Graph both equations. How far is Steve going to travel and how much will he pay?

_____

_____

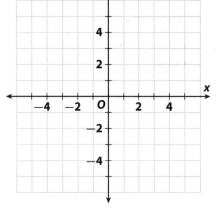

MODULE 13 Writing Linear Equations

? **ESSENTIAL QUESTION**

How can you use linear equations to solve real-world problems?

EXAMPLE 1

Jose is renting a backhoe for a construction job. The rental charge for a month is based on the number of days in the month and a set charge per month. In September, which has 30 days, Jose paid $700. In August, which has 31 days, he paid $715. Write an equation in slope-intercept form that represents this situation.

$(x_1, y_1), (x_2, y_2) \rightarrow (30, 700), (31, 715)$ Write the information given as ordered pairs.

$m = \dfrac{y_2 - y_1}{x_2 - x_1} = \dfrac{715 - 700}{31 - 30} = 15$ Find the slope.

$y = mx + b$ Slope-intercept form

$715 = 15(31) + b$ Substitute for y, m, and x to find b.

$250 = b$ Solve for b.

$y = 15x + 250$ Write the equation.

EXAMPLE 2

Determine if the graph shown represents a linear or nonlinear relationship.

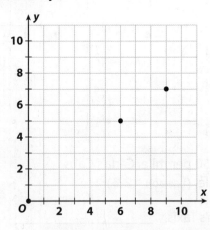

Points	Rate of Change
(0, 0) and (6, 5)	$m = \dfrac{5 - 0}{6 - 0} = \dfrac{5}{6}$
(6, 5) and (9, 7)	$m = \dfrac{7 - 5}{9 - 6} = \dfrac{2}{3}$
(0, 0) and (9, 7)	$m = \dfrac{7 - 0}{9 - 0} = \dfrac{7}{9}$

The rates of change are not constant. The graph represents a nonlinear relationship.

EXERCISES

1. Ms. Thompson is grading math tests. She is giving everyone that took the test a 10-point bonus. Each correct answer is worth 5 points. Write an equation in slope-intercept form that represents the scores on the tests. (Lesson 13.1) _____

The table shows a pay scale based on years of experience. (Lessons 13.1, 13.2)

Experience (years), x	0	2	4	6	8
Hourly pay ($), y	9	14	19	24	29

2. Find the slope for this relationship. _____

3. Find the y-intercept. _____

4. Write an equation in slope-intercept form that represents this

   relationship. _____

5. Graph the equation, and use it to predict the hourly pay of someone with 10 years of experience.

   _____

   _____

   _____

   _____

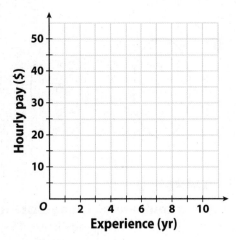

Does each of the following graphs represent a linear relationship? Why or why not? (Lesson 13.3)

6.

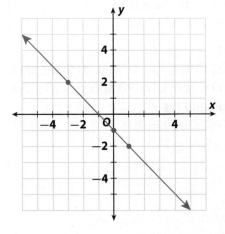

_____

_____

_____

7.

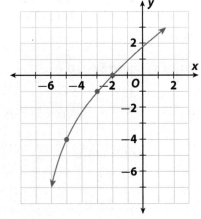

_____

_____

_____

? **ESSENTIAL QUESTION**

How can you use functions to solve real-world problems?

EXAMPLE 1

Determine whether each relationship is a function.

A

Input	Output
3	10
4	4
5	2
4	0
6	5

The relationship is not a function, because an input, 4, is paired with 2 different outputs, 4 and 0.

B

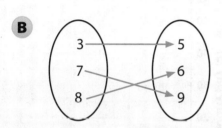

Since each input value is paired with only one output value, the relationship is a function.

EXAMPLE 2

Sally and Louis are on a long-distance bike ride. Sally bikes at a steady rate of 18 miles per hour. The distance y that Sally covers in x hours is given by the equation $y = 18x$. Louis's speed can be found by using the numbers in the table. Who will travel farther in 4 hours and by how much?

Louis's Biking Speed			
Time (h), x	3	5	7
Distance (mi), y	60	100	140

Each distance in the table is 20 times each number of hours. Louis's speed is 20 miles per hour, and his distance covered is represented by $y = 20x$.

Sally's ride:

$y = 18x$

$y = 18(4)$

$y = 72$

Louis's ride:

$y = 20x$

$y = 20(4)$

$y = 80$

Sally will ride 72 miles in 4 hours. Louis will ride 80 miles in 4 hours. Louis will go 8 miles farther.

EXERCISES

Determine whether each relationship is a function. (Lesson 14.1)

1.

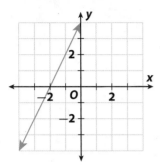

2.

Input	Output
−1	8
0	4
1	8
2	16

_____

_____

Tell whether the function is linear or nonlinear. (Lesson 14.2)

3. $y = 5x + \dfrac{1}{2}$ _____

4. $y = x^2 + 3$ _____

5. Elaine has a choice of two health club memberships. The first membership option is to pay $500 now and then pay $150 per month. The second option is shown in the table. Elaine plans to go to the club for 12 months. Which option is cheaper? Explain. (Lesson 14.3)

Months, x	1	2	3
Total paid ($), y	215	430	645

_____

_____

_____

6. Jenny rode her bike around her neighborhood. Use the graph to describe Jenny's bike ride. (Lesson 14.4)

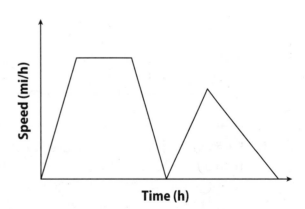

_____

_____

_____

_____

_____

_____

_____

1. **CAREERS IN MATH** | Cost Estimator To make MP3 players, a cost estimator determined it costs a company $1500 per week for overhead and $45 for each MP3 player made.

   a. Define a variable to represent the number of players made. Then write an equation to represent the company's total cost c.

   _____

   b. One week, the company spends $5460 making MP3 players. How many players were made that week? Show your work.

   _____

   _____

   c. If the company sells MP3 players for $120, how much profit would it make if it sold 80 players in one week? Explain how you found your answer.

   _____

   _____

2. A train from Portland, Oregon, to Los Angeles, California, travels at an average speed of 60 miles per hour and covers a distance of 963 miles. Susanna is taking the train from Portland to Los Angeles to see her aunt. She needs to arrive at her aunt's house by 8 p.m. It takes 30 minutes to get from the train station to her aunt's house.

   a. By what time does the train need to leave Portland for Susanna to arrive by 8 p.m.? Explain how you got your answer. As part of your explanation, write a function that you used in your work.

   _____

   _____

   _____

   _____

   b. Susanna does not want to leave Portland later than 10 p.m. or earlier than 6 a.m. Does the train in part **a** meet her requirements? If not, give a new departure time that would allow her to still get to her aunt's house on time, and find the arrival time of that train.

   _____

   _____

   _____

Selected Response

1. Rickie earns $7 an hour babysitting. Which table represents this proportional relationship?

Ⓐ
Hours	4	6	8
Earnings ($)	28	42	56

Ⓑ
Hours	4	6	8
Earnings ($)	28	35	42

Ⓒ
Hours	2	3	4
Earnings ($)	7	14	21

Ⓓ
Hours	2	3	4
Earnings ($)	14	21	42

2. Which of the relationships below is a function?

Ⓐ $(6, 3), (5, 2), (6, 8), (0, 7)$

Ⓑ $(8, 2), (1, 7), (-1, 2), (1, 9)$

Ⓒ $(4, 3), (3, 0), (-1, 3), (2, 7)$

Ⓓ $(7, 1), (0, 0), (6, 2), (0, 4)$

3. Which set best describes the numbers used on the scale for a standard thermometer?

Ⓐ whole numbers

Ⓑ rational numbers

Ⓒ real numbers

Ⓓ integers

4. Which term refers to slope?

Ⓐ rate of change   Ⓒ y-intercept

Ⓑ equation   Ⓓ coordinate

5. The graph of which equation is shown below?

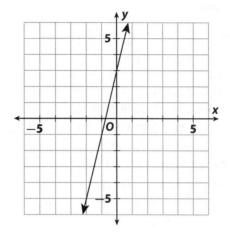

Ⓐ $y = 4x + 3$

Ⓑ $y = -4x - 0.75$

Ⓒ $y = -4x + 3$

Ⓓ $y = 4x - 0.75$

6. Which equation represents a nonproportional relationship?

Ⓐ $y = 5x$

Ⓑ $y = -5x$

Ⓒ $y = 5x + 3$

Ⓓ $y = -\frac{1}{5}x$

7. Which number is 7.0362×10^{-4} written in standard notation?

Ⓐ 0.000070362

Ⓑ 0.00070362

Ⓒ 7.0362

Ⓓ 7036.2

8. Which term does not correctly describe the relationship shown in the table?

x	0	2	4
y	0	70	140

- (A) function
- (B) linear
- (C) proportional
- (D) nonproportional

9. As part of a science experiment, Greta measured the amount of water flowing from Container A to Container B. Container B had half a gallon of water in it to start the experiment. Greta found that the water was flowing at a rate of two gallons per hour. Which equation represents the amount of water in Container B?

- (A) $y = 2x$
- (B) $y = 0.5x$
- (C) $y = 2x + 0.5$
- (D) $y = 0.5x + 2$

10. Carl and Jeannine both work at appliance stores. Carl earns a weekly salary of $600 plus $40 for each appliance he sells. The equation $p = 50n + 550$ represents the amount of money Jeannine earns in a week, p ($), as a function of the number of appliances she sells, n. Which of the following statements is true?

- (A) Carl has a greater salary and a greater rate per appliance sold.
- (B) Jeannine has a greater salary and a greater rate per appliance sold.
- (C) Carl will earn more than Jeannine if they each sell 10 appliances in a given week.
- (D) Both Carl and Jeannine earn the same amount if they each sell 5 appliances in a given week.

Mini-Task

11. The table below represents a linear relationship.

x	2	3	4	5
y	14	17	20	23

a. Find the slope for this relationship.

_____

b. Find the y-intercept. Explain how you found it.

_____

_____

_____

_____

c. Write an equation in slope-intercept form that represents this relationship.

_____

Hot Tip! Estimate your answer before solving the problem. Use your estimate to check the reasonableness of your answer.

12. Jacy has a choice of cell phone plans. Plan A is to pay $260 for the phone and then pay $70 per month for service. Plan B is to get the phone for free and pay $82 per month for service.

a. Write an equation to represent the total cost, c, of Plan A for m months.

_____

b. Write an equation to represent the total cost, c, of Plan B for m months.

_____

c. If Jacy plans to keep the phone for 24 months, which plan is cheaper? Explain.

_____

_____

_____

Solving Equations and Systems of Equations

MODULE 15
Solving Linear Equations
COMMON CORE 8.EE.7, 8.EE.7a, 8.EE.7b

MODULE 16
Solving Systems of Linear Equations
COMMON CORE 8.EE.8, 8.EE.8a, 8.EE.8b, 8.EE.8c

CAREERS IN MATH

Hydraulic Engineer A hydraulic engineer specializes in the behavior of fluids, mainly water. A hydraulic engineer applies the mathematics of fluid dynamics to the collection, transport, measurement, and regulation of water and other fluids.

If you are interested in a career in hydraulic engineering, you should study the following mathematical subjects:
- Algebra
- Geometry
- Trigonometry
- Probability and Statistics
- Calculus

Research other careers that require the understanding of the mathematics of fluid dynamics.

Unit 7 Performance Task

At the end of the unit, check out how **hydraulic engineers** use math.

Use the puzzle to preview key vocabulary from this unit. Unscramble the circled letters to answer the riddle at the bottom of the page.

1. FIACALRONT INFEOCIECTF

2. LCMADEI CINETFOEFIC

3. UQAOTENI

4. ROPWE

5. TNUSITBUOSIT DOHMTE

1. A number that is multiplied by the variable in an algebraic expression, where the number is a fraction. (Lesson 15.2)

2. A number that is multiplied by the variable in an algebraic expression, where the number is a decimal. (Lesson 15.2)

3. A mathematical statement that two expressions are equal. (Lesson 15.1)

4. A number that is formed by repeated multiplication of the same factor. Multiply by this to remove decimals from an unsolved equation. (Lesson 15.2)

5. A process used to solve systems of linear equations by solving an equation for one variable and then substituting the resulting expression for that variable into the other equation. (Lesson 16.2)

Q: What is the best time to divide a half dollar between two people?

A: at a ___ ___ ___ ___ ___ ___ ___ ___ ___ ___ ___ ___ ___!

Solving Linear Equations

 ESSENTIAL QUESTION

How can you use equations with the variable on both sides to solve real-world problems?

 my.hrw.com

Real-World Video

Some employees earn commission plus their salary when they make a sale. There may be options about their pay structure. They can find the best option by solving an equation with the variable on both sides.

 GO DIGITAL

my.hrw.com

 my.hrw.com

Go digital with your write-in student edition, accessible on any device.

 Math On the Spot

Scan with your smart phone to jump directly to the online edition, video tutor, and more.

 Animated Math

Interactively explore key concepts to see how math works.

 Personal Math Trainer

Get immediate feedback and help as you work through practice sets.

Are YOU Ready?

Complete these exercises to review skills you will need for this module.

Personal Math Trainer

Online Assessment and Intervention

my.hrw.com

Find Common Denominators

EXAMPLE   Find the LCD of 3, 5, and 10.

3: 3, 6, 9, 12, 15, 18, 21, 24, 27, 30,...   List the multiples of each number.
5: 5, 10, 15, 20, 25, 30, 35,...   Choose the least multiple the
10: 10, 20, 30, 40, 50,...   lists have in common.
                                                 LCD(3, 5, 10) = 30

Find the LCD.

1. 8, 12 _____   **2.** 9, 12 _____   **3.** 15, 20 _____   **4.** 8, 10 _____

Multiply Decimals by Powers of 10

EXAMPLE 3.719×100 Count the zeros in 100: 2 zeros
               $3.719 \times 100 = 371.9$ Move the decimal point 2 places to the right.

Find the product.

5. 0.683×100 **6.** $9.15 \times 1,000$ **7.** 0.005×100 **8.** $1,000 \times 1,000$

_____   _____   _____   _____

Connect Words and Equations

EXAMPLE   Two times a number decreased by 5 is −6.

Two times x decreased by 5 is −6.   Represent the unknown with
$2x - 5$ is −6   a variable.
$2x - 5 = -6$ *Times* means multiplication.
                                        Decreased by means subtraction.
                                        Place the equal sign.

Write an algebraic equation for the sentence.

9. The difference between three times a number and 7 is 14. _____

10. The quotient of five times a number and 7 is no more than 10. _____

11. 14 less than 3 times a number is 5 more than half of the number. _____

Reading Start-Up

Vocabulary

Review Words
- ✔ algebraic expression *(expresión algebraica)*
- coefficient *(coeficiente)*
- common denominator *(denominador común)*
- ✔ constant *(constante)*
- ✔ equation *(ecuación)*
- integers *(entero)*
- least common multiple *(mínimo común múltiplo)*
- operations *(operaciones)*
- solution *(solución)*
- ✔ variable *(variable)*

Visualize Vocabulary

Use the ✔ words to complete the bubble map. You may put more than one word in each oval.

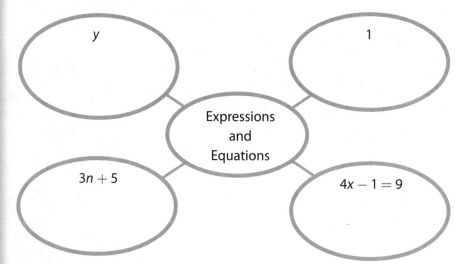

- y
- 1
- Expressions and Equations
- $3n + 5$
- $4x - 1 = 9$

Understand Vocabulary

Complete the sentences using the review words.

1. A value of the variable that makes an equation true is a _____.

2. The set of all whole numbers and their opposites are _____.

3. An _____ is an expression that contains at least one variable.

Active Reading

Layered Book Before beginning the module, create a layered book to help you learn the concepts in this module. At the top of the first flap, write the title of the book, "Solving Linear Equations." Then label each flap with one of the lesson titles in this module. As you study each lesson, write important ideas, such as vocabulary and formulas, under the appropriate flap.

Unpacking the Standards

Understanding the standards and the vocabulary terms in the standards will help you know exactly what you are expected to learn in this module.

COMMON CORE **8.EE.7a**

Give examples of linear equations in one variable with one solution, infinitely many solutions, or no solutions. Show which of these possibilities is the case by successively transforming the given equation into simpler forms, until an equivalent equation of the form $x = a$, $a = a$, or $a = b$ results (where a and b are different numbers).

Key Vocabulary

linear equation in one variable
(ecuación lineal en una variable)
An equation that can be written in the form $ax = b$ where a and b are constants and $a \neq 0$.

What It Means to You

You will identify the number of solutions an equation has.

UNPACKING EXAMPLE 8.EE.7a

Your gym charges $50 per month. Find the number of months for which your costs will equal the cost of membership at each gym shown.

A: $40 per month plus $100 one-time fee
$50x = 40x + 100 \rightarrow x = 10$
Equal in 10 months → one solution

B: $50 per month plus $25 one-time fee
$50x = 50x + 25 \rightarrow 0 = 25$
Never equal → no solution

C: $40 per month plus $10 monthly garage fee
$50x = 40x + 10x \rightarrow x = x$
Equal for any number of months → infinitely many solutions

COMMON CORE **8.EE.7b**

Solve linear equations with rational number coefficients, including equations whose solutions require expanding expressions using the distributive property and collecting like terms.

Key Vocabulary

solution *(solución)*
In an equation, the value for the variable that makes the equation true.

Visit **my.hrw.com**
to see all the
Common Core Standards unpacked.

ⓜ my.hrw.com

What It Means to You

You can write and solve an equation that has a variable on both sides of the equal sign.

UNPACKING EXAMPLE 8.EE.7b

Yellow Taxi has no pickup fee but charges $0.25 per mile. AAA Taxi charges $3 for pickup and $0.15 per mile. Find the number of miles for which the cost of the two taxis is the same.

$$0.25x = 3 + 0.15x$$
$$100(0.25x) = 100(3) + 100(0.15x)$$
$$25x = 300 + 15x$$
$$10x = 300$$
$$x = 30$$

The cost is the same for 30 miles.

Equations with the Variable on Both Sides

COMMON CORE **8.EE.7**
Solve linear equations in one variable. *Also 8.EE.7b*

ESSENTIAL QUESTION

How can you represent and solve equations with the variable on both sides?

EXPLORE ACTIVITY COMMON CORE **8.EE.7, 8.EE.7b**

Modeling an Equation with a Variable on Both Sides

Algebra tiles can model equations with a variable on both sides.

KEY

= 1
= −1
+ = 0
+ = x

Use algebra tiles to model and solve $x + 5 = 3x - 1$.

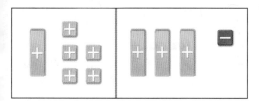

Model $x + 5$ on the left side of the mat and $3x - 1$ on the right side.
Remember that $3x - 1$ is the same as

$3x +$ _____ .

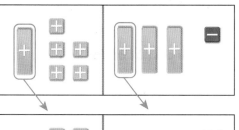

Remove one x-tile from both sides. This

represents subtracting _____ from both sides of the equation.

> **Math Talk**
> Mathematical Practices
>
> Why is a positive unit tile added to both sides in the third step?

Place one +1-tile on both sides. This

represents adding _____ to both sides of the equation. Remove zero pairs.

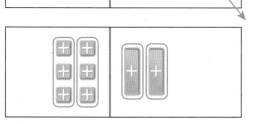

Separate each side into 2 equal groups.

One x-tile is equivalent to _____ +1-tiles.

The solution is _____ = _____ .

Reflect

1. How can you check the solution to $x + 5 = 3x - 1$ using algebra tiles?

_____

_____

Math On the Spot

⏻ my.hrw.com

Animated Math

⏻ my.hrw.com

Solving an Equation with the Variable on Both Sides

Equations with the variable on both sides can be used to compare costs of real-world situations. To solve these equations, use inverse operations to get the variable terms on one side of the equation.

EXAMPLE 1   COMMON CORE 8.EE.7, 8.EE.7b

Andy's Rental Car charges an initial fee of $20 plus an additional $30 per day to rent a car. Buddy's Rental Car charges an initial fee of $36 plus an additional $28 per day. For what number of days is the total cost charged by the companies the same?

 STEP 1 Write an expression representing the total cost of renting a car from Andy's Rental Car.

$$\text{Initial fee} \quad + \quad \text{Cost for } x \text{ days}$$
$$20 \quad + \quad 30x$$

 STEP 2 Write an expression representing the total cost of renting a car from Buddy's Rental Car.

$$\text{Initial fee} \quad + \quad \text{Cost for } x \text{ days}$$
$$36 \quad + \quad 28x$$

 STEP 3 Write an equation that can be solved to find the number of days for which the total cost charged by the companies would be the same.

$$\text{Total cost at Andy's} \quad = \quad \text{Total cost at Buddy's}$$
$$20 + 30x \quad = \quad 36 + 28x$$

 STEP 4 Solve the equation for x.

Math Talk
Mathematical Practices

When is it more economical to rent from Andy's Rental Car? When is it more economical to rent from Buddy's?

$20 + 30x =$	$36 + 28x$	*Write the equation.*
$-28x$	$-28x$	*Subtract 28x from both sides.*
$20 + 2x =$	36	
-20	-20	*Subtract 20 from both sides.*
$2x =$	16	
$\dfrac{2x}{2} =$	$\dfrac{16}{2}$	*Divide both sides by 2.*
$x =$	8	

The total cost is the same if the rental is for 8 days.

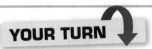

2. A water tank holds 256 gallons but is leaking at a rate of 3 gallons per week. A second water tank holds 384 gallons but is leaking at a rate of 5 gallons per week. After how many weeks will the amount of water in the two tanks be the same?

_____

Personal Math Trainer

Online Assessment and Intervention

⏻ my.hrw.com

Writing a Real-World Situation from an Equation

As shown in Example 1, an equation with the variable on both sides can be used to represent a real-world situation. You can reverse this process by writing a real-world situation for a given equation.

Math On the Spot

⏻ my.hrw.com

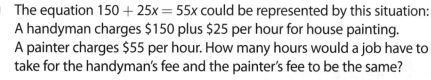

EXAMPLE 2

COMMON CORE 8.EE.7

My Notes

Write a real-world situation that could be modeled by the equation 150 + 25x = 55x.

STEP 1 The left side of the equation consists of a constant plus a variable term. It could represent the total cost for doing a job where there is an initial fee plus an hourly charge.

STEP 2 The right side of the equation consists of a variable term. It could represent the cost for doing the same job based on an hourly charge only.

STEP 3 The equation 150 + 25x = 55x could be represented by this situation: A handyman charges $150 plus $25 per hour for house painting. A painter charges $55 per hour. How many hours would a job have to take for the handyman's fee and the painter's fee to be the same?

YOUR TURN

3. Write a real-world situation that could be modeled by the equation 30x = 48 + 22x.

_____

_____

_____

_____

Personal Math Trainer

Online Assessment and Intervention

⏻ my.hrw.com

Guided Practice

Use algebra tiles to model and solve each equation. (Explore Activity)

1. $x + 4 = -x - 4$ _____ **2.** $2 - 3x = -x - 8$ _____

3. At Silver Gym, membership is \$25 per month, and personal training sessions are \$30 each. At Fit Factor, membership is \$65 per month, and personal training sessions are \$20 each. In one month, how many personal training sessions would Sarah have to buy to make the total cost at the two gyms equal? (Example 1)

_____

4. Write a real-world situation that could be modeled by the equation $120 + 25x = 45x$. (Example 2)

_____

_____

_____

_____

5. Write a real-world situation that could be modeled by the equation $100 - 6x = 160 - 10x$. (Example 2)

_____

_____

_____

_____

_____

? ESSENTIAL QUESTION CHECK-IN

6. How can you solve an equation with the variable on both sides?

_____

_____

_____

_____

_____

15.1 Independent Practice

COMMON CORE 8.EE.7, 8.EE.7b

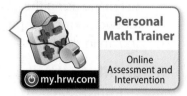

Personal Math Trainer

Online Assessment and Intervention

my.hrw.com

7. Derrick's Dog Sitting and Darlene's Dog Sitting are competing for new business. The companies ran the ads shown.

a. Write and solve an equation to find the number of hours for which the total cost will be the same for the two services.

_____

b. Analyze Relationships Which dog sitting service is more economical to use if you need 5 hours of service? Explain.

_____

_____

Derrick's Dog Sitting

$12 plus $5 per hour

Darlene's Dog Sitting

$18 plus $3 per hour

8. Country Carpets charges $22 per square yard for carpeting, and an additional installation fee of $100. City Carpets charges $25 per square yard for the same carpeting, and an additional installation fee of $70.

a. Write and solve an equation to find the number of square yards of carpeting for which the total cost charged by the two companies will be the same.

_____

b. Justify Reasoning Mr. Shu wants to hire one of the two carpet companies to install carpeting in his basement. Is he more likely to hire Country Carpets or City Carpets? Explain your reasoning.

_____

_____

_____

_____

Write an equation to represent each relationship. Then solve the equation.

9. Two less than 3 times a number is the same as the number plus 10.

_____

10. A number increased by 4 is the same as 19 minus 2 times the number.

_____

11. Twenty less than 8 times a number is the same as 15 more than the number.

_____

12. The charges for an international call made using the calling card for two phone companies are shown in the table.

Phone Company	Charges
Company A	35¢ plus 3¢ per minute
Company B	45¢ plus 2¢ per minute

a. What is the length of a phone call that would cost the same no matter which company is used?

_____

b. **Analyze Relationships** When is it better to use the card from Company B?

_____

_____

 **FOCUS ON HIGHER ORDER THINKING**

Work Area

13. **Draw Conclusions** Liam is setting up folding chairs for a meeting. If he arranges the chairs in 9 rows of the same length, he has 3 chairs left over. If he arranges the chairs in 7 rows of that same length, he has 19 left over. How many chairs does Liam have?

_____

14. **Explain the Error** Rent-A-Tent rents party tents for a flat fee of $365 plus $125 a day. Capital Rentals rents party tents for a flat fee of $250 plus $175 a day. Delia wrote the following equation to find the number of days for which the total cost charged by the two companies would be the same:

$$365x + 125 = 250x + 175$$

Find and explain the error in Delia's work. Then write the correct equation.

_____

_____

_____

_____

15. **Persevere in Problem Solving** Lilliana is training for a marathon. She runs the same distance every day for a week. On Monday, Wednesday, and Friday, she runs 3 laps on a running trail and then runs 6 more miles. On Tuesday and Sunday, she runs 5 laps on the trail and then runs 2 more miles. On Saturday, she just runs laps. How many laps does Lilliana run on Saturday?

_____

Equations with Rational Numbers

COMMON CORE **8.EE.7b**

Solve linear equations with rational number coefficients, ... *Also 8.EE.7*

ESSENTIAL QUESTION

How can you solve equations with rational number coefficients and constants?

EXPLORE ACTIVITY COMMON CORE **8.EE.7b, 8.EE.7**

Solving an Equation That Involves Fractions

To solve an equation with the variable on both sides that involves fractions, start by eliminating the fractions from the equation.

Math On the Spot
⏻ my.hrw.com

EXAMPLE 1 Solve $\frac{7}{10}n + \frac{3}{2} = \frac{3}{5}n + 2$.

STEP 1 Determine the least common multiple of the denominators: _____

STEP 2 Multiply both sides of the equation by the LCM.

$$\boxed{}\left(\frac{7}{10}n + \frac{3}{2}\right) = \boxed{}\left(\frac{3}{5}n + 2\right)$$

$$\boxed{}\,10\left(\frac{7}{10_1}n\right) + \boxed{}\,10\left(\frac{3}{2_1}\right) = \boxed{}\,10\left(\frac{3}{5_1}n\right) + 10(2)$$

$$\boxed{}n + \boxed{} = \boxed{}n + \boxed{}$$

STEP 3 Use inverse operations to solve the equation.

$$7n + 15 = 6n + 20$$

Subtract 15 from both sides.

$$-\boxed{} \qquad -\boxed{}$$

$$\boxed{} = 6n + \boxed{}$$

$$-\boxed{} \qquad -\boxed{}$$

Subtract 6n from both sides.

$$n = \boxed{}$$

Reflect

1. What is the advantage of multiplying both sides of the equation by the least common multiple of the denominators in the first step?

_____

2. **What If?** What happens in the first step if you multiply both sides by a common multiple of the denominators that is not the LCM?

_____

_____

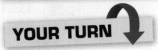

YOUR TURN

Solve.

3. $\frac{1}{7}k - 6 = \frac{3}{7}k + 4$ _____

4. $\frac{5}{6}y + 1 = -\frac{1}{2}y + \frac{1}{4}$ _____

Personal
Math Traine

Online Assessmen
and Intervention

my.hrw.com

Math On the Spot

my.hrw.com

Solving an Equation that Involves Decimals

Solving an equation with the variable on both sides that involves decimals is similar to solving an equation with fractions. But instead of first multiplying both sides by the LCM, multiply by a power of 10 to eliminate the decimals.

EXAMPLE 2

COMMON CORE   8.EE.7, 8.EE.7b

Javier walks from his house to the zoo at a constant rate. After walking 0.75 mile, he meets his brother, Raul, and they continue walking at the same constant rate. When they arrive at the zoo, Javier has walked for 0.5 hour and Raul has walked for 0.2 hour. What is the rate in miles per hour at which the brothers walked to the zoo?

STEP 1 Write an equation for the distance from the brothers' house to the zoo, using the fact that distance equals rate times time. Let $r =$ the brothers' walking rate.

$$\underbrace{0.2r + 0.75}_{\text{distance to zoo}} = \underbrace{0.5r}_{\text{distance to zoo}}$$

STEP 2 Multiply both sides of the equation by $10^2 = 100$.

$$100(0.2r) + 100(0.75) = 100(0.5r)$$
$$20r + 75 = 50r$$

> Multiplying by 100 clears the equation of decimals. Multiplying by 10 does not: $10 \times 0.75 = 7.5$.

STEP 3 Use inverse operations to solve the equation.

$$
\begin{array}{rll}
20r + 75 &= 50r & \text{Write the equation.} \\
\underline{-20r} & \underline{ -20r} & \text{Subtract } 20r \text{ from both sides.} \\
75 &= 30r & \\
\dfrac{75}{30} &= \dfrac{30r}{30} & \text{Divide both sides by 30.} \\
2.5 &= r &
\end{array}
$$

So, the brothers' constant rate of speed was 2.5 miles per hour.

5. Logan has two aquariums. One aquarium contains 1.3 cubic feet of water and the other contains 1.9 cubic feet of water. The water in the larger aquarium weighs 37.44 pounds more than the water in the smaller aquarium. Write an equation with a variable on both sides to represent the situation. Then find the weight of 1 cubic foot of water.

_____

Writing a Real-World Situation from an Equation

Real-world situations can often be represented by equations involving fractions and decimals. Fractions and decimals can represent quantities such as weight, volume, capacity, time, and temperature. Decimals can also be used to represent dollars and cents.

EXAMPLE 3 COMMON CORE 8.EE.7

Write a real-world situation that can be modeled by the equation 0.95x = 0.55x + 60.

The left side of the equation consists of a variable term. It could represent the total cost for *x* items.

The right side of the equation consists of a variable term plus a constant. It could represent the total cost for *x* items plus a flat fee.

The equation $0.95x = 0.55x + 60$ could be represented by this situation: Toony Tunes charges $0.95 for each song you download. Up With Downloads charges $0.55 for each song but also charges an annual membership fee of $60. How many songs must a customer download in a year so that the cost will be the same at both websites?

My Notes

YOUR TURN

6. Write a real-world problem that can be modeled by the equation $\frac{1}{3}x + 10 = \frac{3}{5}x$.

_____

_____

_____

_____

1. Sandy is upgrading her Internet service. Fast Internet charges $60 for installation and $50.45 per month. Quick Internet has free installation but charges $57.95 per month. (Example 2)

   a. Write an equation that can be used to find the number of months at which the Internet service would cost the same.

   _____

   b. Solve the equation.

   _____

Solve. (Explore Activity Example 1 and Example 2)

2. $\frac{3}{4}n - 18 = \frac{1}{4}n - 4$

3. $6 + \frac{4}{5}b = \frac{9}{10}b$

4. $\frac{2}{11}m + 16 = 4 + \frac{6}{11}m$

5. $2.25t + 5 = 13.5t + 14$

6. $3.6w = 1.6w + 24$

7. $-0.75p - 2 = 0.25p$

8. Write a real-world problem that can be modeled by the equation $1.25x = 0.75x + 50$. (Example 3)

   _____

   _____

   _____

   _____

   _____

? ESSENTIAL QUESTION CHECK-IN

9. How does the method for solving equations with fractional or decimal coefficients and constants compare with the method for solving equations with integer coefficients and constants?

   _____

   _____

   _____

15.2 Independent Practice

COMMON CORE 8.EE.7, 8.EE.7b

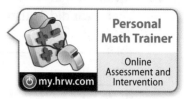

Personal Math Trainer

Online Assessment and Intervention

my.hrw.com

10. Members of the Wide Waters Club pay $105 per summer season, plus $9.50 each time they rent a boat. Nonmembers must pay $14.75 each time they rent a boat. How many times would a member and a non-member have to rent a boat in order to pay the same amount?

_____

11. Margo can purchase tile at a store for $0.79 per tile and rent a tile saw for $24. At another store she can borrow the tile saw for free if she buys tiles there for $1.19 per tile. How many tiles must she buy for the cost to be the same at both stores?

_____

12. The charges for two shuttle services are shown in the table. Find the number of miles for which the cost of both shuttles is the same.

	Pickup Charge ($)	Charge per Mile ($)
Easy Ride	10	0.10
Best	0	0.35

_____

13. Multistep Rapid Rental Car charges a $40 rental fee, $15 for gas, and $0.25 per mile driven. For the same car, Capital Cars charges $45 for rental and gas and $0.35 per mile.

a. For how many miles is the rental cost at both companies the same?

_____

b. What is that cost?

14. Write an equation with the solution $x = 20$. The equation should have the variable on both sides, a fractional coefficient on the left side, and a fraction anywhere on the right side.

_____

15. Write an equation with the solution $x = 25$. The equation should have the variable on both sides, a decimal coefficient on the left side, and a decimal anywhere on the right side. One of the decimals should be written in tenths, the other in hundredths.

_____

16. Geometry The perimeters of the rectangles shown are equal. What is the perimeter of each rectangle?

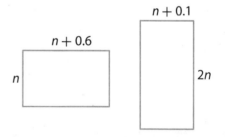

$n + 0.6$

n

$n + 0.1$

$2n$

_____

17. Analyze Relationships The formula $F = 1.8C + 32$ gives the temperature in degrees Fahrenheit (F) for a given temperature in degrees Celsius (C). There is one temperature for which the number of degrees Fahrenheit is equal to the number of degrees Celsius. Write an equation you can solve to find that temperature and then use it to find the temperature.

_____

18. Explain the Error Agustin solved an equation as shown. What error did Agustin make? What is the correct answer?

$$\frac{1}{3}x - 4 = \frac{3}{4}x + 1$$

$$12\left(\frac{1}{3}x\right) - 4 = 12\left(\frac{3}{4}x\right) + 1$$

$$4x - 4 = 9x + 1$$

$$-5 = 5x$$

$$x = -1$$

_____

_____

_____

_____

 FOCUS ON HIGHER ORDER THINKING

Work Area

19. Draw Conclusions Solve the equation $\frac{1}{2}x - 5 + \frac{2}{3}x = \frac{7}{6}x + 4$. Explain your results.

_____

_____

_____

_____

20. Look for a Pattern Describe the pattern in the equation. Then solve the equation.

$$0.3x + 0.03x + 0.003x + 0.0003x + \ldots = 3$$

_____

_____

_____

_____

21. Critique Reasoning Jared wanted to find three consecutive even integers whose sum was 4 times the first of those integers. He let k represent the first integer, then wrote and solved this equation: $k + (k + 1) + (k + 2) = 4k$. Did he get the correct answer? Explain.

_____

_____

_____

_____

_____

_____

Equations with the Distributive Property

COMMON CORE 8.EE.7b

Solve linear equations with rational number coefficients, including equations whose solutions require expanding expressions using the distributive property and collecting like terms.

ESSENTIAL QUESTION

How do you use the Distributive Property to solve equations?

EXPLORE ACTIVITY COMMON CORE 8.EE.7b

Math On the Spot

⊙ my.hrw.com

Using the Distributive Property

The Distributive Property can be useful in solving equations.

EXAMPLE 1 Solve each equation.

A $3(x - 5) + 1 = 2 + x$

STEP 1 Use the Distributive Property.

Distribute 3 to the terms inside the parentheses. $3x - \boxed{} + 1 = 2 + x$

Simplify. $\boxed{} = 2 + x$

STEP 2 Use inverse operations to solve the equation. $3x - 14 = 2 + x$

Subtract _____ from both sides. $\dfrac{-\boxed{}}{2x - 14} \quad \dfrac{-\boxed{}}{= 2}$

Add _____ to both sides. $\dfrac{+\boxed{}}{2x} \quad = \dfrac{+\boxed{}}{16}$

Divide both sides by 2.

$x = \boxed{}$

B $5 - 7k = -4(k + 1) - 3$

STEP 1 Use the Distributive Property.

Distribute _____ to the terms inside the parentheses. $5 - 7k = \boxed{} - 4 - 3$

Simplify. $5 - 7k = \boxed{}$

STEP 2 Use inverse operations to solve the equation. $5 - 7k = -4k - 7$

Add _____ to both sides. $\dfrac{+4k \quad +\boxed{}}{5 - 3k = \quad -7}$

Subtract _____ from both sides. $\dfrac{-\boxed{} \quad -\boxed{}}{-3k = \quad -12}$

Divide both sides by _____.

$k = \boxed{}$

YOUR TURN

Solve each equation.

1. $y - 5 = 3 - 9(y + 2)$ _____

2. $2(x - 7) - 10 = 12 - 4x$ _____

Personal Math Trainer

Online Assessment and Intervention

⏻ my.hrw.com

Math On the Spot

⏻ my.hrw.com

Using the Distributive Property on Both Sides

Some equations require the use of the Distributive Property on both sides.

EXAMPLE 2

COMMON CORE 8.EE.7b

Solve: $\frac{3}{4}(x - 13) = -2(9 + x)$

STEP 1 Eliminate the fraction.

$\frac{3}{4}(x - 13) = -2(9 + x)$

$4 \times \frac{3}{4}(x - 13) = 4 \times [-2(9 + x)]$ Multiply both sides by 4.

$3(x - 13) = -8(9 + x)$

STEP 2 Use the Distributive Property.

$3x - 39 = -72 - 8x$ Distribute 3 and −8 to the terms within the parentheses.

STEP 3 Use inverse operations to solve the equation.

$$
\begin{array}{rl}
3x - 39 = & -72 - 8x \\
\underline{+ 8x} \quad\quad & \underline{+ 8x} \\
11x - 39 = & -72 \\
\underline{+ 39} \quad & \underline{+ 39} \\
11x = & -33 \\
\frac{11x}{11} = & \frac{-33}{11} \\
x = & -3
\end{array}
$$

Add 8x to both sides.

Add 39 to both sides.

Divide both sides by 11.

Math Talk

Mathematical Practices

How can you eliminate fractions if there is a fraction being distributed on both sides of an equation?

Personal Math Trainer

Online Assessment and Intervention

⏻ my.hrw.com

YOUR TURN

Solve each equation.

3. $-4(-5 - b) = \frac{1}{3}(b + 16)$ _____

4. $\frac{3}{5}(t + 18) = -3(2 - t)$ _____

Solving a Real-World Problem Using the Distributive Property

Solving a real-world problem may involve using the Distributive Property.

Math On the Spot
my.hrw.com

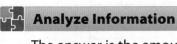

EXAMPLE 3   Problem Solving

COMMON CORE 8.EE.7b

The Coleman family had their bill at a restaurant reduced by $7.50 because of a special discount. They left a tip of $8.90, which was 20% of the reduced amount. How much was their bill before the discount?

Analyze Information

The answer is the amount before the discount.

Formulate a Plan

Use an equation to find the amount before the discount.

Solve

STEP 1 Write the equation $0.2(x - 7.5) = 8.9$, where x is the amount of the Coleman family's bill before the discount.

STEP 2 Use the Distributive Property: $0.2x - 1.5 = 8.9$

STEP 3 Use inverse operations to solve the equation.

$$0.2x - 1.5 = 8.9$$
$$\underline{+ 1.5 \quad + 1.5} \qquad \text{Add 1.5 to both sides.}$$
$$0.2x = 10.4$$
$$\frac{0.2x}{0.2} = \frac{10.4}{0.2} \qquad \text{Divide both sides by 0.2.}$$
$$x = 52$$

The Coleman family's bill before the discount was $52.00.

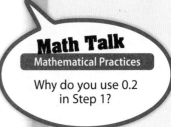

Math Talk
Mathematical Practices

Why do you use 0.2 in Step 1?

Justify and Evaluate

$52.00 - $7.50 = $44.50 and 0.2($44.50) = $8.90. This is the amount of the tip the Colemans left. The answer is reasonable.

YOUR TURN

5. The Smiths spend 8% of their budget on entertainment. Their total budget this year is $2,000 more than last year, and this year they plan to spend $3,840 on entertainment. What was their total budget last year? _____

Personal Math Trainer

Online Assessment and Intervention

my.hrw.com

Solve each equation.

1. $4(x + 8) - 4 = 34 - 2x$
(Explore Activity Ex. 1)

$$\boxed{}\,x + \boxed{} - 4 = 34 - 2x$$

$$\boxed{}\,x + \boxed{} = 34 - 2x$$

$$\boxed{}\,x + \boxed{} = 34$$

$$\boxed{}\,x = \boxed{}$$

$$\frac{\boxed{}\,x}{\boxed{}} = \frac{\boxed{}}{\boxed{}}$$

$$x = \boxed{}$$

2. $\frac{2}{3}(9 + x) = -5(4 - x)$ (Ex. 2)

$$\boxed{} \times \frac{2}{3}(9 + x) = \boxed{} \times [-5(4 - x)]$$

$$\boxed{}(9 + x) = \boxed{}(4 - x)$$

$$\boxed{} + \boxed{}\,x = \boxed{}\;\bigcirc\;\boxed{}\,x$$

$$\boxed{}\,x = \boxed{}$$

$$\frac{\boxed{}\,x}{\boxed{}} = \frac{\boxed{}}{\boxed{}}$$

$$x = \boxed{}$$

3. $-3(x + 4) + 15 = 6 - 4x$
(Explore Activity Ex. 1)

_____

4. $10 + 4x = 5(x - 6) + 33$
(Explore Activity Ex. 1)

_____

5. $x - 9 = 8(2x + 3) - 18$
(Explore Activity Ex. 1)

_____

6. $-6(x - 1) - 7 = -7x + 2$
(Explore Activity Ex. 1)

_____

7. $\frac{1}{10}(x + 11) = -2(8 - x)$ (Ex. 2)

_____

8. $-(4 - x) = \frac{3}{4}(x - 6)$ (Ex. 2)

_____

9. $-8(8 - x) = \frac{4}{5}(x + 10)$ (Ex. 2)

_____

10. $\frac{1}{2}(16 - x) = -12(x + 7)$ (Ex. 2)

_____

11. Sandra saves 12% of her salary for retirement. This year her salary
was $3,000 more than in the previous year, and she saved $4,200.
What was her salary in the previous year? (Example 3)

Write an equation. _____

Sandra's salary in the previous year was _____.

? **ESSENTIAL QUESTION CHECK-IN**

12. When solving an equation using the Distributive Property, if the
numbers being distributed are fractions, what is your first step? Why?

_____

15.3 Independent Practice

COMMON CORE 8.EE.7b

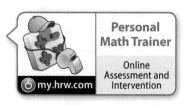

Personal Math Trainer

Online Assessment and Intervention

my.hrw.com

13. Multistep Martina is currently 14 years older than her cousin Joey. In 5 years she will be 3 times as old as Joey. Use this information to answer the following questions.

a. If you let x represent Joey's current age, what expression can you use to represent Martina's current age?

_____

b. Based on your answer to part a, what expression represents Joey's age in 5 years? What expression represents Martina's age in 5 years?

_____

c. What equation can you write based on the information given?

_____

d. What is Joey's current age? What is Martina's current age?

_____

14. As part of a school contest, Sarah and Luis are playing a math game. Sarah must pick a number between 1 and 50 and give Luis clues so he can write an equation to find her number. Sarah says, "If I subtract 5 from my number, multiply that quantity by 4, and then add 7 to the result, I get 35." What equation can Luis write based on Sarah's clues and what is Sarah's number?

_____

15. Critical Thinking When solving an equation using the Distributive Property that involves distributing fractions, usually the first step is to multiply by the LCD to eliminate the fractions in order to simplify computation. Is it necessary to do this to solve $\frac{1}{2}(4x + 6) = \frac{1}{3}(9x - 24)$? Why or why not?

_____

_____

16. Solve the equation given in Exercise 15 with and without using the LCD of the fractions. Are your answers the same?

_____

17. Represent Real-World Problems A chemist mixed x milliliters of 25% acid solution with some 15% acid solution to produce 100 milliliters of a 19% acid solution. Use this information to fill in the missing information in the table and answer the questions that follow.

	ml of Solution	Percent Acid as a Decimal	ml of Acid
25% Solution	x		
15% Solution			
Mixture (19% Solution)	100		

a. What is the relationship between the milliliters of acid in the 25% solution, the milliliters of acid in the 15% solution, and the milliliters of acid in the mixture? _____

_____

_____

b. What equation can you use to solve for x based on your answer to part a? _____

c. How many milliliters of the 25% solution and the 15% solution did the chemist use in the mixture? _____

_____

H.O.T. FOCUS ON HIGHER ORDER THINKING

Work Area

18. Explain the Error Anne solved $5(2x) - 3 = 20x + 15$ for x by first distributing 5 on the left side of the equation. She got the answer $x = -3$. However, when she substituted -3 into the original equation for x, she saw that her answer was wrong. What did Anne do wrong, and what is the correct answer? _____

_____

_____

19. Communicate Mathematical Ideas Explain a procedure that can be used to solve $5[3(x + 4) - 2(1 - x)] - x - 15 = 14x + 45$. Then solve the equation. _____

_____

_____

_____

Equations with Many Solutions or No Solution

COMMON CORE 8.EE.7a

Give examples of linear equations ... with one solution, infinitely many solutions, or no solutions. Show which of these ... is the case by ... transforming the given equation into ... $x = a$, $a = a$, or $a = b$ ... .

ESSENTIAL QUESTION

How can you give examples of equations with a given number of solutions?

EXPLORE ACTIVITY COMMON CORE 8.EE.7a

Determining the Number of Solutions

So far, when you solved a linear equation in one variable, you found one value of x that makes the equation a true statement. When you simplify some equations, you may find that they do not have one solution.

Math On the Spot
my.hrw.com

EXAMPLE 1 Use the properties of equality to simplify each equation. Tell whether the final equation is a true statement.

A $4x - 3 = 2x + 13$

Add _____ to both sides.

Subtract _____ from both sides.

Divide both sides by _____.

The statement is true. There is one solution.

$$4x - 3 = 2x + 13$$

$$+ \boxed{} = + \boxed{}$$

$$\overline{4x = 2x + 16}$$

$$- \boxed{} \qquad - \boxed{}$$

$$\overline{2x = 16}$$

$$\frac{2x}{\boxed{}} = \frac{16}{\boxed{}}$$

$$x = \boxed{}$$

B $4x - 5 = 2(2x - 1) - 3$

Apply the Distributive Property.

Simplify.

Subtract _____ from both sides.

The statement is true. There are many solutions.

$$4x - 5 = 2(2x - 1) - 3$$

$$4x - 5 = \boxed{} - \boxed{} - 3$$

$$4x - 5 = 4x - \boxed{}$$

$$- \boxed{} \qquad - \boxed{}$$

$$\overline{-5 = -5}$$

C $4x + 2 = 4x - 5$

$$4x + 2 = 4x - 5$$

Subtract _____ from both sides.

$$- \boxed{} \qquad - \boxed{}$$

$$4x = 4x - 7$$

Subtract _____ from both sides.

$$- \boxed{} \qquad - \boxed{}$$

$$0 = -7$$

The statement is false. There is no solution.

Reflect

Math Talk
Mathematical Practices

Why do you substitute values for *x* into the *original* equation?

1. What happens when you substitute any value for *x* in the original equation in part B? in the original equation in part C?

_____

_____

YOUR TURN

Use the properties of equality to simplify each equation. Tell whether the final equation is a true statement.

2. $2x + 1 = 5x - 8$ **3.** $3(4x + 3) - 2 = 12x + 7$ **4.** $3x - 9 = 5 + 3x$

_____   _____   _____

Personal Math Trainer

Online Assessment and Intervention

⊙ my.hrw.com

Math On the Spot

⊙ my.hrw.com

Writing Equations with a Given Number of Solutions

When you simplify an equation using the properties of equality, you will find one of three results.

Result	What does this mean?	How many solutions?
$x = a$	When the value of *x* is *a*, the equation is a true statement.	1
$a = a$	Any value of *x* makes the equation a true statement.	Infinitely many
$a = b$, where $a \neq b$	There is no value of *x* that makes the equation a true statement.	0

You can use these results to write a linear equation that has a given number of solutions.

EXAMPLE 2

COMMON CORE 8.EE.7a

Write a linear equation in one variable that has no solution.

You can use the strategy of working backward:

STEP 1 Start with a false statement such as $3 = 5$. Add the same variable term to both sides.

$3 + x = 5 + x$ Add x to both sides.

STEP 2 Next, add the same constant to both sides and combine like terms on each side of the equation.

$10 + x = 12 + x$ Add 7 to both sides.

STEP 3 Verify that your equation has no solutions by using properties of equality to simplify your equation.

$$10 + x = 12 + x$$
$$\underline{-x = -x}$$
$$10 = 12$$

> **Math Talk**
> **Mathematical Practices**
>
> What type of statement do you start with to write an equation with infinitely many solutions? Give an example.

Reflect

5. Explain why the result of the process above is an equation with no solution.

_____

_____

_____

_____

YOUR TURN

Tell whether each equation has one, zero, or infinitely many solutions.

6. $6 + 3x = x - 8$ _____

7. $8x + 4 = 4(2x + 1)$ _____

Complete each equation so that it has the indicated number of solutions.

8. No solution: $3x + 1 = 3x +$ _____

9. Infinitely many: $2x - 4 = 2x -$ _____

Personal Math Trainer

Online Assessment and Intervention

⏻ my.hrw.com

Guided Practice

Use the properties of equality to simplify each equation. Tell whether the final equation is a true statement. (Explore Activity Example 1)

1. $3x - 2 = 25 - 6x$

$$\underline{+6x} \qquad \underline{+6x}$$

$\boxed{} - 2 = \boxed{}$

$\boxed{} = \boxed{}$

$\boxed{}\,x = \boxed{}$

$\dfrac{\boxed{}\,x}{\boxed{}} = \dfrac{\boxed{}}{\boxed{}}$

$x = \boxed{}$

The statement is $\boxed{}$.

2. $2x - 4 = 2(x - 1) + 3$

$2x - 4 = \boxed{} + 3$

$2x - 4 = 2x + \boxed{}$

$-\boxed{} = -\boxed{}$

$\boxed{} = \boxed{}$

The statement is $\boxed{}$.

3. How many solutions are there to the equation in Exercise 2? _____
(Explore Activity Example 1)

4. After simplifying an equation, Juana gets $6 = 6$. Explain what this means.
(Explore Activity Example 1)

_____

Write a linear equation in one variable that has infinitely many solutions. (Example 2)

5. Start with a _____ statement.

Add the _____ to both sides.

Add the _____ to both sides.

Combine _____ terms.

$10 = \boxed{}$

$10 + x = \boxed{}$

$10 + x + 5 = \boxed{}$

$\boxed{} = \boxed{}$

? ESSENTIAL QUESTION CHECK-IN

6. Give an example of an equation with an infinite number of solutions.
Then make one change to the equation so that it has no solution.

_____

_____

15.4 Independent Practice

COMMON CORE 8.EE.7a

Personal Math Trainer

Online Assessment and Intervention

my.hrw.com

Tell whether each equation has one, zero, or infinitely many solutions.

7. $-(2x + 2) - 1 = -x - (x + 3)$

_____

8. $-2(z + 3) - z = -z - 4(z + 2)$

_____

Create an equation with the indicated number of solutions.

9. No solution:

$$3\left(x - \frac{4}{3}\right) = 3x + \boxed{}$$

10. Infinitely many solutions:

$$2(x - 1) + 6x = 4\left(\boxed{} - 1\right) + 2$$

11. One solution of $x = -1$:

$$5x - (x - 2) = 2x - \left(\boxed{}\right)$$

12. Infinitely many solutions:

$$-(x - 8) + 4x = 2\left(\boxed{}\right) + x$$

13. Persevere in Problem Solving The Dig It Project is designing two gardens that have the same perimeter. One garden is a trapezoid whose nonparallel sides are equal. The other is a quadrilateral. Two possible designs are shown at the right.

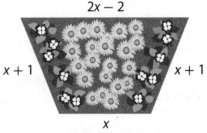

$2x - 2$

$x + 1$ $x + 1$

x

a. Based on these designs, is there more than one value for x? Explain how you know this.

_____

_____

_____

_____

_____

$2x - 9$

x $x + 1$

$x + 8$

b. Why does your answer to part a make sense in this context?

_____

_____

_____

c. Suppose the Dig It Project wants the perimeter of each garden to be 60 meters. What is the value of x in this case? How did you find this?

_____

_____

14. Critique Reasoning Lisa says that the indicated angles cannot have the same measure. Marita disagrees and says she can prove that they can have the same measure. Who do you agree with? Justify your answer.

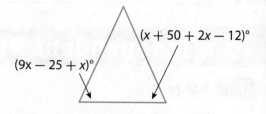

$(x + 50 + 2x - 12)°$

$(9x - 25 + x)°$

_____

_____

_____

_____

15. Represent Real-World Problems Adele opens an account with $100 and deposits $35 a month. Kent opens an account with $50 and also deposits $35 a month. Will they have the same amount in their accounts at any point? If so, in how many months and how much will be in each account? Explain.

_____

_____

_____

H.O.T. FOCUS ON HIGHER ORDER THINKING

Work Area

16. Communicate Mathematical Ideas Frank solved an equation and got the result $x = x$. Sarah solved the same equation and got $12 = 12$. Frank says that one of them is incorrect because you cannot get different results for the same equation. What would you say to Frank? If both results are indeed correct, explain how this happened.

_____

_____

_____

17. Critique Reasoning Matt said $2x - 7 = 2(x - 7)$ has infinitely many solutions. Is he correct? Justify Matt's answer or show how he is incorrect.

_____

_____

_____

Mathy Plants

INSTRUCTIONS

STEP 1 Solve each equation for the variable.

A _____ $3a + 17 = -25$

B _____ $2b - 25 + 5b = 7 - 32$

C _____ $2.7c - 4.5 = 3.6c - 9$

D _____ $\frac{5}{12}d + \frac{1}{6}d + \frac{1}{3}d + \frac{1}{12}d = 6$

E _____ $4e - 6e - 5 = 15$

F _____ $420 = 29f - 73$

G _____ $2(g + 6) = -20$

H _____ $2h + 7 = -3h + 52$

I _____ $96i + 245 = 53$

J _____ $3j + 7 = 46$

K _____ $\frac{1}{2}k = \frac{3}{4}k - \frac{1}{2}$

L _____ $30l + 240 = 50l - 160$

M _____ $4m + \frac{3}{8} = \frac{67}{8}$

N _____ $24 - 6n = 54$

O _____ $8.4o - 6.8 = 14.2 + 6.3o$

P _____ $4p - p + 8 = 2p + 5$

Q _____ $16 - 3q = 3q + 40$

R _____ $4 + \frac{1}{3}r = r - 8$

S _____ $\frac{2}{3}s - \frac{5}{6}s + \frac{1}{2} = -\frac{3}{2}$

T _____ $4 - 15 = 4t + 17$

U _____ $45 + 36u = 66 + 23u + 31$

V _____ $6v + 8 = -4 - 6v$

W _____ $4w + 3w - 6w = w + 15 + 2w - 3w$

X _____ $x + 2x + 3x + 4x + 5 = 75$

Y _____ $\dfrac{4 - y}{5} = \dfrac{2 - 2y}{8}$

Z _____ $-11 = 25 - 4.5z$

STEP 2 Use the value of each variable to decode the answer to the riddle.

What happens to plants that live in a math classroom?

☐	☐	☐	☐
−7	9	−10	−11

☐	☐	☐	☐
−16	18	10	15

☐	☐	☐	☐	☐	☐
12	−4	4	−14	18	−10

☐	☐	☐	☐	☐
18	10	10	−7	12

Ready to Go On?

Personal
Math Trainer

Online Assessment
and Intervention

my.hrw.com

15.1 Equations with the Variable on Both Sides

Solve.

1. $4a - 4 = 8 + a$ _____

2. $4x + 5 = x + 8$ _____

3. Hue is arranging chairs. She can form 6 rows of a given length with 3 chairs left over, or 8 rows of that same length if she gets 11 more chairs. Write and solve an equation to find how many chairs are in that row length.

_____

15.2 Equations with Rational Numbers

Solve.

4. $\frac{2}{3}n - \frac{2}{3} = \frac{n}{6} + \frac{4}{3}$ _____

5. $1.5d + 3.25 = 1 + 2.25d$ _____

6. Happy Paws charges $19.00 plus $1.50 per hour to keep a dog during the day. Woof Watchers charges $14.00 plus $2.75 per hour. Write and solve an equation to find for how many hours the total cost of the services is equal.

_____

15.3 Equations with the Distributive Property

Solve.

7. $14 + 5x = 3(-x + 3) - 11$ _____

8. $\frac{1}{4}(x - 7) = 1 + 3x$ _____

9. $-5(2x - 9) = 2(x - 8) - 11$ _____

10. $3(x + 5) = 2(3x + 12)$ _____

15.4 Equations with Many Solutions or No Solution

Tell whether each equation has one, zero, or infinitely many solutions.

11. $5(x - 3) + 6 = 5x - 9$ _____

12. $5(x - 3) + 6 = 5x - 10$ _____

13. $5(x - 3) + 6 = 4x + 3$ _____

Selected Response

1. Two cars are traveling in the same direction. The first car is going 40 mi/h, and the second car is going 55 mi/h. The first car left 3 hours before the second car. Which equation could you solve to find how many hours it will take for the second car to catch up to the first car?

Ⓐ $55t + 3 = 40t$

Ⓑ $55t + 165 = 40t$

Ⓒ $40t + 3 = 55t$

Ⓓ $40t + 120 = 55t$

2. Which linear equation is represented by the table?

x	−2	1	3	6
y	7	4	2	−1

Ⓐ $y = -x + 5$ Ⓒ $y = x + 3$

Ⓑ $y = 2x - 1$ Ⓓ $y = -3x + 11$

3. Shawn's Rentals charges $27.50 per hour to rent a surfboard and a wetsuit. Darla's Surf Shop charges $23.25 per hour to rent a surfboard plus $17 extra for a wetsuit. For what total number of hours are the charges for Shawn's Rentals the same as the charges for Darla's Surf Shop?

Ⓐ 3   Ⓒ 5

Ⓑ 4   Ⓓ 6

4. Which of the following is irrational?

Ⓐ −8   Ⓒ $\sqrt{11}$

Ⓑ 4.63   Ⓓ $\frac{1}{3}$

5. Greg and Jane left a 15% tip after dinner. The amount of the tip was $9. Greg's dinner cost $24. Which equation can you use to find x, the cost of Jane's dinner?

Ⓐ $0.15x + 24 = 9$

Ⓑ $0.15(x + 24) = 9$

Ⓒ $15(x + 24) = 9$

Ⓓ $0.15x = 24 + 9$

6. For the equation $3(2x - 5) = 6x + k$, which value of k will create an equation with infinitely many solutions?

Ⓐ 15   Ⓒ 5

Ⓑ −5   Ⓓ −15

7. Which of the following is equivalent to 2^{-4}?

Ⓐ $\frac{1}{16}$ Ⓒ −2

Ⓑ $\frac{1}{8}$ Ⓓ −16

Mini-Task

8. Use the figures below for parts *a* and *b*.

 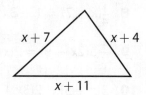

a. Both figures have the same perimeter. Solve for *x*.

_____

b. What is the perimeter of each figure?

_____

Solving Systems of Linear Equations

? **ESSENTIAL QUESTION**

How can you use systems of equations to solve real-world problems?

Real-World Video

The distance contestants in a race travel over time can be modeled by a system of equations. Solving such a system can tell you when one contestant will overtake another who has a head start, as in a boating race or marathon.

my.hrw.com

GO DIGITAL

my.hrw.com

my.hrw.com

Go digital with your write-in student edition, accessible on any device.

Math On the Spot

Scan with your smart phone to jump directly to the online edition, video tutor, and more.

Animated Math

Interactively explore key concepts to see how math works.

Personal Math Trainer

Get immediate feedback and help as you work through practice sets.

Are YOU Ready?

Complete these exercises to review skills you will need for this module.

Simplify Algebraic Expressions

> **EXAMPLE** Simplify $5 - 4y + 2x - 6 + y$.
>
> $-4y + y + 2x - 6 + 5$ Group like terms.
>
> $-3y + 2x - 1$ Combine like terms.

Simplify.

1. $14x - 4x + 21$

2. $-y - 4x + 4y$

3. $5.5a - 1 + 21b + 3a$

4. $2y - 3x + 6x - y$

Graph Linear Equations

> **EXAMPLE** Graph $y = -\frac{1}{3}x + 2$.
>
> Step 1: Make a table of values.
>
> | x | $y = -\frac{1}{3}x + 2$ | (x, y) |
> |---|---|---|
> | 0 | $y = -\frac{1}{3}(0) + 2 = 2$ | $(0, 2)$ |
> | 3 | $y = -\frac{1}{3}(3) + 2 = 1$ | $(3, 1)$ |
>
> Step 2: Plot the points.
> Step 3: Connect the points with a line.

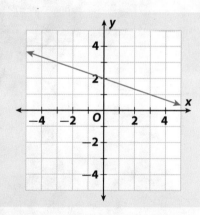

Graph each equation.

5. $y = 4x - 1$

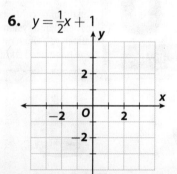

6. $y = \frac{1}{2}x + 1$

7. $y = -x$

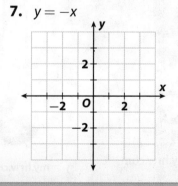

Reading Start-Up

Visualize Vocabulary

Use the ✔ words to complete the graphic.

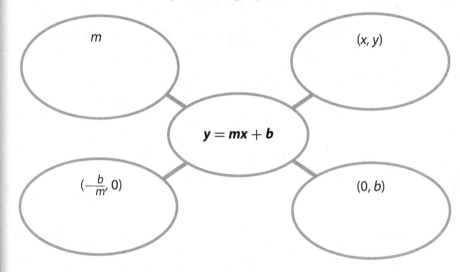

Diagram center: $y = mx + b$

Surrounding ovals:
- m
- (x, y)
- $(-\frac{b}{m}, 0)$
- $(0, b)$

Understand Vocabulary

Complete the sentences using the preview words.

1. A _____ is any ordered pair

   that satisfies all the equations in a system.

2. A set of two or more equations that contain two or more variables is

   called a _____.

Active Reading

Four-Corner Fold Before beginning the module, create a four-corner fold to help you organize what you learn about solving systems of equations. Use the categories "Solving by Graphing," "Solving by Substitution," "Solving by Elimination," and "Solving by Multiplication." As you study this module, note similarities and differences among the four methods. You can use your four-corner fold later to study for tests and complete assignments.

COMMON CORE
Unpacking the Standards

Understanding the standards and the vocabulary terms in the standards will help you know exactly what you are expected to learn in this module.

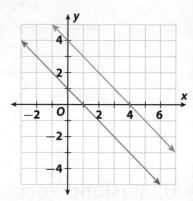

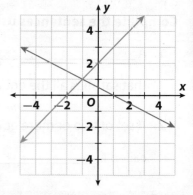

COMMON CORE 8.EE.8a

Understand that solutions to a system of two linear equations in two variables correspond to points of intersection of their graphs, because points of intersection satisfy both equations simultaneously.

COMMON CORE 8.EE.8b

Solve systems of two linear equations in two variables algebraically, and estimate solutions by graphing the equations. Solve simple cases by inspection.

Key Vocabulary

solution of a system of equations *(solución de un sistema de ecuaciones)* A set of values that make all equations in a system true.

system of equations *(sistema de ecuaciones)* A set of two or more equations that contain two or more variables.

Visit **my.hrw.com** to see all the **Common Core Standards** unpacked.

my.hrw.com

What It Means to You

You will understand that the points of intersection of two or more graphs represent the solution to a system of linear equations.

UNPACKING EXAMPLE 8.EE.8a, 8.EE.8b

Use the elimination method.

A.
$$-x = -1 + y$$
$$\underline{x + y = 4}$$
$$y = y + 3$$

This is never true, so the system has no solution.

The lines never intersect.

B.
$$2y + x = 1$$
$$y - 2 = x$$

Use the substitution method.
$$2y + (y - 2) = 1$$
$$3y - 2 = 1$$
$$y = 1$$
$$x = y - 2$$
$$x = 1 - 2$$
$$= -1$$

There is only one solution: $x = -1, y = 2$.

The lines intersect at a single point: $(-1, 2)$.

C.
$$3y - 6x = 3$$
$$y - 2x = 1$$

Use the multiplication method.
$$3y - 6x = 3$$
$$\underline{3y - 6x = 3}$$
$$0 = 0$$

This is always true. So the system has infinitely many solutions.

The graphs overlap completely. They are the same line.

LESSON 16.1

Solving Systems of Linear Equations by Graphing

COMMON CORE 8.EE.8a

Understand that solutions to a system of two linear equations in two variables correspond to points of intersection of their graphs, because points of intersection satisfy both equations simultaneously. *Also 8.EE.8, 8.EE.8c*

ESSENTIAL QUESTION

How can you solve a system of equations by graphing?

EXPLORE ACTIVITY **COMMON CORE** 8.EE.8a

> Slope-intercept form is $y = mx + b$, where m is the slope and b is the y-intercept.

Investigating Systems of Equations

You have learned several ways to graph a linear equation in slope-intercept form. For example, you can use the slope and y-intercept or you can find two points that satisfy the equation and connect them with a line.

A Graph the pair of equations together: $\begin{cases} y = 3x - 2 \\ y = -2x + 3 \end{cases}$.

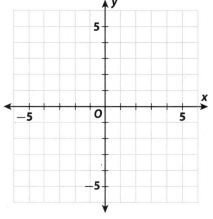

B Explain how to tell whether $(2, -1)$ is a solution of the equation $y = 3x - 2$ without using the graph.

_____

_____

C Explain how to tell whether $(2, -1)$ is a solution of the equation $y = -2x + 3$ without using the graph.

_____

_____

D Use the graph to explain whether $(2, -1)$ is a solution of each equation.

_____

_____

E Determine if the point of intersection is a solution of both equations.

Point of intersection: $\left(\boxed{}, \boxed{} \right)$

$y = 3x - 2$

$\boxed{} = 3\boxed{} - 2$

$1 = \boxed{}$

$y = -2x + 3$

$\boxed{} = -2\boxed{} + 3$

$1 = \boxed{}$

The point of intersection $\boxed{\text{is / is not}}$ the solution of both equations.

Solving Systems Graphically

An ordered pair (x, y) is a solution of an equation in two variables if substituting the x- and y-values into the equation results in a true statement. A **system of equations** is a set of equations that have the same variables. An ordered pair is a **solution of a system of equations** if it is a solution of every equation in the set.

Since the graph of an equation represents all ordered pairs that are solutions of the equation, if a point lies on the graphs of two equations, the point is a solution of both equations and is, therefore, a solution of the system.

EXAMPLE 1

COMMON CORE 8.EE.8

Solve each system by graphing.

A $\begin{cases} y = -x + 4 \\ y = 3x \end{cases}$

My Notes

STEP 1 Start by graphing each equation.

STEP 2 Find the point of intersection of the two lines. It appears to be (1, 3). Check by substitution to determine if it is a solution to both equations.

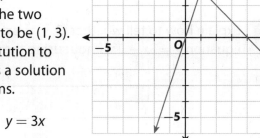

$y = -x + 4 \qquad y = 3x$

$3 \overset{?}{=} -(1) + 4 \qquad 3 \overset{?}{=} 3(1)$

$3 = 3 \checkmark \qquad 3 = 3 \checkmark$

The solution of the system is (1, 3).

B $\begin{cases} y = 3x - 3 \\ y = 3(x - 1) \end{cases}$

STEP 1 Start by graphing each equation.

STEP 2 Identify any ordered pairs that are solutions of both equations.

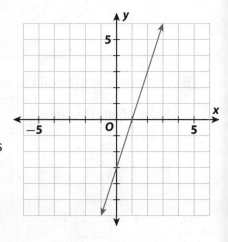

The graphs of the equations are the same line. So, every ordered pair that is a solution of one equation is also a solution of the other equation. The system has infinitely many solutions.

Reflect

1. A system of linear equations has infinitely many solutions. Does that mean any ordered pair in the coordinate plane is a solution?

_____

_____

2. Can you show algebraically that both equations in part B represent the same line? If so, explain how.

_____

_____

_____

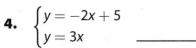

Solve each system by graphing. Check by substitution.

3. $\begin{cases} y = -x + 2 \\ y = -4x - 1 \end{cases}$ _____

Check:

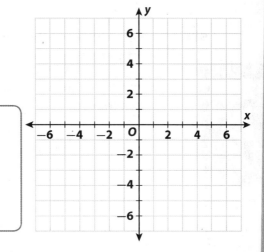

4. $\begin{cases} y = -2x + 5 \\ y = 3x \end{cases}$ _____

Check:

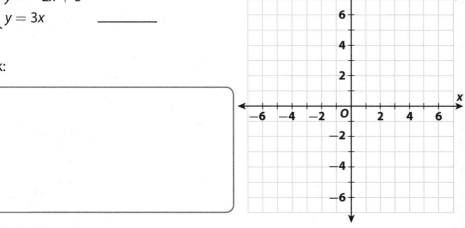

Personal Math Trainer

Online Assessment and Intervention

my.hrw.com

Solving Problems Using Systems of Equations

When using graphs to solve a system of equations, it is best to rewrite both equations in slope-intercept form for ease of graphing.

To write an equation in slope-intercept form starting from $ax + by = c$:

$ax + by = c$

$by = c - ax$ Subtract ax from both sides.

$y = \dfrac{c}{b} - \dfrac{ax}{b}$ Divide both sides by b.

$y = -\dfrac{a}{b}x + \dfrac{c}{b}$ Rearrange the equation.

EXAMPLE 2   **8.EE.8c, 8.EE.8**

Keisha and her friends visit the concession stand at a football game. The stand charges $2 for a hot dog and $1 for a drink. The friends buy a total of 8 items for $11. Tell how many hot dogs and how many drinks they bought.

STEP 1   Let x represent the number of hot dogs they bought and let y represent the number of drinks they bought.

Write an equation representing the **number of items they purchased.**

Number of hot dogs	+	Number of drinks	=	Total items
x	+	y	=	8

Write an equation representing the **money spent on the items.**

Cost of 1 hot dog times number of hot dogs	+	Cost of 1 drink times number of drinks	=	Total cost
$2x$	+	$1y$	=	11

STEP 2   Write the equations in slope-intercept form. Then graph.

$x + y = 8$

$y = 8 - x$

$y = -x + 8$

$2x + 1y = 11$

$1y = 11 - 2x$

$y = -2x + 11$

Graph the equations $y = -x + 8$ and $y = -2x + 11$.

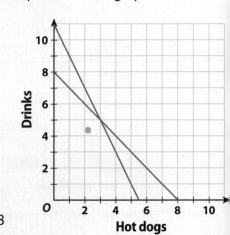

STEP 3　Use the graph to identify the solution of the system of equations. Check your answer by substituting the ordered pair into both equations.

Apparent solution: (3, 5)
Check:

$$x + y = 8 \qquad 2x + y = 11$$
$$3 + 5 \overset{?}{=} 8 \qquad 2(3) + 5 \overset{?}{=} 11$$
$$8 = 8 \checkmark \qquad 11 = 11 \checkmark$$

The point (3, 5) is a solution of both equations.

STEP 4　Interpret the solution in the original context.

Keisha and her friends bought 3 hot dogs and 5 drinks.

Animated Math

my.hrw.com

Reflect

5. Conjecture Why do you think the graph is limited to the first quadrant?

_____

_____

YOUR TURN

6. During school vacation, Marquis wants to go bowling and to play laser tag. He wants to play 6 total games but needs to figure out how many of each he can play if he spends exactly $20. Each game of bowling is $2 and each game of laser tag is $4.

a. Let *x* represent the number of games Marquis bowls and let *y* represent the number of games of laser tag Marquis plays. Write a system of equations that describes the situation. Then write the equations in slope-intercept form.

_____

_____

b. Graph the solutions of both equations.

c. How many games of bowling and how many games of laser tag will Marquis play?

_____

_____

_____

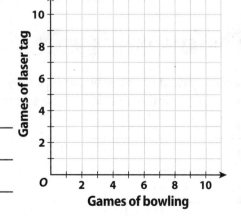

Personal Math Trainer

Online Assessment and Intervention

my.hrw.com

Solve each system by graphing. (Example 1)

1. $\begin{cases} y = 3x - 4 \\ y = x + 2 \end{cases}$ _____

2. $\begin{cases} x - 3y = 2 \\ -3x + 9y = -6 \end{cases}$ _____

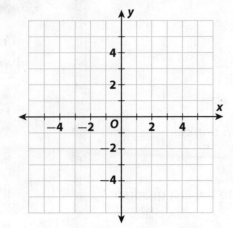

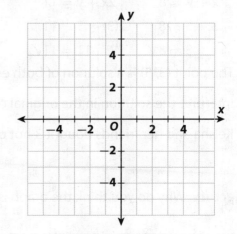

3. **Mrs. Morales wrote a test with 15 questions covering spelling and vocabulary. Spelling questions (x) are worth 5 points and vocabulary questions (y) are worth 10 points. The maximum number of points possible on the test is 100.** (Example 2)

   a. Write an equation in slope-intercept form to represent the number of questions on the test.

   _____

   b. Write an equation in slope-intercept form to represent the total number of points on the test.

   _____

   c. Graph the solutions of both equations.

   d. Use your graph to tell how many of each question type are on the test.

   _____

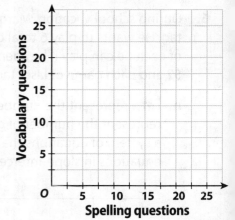

![Spelling questions vs Vocabulary questions graph]

? **ESSENTIAL QUESTION CHECK-IN**

4. When you graph a system of linear equations, why does the intersection of the two lines represent the solution of the system?

_____

_____

_____

16.1 Independent Practice

COMMON CORE 8.EE.8, 8.EE.8a, 8.EE.8c

Personal Math Trainer

Online Assessment and Intervention
my.hrw.com

5. Vocabulary A _____ is a set of equations that have the same variables.

6. Eight friends started a business. They will wear either a baseball cap or a shirt imprinted with their logo while working. They want to spend exactly $36 on the shirts and caps. Shirts cost $6 each and caps cost $3 each.

a. Write a system of equations to describe the situation. Let *x* represent the number of shirts and let *y* represent the number of caps.

_____

_____

b. Graph the system. What is the solution and what does it represent?

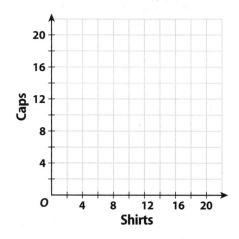

Business Logo Wear

_____

_____

_____

_____

7. Multistep The table shows the cost for bowling at two bowling alleys.

	Shoe Rental Fee	Cost per Game
Bowl-o-Rama	$2.00	$2.50
Bowling Pinz	$4.00	$2.00

a. Write a system of equations, with one equation describing the cost to bowl at Bowl-o-Rama and the other describing the cost to bowl at Bowling Pinz. For each equation, let *x* represent the number of games played and let *y* represent the total cost.

_____

_____

b. Graph the system. What is the solution and what does it represent?

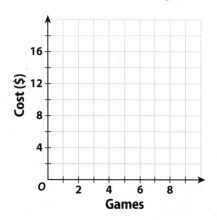

Cost of Bowling

_____

_____

_____

_____

8. **Multi-Step** Jeremy runs 7 miles per week and increases his distance by 1 mile each week. Tony runs 3 miles per week and increases his distance by 2 miles each week. In how many weeks will Jeremy and Tony be running the same distance? What will that distance be?

_____

9. **Critical Thinking** Write a real-world situation that could be represented by the system of equations shown below.

$$\begin{cases} y = 4x + 10 \\ y = 3x + 15 \end{cases}$$

_____

_____

_____

 **FOCUS ON HIGHER ORDER THINKING**

Work Area

10. **Multistep** The table shows two options provided by a high-speed Internet provider.

	Setup Fee ($)	Cost per Month ($)
Option 1	50	30
Option 2	No setup fee	$40

a. In how many months will the total cost of both options be the same? What will that cost be?

_____

b. If you plan to cancel your Internet service after 9 months, which is the cheaper option? Explain.

_____

_____

_____

11. **Draw Conclusions** How many solutions does the system formed by $x - y = 3$ and $ay - ax + 3a = 0$ have for a nonzero number a? Explain.

_____

_____

_____

_____

Solving Systems by Substitution

COMMON CORE 8.EE.8b

Solve systems of two linear equations in two variables algebraically, and estimate solutions by graphing the equations. ... *Also 8.EE.8c*

ESSENTIAL QUESTION How do you use substitution to solve a system of linear equations?

EXPLORE ACTIVITY

COMMON CORE 8.EE.8b

Math On the Spot
⊙ my.hrw.com

Solving a Linear System by Substitution

The **substitution method** is used to solve systems of linear equations by solving an equation for one variable and then substituting the resulting expression for that variable into the other equation. The steps for this method are as follows:

1. Solve one of the equations for one of its variables.

2. Substitute the expression from Step 1 into the other equation and solve for the other variable.

3. Substitute the value from Step 2 into either original equation and solve to find the value of the variable in Step 1.

EXAMPLE 1 **Solve the system of linear equations by substitution. Check your answer.**

$$\begin{cases} -3x + y = 1 \\ 4x + y = 8 \end{cases}$$

STEP 1 Solve an equation for one variable.

Select one of the equations. $\qquad -3x + y = 1$

Solve for the variable y. $\qquad y = \boxed{}$

STEP 2 Substitute the expression for y in the other equation, and solve for x.

Substitute _____ for y. $\qquad 4x + \left(\boxed{} \right) = 8$

Combine like terms. $\qquad \boxed{} + 1 = 8$

Subtract _____ from each side. $\qquad 7x = \boxed{}$

Solve for x. $\qquad x = \boxed{}$

STEP 3 Substitute the value of x you found into one of the equations, and solve for the other variable, y.

$$-3x + y = 1$$

Substitute _____ for x. $\qquad -3\left(\boxed{} \right) + y = 1$

Simplify. $\qquad \boxed{} + y = 1$

Solve for y. $\qquad y = \boxed{}$

So (____, ____) is the solution of the system.

STEP 4 Check the solution by graphing.

$$-3x + y = 1$$

x-intercept: $-3x + 0 = 1 \rightarrow x = $ ☐

y-intercept: $3(0) + y = 1 \rightarrow y = $ ☐

$$4x + y = 8$$

x-intercept: $4x + 0 = 8 \rightarrow x = $ ☐

y-intercept: $4(0) + y = 8 \rightarrow y = $ ☐

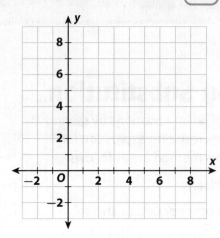

The graph confirms that the

solution is (____, ____).

Reflect

1. Is it more efficient to solve $-3x + y = 1$ for *x*? Why or why not?

_____

_____

2. Is there another way to solve the system?

_____

_____

3. What is another way to check your solution?

_____

_____

YOUR TURN

Solve each system of linear equations by substitution.

4. $\begin{cases} 3x + y = 11 \\ -2x + y = 1 \end{cases}$

5. $\begin{cases} 2x - 3y = -24 \\ x + 6y = 18 \end{cases}$

6. $\begin{cases} x - 2y = 5 \\ 3x - 5y = 8 \end{cases}$

_____   _____   _____

Personal Math Trainer

Online Assessment and Intervention

⊙ my.hrw.com

Using a Graph to Estimate the Solution of a System

You can use a graph to estimate the solution of a system of equations before solving the system algebraically.

Math On the Spot

⏻ my.hrw.com

EXAMPLE 2

COMMON CORE 8.EE.8b

Solve the system $\begin{cases} x - 4y = 4 \\ 2x - 3y = -3 \end{cases}$.

STEP 1 Sketch a graph of each equation by substituting values for x and generating values of y.

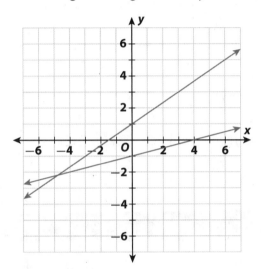

STEP 2 Find the intersection of the lines. The lines appear to intersect near $(-5, -2)$.

Math Talk
Mathematical Practices

In Step 2, how can you tell that $(-5, -2)$ is not the solution?

STEP 3 Solve the system algebraically.

Solve $x - 4y = 4$ for x.
$$x - 4y = 4$$
$$x = 4 + 4y$$

Substitute to find y.
$$2(4 + 4y) - 3y = -3$$
$$8 + 8y - 3y = -3$$
$$8 + 5y = -3$$
$$5y = -11$$
$$y = -\frac{11}{5}$$

Substitute to find x.
$$x = 4 + 4y$$
$$= 4 + 4\left(-\frac{11}{5}\right)$$
$$= \frac{20 - 44}{5}$$
$$= -\frac{24}{5}$$

The solution is $\left(-\frac{24}{5}, -\frac{11}{5}\right)$.

STEP 4 Use the estimate you made using the graph to judge the reasonableness of your solution.

$-\frac{24}{5}$ is close to the estimate of -5, and $-\frac{11}{5}$ is close to the estimate of -2, so the solution seems reasonable.

YOUR TURN

7. Estimate the solution of the system $\begin{cases} x + y = 4 \\ 2x - y = 6 \end{cases}$ by sketching a graph of each linear function. Then solve the system algebraically. Use your estimate to judge the reasonableness of your solution.

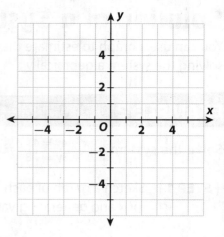

The estimated solution is _____.

The algebraic solution is _____.

The solution ⟨ is/is not ⟩ reasonable because

_____

_____

Solving Problems with Systems of Equations

EXAMPLE 3 Real World

COMMON CORE **8.EE.8c**

As part of Class Day, the eighth grade is doing a treasure hunt. Each team is given the following riddle and map. At what point is the treasure located?

There's pirate treasure to be found. So search on the island, all around. Draw a line through *A* and *B*. Then another through *C* and *D*. Dance a jig, "X" marks the spot. Where the lines intersect, that's the treasure's plot!

 STEP 1 Give the coordinates of each point and find the slope of the line through each pair of points.

A: $(-2, -1)$ C: $(-1, 4)$

B: $(2, 5)$ D: $(1, -4)$

Slope: Slope:

$$\frac{5 - (-1)}{2 - (-2)} = \frac{6}{4}$$ $$\frac{-4 - 4}{1 - (-1)} = \frac{-8}{2}$$

$$= \frac{3}{2}$$ $$= -4$$

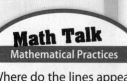

STEP 2 Write equations in slope-intercept form describing the line through points A and B and the line through points C and D.

Line through A and B:

Use the slope and a point to find b.

$5 = \left(\frac{3}{2}\right)2 + b$

$b = 2$

The equation is $y = \frac{3}{2}x + 2$.

Line through C and D:

Use the slope and a point to find b.

$4 = -4(-1) + b$

$b = 0$

The equation is $y = -4x$.

STEP 3 Solve the system algebraically.

Substitute $\frac{3}{2}x + 2$ for y in $y = -4x$ to find x.

$\frac{3}{2}x + 2 = -4x$

$\frac{11}{2}x = -2$

$x = -\frac{4}{11}$

Substitute to find y.

$y = -4\left(-\frac{4}{11}\right) = \frac{16}{11}$

The solution is $\left(-\frac{4}{11}, \frac{16}{11}\right)$.

YOUR TURN

8. Ace Car Rental rents cars for x dollars per day plus y dollars for each mile driven. Carlos rented a car for 4 days, drove it 160 miles, and spent $120. Vanessa rented a car for 1 day, drove it 240 miles, and spent $80. Write equations to represent Carlos's expenses and Vanessa's expenses. Then solve the system and tell what each number represents.

_____

_____

_____

_____

_____

Personal Math Trainer

Online Assessment and Intervention

my.hrw.com

Solve each system of linear equations by substitution. (Explore Activity Example 1)

1. $\begin{cases} 3x - 2y = 9 \\ y = 2x - 7 \end{cases}$ _____

2. $\begin{cases} y = x - 4 \\ 2x + y = 5 \end{cases}$ _____

3. $\begin{cases} x + 4y = 6 \\ y = -x + 3 \end{cases}$ _____

4. $\begin{cases} x + 2y = 6 \\ x - y = 3 \end{cases}$ _____

Solve each system. Estimate the solution first. (Example 2)

5. $\begin{cases} 6x + y = 4 \\ x - 4y = 19 \end{cases}$

Estimate _____

Solution _____

6. $\begin{cases} x + 2y = 8 \\ 3x + 2y = 6 \end{cases}$

Estimate _____

Solution _____

7. $\begin{cases} 3x + y = 4 \\ 5x - y = 22 \end{cases}$

Estimate _____

Solution _____

8. $\begin{cases} 2x + 7y = 2 \\ x + y = -1 \end{cases}$

Estimate _____

Solution _____

9. Adult tickets to Space City amusement park cost x dollars. Children's tickets cost y dollars. The Henson family bought 3 adult and 1 child tickets for $163. The Garcia family bought 2 adult and 3 child tickets for $174. (Example 3)

   a. Write equations to represent the Hensons' cost and the Garcias' cost.

      Hensons' cost: _____   Garcias' cost: _____

   b. Solve the system.

      adult ticket price: _____   child ticket price: _____

? **ESSENTIAL QUESTION CHECK-IN**

10. How can you decide which variable to solve for first when you are solving a linear system by substitution?

_____

_____

_____

16.2 Independent Practice

COMMON CORE 8.EE.8b, 8.EE.8c

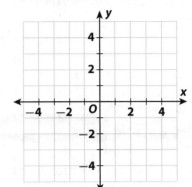

Personal
Math Trainer

Online
Assessment and
Intervention

my.hrw.com

11. Check for Reasonableness Zach solves the system $\begin{cases} x+y=-3 \\ x-y=1 \end{cases}$ and finds the solution $(1, -2)$. Use a graph to explain whether Zach's solution is reasonable.

_____

_____

12. Represent Real-World Problems Angelo bought apples and bananas at the fruit stand. He bought 20 pieces of fruit and spent $11.50. Apples cost $0.50 and bananas cost $0.75 each.

a. Write a system of equations to model the problem. (Hint: One equation will represent the number of pieces of fruit. A second equation will represent the money spent on the fruit.)

_____

b. Solve the system algebraically. Tell how many apples and bananas Angelo bought.

_____

Apples $0.50
Bananas $0.75

13. Represent Real-World Problems A jar contains n nickels and d dimes. There is a total of 200 coins in the jar. The value of the coins is $14.00. How many nickels and how many dimes are in the jar?

_____

14. Multistep The graph shows a triangle formed by the x-axis, the line $3x - 2y = 0$, and the line $x + 2y = 10$. Follow these steps to find the area of the triangle.

a. Find the coordinates of point A by solving the system $\begin{cases} 3x - 2y = 0 \\ x + 2y = 10 \end{cases}$.

Point A: _____

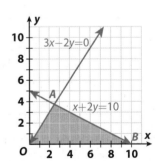

b. Use the coordinates of point A to find the height of the triangle.

height: _____

c. What is the length of the base of the triangle?

base: _____

d. What is the area of the triangle? _____

15. Jed is graphing the design for a kite on a coordinate grid. The four vertices of the kite are at $A\left(-\frac{4}{3}, \frac{2}{3}\right)$, $B\left(\frac{14}{3}, -\frac{4}{3}\right)$, $C\left(\frac{14}{3}, -\frac{16}{3}\right)$, and $D\left(\frac{2}{3}, -\frac{16}{3}\right)$. One kite strut will connect points A and C. The other will connect points B and D. Find the point where the struts cross.

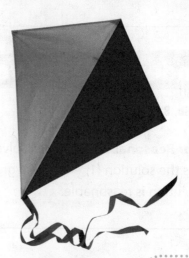

_____

 **FOCUS ON HIGHER ORDER THINKING**

Work Area

16. Analyze Relationships Consider the system $\begin{cases} 6x - 3y = 15 \\ x + 3y = -8 \end{cases}$. Describe three different substitution methods that can be used to solve this system. Then solve the system.

_____

_____

_____

_____

_____

_____

17. Communicate Mathematical Ideas Explain the advantages, if any, that solving a system of linear equations by substitution has over solving the same system by graphing.

_____

_____

_____

_____

18. Persevere in Problem Solving Create a system of equations of the form $\begin{cases} Ax + By = C \\ Dx + Ey = F \end{cases}$ that has $(7, -2)$ as its solution. Explain how you found the system.

_____

_____

_____

_____

Solving Systems by Elimination

COMMON CORE 8.EE.8b

Solve systems of two linear equations in two variables algebraically, ... *Also* 8.EE.8c

ESSENTIAL QUESTION

How do you solve a system of linear equations by adding or subtracting?

EXPLORE ACTIVITY

COMMON CORE 8.EE.8b

Solving a Linear System by Adding

The **elimination method** is another method used to solve a system of linear equations. In this method, one variable is *eliminated* by adding or subtracting the two equations of the system to obtain a single equation in one variable. The steps for this method are as follows:

Math On the Spot

⊙ my.hrw.com

1. Add or subtract the equations to eliminate one variable.

2. Solve the resulting equation for the other variable.

3. Substitute the value into either original equation to find the value of the eliminated variable.

EXAMPLE 1 Solve the system of equations by adding. Check your answer.

$$\begin{cases} 2x - 3y = 12 \\ x + 3y = 6 \end{cases}$$

STEP 1

Add the equations.

Write the equations so that like terms are aligned.

Notice that the terms $-3y$ and _____ are opposites.

Add to eliminate the variable _____.

Simplify.

$$2x - 3y = 12$$
$$+ x + \boxed{} = 6$$
$$\overline{3x + \boxed{} = 18}$$

$$3x = 18$$

Divide each side by _____.

$$\frac{3x}{\boxed{}} = \frac{18}{\boxed{}}$$

Simplify.

$$x = \boxed{}$$

STEP 2

Substitute the solution into one of the original equations, and solve for y.

Use the second equation.

Substitute _____ for the variable x.

Subtract _____ from each side.

Divide each side by _____ and simplify.

$$x + 3y = 6$$
$$\boxed{} + 3y = 6$$
$$3y = \boxed{}$$
$$y = \boxed{}$$

STEP 3 Write the solution as an ordered pair: (____, ____)

STEP 4 Check the solution by graphing.

$$2x - 3y = 12$$

x-intercept: $2x - 3(0) = 12 \rightarrow x =$ ☐

y-intercept: $2(0) - 3y = 12 \rightarrow y =$ ☐

$$x + 3y = 6$$

x-intercept: $x + 3(0) = 6 \rightarrow x =$ ☐

y-intercept: $0 + 3y = 6 \rightarrow y =$ ☐

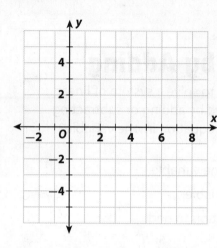

The graph confirms that the solution is (____, ____).

Reflect

1. Can this linear system be solved by subtracting one of the original equations from the other? Why or why not?

   _____

   _____

   _____

2. What is another way to check your solution?

   _____

   _____

   _____

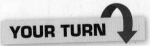

Solve each system of equations by adding. Check your answers.

3. $\begin{cases} x + y = -1 \\ x - y = 7 \end{cases}$

4. $\begin{cases} 2x + 2y = -2 \\ 3x - 2y = 12 \end{cases}$

5. $\begin{cases} 6x + 5y = 4 \\ -6x + 7y = 20 \end{cases}$

_____   _____   _____

Personal Math Trainer

Online Assessment and Intervention

⏻ my.hrw.com

Solving a Linear System by Subtracting

If both equations contain the same *x*- or *y*-term, you can solve by subtracting.

EXAMPLE 2

COMMON CORE 8.EE.8b

Math On the Spot

my.hrw.com

Solve the system of equations by subtracting. Check your answer.

$$\begin{cases} 3x + 3y = 6 \\ 3x - y = -6 \end{cases}$$

STEP 1 Subtract the equations.

$3x + 3y = 6$ *Write the equations so that like terms are aligned.*

$-(3x - y = -6)$ *Notice that both equations contain the term 3x.*

$0 + 4y = 12$ *Subtract to eliminate the variable x.*

$4y = 12$ *Simplify and solve for y.*

$y = 3$ *Divide each side by 4 and simplify.*

STEP 2 Substitute the solution into one of the original equations and solve for *x*.

$3x - y = -6$ *Use the second equation.*

$3x - 3 = -6$ *Substitute 3 for the variable y.*

$3x = -3$ *Add 3 to each side.*

$x = -1$ *Divide each side by 3 and simplify.*

STEP 3 Write the solution as an ordered pair: $(-1, 3)$

STEP 4 Check the solution by graphing.

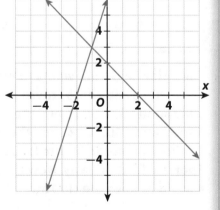

$3x + 3y = 6$	$3x - y = -6$
x-intercept: 2	*x*-intercept: −2
y-intercept: 2	*y*-intercept: 6

The point of intersection is $(-1, 3)$.

Reflect

6. What would happen if you added the original equations?

_____

_____

My Notes

7. How can you decide whether to add or subtract to eliminate a variable in a linear system? Explain your reasoning.

_____

_____

_____

_____

_____

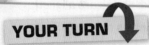

Solve each system of equations by subtracting. Check your answers.

8. $\begin{cases} 6x - 3y = 6 \\ 6x + 8y = -16 \end{cases}$

9. $\begin{cases} 4x + 3y = 19 \\ 6x + 3y = 33 \end{cases}$

10. $\begin{cases} 2x + 6y = 17 \\ 2x - 10y = 9 \end{cases}$

_____   _____   _____

Solving Problems with Systems of Equations

Many real-world situations can be modeled and solved with a system of equations.

EXAMPLE 3 COMMON CORE **8.EE.8c**

The Polar Bear Club wants to buy snowshoes and camp stoves. The club will spend $554.50 to buy them at Top Sports and $602.00 to buy them at Outdoor Explorer, before taxes, but Top Sports is farther away. How many of each item does the club intend to buy?

	Snowshoes	Camp Stoves
Top Sports	$79.50 per pair	$39.25
Outdoor Explorer	$89.00 per pair	$39.25

STEP 1 Choose variables and write a system of equations.
Let x represent the number of pairs of snowshoes.
Let y represent the number of camp stoves.

Top Sports cost: $79.50x + 39.25y = 554.50$
Outdoor Explorer cost: $89.00x + 39.25y = 602.00$

STEP 2 Subtract the equations.

$$79.50x + 39.25y = 554.50$$
$$-(89.00x + 39.25y = 602.00)$$
$$\overline{}$$
$$-9.50x + 0 = -47.50$$

Both equations contain the term $39.25y$.

Subtract to eliminate the variable y.

$$-9.50x = -47.50$$
Simplify and solve for x.

$$\frac{-9.50x}{-9.50} = \frac{-47.50}{-9.50}$$
Divide each side by -9.50.

$$x = 5$$
Simplify.

STEP 3 Substitute the solution into one of the original equations and solve for y.

$$79.50x + 39.25y = 554.50$$
Use the first equation.

$$79.50(5) + 39.25y = 554.50$$
Substitute 5 for the variable x.

$$397.50 + 39.25y = 554.50$$
Multiply.

$$39.25y = 157.00$$
Subtract 397.50 from each side.

$$\frac{39.25y}{39.25} = \frac{157.00}{39.25}$$
Divide each side by 39.25.

$$y = 4$$
Simplify.

STEP 4 Write the solution as an ordered pair: (5, 4)

The club intends to buy 5 pairs of snowshoes and 4 camp stoves.

YOUR TURN

11. At the county fair, the Baxter family bought 6 hot dogs and 4 juice drinks for $16.70. The Farley family bought 3 hot dogs and 4 juice drinks for $10.85. Find the price of a hot dog and the price of a juice drink.

_____

_____

Personal Math Trainer

Online Assessment and Intervention

my.hrw.com

Guided Practice

1. Solve the system $\begin{cases} 4x + 3y = 1 \\ x - 3y = -11 \end{cases}$ by adding. (Explore Activity Example 1)

STEP 1 Add the equations.

$$4x + 3y = 1$$

Write the equations so that like terms are aligned.

$$+\ \underline{x - 3y = -11}$$

$$5x + \boxed{} = \boxed{}$$ Add to eliminate the variable $\boxed{}$.

$$5x = \boxed{}$$ Simplify and solve for x.

$$x = \boxed{}$$ Divide both sides by $\boxed{}$ and simplify.

STEP 2 Substitute into one of the original equations and solve for y.

$$y = \boxed{}$$ So, $\boxed{}$ is the solution of the system.

Solve each system of equations by adding or subtracting.
(Explore Activity Example 1, Example 2)

2. $\begin{cases} x + 2y = -2 \\ -3x + 2y = -10 \end{cases}$

3. $\begin{cases} 3x + y = 23 \\ 3x - 2y = 8 \end{cases}$

4. $\begin{cases} -4x - 5y = 7 \\ 3x + 5y = -14 \end{cases}$

_____

5. $\begin{cases} x - 2y = -19 \\ 5x + 2y = 1 \end{cases}$

6. $\begin{cases} 3x + 4y = 18 \\ -2x + 4y = 8 \end{cases}$

7. $\begin{cases} -5x + 7y = 11 \\ -5x + 3y = 19 \end{cases}$

_____

8. The Green River Freeway has a minimum and a maximum speed limit. Tony drove for 2 hours at the minimum speed limit and 3.5 hours at the maximum limit, a distance of 355 miles. Rae drove 2 hours at the minimum speed limit and 3 hours at the maximum limit, a distance of 320 miles. What are the two speed limits? (Example 3)

a. Write equations to represent Tony's distance and Rae's distance.

Tony: _____ Rae: _____

b. Solve the system.

minimum speed limit: _____ maximum speed limit: _____

? ESSENTIAL QUESTION CHECK-IN

9. Can you use addition or subtraction to solve any system? Explain.

_____

_____

16.3 Independent Practice

 8.EE.8b, 8.EE.8c

10. Represent Real-World Problems Marta bought new fish for her home aquarium. She bought 3 guppies and 2 platies for a total of $13.95. Hank also bought guppies and platies for his aquarium. He bought 3 guppies and 4 platies for a total of $18.33. Find the price of a guppy and the price of a platy.

_____

11. Represent Real-World Problems The rule for the number of fish in a home aquarium is 1 gallon of water for each inch of fish length. Marta's aquarium holds 13 gallons and Hank's aquarium holds 17 gallons. Based on the number of fish they bought in Exercise 10, how long is a guppy and how long is a platy?

_____

12. Line m passes through the points (6, 1) and (2, −3). Line n passes through the points (2, 3) and (5, −6). Find the point of intersection of these lines.

_____

13. Represent Real-World Problems Two cars got an oil change at the same auto shop. The shop charges customers for each quart of oil plus a flat fee for labor. The oil change for one car required 5 quarts of oil and cost $22.45. The oil change for the other car required 7 quarts of oil and cost $25.45. How much is the labor fee and how much is each quart of oil?

_____

14. Represent Real-World Problems A sales manager noticed that the number of units sold for two T-shirt styles, style A and style B, was the same during June and July. In June, total sales were $2779 for the two styles, with A selling for $15.95 per shirt and B selling for $22.95 per shirt. In July, total sales for the two styles were $2385.10, with A selling at the same price and B selling at a discount of 22% off the June price. How many T-shirts of each style were sold in June and July combined?

_____

_____

15. Represent Real-World Problems Adult tickets to a basketball game cost $5. Student tickets cost $1. A total of $2,874 was collected on the sale of 1,246 tickets. How many of each type of ticket were sold?

_____

FOCUS ON HIGHER ORDER THINKING

16. Communicate Mathematical Ideas Is it possible to solve the system $\begin{cases} 3x - 2y = 10 \\ x + 2y = 6 \end{cases}$ by using substitution? If so, explain how. Which method, substitution or elimination, is more efficient? Why?

_____

_____

_____

_____

_____

_____

17. Jenny used substitution to solve the system $\begin{cases} 2x + y = 8 \\ x - y = 1 \end{cases}$. Her solution is shown below.

Step 1 $y = -2x + 8$ Solve the first equation for y.

Step 2 $2x + (-2x + 8) = 8$ Substitute the value of y in an original equation.

Step 3 $2x - 2x + 8 = 8$ Use the Distributive Property.

Step 4 $8 = 8$ Simplify.

a. Explain the Error Explain the error Jenny made. Describe how to correct it.

_____

_____

_____

_____

b. Communicate Mathematical Ideas Would adding the equations have been a better method for solving the system? If so, explain why.

_____

_____

_____

_____

_____

Solving Systems by Elimination with Multiplication

COMMON CORE 8.EE.8b

Solve systems of two linear equations in two variables algebraically, ... *Also 8.EE.8c*

ESSENTIAL QUESTION

How do you solve a system of linear equations by multiplying?

EXPLORE ACTIVITY **COMMON CORE** 8.EE.8b

Solving a System by Multiplying and Adding

Math On the Spot
⊙ my.hrw.com

In some linear systems, neither variable can be eliminated by adding or subtracting the equations directly. In systems like these, you need to multiply one of the equations by a constant so that adding or subtracting the equations will eliminate one variable. The steps for this method are as follows:

1. Decide which variable to eliminate.

2. Multiply one equation by a constant so that adding or subtracting will eliminate that variable.

3. Solve the system using the elimination method.

EXAMPLE 1 Solve the system of equations by multiplying and adding.

$$\begin{cases} 2x + 10y = 2 \\ 3x - 5y = -17 \end{cases}$$

 STEP 1

The coefficient of y in the first equation, 10, is 2 times the coefficient of y, 5, in the second equation. Also, the y-term in the first equation is being added, while the y-term in the second equation is being subtracted. To eliminate the _____, multiply the second equation by 2 and add this new equation to the first equation.

$\boxed{}(3x - 5y = -17)$

$\boxed{}x - \boxed{}y = -34$

Multiply each term in the second equation by _____ to get opposite coefficients for the _____, and simplify.

$6x - 10y = -34$

$+ 2x + \boxed{} = 2$

Add the first equation to the new equation.

Add to eliminate the variable _____.

$8x + \boxed{}y = -32$

$8x = -32$

Simplify.

Divide each side by _____.

$\dfrac{8x}{\boxed{}} = \dfrac{-32}{\boxed{}}$

Simplify.

$x = \boxed{}$

STEP 2   Substitute the solution into one of the original equations, and solve for *y*.

Use the first equation. $2x + 10y = 2$

Substitute _____ for the variable *x*. $2\left(\boxed{}\right) + 10y = 2$

Simplify. $\boxed{} + 10y = 2$

Add _____ to each side. $10y = \boxed{}$

Divide each side by _____, and simplify. $y = \boxed{}$

STEP 3   Write the solution as an ordered pair: (____, ____).

STEP 4   Check your answer algebraically.

Substitute _____ for *x* and _____ for *y* in the original system.

$$\begin{cases} 2x + 10y = 2 \rightarrow 2\left(\boxed{}\right) + 10\left(\boxed{}\right) = \boxed{} \checkmark \\ 3x - 5y = -17 \rightarrow 3\left(\boxed{}\right) - 5\left(\boxed{}\right) = \boxed{} \checkmark \end{cases}$$

The solution is correct.

Reflect

1. How can you solve this linear system by subtracting? Which is more efficient, adding or subtracting? Explain your reasoning.

   _____

   _____

2. Can this linear system be solved by adding or subtracting without multiplying? Why or why not?

   _____

3. What would you need to multiply the second equation by to eliminate *x* by adding? Why might you choose to eliminate *y* instead of *x*?

   _____

   _____

YOUR TURN

Solve each system of equations by multiplying and adding.

4. $\begin{cases} 5x + 2y = -10 \\ 3x + 6y = 66 \end{cases}$

5. $\begin{cases} 4x + 2y = 6 \\ 3x - y = -8 \end{cases}$

6. $\begin{cases} -6x + 9y = -12 \\ 2x + y = 0 \end{cases}$

Personal Math Trainer

Online Assessment and Intervention

my.hrw.com

_____   _____   _____

Solving a System by Multiplying and Subtracting

You can solve some systems of equations by multiplying one equation by a constant and then subtracting.

Math On the Spot

⏻ my.hrw.com

EXAMPLE 2

COMMON CORE 8.EE.8b

Solve the system of equations by multiplying and subtracting.

$$\begin{cases} 6x + 5y = 7 \\ 2x - 4y = -26 \end{cases}$$

My Notes

STEP 1 Multiply the second equation by 3 and subtract this new equation from the first equation.

$3(2x - 4y) = -26$ Multiply each term in the second equation by 3 to get the same coefficients for the x-terms.

$6x - 12y = -78$ Simplify.

$\begin{array}{r} 6x + 5y = 7 \\ -(6x - 12y = -78) \\ \hline \end{array}$ Subtract the new equation from the first equation.

$0x + 17y = 85$ Subtract to eliminate the variable x.

$17y = 85$ Simplify and solve for y.

$\dfrac{17y}{17} = \dfrac{85}{17}$ Divide each side by 17.

$y = 5$ Simplify.

STEP 2 Substitute the solution into one of the original equations and solve for *x*.

$6x + 5y = 7$ Use the first equation.

$6x + 5(5) = 7$ Substitute 5 for the variable y.

$6x + 25 = 7$ Simplify.

$6x = -18$ Subtract 25 from each side.

$x = -3$ Divide each side by 6 and simplify.

STEP 3 Write the solution as an ordered pair: $(-3, 5)$

STEP 4 Check your answer algebraically.
Substitute -3 for *x* and 5 for *y* in the original system.

$$\begin{cases} 6x + 5y = 7 \rightarrow 6(-3) + 5(5) = -18 + 25 = 7 \ \checkmark \\ 2x - 4y = -26 \rightarrow 2(-3) - 4(5) = -6 - 20 = -26 \ \checkmark \end{cases}$$

The solution is correct.

My Notes

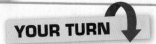

YOUR TURN

Solve each system of equations by multiplying and subtracting.

7. $\begin{cases} 3x - 7y = 2 \\ 6x - 9y = 9 \end{cases}$

8. $\begin{cases} -3x + y = 11 \\ 2x + 3y = -11 \end{cases}$

9. $\begin{cases} 9x + y = 9 \\ 3x - 2y = -11 \end{cases}$

Solving Problems with Systems of Equations

Many real-world situations can be modeled with a system of equations.

EXAMPLE 3 Problem Solving

COMMON CORE **8.EE.8c**

The Simon family attended a concert and visited an art museum. Concert tickets were $24.75 for adults and $16.00 for children, for a total cost of $138.25. Museum tickets were $8.25 for adults and $4.50 for children, for a total cost of $42.75. How many adults and how many children are in the Simon family?

 Analyze Information

The answer is the number of adults and children.

 Formulate a Plan

Solve a system to find the number of adults and children.

 Solve

STEP 1 Choose variables and write a system of equations. Let x represent the number of adults. Let y represent the number of children.

Concert cost: $24.75x + 16.00y = 138.25$
Museum cost: $8.25x + 4.50y = 42.75$

STEP 2 Multiply both equations by 100 to eliminate the decimals.

$100(24.75x + 16.00y = 138.25) \rightarrow 2{,}475x + 1{,}600y = 13{,}825$

$100(8.25x + 4.50y = 42.75) \rightarrow 825x + 450y = 4{,}275$

STEP 3 Multiply the second equation by 3 and subtract this new equation from the first equation.

$3(825x + 450y = 4{,}275)$ Multiply each term in the second equation by 3 to get the same coefficients for the x-terms.

$2{,}475x + 1{,}350y = 12{,}825$ Simplify.

$2{,}475x + 1{,}600y = 13{,}825$
$-(2{,}475x + 1{,}350y = 12{,}825)$ Subtract the new equation from the first equation.

$0x + 250y = 1{,}000$ Subtract to eliminate the variable x.

$250y = 1{,}000$ Simplify and solve for y.

$\dfrac{250y}{250} = \dfrac{1{,}000}{250}$ Divide each side by 250.

$y = 4$ Simplify.

STEP 4 Substitute the solution into one of the original equations and solve for x.

$8.25x + 4.50y = 42.75$ Use the second equation.

$8.25x + 4.50(4) = 42.75$ Substitute 4 for the variable y.

$8.25x + 18 = 42.75$ Simplify.

$8.25x = 24.75$ Subtract 18 from each side.

$x = 3$ Divide each side by 8.25 and simplify.

STEP 5 Write the solution as an ordered pair: (3, 4).
There are 3 adults and 4 children in the family.

 Justify and Evaluate

Substituting $x = 3$ and $y = 4$ into the original equations results in true statements. The answer is correct.

YOUR TURN

10. Contestants in the Run-and-Bike-a-thon run for a specified length of time, then bike for a specified length of time. Jason ran at an average speed of 5.2 mi/h and biked at an average speed of 20.6 mi/h, going a total of 14.2 miles. Seth ran at an average speed of 10.4 mi/h and biked at an average speed of 18.4 mi/h, going a total of 17 miles. For how long do contestants run and for how long do they bike?

_____

_____

Personal Math Trainer

Online Assessment and Intervention

my.hrw.com

1. Solve the system $\begin{cases} 3x - y = 8 \\ -2x + 4y = -12 \end{cases}$ by multiplying and adding. (Explore Activity Example 1)

STEP 1 Multiply the first equation by 4. Add to the second equation.

$4(3x - y = 8)$ Multiply each term in the first equation by 4 to get opposite coefficients for the y-terms.

$\boxed{}x - \boxed{}y = \boxed{}$ Simplify.

$+ \, (-2x) + \, 4y \; = -12$ Add the second equation to the new equation.

$10x = \boxed{}$ Add to eliminate the variable $\boxed{}$.

$x = \boxed{}$ Divide both sides by $\boxed{}$ and simplify.

STEP 2 Substitute into one of the original equations and solve for y.

$y = \boxed{}$ So, $\boxed{}$ is the solution of the system.

Solve each system of equations by multiplying first. (Explore Activity Example 1, Example 2)

2. $\begin{cases} x + 4y = 2 \\ 2x + 5y = 7 \end{cases}$ _____

3. $\begin{cases} 3x + y = -1 \\ 2x + 3y = 18 \end{cases}$ _____

4. $\begin{cases} 2x + 8y = 21 \\ 6x - 4y = 14 \end{cases}$ _____

5. $\begin{cases} 2x + y = 3 \\ -x + 3y = -12 \end{cases}$ _____

6. $\begin{cases} 6x + 5y = 19 \\ 2x + 3y = 5 \end{cases}$ _____

7. $\begin{cases} 2x + 5y = 16 \\ -4x + 3y = 20 \end{cases}$ _____

8. Bryce spent $5.26 on some apples priced at $0.64 each and some pears priced at $0.45 each. At another store he could have bought the same number of apples at $0.32 each and the same number of pears at $0.39 each, for a total cost of $3.62. How many apples and how many pears did Bryce buy? (Example 3)

  a. Write equations to represent Bryce's expenditures at each store.

    First store: _____   Second store: _____

  b. Solve the system.

    Number of apples: _____   Number of pears: _____

? ESSENTIAL QUESTION CHECK-IN

9. When solving a system by multiplying and then adding or subtracting, how do you decide whether to add or subtract?

_____

_____

16.4 Independent Practice

 COMMON CORE 8.EE.8b, 8.EE.8c

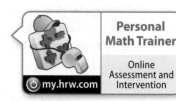
Personal Math Trainer

Online Assessment and Intervention

⏻ my.hrw.com

10. Explain the Error Gwen used elimination with multiplication to solve the system $\begin{cases} 2x + 6y = 3 \\ x - 3y = -1 \end{cases}$. Her work to find x is shown. Explain her error. Then solve the system.

$$2(x - 3y) = -1$$
$$2x - 6y = -1$$
$$\underline{+2x + 6y = 3}$$
$$4x + 0y = 2$$
$$x = \frac{1}{2}$$

_____

11. Represent Real-World Problems At Raging River Sports, polyester-fill sleeping bags sell for $79. Down-fill sleeping bags sell for $149. In one week the store sold 14 sleeping bags for $1,456.

Sleeping Bags

Nylon
Down-filled, 35°
$149

Flannel-lined
Polyester-filled, 40°
$79

a. Let x represent the number of polyester-fill bags sold and let y represent the number of down-fill bags sold. Write a system of equations you can solve to find the number of each type sold.

_____

b. Explain how you can solve the system for y by multiplying and subtracting.

_____

_____

c. Explain how you can solve the system for y using substitution.

_____

_____

_____

d. How many of each type of bag were sold?

_____

12. Twice a number plus twice a second number is 310. The difference between the numbers is 55. Find the numbers by writing and solving a system of equations. Explain how you solved the system.

_____

_____

_____

13. Represent Real-World Problems A farm stand sells apple pies and jars of applesauce. The table shows the number of apples needed to make a pie and a jar of applesauce. Yesterday, the farm picked 169 Granny Smith apples and 95 Red Delicious apples. How many pies and jars of applesauce can the farm make if every apple is used?

Type of apple	Granny Smith	Red Delicious
Needed for a pie	5	3
Needed for a jar of applesauce	4	2

_____

14. Make a Conjecture Lena tried to solve a system of linear equations algebraically and in the process found the equation $5 = 9$. Lena thought something was wrong, so she graphed the equations and found that they were parallel lines. Explain what Lena's graph and equation could mean.

_____

_____

_____

_____

_____

15. Consider the system $\begin{cases} 2x + 3y = 6 \\ 3x + 7y = -1 \end{cases}$.

a. Communicate Mathematical Ideas Describe how to solve the system by multiplying the first equation by a constant and subtracting. Why would this method be less than ideal?

_____

_____

_____

b. Draw Conclusions Is it possible to solve the system by multiplying both equations by integer constants? If so, explain how.

_____

_____

_____

c. Use your answer from part b to solve the system.

_____

LESSON 16.5 Solving Special Systems

COMMON CORE **8.EE.8b**
Solve systems of two linear equations in two variables algebraically, ... Solve simple cases by inspection. *Also 8.EE.8c*

ESSENTIAL QUESTION

How do you solve systems with no solution or infinitely many solutions?

EXPLORE ACTIVITY

 COMMON CORE 8.EE.8b

Solving Special Systems by Graphing

As with equations, some systems may have no solution or infinitely many solutions. One way to tell how many solutions a system has is by inspecting its graph.

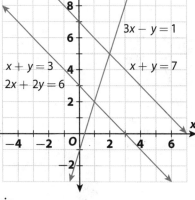

Use the graph to solve each system of linear equations.

 A $\begin{cases} x + y = 7 \\ 2x + 2y = 6 \end{cases}$

Is there a point of intersection? Explain.

_____

_____

Does this linear system have a solution? Use the graph to explain.

_____

_____

 B $\begin{cases} 2x + 2y = 6 \\ x + y = 3 \end{cases}$

Is there a point of intersection? Explain.

_____

Does this linear system have a solution? Use the graph to explain.

_____

_____

Reflect

1. Use the graph to identify two lines that represent a linear system with exactly one solution. What are the equations of the lines? Explain your reasoning.

_____

2. If each equation in a system of two linear equations is represented by a different line when graphed, what is the greatest number of solutions the system can have? Explain your reasoning.

_____

_____

3. Identify the three possible numbers of solutions for a system of linear equations. Explain when each type of solution occurs.

_____

_____

_____

Math On the Spot

⏻ my.hrw.com

Solving Special Systems Algebraically

As with equations, if you solve a system of equations with no solution, you get a false statement, and if you solve a system with infinitely many solutions, you get a true statement.

EXAMPLE 1 COMMON CORE 8.EE.8b

My Notes

A Solve the system of linear equations by substitution.

$$\begin{cases} x - y = -2 \\ -x + y = 4 \end{cases}$$

STEP 1 Solve $x - y = -2$ for x:
$$x = y - 2$$

STEP 2 Substitute the resulting expression into the other equation and solve.

$$-(y - 2) + y = 4 \qquad \text{Substitute the expression for the variable } x.$$

$$2 = 4 \qquad \text{Simplify.}$$

STEP 3 Interpret the solution. The result is the false statement $2 = 4$, which means there is no solution.

STEP 4 Graph the equations to check your answer. The graphs do not intersect, so there is no solution.

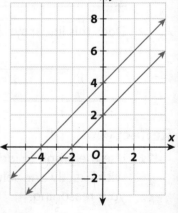

B Solve the system of linear equations by elimination.

$$\begin{cases} 2x + y = -2 \\ 4x + 2y = -4 \end{cases}$$

Math Talk

Mathematical Practices

What solution do you get when you solve the system in part B by substitution? Does this result change the number of solutions? Explain.

STEP 1 Multiply the first equation by -2.

$$-2(2x + y = -2) \rightarrow -4x + (-2y) = 4$$

STEP 2 Add the new equation from Step 1 to the original second equation.

$$\begin{array}{r} -4x + (-2y) = 4 \\ +4x + 2y = -4 \\ \hline 0x + 0y = 0 \\ 0 = 0 \end{array}$$

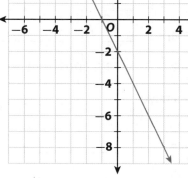

STEP 3 Interpret the solution. The result is the statement $0 = 0$, which is always true. This means that the system has infinitely many solutions.

STEP 4 Graph the equations to check your answer. The graphs are the same line, so there are infinitely many solutions.

Reflect

4. If x represents a variable and a and b represent constants so that $a \neq b$, interpret what each result means when solving a system of equations.

$x = a$ _____

$a = b$ _____

$a = a$ _____

5. In part B, can you tell without solving that the system has infinitely many solutions? If so, how?

_____

_____

_____

YOUR TURN

Solve each system. Tell how many solutions each system has.

6. $\begin{cases} 4x - 6y = 9 \\ -2x + 3y = 4 \end{cases}$ **7.** $\begin{cases} x + 2y = 6 \\ 2x - 3y = 26 \end{cases}$ **8.** $\begin{cases} 12x - 8y = -4 \\ -3x + 2y = 1 \end{cases}$

_____   _____   _____

_____   _____   _____

Personal Math Trainer

Online Assessment and Intervention

my.hrw.com

1. Use the graph to solve each system of linear equations. (Explore Activity)

A. $\begin{cases} 4x - 2y = -6 \\ 2x - y = 4 \end{cases}$ **B.** $\begin{cases} 4x - 2y = -6 \\ x + y = 6 \end{cases}$ **C.** $\begin{cases} 2x - y = 4 \\ 6x - 3y = 12 \end{cases}$

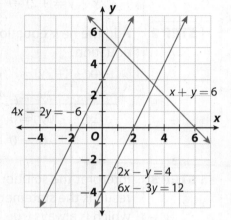

STEP 1 Decide if the graphs of the equations in each system intersect, are parallel, or are the same line.

System A: The graphs _____ .

System B: The graphs _____ .

System C: The graphs _____ .

STEP 2 Decide how many points the graphs have in common.

Intersecting lines have _____ point(s) in common.

Parallel lines have _____ point(s) in common.

The same lines have _____ point(s) in common.

STEP 3 Solve each system.

System A has _____ points in common, so it has _____ solution.

System B has _____ point in common. That point is the solution, _____ .

System C has _____ points in common. _____ ordered pairs on the line will make both equations true.

Solve each system. Tell how many solutions each system has. (Example 1)

2. $\begin{cases} x - 3y = 4 \\ -5x + 15y = -20 \end{cases}$ **3.** $\begin{cases} 6x + 2y = -4 \\ 3x + y = 4 \end{cases}$ **4.** $\begin{cases} 6x - 2y = -10 \\ 3x + 4y = -25 \end{cases}$

_____   _____   _____

? ESSENTIAL QUESTION CHECK-IN

5. When you solve a system of equations algebraically, how can you tell whether the system has zero, one, or an infinite number of solutions?

_____

_____

_____

_____

16.5 Independent Practice

COMMON CORE 8.EE.8b, 8.EE.8c

Personal Math Trainer

Online Assessment and Intervention

my.hrw.com

Solve each system by graphing. Check your answer algebraically.

6. $\begin{cases} -2x + 6y = 12 \\ x - 3y = 3 \end{cases}$

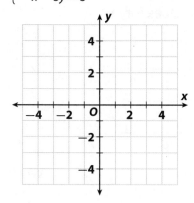

7. $\begin{cases} 15x + 5y = 5 \\ 3x + y = 1 \end{cases}$

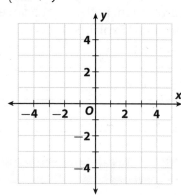

Solution: _____

Solution: _____

For Exs. 8–14, state the number of solutions for each system of linear equations.

8. a system whose graphs have the same slope but different y-intercepts

_____

9. a system whose graphs have the same y-intercepts but different slopes

_____

10. a system whose graphs have the same y-intercepts and the same slopes

_____

11. a system whose graphs have different y-intercepts and different slopes

_____

12. the system $\begin{cases} y = 2 \\ y = -3 \end{cases}$ _____

13. the system $\begin{cases} x = 2 \\ y = -3 \end{cases}$ _____

14. the system whose graphs were drawn using these tables of values:

Equation 1

x	0	1	2	3
y	1	3	5	7

Equation 2

x	0	1	2	3
y	3	5	7	9

_____

15. Draw Conclusions The graph of a linear system appears in a textbook. You can see that the lines do not intersect on the graph, but also they do not appear to be parallel. Can you conclude that the system has no solution? Explain.

_____

_____

_____

16. Represent Real-World Problems Two school groups go to a roller skating rink. One group pays $243 for 36 admissions and 21 skate rentals. The other group pays $81 for 12 admissions and 7 skate rentals. Let x represent the cost of admission and let y represent the cost of a skate rental. Is there enough information to find values for x and y? Explain.

_____

17. Represent Real-World Problems Juan and Tory are practicing for a track meet. They start their practice runs at the same point, but Tory starts 1 minute after Juan. Both run at a speed of 704 feet per minute. Does Tory catch up to Juan? Explain.

_____

_____

_____

H.O.T. FOCUS ON HIGHER ORDER THINKING

Work Area

18. Justify Reasoning A linear system with no solution consists of the equation $y = 4x - 3$ and a second equation of the form $y = mx + b$. What can you say about the values of m and b? Explain your reasoning.

_____

_____

_____

_____

_____

19. Justify Reasoning A linear system with infinitely many solutions consists of the equation $3x + 5 = 8$ and a second equation of the form $Ax + By = C$. What can you say about the values of A, B, and C? Explain your reasoning.

_____

_____

_____

_____

20. Draw Conclusions Both the points $(2, -2)$ and $(4, -4)$ are solutions of a system of linear equations. What conclusions can you make about the equations and their graphs?

_____

_____

Ready to Go On?

16.1 Solving Systems of Linear Equations by Graphing

Solve each system by graphing.

1. $\begin{cases} y = x - 1 \\ y = 2x - 3 \end{cases}$

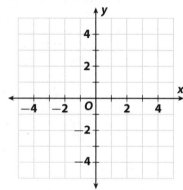

2. $\begin{cases} x + 2y = 1 \\ -x + y = 2 \end{cases}$

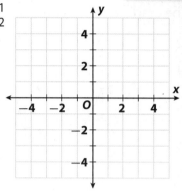

16.2 Solving Systems by Substitution

Solve each system of equations by substitution.

3. $\begin{cases} y = 2x \\ x + y = -9 \end{cases}$ _____

4. $\begin{cases} 3x - 2y = 11 \\ x + 2y = 9 \end{cases}$ _____

16.3 Solving Systems by Elimination

Solve each system of equations by adding or subtracting.

5. $\begin{cases} 3x + y = 9 \\ 2x + y = 5 \end{cases}$ _____

6. $\begin{cases} -x - 2y = 4 \\ 3x + 2y = 4 \end{cases}$ _____

16.4 Solving Systems by Elimination with Multiplication

Solve each system of equations by multiplying first.

7. $\begin{cases} x + 3y = -2 \\ 3x + 4y = -1 \end{cases}$ _____

8. $\begin{cases} 2x + 8y = 22 \\ 3x - 2y = 5 \end{cases}$ _____

16.5 Solving Special Systems

Solve each system. Tell how many solutions each system has.

9. $\begin{cases} -2x + 8y = 5 \\ x - 4y = -3 \end{cases}$ _____

10. $\begin{cases} 6x + 18y = -12 \\ x + 3y = -2 \end{cases}$ _____

? ESSENTIAL QUESTION

11. What are the possible solutions to a system of linear equations, and what do they represent graphically?

_____

_____

MODULE 16 MIXED REVIEW

COMMON CORE

Assessment Readiness

Personal Math Trainer

Online Assessment and Intervention

my.hrw.com

Selected Response

1. The graph of which equation is shown?

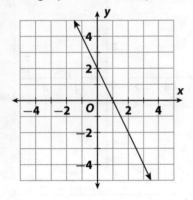

Ⓐ $y = -2x + 2$ Ⓒ $y = 2x + 2$

Ⓑ $y = -x + 2$ Ⓓ $y = 2x + 1$

2. Which best describes the solutions to the system $\begin{cases} x + y = -4 \\ -2x - 2y = 0 \end{cases}$?

Ⓐ one solution   Ⓒ infinitely many

Ⓑ no solution   Ⓓ $(0, 0)$

3. Which of the following represents 0.000056023 written in scientific notation?

Ⓐ 5.6023×10^5 Ⓒ 5.6023×10^{-4}

Ⓑ 5.6023×10^4 Ⓓ 5.6023×10^{-5}

4. Which is the solution to $\begin{cases} 2x - y = 1 \\ 4x + y = 11 \end{cases}$?

Ⓐ $(2, 3)$ Ⓒ $(-2, 3)$

Ⓑ $(3, 2)$ Ⓓ $(3, -2)$

5. Which expression can you substitute in the indicated equation to solve $\begin{cases} 3x - y = 5 \\ x + 2y = 4 \end{cases}$?

Ⓐ $2y - 4$ for x in $3x - y = 5$

Ⓑ $4 - x$ for y in $3x - y = 5$

Ⓒ $3x - 5$ for y in $3x - y = 5$

Ⓓ $3x - 5$ for y in $x + 2y = 4$

6. What is the solution to the system of linear equations shown on the graph?

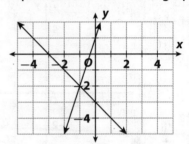

Ⓐ -1 Ⓒ $(-1, -2)$

Ⓑ -2 Ⓓ $(-2, -1)$

7. Which step could you use to start solving $\begin{cases} x - 6y = 8 \\ 2x - 5y = 3 \end{cases}$?

Ⓐ Add $2x - 5y = 3$ to $x - 6y = 8$.

Ⓑ Multiply $x - 6y = 8$ by 2 and add it to $2x - 5y = 3$.

Ⓒ Multiply $x - 6y = 8$ by 2 and subtract it from $2x - 5y = 3$.

Ⓓ Substitute $x = 6y - 8$ for x in $2x - 5y = 3$.

Mini-Task

8. A hot-air balloon begins rising from the ground at 4 meters per second at the same time a parachutist's chute opens at a height of 200 meters. The parachutist descends at 6 meters per second.

a. Define the variables and write a system that represents the situation.

_____

_____

b. Find the solution. What does it mean?

_____

_____

MODULE 15 Solving Linear Equations

? ESSENTIAL QUESTION

How can you use equations with variables on both sides to solve real-world problems?

EXAMPLE 1

A tutor gives students a choice of how to pay: a base rate of $20 plus $8 per hour, or a set rate of $13 per hour. Find the number of hours of tutoring for which the cost is the same for either choice.

Plan 1 cost: $20 + 8x$ Plan 2 cost: $13x$

$$20 + 8x = 13x \qquad \text{Write the equation.}$$
$$\underline{-8x \quad -8x} \qquad \text{Subtract 8x from both sides.}$$
$$20 = 5x \qquad \text{Divide both sides by 5.}$$
$$x = 4$$

The cost is the same for 4 hours of tutoring.

EXAMPLE 2

Solve $-2.4(3x + 5) = 0.8(x + 3.5)$.

$$-2.4(3x + 5) = 0.8(x + 3.5)$$

$$10(-2.4)(3x + 5) = 10(0.8)(x + 3.5) \qquad \text{Multiply each side by 10 to clear some decimals.}$$

$$-24(3x + 5) = 8(x + 3.5)$$

$$-24(3x) - 24(5) = 8(x) + 8(3.5) \qquad \text{Apply the Distributive Property.}$$

$$-72x - 120 = 8x + 28$$

$$\underline{-8x \qquad\qquad -8x} \qquad \text{Subtract 8x from both sides of the equation.}$$

$$-80x - 120 = 28$$

$$\underline{+120 \quad +120} \qquad \text{Add 120 to both sides of the equation.}$$

$$-80x = 148$$

$$\frac{-80x}{-80} = \frac{148}{-80} \qquad \text{Divide both sides of the equation by } -80.$$

$$x = -1.85$$

EXAMPLE 3

Solve $4(3x - 6) = 2(6x - 5)$.

$$4(3x - 6) = 2(6x - 5)$$

$12x - 24 =$	$12x - 10$	Apply the Distributive Property.
$-12x$	$-12x$	Subtract 8x from both sides of the equation.
$-24 = -10$		The statement is false.

There is no value of x that makes a true statement. Therefore, this equation has no solution.

EXERCISES

Solve. (Lessons 15.1, 15.2, 15.3, 15.4)

1. $13.02 - 6y = 8y$ _____

2. $\frac{1}{5}x + 5 = 19 - \frac{1}{2}x$ _____

3. $7.3t + 22 = 2.1t - 22.2$ _____

4. $1.4 + \frac{2}{5}e = \frac{3}{15}e - 0.8$ _____

5. $5(x - 4) = 2(x + 5)$ _____

6. $-7(3 + t) = 4(2t + 6)$ _____

7. $\frac{3}{4}(x + 8) = \frac{1}{3}(x + 27)$ _____

8. $3(4x - 8) = \frac{1}{5}(35x + 30)$ _____

9. $-1.6(2y + 15) = -1.2(2y - 10)$

10. $9(4a - 2) = 12(3a + 8)$

_____

_____

11. $6(x - \frac{1}{3}) = -2(x + 23)$

12. $8(p - 0.25) = 4(2p - 0.5)$

_____

_____

13. Write a real-world situation that could be modeled by the equation $650 + 10m = 60m + 400$. (Lesson 15.1)

_____

_____

_____

_____

? ESSENTIAL QUESTION

How can you use systems of equations to solve real-world problems?

EXAMPLE 1 Solve the system of equations by substitution.

$$\begin{cases} 3x + y = 7 \\ x + y = 3 \end{cases}$$

Step 1 Solve an equation for one variable.

$3x + y = 7$

$y = -3x + 7$

Step 2 Substitute the expression for y in the other equation and solve.

$x + y = 3$

$x + (-3x + 7) = 3$

$-2x + 7 = 3$

$-2x = -4$

$x = 2$

Step 3 Substitute the value of x into one of the equations and solve for the other variable, y.

$x + y = 3$

$2 + y = 3$

$y = 1$

(2, 1) is the solution of the system.

EXAMPLE 2 Solve the system of equations by elimination.

$$\begin{cases} x + y = 8 \\ 2x - 3y = 1 \end{cases}$$

Step 1 Multiply the first equation by 3 and add this new equation to the second equation.

$3(x + y = 8) = 3x + 3y = 24$

$3x + 3y = 24$

$\underline{2x - 3y = 1}$

$5x + 0y = 25$

$5x \quad\;\; = 25$

$x \quad\;\; = 5$

Step 2 Substitute the solution into one of the original equations and solve for y.

$x + y = 8$

$5 + y = 8$

$y = 3$

(5, 3) is the solution of the system.

EXERCISES

Solve each system of linear equations. (Lessons 16.1, 16.2, 16.3, 16.4, and 16.5)

14. $\begin{cases} x + y = -2 \\ 2x - y = 5 \end{cases}$

15. $\begin{cases} y = 2x + 1 \\ x + 2y = 17 \end{cases}$

16. $\begin{cases} y = -2x - 3 \\ 2x + y = 9 \end{cases}$

_____

_____

_____

17. $\begin{cases} y = 5 - x \\ 2x + 2y = 10 \end{cases}$

18. $\begin{cases} 2x - y = 26 \\ 3x - 2y = 42 \end{cases}$

19. $\begin{cases} 2x + 3y = 11 \\ 5x - 2y = 18 \end{cases}$

_____

_____

_____

20. Last week Andrew bought 3 pounds of zucchini and 2 pounds of tomatoes for $7.05 at a farm stand. This week he bought 4 pounds of zucchini and 3 pounds of tomatoes, at the same prices, for $9.83. What is the cost of 1 pound of zucchini and 1 pound of tomatoes at the farm stand?

_____

Unit 7 Performance Tasks

1. **CAREERS IN MATH** **Hydraulic Engineer** A hydraulic engineer is studying the pressure in a particular fluid. The pressure is equal to the atmospheric pressure 101 kN/m plus 8 kN/m for every meter below the surface, where kN/m is kilonewtons per meter, a unit of pressure.

a. Write an expression for the pressure at a depth of d_1 meters below the liquid surface.

_____

b. Write and solve an equation to find the depth at which the pressure is 200 kN/m.

_____

c. The hydraulic engineer alters the density of the fluid so that the pressure at depth d_2 below the surface is atmospheric pressure 101 kN/m plus 9 kN/m for every meter below the surface. Write an expression for the pressure at depth d_2.

_____

d. If the pressure at depth d_1 in the first fluid is equal to the pressure at depth d_2 in the second fluid, what is the relationship between d_1 and d_2? Explain how you found your answer.

_____

_____

_____

UNIT 7 MIXED REVIEW

Assessment Readiness

COMMON CORE

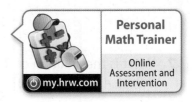

Personal Math Trainer

Online Assessment and Intervention

my.hrw.com

Selected Response

1. Ricardo and John start swimming from the same location. Ricardo starts 15 seconds before John and swims at a rate of 3 feet per second. John swims at a rate of 4 feet per second in the same direction as Ricardo. Which equation could you solve to find how long it will take John to catch up with Ricardo?

ⓐ $4t + 3 = 3t$

ⓑ $4t + 60 = 3t$

ⓒ $3t + 3 = 4t$

ⓓ $3t + 45 = 4t$

2. Gina and Rhonda work for different real estate agencies. Gina earns a monthly salary of $5,000 plus a 6% commission on her sales. Rhonda earns a monthly salary of $6,500 plus a 4% commission on her sales. How much must each sell to earn the same amount in a month?

ⓐ $1,500   ⓒ $75,000

ⓑ $15,000   ⓓ $750,000

3. What is the slope of the line?

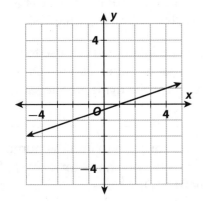

ⓐ -3 ⓒ $\frac{1}{3}$

ⓑ $-\frac{1}{3}$ ⓓ 3

4. What is the solution of the system of equations?

$$\begin{cases} y = 2x - 3 \\ 5x + y = 11 \end{cases}$$

ⓐ $(2, 1)$

ⓑ $(1, 2)$

ⓒ $(3, -4)$

ⓓ $(1, -1)$

5. Alana is having a party. She bought 3 rolls of streamers and 2 packages of balloons for $10.00. She realized she needed more supplies and went back to the store and bought 2 more rolls of streamers and 1 more package of balloons for $6.25. How much did each roll of streamers and each package of balloons cost?

ⓐ streamers: $3.00, balloons: $2.00

ⓑ streamers: $2.00, balloons: $1.00

ⓒ streamers: $1.25, balloons: $2.50

ⓓ streamers: $2.50, balloons: $1.25

6. The triangle and the rectangle have the same perimeter.

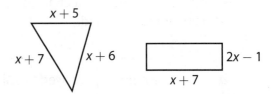

Find the value of x.

ⓐ 2

ⓑ 10

ⓒ 18

ⓓ 24

7. What is the solution of the equation $8(3x + 4) = 2(12x − 8)$?

Ⓐ $x = −2$

Ⓑ $x = 2$

Ⓒ no solution

Ⓓ infinitely many solutions

8. A square wall tile has an area of 58,800 square millimeters. Between which two measurements is the length of one side?

Ⓐ between 24 and 25 millimeters

Ⓑ between 76 and 77 millimeters

Ⓒ between 242 and 243 millimeters

Ⓓ between 766 and 767 millimeters

Mini-Task

9. Lily and Alex went to a Mexican restaurant. Lily paid $9 for 2 tacos and 3 enchiladas, and Alex paid $12.50 for 3 tacos and 4 enchiladas.

a. Write a system of equations that represents this situation.

_____

_____

b. Use the system of equations to find how much the restaurant charges for a taco and for an enchilada.

_____

c. Describe the method you used to solve the system of equations.

_____

_____

_____

_____

Solutions of a system of two equations must make both equations true. Check solutions in both equations.

10. Use the system of equations to answer the questions below.

$$\begin{cases} 4x + 2y = −8 \\ 2x + y = 4 \end{cases}$$

a. Graph the equations on the grid.

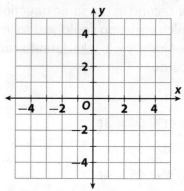

b. How many solutions does the system of equations have? Explain your answer.

_____

_____

11. Isaac wants to join a gym. He checked out the membership fees at two gyms.

Gym A charges a new member fee of $65 and $20 per month.

Gym B charges a new member fee of $25 and $35 per month, but Isaac will get a discount of 20% on the monthly fee.

a. Write an equation you can use to find the number of months for which the total costs at the gyms are the same.

_____

b. Solve the equation to find the number of months for which the total costs of the gyms are the same.

_____

_____

_____

Transformational Geometry

MODULE **17**

Transformations and Congruence

COMMON CORE 8.G.1, 8.G.2, 8.G.3

MODULE **18**

Transformations and Similarity

COMMON CORE 8.G.3, 8.G.4

CAREERS IN MATH

Contractor A contractor is engaged in the construction, repair, and dismantling of structures such as buildings, bridges, and roads. Contractors use math when researching and implementing building codes, making measurements and scaling models, and in financial management.

If you are interested in a career as a contractor, you should study the following mathematical subjects:
- Business Math
- Geometry
- Algebra
- Trigonometry

Research other careers that require the use of business math and scaling.

Unit 8 Performance Task

At the end of the unit, check out how **contractors** use math.

Vocabulary Preview

Use the puzzle to preview key vocabulary from this unit. Unscramble the circled letters within found words to answer the riddle at the bottom of the page.

```
W T C F V A F I L I T U G N S
M U J L O C Z H B R S D E O W
F E Q V H B T (E)(A) N T P X I A
M Y J G B O G N P K G G B (T) Q
N X L H A A S E V Z R U B C W
L O X D M L A G R H H L R U A
G P I I A E M X K V A K X D K
B D E T N E M E (G) R A L N (E) A
W R I E (C) A N R E Y M A T R P
P O G (L) K E R O T A T I O (N) R
N Z Y E A C L R O V Z S P I U
U Y T J N T Q F N B X G G C J
O N E R Z I I P E I Y F A B W
I F V U C M S O G (R) P Q K B W
C Q T U I C C U N L N T L D Y
```

The input of a transformation. (Lesson 17.1)

A transformation that flips a figure across a line. (Lesson 17.2)

A transformation that slides a figure along a straight line. (Lesson 17.1)

A transformation that turns a figure around a given point. (Lesson 17.3)

The product of a figure made larger by dilation. (Lesson 18.1)

The product of a figure made smaller by dilation. (Lesson 18.1)

Scaled replicas that change the size but not the shape of a figure. (Lesson 18.1)

Q: What do you call an angle that's broken?

A: A __ __ __ __ __ __ __ __ __!

Transformations and Congruence

 ESSENTIAL QUESTION

How can you use transformations and congruence to solve real-world problems?

Real-World Video

When a marching band lines up and marches across the field, they are modeling a translation. As they march, they maintain size and orientation. A translation is one type of transformation.

my.hrw.com

GO DIGITAL
my.hrw.com

my.hrw.com

Go digital with your write-in student edition, accessible on any device.

Math On the Spot

Scan with your smart phone to jump directly to the online edition, video tutor, and more.

Animated Math

Interactively explore key concepts to see how math works.

Personal Math Trainer

Get immediate feedback and help as you work through practice sets.

Are YOU Ready?

Complete these exercises to review skills you will need for this module.

Integer Operations

EXAMPLE

$-3 - (-6) = -3 + 6$

$= |-3| - |6|$

$= 3$

To subtract an integer, add its opposite. The signs are different, so find the difference of the absolute values: $6 - 3 = 3$. Use the sign of the number with the greater absolute value.

Find each difference.

1. $5 - (-9)$ _____

2. $-6 - 8$ _____

3. $2 - 9$ _____

4. $-10 - (-6)$ _____

5. $3 - (-11)$ _____

6. $12 - 7$ _____

7. $-4 - 11$ _____

8. $0 - (-12)$ _____

Measure Angles

EXAMPLE

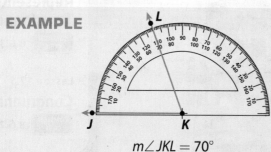

$m\angle JKL = 70°$

Place the center point of the protractor on the angle's vertex.

Align one ray with the base of the protractor.

Read the angle measure where the other ray intersects the semicircle.

Use a protractor to measure each angle.

9.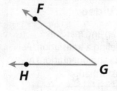

10.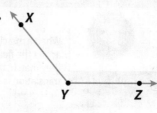

11.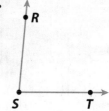

_____ _____ _____

Reading Start-Up

Vocabulary

Review Words

coordinate plane (*plano cartesiano*)

✔ parallelogram (*paralelogramo*)

quadrilateral (*cuadrilátero*)

✔ rhombus (*rombo*)

✔ trapezoid (*trapecio*)

Preview Words

center of rotation (*centro de rotación*)

congruent (*congruente*)

image (*imagen*)

line of reflection (*línea de reflexión*)

preimage (*imagen original*)

reflection (*reflexión*)

rotation (*rotación*)

transformation (*transformación*)

translation (*traslación*)

Visualize Vocabulary

Use the ✔ words to complete the graphic organizer. You will put one word in each oval.

Types of Quadrilaterals

A quadrilateral in which all sides are congruent and opposite sides are parallel.

A quadrilateral in which opposite sides are parallel and congruent.

A quadrilateral in which at least two sides are parallel.

Understand Vocabulary

Match the term on the left to the correct expression on the right.

1. transformation

2. reflection

3. translation

A. A function that describes a change in the position, size, or shape of a figure.

B. A function that slides a figure along a straight line.

C. A transformation that flips a figure across a line.

Active Reading

Booklet Before beginning the module, create a booklet to help you learn the concepts in this module. Write the main idea of each lesson on each page of the booklet. As you study each lesson, write important details that support the main idea, such as vocabulary and formulas. Refer to your finished booklet as you work on assignments and study for tests.

Unpacking the Standards

Understanding the standards and the vocabulary terms in the standards will help you know exactly what you are expected to learn in this module.

COMMON CORE 8.G.2

Understand that a two-dimensional figure is congruent to another if the second can be obtained from the first by a sequence of rotations, reflections, and translations; given two congruent figures, describe a sequence that exhibits the congruence between them.

What It Means to You

You will identify a rotation, a reflection, a translation, and a sequence of transformations, and understand that the image has the same shape and size as the preimage.

UNPACKING EXAMPLE 8.G.2

The figure shows triangle *ABC* and its image after three different transformations. Identify and describe the translation, the reflection, and the rotation of triangle *ABC*.

Figure 1 is a translation 4 units down. Figure 2 is a reflection across the *y*-axis. Figure 3 is a rotation of 180°.

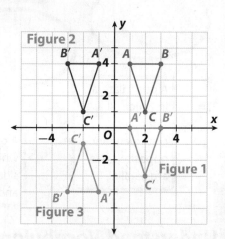

COMMON CORE 8.G.3

Describe the effect of dilations, translations, rotations, and reflections on two-dimensional figures using coordinates.

What It Means to You

You can use an algebraic representation to translate, reflect, or rotate a two-dimensional figure.

UNPACKING EXAMPLE 8.G.3

Rectangle *RSTU* with vertices $(-4, 1)$, $(-1, 1)$, $(-1, -3)$, and $(-4, -3)$ is reflected across the *y*-axis. Find the coordinates of the image.

The rule to reflect across the *y*-axis is to change the sign of the *x*-coordinate.

Coordinates	Reflect across the y-axis $(-x, y)$	Coordinates of image
$(-4, 1)$, $(-1, 1)$, $(-1, -3)$, $(-4, -3)$	$(-(-4), 1)$, $(-(-1), 1)$, $(-(-1), -3)$, $(-(-4), -3)$	$(4, 1)$, $(1, 1)$, $(1, -3)$, $(4, -3)$

The coordinates of the image are $(4, 1)$, $(1, 1)$, $(1, -3)$, and $(4, -3)$.

Visit **my.hrw.com** to see all the **Common Core Standards** unpacked.

my.hrw.com

Properties of Translations

COMMON CORE 8.G.1

Verify experimentally the properties of...translations. *Also 8.G.1a, 8.G.1b, 8.G.1c, 8.G.3*

ESSENTIAL QUESTION How do you describe the properties of translation and their effect on the congruence and orientation of figures?

EXPLORE ACTIVITY 1 COMMON CORE 8.G.1

Exploring Translations

You learned that a function is a rule that assigns exactly one output to each input. A **transformation** is a function that describes a change in the position, size, or shape of a figure. The input of a transformation is the **preimage**, and the output of a transformation is the **image**.

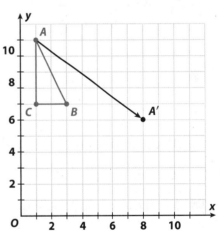

A **translation** is a transformation that slides a figure along a straight line.

The triangle shown on the grid is the preimage (input). The arrow shows the motion of a translation and how point *A* is translated to point *A′*.

A Trace triangle *ABC* onto a piece of paper. Cut out your traced triangle.

B Slide your triangle along the arrow to model the translation that maps point *A* to point *A′*.

C The image of the translation is the triangle produced by the translation. Sketch the image of the translation.

D The vertices of the image are labeled using prime notation. For example, the image of *A* is *A′*. Label the images of points *B* and *C*.

E Describe the motion modeled by the translation.

Move _____ units right and _____ units down.

F Check that the motion you described in part **E** is the same motion that maps point *A* onto *A′*, point *B* onto *B′*, and point *C* onto *C′*.

Reflect

1. How is the orientation of the triangle affected by the translation?

_____

EXPLORE ACTIVITY 2 COMMON CORE 8.G.1

Properties of Translations

Use trapezoid *TRAP* to investigate the properties of translations.

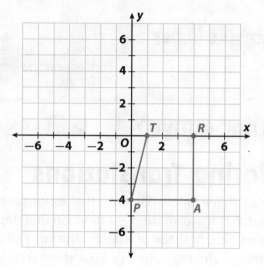

A Trace the trapezoid onto a piece of paper. Cut out your traced trapezoid.

B Place your trapezoid on top of the trapezoid in the figure. Then translate your trapezoid 5 units to the left and 3 units up. Sketch the image of the translation by tracing your trapezoid in this new location. Label the vertices of the image T', R', A', and P'.

C Use a ruler to measure the sides of trapezoid *TRAP* in centimeters.

$TR =$ ________ $RA =$ ________ $AP =$ ________ $TP =$ ________

D Use a ruler to measure the sides of trapezoid $T'R'A'P'$ in centimeters.

$T'R' =$ ________ $R'A' =$ ________ $A'P' =$ ________ $T'P' =$ ________

E What do you notice about the lengths of corresponding sides of the two figures?

____

F Use a protractor to measure the angles of trapezoid *TRAP*.

$m\angle T =$ ________ $m\angle R =$ ________ $m\angle A =$ ________ $m\angle P =$ ________

G Use a protractor to measure the angles of trapezoid $T'R'A'P'$.

$m\angle T' =$ ________ $m\angle R' =$ ________ $m\angle A' =$ ________ $m\angle P' =$ ________

H What do you notice about the measures of corresponding angles of the two figures?

____

I Which sides of trapezoid *TRAP* are parallel? How do you know?

____

Which sides of trapezoid $T'R'A'P'$ are parallel? ________________

What do you notice? ________________________________

____

Reflect

2. Make a Conjecture Use your results from parts **E**, **H**, and **I** to make a conjecture about translations.

_____

_____

3. Two figures that have the same size and shape are called *congruent*. What can you say about translations and congruence?

_____

Graphing Translations

To translate a figure in the coordinate plane, translate each of its vertices. Then connect the vertices to form the image.

EXAMPLE 1

COMMON CORE   8.G.3

The figure shows triangle *XYZ*. Graph the image of the triangle after a translation of 4 units to the right and 1 unit up.

STEP 1 Translate point *X*.

Count right 4 units and up 1 unit and plot point *X'*.

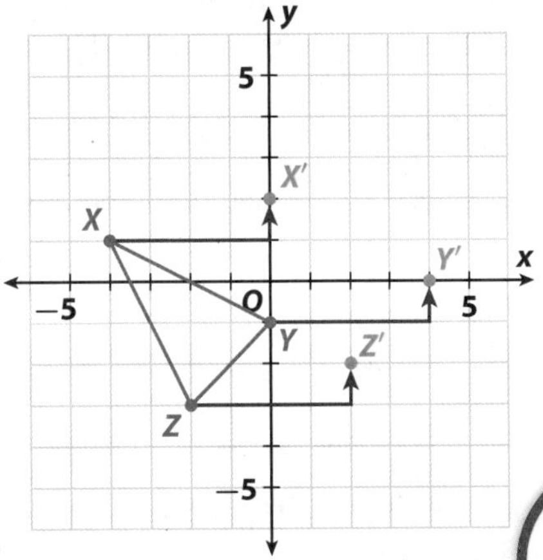

STEP 2 Translate point *Y*.

Count right 4 units and up 1 unit and plot point *Y'*.

STEP 3 Translate point *Z*.

Count right 4 units and up 1 unit and plot point *Z'*.

STEP 4 Connect *X'*, *Y'*, and *Z'* to form triangle *X'Y'Z'*.

Each vertex is moved 4 units right and 1 unit up.

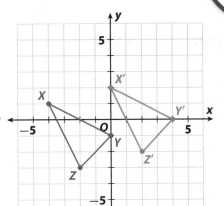

Math Talk
Mathematical Practices

Is the image congruent to the preimage? How do you know?

4. The figure shows parallelogram *ABCD*. Graph the image of the parallelogram after a translation of 5 units to the left and 2 units down.

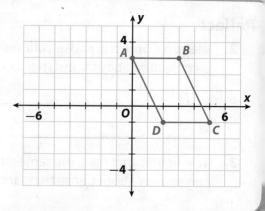

Guided Practice

1. **Vocabulary** A _____ is a change in the position, size, or shape of a figure.

2. **Vocabulary** When you perform a transformation of a figure on the coordinate plane, the input of the transformation is called

   the _____, and the output of the transformation is

   called the _____.

3. Joni translates a right triangle 2 units down and 4 units to the right. How does the orientation of the image of the triangle compare with the orientation of the preimage? (Explore Activity 1)

   _____

4. Rashid drew rectangle *PQRS* on a coordinate plane. He then translated the rectangle 3 units up and 3 units to the left and labeled the image *P'Q'R'S'*. How do rectangle *PQRS* and rectangle *P'Q'R'S'* compare? (Explore Activity 2)

   _____

5. The figure shows trapezoid *WXYZ*. Graph the image of the trapezoid after a translation of 4 units up and 2 units to the left. (Example 1)

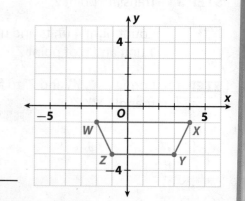

❓ ESSENTIAL QUESTION CHECK-IN

6. What are the properties of translations?

   _____

   _____

17.1 Independent Practice

 8.G.1, 8.G.3

Personal Math Trainer

Online Assessment and Intervention

my.hrw.com

7. The figure shows triangle *DEF*.

   a. Graph the image of the triangle after the translation that maps point *D* to point *D'*.

   b. How would you describe the translation?

   _____

   _____

   c. How does the image of triangle *DEF* compare with the preimage?

   _____

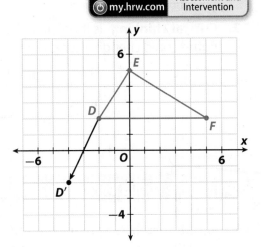

8. a. Graph quadrilateral *KLMN* with vertices *K*(−3, 2), *L*(2, 2), *M*(0, −3), and *N*(−4, 0) on the coordinate grid.

   b. On the same coordinate grid, graph the image of quadrilateral *KLMN* after a translation of 3 units to the right and 4 units up.

   c. Which side of the image is congruent to side $\overline{LM}$?

   _____

   Name three other pairs of congruent sides.

   _____

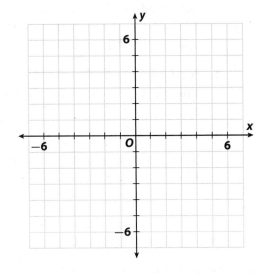

Draw the image of the figure after each translation.

9. 4 units left and 2 units down

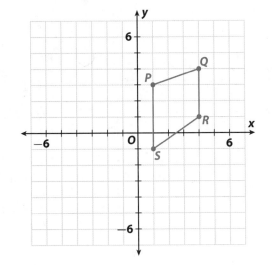

10. 5 units right and 3 units up

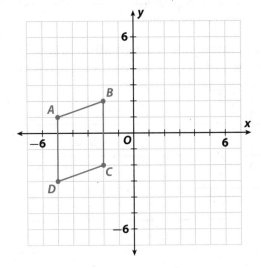

11. The figure shows the ascent of a hot air balloon. How would you describe the translation?

_____

_____

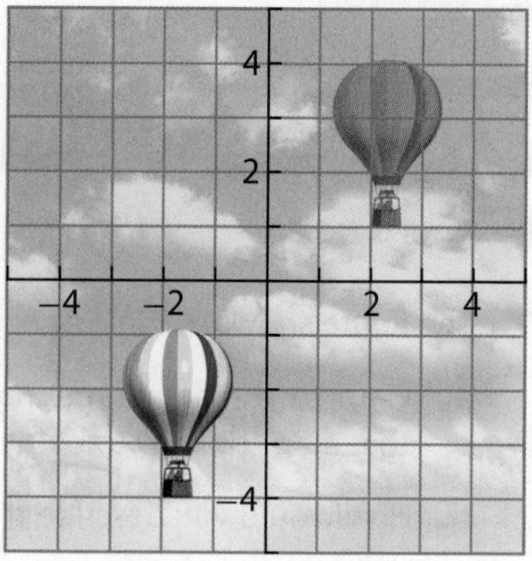

12. Critical Thinking Is it possible that the orientation of a figure could change after it is translated? Explain.

_____

_____

_____

H.O.T.(FOCUS ON HIGHER ORDER THINKING

13. a. Multistep Graph triangle XYZ with vertices $X(-2, -5)$, $Y(2, -2)$, and $Z(4, -4)$ on the coordinate grid.

b. On the same coordinate grid, graph and label triangle $X'Y'Z'$, the image of triangle XYZ after a translation of 3 units to the left and 6 units up.

c. Now graph and label triangle $X''Y''Z''$, the image of triangle $X'Y'Z'$ after a translation of 1 unit to the left and 2 units down.

d. Analyze Relationships How would you describe the translation that maps triangle XYZ onto triangle $X''Y''Z''$?

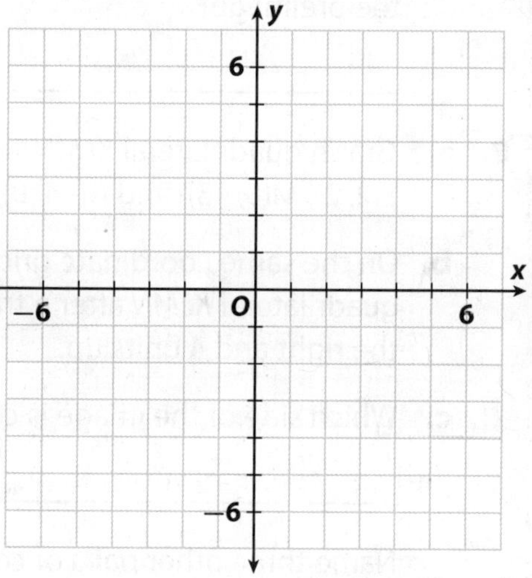

_____

_____

14. Critical Thinking The figure shows rectangle $P'Q'R'S'$, the image of rectangle PQRS after a translation of 5 units to the right and 7 units up. Graph and label the preimage PQRS.

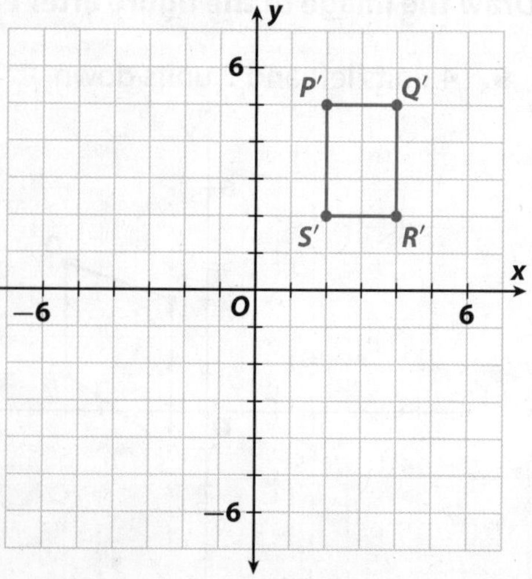

15. Communicate Mathematical Ideas Explain why the image of a figure after a translation is congruent to its preimage.

_____

_____

_____

_____

Properties of Reflections

COMMON CORE **8.G.1**
Verify experimentally the properties of . . . reflections. . . .
Also 8.G.1a, 8.G.1b, 8.G.1c, 8.G.3

ESSENTIAL QUESTION

How do you describe the properties of reflection and their effect on the congruence and orientation of figures?

EXPLORE ACTIVITY 1   COMMON CORE 8.G.1

Exploring Reflections

A **reflection** is a transformation that flips a figure across a line. The line is called the **line of reflection**. Each point and its image are the same distance from the line of reflection.

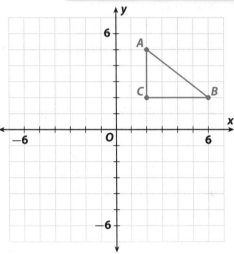

The triangle shown on the grid is the preimage. You will explore reflections across the x- and y-axes.

A Trace triangle ABC and the x- and y-axes onto a piece of paper.

B Fold your paper along the x-axis and trace the image of the triangle on the opposite side of the x-axis. Unfold your paper and label the vertices of the image A', B', and C'.

C What is the line of reflection for this transformation?

_____

D Find the perpendicular distance from each point to the line of reflection.

Point A _____   Point B _____   Point C _____

E Find the perpendicular distance from each point to the line of reflection.

Point A' _____   Point B' _____   Point C' _____

F What do you notice about the distances you found in **D** and **E**?

_____

Reflect

1. Fold your paper from **A** along the y-axis and trace the image of triangle ABC on the opposite side. Label the vertices of the image A'', B'', and C''. What is the line of reflection for this transformation? _____

2. How does each image in your drawings compare with its preimage?

_____

Properties of Reflections

Use trapezoid *TRAP* to investigate the properties of reflections.

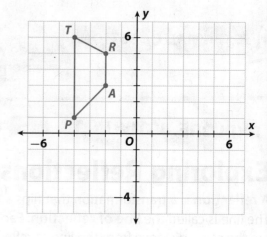

A Trace the trapezoid onto a piece of paper. Cut out your traced trapezoid.

B Place your trapezoid on top of the trapezoid in the figure. Then reflect your trapezoid across the *y*-axis. Sketch the image of the reflection by tracing your trapezoid in this new location. Label the vertices of the image *T′*, *R′*, *A′*, and *P′*.

C Use a ruler to measure the sides of trapezoid *TRAP* in centimeters.

TR = _____   *RA* = _____   *AP* = _____   *TP* = _____

D Use a ruler to measure the sides of trapezoid *T′R′A′P′* in centimeters.

T′R′ = _____   *R′A′* = _____   *A′P′* = _____   *T′P′* = _____

E What do you notice about the lengths of corresponding sides of the two figures?

_____

F Use a protractor to measure the angles of trapezoid *TRAP*.

m∠T = _____   *m∠R* = _____   *m∠A* = _____   *m∠P* = _____

G Use a protractor to measure the angles of trapezoid *T′R′A′P′*.

m∠T′ = _____   *m∠R′* = _____   *m∠A′* = _____   *m∠P′* = _____

H What do you notice about the measures of corresponding angles of the two figures?

_____

I Which sides of trapezoid *TRAP* are parallel? _____

Which sides of trapezoid *T′R′A′P′* are parallel? _____
What do you notice?

_____

_____

Reflect

3. Make a Conjecture Use your results from 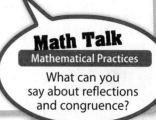 **E** , **H** , and **I** to make a conjecture about reflections.

_____

_____

_____

Math Talk

Mathematical Practices

What can you say about reflections and congruence?

Graphing Reflections

To reflect a figure across a line of reflection, reflect each of its vertices. Then connect the vertices to form the image. Remember that each point and its image are the same distance from the line of reflection.

Math On the Spot

my.hrw.com

EXAMPLE 1

COMMON CORE 8.G.3

The figure shows triangle *XYZ*. Graph the image of the triangle after a reflection across the *x*-axis.

My Notes

STEP 1 Reflect point *X*.

Point *X* is 3 units below the *x*-axis. Count 3 units above the *x*-axis and plot point *X′*.

STEP 2 Reflect point *Y*.

Point *Y* is 1 unit below the *x*-axis. Count 1 unit above the *x*-axis and plot point *Y′*.

STEP 3 Reflect point *Z*.

Point *Z* is 5 units below the *x*-axis. Count 5 units above the *x*-axis and plot point *Z′*.

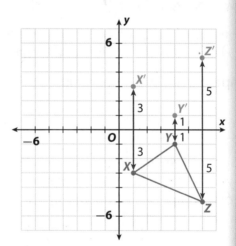

STEP 4 Connect *X′*, *Y′*, and *Z′* to form triangle *X′Y′Z′*.

Each vertex of the image is the same distance from the *x*-axis as the corresponding vertex in the original figure.

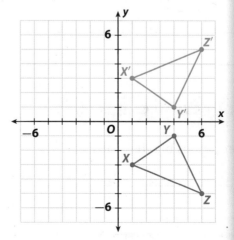

YOUR TURN

4. The figure shows pentagon *ABCDE*. Graph the image of the pentagon after a reflection across the *y*-axis.

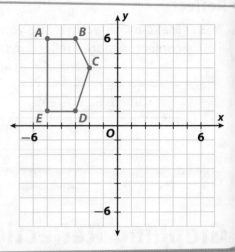

Guided Practice

1. **Vocabulary** A reflection is a transformation that flips a figure across

   a line called the _____.

2. The figure shows trapezoid *ABCD*. (Explore Activities 1 and 2 and Example 1)

   a. Graph the image of the trapezoid after a reflection across the *x*-axis. Label the vertices of the image.

   b. How do trapezoid *ABCD* and trapezoid *A'B'C'D'* compare?

      _____

   c. **What If?** Suppose you reflected trapezoid *ABCD* across the *y*-axis. How would the orientation of the image of the trapezoid compare with the orientation of the preimage?

      _____

      _____

      _____

      _____

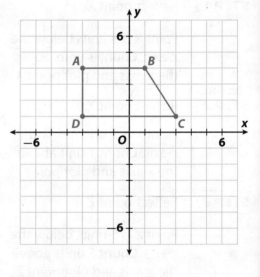

❓ ESSENTIAL QUESTION CHECK-IN

3. What are the properties of reflections?

   _____

   _____

17.2 Independent Practice

COMMON CORE 8.G.1, 8.G.3

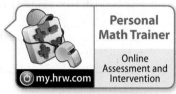

Personal
Math Trainer

Online
Assessment and
Intervention

my.hrw.com

The graph shows four right triangles. Use the graph for Exercises 4–7.

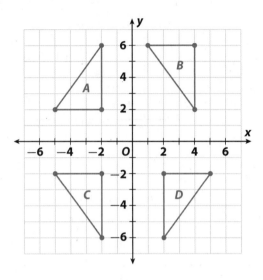

8. a. Graph quadrilateral *WXYZ* with vertices *W*(−2, −2), *X*(3, 1), *Y*(5, −1), and *Z*(4, −6) on the coordinate grid.

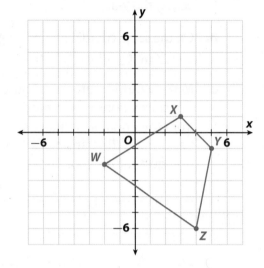

4. Which two triangles are reflections of each other across the *x*-axis?

_____

5. For which two triangles is the line of reflection the *y*-axis?

_____

6. Which triangle is a translation of triangle *C*? How would you describe the translation?

_____

_____

7. Which triangles are congruent? How do you know?

_____

_____

_____

_____

_____

b. On the same coordinate grid, graph quadrilateral *W′X′Y′Z′*, the image of quadrilateral *WXYZ* after a reflection across the *x*-axis.

c. Which side of the image is congruent to side $\overline{YZ}$?

_____

Name three other pairs of congruent sides.

_____

_____

d. Which angle of the image is congruent to ∠*X*?

_____

Name three other pairs of congruent angles.

_____

_____

9. Critical Thinking Is it possible that the image of a point after a reflection could be the same point as the preimage? Explain.

_____

_____

10. a. Graph the image of the figure shown after a reflection across the *y*-axis.

b. On the same coordinate grid, graph the image of the figure you drew in part **a** after a reflection across the *x*-axis.

c. Make a Conjecture What other sequence of transformations would produce the same final image from the original preimage? Check your answer by performing the transformations. Then make a conjecture that generalizes your findings.

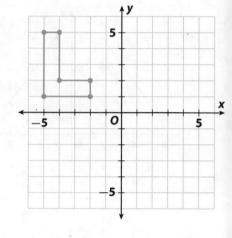

_____

_____

_____

_____

_____

11. a. Graph triangle *DEF* with vertices *D*(2, 6), *E*(5, 6), and *F*(5, 1) on the coordinate grid.

b. Next graph triangle *D′E′F′*, the image of triangle *DEF* after a reflection across the *y*-axis.

c. On the same coordinate grid, graph triangle *D″E″F″*, the image of triangle *D′E′F′* after a translation of 7 units down and 2 units to the right.

d. Analyze Relationships Find a different sequence of transformations that will transform triangle *DEF* to triangle *D″E″F″*.

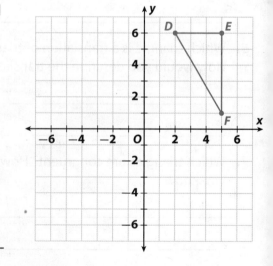

_____

_____

_____

_____

LESSON
17.3 Properties of Rotations

COMMON CORE 8.G.1

Verify experimentally the properties of rotations.... Also 8.G.1a, 8.G.1b, 8.G.1c, 8.G.3

ESSENTIAL QUESTION

How do you describe the properties of rotation and their effect on the congruence and orientation of figures?

EXPLORE ACTIVITY 1 **COMMON CORE** 8.G.1

Exploring Rotations

A **rotation** is a transformation that turns a figure around a given point called the **center of rotation**. The image has the same size and shape as the preimage.

The triangle shown on the grid is the preimage. You will use the origin as the center of rotation.

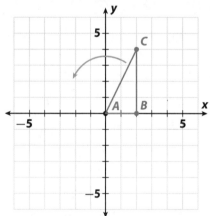

A Trace triangle *ABC* onto a piece of paper. Cut out your traced triangle.

B Rotate your triangle 90° counterclockwise about the origin. The side of the triangle that lies along the *x*-axis should now lie along the *y*-axis.

C Sketch the image of the rotation. Label the images of points *A*, *B*, and *C* as *A′*, *B′*, and *C′*.

D Describe the motion modeled by the rotation.

Rotate _____ degrees _____ about the origin.

E Check that the motion you described in **D** is the same motion that maps point *A* onto *A′*, point *B* onto *B′*, and point *C* onto *C′*.

Reflect

1. **Communicate Mathematical Ideas** How are the size and the orientation of the triangle affected by the rotation?

   _____

   _____

   _____

2. Rotate triangle *ABC* 90° clockwise about the origin. Sketch the result on the coordinate grid above. Label the image vertices *A″*, *B″*, and *C″*.

Properties of Rotations

Use trapezoid *TRAP* to investigate the properties of rotations.

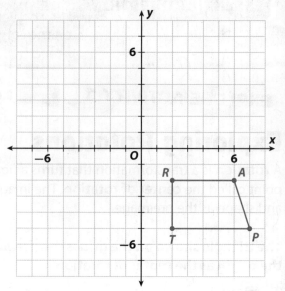

A   Trace the trapezoid onto a piece of paper. Include the portion of the x- and y-axes bordering the third quadrant. Cut out your tracing.

B   Place your trapezoid and axes on top of those in the figure. Then use the axes to help rotate your trapezoid 180° counterclockwise about the origin. Sketch the image of the rotation of your trapezoid in this new location. Label the vertices of the image T′, R′, A′, and P′.

C   Use a ruler to measure the sides of trapezoid *TRAP* in centimeters.

    $TR =$ _____ $RA =$ _____

    $AP =$ _____ $TP =$ _____

D   Use a ruler to measure the sides of trapezoid *T′R′A′P′* in centimeters.

    $T′R′ =$ _____ $R′A′ =$ _____

    $A′P′ =$ _____ $T′P′ =$ _____

E   What do you notice about the lengths of corresponding sides of the two figures?

_____

F   Use a protractor to measure the angles of trapezoid *TRAP*.

    $m\angle T =$ _____ $m\angle R =$ _____ $m\angle A =$ _____ $m\angle P =$ _____

G   Use a protractor to measure the angles of trapezoid *T′R′A′P′*.

    $m\angle T′ =$ _____ $m\angle R′ =$ _____ $m\angle A′ =$ _____ $m\angle P′ =$ _____

H   What do you notice about the measures of corresponding angles of the two figures?

_____

I   Which sides of trapezoid *TRAP* are parallel? _____

    Which sides of trapezoid *T′R′A′P′* are parallel? _____

    What do you notice? _____

_____

Reflect

3. **Make a Conjecture** Use your results from ⓔ, ⓗ, and ⓘ to make a conjecture about rotations.

_____

_____

4. Place your tracing back in its original position. Then perform a 180° _clockwise_ rotation about the origin. Compare the result with the result of the transformation in ⓑ.

_____

_____

Graphing Rotations

To rotate a figure in the coordinate plane, rotate each of its vertices. Then connect the vertices to form the image.

Math On the Spot

my.hrw.com

EXAMPLE 1

COMMON CORE 8.G.3

The figure shows triangle _ABC_. Graph the image of triangle _ABC_ after a rotation of 90° clockwise.

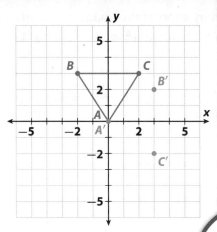

STEP 1 Rotate the figure clockwise from the _y_-axis to the _x_-axis. Point _A_ will still be at (0, 0).

Point _B_ is 2 units to the left of the _y_-axis, so point _B′_ is 2 units above the _x_-axis.

Point _C_ is 2 units to the right of the _y_-axis, so point _C′_ is 2 units below the _x_-axis.

STEP 2 Connect _A′_, _B′_, and _C′_ to form the image triangle _A′B′C′_.

Math Talk
Mathematical Practices

How is the orientation of the triangle affected by the rotation?

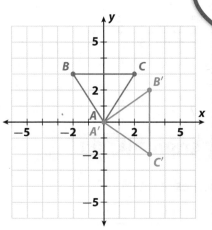

Reflect

5. Is the image congruent to the preimage? How do you know?

_____

_____

_____

_____

YOUR TURN

Graph the image of quadrilateral *ABCD* after each rotation.

6. 180°

7. 270° clockwise

8. Find the coordinates of Point *C* after a 90° counterclockwise rotation followed by a 180° rotation.

_____

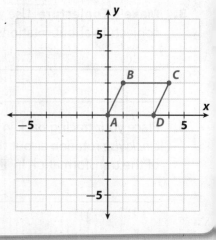

Guided Practice

1. **Vocabulary** A rotation is a transformation that turns a figure around a

   given _____ called the center of rotation.

Siobhan rotates a right triangle 90° counterclockwise about the origin.

2. How does the orientation of the image of the triangle compare with the orientation of the preimage? (Explore Activity 1)

   _____

3. Is the image of the triangle congruent to the preimage? (Explore Activity 2)

   _____

Draw the image of the figure after the given rotation about the origin. (Example 1)

4. 90° counterclockwise

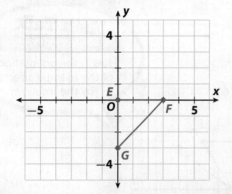

5. 180°

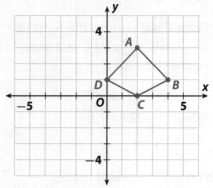

? ESSENTIAL QUESTION CHECK-IN

6. What are the properties of rotations?

_____

17.3 Independent Practice

 8.G.1, 8.G.3

7. The figure shows triangle *ABC* and a rotation of the triangle about the origin.

   a. How would you describe the rotation?

   _____

   _____

   b. What are the coordinates of the image?

   _____ , _____ , _____

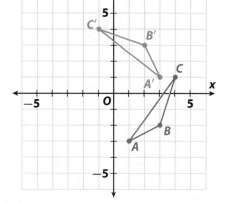

8. The graph shows a figure and its image after a transformation.

   a. How would you describe this as a rotation?

   _____

   _____

   b. Can you describe this as a transformation other than a rotation? Explain.

   _____

   _____

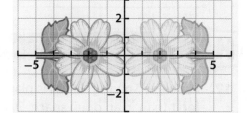

9. What type of rotation will preserve the orientation of the H-shaped figure in the grid?

   _____

10. A point with coordinates $(-2, -3)$ is rotated 90° clockwise about the origin. What are the coordinates of its image?

   _____

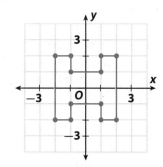

Complete the table with rotations of 180° or 90°. Include the direction of rotation for rotations of 90°.

	Shape in quadrant	Image in quadrant	Rotation
11.	I	IV	
12.	III	I	
13.	IV	III	

Draw the image of the figure after the given rotation about the origin.

14. 180°

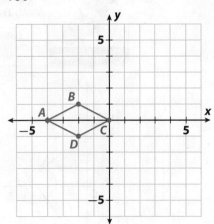

15. 270° counterclockwise

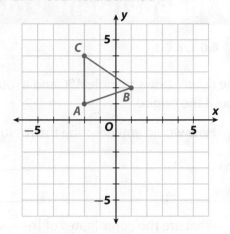

16. Is there a rotation for which the orientation of the image is always the same as that of the preimage? If so, what?

_____

 **FOCUS ON HIGHER ORDER THINKING**

Work Area

17. Problem Solving Lucas is playing a game where he has to rotate a figure for it to fit in an open space. Every time he clicks a button, the figure rotates 90 degrees clockwise. How many times does he need to click the button so that each figure returns to its original orientation?

Figure A _____

Figure B _____

Figure C _____

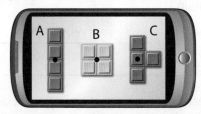

18. Make a Conjecture Triangle *ABC* is reflected across the *y*-axis to form the image *A'B'C'*. Triangle *A'B'C'* is then reflected across the *x*-axis to form the image *A"B"C"*. What type of rotation can be used to describe the relationship between triangle *A"B"C"* and triangle *ABC*?

_____

19. Communicate Mathematical Ideas Point *A* is on the *y*-axis. Describe all possible locations of image *A'* for rotations of 90°, 180°, and 270°. Include the origin as a possible location for *A*.

_____

_____

_____

_____

LESSON
17.4

COMMON CORE 8.G.3
Describe the effect of . . . , translations, rotations, and reflections on two-dimensional figures using coordinates.

Algebraic Representations of Transformations

ESSENTIAL QUESTION

How can you describe the effect of a translation, rotation, or reflection on coordinates using an algebraic representation?

EXPLORE ACTIVITY   **8.G.3**

Algebraic Representations of Translations

The rules shown in the table describe how coordinates change when a figure is translated up, down, right, and left on the coordinate plane.

Math On the Spot
ⓦ my.hrw.com

Translations	
Right *a* units	Add *a* to the *x*-coordinate: $(x, y) \rightarrow (x + a, y)$
Left *a* units	Subtract *a* from the *x*-coordinate: $(x, y) \rightarrow (x - a, y)$
Up *b* units	Add *b* to the *y*-coordinate: $(x, y) \rightarrow (x, y + b)$
Down *b* units	Subtract *b* from the *y*-coordinate: $(x, y) \rightarrow (x, y - b)$

EXAMPLE 1 Triangle *XYZ* has vertices *X*(0, 0), *Y*(2, 3), and *Z*(4, −1). Find the vertices of triangle *X′Y′Z′* after a translation of 3 units to the right and 1 unit down. Then graph the triangle and its image.

> Add 3 to the *x*-coordinate of each vertex, and subtract 1 from the *y*-coordinate of each vertex.

STEP 1 Apply the rule to find the vertices of the image.

Vertices of △*XYZ*	Rule: $(x + 3, y − 1)$	Vertices of △*X′Y′Z′*
X(0, 0)	$(0 + 3, 0 − 1)$	*X′*(____ , ____)
Y(2, 3)	$(\_\_\_\_ + 3, \_\_\_\_ − 1)$	*Y′*(____ , ____)
Z(4, −1)	$(4 + \_\_\_\_ , −1 − \_\_\_\_)$	*Z′*(____ , ____)

STEP 2 Graph the image with triangle *XYZ* on the coordinate plane.

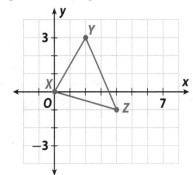

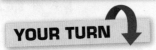

YOUR TURN

1. A rectangle has vertices at (0, −2), (0, 3), (3, −2), and (3, 3). What are the coordinates of the vertices of the image after the translation $(x, y) \rightarrow (x - 6, y - 3)$? Describe the translation.

Personal Math Trainer

Online Assessment and Intervention

○ my.hrw.com

Math On the Spot

○ my.hrw.com

Algebraic Representations of Reflections

The signs of the coordinates of a figure change when the figure is reflected across the *x*-axis and *y*-axis. The table shows the rules for changing the signs of the coordinates after a reflection.

Reflections	
Across the *x*-axis	Multiply each *y*-coordinate by −1: $(x, y) \rightarrow (x, -y)$
Across the *y*-axis	Multiply each *x*-coordinate by −1: $(x, y) \rightarrow (-x, y)$

EXAMPLE 2

COMMON CORE 8.G.3

My Notes

Rectangle *RSTU* has vertices *R*(−4, −1), *S*(−1, −1), *T*(−1, −3), and *U*(−4, −3). Find the vertices of rectangle *R'S'T'U'* after a reflection across the *y*-axis. Then graph the rectangle and its image.

Multiply the x-coordinate o each vertex by

STEP 1 Apply the rule to find the vertices of the image.

Vertices of *RSTU*	Rule: $(-1 \cdot x, y)$	Vertices of *R'S'T'U'*
R(−4, −1)	$(-1 \cdot (-4), -1)$	*R'*(4, −1)
S(−1, −1)	$(-1 \cdot (-1), -1)$	*S'*(1, −1)
T(−1, −3)	$(-1 \cdot (-1), -3)$	*T'*(1, −3)
U(−4, −3)	$(-1 \cdot (-4), -3)$	*U'*(4, −3)

STEP 2 Graph rectangle *RSTU* and its image.

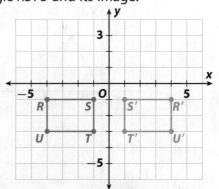

2. Triangle *ABC* has vertices *A*(−2, 6), *B*(0, 5), and *C*(3, −1). Find the vertices of triangle *A'B'C'* after a reflection across the *x*-axis.

Math On the Spot

ⓑ my.hrw.com

Algebraic Representations of Rotations

When points are rotated about the origin, the coordinates of the image can be found using the rules shown in the table.

Rotations	
90° clockwise	Multiply each *x*-coordinate by −1; then switch the *x*- and *y*-coordinates: $(x, y) \rightarrow (y, -x)$
90° counterclockwise	Multiply each *y*-coordinate by −1; then switch the *x*- and *y*-coordinates: $(x, y) \rightarrow (-y, x)$
180°	Multiply both coordinates by −1: $(x, y) \rightarrow (-x, -y)$

EXAMPLE 3

COMMON CORE 8.G.3

Quadrilateral *ABCD* has vertices at *A*(−4, 2), *B*(−3, 4), *C*(2, 3), and *D*(0, 0). Find the vertices of quadrilateral *A'B'C'D'* after a 90° clockwise rotation. Then graph the quadrilateral and its image.

> Multiply the *x*-coordinate of each vertex by −1, and then switch the *x*- and *y*-coordinates.

STEP 1 Apply the rule to find the vertices of the image.

Vertices of *ABCD*	Rule: (*y*, −*x*)	Vertices of *A'B'C'D'*
A(−4, 2)	(2, −1 · (−4))	*A'*(2, 4)
B(−3, 4)	(4, −1 · (−3))	*B'*(4, 3)
C(2, 3)	(3, −1 · 2)	*C'*(3, −2)
D(0, 0)	(0, −1 · 0)	*D'*(0, 0)

STEP 2 Graph the quadrilateral and its image.

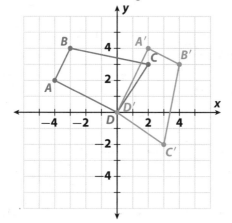

Reflect

3. Communicate Mathematical Ideas How would you find the vertices of an image if a figure were rotated 270° clockwise? Explain.

_____

_____

_____

YOUR TURN

4. A triangle has vertices at $J(-2, -4)$, $K(1, 5)$, and $L(2, 2)$. What are the coordinates of the vertices of the image after the triangle is rotated 90° counterclockwise?

_____

Guided Practice

1. Triangle XYZ has vertices $X(-3, -2)$, $Y(-1, 0)$, and $Z(1, -6)$. Find the vertices of triangle $X'Y'Z'$ after a translation of 6 units to the right. Then graph the triangle and its image. (Explore Activity Example 1)

_____

2. Describe what happens to the x- and y-coordinates after a point is reflected across the x-axis. (Example 2)

_____

_____

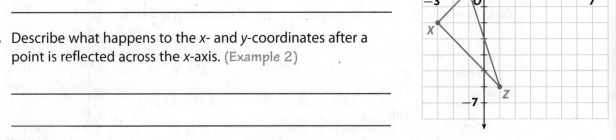

3. Use the rule $(x, y) \rightarrow (y, -x)$ to graph the image of the triangle at right. Then describe the transformation. (Example 3)

_____

❓ ESSENTIAL QUESTION CHECK-IN

4. How do the x- and y-coordinates change when a figure is translated right a units and down b units?

_____

_____

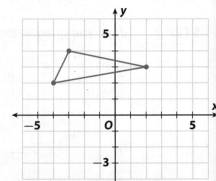

17.4 Independent Practice

Personal Math Trainer

my.hrw.com

Online Assessment and Intervention

COMMON CORE 8.G.3

Write an algebraic rule to describe each transformation. Then describe the transformation.

5.

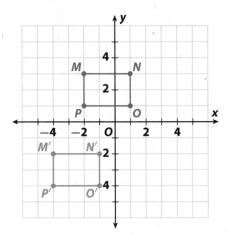

_____

_____

6.

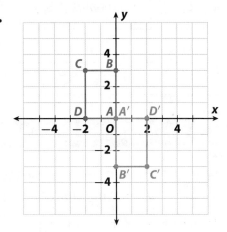

_____

_____

7. Triangle *XYZ* has vertices *X*(6, −2.3), *Y*(7.5, 5), and *Z*(8, 4). When translated, *X'* has coordinates (2.8, −1.3). Write a rule to describe this transformation. Then find the coordinates of *Y'* and *Z'*.

_____

8. Point *L* has coordinates (3, −5). The coordinates of point *L'* after a reflection are (−3, −5). Without graphing, tell which axis point *L* was reflected across. Explain your answer.

_____

_____

_____

9. Use the rule $(x, y) \rightarrow (x − 2, y − 4)$ to graph the image of the rectangle. Then describe the transformation.

_____

_____

10. Parallelogram *ABCD* has vertices $A(−2, −5\frac{1}{2})$, $B(−4, −5\frac{1}{2})$, $C(−3, −2)$, and $D(−1, −2)$. Find the vertices of parallelogram *A'B'C'D'* after a translation of $2\frac{1}{2}$ units down.

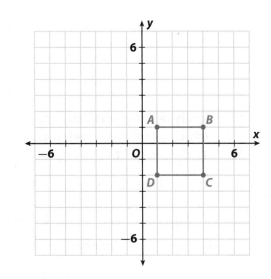

_____

_____

11. Alexandra drew the logo shown on half-inch graph paper. Write a rule that describes the translation Alexandra used to create the shadow on the letter A.

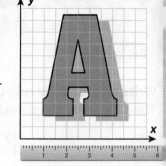

_____

12. Kite *KLMN* has vertices at *K*(1, 3), *L*(2, 4), *M*(3, 3), and *N*(2, 0). After the kite is rotated, *K′* has coordinates (−3, 1). Describe the rotation, and include a rule in your description. Then find the coordinates of *L′*, *M′*, and *N′*.

_____

_____

 **FOCUS ON HIGHER ORDER THINKING**

13. Make a Conjecture Graph the triangle with vertices (−3, 4), (3, 4), and (−5, −5). Use the transformation (*y*, *x*) to graph its image.

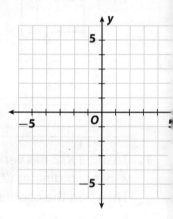

a. Which vertex of the image has the same coordinates as a vertex of the original figure? Explain why this is true.

_____

_____

b. What is the equation of a line through the origin and this point?

_____

c. Describe the transformation of the triangle.

_____

14. Critical Thinking Mitchell says the point (0, 0) does not change when reflected across the *x*- or *y*-axis or when rotated about the origin. Do you agree with Mitchell? Explain why or why not.

_____

_____

_____

15. Analyze Relationships Triangle *ABC* with vertices *A*(−2, −2), *B*(−3, 1), and *C*(1, 1) is translated by (*x*, *y*) → (*x* − 1, *y* + 3). Then the image, triangle *A′B′C′*, is translated by (*x*, *y*) → (*x* + 4, *y* − 1), resulting in *A″B″C″*.

a. Find the coordinates for the vertices of triangle *A″B″C″*.

_____

b. Write a rule for one translation that maps triangle *ABC* to triangle *A″B″C″*.

_____

Work Area

17.5 Congruent Figures

COMMON CORE 8.G.2

Understand that a two-dimensional figure is congruent to another if the second can be obtained from the first by a sequence of rotations, reflections, and translations; given two congruent figures, describe a sequence that exhibits the congruence between them.

ESSENTIAL QUESTION

What is the connection between transformations and figures that have the same shape and size?

EXPLORE ACTIVITY   8.G.2

Combining Transformations

Apply the indicated series of transformations to the triangle. Each transformation is applied to the image of the previous transformation, not the original figure. Label each image with the letter of the transformation applied.

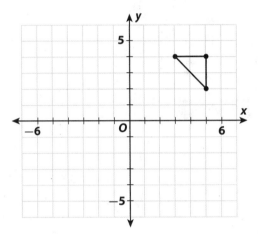

A Reflection across the x-axis

B $(x, y) \rightarrow (x - 3, y)$

C Reflection across the y-axis

D $(x, y) \rightarrow (x, y + 4)$

E Rotation 90° clockwise around the origin

F Compare the size and shape of the final image to that of the original figure.

_____

_____

Reflect

1. Which transformation(s) change the orientation of figures? Which do not?

_____

2. **Make a Conjecture**   Two figures have the same size and shape. What does this indicate about the figures?

_____

_____

_____

Congruent Figures

Recall that segments and their images have the same length and angles and their images have the same measure under a translation, reflection, or rotation. Two figures are said to be **congruent** if one can be obtained from the other by a sequence of translations, reflections, and rotations. Congruent figures have the same size and shape.

When you are told that two figures are congruent, there must be a sequence of translations, reflections, and/or rotations that transforms one into the other.

EXAMPLE 1   COMMON CORE   8.G.2

A Identify a sequence of transformations that will transform figure A into figure B.

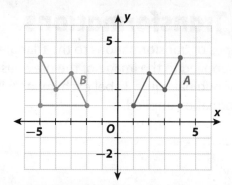

To transform figure A into figure B, you need to reflect it over the y-axis and translate one unit to the left. A sequence of transformations that will accomplish this is $(x, y) \rightarrow (-x, y)$ and $(x, y) \rightarrow (x - 1, y)$.

B Identify a sequence of transformations that will transform figure B into figure C.

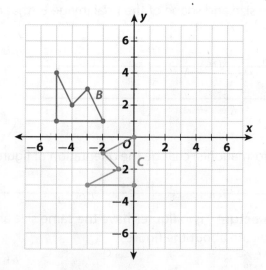

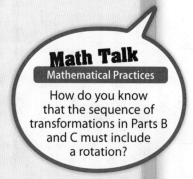
Any sequence of transformations that changes figure B into figure C will need to include a rotation. A 90° counterclockwise rotation around the origin would result in the figure being oriented as figure C.

However, the rotated figure would be 2 units below and 1 unit to the left of where figure C is. You would need to translate the rotated figure up 2 units and right 1 unit.

The sequence of transformations is a 90° counterclockwise rotation about the origin, $(x, y) \rightarrow (-y, x)$, followed by $(x, y) \rightarrow (x + 1, y + 2)$.

C Identify a sequence of transformations that will transform figure *D* into figure *E*.

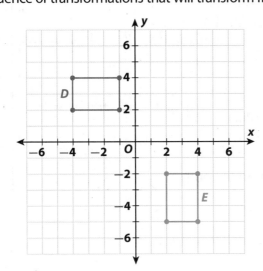

A sequence of transformations that changes figure *D* to figure *E* will need to include a rotation. A 90º clockwise rotation around the origin would result in the figure being oriented as figure *E*.

However, the rotated figure would be 6 units above where figure *E* is. You would need to translate the rotated figure down 6 units.

The sequence of transformations is a 90º clockwise rotation about the origin, $(x, y) \rightarrow (y, -x)$, followed by $(x, y) \rightarrow (x, y - 6)$.

YOUR TURN

3. Identify a sequence of transformations that will transform figure *A* into figure *B*.

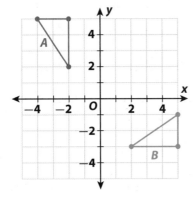

_____

_____

_____

Personal Math Trainer

Online Assessment and Intervention

my.hrw.com

1. Apply the indicated series of transformations to the rectangle. Each transformation is applied to the image of the previous transformation, not the original figure. Label each image with the letter of the transformation applied. (Explore Activity)

   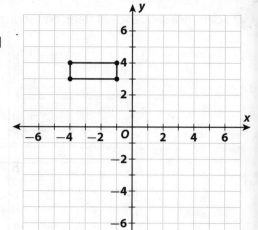

   a. Reflection across the *y*-axis

   b. Rotation 90° clockwise around the origin

   c. $(x, y) \rightarrow (x - 2, y)$

   d. Rotation 90° counterclockwise around the origin

   e. $(x, y) \rightarrow (x - 7, y - 2)$

Identify a sequence of transformations that will transform figure *A* into figure *C*. (Example 1)

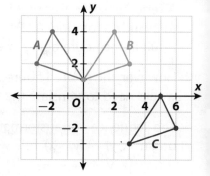

2. What transformation is used to transform figure *A* into figure *B*?

   _____

   _____

3. What transformation is used to transform figure *B* into figure *C*?

   _____

   _____

4. What sequence of transformations is used to transform figure *A* into figure *C*? Express the transformations algebraically.

   _____

   _____

5. **Vocabulary** What does it mean for two figures to be congruent?

   _____

   _____

ESSENTIAL QUESTION CHECK-IN

6. After a sequence of translations, reflections, and rotations, what is true about the first figure and the final figure?

   _____

   _____

17.5 Independent Practice

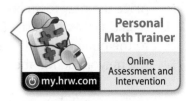

Personal Math Trainer

Online Assessment and Intervention

my.hrw.com

For each given figure *A*, graph figures *B* and *C* using the given sequence of transformations. State whether figures *A* and *C* have the same or different orientation.

7.

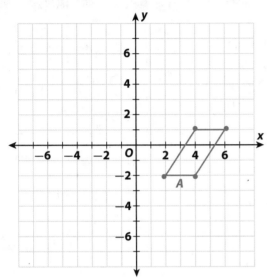

Figure *B*: a translation of 1 unit to the right and 3 units up

Figure *C*: a 90° clockwise rotation around the origin

_____

8.

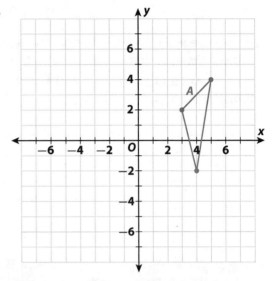

Figure *B*: a reflection across the *y*-axis

Figure *C*: a 180° rotation around the origin

_____

9.

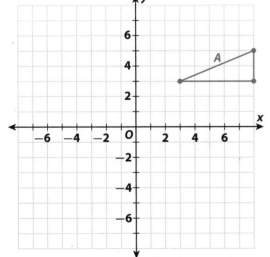

Figure *B*: a reflection across the *y*-axis

Figure *C*: a translation 2 units down

_____

10.

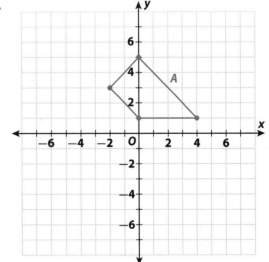

Figure *B*: a translation 2 units up

Figure *C*: a rotation of 180° around the origin

_____

11. Represent Real-World Problems A city planner wanted to place the new town library at site *A*. The mayor thought that it would be better at site *B*. What transformations were applied to the building at site *A* to relocate the building to site *B*? Did the mayor change the size or orientation of the library?

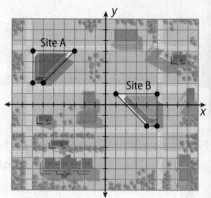

_____

_____

_____

12. Persevere in Problem Solving Find a sequence of three transformations that can be used to obtain figure *D* from figure *A*. Graph the figures *B* and *C* that are created by the transformations.

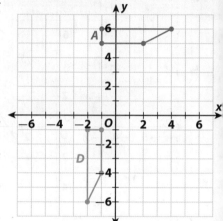

_____

_____

_____

_____

 **FOCUS ON HIGHER ORDER THINKING**

13. Counterexamples The Commutative Properties for Addition and Multiplication state that the order of two numbers being added or multiplied does not change the sum or product. Are translations and rotations commutative? If not, give a counterexample.

_____

_____

_____

_____

_____

14. Multiple Representations For each representation, describe a possible sequence of transformations.

a. $(x, y) \rightarrow (-x - 2, y + 1)$

_____

_____

b. $(x, y) \rightarrow (y, -x - 3)$

_____

_____

Work Area

Ready to Go On?

Personal Math Trainer

Online Assessment and Intervention

⏻ my.hrw.com

17.1–17.3 Properties of Translations, Reflections, and Rotations

1. Graph the image of triangle *ABC* after a translation of 6 units to the right and 4 units down. Label the vertices of the image *A′*, *B′*, and *C′*.

2. On the same coordinate grid, graph the image of triangle *ABC* after a reflection across the *x*-axis. Label the vertices of the image *A″*, *B″*, and *C″*.

3. Graph the image of *HIJK* after it is rotated 180° about the origin. Label the vertices of the image *H′I′J′K′*.

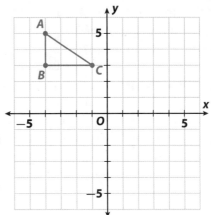

17.4 Algebraic Representations of Transformations

4. A triangle has vertices at (2, 3), (−2, 2), and (−3, 5). What are the coordinates of the vertices of the image after the translation $(x, y) \rightarrow (x + 4, y - 3)$?

_____

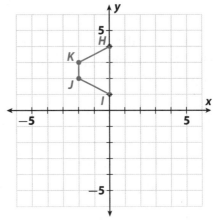

17.5 Congruent Figures

5. **Vocabulary** Translations, reflections, and rotations produce a figure

   that is _____ to the original figure.

6. Use the coordinate grid for Exercise 3. Reflect *H′I′J′K′* over the *y*-axis, then rotate it 180° about the origin. Label the new figure *H″I″J″K″*.

? ESSENTIAL QUESTION

7. How can you use transformations to solve real-world problems?

   _____

   _____

MODULE 17 MIXED REVIEW

Assessment Readiness

COMMON CORE

Personal Math Trainer

Online Assessment and Intervention

my.hrw.com

Selected Response

1. What would be the orientation of the figure L after a translation of 8 units to the right and 3 units up?

Ⓐ

Ⓒ

Ⓑ

Ⓓ

2. Figure A is reflected over the *y*-axis and then lowered 6 units. Which sequence describes these transformations?

Ⓐ $(x, y) \rightarrow (x, -y)$ and $(x, y) \rightarrow (x, y - 6)$

Ⓑ $(x, y) \rightarrow (-x, y)$ and $(x, y) \rightarrow (x, y - 6)$

Ⓒ $(x, y) \rightarrow (x, -y)$ and $(x, y) \rightarrow (x - 6, y)$

Ⓓ $(x, y) \rightarrow (-x, y)$ and $(x, y) \rightarrow (x - 6, y)$

3. What quadrant would the triangle be in after a rotation of 90° counterclockwise about the origin?

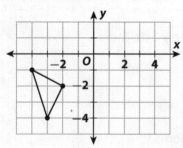

Ⓐ I   Ⓑ II   Ⓒ III   Ⓓ IV

4. Which rational number is greater than $-3\frac{1}{3}$ but less than $-\frac{4}{5}$?

Ⓐ −0.4   Ⓒ −0.19

Ⓑ $-\frac{9}{7}$ Ⓓ $-\frac{22}{5}$

5. Which of the following is **not** true of a trapezoid that has been reflected across the *x*-axis?

Ⓐ The new trapezoid is the same size as the original trapezoid.

Ⓑ The new trapezoid is the same shape as the original trapezoid.

Ⓒ The new trapezoid is in the same orientation as the original trapezoid.

Ⓓ The *x*-coordinates of the new trapezoid are the same as the *x*-coordinates of the original trapezoid.

6. A triangle with coordinates (6, 4), (2, −1), and (−3, 5) is translated 4 units left and rotated 180° about the origin. What are the coordinates of its image?

Ⓐ (2, 4), (−2, −1), (−7, 5)

Ⓑ (4, 6), (−1, 2), (5, −3)

Ⓒ (4, −2), (−1, 2), (5, 7)

Ⓓ (−2, −4), (2, 1), (7, −5)

Mini-Task

7. A rectangle with vertices (3, −2), (3, −4), (7, −2), (7, −4) is reflected across the *x*-axis and then rotated 90° counterclockwise.

a. In what quadrant does the image lie?

_____

b. What are the vertices of the image?

_____

c. What other transformations produce the same image?

_____

_____

Transformations and Similarity

ESSENTIAL QUESTION

How can you use dilations and similarity to solve real-world problems?

Real-World Video

To plan a mural, the artist first makes a smaller drawing showing what the mural will look like. Then the image is enlarged by a scale factor on the mural canvas. This enlargement is called a dilation.

my.hrw.com

GO DIGITAL
my.hrw.com

my.hrw.com

Go digital with your write-in student edition, accessible on any device.

Math On the Spot

Scan with your smart phone to jump directly to the online edition, video tutor, and more.

Animated Math

Interactively explore key concepts to see how math works.

Personal Math Trainer

Get immediate feedback and help as you work through practice sets.

575

Are YOU Ready?

Complete these exercises to review skills you will need for this module.

Simplify Ratios

EXAMPLE $\frac{35}{21} = \frac{35 \div 7}{21 \div 7}$

$= \frac{5}{3}$

To write a ratio in simplest form, find the greatest common factor of the numerator and denominator. Divide the numerator and denominator by the GCF.

Write each ratio in simplest form.

1. $\frac{6}{15}$ _____

2. $\frac{8}{20}$ _____

3. $\frac{30}{18}$ _____

4. $\frac{36}{30}$ _____

Multiply with Fractions and Decimals

EXAMPLE $2\frac{3}{5} \times 20$

$= \frac{13 \times 20}{5 \times 1}$

$= \frac{13 \times \overset{4}{\cancel{20}}}{\underset{1}{\cancel{5}} \times 1}$

$= 52$

Write numbers as fractions and multiply.

Simplify.

$$\begin{array}{r} 68 \\ \times 4.5 \\ \hline 340 \\ +272 \\ \hline 306.0 \end{array}$$

Multiply as you would with whole numbers.

Place the decimal point in the answer based on the total number of decimal places in the two factors.

Multiply.

5. $60 \times \frac{25}{100}$

6. 3.5×40

7. 4.4×44

8. $24 \times \frac{8}{9}$

_____ _____ _____ _____

Graph Ordered Pairs (First Quadrant)

EXAMPLE

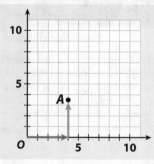

Graph the point A(4, 3.5).
Start at the origin.
Move 4 units right.
Then move 3.5 units up.
Graph point A(4, 3.5).

Graph each point on the coordinate grid above.

9. $B\,(9, 0)$

10. $C\,(2, 7)$

11. $D\,(0, 4.5)$

12. $E\,(6, 2.5)$

Reading Start-Up

Visualize Vocabulary

**Use the ✔ words to complete the graphic organizer.
You will put one word in each rectangle.**

The four regions on a coordinate plane.	The point where the axes intersect to form the coordinate plane.

Reviewing the Coordinate Plane

The horizontal axis of a coordinate plane.	The vertical axis of a coordinate plane.

Understand Vocabulary

Complete the sentences using the preview words.

1. A figure larger than the original, produced through dilation, is

   an _____.

2. A figure smaller than the original, produced through dilation, is

   a _____.

Vocabulary

Review Words

coordinate plane (*plano cartesiano*)

image (*imagen*)

✔ origin (*origen*)

preimage (*imagen original*)

✔ quadrants (*cuadrante*)

ratio (*razón*)

scale (*escala*)

✔ x-axis (*eje x*)

✔ y-axis (*eje y*)

Preview Words

center of dilation (*centro de dilatación*)

dilation (*dilatación*)

enlargement (*agrandamiento*)

reduction (*reducción*)

scale factor (*factor de escala*)

similar (*similar*)

Active Reading

Key-Term Fold Before beginning the module, create a key-term fold to help you learn the vocabulary in this module. Write the highlighted vocabulary words on one side of the flap. Write the definition for each word on the other side of the flap. Use the key-term fold to quiz yourself on the definitions used in this module.

Unpacking the Standards

Understanding the standards and the vocabulary terms in the standards will help you know exactly what you are expected to learn in this module.

COMMON CORE 8.G.3

Describe the effect of dilations, translations, rotations, and reflections on two-dimensional figures using coordinates.

What It Means to You

You will use an algebraic representation to describe a dilation.

UNPACKING EXAMPLE 8.G.3

The blue square *ABCD* is the preimage. Write two algebraic representations, one for the dilation to the green square and one for the dilation to the purple square.

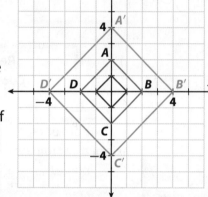

The coordinates of the vertices of the original image are multiplied by 2 for the green square.

Green square: $(x, y) \rightarrow (2x, 2y)$

The coordinates of the vertices of the original image are multiplied by $\frac{1}{2}$ for the purple square.

Purple square: $(x, y) \rightarrow \left(\frac{1}{2}x, \frac{1}{2}y\right)$

COMMON CORE 8.G.4

Understand that a two-dimensional figure is similar to another if the second can be obtained from the first by a sequence of rotations, reflections, translations, and dilations; given two similar two-dimensional figures, describe a sequence that exhibits the similarity between them.

What It Means to You

You will describe a sequence of transformations between two similar figures.

UNPACKING EXAMPLE 8.G.4

Identify a sequence of two transformations that will transform figure *A* into figure *B*.

Dilate with center at the origin by a scale factor of $\frac{1}{2}$.

Then translate right 3 units and up 2 units.

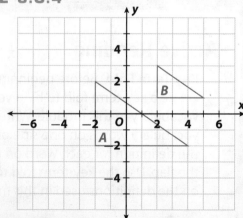

Visit **my.hrw.com** to see all the **Common Core Standards** unpacked.

my.hrw.com

LESSON 18.1 Properties of Dilations

COMMON CORE 8.G.4
Understand that a two-dimensional figure is similar to another if the second can be obtained from the first by a sequence of ... dilations; ... *Also 8.G.3*

ESSENTIAL QUESTION

How do you describe the properties of dilations?

EXPLORE ACTIVITY 1 **COMMON CORE 8.G.4**

Exploring Dilations

The missions that placed 12 astronauts on the moon were controlled at the Johnson Space Center in Houston. The toy models at the right are scaled-down replicas of the Saturn V rocket that powered the moon flights. Each replica is a transformation called a **dilation**. Unlike the other transformations you have studied—translations, rotations, and reflections—dilations change the size (but not the shape) of a figure.

Every dilation has a fixed point called the **center of dilation** located where the lines connecting corresponding parts of figures intersect.

Triangle *R′S′T′* is a dilation of triangle *RST*. Point *C* is the center of dilation.

A Use a ruler to measure segments $\overline{CR}$, $\overline{CR'}$, $\overline{CS}$, $\overline{CS'}$, $\overline{CT}$, and $\overline{CT'}$ to the nearest millimeter. Record the measurements and ratios in the table.

CR′	*CR*	$\frac{CR'}{CR}$	*CS′*	*CS*	$\frac{CS'}{CS}$	*CT′*	*CT*	$\frac{CT'}{CT}$

B Write a conjecture based on the ratios in the table.

_____

C Measure and record the corresponding side lengths of the triangles.

R′S′	*RS*	$\frac{R'S'}{RS}$	*S′T′*	*ST*	$\frac{S'T'}{ST}$	*R′T′*	*RT*	$\frac{R'T'}{RT}$

D Write a conjecture based on the ratios in the table.

_____

E Measure the corresponding angles and describe your results.

_____

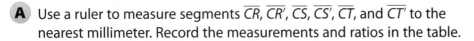

Reflect

1. Two figures that have the same shape but different sizes are called *similar*. Are triangles *RST* and *R'S'T'* similar? Why or why not?

_____

_____

2. Compare the orientation of a figure with the orientation of its dilation.

_____

EXPLORE ACTIVITY 2 | COMMON CORE | 8.G.3

Exploring Dilations on a Coordinate Plane

In this activity you will explore how the coordinates of a figure on a coordinate plane are affected by a dilation.

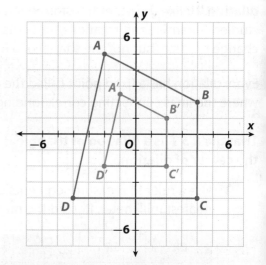

A Complete the table. Record the *x*- and *y*-coordinates of the points in the two figures and the ratios of the *x*-coordinates and the *y*-coordinates.

Vertex	x	y	Vertex	x	y	Ratio of x-coordinates (A'B'C'D' ÷ ABCD)	Ratio of y-coordinates (A'B'C'D' ÷ ABCD)
A'			A				
B'			B				
C'			C				
D'			D				

B Write a conjecture about the ratios of the coordinates of a dilation image to the coordinates of the original figure.

_____

_____

Reflect

3. In Explore Activity 1, triangle *R'S'T'* was larger than triangle *RST*. How is the relationship between quadrilateral *A'B'C'D'* and quadrilateral *ABCD* different?

_____

Math Talk
Mathematical Practices

How are dilations different from the other transformations you have learned about?

Finding a Scale Factor

As you have seen in the two activities, a dilation can produce a larger figure (an **enlargement**) or a smaller figure (a **reduction**). The **scale factor** describes how much the figure is enlarged or reduced. The scale factor is the ratio of a length of the image to the corresponding length on the original figure.

Math On the Spot
⏻ my.hrw.com

In Explore Activity 1, the side lengths of triangle *R'S'T'* were twice the length of those of triangle *RST*, so the scale factor was 2. In Explore Activity 2, the side lengths of quadrilateral *A'B'C'D'* were half those of quadrilateral *ABCD*, so the scale factor was 0.5.

EXAMPLE 1 Real World

COMMON CORE 8.G.4

An art supply store sells several sizes of drawing triangles. All are dilations of a single basic triangle. The basic triangle and one of its dilations are shown on the grid. Find the scale factor of the dilation.

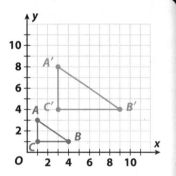

 STEP 1 Use the coordinates to find the lengths of the sides of each triangle.

Triangle *ABC*: *AC* = 2   *CB* = 3

Triangle *A'B'C'*: *A'C'* = 4   *C'B'* = 6

Since the scale factor is the same for all corresponding sides, you can record just two pairs of side lengths. Use one pair as a check on the other.

STEP 2 Find the ratios of the corresponding sides.

$\frac{A'C'}{AC} = \frac{4}{2} = 2$ $\frac{C'B'}{CB} = \frac{6}{3} = 2$

The scale factor of the dilation is 2.

Animated Math
⏻ my.hrw.com

Reflect

4. Is the dilation an enlargement or a reduction? How can you tell?

_____

_____

YOUR TURN

5. Find the scale factor of the dilation.

_____

_____

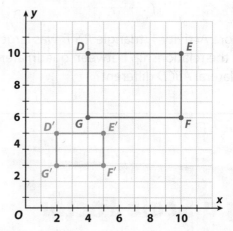

Math Talk

Mathematical Practices

Which scale factors lead to enlargements? Which scale factors lead to reductions?

Guided Practice

Use triangles ABC and A′B′C′ for 1–5. (Explore Activities 1 and 2, Example 1)

1. For each pair of corresponding vertices, find the ratio of the x-coordinates and the ratio of the y-coordinates.

   ratio of x-coordinates = _____

   ratio of y-coordinates = _____

2. I know that triangle A′B′C′ is a dilation of triangle ABC because the ratios of the corresponding

   x-coordinates are _____ and the ratios of the

   corresponding y-coordinates are _____.

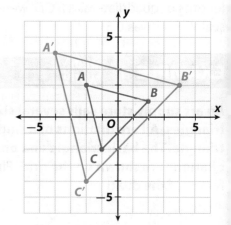

3. The ratio of the lengths of the corresponding sides of triangle A′B′C′ and

   triangle ABC equals _____.

4. The corresponding angles of triangle ABC and triangle A′B′C′

   are _____.

5. The scale factor of the dilation is _____.

? ESSENTIAL QUESTION CHECK-IN

6. How can you find the scale factor of a dilation?

   _____

   _____

18.1 Independent Practice

COMMON CORE 8.G.3, 8.G.4

Personal
Math Trainer

Online
Assessment and
Intervention

my.hrw.com

For 7–11, tell whether one figure is a dilation of the other or not. Explain your reasoning.

7. Quadrilateral *MNPQ* has side lengths of 15 mm, 24 mm, 21 mm, and 18 mm. Quadrilateral *M'N'P'Q'* has side lengths of 5 mm, 8 mm, 7 mm, and 4 mm.

_____

_____

_____

8. Triangle *RST* has angles measuring 38° and 75°. Triangle *R'S'T'* has angles measuring 67° and 38°. The sides are proportional.

_____

_____

_____

_____

9. Two triangles, Triangle 1 and Triangle 2, are similar.

_____

_____

10. Quadrilateral *MNPQ* is the same shape but a different size than quadrilateral *M'N'P'Q*.

_____

_____

_____

_____

_____

11. On a coordinate plane, triangle *UVW* has coordinates *U*(20, −12), *V*(8, 6), and *W*(−24, −4). Triangle *U'V'W'* has coordinates *U'*(15, −9), *V'*(6, 4.5), and *W'*(−18, −3).

_____

_____

_____

_____

Complete the table by writing "same" or "changed" to compare the image with the original figure in the given transformation.

	Image Compared to Original Figure		
	Orientation	**Size**	**Shape**
12. Translation			
13. Reflection			
14. Rotation			
15. Dilation			

16. Describe the image of a dilation with a scale factor of 1.

_____

_____

Identify the scale factor used in each dilation.

17.

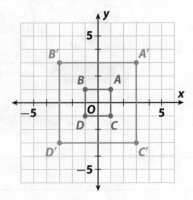

_____

18.

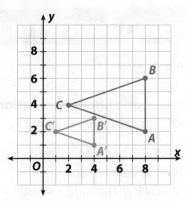

_____

 **FOCUS ON HIGHER ORDER THINKING**

Work Area

19. Critical Thinking Explain how you can find the center of dilation of a triangle and its dilation.

_____

_____

_____

20. Make a Conjecture

a. A square on the coordinate plane has vertices at $(-2, 2)$, $(2, 2)$, $(2, -2)$, and $(-2, -2)$. A dilation of the square has vertices at $(-4, 4)$, $(4, 4)$, $(4, -4)$, and $(-4, -4)$. Find the scale factor and the perimeter of each square.

_____

_____

b. A square on the coordinate plane has vertices at $(-3, 3)$, $(3, 3)$, $(3, -3)$, and $(-3, -3)$. A dilation of the square has vertices at $(-6, 6)$, $(6, 6)$, $(6, -6)$, and $(-6, -6)$. Find the scale factor and the perimeter of each square.

_____

_____

c. Make a conjecture about the relationship of the scale factor to the perimeter of a square and its image.

_____

_____

Algebraic Representations of Dilations

COMMON CORE 8.G.3

Describe the effect of dilations, ... on two-dimensional figures using coordinates.

ESSENTIAL QUESTION

How can you describe the effect of a dilation on coordinates using an algebraic representation?

EXPLORE ACTIVITY 1
COMMON CORE 8.G.3

Graphing Enlargements

When a dilation in the coordinate plane has the origin as the center of dilation, you can find points on the dilated image by multiplying the x- and y-coordinates of the original figure by the scale factor. For scale factor k, the algebraic representation of the dilation is $(x, y) \rightarrow (kx, ky)$. For enlargements, $k > 1$.

The figure shown on the grid is the preimage. The center of dilation is the origin.

A List the coordinates of the vertices of the preimage in the first column of the table.

Preimage (x, y)	Image $(3x, 3y)$
(2, 2)	(6, 6)

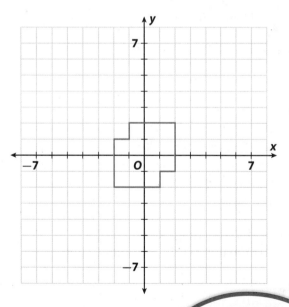

B What is the scale factor for the dilation? _____

C Apply the dilation to the preimage and write the coordinates of the vertices of the image in the second column of the table.

D Sketch the image after the dilation on the coordinate grid.

Math Talk
Mathematical Practices

What effect would the dilation $(x, y) \rightarrow (4x, 4y)$ have on the radius of a circle?

Reflect

1. How does the dilation affect the length of line segments?

_____

_____

2. How does the dilation affect angle measures?

_____

EXPLORE ACTIVITY 2   COMMON CORE   8.G.3

Graphing Reductions

For scale factors between 0 and 1, the image is smaller than the preimage. This is called a reduction.

The arrow shown is the preimage. The center of dilation is the origin.

A List the coordinates of the vertices of the preimage in the first column of the table.

B What is the scale factor for the dilation? _____

C Apply the dilation to the preimage and write the coordinates of the vertices of the image in the second column of the table.

Preimage (x, y)	Image $\left(\frac{1}{2}x, \frac{1}{2}y\right)$

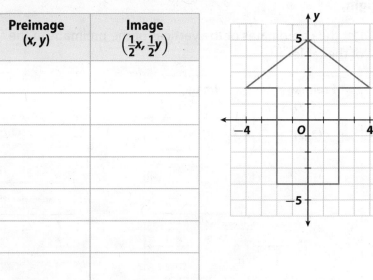

D Sketch the image after the dilation on the coordinate grid.

Reflect

3. How does the dilation affect the length of line segments?

_____

4. How would a dilation with scale factor 1 affect the preimage?

_____

Center of Dilation Outside the Image

The center of dilation can be inside *or* outside the original image and the dilated image. The center of dilation can be anywhere on the coordinate plane as long as the lines that connect each pair of corresponding vertices between the original and dilated image intersect at the center of dilation.

EXAMPLE 1

COMMON CORE 8.G.3

Graph the image of △ABC after a dilation with the origin as its center and a scale factor of 3. What are the vertices of the image?

STEP 1 Multiply each coordinate of the vertices of △ABC by 3 to find the vertices of the dilated image.

$$\triangle ABC\ (x, y) \rightarrow (3x, 3y)\ \triangle A'B'C'$$

$$A(1, 1) \rightarrow A'(1 \cdot 3, 1 \cdot 3) \rightarrow A'(3, 3)$$

$$B(3, 1) \rightarrow B'(3 \cdot 3, 1 \cdot 3) \rightarrow B'(9, 3)$$

$$C(1, 3) \rightarrow C'(1 \cdot 3, 3 \cdot 3) \rightarrow C'(3, 9)$$

The vertices of the dilated image are $A'(3, 3)$, $B'(9, 3)$, and $C'(3, 9)$.

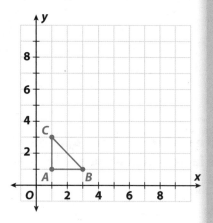

STEP 2 Graph the dilated image.

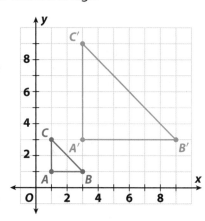

Math Talk
Mathematical Practices

Describe how you can check graphically that you have drawn the image triangle correctly.

YOUR TURN

5. Graph the image of △XYZ after a dilation with a scale factor of $\frac{1}{3}$ and the origin as its center. Then write an algebraic rule to describe the dilation.

_____

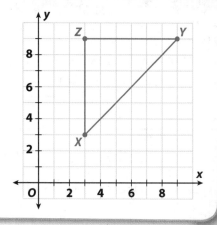

1. The grid shows a diamond-shaped preimage. Write the coordinates of the vertices of the preimage in the first column of the table. Then apply the dilation $(x, y) \rightarrow \left(\frac{3}{2}x, \frac{3}{2}y\right)$ and write the coordinates of the vertices of the image in the second column. Sketch the image of the figure after the dilation. (Explore Activities 1 and 2)

Preimage	Image
(2, 0)	(3, 0)

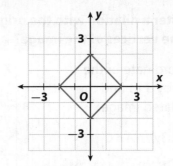

Graph the image of each figure after a dilation with the origin as its center and the given scale factor. Then write an algebraic rule to describe the dilation. (Example 1)

2. scale factor of 1.5

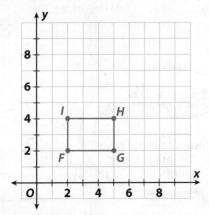

_____

3. scale factor of $\frac{1}{3}$

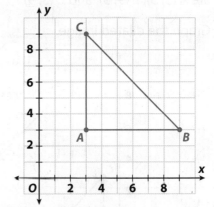

_____

? **ESSENTIAL QUESTION CHECK-IN**

4. A dilation of $(x, y) \rightarrow (kx, ky)$ when $0 < k < 1$ has what effect on the figure? What is the effect on the figure when $k > 1$?

_____

_____

_____

18.2 Independent Practice

COMMON CORE 8.G.3

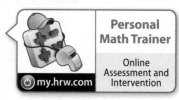

Personal Math Trainer

Online Assessment and Intervention

my.hrw.com

5. The blue square is the preimage. Write two algebraic representations, one for the dilation to the green square and one for the dilation to the purple square.

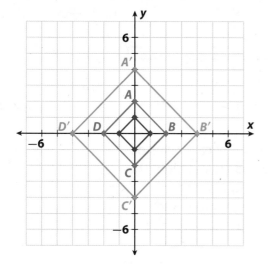

_____

_____

6. Critical Thinking A triangle has vertices $A(-5, -4)$, $B(2, 6)$, and $C(4, -3)$. The center of dilation is the origin and $(x, y) \rightarrow (3x, 3y)$. What are the vertices of the dilated image?

_____

_____

7. Critical Thinking $M'N'O'P'$ has vertices at $M'(3, 4)$, $N'(6, 4)$, $O'(6, 7)$, and $P'(3, 7)$. The center of dilation is the origin. $MNOP$ has vertices at $M(4.5, 6)$, $N(9, 6)$, $O'(9, 10.5)$, and $P'(4.5, 10.5)$. What is the algebraic representation of this dilation?

_____

8. Critical Thinking A dilation with center $(0,0)$ and scale factor k is applied to a polygon. What dilation can you apply to the image to return it to the original preimage?

_____

9. Represent Real-World Problems The blueprints for a new house are scaled so that $\frac{1}{4}$ inch equals 1 foot. The blueprint is the preimage and the house is the dilated image. The blueprints are plotted on a coordinate plane.

a. What is the scale factor in terms of inches to inches?

_____

b. One inch on the blueprint represents how many inches in the actual house? How many feet?

_____

c. Write the algebraic representation of the dilation from the blueprint to the house.

_____

d. A rectangular room has coordinates $Q(2, 2)$, $R(7, 2)$, $S(7, 5)$, and $T(2, 5)$ on the blueprint. The homeowner wants this room to be 25% larger. What are the coordinates of the new room?

_____

_____

e. What are the dimensions of the new room, in inches, on the blueprint? What will the dimensions of the new room be, in feet, in the new house?

_____

_____

_____

_____

10. Write the algebraic representation of the dilation shown.

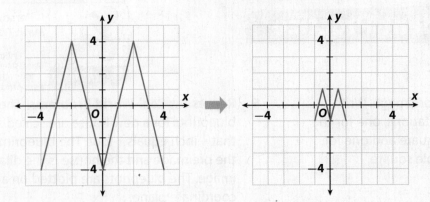

_____

Work Area

11. Critique Reasoning The set for a school play needs a replica of a historic building painted on a backdrop that is 20 feet long and 16 feet high. The actual building measures 400 feet long and 320 feet high. A stage crewmember writes $(x, y) \rightarrow \left(\frac{1}{12}x, \frac{1}{12}y\right)$ to represent the dilation. Is the crewmember's calculation correct if the painted replica is to cover the entire backdrop? Explain.

_____

_____

12. Communicate Mathematical Ideas Explain what each of these algebraic transformations does to a figure.

a. $(x, y) \rightarrow (y, -x)$ _____

b. $(x, y) \rightarrow (-x, -y)$ _____

c. $(x, y) \rightarrow (x, 2y)$ _____

_____

d. $(x, y) \rightarrow \left(\frac{2}{3}x, y\right)$ _____

_____

e. $(x, y) \rightarrow (0.5x, 1.5y)$ _____

_____

13. Communicate Mathematical Ideas Triangle ABC has coordinates $A(1, 5)$, $B(-2, 1)$, and $C(-2, 4)$. Sketch triangle ABC and $A'B'C'$ for the dilation $(x, y) \rightarrow (-2x, -2y)$. What is the effect of a negative scale factor?

_____

_____

18.3 Similar Figures

COMMON CORE 8.G.4

Understand that a ... figure is similar to another if the second can be obtained ... by a sequence of rotations, reflections, translations, and dilations; given two similar ... figures, describe a sequence that exhibits the similarity between them.

ESSENTIAL QUESTION

What is the connection between transformations and similar figures?

EXPLORE ACTIVITY COMMON CORE 8.G.4

Combining Transformations with Dilations

When creating an animation, figures need to be translated, reflected, rotated, and sometimes dilated. As an example of this, apply the indicated sequence of transformations to the rectangle. Each transformation is applied to the image of the previous transformation, not to the original figure. Label each image with the letter of the transformation applied.

A $(x, y) \rightarrow (x + 7, y - 2)$

B $(x, y) \rightarrow (x, -y)$

C rotation 90° clockwise around the origin

D $(x, y) \rightarrow (x + 5, y + 3)$

E $(x, y) \rightarrow (3x, 3y)$

F List the coordinates of the vertices of rectangle E.

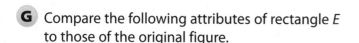

G Compare the following attributes of rectangle E to those of the original figure.

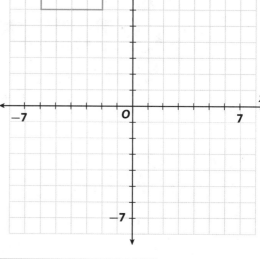

Shape	
Size	
Angle Measures	

Reflect

1. Which transformation represents the dilation? How can you tell?

_____

_____

2. A sequence of transformations containing a single dilation is applied to a figure. Are the original figure and its final image congruent? Explain.

_____

_____

Math On the Spot

⏱ my.hrw.com

Similar Figures

Two figures are **similar** if one can be obtained from the other by a sequence of translations, reflections, rotations, and dilations. Similar figures have the same shape but may be different sizes.

When you are told that two figures are similar, there must be a sequence of translations, reflections, rotations, and/or dilations that can transform one to the other.

EXAMPLE 1

COMMON CORE 8.G.4

A Identify a sequence of transformations that will transform figure *A* into figure *B*. Tell whether the figures are congruent. Tell whether they are similar.

My Notes

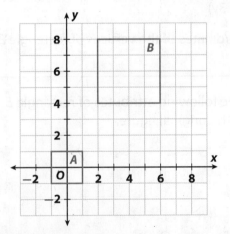

Both figures are squares whose orientations are the same, so no reflection or rotation is needed. Figure *B* has sides twice as long as figure *A*, so a dilation with a scale factor of 2 is needed. Figure *B* is moved to the right and above figure *A*, so a translation is needed. A sequence of transformations that will accomplish this is a dilation by a scale factor of 2 centered at the origin followed by the translation $(x, y) \rightarrow (x + 4, y + 6)$. The figures are not congruent, but they are similar.

B Identify a sequence of transformations that will transform figure *C* into figure *D*. Include a reflection. Tell whether the figures are congruent. Tell whether they are similar.

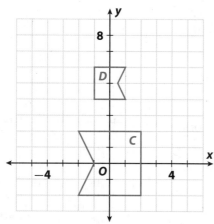

The orientation of figure *D* is reversed from that of figure *C*, so a reflection over the *y*-axis is needed. Figure *D* has sides that are half as long as figure *C*, so a dilation with a scale factor of $\frac{1}{2}$ is needed. Figure *D* is moved above figure *C*, so a translation is needed. A sequence of transformations that will accomplish this is a dilation by a scale factor of $\frac{1}{2}$ centered at the origin, followed by the reflection $(x, y) \rightarrow (-x, y)$, followed by the translation $(x, y) \rightarrow (x, y + 5)$. The figures are not congruent, but they are similar.

Math Talk
Mathematical Practices

A figure and its image have different sizes and orientations. What do you know about the sequence of transformations that generated the image?

C Identify a sequence of transformations that will transform figure *C* into figure *D*. Include a rotation.

The orientation of figure *D* is reversed from that of figure *C*, so a rotation of 180° is needed. Figure *D* has sides that are half as long as figure *C*, so a dilation with a scale factor of $\frac{1}{2}$ is needed. Figure *D* is moved above figure *C*, so a translation is needed. A sequence of transformations that will accomplish this is a rotation of 180° about the origin, followed by a dilation by a scale factor of $\frac{1}{2}$ centered at the origin, followed by the translation $(x, y) \rightarrow (x, y + 5)$.

YOUR TURN

3. Look again at the Explore Activity. Start with the original figure. Create a new sequence of transformations that will yield figure *E*, the final image. Your transformations do not need to produce the images in the same order in which they originally appeared.

_____

_____

_____

Personal Math Trainer

Online Assessment and Intervention

ⓒ my.hrw.com

1. Apply the indicated sequence of transformations to the square. Apply each transformation to the image of the previous transformation. Label each image with the letter of the transformation applied.
(Explore Activity)

A $(x, y) \rightarrow (-x, y)$

B Rotate the square 180° around the origin.

C $(x, y) \rightarrow (x - 5, y - 6)$

D $(x, y) \rightarrow \left(\frac{1}{2}x, \frac{1}{2}y\right)$

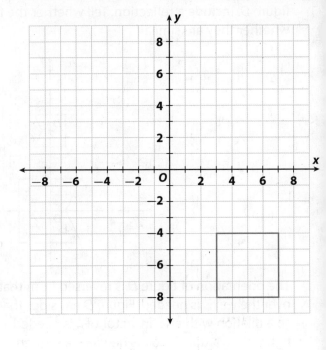

Identify a sequence of two transformations that will transform figure A into the given figure. (Example 1)

2. figure B

_____

_____

3. figure C

_____

_____

4. figure D

_____

_____

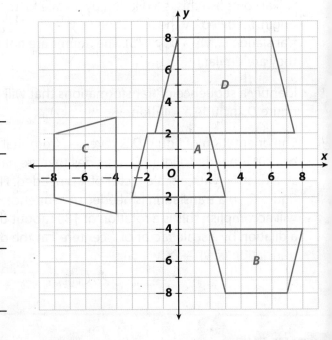

? ESSENTIAL QUESTION CHECK-IN

5. If two figures are similar but not congruent, what do you know about the sequence of transformations used to create one from the other?

_____

_____

18.3 Independent Practice

 8.G.4

Personal
Math Trainer

Online
Assessment and
Intervention

my.hrw.com

6. A designer creates a drawing of a triangular sign on centimeter grid paper for a new business. The drawing has sides measuring 6 cm, 8 cm, and 10 cm, and angles measuring 37°, 53°, and 90°. To create the actual sign shown, the drawing must be dilated using a scale factor of 40.

a. Find the lengths of the sides of the actual sign.

_____

b. Find the angle measures of the actual sign.

_____

c. The drawing has the hypotenuse on the bottom. The business owner would like it on the top. Describe two transformations that will do this.

_____

_____

d. The shorter leg of the drawing is currently on the left. The business owner wants it to remain on the left after the hypotenuse goes to the top. Which transformation in part c will accomplish this?

_____

In Exercises 7–10, the transformation of a figure into its image is described. Describe the transformations that will transform the image back into the original figure. Then write them algebraically.

7. The figure is reflected across the *x*-axis and dilated by a scale factor of 3.

_____

_____

8. The figure is dilated by a scale factor of 0.5 and translated 6 units left and 3 units up.

_____

_____

9. The figure is dilated by a scale factor of 5 and rotated 90° clockwise.

_____

_____

10. The figure is reflected across the y-axis and dilated by a scale factor of 4.

H.O.T. FOCUS ON HIGHER ORDER THINKING

Work Area

11. **Draw Conclusions** A figure undergoes a sequence of transformations that include dilations. The figure and its final image are congruent. Explain how this can happen.

12. **Multistep** As with geometric figures, graphs can be transformed through translations, reflections, rotations, and dilations. Describe how the graph of $y = x$ shown at the right is changed through each of the following transformations.

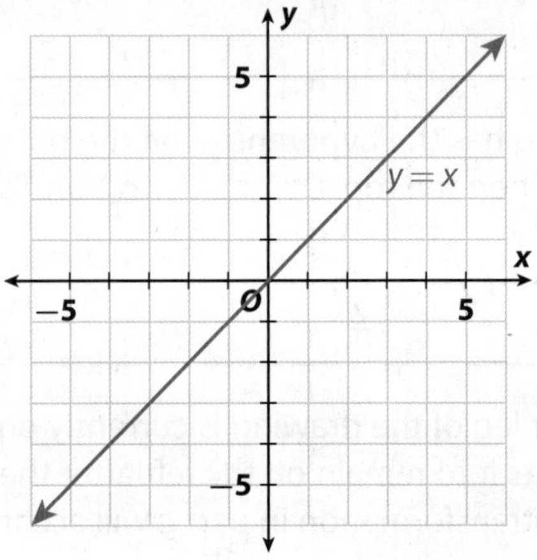

a. a dilation by a scale factor of 4

b. a translation down 3 units

c. a reflection across the y-axis

13. **Justify Reasoning** The graph of the line $y = x$ is dilated by a scale factor of 3 and then translated up 5 units. Is this the same as translating the graph up 5 units and then dilating by a scale factor of 3? Explain.

Copy-Cat

INSTRUCTIONS

STEP 1 Use tape to secure the tracing paper onto the grid. Then trace the grid lines onto the tracing paper.

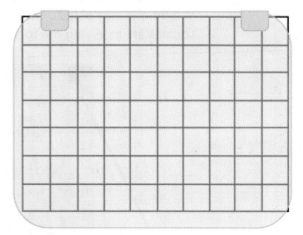

STEP 2 Remove the tracing paper from the grid paper and securely tape the tracing paper over the image that will be copied. Leave the tracing paper attached when you submit your work.

STEP 3 Create a blank grid on your large blank piece of paper or poster board. The blank grid should have the same number of squares as the grid on the tracing paper over the original image. The squares do not need to be the same size as those on the tracing paper.

STEP 4 Copy exactly the appearance of each square from the original image onto the corresponding square of the blank grid on the large piece of paper or poster board.

Be careful not to focus on the overall picture, only focus on one square at a time. It may help to do the squares in random order so that the squares are receiving the focus instead of the overall image.

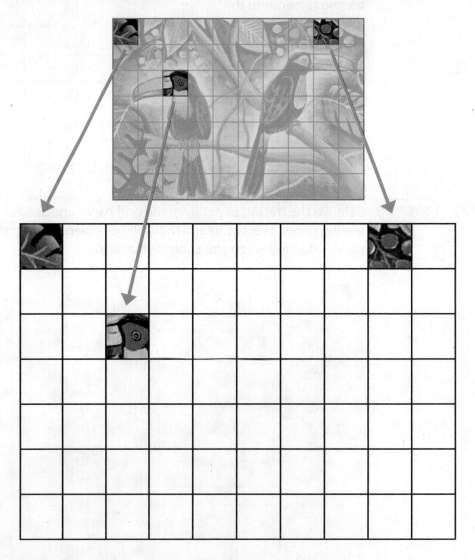

STEP 5 When you have copied all of the squares, the drawing on your finished grid should look like a dilation or copy of the original image.

Ready to Go On?

Personal Math Trainer

Online Assessment and Intervention

my.hrw.com

18.1 Properties of Dilations

Determine whether one figure is a dilation of the other. Justify your answer.

1. Triangle *XYZ* has angles measuring 54° and 29°. Triangle *X'Y'Z'* has angles measuring 29° and 92°.

_____

2. Quadrilateral *DEFG* has sides measuring 16 m, 28 m, 24 m, and 20 m. Quadrilateral *D'E'F'G'* has sides measuring 20 m, 35 m, 30 m, and 25 m.

_____

_____

18.2 Algebraic Representations of Dilations

Dilate each figure with the origin as the center of dilation.

3. $(x, y) \rightarrow (0.8x, 0.8y)$

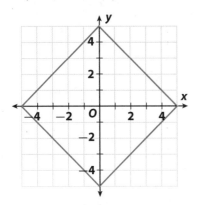

4. $(x, y) \rightarrow (2.5x, 2.5y)$

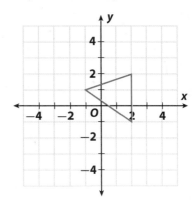

18.3 Similar Figures

5. Describe what happens to a figure when the given sequence of transformations is applied to it: $(x, y) \rightarrow (-x, y)$; $(x, y) \rightarrow (0.5x, 0.5y)$; $(x, y) \rightarrow (x - 2, y + 2)$

_____

_____

? ESSENTIAL QUESTION

6. How can you use dilations to solve real-world problems?

_____

Assessment Readiness

Selected Response

1. A rectangle has vertices (6, 4), (2, 4), (6, −2), and (2, −2). What are the coordinates of the vertices of the image after a dilation with the origin as its center and a scale factor of 1.5?

Ⓐ (9, 6), (3, 6), (9, −3), (3, −3)

Ⓑ (3, 2), (1, 2), (3, −1), (1, −1)

Ⓒ (12, 8), (4, 8), (12, −4), (4, −4)

Ⓓ (15, 10), (5, 10), (15, −5), (5, −5)

2. Which represents the dilation shown where the black figure is the preimage?

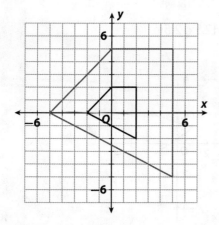

Ⓐ $(x, y) \rightarrow (1.5x, 1.5y)$

Ⓑ $(x, y) \rightarrow (2.5x, 2.5y)$

Ⓒ $(x, y) \rightarrow (3x, 3y)$

Ⓓ $(x, y) \rightarrow (6x, 6y)$

3. Identify the sequence of transformations that will reflect a figure over the x-axis and then dilate it by a scale factor of 3.

Ⓐ $(x, y) \rightarrow (−x, y); (x, y) \rightarrow (3x, 3y)$

Ⓑ $(x, y) \rightarrow (−x, y); (x, y) \rightarrow (x, 3y)$

Ⓒ $(x, y) \rightarrow (x, −y); (x, y) \rightarrow (3x, y)$

Ⓓ $(x, y) \rightarrow (x, −y); (x, y) \rightarrow (3x, 3y)$

4. Solve $−a + 7 = 2a − 8$.

Ⓐ $a = −3$　　　Ⓒ $a = 5$

Ⓑ $a = −\frac{1}{3}$　　Ⓓ $a = 15$

5. Which equation does **not** represent a line with an x-intercept of 3?

Ⓐ $y = −2x + 6$　　Ⓒ $y = \frac{2}{3}x − 2$

Ⓑ $y = −\frac{1}{3}x + 1$　　Ⓓ $y = 3x − 1$

Mini-Task

6. The square is dilated under the dilation $(x, y) \rightarrow (0.25x, 0.25y)$.

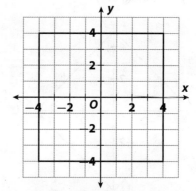

a. Graph the image. What are the coordinates?

_____

b. What is the length of a side of the image?

_____

c. What are the perimeter and area of the preimage?

_____

d. What are the perimeter and area of the image?

_____

Study Guide Review

MODULE 17 **Transformations and Congruence**

? **ESSENTIAL QUESTION**

How can you use transformations and congruence to solve real-world problems?

EXAMPLE

Translate triangle *XYZ* left 4 units and down 2 units. Graph the image and label the vertices.

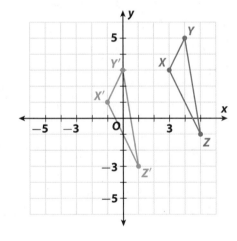

Translate the vertices by subtracting 4 from each *x*-coordinate and 2 from each *y*-coordinate. The new vertices are $X'(-1, 1)$, $Y'(0, 3)$, and $Z'(1, -3)$.

Connect the vertices to draw triangle $X'Y'Z'$.

EXERCISES

Perform the transformation shown. (Lessons 17.1, 17.2, 17.3)

1. Reflection over the *x*-axis

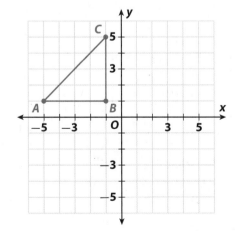

2. Translation 5 units right

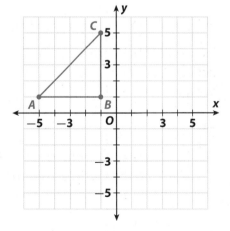

3. Rotation 90° counterclockwise about the origin

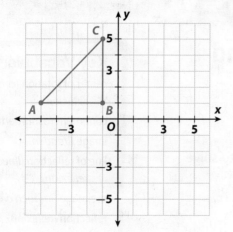

4. Translation 4 units right and 4 units down

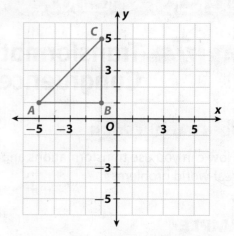

5. Quadrilateral ABCD with vertices A(4, 4), B(5, 1), C(5, −1) and D(4, −2) is translated left 2 units and down 3 units. Graph the preimage and the image. (Lesson 17.4)

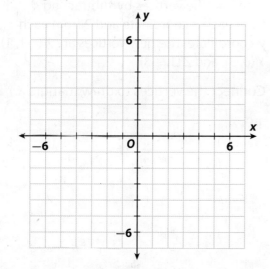

6. Triangle ABC with vertices A(1, 2), B(1, 4), and C(3, 3) is translated by $(x, y) \rightarrow (x − 4, y)$, and the result is reflected by $(x, y) \rightarrow (x, −y)$. Graph the preimage and the image. (Lesson 17.5)

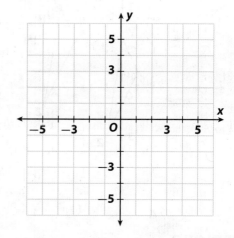

7. Triangle RST has vertices at (−8, 2), (−4, 0), and (−12, 8). Find the vertices after the triangle has been reflected over the y-axis. (Lesson 17.4)

_____

8. Triangle XYZ has vertices at (3, 7), (9, 14), and (12, −1). Find the vertices after the triangle has been rotated 180° about the origin. (Lesson 17.4)

_____

9. Triangle MNP has its vertices located at (−1, −4), (−2, −5), and (−3, −3). Find the vertices after the triangle has been reflected by $(x, y) \rightarrow (x, −y)$ and translated by $(x, y) \rightarrow (x + 6, y)$. (Lesson 17.5)

_____

Transformations and Similarity

Key Vocabulary

center of dilation (*centro de dilatación*)

dilation (*dilatación*)

enlargement (*agrandamiento*)

reduction (*reducción*)

scale factor (*factor de escala*)

similar (*semejantes*)

? ESSENTIAL QUESTION

How can you use dilations, similarity, and proportionality to solve real-world problems?

EXAMPLE

Dilate triangle *ABC* with the origin as the center of dilation and scale factor $\frac{1}{2}$. Graph the dilated image.

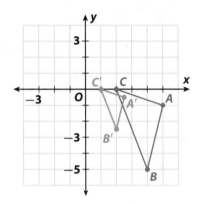

Multiply each coordinate of the vertices of *ABC* by $\frac{1}{2}$ to find the vertices of the dilated image.

$$A(5, -1) \rightarrow A'\left(5 \cdot \frac{1}{2}, -1 \cdot \frac{1}{2}\right) \rightarrow A'\left(2\frac{1}{2}, -\frac{1}{2}\right)$$

$$B(4, -5) \rightarrow B'\left(4 \cdot \frac{1}{2}, -5 \cdot \frac{1}{2}\right) \rightarrow B'\left(2, -2\frac{1}{2}\right)$$

$$C(2, 0) \rightarrow C'\left(2 \cdot \frac{1}{2}, 0 \cdot \frac{1}{2}\right) \rightarrow C'(1, 0)$$

EXERCISES

1. For each pair of corresponding vertices, find the ratio of the *x*-coordinates and the ratio of the *y*-coordinates. (Lesson 18.1)

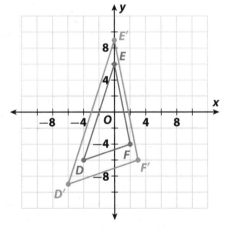

Ratio of *x*-coordinates: _____

Ratio of *y*-coordinates: _____

What is the scale factor of the dilation? _____

2. Rectangle *WXYZ* has vertices at $(-2, -1)$, $(-2, 1)$, $(2, -1)$, and $(2, 1)$. It is first dilated by $(x, y) \rightarrow (2x, 2y)$, and then translated by $(x, y) \rightarrow (x, y + 3)$. (Lesson 18.3)

   a. What are the vertices of the image? _____

   b. Are the preimage and image congruent? Are they similar? Explain.

   _____

   _____

Dilate each figure with the origin as the center of the dilation. List the vertices of the dilated figure then graph the figure. (Lesson 18.2)

3. $(x, y) \rightarrow \left(\frac{1}{4}x, \frac{1}{4}y \right)$

4. $(x, y) \rightarrow (2x, 2y)$

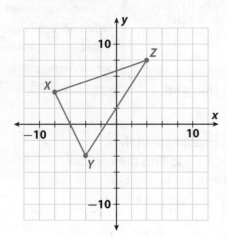

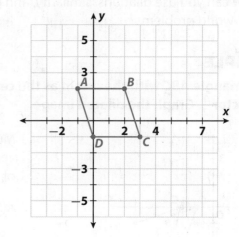

Unit 8 Performance Tasks

1. **CAREERS IN MATH** Contractor Fernando is expanding his dog's play yard. The original yard has a fence represented by rectangle *LMNO* on the coordinate plane. Fernando hires a contractor to construct a new fence that should enclose 6 times as much area as the current fence. The shape of the fence must remain the same. The contractor constructs the fence shown by rectangle *L'M'N'O'*.

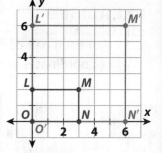

   a. Did the contractor increase the area by the amount Fernando wanted? Explain.

_____

_____

   b. Does the new fence maintain the shape of the old fence? How do you know?

_____

_____

2. A sail for a sailboat is represented by a triangle on the coordinate plane with vertices (0, 0), (5, 0), and (5, 4). The triangle is dilated by a scale factor of 1.5 with the origin as the center of dilation. Find the coordinates of the dilated triangle. Are the triangles similar? Explain.

_____

_____

UNIT 8 MIXED REVIEW

COMMON CORE

Assessment Readiness

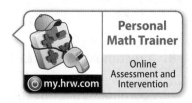

Personal Math Trainer

Online Assessment and Intervention

my.hrw.com

Selected Response

1. What would be the orientation of the figure below after a reflection over the *x*-axis?

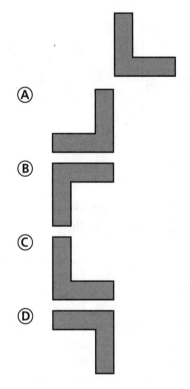

Ⓐ

Ⓑ

Ⓒ

Ⓓ

2. A triangle with coordinates (4, 2), (0, −3), and (−5, 3) is translated 5 units right and rotated 180° about the origin. What are the coordinates of its image?

Ⓐ (9, 2), (−1, −2), (5, −7)

Ⓑ (−10, 3), (−1, 2), (−5, −3)

Ⓒ (2, −1), (−3, −5), (3, −10)

Ⓓ (−9, −2), (−5, 3), (0, −3)

3. Quadrilateral *LMNP* has sides measuring 16, 28, 12, and 32. Which could be the side lengths of a dilation of *LMNP*?

Ⓐ 24, 40, 18, 90

Ⓑ 32, 60, 24, 65

Ⓒ 20, 35, 15, 40

Ⓓ 40, 70, 30, 75

4. The table below represents which equation?

x	−1	0	1	2
y	1	−2	−5	−8

Ⓐ $y = x + 2$

Ⓑ $y = -x$

Ⓒ $y = 3x + 6$

Ⓓ $y = -3x - 2$

5. Which of the following is **not** true of a trapezoid that has been translated 8 units down?

Ⓐ The new trapezoid is the same size as the original trapezoid.

Ⓑ The new trapezoid is the same shape as the original trapezoid.

Ⓒ The new trapezoid is in the same orientation as the original trapezoid.

Ⓓ The *y*-coordinates of the new trapezoid are the same as the *y*-coordinates of the original trapezoid.

6. Which represents a reduction?

Ⓐ $(x, y) \rightarrow (0.9x, 0.9y)$

Ⓑ $(x, y) \rightarrow (1.4x, 1.4y)$

Ⓒ $(x, y) \rightarrow (0.7x, 0.3y)$

Ⓓ $(x, y) \rightarrow (2.5x, 2.5y)$

7. Which is the solution for $4(x + 1) = 2(3x - 2)$?

Ⓐ $x = -4$

Ⓑ $x = -1$

Ⓒ $x = 0$

Ⓓ $x = 4$

8. A rectangle has vertices (8, 6), (4, 6), (8, −4), and (4, −4). What are the coordinates after dilating from the origin by a scale factor of 1.5?

Ⓐ (9, 6), (3, 6), (9, −3), (3, −3)

Ⓑ (10, 8), (5, 8), (10, −5), (5, −5)

Ⓒ (16, 12), (8, 12), (16, −8), (8, −8)

Ⓓ (12, 9), (6, 9), (12, −6), (6, −6)

 Make sure you look at all answer choices before making your decision. Try substituting each answer choice into the problem if you are unsure of the answer.

9. Two apples plus four bananas cost $2.00. An apple costs twice as much as a banana. Using the equations $2a + 4b = 2.00$ and $a = 2b$, where a is the cost of one apple and b is the cost of one banana, what are a and b?

Ⓐ $a = \$0.25$; $b = \$0.25$

Ⓑ $a = \$0.25$; $b = \$0.50$

Ⓒ $a = \$0.50$; $b = \$0.25$

Ⓓ $a = \$0.50$; $b = \$0.50$

10. Which statement is false?

Ⓐ No integers are irrational numbers.

Ⓑ All whole numbers are integers.

Ⓒ No real numbers are rational numbers.

Ⓓ All integers greater than or equal to 0 are whole numbers.

11. Consider the system of equations $3x + 4y = 2$ and $2x − 4y = 8$. Which is its solution?

Ⓐ $x = −1, y = −2$

Ⓑ $x = 1, y = 2$

Ⓒ $x = −2, y = 1$

Ⓓ $x = 2, y = −1$

12. A triangle with vertices (−2, −3), (−4, 0), and (0, 0) is congruent to a second triangle located in quadrant I with two of its vertices at (3, 2) and (1, 5).

a. Graph the two triangles on the same coordinate grid.

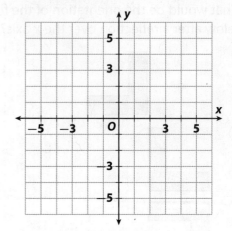

b. What are the coordinates of the third vertex of the second triangle?

_____

13. Tamiko is planning a stone wall shaped like a triangle, with vertices at (−1, −2), (2, 2), and (−2, 2) on a coordinate grid. She plans to add a second wall, in the same shape, enclosing the first wall, with the origin as the center of dilation. The vertices of the second wall are (−3, −6), (6, 6), and (−6, 6).

a. What scale factor did Tamiko use for the second wall?

_____

b. Are the two walls similar? Explain.

_____

_____

_____

_____

Measurement Geometry

CAREERS IN MATH

Hydrologist A hydrologist is a scientist who studies and solves water-related issues. A hydrologist might work to prevent or clean up polluted water sources, locate water supplies for urban or rural needs, or control flooding and erosion. A hydrologist uses math to assess water resources and mathematical models to understand water systems, as well as statistics to analyze phenomena such as rainfall patterns. If you are interested in a career as a hydrologist, you should study the following mathematical subjects:

- Algebra
- Trigonometry
- Calculus
- Statistics

Research other careers that require creating and using mathematical models to understand physical phenomena.

Unit 9 Performance Task

At the end of the unit, check out how **hydrologists** use math.

Vocabulary Preview

Use the puzzle to preview key vocabulary from this unit. Unscramble the circled letters to answer the riddle at the bottom of the page.

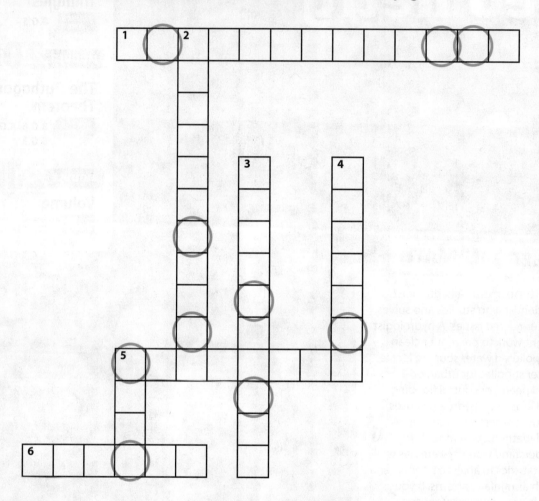

Across

1. The angle formed by two sides of a triangle (2 words) (Lesson 19.2)

5. A three-dimensional figure that has two congruent circular bases. (Lesson 21.1)

6. A three-dimensional figure with all points the same distance from the center. (Lesson 21.3)

Down

2. The line that intersects two or more lines. (Lesson 19.1)

3. The side opposite the right angle in a right triangle. (Lesson 20.1)

4. Figures with the same shape but not necessarily the same size. (Lesson 19.3)

5. A three-dimensional figure that has one vertex and one circular base. (Lesson 21.2)

Q: What do you call an angle that is adorable?

A: __ __ __ __ __ __ __ __ __ __ __ __ __!

Angle Relationships in Parallel Lines and Triangles

ESSENTIAL QUESTION

How can you use angle relationships in parallel lines and triangles to solve real-world problems?

Real-World Video

Many cities are designed on a grid with parallel streets. If another street runs across the parallel lines, it is a transversal. Special relationships exist between parallel lines and transversals.

 my.hrw.com

GO DIGITAL
my.hrw.com

my.hrw.com

Go digital with your write-in student edition, accessible on any device.

Math On the Spot

Scan with your smart phone to jump directly to the online edition, video tutor, and more.

Animated Math

Interactively explore key concepts to see how math works.

Personal Math Trainer

Get immediate feedback and help as you work through practice sets.

Are YOU Ready?

Complete these exercises to review skills you will need for this module.

Personal Math Trainer

Online Assessment and Intervention

my.hrw.com

Solve Two-Step Equations

EXAMPLE

$$7x + 9 = 30$$ Write the equation.

$$7x + 9 - 9 = 30 - 9$$ Subtract 9 from both sides.

$$7x = 21$$ Simplify.

$$\frac{7x}{7} = \frac{21}{7}$$ Divide both sides by 7.

$$x = 3$$ Simplify.

Solve for x.

1. $6x + 10 = 46$

2. $7x - 6 = 36$

3. $3x + 26 = 59$

4. $2x + 5 = -25$

5. $6x - 7 = 41$

6. $\frac{1}{2}x + 9 = 30$

7. $\frac{1}{3}x - 7 = 15$

8. $0.5x - 0.6 = 8.4$

Name Angles

EXAMPLE

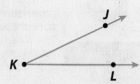

Use three points of an angle, including the vertex, to name the angle. Write the vertex between the other two points: $\angle JKL$ or $\angle LKJ$. You can also use just the vertex letter to name the angle if there is no danger of confusing the angle with another. This is also $\angle K$.

Give two names for the angle formed by the dashed rays.

9. _____

10. _____

11. _____

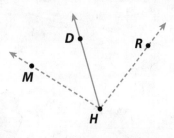

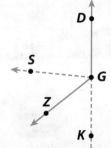

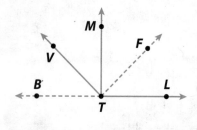

Reading Start-Up

Visualize Vocabulary

Use the ✔ words to complete the graphic. You can put more than one word in each section of the triangle.

Reviewing Angles

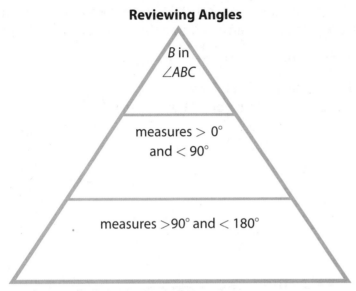

B in ∠*ABC*

measures > 0° and < 90°

measures >90° and < 180°

Understand Vocabulary

Complete the sentences using preview words.

1. A line that intersects two or more lines is a _____.

2. Figures with the same shape but not necessarily the same size are _____.

3. An _____ is an angle formed by one side of the triangle and the extension of an adjacent side.

Active Reading

Pyramid Before beginning the module, create a pyramid to help you organize what you learn. Label each side with one of the lesson titles from this module. As you study each lesson, write important ideas like vocabulary, properties, and formulas on the appropriate side.

Unpacking the Standards

Understanding the standards and the vocabulary terms in the standards will help you know exactly what you are expected to learn in this module.

COMMON CORE 8.G.5

Use informal arguments to establish facts about the angle sum and exterior angle of triangles, about the angles created when parallel lines are cut by a transversal, and the angle-angle criterion for similarity of triangles.

Key Vocabulary

transversal *(transversal)*
  A line that intersects two or more lines.

What It Means to You

You will learn about the special angle relationships formed when parallel lines are intersected by a third line called a transversal.

UNPACKING EXAMPLE 8.G.5

Which angles formed by the transversal and the parallel lines seem to be congruent?

It appears that the angles below are congruent.

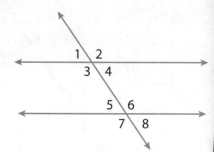

$\angle 1 \cong \angle 4 \cong \angle 5 \cong \angle 8$

$\angle 2 \cong \angle 3 \cong \angle 6 \cong \angle 7$

COMMON CORE 8.G.5

Use informal arguments to establish facts about the angle sum and exterior angle of triangles, about the angles created when parallel lines are cut by a transversal, and the angle-angle criterion for similarity of triangles.

What It Means to You

You will use the angle-angle criterion to determine similarity of two triangles.

UNPACKING EXAMPLE 8.G.5

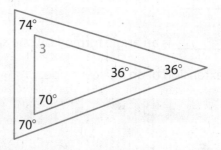

Explain whether the triangles are similar.

Two angles in the large triangle are congruent to two angles in the smaller triangle, so the third pair of angles must also be congruent, which makes the triangles similar.

$70° + 36° + m\angle 3 = 180°$

$m\angle 3 = 74°$

Parallel Lines Cut by a Transversal

COMMON CORE 8.G.5

Use informal arguments to establish facts about... the angles created when parallel lines are cut by a transversal....

ESSENTIAL QUESTION

What can you conclude about the angles formed by parallel lines that are cut by a transversal?

EXPLORE ACTIVITY 1   8.G.5

Parallel Lines and Transversals

A **transversal** is a line that intersects two lines in the same plane at two different points. Transversal *t* and lines *a* and *b* form eight angles.

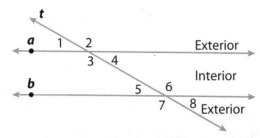

Angle Pairs Formed by a Transversal	
Term	**Example**
Corresponding angles lie on the same side of the transversal *t*, on the same side of lines *a* and *b*.	∠1 and ∠5
Alternate interior angles are nonadjacent angles that lie on opposite sides of the transversal *t*, between lines *a* and *b*.	∠3 and ∠6
Alternate exterior angles lie on opposite sides of the transversal *t*, outside lines *a* and *b*.	∠1 and ∠8
Same-side interior angles lie on the same side of the transversal *t*, between lines *a* and *b*.	∠3 and ∠5

Use geometry software to explore the angles formed when a transversal intersects parallel lines.

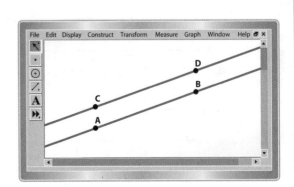

A Construct a line and label two points on the line *A* and *B*.

B Create point *C* not on $\overleftrightarrow{AB}$. Then construct a line parallel to $\overleftrightarrow{AB}$ through point *C*. Create another point on this line and label it *D*.

C Create two points outside the two parallel lines and label them *E* and *F*. Construct transversal $\overleftrightarrow{EF}$. Label the points of intersection *G* and *H*.

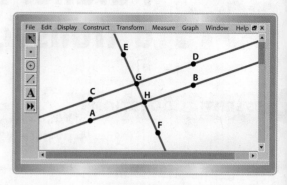

D Measure the angles formed by the parallel lines and the transversal. Write the angle measures in the table below.

E Drag point *E* or point *F* to a different position. Record the new angle measures in the table.

Angle	∠CGE	∠DGE	∠CGH	∠DGH	∠AHG	∠BHG	∠AHF	∠BHF
Measure								
Measure								

Reflect

Make a Conjecture Identify the pairs of angles in the diagram. Then make a conjecture about their angle measures. Drag a point in the diagram to confirm your conjecture.

1. corresponding angles

    _____

    _____

    _____

2. alternate interior angles

    _____

    _____

3. alternate exterior angles

    _____

    _____

4. same-side interior angles

    _____

    _____

Justifying Angle Relationships

You can use tracing paper to informally justify your conclusions from the first Explore Activity.

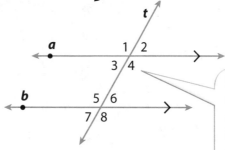

Lines *a* and *b* are parallel. (The black arrows on the diagram indicate parallel lines.)

> Recall that vertical angles are the opposite angles formed by two intersecting lines.
> ∠1 and ∠4 are vertical angles.

A Trace the diagram onto tracing paper.

B Position the tracing paper over the original diagram so that ∠1 on the tracing is over ∠5 on the original diagram. Compare the two angles. Do they appear to be congruent?

_____

_____

C Use the tracing paper to compare all eight angles in the diagram to each other. List all of the congruent angle pairs.

_____

_____

_____

> **Math Talk**
> Mathematical Practices
>
> What do you notice about the special angle pairs formed by the transversal?

Finding Unknown Angle Measures

You can find any unknown angle measure when two parallel lines are cut by a transversal if you are given at least one other angle measure.

Math On the Spot
⊙ my.hrw.com

EXAMPLE 1   COMMON CORE 8.G.5

A **Find m∠2 when m∠7 = 125°.**

∠2 is congruent to ∠7 because they are alternate exterior angles.

Therefore, m∠2 = 125°.

B **Find m∠VWZ.**

∠VWZ is supplementary to ∠YVW because they are same-side interior angles.

m∠VWZ + m∠YVW = 180°

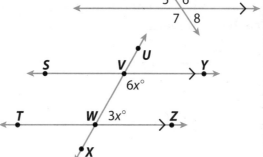

Animated Math
⊙ my.hrw.com

From the previous page, m∠VWZ + m∠YVW = 180°, m∠VWZ = 3x°, and m∠YVW = 6x°.

$$m\angle VWZ + m\angle YVW = 180°$$

$$3x° + 6x° = 180°$$ Replace m∠VWZ with 3x° and m∠YVW with 6x°.

$$9x = 180$$ Combine like terms.

$$\frac{9x}{9} = \frac{180}{9}$$ Divide both sides by 9.

Simplify.

$$x = 20$$

$$m\angle VWZ = 3x° = (3 \cdot 20)° = 60°$$

Personal Math Trainer

Online Assessment and Intervention

⏻ my.hrw.com

YOUR TURN

Find each angle measure.

5. m∠GDE = _____

6. m∠BEF = _____

7. m∠CDG = _____

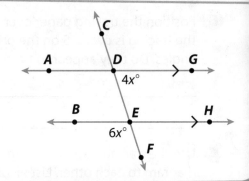

Guided Practice

Use the figure for Exercises 1–4. (Explore Activity 1 and Example 1)

1. ∠UVY and _____ are a pair of corresponding angles.

2. ∠WVY and ∠VWT are _____ angles.

3. Find m∠SVW. _____

4. Find m∠VWT. _____

5. **Vocabulary** When two parallel lines are cut by a transversal,

_____ angles are supplementary. (Explore Activity 1)

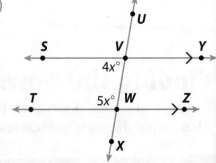

❓ ESSENTIAL QUESTION CHECK-IN

6. What can you conclude about the interior angles formed when two parallel lines are cut by a transversal?

_____

_____

19.1 Independent Practice

 8.G.5

Vocabulary Use the figure for Exercises 7–10.

7. Name all pairs of corresponding angles.

_____

8. Name both pairs of alternate exterior angles.

_____

9. Name the relationship between ∠3 and ∠6.

_____

10. Name the relationship between ∠4 and ∠6.

_____

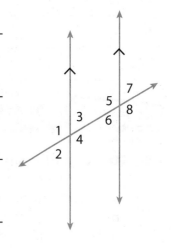

Find each angle measure.

11. m∠AGE when m∠FHD = 30° _____

12. m∠AGH when m∠CHF = 150° _____

13. m∠CHF when m∠BGE = 110° _____

14. m∠CHG when m∠HGA = 120° _____

15. m∠BGH = _____

16. m∠GHD = _____

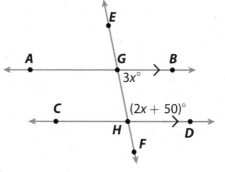

17. The Cross Country Bike Trail follows a straight line where it crosses 350th and 360th Streets. The two streets are parallel to each other. What is the measure of the larger angle formed at the intersection of the bike trail and 360th Street? Explain.

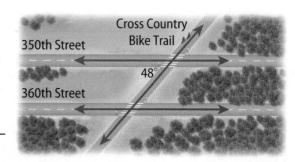

_____

_____

_____

18. Critical Thinking How many different angles would be formed by a transversal intersecting three parallel lines? How many different angle measures would there be?

_____

_____

19. Communicate Mathematical Ideas In the diagram at the right, suppose m∠6 = 125°. Explain how to find the measures of each of the other seven numbered angles.

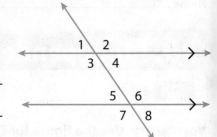

_____

_____

_____

_____

_____

_____

Work Area

20. Draw Conclusions In a diagram showing two parallel lines cut by a transversal, the measures of two same-side interior angles are both given as $3x°$. Without writing and solving an equation, can you determine the measures of both angles? Explain. Then write and solve an equation to find the measures.

_____

_____

_____

21. Make a Conjecture Draw two parallel lines and a transversal. Choose one of the eight angles that are formed. How many of the other seven angles are congruent to the angle you selected? How many of the other seven angles are supplementary to your angle? Will your answer change if you select a different angle?

_____

22. Critique Reasoning In the diagram at the right, ∠2, ∠3, ∠5, and ∠8 are all congruent, and ∠1, ∠4, ∠6, and ∠7 are all congruent. Aiden says that this is enough information to conclude that the diagram shows two parallel lines cut by a transversal. Is he correct? Justify your answer.

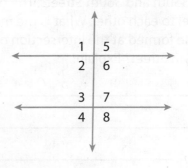

_____

_____

_____

_____

Angle Theorems for Triangles

COMMON CORE **8.G.5**

Use informal arguments to establish facts about the angle sum and exterior angle of triangles.... *Also 8.EE.7, 8.EE.7b*

ESSENTIAL QUESTION

What can you conclude about the measures of the angles of a triangle?

EXPLORE ACTIVITY 1 COMMON CORE 8.G.5

Sum of the Angle Measures in a Triangle

There is a special relationship between the measures of the interior angles of a triangle.

A Draw a triangle and cut it out. Label the angles *A, B,* and *C.*

B Tear off each "corner" of the triangle. Each corner includes the vertex of one angle of the triangle.

C Arrange the vertices of the triangle around a point so that none of your corners overlap and there are no gaps between them.

D What do you notice about how the angles fit together around a point?

_____

E What is the measure of a straight angle? _____

F Describe the relationship among the measures of the angles of △*ABC.*

_____

The Triangle Sum Theorem states that for △*ABC,* m∠*A* + m∠*B* + m∠*C* = _____.

Reflect

1. **Justify Reasoning** Can a triangle have two right angles? Explain.

_____

_____

_____

2. **Analyze Relationships** Describe the relationship between the two acute angles in a right triangle. Explain your reasoning.

_____

_____

_____

Justifying the Triangle Sum Theorem

You can use your knowledge of parallel lines intersected by a transversal to informally justify the Triangle Sum Theorem.

Follow the steps to informally prove the Triangle Sum Theorem. You should draw each step on your own paper. The figures below are provided for you to check your work.

A Draw a triangle and label the angles as ∠1, ∠2, and ∠3 as shown.

B Draw line *a* through the base of the triangle.

C The Parallel Postulate states that through a point not on a line ℓ, there is exactly one line parallel to line ℓ. Draw line *b* parallel to line *a*, through the vertex opposite the base of the triangle.

D Extend each of the non-base sides of the triangle to form transversal *s* and transversal *t*. Transversals *s* and *t* intersect parallel lines *a* and *b*.

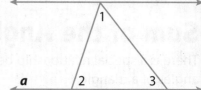

E Label the angles formed by line *b* and the transversals as ∠4 and ∠5.

F Because ∠4 and _____ are alternate interior

angles, they are _____.

Label ∠4 with the number of the angle to which it is congruent.

G Because ∠5 and _____ are alternate interior angles,

they are _____.

Label ∠5 with the number of the angle to which it is congruent.

H The three angles that lie along line *b* at the vertex of the triangle are ∠1, ∠4, and ∠5. Notice that these three angles lie along a line.

So, m∠1 + m∠4 + m∠5 = _____.

Because angles 2 and 4 are congruent and angles 3 and 5 are congruent, you can substitute m∠2 for m∠4 and m∠3 for m∠5 in the equation above.

So, m∠1 + m∠2 + m∠3 = _____.

This shows that the sum of the angle measures in a triangle is

always _____.

Reflect

3. Analyze Relationships How can you use the fact that m∠4 + m∠1 + m∠5 = 180° to show that m∠2 + m∠1 + m∠3 = 180°?

_____

_____

_____

Finding Missing Angle Measures in Triangles

If you know the measures of two angles in a triangle, you can use the Triangle Sum Theorem to find the measure of the third angle.

EXAMPLE 1

COMMON CORE **8.EE.7**

Find the missing angle measure.

My Notes

STEP 1 Write the Triangle Sum Theorem for this triangle.

$$m\angle D + m\angle E + m\angle F = 180°$$

STEP 2 Substitute the given angle measures.

$$55° + m\angle E + 100° = 180°$$

STEP 3 Solve the equation for m∠E.

$$55° + m\angle E + 100° = 180°$$

$$155° + m\angle E = 180°$$

$$\underline{-155°} \qquad \underline{-155°} \qquad \text{Subtract 155° from both sides.}$$

$$m\angle E = \quad 25° \qquad \text{Simplify.}$$

So, m∠E = 25°.

YOUR TURN

Find the missing angle measure.

4.

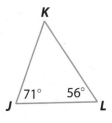

m∠K = _____

5.

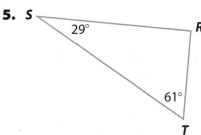

m∠R = _____

Exterior Angles and Remote Interior Angles

An **interior angle** of a triangle is formed by two sides of the triangle. An **exterior angle** is formed by one side of the triangle and the extension of an adjacent side. Each exterior angle has two remote interior angles. A **remote interior angle** is an interior angle that is not adjacent to the exterior angle.

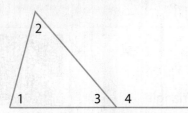

- $\angle 1$, $\angle 2$, and $\angle 3$ are interior angles.

- $\angle 4$ is an exterior angle.

- $\angle 1$ and $\angle 2$ are remote interior angles to $\angle 4$.

There is a special relationship between the measure of an exterior angle and the measures of its remote interior angles.

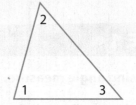

A Extend the base of the triangle and label the exterior angle as $\angle 4$.

B The Triangle Sum Theorem states:

$m\angle 1 + m\angle 2 + m\angle 3 =$ _____.

C $\angle 3$ and $\angle 4$ form a _____,

so $m\angle 3 + m\angle 4 =$ _____.

D Use the equations in **B** and **C** to complete the following equation:

$m\angle 1 + m\angle 2 +$ _____ $=$ _____ $+ m\angle 4$

E Use properties of equality to simplify the equation in **D**:

_____

The Exterior Angle Theorem states that the measure of an _____ angle

is equal to the sum of its _____ angles.

Reflect

6. Sketch a triangle and draw all of its exterior angles. How many exterior angles does a triangle have at each vertex?

_____

7. How many total exterior angles does a triangle have?

_____

Using the Exterior Angle Theorem

You can use the Exterior Angle Theorem to find the measures of the interior angles of a triangle.

EXAMPLE 2

COMMON CORE 8.EE.7b

Find m∠A and m∠B.

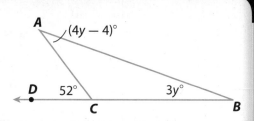

STEP 1 Write the Exterior Angle Theorem as it applies to this triangle.

$$m\angle A + m\angle B = m\angle ACD$$

STEP 2 Substitute the given angle measures.

$$(4y - 4)° + 3y° = 52°$$

Math Talk

Mathematical Practices

Describe two ways to find m∠ACB.

STEP 3 Solve the equation for y.

$$(4y - 4)° + 3y° = 52°$$

$$4y° - 4° + 3y° = 52° \quad \text{Remove parentheses.}$$

$$7y° - 4° = 52° \quad \text{Simplify.}$$

$$\underline{+4° \qquad +4°} \quad \text{Add 4° to both sides.}$$

$$7y° = 56° \quad \text{Simplify.}$$

$$\frac{7y°}{7} = \frac{56°}{7} \quad \text{Divide both sides by 7.}$$

$$y = 8 \quad \text{Simplify.}$$

STEP 4 Use the value of y to find m∠A and m∠B.

$$m\angle A = 4y - 4 \qquad\qquad m\angle B = 3y$$
$$= 4(8) - 4 \qquad\qquad = 3(8)$$
$$= 32 - 4 \qquad\qquad = 24$$
$$= 28$$

So, m∠A = 28° and m∠B = 24°.

YOUR TURN

8. Find m∠M and m∠N.

m∠M = _____

m∠N = _____

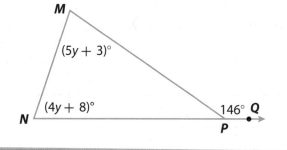

Find each missing angle measure. (Explore Activity 1 and Example 1)

1.

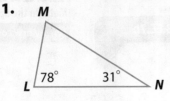

m∠M = _____

2.

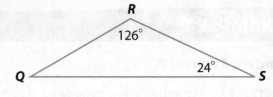

m∠Q = _____

Use the Triangle Sum Theorem to find the measure of each angle in degrees. (Explore Activity 2 and Example 1)

3.

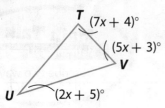

m∠T = _____, m∠U = _____,

m∠V = _____

4.

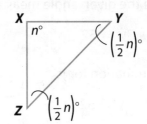

m∠X = _____, m∠Y = _____,

m∠Z = _____

Use the Exterior Angle Theorem to find the measure of each angle in degrees. (Explore Activity 3 and Example 2)

5.

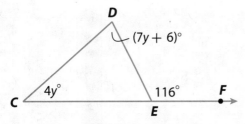

m∠C = _____, m∠D = _____,

m∠DEC = _____

6.

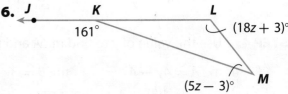

m∠L = _____, m∠M = _____,

m∠LKM = _____

ESSENTIAL QUESTION CHECK-IN

7. Describe the relationships among the measures of the angles of a triangle.

_____

_____

_____

Name _____ Class _____ Date _____

19.2 Independent Practice

 8.EE.7, 8.EE.7b, 8.G.5

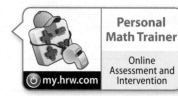

Find the measure of each angle.

8.

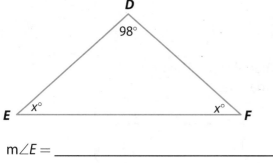

m∠E = _____

m∠F = _____

9.

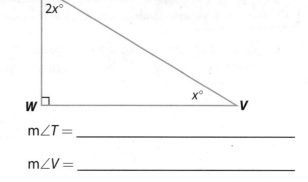

m∠T = _____

m∠V = _____

10.

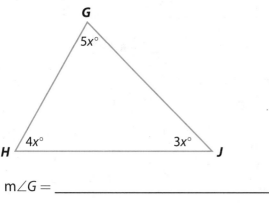

m∠G = _____

m∠H = _____

m∠J = _____

11.

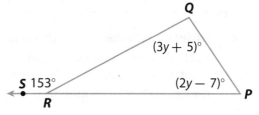

m∠Q = _____

m∠P = _____

m∠QRP = _____

12.

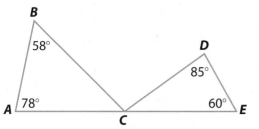

m∠ACB = _____

m∠BCD = _____

m∠DCE = _____

13.

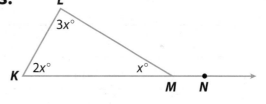

m∠K = _____

m∠L = _____

m∠KML = _____

m∠LMN = _____

14. Multistep The second angle in a triangle is five times as large as the first. The third angle is two-thirds as large as the first. Find the angle measures. _____

15. Analyze Relationships Can a triangle have two obtuse angles? Explain.

_____

_____

_____

_____

H.O.T. FOCUS ON HIGHER ORDER THINKING

16. Critical Thinking Explain how you can use the Triangle Sum Theorem to find the measures of the angles of an equilateral triangle.

_____

_____

_____

_____

17. a. Draw Conclusions Find the sum of the measures of the angles in quadrilateral *ABCD*. (Hint: Draw diagonal $\overline{AC}$. How can you use the figures you have formed to find the sum?)

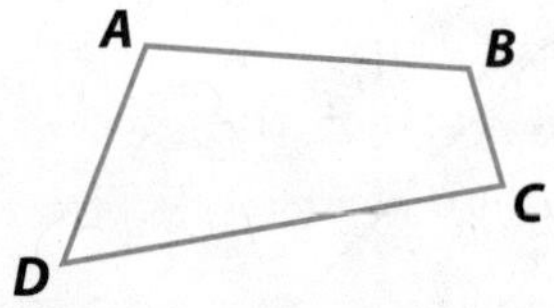

Sum = _____

b. Make a Conjecture Write a "Quadrilateral Sum Theorem." Explain why you think it is true.

_____

_____

_____

_____

_____

18. Communicate Mathematical Ideas Describe two ways that an exterior angle of a triangle is related to one or more of the interior angles.

_____

_____

_____

_____

LESSON
19.3

COMMON CORE 8.G.5

Use informal arguments to establish facts about . . . the angle-angle criterion for similarity of triangles. *Also* 8.EE.6, 8.EE.7

Angle-Angle Similarity

ESSENTIAL QUESTION

How can you determine when two triangles are similar?

EXPLORE ACTIVITY 1   COMMON CORE 8.G.5

Discovering Angle-Angle Similarity

Similar figures have the same shape but may have different sizes. Two triangles are **similar** if their corresponding angles are congruent and the lengths of their corresponding sides are proportional.

A Use your protractor and a straightedge to draw a triangle. Make one angle measure 45° and another angle measure 60°.

B Compare your triangle to those drawn by your classmates. How are the triangles the same?

_____

How are they different?

_____

C Use the Triangle Sum Theorem to find the measure of the third angle of your triangle.

_____

Reflect

1. If two angles in one triangle are congruent to two angles in another triangle, what do you know about the third pair of angles?

_____

2. **Make a Conjecture** Are two pairs of congruent angles enough information to conclude that two triangles are similar? Explain.

_____

_____

_____

Using the AA Similarity Postulate

Angle-Angle (AA) Similarity Postulate

If two angles of one triangle are congruent to two angles of another triangle, then the triangles are similar.

EXAMPLE 1

COMMON CORE 8.G.5

Explain whether the triangles are similar.

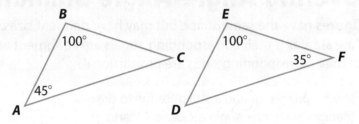

The figure shows only one pair of congruent angles. Find the measure of the third angle in each triangle.

$$45° + 100° + m\angle C = 180° \qquad 100° + 35° + m\angle D = 180°$$

$$145° + m\angle C = 180° \qquad 135° + m\angle D = 180°$$

$$145° + m\angle C - 145° = 180° - 145° \qquad 135° + m\angle D - 135° = 180° - 135°$$

$$m\angle C = 35° \qquad m\angle D = 45°$$

Because two angles in one triangle are congruent to two angles in the other triangle, the triangles are similar.

YOUR TURN

3. **Explain whether the triangles are similar.**

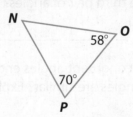
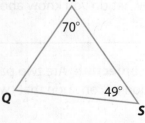

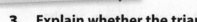

_____

_____

_____

Finding Missing Measures in Similar Triangles

Because corresponding angles are congruent and corresponding sides are proportional in similar triangles, you can use similar triangles to solve real-world problems.

EXAMPLE 2

COMMON CORE 8.EE.7

While playing tennis, Matt is 12 meters from the net, which is 0.9 meter high. He needs to hit the ball so that it just clears the net and lands 6 meters beyond the base of the net. At what height should Matt hit the tennis ball?

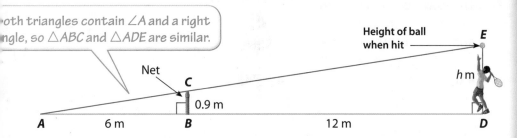

Both triangles contain $\angle A$ and a right angle, so $\triangle ABC$ and $\triangle ADE$ are similar.

Height of ball when hit

Net

C

0.9 m

A 6 m B 12 m D

E

h m

In similar triangles, corresponding side lengths are proportional.

$$\frac{AD}{AB} = \frac{DE}{BC} \longrightarrow \frac{6+12}{6} = \frac{h}{0.9}$$

Substitute the lengths from the figure.

$$0.9 \times \frac{18}{6} = \frac{h}{0.9} \times 0.9$$

Use properties of equality to get h by itself.

$$0.9 \times 3 = h$$

Simplify.

$$2.7 = h$$

Multiply.

Matt should hit the ball at a height of 2.7 meters.

Reflect

4. **What If?** Suppose you set up a proportion so that each ratio compares parts of one triangle, as shown below.

height of $\triangle ABC$ ⟶ $\dfrac{BC}{AB} = \dfrac{DE}{AD}$ ⟵ height of $\triangle ADE$
base of $\triangle ABC$ ⟶ ⟵ base of $\triangle ADE$

Show that this proportion leads to the same value for h as in Example 2.

YOUR TURN

5. Rosie is building a wheelchair ramp that is 24 feet long and 2 feet high. She needs to install a vertical support piece 8 feet from the end of the ramp. What is the length of the support piece in inches?

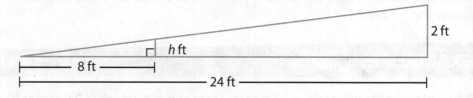

2 ft

h ft

8 ft

24 ft

_____

6. The lower cable meets the tree at a height of 6 feet and extends out 16 feet from the base of the tree. If the triangles are similar, how tall is the tree?

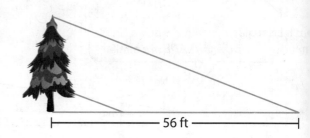

56 ft

_____

EXPLORE ACTIVITY 2 COMMON CORE 8.EE.6

Using Similar Triangles to Explain Slope

You can use similar triangles to show that the slope of a line is constant.

A Draw a line ℓ that is not a horizontal line. Label four points on the line as *A*, *B*, *C*, and *D*.

You need to show that the slope between points *A* and *B* is the same as the slope between points *C* and *D*.

B Draw the rise and run for the slope between points A and B. Label the intersection as point E. Draw the rise and run for the slope between points C and D. Label the intersection as point F.

C Write expressions for the slope between A and B and between C and D.

Slope between A and B: $\dfrac{BE}{\boxed{}}$ Slope between C and D: $\dfrac{\boxed{}}{CF}$

D Extend $\overleftrightarrow{AE}$ and $\overleftrightarrow{CF}$ across your drawing. $\overleftrightarrow{AE}$ and $\overleftrightarrow{CF}$ are both horizontal lines, so they are parallel.

Line ℓ is a _____ that intersects parallel lines.

E Complete the following statements:

$\angle BAE$ and _____ are corresponding angles and are _____.

$\angle BEA$ and _____ are right angles and are _____.

F By Angle–Angle Similarity, $\triangle ABE$ and _____ are similar triangles.

G Use the fact that the lengths of corresponding sides of similar triangles are proportional to complete the following ratios: $\dfrac{BE}{DF} = \dfrac{\boxed{}}{CF}$

H Recall that you can also write the proportion so that the ratios compare parts of the same triangle: $\dfrac{\boxed{}}{AE} = \dfrac{DF}{\boxed{}}$.

I The proportion you wrote in step **H** shows that the ratios you wrote in **C** are equal. So, the slope of line ℓ is constant.

Reflect

7. What If? Suppose that you label two other points on line ℓ as G and H. Would the slope between these two points be different than the slope you found in the Explore Activity? Explain.

_____

_____

_____

1. Explain whether the triangles are similar. Label the angle measures in the figure. (Explore Activity 1 and Example 1)

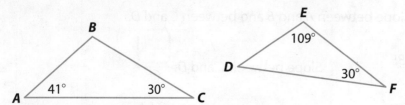

△ABC has angle measures _____ and △DEF has angle

measures _____. Because _____ in one

triangle are congruent to _____ in the other triangle, the

triangles are _____.

2. A flagpole casts a shadow 23.5 feet long. At the same time of day, Mrs. Gilbert, who is 5.5 feet tall, casts a shadow that is 7.5 feet long. How tall in feet is the flagpole? Round your answer to the nearest tenth. (Example 2)

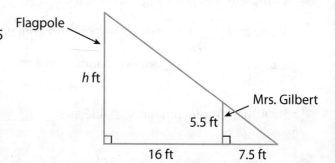

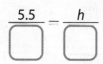

$$\dfrac{5.5}{\boxed{}} = \dfrac{h}{\boxed{}}$$

$h =$ _____ feet

3. Two transversals intersect two parallel lines as shown. Explain whether △ABC and △DEC are similar. (Example 1)

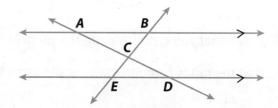

∠BAC and ∠EDC are _____ since they are _____.

∠ABC and ∠DEC are _____ since they are _____.

By _____, △ABC and △DEC are _____.

4. How can you determine when two triangles are similar?

_____

_____

_____

19.3 Independent Practice

COMMON CORE 8.EE.6, 8.EE.7, 8.G.5

Personal Math Trainer

Online Assessment and Intervention

my.hrw.com

Use the diagrams for Exercises 5–7.

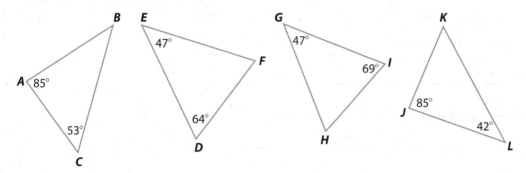

5. Find the missing angle measures in the triangles.

_____

6. Which triangles are similar?

_____

7. Analyze Relationships Determine which angles are congruent to the angles in △ABC.

_____

8. Multistep A tree casts a shadow that is 20 feet long. Frank is 6 feet tall, and while standing next to the tree he casts a shadow that is 4 feet long.

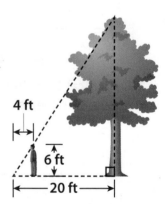

a. How tall is the tree? _____

b. How much taller is the tree than Frank? _____

9. Represent Real-World Problems Sheila is climbing on a ladder that is attached against the side of a jungle gym wall. She is 5 feet off the ground and 3 feet from the base of the ladder, which is 15 feet from the wall. Draw a diagram to help you solve the problem. How high up the wall is the top of the ladder?

_____

10. Justify Reasoning Are two equilateral triangles always similar? Explain.

_____

_____

_____

11. **Critique Reasoning** Ryan calculated the missing measure in the diagram shown. What was his mistake?

$$\frac{3.4}{6.5} = \frac{h}{19.5}$$

$$19.5 \times \frac{3.4}{6.5} = \frac{h}{19.5} \times 19.5$$

$$\frac{66.3}{6.5} = h$$

$$10.2 \text{ cm} = h$$

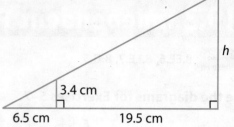

3.4 cm

6.5 cm   19.5 cm

h

_____

_____

_____

Work Area

12. **Communicate Mathematical Ideas** For a pair of triangular earrings, how can you tell if they are similar? How can you tell if they are congruent?

_____

_____

_____

_____

13. **Critical Thinking** When does it make sense to use similar triangles to measure the height and length of objects in real life?

_____

_____

_____

14. **Justify Reasoning** Two right triangles on a coordinate plane are similar but not congruent. Each of the legs of both triangles are extended by 1 unit, creating two new right triangles. Are the resulting triangles similar? Explain using an example.

_____

_____

_____

_____

_____

_____

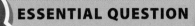

Similar Triangles and Slope

COMMON CORE 8.EE.6

Use similar triangles to explain why the slope *m* is the same between any two distinct points on a non-vertical line in the coordinate plane; ...

> ### ESSENTIAL QUESTION
>
> How can you apply the concept of similar triangles to prove that the slope of a line is constant between any two points on the line?

EXPLORE ACTIVITY **COMMON CORE** 8.EE.6

Using Similar Triangles to Prove a Constant Slope

The R-value of insulation gives the material's resistance to heat flow. The graph shows the proportional relationship between the R-value and the thickness of fiberglass insulation.

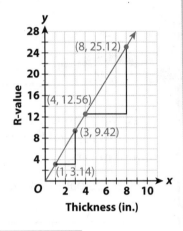

A The graph shows four points on the line and the triangles resulting from sketching the rise and run from one point to the next. Viewing the graph of R-value as a transversal to the rise and run segments, are the two pairs of corresponding angles along the transversal congruent? Explain.

_____

_____

_____

B What is the relationship between the two resulting triangles? Explain your answer.

_____

C Use the relationship from Part B to state the relationship between corresponding sides of the resulting triangles.

_____

D Use the properties of similar triangles to explain why the slope, or rise-to-run ratio, is constant between any two points on the line.

_____

_____

_____

E Use any two points to find the unit rate for this proportional relationship. Show your work.

_____

Reflect

1. Communicate Mathematical Ideas How can you use properties of similar triangles to show that the unit rate of a real-world proportional relationship is the same as the slope of its graph?

_____

_____

_____

_____

2. Critical Thinking What can you say about the y-value of the point (1, y) on the graph of a proportional relationship?

_____

Practice

The graph shows two pairs of points on a line and similar right triangles formed by drawing the rise and run segments for each pair of points.

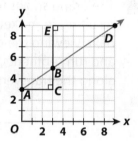

1. List the pairs of congruent angles and the similar triangles.

_____

_____

2. Use proportional corresponding side lengths to show that the slope of $\overline{AB}$ is equal to the slope of $\overline{BD}$.

_____

Use the graph at right for Exercises 3–8.

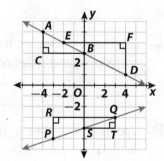

3. Name the pairs of congruent angles and similar triangles from the line containing A and D.

_____

_____

4. Name the pairs of congruent angles and similar triangles from the line containing P and Q.

_____

Complete each ratio.

5. $\dfrac{AC}{CB} = \dfrac{\boxed{}}{FE}$

6. $\dfrac{AB}{\boxed{}} = \dfrac{CB}{FE}$

7. $\dfrac{\boxed{}}{RP} = \dfrac{ST}{TQ}$

8. $\dfrac{PQ}{QS} = \dfrac{PR}{\boxed{}}$

Ready to Go On?

Personal Math Trainer

Online Assessment and Intervention

⊙ my.hrw.com

19.1 Parallel Lines Cut by a Transversal

In the figure, line $p \parallel$ line q. Find the measure of each angle if m$\angle 8 = 115°$.

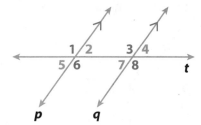

1. m$\angle 7 =$ _____

2. m$\angle 6 =$ _____

3. m$\angle 1 =$ _____

19.2 Angle Theorems for Triangles

Find the measure of each angle.

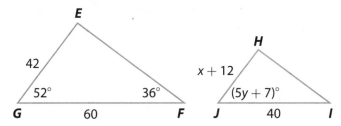

4. m$\angle A =$ _____

5. m$\angle B =$ _____

6. m$\angle BCA =$ _____

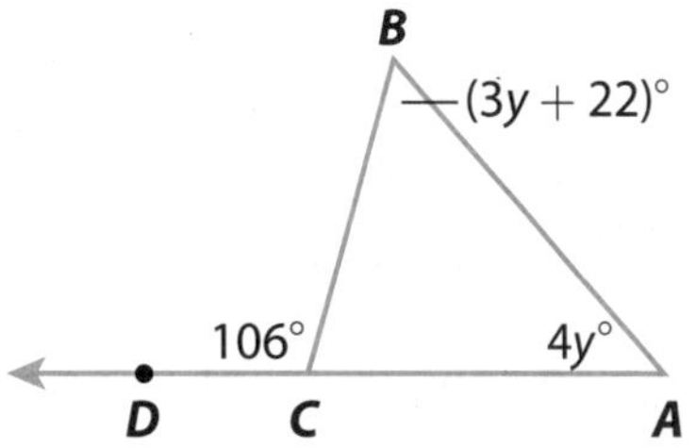

19.3 Angle-Angle Similarity

Triangle *FEG* is similar to triangle *IHJ*. Find the missing values.

7. $x =$ _____   **8.** $y =$ _____   **9.** m$\angle H =$ _____

❓ ESSENTIAL QUESTION

10. How can you use similar triangles to solve real-world problems?

_____

_____

Selected Response

Use the figure for Exercises 1 and 2.

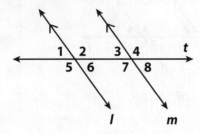

1. Which angle pair is a pair of alternate exterior angles?

Ⓐ ∠5 and ∠6

Ⓑ ∠6 and ∠7

Ⓒ ∠5 and ∠4

Ⓓ ∠5 and ∠2

2. Which of the following angles is **not** congruent to ∠3?

Ⓐ ∠1

Ⓑ ∠2

Ⓒ ∠6

Ⓓ ∠8

3. The measures, in degrees, of the three angles of a triangle are given by $2x + 1$, $3x - 3$, and $9x$. What is the measure of the smallest angle?

Ⓐ 13°

Ⓑ 27°

Ⓒ 36°

Ⓓ 117°

4. Which is a possible measure of ∠DCA in the triangle below?

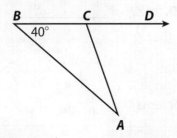

Ⓐ 36°

Ⓑ 38°

Ⓒ 40°

Ⓓ 70°

5. Kaylee wrote in her dinosaur report that the Jurassic period was 1.75×10^8 years ago. What is this number written in standard form?

Ⓐ 1,750,000

Ⓑ 17,500,000

Ⓒ 175,000,000

Ⓓ 17,500,000,000

6. Given that y is proportional to x, what linear equation can you write if y is 16 when x is 20?

Ⓐ $y = 20x$

Ⓑ $y = \frac{5}{4}x$

Ⓒ $y = \frac{4}{5}x$

Ⓓ $y = 0.6x$

Mini-Task

7. Two transversals intersect two parallel lines as shown.

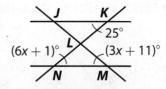

a. What is the value of x?

_____

b. What is the measure of ∠LMN?

_____

c. What is the measure of ∠KLM?

_____

d. Which two triangles are similar? How do you know?

_____

_____

_____

The Pythagorean Theorem

ESSENTIAL QUESTION

How can you use the Pythagorean Theorem to solve real-world problems?

Real-World Video

The sizes of televisions are usually described by the length of the diagonal of the screen. To find this length of the diagonal of a rectangle, you can use the Pythagorean Theorem.

my.hrw.com

GO DIGITAL

my.hrw.com

my.hrw.com

Go digital with your write-in student edition, accessible on any device.

Math On the Spot

Scan with your smart phone to jump directly to the online edition, video tutor, and more.

Animated Math

Interactively explore key concepts to see how math works.

Personal Math Trainer

Get immediate feedback and help as you work through practice sets.

Are YOU Ready?

Complete these exercises to review skills you will need for this module.

Find the Square of a Number

EXAMPLE   Find the square of 2.7.

$$\begin{array}{r} 2.7 \\ \times\, 2.7 \\ \hline 189 \\ 54 \\ \hline 7.29 \end{array}$$

Multiply the number by itself.

So, $2.7^2 = 7.29$.

Find the square of each number.

1. 5 _____
2. 16 _____
3. −11 _____
4. $\frac{2}{7}$ _____

Order of Operations

EXAMPLE $\sqrt{(5-2)^2 + (8-4)^2}$ First, operate within parentheses.

$\sqrt{(3)^2 + (4)^2}$ Next, simplify exponents.

$\sqrt{9 + 16}$ Then add and subtract left to right.

$\sqrt{25}$ Finally, take the square root.

5

Evaluate each expression.

5. $\sqrt{(6+2)^2 + (3+3)^2}$ _____
6. $\sqrt{(9-4)^2 + (5+7)^2}$ _____

7. $\sqrt{(10-6)^2 + (15-12)^2}$ _____
8. $\sqrt{(6+9)^2 + (10-2)^2}$ _____

Simplify Numerical Expressions

EXAMPLE $\frac{1}{2}(2.5)^2(4) = \frac{1}{2}(6.25)(4)$ Simplify the exponent.

$= 12.5$ Multiply from left to right.

Simplify each expression.

9. $5(8)(10)$ _____
10. $\frac{1}{2}(6)(12)$ _____
11. $\frac{1}{3}(3)(12)$ _____

12. $\frac{1}{2}(8)^2(4)$ _____
13. $\frac{1}{4}(10)^2(15)$ _____
14. $\frac{1}{3}(9)^2(6)$ _____

Reading Start-Up

Visualize Vocabulary

Use the ✔ words to complete the graphic.

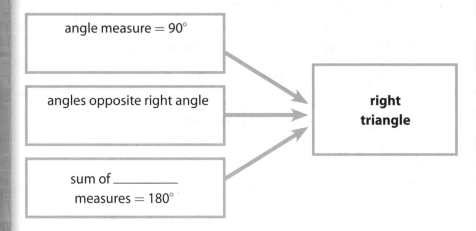

angle measure = 90°

angles opposite right angle

sum of _____ measures = 180°

right triangle

Vocabulary

Review Words

✔ acute angles (*ángulos agudos*)

✔ angles (*ángulos*)

area (*área*)

ordered pair (*par ordenado*)

✔ right angle (*ángulo recto*)

✔ right triangle (*triángulo recto*)

square root (*raíz cuadrada*)

x-coordinate (*coordenada x*)

y-coordinate (*coordenada y*)

Preview Words

hypotenuse (*hipotenusa*)

legs (*catetos*)

theorem (*teorema*)

vertex (*vértice*)

Understand Vocabulary

Match the term on the left to the correct expression on the right.

1. hypotenuse

2. theorem

3. legs

A. An idea that has been demonstrated as true.

B. The two sides that form the right angle of a right triangle.

C. The side opposite the right angle in a right triangle.

Active Reading

Booklet Before beginning the module, create a booklet to help you learn about the Pythagorean Theorem. Write the main idea of each lesson on each page of the booklet. As you study each lesson, write important details that support the main idea, such as vocabulary and formulas. Refer to your finished booklet as you work on assignments and study for tests.

Unpacking the Standards

COMMON CORE Understanding the standards and the vocabulary terms in the standards will help you know exactly what you are expected to learn in this module.

COMMON CORE 8.G.7

Apply the Pythagorean Theorem to determine unknown side lengths in right triangles in real-world and mathematical problems in two and three dimensions.

Key Vocabulary

Pythagorean Theorem
(Teorema de Pitágoras)
In a right triangle, the square of the length of the hypotenuse is equal to the sum of the squares of the lengths of the legs.

What It Means to You

You will find a missing length in a right triangle, or use side lengths to see whether a triangle is a right triangle.

UNPACKING EXAMPLE 8.G.7

Mark and Sarah start walking at the same point, but Mark walks 50 feet north while Sarah walks 75 feet east. How far apart are Mark and Sarah when they stop?

50 ft · · · c · · · 75 ft

$$a^2 + b^2 = c^2 \qquad \text{Pythagorean Theorem}$$
$$50^2 + 75^2 = c^2 \qquad \text{Substitute.}$$
$$2500 + 5625 = c^2$$
$$8125 = c^2$$
$$90.1 \approx c$$

Mark and Sarah are approximately 90.1 feet apart.

COMMON CORE 8.G.8

Apply the Pythagorean Theorem to find the distance between two points in a coordinate system.

Key Vocabulary

coordinate plane
(plano cartesiano)
A plane formed by the intersection of a horizontal number line called the x-axis and a vertical number line called the y-axis.

What It Means to You

You can use the Pythagorean Theorem to find the distance between two points.

UNPACKING EXAMPLE 8.G.8

Find the distance between points A and B.

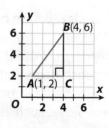

$$(AC)^2 + (BC)^2 = (AB)^2$$
$$(4 - 1)^2 + (6 - 2)^2 = (AB)^2$$
$$3^2 + 4^2 = (AB)^2$$
$$9 + 16 = (AB)^2$$
$$25 = (AB)^2$$
$$5 = AB$$

The distance is 5 units.

Visit **my.hrw.com** to see all the **Common Core Standards** unpacked.

⏻ my.hrw.com

LESSON 20.1 The Pythagorean Theorem

COMMON CORE 8.G.7

Apply the Pythagorean Theorem to determine unknown side lengths in right triangles in real-world and mathematical problems in two and three dimensions.
Also 8.G.6

💬 **ESSENTIAL QUESTION**

How can you prove the Pythagorean Theorem and use it to solve problems?

EXPLORE ACTIVITY   **COMMON CORE** 8.G.6

Proving the Pythagorean Theorem

In a right triangle, the two sides that form the right angle are the **legs**.
The side opposite the right angle is the **hypotenuse**.

Leg   Hypotenuse

Leg

> ### The Pythagorean Theorem
>
> In a right triangle, the sum of the squares of the lengths of the legs is equal to the square of the length of the hypotenuse.
>
> If a and b are legs and c is the hypotenuse, $a^2 + b^2 = c^2$.

A   Draw a right triangle on a piece of paper and cut it out. Make one leg shorter than the other.

B   Trace your triangle onto another piece of paper four times, arranging them as shown. For each triangle, label the shorter leg a, the longer leg b, and the hypotenuse c.

C   What is the area of the unshaded square?

_____

Label the unshaded square with its area.

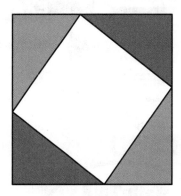

D   Trace your original triangle onto a piece of paper four times again, arranging them as shown. Draw a line outlining a larger square that is the same size as the figure you made in **B**.

E   What is the area of the unshaded square at the top right of the figure in **D**? at the top left?

_____

Label the unshaded squares with their areas.

F   What is the total area of the unshaded regions in **D**?

_____

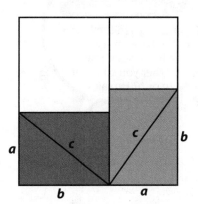

Reflect

1. Explain whether the figures in **B** and **D** have the same area.

   _____

2. Explain whether the unshaded regions of the figures in **B** and **D** have the same area.

   _____

   _____

   _____

3. **Analyze Relationships** Write an equation relating the area of the unshaded region in step **B** to the unshaded region in **D**.

   _____

Math On the Spot

⏻ my.hrw.com

Animated Math

⏻ my.hrw.com

Using the Pythagorean Theorem

You can use the Pythagorean Theorem to find the length of a side of a right triangle when you know the lengths of the other two sides.

EXAMPLE 1

COMMON CORE **8.G.7**

Find the length of the missing side.

A

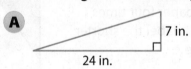

7 in.

24 in.

$a^2 + b^2 = c^2$

$24^2 + 7^2 = c^2$ Substitute into the formula.

$576 + 49 = c^2$ Simplify.

$625 = c^2$ Add.

$25 = c$ Take the square root of both sides.

The length of the hypotenuse is 25 inches.

Math Talk

Mathematical Practices

If you are given the length of the hypotenuse and one leg, does it matter whether you solve for *a* or *b*? Explain.

B

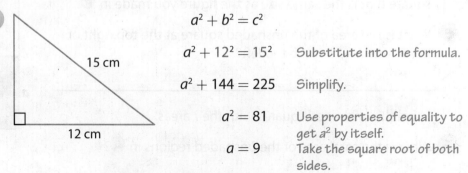

15 cm

12 cm

$a^2 + b^2 = c^2$

$a^2 + 12^2 = 15^2$ Substitute into the formula.

$a^2 + 144 = 225$ Simplify.

$a^2 = 81$ Use properties of equality to get a^2 by itself.

$a = 9$ Take the square root of both sides.

The length of the leg is 9 centimeters.

YOUR TURN

Find the length of the missing side.

4.

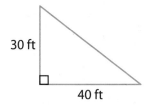

30 ft

40 ft

5.

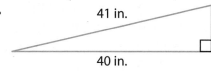

41 in.

40 in.

Pythagorean Theorem in Three Dimensions

You can use the Pythagorean Theorem to solve problems in three dimensions.

EXAMPLE 2

COMMON CORE **8.G.7**

A box used for shipping narrow copper tubes measures 6 inches by 6 inches by 20 inches. What is the length of the longest tube that will fit in the box, given that the length of the tube must be a whole number of inches?

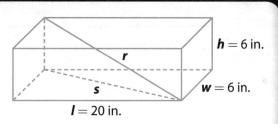

$h = 6$ in.

r

$w = 6$ in.

s

$l = 20$ in.

STEP 1 You want to find r, the length from a bottom corner to the opposite top corner. First, find s, the length of the diagonal across the bottom of the box.

$$w^2 + l^2 = s^2$$

$$6^2 + 20^2 = s^2 \qquad \text{Substitute into the formula.}$$

$$36 + 400 = s^2 \qquad \text{Simplify.}$$

$$436 = s^2 \qquad \text{Add.}$$

STEP 2 Use your expression for s to find r.

$$h^2 + s^2 = r^2$$

$$6^2 + 436 = r^2 \qquad \text{Substitute into the formula.}$$

$$472 = r^2 \qquad \text{Add.}$$

$$\sqrt{472} = r \qquad \text{Take the square root of both sides.}$$

$$21.7 \approx r \qquad \text{Use a calculator to round to the nearest tenth.}$$

The length of the longest tube that will fit in the box is 21 inches.

> **Math Talk**
> **Mathematical Practices**
>
> Looking at Step 2, why did the calculations in Step 1 stop before taking the square root of both sides of the final equation?

YOUR TURN

6. Tina ordered a replacement part for her desk. It was shipped in a box that measures 4 in. by 4 in. by 14 in. What is the greatest length in whole inches that the part could have been?

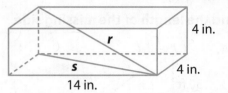

Guided Practice

1. Find the length of the missing side of the triangle. (Explore Activity 1 and Example 1)

$$a^2 + b^2 = c^2 \rightarrow 24^2 + \boxed{} = c^2 \rightarrow \boxed{} = c^2$$

The length of the hypotenuse is $\boxed{}$ feet.

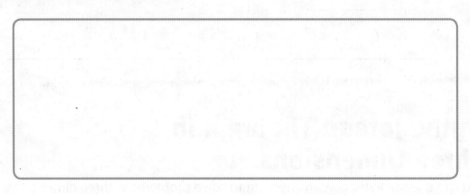

2. Mr. Woo wants to ship a fishing rod that is 42 inches long to his son. He has a box with the dimensions shown. (Example 2)

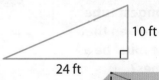

   a. Find the square of the length of the diagonal across the bottom of the box.

   _____

   b. Find the length from a bottom corner to the opposite top corner to the nearest tenth. Will the fishing rod fit?

   _____

? ESSENTIAL QUESTION CHECK-IN

3. State the Pythagorean Theorem and tell how you can use it to solve problems.

_____

_____

_____

_____

20.1 Independent Practice

 COMMON CORE 8.G.6, 8.G.7

Personal
Math Trainer

Online
Assessment and
Intervention

my.hrw.com

Find the length of the missing side of each triangle. Round your answers to the nearest tenth.

4.

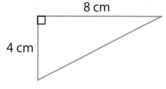

8 cm

4 cm

_____

5.

14 in.

8 in.

_____

6. The diagonal of a rectangular big-screen TV screen measures 152 cm. The length measures 132 cm. What is the height of the screen?   _____

7. Dylan has a square piece of metal that measures 10 inches on each side. He cuts the metal along the diagonal, forming two right triangles. What is the length of the hypotenuse of each right triangle to the nearest tenth of an inch?   _____

8. **Represent Real-World Problems** A painter has a 24-foot ladder that he is using to paint a house. For safety reasons, the ladder must be placed at least 8 feet from the base of the side of the house. To the nearest tenth of a foot, how high can the ladder safely reach?   _____

9. What is the longest flagpole (in whole feet) that could be shipped in a box that measures 2 ft by 2 ft by 12 ft? _____

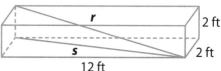

r

2 ft

s

2 ft

12 ft

10. **Sports** American football fields measure 100 yards long between the end zones, and are $53\frac{1}{3}$ yards wide. Is the length of the diagonal across this field more or less than 120 yards? Explain.

_____

11. **Justify Reasoning** A tree struck by lightning broke at a point 12 ft above the ground as shown. What was the height of the tree to the nearest tenth of a foot? Explain your reasoning.

12 ft

39 ft

_____

_____

_____

Work Area

12. Multistep Main Street and Washington Avenue meet at a right angle. A large park begins at this corner. Joe's school lies at the opposite corner of the park. Usually Joe walks 1.2 miles along Main Street and then 0.9 miles up Washington Avenue to get to school. Today he walked in a straight path across the park and returned home along the same path. What is the difference in distance between the two round trips? Explain.

_____

_____

_____

13. Analyze Relationships An isosceles right triangle is a right triangle with congruent legs. If the length of each leg is represented by x, what algebraic expression can be used to represent the length of the hypotenuse? Explain your reasoning.

_____

_____

14. Persevere in Problem Solving A square hamburger is centered on a circular bun. Both the bun and the burger have an area of 16 square inches.

a. How far, to the nearest hundredth of an inch, does each corner of the burger stick out from the bun? Explain.

_____

_____

_____

_____

b. How far does each bun stick out from the center of each side of the burger?

_____

_____

c. Are the distances in part **a** and part **b** equal? If not, which sticks out more, the burger or the bun? Explain.

_____

_____

_____

LESSON
20.2

COMMON CORE 8.G.6
Explain a proof of the
Pythagorean Theorem and its
converse.

Converse of the Pythagorean Theorem

How can you test the converse of the Pythagorean Theorem
and use it to solve problems?

EXPLORE ACTIVITY **8.G.6**

Testing the Converse of the Pythagorean Theorem

The Pythagorean Theorem states that if a triangle is a right
triangle, then $a^2 + b^2 = c^2$.

The *converse* of the Pythagorean Theorem states that
if $a^2 + b^2 = c^2$, then the triangle is a right triangle.

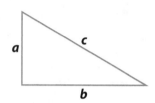

Decide whether the converse of the Pythagorean Theorem is true.

A Verify that the following sets of lengths make the equation $a^2 + b^2 = c^2$
true. Record your results in the table.

a	b	c	Is $a^2 + b^2 = c^2$ true?	Makes a right triangle?
3	4	5		
5	12	13		
7	24	25		
8	15	17		
20	21	29		

B For each set of lengths in the table, cut strips of grid paper with a width
of one square and lengths that correspond to the values of a, b, and c.

C For each set of lengths, use the strips of grid paper to try to form
a right triangle. An example using the first set of lengths is shown.
Record your findings in the table.

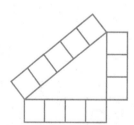

Reflect

1. **Draw Conclusions** Based on your observations, explain whether you
   think the converse of the Pythagorean Theorem is true.

   _____

   _____

Identifying a Right Triangle

The converse of the Pythagorean Theorem gives you a way to tell if a triangle is a right triangle when you know the side lengths.

EXAMPLE 1

 8.G.6

Tell whether each triangle with the given side lengths is a right triangle.

A 9 inches, 40 inches, and 41 inches

Let $a = 9$, $b = 40$, and $c = 41$.

$$a^2 + b^2 = c^2$$
$$9^2 + 40^2 \overset{?}{=} 41^2 \qquad \text{Substitute into the formula.}$$
$$81 + 1600 \overset{?}{=} 1681 \qquad \text{Simplify.}$$
$$1681 = 1681 \qquad \text{Add.}$$

Since $9^2 + 40^2 = 41^2$, the triangle is a right triangle by the converse of the Pythagorean Theorem.

B 8 meters, 10 meters, and 12 meters

Let $a = 8$, $b = 10$, and $c = 12$.

$$a^2 + b^2 = c^2$$
$$8^2 + 10^2 \overset{?}{=} 12^2 \qquad \text{Substitute into the formula.}$$
$$64 + 100 \overset{?}{=} 144 \qquad \text{Simpify.}$$
$$164 \neq 144 \qquad \text{Add.}$$

Since $8^2 + 10^2 \neq 12^2$, the triangle is not a right triangle by the converse of the Pythagorean Theorem.

YOUR TURN

Tell whether each triangle with the given side lengths is a right triangle.

2. 14 cm, 23 cm, and 25 cm

3. 16 in., 30 in., and 34 in.

4. 27 ft, 36 ft, 45 ft

5. 11 mm, 18 mm, 21 mm

Using the Converse of the Pythagorean Theorem

You can use the converse of the Pythagorean Theorem to solve real-world problems.

Math On the Spot
ⓞ my.hrw.com

EXAMPLE 2

COMMON CORE 8.G.6

Katya is buying edging for a triangular flower garden she plans to build in her backyard. If the lengths of the three pieces of edging that she purchases are 13 feet, 10 feet, and 7 feet, will the flower garden be in the shape of a right triangle?

Use the converse of the Pythagorean Theorem. Remember to use the longest length for c.

Let $a = 7$, $b = 10$, and $c = 13$.

$$a^2 + b^2 = c^2$$

$$7^2 + 10^2 \overset{?}{=} 13^2 \qquad \text{Substitute into the formula.}$$

$$49 + 100 \overset{?}{=} 169 \qquad \text{Simpify.}$$

$$149 \neq 169 \qquad \text{Add.}$$

Since $7^2 + 10^2 \neq 13^2$, the garden will not be in the shape of a right triangle.

> **Math Talk**
> **Mathematical Practices**
>
> To what length, to the nearest tenth, can Katya trim the longest piece of edging to form a right triangle?

YOUR TURN

6. A blueprint for a new triangular playground shows that the sides measure 480 ft, 140 ft, and 500 ft. Is the playground in the shape of a right triangle? Explain.

_____

_____

7. A triangular piece of glass has sides that measure 18 in., 19 in., and 25 in. Is the piece of glass in the shape of a right triangle? Explain.

_____

8. A corner of a fenced yard forms a right angle. Can you place a 12 foot long board across the corner to form a right triangle for which the leg lengths are whole numbers? Explain.

_____

_____

1. Lashandra used grid paper to construct the triangle shown. (Explore Activity)

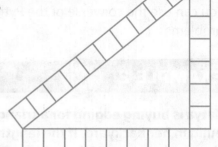

   a. What are the lengths of the sides of Lashandra's triangle?

   _____units, _____units, _____units

   b. Use the converse of the Pythagorean Theorem
   to determine whether the triangle is a right triangle.

   $$a^2 + b^2 = c^2$$

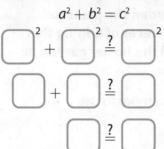

   The triangle that Lashandra constructed | **is / is not** | a right triangle.

2. A triangle has side lengths 9 cm, 12 cm, and 16 cm. Tell whether the triangle
   is a right triangle. (Example 1)

   Let $a =$ _____ , $b =$ _____ , and $c =$ _____ .

   $$a^2 + b^2 = c^2$$

   By the converse of the Pythagorean Theorem, the triangle | **is / is not** |
   a right triangle.

3. The marketing team at a new electronics company is designing a logo that
   contains a circle and a triangle. On one design, the triangle's side lengths are
   2.5 in., 6 in., and 6.5 in. Is the triangle a right triangle? Explain. (Example 2)

   _____

   _____

? ESSENTIAL QUESTION CHECK-IN

4. How can you use the converse of the Pythagorean Theorem
   to tell if a triangle is a right triangle?

   _____

   _____

20.2 Independent Practice

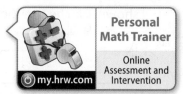

Personal
Math Trainer

Online
Assessment and
Intervention

my.hrw.com

Tell whether each triangle with the given side lengths is a right triangle.

5. 11 cm, 60 cm, 61 cm

_____

6. 5 ft, 12 ft, 15 ft

_____

7. 9 in., 15 in., 17 in.

_____

8. 15 m, 36 m, 39 m

_____

9. 20 mm, 30 mm, 40 mm

_____

10. 20 cm, 48 cm, 52 cm

_____

11. 18.5 ft, 6 ft, 17.5 ft

_____

12. 2 mi, 1.5 mi, 2.5 mi

_____

13. 35 in., 45 in., 55 in.

_____

14. 25 cm, 14 cm, 23 cm

_____

15. The emblem on a college banner consists of the face of a tiger inside a triangle. The lengths of the sides of the triangle are 13 cm, 14 cm, and 15 cm. Is the triangle a right triangle? Explain.

_____

16. Kerry has a large triangular piece of fabric that she wants to attach to the ceiling in her bedroom. The sides of the piece of fabric measure 4.8 ft, 6.4 ft, and 8 ft. Is the fabric in the shape of a right triangle? Explain.

_____

17. A mosaic consists of triangular tiles. The smallest tiles have side lengths 6 cm, 10 cm, and 12 cm. Are these tiles in the shape of right triangles? Explain.

_____

18. History In ancient Egypt, surveyors made right angles by stretching a rope with evenly spaced knots as shown. Explain why the rope forms a right angle.

_____

_____

_____

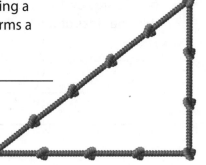

19. Justify Reasoning Yoshi has two identical triangular boards as shown. Can he use these two boards to form a rectangle? Explain.

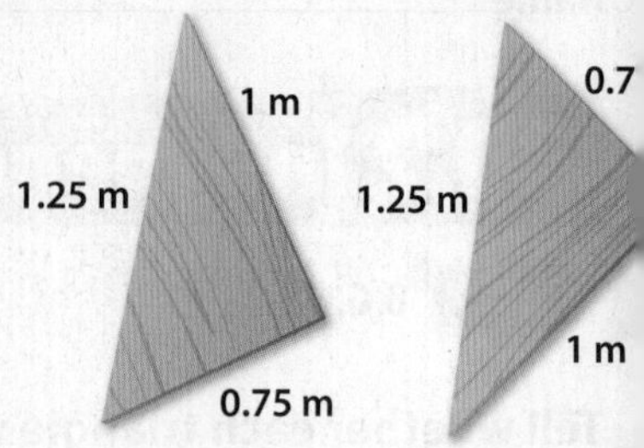

_____

_____

_____

1 m
0.7
1.25 m   1.25 m
1 m
0.75 m

20. Critique Reasoning Shoshanna says that a triangle with side lengths 17 m, 8 m, and 15 m is not a right triangle because $17^2 + 8^2 = 353$, $15^2 = 225$, and $353 \neq 225$. Is she correct? Explain.

_____

_____

H.O.T. **FOCUS ON HIGHER ORDER THINKING**

Work Area

21. Make a Conjecture Diondre says that he can take any right triangle and make a new right triangle just by doubling the side lengths. Is Diondre's conjecture true? Test his conjecture using three different right triangles.

_____

_____

_____

_____

22. Draw Conclusions A diagonal of a parallelogram measures 37 inches. The sides measure 35 inches and 1 foot. Is the parallelogram a rectangle? Explain your reasoning.

_____

_____

_____

23. Represent Real-World Problems A soccer coach is marking the lines for a soccer field on a large recreation field. The dimensions of the field are to be 90 yards by 48 yards. Describe a procedure she could use to confirm that the sides of the field meet at right angles.

_____

_____

_____

Triple Concentration

INSTRUCTIONS

Playing the Game

STEP 1 Complete the Pythagorean Triples Worksheet to use as a reference for Pythagorean triples throughout the game.

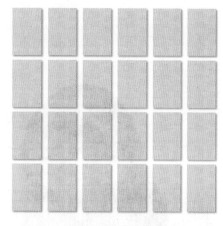

Pythagorean Triples Worksheet A

Find the missing third number in each Pythagorean triple to complete the table. *HINT*: Multiples of Pythagorean triple are also Pythagorean triples.

$a^2 + b^2 = c^2$	a	b	c
$3^2 + 4^2 = \boxed{}^2$	3	4	
$6^2 + \boxed{}^2 = 10^2$	6		10
$\boxed{}^2 + 12^2 = 15^2$		12	15
$12^2 + 16^2 = \boxed{}^2$	12	16	
$5^2 + \boxed{}^2 = 13^2$	5		13
$\boxed{}^2 + 24^2 = 26^2$		24	26
$7^2 + 24^2 = \boxed{}^2$	7	24	
$8^2 + \boxed{}^2 = 17^2$	8		17

STEP 2 Arrange the 24 game cards randomly facedown in rows.

STEP 3 To start the game, each player turns over one card. The player whose card shows the largest number is Player 1, and will go first. Players observe the numbers showing, and then the cards are turned facedown again.

This is Player 1.

STEP 4 Players take turns moving clockwise.

When it is your turn, flip over any three cards, one at a time. Make sure that all players observe the cards. If the numbers shown form a Pythagorean triple, then pick up the cards, keep them, and take another turn. If they do not form a Pythagorean triple, then turn the cards facedown again in their original positions, and continue playing the game.

Is this a Pythagorean Triple?

STEP 5 Continue until all of the cards are removed.

 ## Winning the Game

The player with the most triples at the end of the game wins.

Distance Between Two Points

COMMON CORE 8.G.8

Apply the Pythagorean Theorem to find the distance between two points in a coordinate system.

ESSENTIAL QUESTION

How can you use the Pythagorean Theorem to find the distance between two points on a coordinate plane?

EXPLORE ACTIVITY 8.G.8

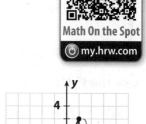

Math On the Spot
⏻ my.hrw.com

Pythagorean Theorem in the Coordinate Plane

EXAMPLE 1 The figure shows a right triangle. Approximate the length of the hypotenuse to the nearest tenth using a calculator.

STEP 1 Find the length of each leg.

The length of the vertical leg is _____ units.

The length of the horizontal leg is _____ units.

STEP 2 Let $a = 4$ and $b = 2$. Let c represent the length of the hypotenuse.

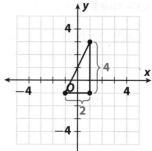

Use the Pythagorean Theorem to find c.　　　$a^2 + b^2 = c^2$

Substitute into the formula.　　$\boxed{}^2 + \boxed{}^2 = c^2$

Simplify.　　$\boxed{} = c^2$

Take the square root of both sides.　　$\sqrt{\boxed{}} = c$

Use a calculator. Round to the nearest tenth.　　$\boxed{} \approx c$

STEP 3 Check for reasonableness by finding perfect squares close to 20.

$\sqrt{20}$ is between $\sqrt{16}$ and $\sqrt{25}$.　　　$\sqrt{16} < \boxed{} < \sqrt{25}$

Simplify.　　$\boxed{} < \boxed{} < 5$

Because 4.5 is between _____ and _____, the answer is reasonable.

The hypotenuse is about 4.5 units long.

YOUR TURN

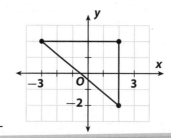

1. Approximate the length of the hypotenuse to the nearest tenth using a calculator.

_____

Personal Math Trainer

Online Assessment and Intervention

⏻ my.hrw.com

Finding the Distance Between Any Two Points

The Pythagorean Theorem can be used to find the distance between any two points (x_1, y_1) and (x_2, y_2) in the coordinate plane. The resulting expression is called the Distance Formula.

> ### Distance Formula
>
> In a coordinate plane, the distance d between two points (x_1, y_1) and (x_2, y_2) is
> $$d = \sqrt{(x_2 - x_1)^2 + (y_2 - y_1)^2}.$$

Use the Pythagorean Theorem to derive the Distance Formula.

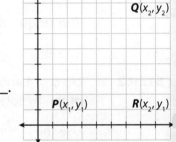

A To find the distance between points P and Q, draw segment $\overline{PQ}$ and label its length d. Then draw horizontal segment $\overline{PR}$ and vertical segment $\overline{QR}$. Label the lengths of these segments a and b. Triangle

    PQR is a _____ triangle, with hypotenuse _____.

B Since $\overline{PR}$ is a horizontal segment, its length, a, is the difference

    between its x-coordinates. Therefore, $a = x_2 -$ _____.

C Since $\overline{QR}$ is a vertical segment, its length, b, is the difference between

    its y-coordinates. Therefore, $b = y_2 -$ _____.

D Use the Pythagorean Theorem to find d, the length of segment $\overline{PQ}$. Substitute the expressions from **B** and **C** for a and b.

$$d^2 = a^2 + b^2$$

$$d = \sqrt{a^2 + b^2}$$

$$d = \sqrt{\left(\bigcirc - \bigcirc\right)^2 + \left(\bigcirc - \bigcirc\right)^2}$$

> ### Math Talk
> **Mathematical Practices**
>
> What do $x_2 - x_1$ and $y_2 - y_1$ represent in terms of the Pythagorean Theorem?

Reflect

2. Why are the coordinates of point R the ordered pair (x_2, y_1)?

_____

_____

_____

Finding the Distance Between Two Points

The Pythagorean Theorem can be used to find the distance between two points in a real-world situation. You can do this by using a coordinate grid that overlays a diagram of the real-world situation.

Math On the Spot

my.hrw.com

EXAMPLE 2 COMMON CORE 8.G.8

Francesca wants to find the distance between her house on one side of a lake and the beach on the other side. She marks off a third point forming a right triangle, as shown. The distances in the diagram are measured in meters.

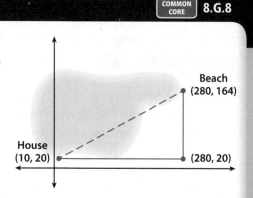

Beach (280, 164)

House (10, 20)

(280, 20)

Use the Pythagorean Theorem to find the straight-line distance from Francesca's house to the beach.

STEP 1 Find the length of the horizontal leg.

The length of the horizontal leg is the absolute value of the difference between the x-coordinates of the points (280, 20) and (10, 20).

$$|280 - 10| = 270$$

The length of the horizontal leg is 270 meters.

STEP 2 Find the length of the vertical leg.

The length of the vertical leg is the absolute value of the difference between the y-coordinates of the points (280, 164) and (280, 20).

$$|164 - 20| = 144$$

The length of the vertical leg is 144 meters.

STEP 3 Let $a = 270$ and $b = 144$. Let c represent the length of the hypotenuse. Use the Pythagorean Theorem to find c.

$$a^2 + b^2 = c^2$$

$270^2 + 144^2 = c^2$ Substitute into the formula.

$72{,}900 + 20{,}736 = c^2$ Simplify.

$93{,}636 = c^2$ Add.

$\sqrt{93{,}636} = c$ Take the square root of both sides.

$306 = c$ Simplify.

The distance from Francesca's house to the beach is 306 meters.

> **Math Talk**
> **Mathematical Practices**
>
> Why is it necessary to take the absolute value of the coordinates when finding the length of a segment?

Reflect

3. Show how you could use the Distance Formula to find the distance from Francesca's house to the beach.

_____

_____

_____

YOUR TURN

4. Camp Sunshine is also on the lake. Use the Pythagorean Theorem to find the distance between Francesca's house and Camp Sunshine to the nearest tenth of a meter.

_____

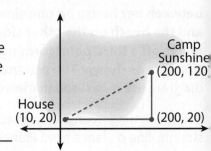

Camp Sunshine (200, 120)

House (10, 20)   (200, 20)

Guided Practice

1. Approximate the length of the hypotenuse of the right triangle to the nearest tenth using a calculator. (Explore Activity Example 1)   _____

2. Find the distance between the points (3, 7) and (15, 12) on the coordinate plane. (Explore Activity 2) _____

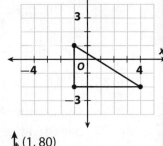

3. A plane leaves an airport and flies due north. Two minutes later, a second plane leaves the same airport flying due east. The flight plan shows the coordinates of the two planes 10 minutes later. The distances in the graph are measured in miles. Use the Pythagorean Theorem to find the distance shown between the two planes.

(Example 2) _____

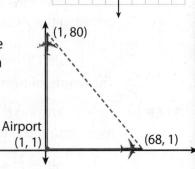

(1, 80)

Airport (1, 1)   (68, 1)

❓ ESSENTIAL QUESTION CHECK-IN

4. Describe two ways to find the distance between two points on a coordinate plane.

_____

_____

_____

20.3 Independent Practice

COMMON CORE 8.G.8

Personal Math Trainer

Online Assessment and Intervention

my.hrw.com

5. A metal worker traced a triangular piece of sheet metal on a coordinate plane, as shown. The units represent inches. What is the length of the longest side of the metal triangle? Approximate the length to the nearest tenth of an inch using a calculator. Check that your answer is reasonable.

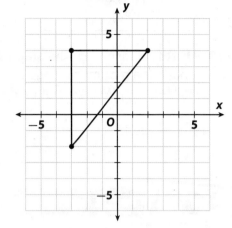

_____

6. When a coordinate grid is superimposed on a map of Harrisburg, the high school is located at (17, 21) and the town park is located at (28, 13). If each unit represents 1 mile, how many miles apart are the high school and the town park? Round your answer to the nearest tenth.

_____

7. The coordinates of the vertices of a rectangle are given by $R(-3, -4)$, $E(-3, 4)$, $C(4, 4)$, and $T(4, -4)$. Plot these points on the coordinate plane at the right and connect them to draw the rectangle. Then connect points E and T to form diagonal $\overline{ET}$.

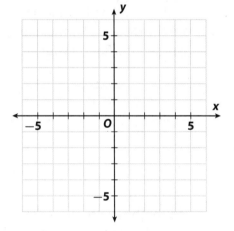

a. Use the Pythagorean Theorem to find the exact length of $\overline{ET}$.

_____

b. How can you use the Distance Formula to find the length of $\overline{ET}$? Show that the Distance Formula gives the same answer.

_____

_____

_____

_____

_____

_____

8. Multistep The locations of three ships are represented on a coordinate grid by the following points: $P(-2, 5)$, $Q(-7, -5)$, and $R(2, -3)$. Which ships are farthest apart?

_____

9. **Make a Conjecture** Find as many points as you can that are 5 units from the origin. Make a conjecture about the shape formed if all the points 5 units from the origin were connected.

_____

_____

10. **Justify Reasoning** The graph shows the location of a motion detector that has a maximum range of 34 feet. A peacock at point *P* displays its tail feathers. Will the motion detector sense this motion? Explain.

_____

_____

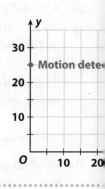

H.O.T. **FOCUS ON HIGHER ORDER THINKING**

Work Area

11. **Persevere in Problem Solving** One leg of an isosceles right triangle has endpoints (1, 1) and (6, 1). The other leg passes through the point (6, 2). Draw the triangle on the coordinate plane. Then show how you can use the Distance Formula to find the length of the hypotenuse. Round your answer to the nearest tenth.

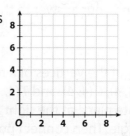

_____

_____

_____

12. **Represent Real-World Problems** The figure shows a representation of a football field. The units represent yards. A sports analyst marks the locations of the football from where it was thrown (point *A*) and where it was caught (point *B*). Explain how you can use the Pythagorean Theorem to find the distance the ball was thrown. Then find the distance.

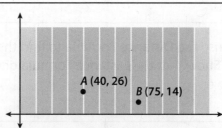

_____

_____

_____

_____

Ready to Go On?

Personal Math Trainer
Online Assessment and Intervention
⏻ my.hrw.com

20.1 The Pythagorean Theorem

Find the length of the missing side.

1.

35 m

21 m

_____

2.

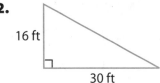

16 ft

30 ft

_____

20.2 Converse of the Pythagorean Theorem

Tell whether each triangle with the given side lengths is a right triangle.

3. 11, 60, 61 _____

4. 9, 37, 40 _____

5. 15, 35, 38 _____

6. 28, 45, 53 _____

7. Keelie has a triangular-shaped card. The lengths of its sides are 4.5 cm, 6 cm, and 7.5 cm. Is the card a right triangle? _____

20.3 Distance Between Two Points

Find the distance between the given points. Round to the nearest tenth.

8. *A* and *B* _____

9. *B* and *C* _____

10. *A* and *C* _____

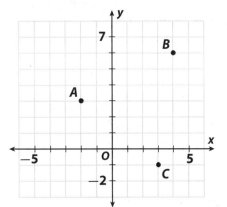

? **ESSENTIAL QUESTION**

11. How can you use the Pythagorean Theorem to solve real-world problems?

_____

_____

_____

Selected Response

1. What is the missing length of the side?

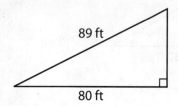

89 ft

80 ft

Ⓐ 9 ft   Ⓒ 39 ft

Ⓑ 30 ft   Ⓓ 120 ft

2. Which relation does **not** represent a function?

Ⓐ (0, 8), (3, 8), (1, 6)

Ⓑ (4, 2), (6, 1), (8, 9)

Ⓒ (1, 20), (2, 23), (9, 26)

Ⓓ (0, 3), (2, 3), (2, 0)

3. Two sides of a right triangle have lengths of 72 cm and 97 cm. The third side is **not** the hypotenuse. How long is the third side?

Ⓐ 25 cm   Ⓒ 65 cm

Ⓑ 45 cm   Ⓓ 121 cm

4. To the nearest tenth, what is the distance between point *F* and point *G*?

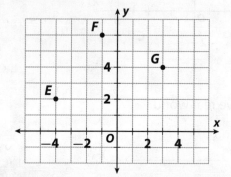

Ⓐ 4.5 units   Ⓒ 7.3 units

Ⓑ 5.0 units   Ⓓ 20 units

5. A flagpole is 53 feet tall. A rope is tied to the top of the flagpole and secured to the ground 28 feet from the base of the flagpole. What is the length of the rope?

Ⓐ 25 feet   Ⓒ 53 feet

Ⓑ 45 feet   Ⓓ 60 feet

6. Which set of lengths are **not** the side lengths of a right triangle?

Ⓐ 36, 77, 85   Ⓒ 27, 120, 123

Ⓑ 20, 99, 101   Ⓓ 24, 33, 42

7. A triangle has one right angle. What could the measures of the other two angles be?

Ⓐ 25° and 65°   Ⓒ 55° and 125°

Ⓑ 30° and 15°   Ⓓ 90° and 100°

Mini-Task

8. A fallen tree is shown on the coordinate grid below. Each unit represents 1 meter.

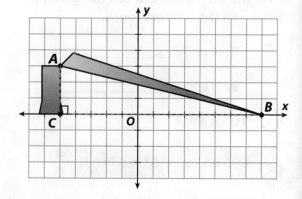

a. What is the distance from *A* to *B*?

_____

b. What was the height of the tree before it fell?

_____

Volume

MODULE

21

COMMON CORE

LESSON 21.1
Volume of Cylinders
COMMON CORE 8.G.9

LESSON 21.2
Volume of Cones
COMMON CORE 8.G.9

LESSON 21.3
Volume of Spheres
COMMON CORE 8.G.9

 ESSENTIAL QUESTION

How can you use volume to solve real-world problems?

Real-World Video

Many foods are in the shape of cylinders, cones, and spheres. To find out how much of the food you are eating, you can use formulas for volume.

⏻ my.hrw.com

 GO DIGITAL

my.hrw.com

 my.hrw.com

Go digital with your write-in student edition, accessible on any device.

 Math On the Spot

Scan with your smart phone to jump directly to the online edition, video tutor, and more.

 Animated Math

Interactively explore key concepts to see how math works.

 Personal Math Trainer

Get immediate feedback and help as you work through practice sets.

659

Are YOU Ready?

Complete these exercises to review skills you will need for this module.

Exponents

> **EXAMPLE** $6^3 = 6 \times 6 \times 6$ Multiply the base (6) by itself the number of times indicated by the exponent (3).
>
> $\qquad = 36 \times 6$ Find the product of the first two terms.
>
> $\qquad = 216$ Find the product of all the terms.

Evaluate each exponential expression.

1. 11^2 _____   2. 2^5 _____   3. $\left(\frac{1}{5}\right)^3$ _____   4. $(0.3)^2$ _____

5. 2.1^3 _____   6. 0.1^3 _____   7. $\left(\frac{9.6}{3}\right)^2$ _____   8. 100^3 _____

Round Decimals

> **EXAMPLE** Round 43.2685 to the underlined place.
>
> $43.2685 \rightarrow 43.27$
>
> The digit to be rounded: 6
> The digit to its right is 8.
> 8 is *5 or greater*, so round *up*.
> The rounded number is 43.27.

Round to the underlined place.

9. 2.3<u>7</u>4 _____   10. 12<u>6</u>.399 _____   11. 13.<u>9</u>577 _____   12. 42.6<u>9</u>0 _____

13. 134.<u>9</u>5 _____   14. 2.<u>0</u>486 _____   15. 63.6<u>3</u>52 _____   16. 98.<u>9</u>499 _____

Simplify Numerical Expressions

> **EXAMPLE** $\frac{1}{3}(3.14)(4)^2(3) = \frac{1}{3}(3.14)(16)(3)$ Simplify the exponent.
>
> $\qquad = 50.24$ Multiply from left to right.

Simplify each expression.

17. $3.14\,(5)^2\,(10)$ _____   18. $\frac{1}{3}(3.14)(3)^2(5)$ _____   19. $\frac{4}{3}(3.14)(3)^3$ _____

20. $\frac{4}{3}(3.14)(6)^3$ _____   21. $3.14\,(4)^2\,(9)$ _____   22. $\frac{1}{3}(3.14)(9)^2\left(\frac{2}{3}\right)$ _____

Reading Start-Up

Visualize Vocabulary

Use the ✔ words to complete the empty columns in the chart. You may use words more than once.

Shape	Distance Around	Attributes	Associated Review Words
circle		r, d	
square		90° corner, sides	
rectangle		90° corner, sides	

Understand Vocabulary

Complete the sentences using the preview words.

1. A three-dimensional figure that has one vertex and one circular base is a _____.

2. A three-dimensional figure with all points the same distance from the center is a _____.

3. A three-dimensional figure that has two congruent circular bases is a _____.

Active Reading

Three-Panel Flip Chart Before beginning the module, create a three-panel flip chart to help you organize what you learn. Label each flap with one of the lesson titles from this module. As you study each lesson, write important ideas like vocabulary, properties, and formulas under the appropriate flap.

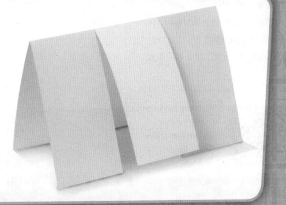

MODULE 21

Unpacking the Standards

Understanding the standards and the vocabulary terms in the standards will help you know exactly what you are expected to learn in this module.

COMMON CORE **8.G.9**

Know the formulas for the volumes of cones, cylinders, and spheres and use them to solve real-world and mathematical problems.

Key Vocabulary

volume *(volumen)*
The number of cubic units needed to fill a given space.

cylinder *(cilindro)*
A three-dimensional figure with two parallel, congruent circular bases connected by a curved lateral surface.

What It Means to You

You will learn the formula for the volume of a cylinder.

UNPACKING EXAMPLE 8.G.9

The Asano Taiko Company of Japan built the world's largest drum in 2000. The drum's diameter is 4.8 meters, and its height is 4.95 meters. Estimate the volume of the drum.

$d = 4.8 \approx 5$

$h = 4.95 \approx 5$

$r = \dfrac{d}{2} \approx \dfrac{5}{2} = 2.5$

$V = (\pi r^2)h$ — Volume of a cylinder

$\approx (3)(2.5)^2 \cdot 5$ — Use 3 for π.

$= (3)(6.25)(5)$

$= 18.75 \cdot 5$

$= 93.75 \approx 94$

The volume of the drum is approximately 94 m³.

COMMON CORE **8.G.9**

Know the formulas for the volumes of cones, cylinders, and spheres and use them to solve real-world and mathematical problems.

Key Vocabulary

cone *(cono)*
A three-dimensional figure with one vertex and one circular base.

sphere *(esfera)*
A three-dimensional figure with all points the same distance from the center.

What It Means to You

You will learn formulas for the volume of a cone and a sphere.

UNPACKING EXAMPLE 8.G.9

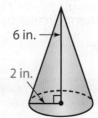

6 in.

2 in.

Find the volume of the cone. Use 3.14 for π.

$B = \pi(2^2) = 4\pi$ in²

$V = \dfrac{1}{3} \cdot 4\pi \cdot 6$ $V = \dfrac{1}{3}Bh$

$V = 8\pi$ Use 3.14 for π.

≈ 25.1 in³

The volume of the cone is approximately 25.1 in³.

The volume of a sphere with the same radius is
$V = \dfrac{4}{3}\pi r^3 \approx \dfrac{4}{3}(3)(2)^3 = 32$ in³.

Visit **my.hrw.com** to see all the **Common Core Standards** unpacked.

my.hrw.com

LESSON
21.1 Volume of Cylinders

COMMON CORE **8.G.9**
Know the formulas for the volumes of…cylinders…and use them to solve real-world and mathematical problems.

> **ESSENTIAL QUESTION**
> How do you find the volume of a cylinder?

EXPLORE ACTIVITY COMMON CORE **8.G.9**

Modeling the Volume of a Cylinder

A **cylinder** is a three-dimensional figure that has two congruent circular bases that lie in parallel planes. The volume of any three-dimensional figure is the number of cubic units needed to fill the space taken up by the solid figure.

One cube represents one cubic unit of volume. You can develop the formula for the volume of a cylinder using an empty soup can or other cylindrical container. First, remove one of the bases.

A Arrange centimeter cubes in a single layer at the bottom of the cylinder. Fit as many cubes into the layer as possible. How many cubes are in this layer?

_____

B To find how many layers of cubes fit in the cylinder, make a stack of cubes along the inside of the cylinder. How many layers fit in the cylinder?

_____

C How can you use what you know to find the approximate number of cubes that would fit in the cylinder?

_____

_____

Reflect

1. **Make a Conjecture** Suppose you know the area of the base of a cylinder and the height of the cylinder. How can you find the cylinder's volume?

_____

2. Let the area of the base of a cylinder be *B* and the height of the cylinder be *h*. Write a formula for the cylinder's volume *V*. _____

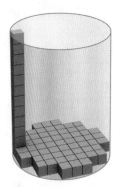

Finding the Volume of a Cylinder Using a Formula

Finding volumes of cylinders is similar to finding volumes of prisms. You find the volume V of both a prism and a cylinder by multiplying the height h by the area of the base B, so $V = Bh$.

The base of a cylinder is a circle, so for a cylinder, $B = \pi r^2$.

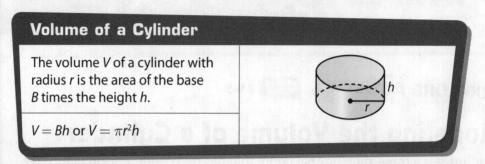

Volume of a Cylinder

The volume V of a cylinder with radius r is the area of the base B times the height h.

$V = Bh$ or $V = \pi r^2 h$

EXAMPLE 1

COMMON CORE 8.G.9

Find the volume of each cylinder. Round your answers to the nearest tenth if necessary. Use 3.14 for π.

My Notes

A

10 in.

3 in.

$V = \pi r^2 h$

$\approx 3.14 \cdot 3^2 \cdot 10$ Substitute.

$\approx 3.14 \cdot 9 \cdot 10$ Simplify.

≈ 282.6 Multiply.

The volume is about 282.6 in³.

B 6.4 cm   13 cm

Since the diameter is 6.4 cm, the radius is 3.2 cm.

$V = \pi r^2 h$

$\approx 3.14 \cdot 3.2^2 \cdot 13$ Substitute.

$\approx 3.14 \cdot 10.24 \cdot 13$ Simplify.

≈ 418 Multiply.

Recall that the diameter of a circle is twice the radius, so $2r = d$ and $r = \frac{d}{2}$.

The volume is about 418 cm³.

Reflect

3. **What If?** If you want a formula for the volume of a cylinder that involves the diameter d instead of the radius r, how can you rewrite it?

_____

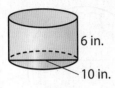

YOUR TURN

Find the volume of each cylinder. Round your answers to the nearest tenth if necessary. Use 3.14 for π.

4.

6 in.

10 in.

_____

5.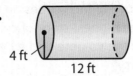

4 ft

12 ft

_____

Finding the Volume of a Cylinder in a Real-World Context

The Longhorn Band at the University of Texas at Austin has one of the world's largest bass drums, known as Big Bertha.

EXAMPLE 2 Real World

COMMON CORE 8.G.9

Big Bertha has a diameter of 8 feet and is 4.5 feet deep. Find the volume of the drum to the nearest tenth. Use 3.14 for π.

STEP 1 Find the radius of the drum.

$$r = \frac{d}{2} = \frac{8}{2} = 4 \text{ ft}$$

STEP 2 Find the volume of the drum.

$V = \pi r^2 h$

$\approx 3.14 \cdot 4^2 \cdot 4.5$ Substitute.

$\approx 3.14 \cdot 16 \cdot 4.5$ Simplify the exponent.

≈ 226.08 Multiply.

The volume of the drum is about 226.1 ft³.

YOUR TURN

6. A drum company advertises a snare drum that is 4 inches high and 12 inches in diameter. Find the volume of the drum to the nearest tenth. Use 3.14 for π.

_____

1. **Vocabulary** Describe the bases of a cylinder. (Explore Activity)

   _____

2. Figure 1 shows a view from above of inch cubes on the bottom of a cylinder. Figure 2 shows the highest stack of cubes that will fit inside the cylinder. Estimate the volume of the cylinder. Explain your reasoning. (Explore Activity)

   _____

   _____

   _____

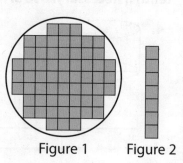

Figure 1   Figure 2

3. Find the volume of the cylinder to the nearest tenth. Use 3.14 for π. (Example 1)

   $V = \pi r^2 h$

   $V = \pi \cdot \boxed{}^2 \cdot \boxed{}$

   $\approx 3.14 \cdot \boxed{} \cdot \boxed{}$

   $\approx \boxed{}$

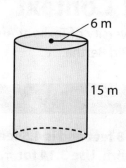

6 m

15 m

   The volume of the cylinder is approximately _____ m³.

4. A Japanese odaiko is a very large drum that is made by hollowing out a section of a tree trunk. A museum in Takayama City has three odaikos of similar size carved from a single tree trunk. The largest measures about 2.7 meters in both diameter and length, and weighs about 4.5 metric tons. Using the volume formula for a cylinder, approximate the volume of the drum to the nearest tenth. (Example 2)

   The radius of the drum is about _____ m.

   The volume of the drum is about _____ m³.

? ESSENTIAL QUESTION CHECK-IN

5. How do you find the volume of a cylinder? Describe which measurements of a cylinder you need to know.

   _____

   _____

   _____

21.1 Independent Practice

 8.G.9

Personal Math Trainer

Online Assessment and Intervention

my.hrw.com

Find the volume of each figure. Round your answers to the nearest tenth if necessary. Use 3.14 for π.

6.

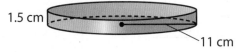

1.5 cm

11 cm

_____

7.

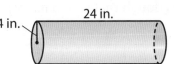

24 in.

4 in.

_____

8.

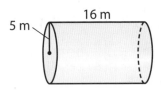

16 m

5 m

_____

9.

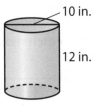

10 in.

12 in.

_____

10. A cylinder has a radius of 4 centimeters and a height of 40 centimeters.

_____

11. A cylinder has a radius of 8 meters and a height of 4 meters.

_____

Round your answer to the nearest tenth, if necessary. Use 3.14 for π.

12. The cylindrical Giant Ocean Tank at the New England Aquarium in Boston is 24 feet deep and has a radius of 18.8 feet. Find the volume of the tank.

_____

13. A standard-size bass drum has a diameter of 22 inches and is 18 inches deep. Find the volume of this drum.

_____

14. Grain is stored in cylindrical structures called silos. Find the volume of a silo with a diameter of 11.1 feet and a height of 20 feet.

_____

15. The Frank Erwin Center, or "The Drum," at the University of Texas in Austin can be approximated by a cylinder that is 120 meters in diameter and 30 meters in height. Find its volume.

_____

16. A barrel of crude oil contains about 5.61 cubic feet of oil. How many barrels of oil are contained in 1 mile (5280 feet) of a pipeline that has an inside diameter of 6 inches and is completely filled with oil? How much is "1 mile" of oil in this pipeline worth at a price of $100 per barrel?

_____

17. A pan for baking French bread is shaped like half a cylinder. It is 12 inches long and 3.5 inches in diameter. What is the volume of uncooked dough that would fill this pan?

3.5 in.

12 in.

_____

H.O.T. FOCUS ON HIGHER ORDER THINKING

18. Explain the Error A student said the volume of a cylinder with a 3-inch diameter is two times the volume of a cylinder with the same height and a 1.5-inch radius. What is the error?

Work Area

_____

_____

_____

19. Communicate Mathematical Ideas Explain how you can find the height of a cylinder if you know the diameter and the volume. Include an example with your explanation.

_____

_____

_____

_____

_____

20. Analyze Relationships Cylinder A has a radius of 6 centimeters. Cylinder B has the same height and a radius half as long as cylinder A. What fraction of the volume of cylinder A is the volume of cylinder B? Explain.

_____

_____

_____

21.2 Volume of Cones

COMMON CORE 8.G.9

Know the formulas for the volumes of cones...and use them to solve real-world and mathematical problems.

ESSENTIAL QUESTION

How do you find the volume of a cone?

EXPLORE ACTIVITY **COMMON CORE** 8.G.9

Modeling the Volume of a Cone

A **cone** is a three-dimensional figure that has one vertex and one circular base.

To explore the volume of a cone, Sandi does an experiment with a cone and a cylinder that have congruent bases and heights. She fills the cone with popcorn kernels and then pours the kernels into the cylinder. She repeats this until the cylinder is full.

Sandi finds that it takes **3 cones** to fill the volume of the cylinder.

STEP 1 What is the formula for the volume V of a cylinder with base area B and height h? _____

STEP 2 What is the area of the base of the cone? _____

STEP 3 Sandi found that, when the bases and height are the same,

_____ times $V_{cone} = V_{cylinder}$.

STEP 4 How does the volume of the cone compare to the volume of the cylinder?

Volume of the cone: $\quad V_{cone} = \dfrac{\Box}{\Box} \cdot V_{cylinder}$

Reflect

1. Use the conclusion from this experiment to write a formula for the volume of a cone in terms of the height and the radius. Explain.

   _____

2. How do you think the formula for the volume of a cone is similar to the formula for the volume of a pyramid?

   _____

Finding the Volume of a Cone Using a Formula

The formulas for the volume of a prism and the volume of a cylinder are the same: multiply the height h by the area of the base B, so $V = Bh$.

In the **Explore Activity**, you saw that the volume of a cone is one third the volume of a cylinder with the same base and height.

Volume of a Cone

The volume V of a cone with radius r is one third the area of the base B times the height h. $V = \frac{1}{3} Bh$ or $V = \frac{1}{3} \pi r^2 h$	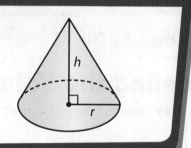

My Notes

EXAMPLE 1

Find the volume of each cone. Round your answers to the nearest tenth. Use 3.14 for π.

A

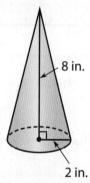

8 in.

2 in.

$V = \frac{1}{3} \pi r^2 h$

$\approx \frac{1}{3} \cdot 3.14 \cdot 2^2 \cdot 8$ Substitute.

$\approx \frac{1}{3} \cdot 3.14 \cdot 4 \cdot 8$ Simplify.

≈ 33.5 Multiply.

The volume is about 33.5 in³.

B Since the diameter is 8 ft, the radius is 4 ft.

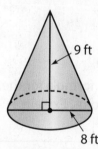

9 ft

8 ft

$V = \frac{1}{3} \pi r^2 h$

$\approx \frac{1}{3} \cdot 3.14 \cdot 4^2 \cdot 9$ Substitute.

$\approx \frac{1}{3} \cdot 3.14 \cdot 16 \cdot 9$ Simplify.

≈ 150.7 Multiply.

The volume is about 150.7 ft³.

Reflect

3. How can you rewrite the formula for the volume of a cone using the diameter d instead of the radius r? _____

YOUR TURN

Find the volume of each cone. Round your answers to the nearest tenth. Use 3.14 for π.

4.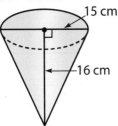
15 cm
16 cm

_____

5.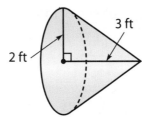
3 ft
2 ft

_____

Finding the Volume of a Volcano

The mountain created by a volcano is often cone-shaped.

EXAMPLE 2 Real World   COMMON CORE 8.G.9

Math On the Spot
⊙ my.hrw.com

For her geography project, Karen built a clay model of a volcano in the shape of a cone. Her model has a diameter of 12 inches and a height of 8 inches. Find the volume of clay in her model to the nearest tenth. Use 3.14 for π.

STEP 1 Find the radius.
$$r = \frac{12}{2} = 6 \text{ in.}$$

STEP 2 Find the volume of clay.

$V = \frac{1}{3}\pi r^2 h$

$\approx \frac{1}{3} \cdot 3.14 \cdot 6^2 \cdot 8$ Substitute.

$\approx \frac{1}{3} \cdot 3.14 \cdot 36 \cdot 8$ Simplify.

≈ 301.44 Multiply.

The volume of the clay is about 301.4 in³.

YOUR TURN

6. The cone of the volcano Parícutin in Mexico had a height of 410 meters and a diameter of 424 meters. Approximate the volume of the cone.

_____

1. The area of the base of a cylinder is 45 square inches and its height is 10 inches. A cone has the same area for its base and the same height. What is the volume of the cone? (Explore Activity)

$$V_{\text{cylinder}} = Bh = \boxed{} \cdot \boxed{} = \boxed{}$$

$$V_{\text{cone}} = \frac{1}{3}V_{\text{cylinder}}$$

$$= \frac{1}{3}\boxed{}$$

$$= \boxed{}$$

The volume of the cone is _____ in³.

2. A cone and a cylinder have congruent height and bases. The volume of the cone is 18 m³. What is the volume of the cylinder? Explain. (Explore Activity)

_____

_____

_____

_____

_____

Find the volume of each cone. Round your answer to the nearest tenth if necessary. Use 3.14 for π. (Example 1)

3.
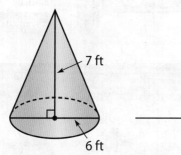
7 ft
6 ft

_____

4.
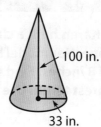
100 in.
33 in.

_____

5. Gretchen made a paper cone to hold a gift for a friend. The paper cone was 15 inches high and had a radius of 3 inches. Find the volume of the paper cone to the nearest tenth. Use 3.14 for π. (Example 2)

_____

6. A cone-shaped building is commonly used to store sand. What would be the volume of a cone-shaped building with a diameter of 50 meters and a height of 20 meters? Round your answer to the nearest tenth. Use 3.14 for π. (Example 2)

_____

 ESSENTIAL QUESTION CHECK-IN

7. How do you find the volume of a cone?

_____

_____

_____

21.2 Independent Practice

COMMON CORE 8.G.9

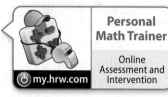

Personal
Math Trainer

Online
Assessment and
Intervention

my.hrw.com

Find the volume of each cone. Round your answers to the nearest tenth if necessary. Use 3.14 for π.

8.

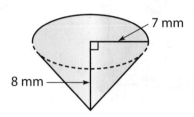

7 mm

8 mm

_____

9.

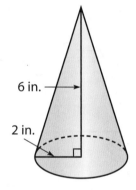

6 in.

2 in.

_____

10. A cone has a diameter of 6 centimeters and a height of 11.5 centimeters.

_____

11. A cone has a radius of 3 meters and a height of 10 meters.

_____

Round your answers to the nearest tenth if necessary. Use 3.14 for π.

12. Antonio is making mini waffle cones. Each waffle cone is 3 inches high and has a radius of $\frac{3}{4}$ inch. What is the volume of a waffle cone?

_____

13. A snack bar sells popcorn in cone-shaped containers. One container has a diameter of 8 inches and a height of 10 inches. How many cubic inches of popcorn does the container hold?

_____

14. A volcanic cone has a diameter of 300 meters and a height of 150 meters. What is the volume of the cone?

_____

15. **Multistep** Orange traffic cones come in a variety of sizes. Approximate the volume, in cubic inches, of a traffic cone that has a height of 2 feet and a diameter of 10 inches. Use 3.14 for π.

_____

Find the missing measure for each cone. Round your answers to the nearest tenth if necessary. Use 3.14 for π.

16. radius = _____

height = 6 in.

volume = 100.48 in³

17. diameter = 6 cm

height = _____

volume = 56.52 cm³

18. The diameter of a cone-shaped container is 4 inches, and its height is 6 inches. How much greater is the volume of a cylinder-shaped container with the same diameter and height? Round your answer to the nearest hundredth. Use 3.14 for π.

_____

19. Alex wants to know the volume of sand in an hourglass. When all the sand is in the bottom, he stands a ruler up beside the hourglass and estimates the height of the cone of sand.

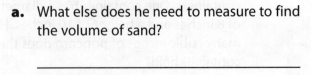

    a. What else does he need to measure to find the volume of sand?

      _____

      _____

    b. **Make a Conjecture** If the volume of sand is increasing at a constant rate, is the height increasing at a constant rate? Explain.

      _____

      _____

      _____

20. **Problem Solving** The diameter of a cone is x cm, the height is 18 cm, and the volume is 301.44 cm³. What is x? Use 3.14 for π.

_____

_____

21. **Analyze Relationships** A cone has a radius of 1 foot and a height of 2 feet. How many cones of liquid would it take to fill a cylinder with a diameter of 2 feet and a height of 2 feet? Explain.

_____

_____

_____

22. **Critique Reasoning** Herb knows that the volume of a cone is one third that of a cylinder with the same base and height. He reasons that a cone with the same height as a given cylinder but 3 times the radius should therefore have the same volume as the cylinder, since $\frac{1}{3} \cdot 3 = 1$. Is Herb correct? Explain.

_____

_____

_____

_____

_____

21.3 Volume of Spheres

COMMON CORE 8.G.9

Know the formulas for the volumes of...spheres and use them to solve real-world and mathematical problems.

ESSENTIAL QUESTION

How do you find the volume of a sphere?

EXPLORE ACTIVITY COMMON CORE 8.G.9

Modeling the Volume of a Sphere

A **sphere** is a three-dimensional figure with all points the same distance from the center. The **radius** of a sphere is the distance from the center to any point on the sphere.

You have seen that a cone fills $\frac{1}{3}$ of a cylinder of the same radius and height h. If you were to do a similar experiment with a sphere of the same radius, you would find that a sphere fills $\frac{2}{3}$ of the cylinder. The cylinder's height is equal to twice the radius of the sphere.

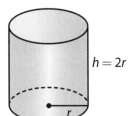 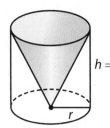 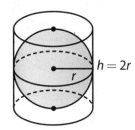

STEP 1 Write the formula $V = Bh$ for each shape. Use $B = \pi r^2$ and substitute the fractions you know for the cone and sphere.

Cylinder	Cone	Sphere
$V = \pi r^2 h$	$V = \frac{1}{3}\pi r^2 h$	$V = \frac{2}{3}\pi r^2 h$

STEP 2 Notice that a sphere always has a height equal to twice the radius. Substitute $2r$ for h.

$V = \frac{2}{3}\pi r^2(2r)$

STEP 3 Simplify this formula for the volume of a sphere.

$V = \boxed{}\pi r^3$

Reflect

1. **Analyze Relationships** A cone has a radius of r and a height of $2r$. A sphere has a radius of r. Compare the volume of the sphere and cone.

_____

_____

_____

Finding the Volume of a Sphere Using a Formula

The Explore Activity illustrates a formula for the volume of a sphere with radius r.

Volume of a Sphere

The volume V of a sphere is $\frac{4}{3}\pi$ times the cube of the radius r.

$$V = \frac{4}{3}\pi r^3$$

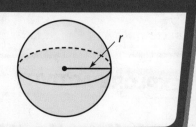

EXAMPLE 1

COMMON CORE 8.G.9

Find the volume of each sphere. Round your answers to the nearest tenth if necessary. Use 3.14 for π.

A

2.1 cm

$$V = \frac{4}{3}\pi r^3$$

$$\approx \frac{4}{3} \cdot 3.14 \cdot 2.1^3 \qquad \text{Substitute.}$$

$$\approx \frac{4}{3} \cdot 3.14 \cdot 9.26 \qquad \text{Simplify.}$$

$$\approx 38.8 \qquad \text{Multiply.}$$

The volume is about 38.8 cm³.

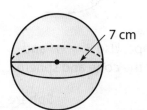

Math Talk

Mathematical Practices

If you know the diameter of a sphere, how would the formula for the volume of a sphere be written in terms of d?

B

7 cm

Since the diameter is 7 cm, the radius is 3.5 cm.

$$V = \frac{4}{3}\pi r^3$$

$$\approx \frac{4}{3} \cdot 3.14 \cdot 3.5^3 \qquad \text{Substitute.}$$

$$\approx \frac{4}{3} \cdot 3.14 \cdot 42.9 \qquad \text{Simplify.}$$

$$\approx 179.6 \qquad \text{Multiply.}$$

The volume is about 179.6 cm³.

 **YOUR TURN**

Find the volume of each sphere. Round your answers to the nearest tenth. Use 3.14 for π.

2. A sphere has a radius of 10 centimeters. _____

3. A sphere has a diameter of 3.4 meters. _____

Finding the Volume of a Sphere in a Real-World Context

Many sports, including golf and tennis, use a ball that is spherical in shape.

Math On the Spot
my.hrw.com

EXAMPLE 2 COMMON CORE 8.G.9

Soccer balls come in several different sizes. One soccer ball has a diameter of 22 centimeters. What is the volume of this soccer ball? Round your answer to the nearest tenth. Use 3.14 for π.

STEP 1 Find the radius.

$$r = \frac{d}{2} = 11 \text{ cm}$$

STEP 2 Find the volume of the soccer ball.

$$V = \frac{4}{3}\pi r^3$$

$\approx \frac{4}{3} \cdot 3.14 \cdot 11^3$ Substitute.

$\approx \frac{4}{3} \cdot 3.14 \cdot 1331$ Simplify.

≈ 5572.4533 Multiply.

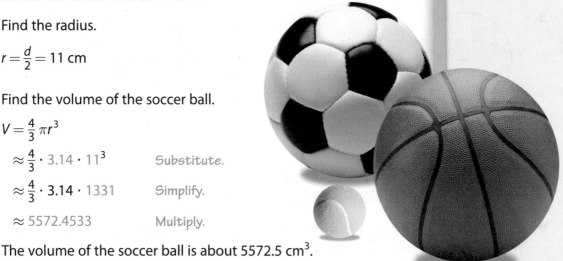

The volume of the soccer ball is about 5572.5 cm³.

Reflect

4. What is the volume of the soccer ball in terms of π, to the nearest whole number multiple? Explain your answer.

_____

_____

5. **Analyze Relationships** The diameter of a basketball is about 1.1 times that of a soccer ball. The diameter of a tennis ball is about 0.3 times that of a soccer ball. How do the volumes of these balls compare to that of a soccer ball? Explain.

_____

_____

_____

6. Val measures the diameter of a ball as 12 inches. How many cubic inches of air does this ball hold, to the nearest tenth? Use 3.14 for π.

_____

Personal Math Trainer

Online Assessment and Intervention

my.hrw.com

Guided Practice

1. **Vocabulary** A sphere is a three-dimensional figure with all points

   _____ from the center. (Explore Activity)

2. **Vocabulary** The _____ is the distance from the center
   of a sphere to a point on the sphere. (Explore Activity)

**Find the volume of each sphere. Round your answers to the nearest tenth
if necessary. Use 3.14 for π.** (Example 1)

3.

   1 in.

   _____

4.

   20 cm

   _____

5. A sphere has a radius of 1.5 feet. _____

6. A sphere has a diameter of 2 yards. _____

7. A baseball has a diameter of 2.9 inches. Find the volume of the baseball. Round
   your answer to the nearest tenth if necessary. Use 3.14 for π. (Example 2) _____

8. A basketball has a radius of 4.7 inches. What is its volume to the nearest
   cubic inch. Use 3.14 for π. (Example 2) _____

9. A company is deciding whether to package a ball
   in a cubic box or a cylindrical box. In either case,
   the ball will touch the bottom, top, and sides.
   (Explore Activity)

   a. What portion of the space inside the cylindrical
      box is empty? Explain.

      _____

   b. Find an expression for the volume of the cubic box. _____

   c. About what portion of the space inside the cubic box is empty? Explain.

      _____

      _____

? ESSENTIAL QUESTION CHECK-IN

10. Explain the steps you use to find the volume of a sphere.

    _____

21.3 Independent Practice

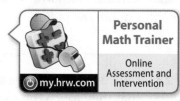

Personal Math Trainer

Online Assessment and Intervention

my.hrw.com

Find the volume of each sphere. Round your answers to the nearest tenth if necessary. Use 3.14 for π.

11. radius of 3.1 meters _____

12. diameter of 18 inches _____

13. $r = 6$ in. _____

14. $d = 36$ m _____

15.

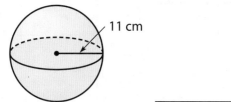

11 cm

_____

16.

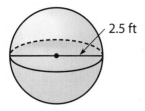

2.5 ft

_____

The eggs of birds and other animals come in many different shapes and sizes. Eggs often have a shape that is nearly spherical. When this is true, you can use the formula for a sphere to find their volume.

17. The green turtle lays eggs that are approximately spherical with an average diameter of 4.5 centimeters. Each turtle lays an average of 113 eggs at one time. Find the total volume of these eggs, to the nearest cubic centimeter.

_____

18. Hummingbirds lay eggs that are nearly spherical and about 1 centimeter in diameter. Find the volume of an egg. Round your answer to the nearest tenth.

_____

19. Fossilized spherical eggs of dinosaurs called titanosaurid sauropods were found in Patagonia. These eggs were 15 centimeters in diameter. Find the volume of an egg. Round your answer to the nearest tenth.

_____

20. **Persevere in Problem Solving** An ostrich egg has about the same volume as a sphere with a diameter of 5 inches. If the eggshell is about $\frac{1}{12}$ inch thick, find the volume of just the shell, not including the interior of the egg. Round your answer to the nearest tenth.

_____

21. **Multistep** Write the steps you would use to find a formula for the volume of the figure at right. Then write the formula.

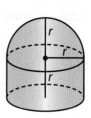

_____

_____

_____

_____

_____

_____

_____

_____

_____

_____

22. Critical Thinking Explain what happens to the volume of a sphere if you double the radius.

_____

23. Multistep A cylindrical can of tennis balls holds a stack of three balls so that they touch the can at the top, bottom, and sides. The radius of each ball is 1.25 inches. Find the volume inside the can that is not taken up by the three tennis balls.

_____

H.O.T. **FOCUS ON HIGHER ORDER THINKING**

24. Critique Reasoning A sphere has a radius of 4 inches, and a cube-shaped box has an edge length of 7.5 inches. J.D. says the box has a greater volume, so the sphere will fit in the box. Is he correct? Explain.

_____

_____

_____

25. Critical Thinking Which would hold the most water: a bowl in the shape of a hemisphere with radius r, a cylindrical glass with radius r and height r, or a cone-shaped drinking cup with radius r and height r? Explain.

_____

_____

_____

26. Analyze Relationships Hari has models of a sphere, a cylinder, and a cone. The sphere's diameter and the cylinder's height are the same, $2r$. The cylinder has radius r. The cone has diameter $2r$ and height $2r$. Compare the volumes of the cone and the sphere to the volume of the cylinder.

_____

_____

_____

27. A spherical helium balloon that is 8 feet in diameter can lift about 17 pounds. What does the diameter of a balloon need to be to lift a person who weighs 136 pounds? Explain.

_____

_____

_____

Ready to Go On?

21.1 Volume of Cylinders

Find the volume of each cylinder. Round your answers to the nearest tenth if necessary. Use 3.14 for π.

1. 6 ft

8 ft

_____

2. A can of juice has a radius of 4 inches and a height of 7 inches. What is the volume of the can?

_____

21.2 Volume of Cones

Find the volume of each cone. Round your answers to the nearest tenth if necessary. Use 3.14 for π.

3.

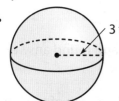

15 cm

6 cm _____

4.

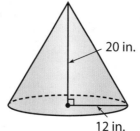

20 in.

12 in. _____

21.3 Volume of Spheres

Find the volume of each sphere. Round your answers to the nearest tenth if necessary. Use 3.14 for π.

5.

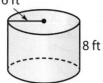

3 ft

_____

6.

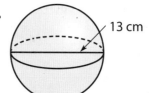

13 cm

_____

? ESSENTIAL QUESTION

7. What measurements do you need to know to find the volume of a cylinder? a cone? a sphere?

_____

_____

MODULE 21 MIXED REVIEW

Assessment Readiness

COMMON CORE

Personal Math Trainer

Online Assessment and Intervention

my.hrw.com

Selected Response

1. The bed of a pickup truck measures 4 feet by 8 feet. To the nearest inch, what is the length of the longest thin metal bar that will lie flat in the bed?

(A) 11 ft 3 in.   (C) 8 ft 11 in.

(B) 10 ft 0 in.   (D) 8 ft 9 in.

2. Using 3.14 for π, what is the volume of the cylinder below to the nearest tenth?

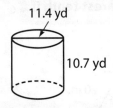

11.4 yd

10.7 yd

(A) 102 cubic yards

(B) 347.6 cubic yards

(C) 1,091.6 cubic yards

(D) 4,366.4 cubic yards

3. Rhett made mini waffle cones for a birthday party. Each waffle cone was 3.5 inches high and had a radius of 0.8 inches. What is the volume of each cone to the nearest hundredth?

(A) 1.70 cubic inches

(B) 2.24 cubic inches

(C) 2.34 cubic inches

(D) 8.79 cubic inches

4. What is the volume of a cone that has a height of 17 meters and a base with a radius of 6 meters? Use 3.14 for π and round to the nearest tenth.

(A) 204 cubic meters

(B) 640.6 cubic meters

(C) 2,562.2 cubic meters

(D) 10,249 cubic meters

5. Using 3.14 for π, what is the volume of the sphere to the nearest tenth?

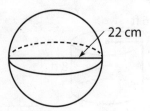

22 cm

(A) 4180 cubic centimeters

(B) 5572.5 cubic centimeters

(C) 33,434.7 cubic centimeters

(D) 44,579.6 cubic centimeters

Mini-Task

6. A diagram of a deodorant container is shown. It is made up of a cylinder and half of a sphere.

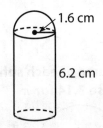

1.6 cm

6.2 cm

Use 3.14 for π and round answers to the nearest tenth.

a. What is the volume of the half sphere?

_____

b. What is the volume of the cylinder?

_____

c. What is the volume of the whole figure?

_____

UNIT 9

Study Guide Review

MODULE 19

Angle Relationships in Parallel Lines and Triangles

ESSENTIAL QUESTION

How can you solve real-world problems that involve angle relationships in parallel lines and triangles?

EXAMPLE 1

Find each angle measure when m∠6 = 81°.

A m∠5 = 180° − 81° = 99°

5 and 6 are supplementary angles.

B m∠1 = 99°

1 and 5 are corresponding angles.

C m∠3 = 180° − 81° = 99°

3 and 6 are same-side interior angles.

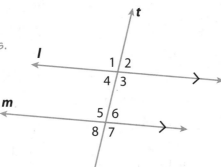

EXAMPLE 2

Are the triangles similar? Explain your answer.

$y = 180° - (67° + 35°)$

$y = 78°$

$x = 180° - (67° + 67°)$

$x = 46°$

The triangles are not similar, because they do not have 2 or more pairs of corresponding congruent angles.

Key Vocabulary

alternate exterior angles *(ángulos alternos externos)*

alternate interior angles *(ángulos alternos internos)*

corresponding angles *(ángulos correspondientes (para líneas))*

exterior angle *(ángulo externo)*

interior angle *(ángulos internos)*

remote interior angle *(ángulo interno remoto)*

same-side interior angles *(ángulos internos del mismo lado)*

similar *(semejantes)*

transversal *(transversal)*

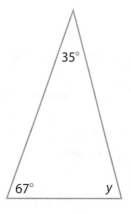

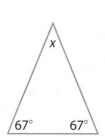

EXERCISES

1. If m∠GHA = 106°, find the measures of the given angles.
   (Lesson 19.1)

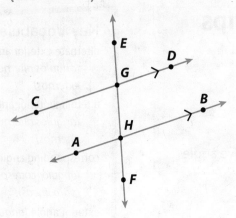

   m∠EGC = _____

   m∠EGD = _____

   m∠BHF = _____

   m∠HGD = _____

2. Find the measure of the missing angles. (Lesson 19.2)

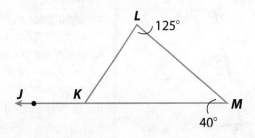

   m∠JKL = _____

   m∠LKM = _____

3. Is the larger triangle similar to the smaller triangle?
   Explain your answer. (Lesson 19.3)

   _____

   _____

   _____

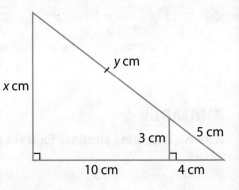

4. Find the value of x and y in the figure. (Lesson 19.3)

   _____

5. If m∠CJI = 132° and m∠EIH = 59°, find the measures of
   the given angles. (Lesson 19.1)

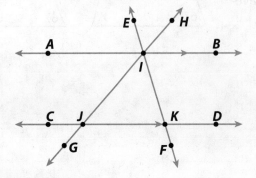

   m∠IKJ = _____

   m∠HIB = _____

   m∠EIJ = _____

   m∠AIK = _____

The Pythagorean Theorem

Key Vocabulary

hypotenuse *(hipotenusa)*

legs *(catetos)*

Pythagorean Theorem
(teorema de Pitágoras)

 ESSENTIAL QUESTION

How can you use the Pythagorean Theorem to solve real-world problems?

EXAMPLE 1

Find the missing side length.
Round your answer to the nearest tenth.

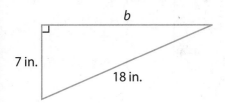

b

7 in.

18 in.

$a^2 + b^2 = c^2$

$7^2 + b^2 = 18^2$

$49 + b^2 = 324$

$b^2 = 275$

$b = \sqrt{275} \approx 16.6$

The length of the leg is about 16.6 inches.

EXAMPLE 2

Thomas drew a diagram to represent the location of his house, the school, and his friend Manuel's house. What is the distance from the school to Manuel's house? Round your answer to the nearest tenth.

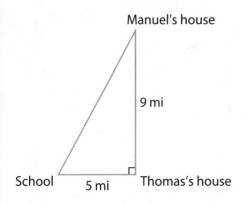

Manuel's house

9 mi

School   5 mi   Thomas's house

$a^2 + b^2 = c^2$

$5^2 + 9^2 = c^2$

$25 + 81 = c^2$

$c^2 = 106$

$c = \sqrt{106} \approx 10.3$

The distance from the school to Manuel's house is about 10.3 miles.

EXERCISES

Find the missing side lengths. Round your answers to the nearest hundredth. *(Lesson 20.1)*

1.

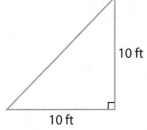

10 ft

10 ft

_____

2.

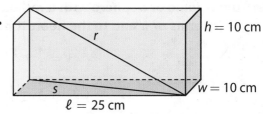

$h = 10$ cm

r

s

$w = 10$ cm

$\ell = 25$ cm

_____

_____

3. Hye Sun has a modern coffee table whose top is a triangle with the following side lengths: 8 feet, 3 feet, and 5 feet. Is Hye Sun's coffee table top a right triangle? (Lesson 20.2)

_____

4. Find the length of each side of triangle *ABC*. If necessary, round your answers to the nearest hundredth. (Lesson 20.3)

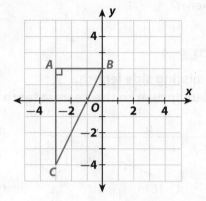

$\overline{AB}$ _____

$\overline{BC}$ _____

$\overline{AC}$ _____

? ESSENTIAL QUESTION

How can you solve real-world problems that involve volume?

EXAMPLE 1

Find the volume of the cistern. Round your answer to the nearest hundredth.

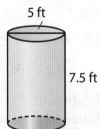

$V = \pi r^2 h$

$\approx 3.14 \cdot 2.5^2 \cdot 7.5$

$\approx 3.14 \cdot 6.25 \cdot 7.5$

≈ 147.19

The cistern has a volume of approximately 147.19 cubic feet.

EXAMPLE 2

Find the volume of a sphere with a radius of 3.7 cm. Write your answer in terms of π and to the nearest hundredth.

$V = \frac{4}{3}\pi r^3$ $V = \frac{4}{3}\pi r^3$

$\approx \frac{4}{3} \cdot \pi \cdot 3.7^3$ $\approx \frac{4}{3} \cdot 3.14 \cdot 3.7^3$

$\approx \frac{4}{3} \cdot \pi \cdot 50.653$ $\approx \frac{4}{3} \cdot 3.14 \cdot 50.653$

$\approx 67.54\pi$ ≈ 212.07

The volume of the sphere is approximately 67.54π cm³, or 212.07 cm³.

EXERCISES

Find the volume of each figure. Round your answers to the nearest hundredth. (Lessons 21.1, 21.2, 21.3)

1.

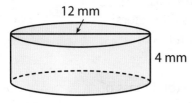

12 mm

4 mm

_____

2.

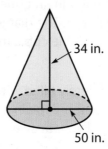

34 in.

50 in.

_____

3. Find the volume of a ball with a radius of 1.68 inches. _____

4.

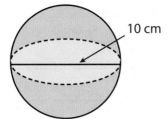

10 cm

_____

5.

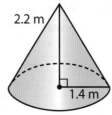

2.2 m

1.4 m

_____

6. A round above-ground swimming pool has a diameter of 15 ft and a height of 4.5 ft. What is the volume of the swimming pool? _____

7.

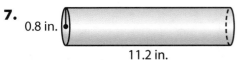

0.8 in.

11.2 in.

8.

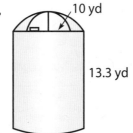

10 yd

13.3 yd

_____   _____

9. A paper cup in the shape of a cone has a height of 4.7 inches and a diameter of 3.6 inches. What is the volume of the paper cup? _____

Unit 9 Performance Tasks

1. **CAREERS IN MATH** | Hydrologist A hydrologist needs to estimate the mass of water in an underground aquifer, which is roughly cylindrical in shape. The diameter of the aquifer is 65 meters, and its depth is 8 meters. One cubic meter of water has a mass of about 1000 kilograms.

   a. The aquifer is completely filled with water. What is the total mass of the water in the aquifer? Explain how you found your answer. Use 3.14 for π and round your answer to the nearest kilogram.

   _____

   _____

   _____

   b. Another cylindrical aquifer has a diameter of 70 meters and a depth of 9 meters. The mass of the water in it is 27×10^7 kilograms. Is the aquifer totally filled with water? Explain your reasoning.

   _____

   _____

   _____

2. From his home, Myles walked his dog north 5 blocks, east 2 blocks, and then stopped at a drinking fountain. He then walked north 3 more blocks and east 4 more blocks. It started to rain so he cut through a field and walked straight home.

   a. Draw a diagram of his path.

   b. How many blocks did Myles walk in all? How much longer was his walk before it started to rain than his walk home?

   _____

UNIT 9 MIXED REVIEW

COMMON
CORE

Assessment Readiness

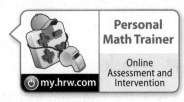

Personal
Math Trainer

Online
Assessment and
Intervention

my.hrw.com

Selected Response

1. Which of the following angle pairs formed by a transversal that intersects two parallel lines are not congruent?

Ⓐ alternate interior angles

Ⓑ adjacent angles

Ⓒ corresponding angles

Ⓓ alternate exterior angles

2. The measures of the three angles of a triangle are given by $3x + 1$, $2x - 3$, and $9x$. What is the measure of the smallest angle?

Ⓐ 13°   Ⓒ 29°

Ⓑ 23°   Ⓓ 40°

3. Using 3.14 for π, what is the volume of the cylinder?

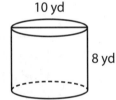

10 yd

8 yd

Ⓐ 200 cubic yards

Ⓑ 628 cubic yards

Ⓒ 1256 cubic yards

Ⓓ 2512 cubic yards

4. Which of the following is **not** true?

Ⓐ $\sqrt{36} + 2 > \sqrt{16} + 5$

Ⓑ $5\pi < 17$

Ⓒ $\sqrt{10} + 1 < \frac{9}{2}$

Ⓓ $5 - \sqrt{35} < 0$

5. A pole is 65 feet tall. A support wire is attached to the top of the pole and secured to the ground 33 feet from the base of the pole. Find the approximate length of the wire.

Ⓐ 32 feet   Ⓒ 56 feet

Ⓑ 73 feet   Ⓓ 60 feet

6. Using 3.14 for π, what is the volume of the sphere to the nearest tenth?

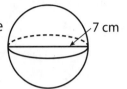

7 cm

Ⓐ 205.1 cm³

Ⓑ 1077 cm³

Ⓒ 179.5 cm³

Ⓓ 4308.1 cm³

7. Which set of lengths are **not** the side lengths of a right triangle?

Ⓐ 28, 45, 53   Ⓒ 36, 77, 85

Ⓑ 13, 84, 85   Ⓓ 16, 61, 65

8. Which statement describes the solution of a system of linear equations for two lines with different slopes and different y-intercepts?

Ⓐ one nonzero solution

Ⓑ infinitely many solutions

Ⓒ no solution

Ⓓ solution of 0

9. What is the side length of a cube that has a volume of 729 cubic inches?

Ⓐ 7 inches   Ⓒ 9 inches

Ⓑ 8 inches   Ⓓ 10 inches

10. What is the solution to the system of equations?

$$\begin{cases} x + 3y = 5 \\ 2x - y = -4 \end{cases}$$

Ⓐ no solution

Ⓑ infinitely many solutions

Ⓒ (2, 1)

Ⓓ (−1, 2)

Mini-Tasks

11. In the figure shown, m∠AGE = (5x − 7)°
and m∠BGH = (3x + 19)°.

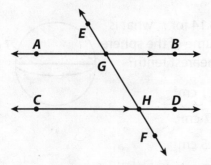

   a. Find the value of x. _____

   b. Find m∠AGE. _____

   c. Find m∠GHD. _____

12. Tom drew two right triangles as shown with
angle measures to the nearest whole unit.

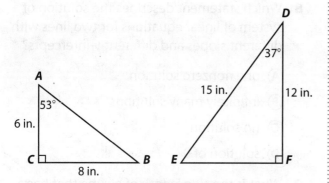

   a. Find the length of $\overline{AB}$ in triangle ABC.

   _____

   b. Find the length of $\overline{EF}$ in triangle DEF.

   _____

   c. Are the triangles similar? Explain your
answer.

   _____

   _____

   _____

   _____

   _____

> **Read graphs and diagrams
> carefully. Look at the labels for
> important information.**

13. In the diagram, the figure at the top of the
cone is a hemisphere.

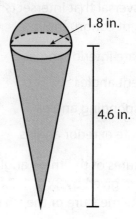

   a. What is the volume of the cone?
Round your answer to the nearest
hundredth.

   _____

   b. What is the volume of the hemisphere
on the top of the cone? Round your
answer to the nearest hundredth.

   _____

   c. What would be the radius of a sphere
with the same total volume as the figure?
Explain how you found your answer.

   _____

   _____

   _____

   _____

   _____

UNIT 1 Selected Answers

MODULE 1

LESSON 1.1

Your Turn

2. $10x - 4$ **3.** $1.25x + 4.4$
5. $0.6b - 3c$ **6.** $x + 6$ **7.** $11.8 -$
$2.6y$ **9.** $2(x + 1)$ **10.** $3(x + 3)$
11. $5(x + 3)$ **12.** $4(x + 4)$

Guided Practice

1. Step 1: baseballs: $14 + 12n$,
tennis balls: $23 + 16n$; Step 2: $14 +$
$12n + 23 + 16n$, $14 + 23 + 12n +$
$16n$, $37 + 28n$, $37 + 28n$ **2.** 289 3.
$0.5(12m) - 0.5(22n)$, $6m - 11n$
4. $2x - 6 - 6x + 4 = 2x + (-6x) +$
$(-6) + 4 = -4x - 2$ **5.** $2(x + 6)$
6. $12(x + 2)$ **7.** $7(x + 5)$

Independent Practice

9. $15(100 + 5d) + 20(50 + 7d) =$
$2{,}500 + 215d$ **11.** 3 and $x + 2$;
$3x + 6$ **13.** The area is the product
of the length and width (6×9).
It is also the sum of the areas of
the rectangles separated by the
dashed line (6×5 and 6×4). So,
$6(9) = 6(5) + 6(4)$.
15. $2x + 6$ **17.** $x^2 + 5x + 6$
19. (1) Think of 997 as $1{,}000 - 3$.
So, $8 \times 997 = 8(1{,}000 - 3)$. By the
Distributive Property,
$8(1{,}000 - 3) = 8{,}000 - 24 =$
$7{,}976$. (2) Think of 997 as $900 +$
$90 + 7$. By the Distributive
Property, $8(900 + 90 + 7) =$
$7{,}200 + 720 + 56 = 7{,}976$.

LESSON 1.2

Your Turn

1. $z = -13.9$ **2.** $r = 12.3$
3. $c = -12$ **5.** $x - 1.5 = 5.25$;
$x = 6.75$; the initial elevation of
the plane is 6.75 miles.
6. $\frac{x}{3.5} = -1.2$; $x = -4.2$; $4.20
7. $2.5x = 7.5$; $x = 3$; 3 hours

Guided Practice

1. Step 1: the number of degrees
warmer the average temperature
is in Nov. than in Jan., $x +$
$(-13.4) = -1.7$ or $x - 13.4 =$
-1.7; Step 2: $11.7°$
2. Step 1: the number of days it
takes the average temperature to
decrease by 9 °F, $-1\frac{1}{2}x = -9$; Step
2: 6 days **3.** $x = -17$ **4.** $y = 1.4$
5. $z = -9$

Independent Practice

7. 29,028.87 ft
9. $28{,}251.31 - x = 11{,}194.21$;
$x = 17{,}057.1$; 17,057.1 ft
11. $26\frac{1}{2}$ ft/min
13. 18.8 °C warmer
15. $36\frac{1}{3}$ yards **17.** Sample answer:
the elevation is the product of
the rate and the time. **19.** (1)
The elevations of the diver and
the reef; both are below sea level.
(2) The change in the plane's
elevation; the plane is moving
from a higher to a lower elevation.
21. Add the deposits and the
withdrawals. Let x represent the
amount of the initial deposit.
Write and solve the equation
$x +$ deposits $-$ withdrawals $=$
$210.85.

LESSON 1.3

Your Turn

4. $150 - 35x = 45$

Guided Practice

1.

2.

3. $6 + 9a = 78$ **4.** the solution;
multiplied by 2; added to 2x; result

Independent Practice

7. three negative variable tiles and
seven $+1$−tiles on one side of a
line and 28 $+1$−tiles on the other
side **9.** $1.25r + 6.75 = 31.75$
11. $\frac{1}{2}n + 45 = 172$ **13.** $500 -$
$20x = 220$ **15a.** $10 + 5c = 25$
b. 3 children **c.** They should
choose Kimmi because she
charges only $25. If they chose
Sandy, they would pay $35.
17. Part of the equation is written in
cents and part in dollars. All of the
numbers in the equation should be
written either in cents or in dollars.

LESSON 1.4

Your Turn

1. $x = 3$ **2.** $n = 3$ **3.** $a = -1$
4. $y = 1$ **6.** $3n + 10 = 37$; the
triplets are 9 years old.
7. $\frac{n}{4} - 5 = 15$; the number is 80.
8. $-20 = \frac{5}{9}(x - 32)$; -4 °F
9. $120 - 4x = 92$; 7 incorrect
answers

Guided Practice

1. one $+1$−tile from both sides;
two equal groups **2.** 4 **3.** $2(18 +$
$w) = 58$; the width is 11 inches
4. $1200 - 25x = 500$; 28 days

Independent Practice

7. $d = 9$ **9.** $k = 42$ **11.** $z = -190$
13. $n = -9$ **15.** $c = 9$ **17.** $t = -9$
19. 13 °F **21.** 12 years old
23. $188 **25.** $x = 0.4$
27. $k = -180.44$ **29.** Sample
answer: $\frac{x}{5} + 10 = 5$
31. The equation says that a
number was divided by 4 and that
6 was then subtracted from the
quotient, giving the result 2. So,
working backward, first add 6 to
2, giving 8. Then multiply 8 by 4,
giving $x = 32$; Algebraic: Add 6
to both sides, then multiply by 4,
giving $x = 32$. The operations are
the same. **33.** $w = \frac{P - 2\ell}{2}$

Selected Answers

LESSON 2.1

Your Turn

4. $y \geq -2$

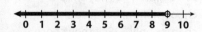

5. $x < 9$

6. $y > -6$

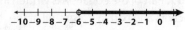

7. $t \geq -42$

8. $m \leq 9$; Tony can pay for no more than 9 months of his gym membership using this account.

Guided Practice

1. $2 \leq 5$ **2.** $2 > 1$ **3.** $0 > -11$
4. $2 \leq 16$ **5.** $n \geq 3$

6. $x < 4$

7. $y \geq -2$

8. $b > -5$

9a. $-4t \geq -80$
b. 20 or fewer hours
c. more than 20 hours

Independent Practice
11. $x > 50$

13. $q \leq 7$

15. $z < 8$ **17.** at most 16 in.
19. at most 7 in. **21.** at least 11 ft
23. $3\frac{1}{3}$ lb **25.** No; $1.25x \leq 3$; $x \leq$ 2.4 so 2.4 lb of onions is the most Florence can buy. $2.4 < 2.5$, so she cannot buy 2.5 lb. **27.** $x > 9$ for each inequality; in each case the number added to x is 9 less than the number on the right side of each inequality, so $x > 9$ is the solution.

LESSON 2.2

Your Turn
3. $1,240 + 45a \geq 6,000$
4. $6 + 3n \leq 40$

Guided Practice

1.

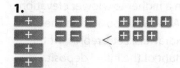

2.

3. \$7,000; \$1,250; 92; $1,250 + 92a \geq 7,000$ **4.** The solution of the problem; the solution multiplied by 7; 18 is subtracted from $7x$; the result can be no greater than 32.

Independent Practice
7. $3a + 28 > 200$; $a =$ possible amounts each friend earned
9. $4a - 25 \leq 75$; $a =$ the maximum amount each shirt can cost

10. $120 + 32n \leq 720$; $n =$ the number of people in each row
13. $7 + 10c \leq 100$; $c =$ the number of CDs she buys **17.** $\leq$
19. $\leq$ **21.** $\geq$ **25.** $n > \frac{1}{n}$ if $n > 1$; $n < \frac{1}{n}$ if $n < 1$; $n = \frac{1}{n}$ if $n = 1$

LESSON 2.3

Your Turn
1. $x > 2$ **2.** $h \geq 3$ **3.** $p \geq 6$; Joshua has to run at a steady pace of at least 6 mi/h. **4.** $v = 11$ **5.** $h = -3$; $h = -4$; $h = -5$

Guided Practice
1. Remove $4 + 1$−tiles from both sides, then divide each side into 3 equal groups; $x < 3$
2. $d < 9$

3. $b \geq 4$

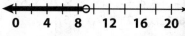

4. $m = -10$ **5.** $y = \frac{1}{2}$; $y = 0$
6. $t \leq 1.25$;

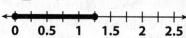

Lizzy can spend from 0 to 1.25 h with each student. No; 1.5 h per student will exceed Lizzy's available time.

Independent Practice
9. $t \leq 10$ **11.** $m < 8$
13. $f < 140$ **15.** $g < -18$
17. $a \geq 16$ **19.** $7n - 25 \geq 65$; $n \geq 12\frac{6}{7}$; Grace must wash at least 13 cars, because n must be a whole number.
21c. There is no number that satisfies both inequalities. **d.** The solution set is all numbers.

 **UNIT 2** **Selected Answers**

LESSON 3.1

Your Turn

4. length: 17.3 feet; width: 13.3 feet; area: 230.1 square feet **5.** length: 22 feet; width: 10 feet; area: 220 square feet

Guided Practice

1a. $y = \frac{5}{3}x$ **b.** $16\frac{2}{3}$ feet
c. 1.5 inches **2.** 28 feet; $\frac{1 \text{ inch} \times 14}{2 \text{ feet} \times 14} = \frac{14 \text{ inches}}{28 \text{ feet}}$; 14 feet; 392 square feet **3.** length: 25 meters; width: 15 meters; area: 375 square meters

4a.

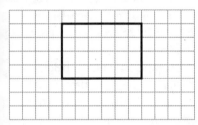

b. Length is 36 m and width is 24 m, using both scales.

Independent Practice

7. The scale drawing is 24 units by 15 units. **9.** Because the scale is 10 cm:1 mm and because 10 cm is longer than 1 mm, the drawing will be larger. **11a.** 6 toothpicks tall **b.** approximately 5 cotton swabs tall

LESSON 3.2

Guided Practice

1. a unique triangle
2. no triangle
3. a unique triangle
4. a unique triangle

Independent Practice

7. The side lengths proposed are 15, 21, and 37 ft, and $15 + 21 < 37$. No such triangle can be created.
9. More than one triangle; two triangles can be created by connecting the top of the 2-in. segment with the dashed line, once in each spot where the arc intersects the dashed line. The triangles are different, but both have sides with lengths of 2 in. and $1\frac{1}{2}$ in., and a 45° angle not included between them.

LESSON 3.3

Guided Practice

1. triangle or equilateral triangle
2. rectangle
3. triangle
4. rainbow-shaped curve

Independent Practice

7. Circles or ovals
9a. It is a circle with a radius of 12 in.
b. The cross sections will still be circles, but their radii will decrease as the plane moves away from the sphere's center.
11. Sample answer: If you think of a building shaped like a rectangular prism, you can think of horizontal planes slicing the prism to form the different floors.

LESSON 3.4

Your Turn

5. Sample answer: $\angle FGA$ and $\angle AGC$ **6.** Sample answer: $\angle FGE$ and $\angle BGC$ **7.** Sample answer: $\angle FGD$ and $\angle DGC$ **8.** Sample answer: $\angle BGC$ and $\angle CGD$
9. 55° **10.** $54° + 3x = 180°$, $x = 42°$, $m\angle JML = 3x = 126°$

11. Sample answer: You can stop at the solution step where you find the value of $3x$ because the measure of $\angle JML$ is equal to $3x$.

Guided Practice

1. complementary **2.** adjacent
3. vertical; 30° **4.** 50°, 30°, 2x; 80°; 100°; 100° **5.** $3x - 13$, 58°, 45°; 45°, 15°; 15°; 45°; 32°

Independent Practice

7. Sample answer: $\angle SUR$ and $\angle QUR$ **9.** Sample answer: $\angle TUS$ and $\angle QUN$ **11.** $m\angle RUQ$
13. 96° **15.** 28°
17. $m\angle A = 47°$, $m\angle B = 43°$
19. 41 degrees, 33 minutes, 52 seconds **21.** Disagree; the sum of the measures of a pair of complementary angles is 90°. So, the measure of each angle must be less than 90°. But $m\angle A = 119°$, and $119° > 90°$.

LESSON 4.1

Your Turn

3. about 34.54 cm **6.** about 2 hours

Guided Practice

1. 3.14(9); 28.26 **2.** 7; 44
3. 78.5 m **4.** 30.14 yd **5.** 47.1 in.
6. 66; 66; 21; $21 + 4 = 25$; 25; $11.25; $11.25 **7.** 0.5 yd; 1 yd
8. 12.55 ft; 25.10 ft **9.** 1.7 in.; 10.68 in.

Independent Practice

11. 18.53 ft **13.** 110 in.
15. $d = 18.8$ ft; $C \approx 59.0$ ft
17. $r = 9$ in.; $C \approx 56.52$ in.
19. about 2,376 ft
21. about 0.14 mi
23. about $713.18
25. 12.56 feet **27.** Pool B; about 0.57 m or 1.84 ft

Selected Answers

LESSON 4.2

Your Turn
4. 314 ft²

Guided Practice
1. 153.9 m² **2.** 452.2 mm²
3. 314 yd² **4.** 200.96 in²
5. 113.04 cm² **6.** 132.67 in² **7.** 4π
square units **8.** 36π square units
9. $\frac{\pi}{16}$ square units **10.** 16π yd

Independent Practice
13. 803.84 cm² **15.** 28.26 square
units **17.** 30.96 m² **19.** No; the
top of the large cake has an area
9 times that of the small cake. The
area of the top of the large cake
is 144π in² and that of the small
cake is 16π in². **21.** The 18-inch
pizza is a better deal because it
costs about 8¢ per square inch
while the 12-inch pizza costs
about 9¢ per square inch. **23.** No;
the combined area is 2πr² while
the area of a circle with twice the
radius is 4πr². **25.** $\frac{\pi (1.5)^2}{\pi (1.75)^2} =$
$\frac{2.25}{56.25} = \frac{1}{25}$ or 0.04 or 4%

LESSON 4.3

Your Turn
2. 51.5 ft² **3.** 139.25 m² **4.** $911.68

Guided Practice
1. rectangle; 4; 15; 15; 4; 15; 15; 34;
34 **2.** Method 1: Divide the figure
into a 12 by 9 rectangle and a 20
by 9 rectangle. Method 2: Divide
the figure into a 9 by 8 rectangle
and a 12 by 18 rectangle. The area
is 288 cm². **3.** $97.88

Independent Practice
5. 941.33 in²
7. 30 square units

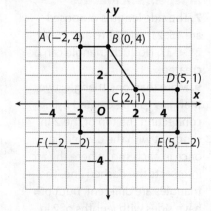

9. 60.56 cm² **11.** 5 ft; 32.5 ft² −
7.5 ft² = 25 ft²; 25 ft² is area of
the square, so each side of the
square is 5 ft because 5 × 5 = 25
15a. 2,228 in² **b.** 3,016 in²

LESSON 4.4

Your Turn
3. 69 in²
4. 976 in²

Guided Practice
1. 18 ft, 7 ft, 12 ft², (18 ft)(7 ft) +
2(12 ft²), 150 ft² **2.** 37.5 m²,
478 m², 6.25 m²,
37.5 + 478 − 2(6.25), 503 m²

Independent Practice
5. 3,720 tiles **7.** 66 ft²
9. 3,264 in²
11. No; they need 3 cans, which will
cost 3($6.79) = $20.37.
13. No; *Ph* doubles, and 2*B*
quadruples. *S* more than doubles.
15. 138.2 in²; 1,440 ft² of cardboard

LESSON 4.5

Your Turn
2. 1,848 m³
5. 2,200 cm³
7. 6,825 in³

Guided Practice
1. 12 ft²; (12 × 7) ft³ = 84 ft³
2. 30 m²; (30 × 11) m³ = 330 m³
3. 288 ft³; 72 ft³; 360 ft³
4. 40,000 ft³
5. 385 cm³

Independent Practice
7. 17.5 in³
9. 384 ft³
11. The units for volume are
incorrect; the volume is 300 cubic
inches.
13. 316.41 m³
15. Triangular prism; you get 192 in³
for the same price you would pay for
180 in³ with the trapezoidal prism.
17. *V* = 30(2.5) = 75 cm³; mass ≈
75(8.6) = 645g
19. Sample answers: (1) height
of trapezoid = 4 cm, base
lengths = 2 cm and 6 cm, height
of prism = 7.5 cm (2) height of
trapezoid = 2.5 cm, base
lengths = 1 cm and 7 cm, height of
prism = 12 cm

UNIT 3 Selected Answers

MODULE 5

LESSON 5.1

Your Turn

4. Yes; every employee had an equal chance of being selected.
5. The question is biased since cats are suggested. **6.** The question is not biased. It does not lead people to pick a particular season.

Guided Practice

2. more; random **3.** less; biased **4.** Yes; Sample answer: What is your favorite color?

Independent Practice

9. It is biased because students who aren't in that class won't be selected. **11.** Yes; the sample is random. **13.** Jae's question is not biased since it does not suggest a type of art to students. **15a.** 60; a random sample **b.** 58%; it appears reasonable because Barbara used a random sample and surveyed a significant percent of the students.

LESSON 5.2

Your Turn

5. 420 damaged MP3s **6.** Sample answer: 6 is a little more than 10% of 50. 10% of 3,500 is 350, and 420 is a little more than that.

Guided Practice

1.

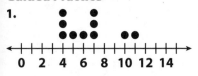

2.

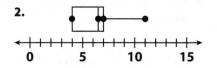

3. 4; 7 **4.** 4; 11 **5.** 6.5 **6.** 280
7. 720 elk

Independent Practice

9. 48 people **11.** 240 puppies
13. Yes, this seems reasonable because 25 is the median of the data. **17.** Kudrey needs to find the median and the lower and upper quartiles and plot those points. He assumed all quartiles would be equally long when each quartile represents an equal number of data values. **19.** a box plot

LESSON 5.3

Guided Practice

1. (1, 600); 20
2. 50; 51, 600
3. No, it has 4 defective batteries, or 20%. For the shipment, $\frac{50}{600}$, or about 8% of the batteries are defective.

Independent Practice

5. Shop A sells 100; Shop B sells 115; Shop C sells 140.
7. Shop A or Shop B; Both samples are large enough to produce a reasonably valid inference. Shop C's sample is too small.
9a. 49.8 palms **b.** about 3,187 palms
11. Sample answer: Roll two six-sided number cubes, with one cube representing the row and the other representing the column. Select the cell represented by the row and column shown on the cubes.

MODULE 6

LESSON 6.1

Your Turn

2. Dot plots for field hockey players and softball players have a similar spread. Center of the field hockey dot plot is less than the center for softball or basketball players. Dot plots for field hockey players and softball players have a similar spread.
3. median: 6 h, range: 10 h; If you remove the outliers, the range is 4 hours. The median is greater than the median for exercise. The range is less than the range for exercise.

Guided Practice

1. Class A: clustered around two areas; Class B: clustered in the middle **2.** Class A: two peaks at 4 and 13 mi; Class B: looks centered around 7 mi **3.** Class A: spread from 4 to 14 mi, a wide gap no data; Class B: spread from 3 to 9 mi **4.** The median for both dot plots is 6 miles. **5.** Range for Class A: 10 mi; range for Class B: 6 mi

Independent Practice

7. The dots have a relatively even spread, with a peak at 8 letters.
9. The dots spread from 3 to 9 letters. **11.** AL: clustered in one small interval with an outlier to the left; VA: relatively uniform in height over the same interval
13. AL: spreads from 1 to 12 days of rain, an outlier at 1; VA: spreads from 8 to 12 days of rain
15. Group A: clustered to the left of size 9; Group B: clustered to the right of size 9 **17.** Group A: range with outlier = 6.5, without outlier = 2.5; Group B: range = 3 **19.** Yes; one group of five students could

have the following number of pets: 1, 2, 3, 4, 5. Another group of five students could have the following number of pets: 1, 3, 3, 3, 5. For both groups of students, the median would be 3 and the range would be 4.

LESSON 6.2

Your Turn

3. Sample: The boxes have similar shapes, although Group B has a shorter box and shorter whiskers. Group B's median is greater than Group A's. Group B's shorter box means the middle 50% of the data are closer together than the middle 50% of Group A's.

4. Sample answer: The shape is similar to Store A's. The median is greater than Store A's and less than Store B's. The interquartile range is about the same as Store A's and longer than B's.

Guided Practice

1. 72; 88 **2.** 79 **3.** 16; 10
4. Volleyball players **5.** Hockey players **6.** Both groups

Independent Practice

9. Both cars have ranges of 45 in. Both cars have interquartile ranges of 25 in. **11.** Car A has less variability in the lowest quarter of its data and greater variability in the highest quarter of its data. The variability is reversed for Car B.
13. City A; $25

LESSON 6.3

Your Turn

1. About 1.1 times the MAD.
2. There is much more overlap between the two distributions.

Guided Practice

1. Class 1: 6, Class 2: 11; Class 1: 3, Class 2: 3 **2.** 1.67 **3.** Both distributions show longer

travel times for school A. The distribution of the medians shows less overlap, so is more convincing.

Independent Practice

5. Mean: 50 °F, MAD: 13 °F
7. 35 °F, 13 °F; the mean for City 2 must be 15 °F less than the mean for City 1, and the MAD must be the same.
9. The variation and overlap in the distributions make it hard to make any convincing comparison.
11. 1.75 × range **13.** Ramon's; the larger the sample size, the less variability there should be in the distributions of the medians and means.

UNIT 4 Selected Answers

MODULE 7

LESSON 7.1

Your Turn

3. as likely as not; $\frac{1}{2}$ **4.** $\frac{1}{2}$ **5.** $\frac{1}{3}$
7. $\frac{7}{8}$ **8.** $\frac{1}{2}$

Guided Practice

1. 8; 5; 7; 1; 3; 2; 4; 6 **2.** impossible;
0 **3.** as likely as not; $\frac{1}{2}$ **4.** certain; 1
5. unlikely; close to 0 **6.** $\frac{2}{5}$ **7.** $\frac{1}{4}$ **8.** $\frac{5}{6}$
9. $\frac{2}{3}$ **10.** $\frac{4}{5}$ **11.** $\frac{12}{13}$

Independent Practice

13. $\frac{2}{13}$; The event can occur in 8
ways. There are 52 outcomes in
the sample space. $\frac{8}{52} = \frac{2}{13}$
15. No, it is unlikely that
she will have oatmeal for
breakfast. **19a.** $\frac{8}{14} = \frac{4}{7}$
b. $8 - 1 = 7$ blue coins and
$6 + 3 = 9$ red coins; $\frac{9}{16}$
c. $8 + 3 = 11$ blue coins and
$6 - 1 = 5$ red coins; $\frac{5}{16}$ **21.** Yes;
Because not selecting red means
black will be selected, and vice
versa. $P(\text{not black}) + P(\text{black}) =$
$P(\text{not black}) + P(\text{not red}) = 1$.

LESSON 7.2

Your Turn

7. red: $\frac{1}{3}$, yellow: $\frac{7}{15}$, blue: $\frac{1}{5}$
8. Let 1 and 2 represent red, let
3 and 4 represent white, and let
5 and 6 represent blue. Toss the
cube 50 times to determine the
experimental probability for each
color. Predict that the next ball
released will be the color with the
greatest experimental probability.

Guided Practice

1. A: $\frac{7}{20}$, 0.35, 35%; B: $\frac{7}{40}$, 0.175,
17.5%; C: $\frac{11}{40}$, 0.275, 27.5%;
D: $\frac{1}{5}$, 0.2, 20%

2. Sample answer: Write "yes" on 6
cards and "no" on 4. Draw a card at
random 50 times. Use the number
of "yes" cards as her prediction.

Independent Practice

5. Sample answer: Compare
the number of wins to the total
number of trials; $\frac{1}{6}$.
7. Yes, because it is based on
actual data of weather patterns.
9. $\frac{2}{5}$; 16 aces; $\frac{2}{5}$ of 40 is 16.
11. No; there were 40 heads in
100 trials; $P(\text{heads}) = \frac{40}{100}$.

LESSON 7.3

Your Turn

1. $\frac{60}{400} = \frac{3}{20} = 15\%$ **3.** $\frac{12}{75} = \frac{4}{25}$

Guided Practice

1. $\frac{50}{400} = \frac{1}{8}$

Independent Practice

5. $\frac{60}{400} = \frac{3}{20}$ **7.** 12; The total is the
product of 3 page count choices
and 4 color choices, which
is 12. **13.** No, because coins are
fair and the probabilities do not
appear to be equally likely.

LESSON 7.4

Your Turn

1. 132 customers **3.** No; about
371 e-mails out of 12,372
will come back undelivered.
The prediction is high. **4.** 84
customers; Yes, 107 > 84, so more
customers than normal bought
two or more pairs.

Guided Practice

1. 15 times **2.** about 55 days
3. No, about 1,009 candles out
of 16,824 will be returned. The
prediction is low. **4.** No, about
746 toys out of 24,850 will be

defective. The prediction is
high. **5.** 39 times; The light-rail's
claim is higher than the actual
85%. **6.** 900 students; The
college's claim is close to the
number actually accepted.

Independent Practice

9. Yes; 6th grade: $\frac{2}{100} = \frac{x}{250} \to x = 5$;
7th grade: $\frac{4}{100} = \frac{x}{200} \to x = 8$; 8th
grade: $\frac{8}{100} = \frac{x}{150} \to x = 12$
11. 36 clients; more than would
be expected on average **13.** He
set up the fraction incorrectly; it
should be $\frac{1}{3} = \frac{x}{180}$. **15.** 14,700
on-time flights

MODULE 8

LESSON 8.1

Your Turn

2. $\frac{1}{3}$ **3.** The total number of
outcomes in the sample space is
the denominator of the formula
for theoretical probability.

Guided Practice

1.

	Basket A	Basket B
Total number of outcomes	16	20
Number of red balls	3	4
$P(\text{win}) = \frac{\text{number of red balls}}{\text{total number of outcomes}}$	$\frac{3}{16}$	$\frac{4}{20} = \frac{1}{5}$

2. Basket B **3.** odd, 6; sections,
11 **4.** even, 5; sections, 11
5. $\frac{2}{6} = \frac{1}{3}$ **6.** Sample answer: No,
but it might be reasonably close.

Independent Practice

9. $\frac{2}{3}$, 0.67, 67% **11.** $\frac{1}{2}$, 0.50,
50% **13.** $\frac{3}{5}$, 0.60, 60% **15.** 9
represents the ways the event can
occur; 13 represents the number
of equally likely outcomes.

LESSON 8.2

Your Turn

3. $\frac{4}{12} = \frac{1}{3}$ **4.** $\frac{6}{12} = \frac{1}{2}$ **5.** $\frac{3}{8}$

Guided Practice

1.

	1	2	3	4	5	6
1	1	2	3	4	5	6
2	2	4	6	8	10	12
3	3	6	9	12	15	18
4	4	8	12	16	20	24
5	5	10	15	20	25	30
6	6	12	18	24	30	36

2. $\frac{15}{16}$ **3.** $\frac{23}{36}$

4.

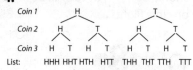

Coin 1: H, T
Coin 2: H, T, H, T
Coin 3: H, T, H, T, H, T, H, T
List: HHH HHT HTH HTT THH THT TTH TTT

5. 8 **6.** TTT **7.** $\frac{1}{8}$ **8.** 3; HTH, THH ; $\frac{3}{8}$

Independent Practice

11. $\frac{1}{2}$ **13.** $\frac{1}{10}$ **15.** $\frac{2}{9}$ **17.** Because there are 3 choices for the first item and 2 for the second, there are $3 \cdot 2 = 6$ possible outcomes. **19.** Neither

LESSON 8.3

Your Turn

1. about 167 times **2.** about 9 times **3.** more likely that he picks a marble of another color **4.** No

Guided Practice

1. $\frac{1}{3}, \frac{1}{3}, \frac{1}{3}, \frac{1}{3}$; 1, 3, 18, 6, 6 **2.** 50 people **3.** brown; $P(\text{hazel}) = \frac{9}{28}$, $P(\text{brown}) = \frac{10}{28}$, $P(\text{blue}) = \frac{7}{28}$, and $P(\text{green}) = \frac{2}{28}$. The event with the greatest probability is choosing a person with brown eyes.

Independent Practice

5. 15 white or gray marbles **7.** It is more likely that she draws 2 red cards. **9.** 500 times **11.** 45 days **17.** Yes, but only theoretically because in reality, nothing can occur 0.5 time.

LESSON 8.4

Guided Practice

1. years with a drought; years without a drought; 4

2.

Trial	Numbers generated	Drought years
1	10, 3, 5, 1	2
2	10, 4, 6, 5	0
3	3, 2, 10, 3	3
4	2, 10, 4, 4	1
5	7, 3, 6, 3	2

Trial	Numbers generated	Drought years
6	8, 4, 8, 5	0
7	6, 2, 2, 8	2
8	6, 5, 2, 4	1
9	2, 2, 3, 2	4
10	6, 3, 1, 5	2

3. 80%

Independent Practice

5. 1 trial **7.** 20%

LESSON 9.1

Your Turn
1. $0.\overline{45}$ 2. 0.125 3. $2.\overline{3}$ 4. $\frac{3}{25}$ 5. $\frac{19}{33}$

6. $1\frac{2}{5}$ 7. $x = \pm 14$ 8. $x = \pm\frac{3}{16}$
9. $x = 8$ 10. $x = \frac{4}{7}$

Guided Practice
1. 0.4 2. $0.\overline{8}$ 3. 3.75 4. 0.7
5. 2.375 6. $0.8\overline{3}$ 7. $\frac{27}{40}$ 8. $5\frac{3}{5}$ 9. $\frac{11}{25}$
10. $4.\overline{4}$; $0.\overline{4}$; 9; 4; $\frac{4}{9}$ 11. $26.\overline{26}$; $0.\overline{26}$;
99; 26; $\frac{26}{99}$ 12. $325.\overline{325}$; $0.\overline{325}$; 999;
325; $\frac{325}{999}$ 13. 144; ± 12 14. $\frac{25}{289}$; $\pm\frac{5}{17}$
15. 216; 6 16. 2.25 17. 1.75
18. 3.15

Independent Practice
21. $0.1\overline{6}$ 23. $98.\overline{6}$ innings
25. $26\frac{1}{5}$ mi 27. $\frac{101}{200}$ cent
29. His estimate is low because
15 is very close to 16, so $\sqrt{15}$ is
very close to $\sqrt{16}$, or 4. A better
estimate would be 3.8 or 3.9.
31. 3 feet
33. $\sqrt{\frac{4}{25}} = \frac{2}{5} = \frac{\sqrt{4}}{\sqrt{25}}$; $\sqrt{\frac{16}{81}} = \frac{4}{9} = \frac{\sqrt{16}}{\sqrt{81}}$;
$\sqrt{\frac{36}{49}} = \frac{6}{7} = \frac{\sqrt{36}}{\sqrt{49}}$; $\frac{\sqrt{a}}{\sqrt{b}} = \sqrt{\frac{a}{b}}$;
$\sqrt{a} \cdot \sqrt{b} = \sqrt{a \cdot b}$

LESSON 9.2

Your Turn
1. rational, real 2. irrational,
real 3. False. Every integer is
a rational number, but every
rational number is not an integer.
Rational numbers such as $\frac{3}{5}$ and
$-\frac{5}{2}$ are not integers. 4. False. Real
numbers are either rational or
irrational numbers. Integers are
rational numbers, so no integers
are irrational numbers. 5. Real
numbers; the amount can be any
number greater than 0. 6. Real
numbers; the number of seconds
left can be any number less than 0.

Guided Practice
1. rational, real 2. whole, integer,
rational, real 3. irrational, real
4. rational, real 5. whole, integer,
rational, real 6. integer, rational,
real 7. rational, real 8. integer,
rational, real 9. True. Whole
numbers are a subset of the set
of rational numbers and can
be written as a ratio of the
whole number to 1. 10. True.
Whole numbers are rational
numbers. 11. Integers; the
change can be a whole dollar
amount and can be positive,
negative, or zero. 12. Rational
numbers; the ruler is marked
every $\frac{1}{16}$th inch.

Independent Practice
15. whole, integer, rational,
real 17. rational, real 19. whole,
integer, rational, real 21. Integers;
the scores are counting numbers,
their opposites, and zero.
23. Whole; the diameter is $\frac{\pi}{\pi} =$
1 mile. 25. rational number
27. Sample answer: If the
calculator shows a terminating
decimal, the number is rational.
Otherwise, you cannot tell
because you see only a few digits.

LESSON 9.3

Your Turn
3. $>$ 4. $<$ 5. $\sqrt{3}$, $\sqrt{5}$, 2.5

$\sqrt{3}$ $\sqrt{5}$
|---|---|---|---|---|---|---|---|---|
0 0.5 1 1.5 2 2.5 3 3.5 4

6. $\sqrt{75}$, π^2, 10

$\sqrt{75}$ π^2
|---|---|---|---|---|
8   9   10   11   12

7. $3\frac{1}{2}$ mi, $3.\overline{45}$ mi, $\frac{10}{3}$ mi, $\sqrt{10}$ mi

Guided Practice
1. $<$ 2. $>$ 3. $<$ 4. $<$ 5. $>$
6. $<$ 7. $>$ 8. $>$ 9. 1.7; 1.8; 1.75;
6.28; 1.5; $\sqrt{3}$; 2π 10. $\left(1 + \frac{\pi}{2}\right)$ km,
2.5 km, $\frac{12}{5}$ km, $(\sqrt{17} - 2)$ km

Independent Practice
13. π, $\sqrt{10}$, 3.5 15. -3.75, $\frac{9}{4}$, $\sqrt{8}$, 3
17a. $\sqrt{60} \approx 7.7.5$, $\frac{58}{8} = 7.25$,
$7.\overline{3} \approx 7.33$, $7\frac{3}{5} = 7.60$, so the
average is 7.4825 km. b. They
are nearly identical. $\sqrt{56}$ is
approximately 7.4833…
19. Sample answer: $\sqrt{31}$
21a. between $\sqrt{7} \approx 2.65$ and
$\sqrt{8} \approx 2.83$ b. between $\sqrt{9} = 3$
and $\sqrt{10} \approx 3.16$ 23. 2 points; A
rational number and an irrational
number cannot be represented
by the same point on the number
line.

LESSON 10.1

Your Turn
6. 5 7. $63\frac{15}{16}$

Guided Practice
1. $\frac{1}{8}$ 2. $\frac{1}{36}$ 3. 1 4. 100 5. 625
6. $\frac{1}{32}$ 7. $\frac{1}{1024}$ 8. 1 9. $\frac{1}{1331}$ 10. 4^3
11. $2^2 \cdot 2^3 = 2^5$ 12. 6^2
13. $8^{12-9} = 8^3$ 14. 5^{12} 15. 7^{13}
16. 4; 6; 6; $(6 \cdot 6)$; 6^8 17. 3; 3; 3;
$(3 \cdot 3 \cdot 3)$; 3^9 18. 1168 19. 343

Independent Practice
21. The exponents cannot be
added because the bases are not
the same.
23. Earth to Neptune; 22^3, or
10,648, times greater. 25. -3
27. 19 29. 10^3 kg, or 1000 kg
31. Both expressions equal x^5,
so $x^7 \cdot x^{-2} = \frac{x^7}{x^2}$. When multiplying
powers with the same base, you
add exponents; $7 + (-2) = 5$.
When dividing powers with

the same base, you subtract exponents; $7 - 2 = 5$. In cases like this, $x^n \cdot x^{-m} = \frac{x^n}{x^m}$.

33. 3^6; 3^3

35. No; $\frac{6^2}{36^2} = \frac{6 \cdot 6}{36 \cdot 36} = \frac{6 \cdot 6}{6 \cdot 6 \cdot 6 \cdot 6} = \frac{1}{6 \cdot 6} = \frac{1}{36}$

37. The number is 5.

LESSON 10.2

Your Turn

3. 6.4×10^3 **4.** 5.7×10^{11}
5. 9.461×10^{12} km **8.** 7,034,000,000
9. 236,000 **10.** 5,000,000 g

Guided Practice

1. 5.8927×10^4 **2.** 1.304×10^9
3. 6.73×10^6 **4.** 1.33×10^4
5. 9.77×10^{22} **6.** 3.84×10^5
7. 400,000 **8.** 1,849,900,00
9. 6,410 **10.** 84,560,00
11. 800,000 **12.** 90,000,000,000
13. 54,00 s **14.** 7,600,000 cans

Independent Practice

17. 2.2×10^5 lb **19.** 4×10^4 lb
21. 5×10^4 lb **23.** $108\frac{1}{3}$ hours or
108 hours and 20 minutes
25. 4.6×10^3 lb **27a.** None of the
girls has the correct answer.
b. Polly and Samantha have the
decimal in the wrong place; Esther
miscounted the number of places
the decimal moved. **29.** The
speed of a car because it is likely
to be less than 100. **31.** Is the first
factor greater than 1 and less than
10? Is the second factor a power
of 10?

LESSON 10.3

Your Turn

4. 8.29×10^{-5} **5.** 3.02×10^{-7}
6. 7×10^{-6} m **9.** 0.000001045
10. 0.000099 **11.** 0.01 m

Guided Practice

1. 4.87×10^{-4} **2.** 2.8×10^{-5}
3. 5.9×10^{-5} **4.** 4.17×10^{-2}
5. 2×10^{-5} **6.** 1.5×10^{-5}
7. 0.00002 **8.** 0.000003582
9. 0.00083 **10.** 0.0297
11. 0.0000906 **12.** 0.00004
13. 1×10^{-4}
14. 0.00000000000000000000000017

Independent Practice

17. 1.3×10^{-3} cm **19.** 4.5×10^{-3} cm **21.** 8×10^{-4} cm
23. 7 cm = 0.07 m, 7 cm = 7×10^0 cm; 0.07 m = 7×10^{-2} m
The first factors are the same; the
exponents differ by 2. **25.** If the
exponent on 10 is nonnegative,
the number is greater than or equal
to 1. **27.** Negative, because a
ladybug would weigh less than
1 ounce. **29.** 0.000000000125
31. 71,490,000 **33.** 3,397,000
35. 5.85×10^{-3} m, 1.5×10^{-2} m,
2.3×10^{-2} m, 9.6×10^{-1} m,
1.2×10^2 m **37.** The result will be
greater than the number with the
positive exponent because the
divisor is less than 1.

LESSON 10.4

Your Turn

1. 7.62×10^7 more people
2. 8.928×10^8 miles
3. 3.14×10^2 minutes **4.** 7.5E5
5. 3E-7 **6.** 2.7E13 **7.** 4.5×10^{-1}
8. 5.6×10^{12} **9.** 6.98×10^{-8}

Guided Practice

1. 0.225; 6; 0.225; 2.8; 7.225×10^6
2. 0.10; 3; 8.5; 5.3; 0.10; 3.1×10^3
3. 5×10^2 **4.** 5.9381×10^5
5. 1.206×10^{22} **6.** 1.73×10^8
7. 1.69×10^{19} **8.** 2×10^7
9. 3.6E11 **10.** 7.25E-5 **11.** 8E-1
12. 7.6×10^{-4} **13.** 1.2×10^{16}
14. 9×10^1

Independent Practice

17. about 1.9×10^3 as many
19. 5.025×10^7 tons **21.** Plastics
23. about 7 people per square
mile **25.** 13 years, 3 months,
22.5 days **27.** 2.94×10^4, or
$29,400 per person. **29.** The
student is off by a power of 10.
The correct product is 40×10^{15},
or 4.0×10^{16}.

 **Selected Answers**

MODULE 11

LESSON 11.1

Your Turn

3. $y = 15x$ **4.** 6 miles hiked in 5 hours **5.** $y = \frac{6}{5}x$

Guided Practice

1. is **2.** constant of proportionality **3a.** The pairs (weeks, days) are (2, 14), (4, 28), (8, 56), (10, 70). **b.** the time in weeks; the time in days; $y = 7x$ **4.** The pairs (oxygen atoms, hydrogen atoms) are (5, 10), (17, 34), (120, 240); $y = 2x$ **5.** $y = 30x$

Independent Practice

7. No; the ratios of the numbers in each column are not equal.
9a. Sample answer: The account had a balance of $100 to begin with. **b.** Sample answer: Have Ralph open the account with no money to begin with and then put $20 in every month. **11.** $y = 105$
13a. The pairs (distance, time) are (10, 1), (20, 2), (30, 3), (40, 4), (50, 5).
b. $y = \frac{1}{10}x$, where y is the time in minutes and x is the distance in inches. **c.** 8.5 minutes **15.** For $S = 1$, $P = 4$ and $A = 1$; For $S = 2$, $P = 8$ and $A = 4$; For $S = 3$, $P = 12$ and $A = 9$; For $S = 4$, $P = 16$ and $A = 16$; For $S = 5$, $P = 20$ and $A = 25$. **a.** Yes. The ratio of the perimeter of a square to its side length is always 4. **b.** No. The ratio of the area of a square to its side length is not constant.

LESSON 11.2

Your Turn

1. 36, 13, −10; variable **4.** +3; +4; $\frac{3}{4}$

Guided Practice

1. constant **2.** variable
3. variable **4.** constant **5.** 200; 1;

200; 1; 200 **6.** 200 ft per min
7. −2 **8.** $\frac{3}{2}$

Independent Practice

11. 15 miles per hour
13a. 1 gallon every 5 minutes, or 0.2 gal/min **b.** 25 minutes
15.

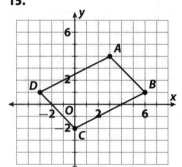

a. slope $\overline{AB} = -1$; slope $\overline{BC} = \frac{1}{2}$; slope $\overline{CD} = -1$; slope $\overline{DA} = \frac{1}{2}$
b. The slopes of the opposite sides are the same. **c.** Yes; opposite sides still have the same slope. **17.** Sample answer: One line has a positive slope and one has a negative slope. The lines are equally steep, but one slants upward left to right and the other slants downward left to right. The lines cross at the origin.

LESSON 11.3

Your Turn

2. His unit rate and the slope of a graph of the ride both equal $\frac{1}{5}$ mi/min.

Tomas's Ride

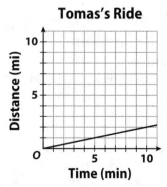

4. A: 375, 375 mi/h; B: 425, 425 mi/h; B is flying faster.

Guided Practice

1. slope = unit rate = $\frac{5}{6}$ mi/h
2. slope = unit rate = $\frac{5}{4}$ mi/h
3. Clark is faster. From the equation, Henry's rate is equal to 0.5, or $\frac{1}{2}$ mile per hour. Clark's rate is the slope of the line, which is $\frac{3}{2}$, or 1.5 miles per hour.
4. $y = 15x$ **5.** $y = \frac{3}{8}x$

Independent Practice

7a. The pairs (time, distance) are (4, 3), (8, 6), (12, 9), (16, 12), (20, 15).
b.

Migration Flight

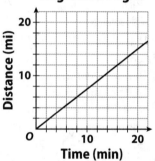

c. $\frac{3}{4}$; The unit rate of migration of the goose and the slope of the graph both equal $\frac{3}{4}$ mi/min.
9a. Machine 1: slope = unit rate = $\frac{0.6}{1}$ = 0.6 gal/s; Machine 2: slope = unit rate = $\frac{3}{4}$ = 0.75 gal/s
b. Machine 2 is working at a faster rate since 0.75 > 0.6. **11.** slope = unit rate = 4.75. If the graph of a proportional relationship passes through the point (1, r), then r equals the slope and the unit rate, which is $4.75/min. **13.** 243 gallons; Sample answer: The unit rate is $\frac{36}{2}$ = 18 gal/min. So, $1\frac{1}{2}$ min after 12 min, an additional $18 \times 1\frac{1}{2}$ = 27 gal will be pumped in. The total is 216 + 27 = 243 gal.

UNIT 6 Selected Answers *(cont'd)*

LESSON 12.1

Your Turn

1. Sample answer: (2, 20), (3, 32), (4, 44), (5, 56) **3.** (−1, 3), (0, 1), (1, −1), (2, −3)

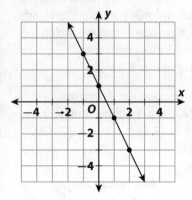

Guided Practice

1. (−2, 1), (−1, 3), (0, 5), (1, 7), (2, 9)
2. (−8, −8), (0, −5), (8, −2), (16, 1), (24, 4) **3.** Undefined, 3.5, 2.75, 2.5, 2.375; The ratio $\frac{y}{x}$ is not constant. **4.** The graph is a line, but it does not pass through the origin. **5.** (−2, −3), (−1, −2), (0, −1), (1, 0), (2, 1)

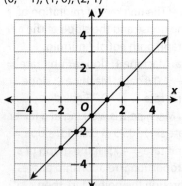

Independent Practice

7. Set of unconnected points; you cannot buy a fractional part of a lunch. **9a.** Sample answer: For (x, y) where x is number of years renewed and y is total cost in dollars: (0, 12), (1, 20), (2, 28), (3, 36), (4, 44)

b.

Magazine Subscription Costs

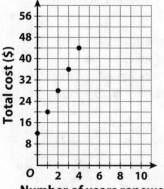

Number of years renewed

c. The graph does not include the origin. Also, the ratio of the total cost and number of years is not constant. **d.** No; the number of years must be a whole number, so total cost goes up in $8 increments. **11.** Sample answer: In a table, the ratios $\frac{y}{x}$ will not be equal; a graph will not pass through the origin; an equation will be in the form $y = mx + b$ where $b \neq 0$. **13.** At most one: A line representing a proportional relationship must pass through the origin. A line parallel to it cannot also pass through the origin.

LESSON 12.2

Your Turn

1. $m = 5$; $b = 12$ **2.** $m = 7$; $b = 1$

Guided Practice

1. −2; 1 **2.** 5; −15 **3.** $\frac{3}{2}$; −2
4. −3; 9 **5.** 3; 1 **6.** −4; 140

Independent Practice

9a. $5 to park; $12 per hour
b. $23.50; (3.5 hours × $12 per hour + $5) ÷ 2 = $23.50
11. Rate of change is constant from 1 to 2 to 3, but not from 3 to 4. **13.** Express the slope m between a random point (x, y) on the line and the point (0, b) where the line crosses the y-axis. Then solve the equation for y.

15. After parking 61 cars; John earns a fixed weekly salary of $300 plus $5 for each car he parks. He earns the same in fees as his fixed salary for parking 300 ÷ 5 = 60 cars.

LESSON 12.3

Your Turn

2.

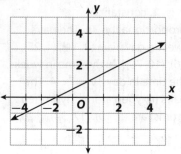

3.

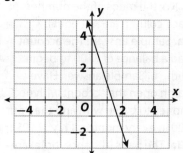

4.

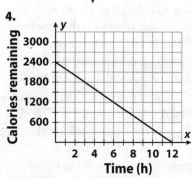

Time (h)

5. The new graph has the same y-intercept but a slope of −200 instead of −300.
6. The calories left to burn will decrease more slowly with each hour of exercise, so it will take longer for Ken to meet his goal.
7. The y-intercept would not change, but the slope would become −600, which is much steeper. The line would intersect the x-axis when x = 4 hours.

Guided Practice

1. $\frac{1}{2}$; -3

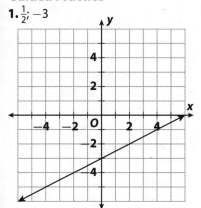

2. -3; 2

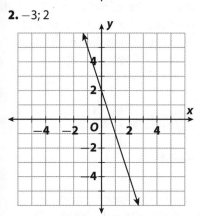

3a. Slope = 4; y-intercept = 2; you start with 2 cards and add 4 cards each week.

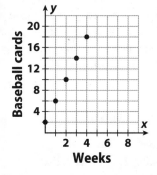

b. The points with coordinates that are not whole numbers; you will not buy part of a baseball card and you are buying only once a week.

Independent Practice

5a.

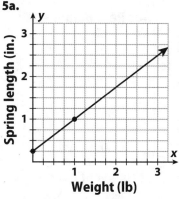

b. The slope, 0.75, means that the spring stretches by 0.75 inch with each additional pound of weight. The y-intercept, 0.25, is the unstretched length of the spring in inches. **c.** 1.75 inches; no; the length with a 4-pound weight is 3.25 in., not 3.5 in. **7.** (0, 8), (1, 7), (2, 6), (3, 5) **9.** (0, −3), (1, −1.5), (2, 0), (3, 1.5) **11.** (0, −5), (3, −3), (6, −1), (9, 1) **13a.** Yes; Since the horizontal and vertical gridlines each represent 25 units, moving up 3 gridlines and right 1 gridline represents a slope of $\frac{75}{25}$, or 3. **b.** $m = 3$ so $3 is the charge per visit; $b = 50$ so the membership fee is $50.

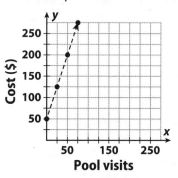

c. 50 visits **15.** Yes; plot the point and use the slope to find a second point. Then draw a line through the two points.

LESSON 12.4

Your Turn

1. nonproportional
2. proportional
5. proportional
6. nonproportional

7. nonproportional
8. nonproportional
9. nonproportional
10. proportional
11. Test-Prep Center A's charges are proportional, but B's are not. Center B offers a coupon for an initial credit, but its hourly rate, $25, is higher than Center A's hourly rate of $20. So, Center B will cost more in the long run.

Guided Practice

1. Proportional; the line includes the origin. **2.** Nonproportional; the line does not include the origin. **3.** Nonproportional; when the equation is written in the form $y = mx + b$, the value of b is not 0. **4.** Proportional; when the equation is written in the form $y = mx + b$, the value of b is 0. **5.** Proportional; the quotient of y and x is constant, 4, for every number pair. **6.** No; the quotient of y and x is not constant for every number pair. **7.** Sample answer: The rating is proportional to the number of households watching: the quotient of the rating and the number of households is always 0.0000008.

Independent Practice

9a. Nonproportional; the graph does not pass through the origin, so $b \neq 0$. **b.** $m = 0.5$, $b = 10$; each cup of sports drink weighs a half pound. The empty cooler weighs 10 pounds. **11.** Proportional; this equation has the form $y = mx + b$ where $b = 0$.
15a. No; from Equation B, the y-intercept is 273.15, not 0, so the graph does not include the origin. From Table C, the quotient of K and C is not constant.
b. No; Equation A is in the form $y = mx + b$, with F instead of y and C instead of x. The value of b is 32, not 0, so the relationship is not proportional.

MODULE 13

LESSON 13.1

Your Turn

3. $y = -2.5x + 25$ **5.** $y = 0.5x + 10$

Guided Practice

1a. the length of the necklace in inches **b.** the total number of beads in the necklace
c. $y = 5x + 27$ **2.** $\frac{0 - 300}{5 - 0} = \frac{-300}{5} = -60$; 300; $y = -60x + 300$
3. temperature; chirps per minute; $\frac{100 - 76}{65 - 59} = \frac{24}{6} = 4$; $100 = 4 \cdot 65 + b$; -160; $y = 4x - 160$

Independent Practice

5. $y = 30x$ **7.** $m = 0.125$; the diver ascends at a rate of 0.125 m/s
9. $y = 0.125x - 10$ **11.** $y = 20x + 12$ **13.** $m = 500$; $b = 1000$
15. The amount of money in the savings account increases by $500 each month. **17.** The rate of change would not be constant. Using different pairs of points in the slope formula would give different results.

LESSON 13.2

Your Turn

1. $m = 15{,}000$; $b = 0$; $y = 15{,}000x$

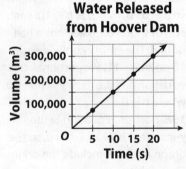

Water Released from Hoover Dam

4. $p = 75n + 250$ **5.** $c = 0.50d + 40$

Guided Practice

1. $m = -1.25$; $b = 20$; $y = -1.25x + 20$

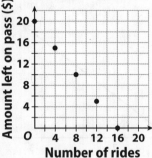

Bus Pass Balance

2. $m = \frac{51 - 59}{2000 - 0} = \frac{-8}{2000} = -0.004$
3. $b = 59$ **4.** $y = -0.004x + 59$
5. $y = -0.004(5000) + 59 = 39°F$

Independent Practice

7. $m = 2$; $b = 8$; $C = 2t + 8$
9a. $y = -1.5x + 30$ **b.** The number of dollars left decreases as the number of car washes increases. **c.** 20; after 20 washes there is no money left on the card.
11. $y = -2x + 6$ **13a.** No, the change between weeks is constant, but the change in the amount of rain is not constant.
b. No; there is no apparent pattern in the table. **15.** 0; Jaíme's graph contained (0, 0). Since Jayla's data were the same, but with x and y switched, her graph also contained (0, 0).

LESSON 13.3

Your Turn

1. $y = 4x + 20$ **2.** $y = 240x$
6. $30 **7.** $48.75 **8.** $600

Guided Practice

1. $y = 30x$ **2.** $y = 2.5x + 2$ **3.** $y = 20x + 30$; $140 **4.** Yes, because the graph has a constant rate of change. **5.** No, because the graph does not have a constant rate of change.

Independent Practice

7. Yes, because the rate of change is constant. **9.** Linear; the rate of change is the cost of a DVD, which is constant. **11.** Not linear;

---

the rate of change in the area of a square increases as the side length increases. **13.** The relationship is linear; the equation of the linear relationship is $y = 0.125x$, so the Mars Rover would travel 7.5 feet in 60 seconds. **15.** Sample answer: Because $x = 6$ lies halfway between $x = 4$ and $x = 8$, so the y-value should lie halfway between the corresponding y-values. **17.** Find the equation of the linear relationship using the slope and given point, and then insert any x-value to find a y-value on the graph of the line.

MODULE 14

LESSON 14.1

Your Turn

4. Function; each input value is paired with only one output value. **5.** Not a function; the input value is paired with more than one output value. **7.** Function; each input value is paired with only one output value. **8.** Not a function; the input value 8 is paired with more than one output value.
10. Not a function; input values are paired with more than one output values; (70, 164) and (70, 174)

Guided Practice

1. $20x$; 200 **2.** $\frac{x}{2}$; 15 **3.** $2.25x$; 27.00 **4.** Function; each input value is paired with only one output value **5.** Not a function; the input value 4 is paired with more than one output value.
6. Yes; each input value is paired with only one output value.

Independent Practice

9. Not a function; the input value 5 is paired with more than one output value. **11a.** There is only one number of bacteria for each number of hours, so each input is paired with only one output.

b. Yes. Each input value would still be paired with only one output value. **13.** Yes. Each input value (the weight) is paired with only one output value (the price). **15.** It does not represent a function. For the input values to be paired with all four output values, at least one of the input values would be paired with more than one output value.

LESSON 14.2

Your Turn
2. proportional
3. $(x, y) = (0, 0), (3, 2), (6, 4), (9, 6)$; linear; proportional

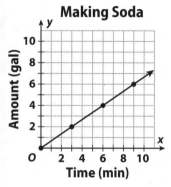

Making Soda

Guided Practice
1. $(-1, 7), (1, 3), (3, -1), (5, -5)$; linear

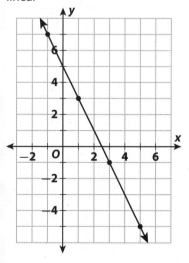

2. $(-2, -2), (-1, 1), (0, 2), (1, 1),$ $(2, -2)$; nonlinear

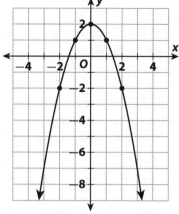

3. No; the equation cannot be written in the form $y = mx + b$, and the graph of the solutions is not a line. **4.** Yes; the equation can be written in the form $y = mx + b$, and the graph of the solutions is a line.

Independent Practice
7. No. The relationship is not linear because x is squared, so it will not be proportional. **9a.** Yes. The graph of the solutions lie in a line.

Drill Team Uniforms

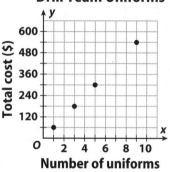

b. $720
11. Disagree; the equation can be written in the form $y = mx + b$ where m is 0, and the graph of the solutions is a horizontal line.
13. The relationship is linear if the points all lie on the same line, and proportional if it is linear and a line through the points passes through the origin. **15.** Applying the Distr. Prop gives $y + 3 = 6x + 3$, or $y = 6x$. This is in the form $y = mx + b$ with $b = 0$, so it is linear and proportional.

LESSON 14.3

Your Turn
1. Buying at the bookstore is more expensive.

Guided Practice
1. The second method (159 bpm vs. 150 bpm) gives the greater heart rate. **2.** Heart rate and age are nonproportional for each method. **3.** Students pay a $40 fee and $5 per hour.
4.

Tutoring Fees

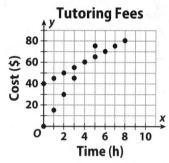

5. With both plans, it costs $60 for 4 hours of tutoring. **6.** Plan 2 ($90 vs. $150) is cheaper for 10 hours of tutoring. **7.** Cost and time are proportional for Plan 1 and nonproportional for Plan 2.

Independent Practice
9. Scooter B (15 gallons vs. 18 gallons) uses fewer gallons of gas. **11.** the first plan **13.** The camera at the second store; the cost at the first store is $290 and the cost at the second store is $260. **15.** Since the rate per visit is the same, the monthly cost of Gym A is always more than Gym B. **17.** $y = -24x + 8$ is changing more quickly because even though -24 is less than -21, the absolute value of -24 is greater than the absolute value of -21.

LESSON 14.4

Guided Practice

1. The graph is increasing quickly. This shows a period of rapid growth.

2. The number of bacteria is decreasing.

3. Graph 2 **4.** Graph 3

5.

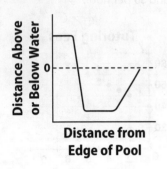

Distance from Edge of Pool

Independent Practice

7. Graph 1

9. Regina left the rental shop and rode for an hour. She took a half-hour rest and then started back. She changed her mind and continued for another half hour. She took a half-hour break and then returned to the rental shop.

11.

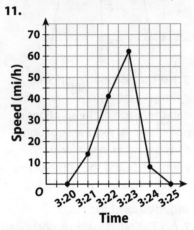

13. 3:23 to 3:24

15.

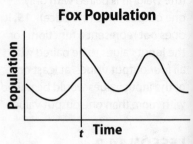

Fox Population

LESSON 15.1

Your Turn

2. 64 weeks

Guided Practice

1. $x = -4$ **2.** $x = 5$ **3.** 4 personal training sessions

Independent Practice

7a. $12 + 5x = 18 + 3x$; $x = 3$; 3 hours **b.** Darlene's Dog Sitting; the cost would be $33, as opposed to $37 at Derrick's Dog Sitting. **9.** $3x - 2 = x + 10$; $x = 6$ **11.** $8x - 20 = x + 15$; $x = 5$ **13.** $9x + 3 = 7x + 19$; $x = 8$; 75 chairs **15.** $3x + 6 = 5x + 2$; $x = 2$; 6 laps

LESSON 15.2

Your Turn

3. $k = -35$ **4.** $y = -\frac{9}{16}$ **5.** $1.9x = 1.3x + 37.44$; 62.4 lb

Guided Practice

1a. $60 + 50.45x = 57.95x$ **b.** $x = 8$; 8 months **2.** $n = 28$ **3.** $b = 60$ **4.** $m = 33$ **5.** $t = -0.8$ **6.** $w = 12$ **7.** $p = -2$

Independent Practice

11. 60 tiles **13a.** 100 mi **b.** $80 **17.** $C = 1.8C + 32$; $-40°F = -40°C$ **19.** When you attempt to solve the equation, you eliminate the variable from both sides of the equation, leaving a false statement such as $-30 = 24$. Since the statement is false, the equation must not have a solution. **21.** No; his equation gives 3, 4, and 5 as the integers. The correct equation is $k + (k + 2) + (k + 4) = 4k$, which gives $k = 6$ and the integers 6, 8, 10.

LESSON 15.3

Your Turn

1. $y = -1$ **2.** $x = 6$ **3.** $b = -4$ **4.** $t = 7$ **5.** $46,000

Guided Practice

1. 4; 32; 4; 28; 6; 28; 6; 6; 6; 6; 6; 6; $x = 1$ **2.** 3; 3; 2; -15; 18; 2; -60; $+$; 15; -13; -78; -13; -78; -13; -13; $x = 6$ **3.** $x = 3$ **4.** $x = 7$ **5.** $x = -1$ **6.** $x = 3$ **7.** $x = 9$ **8.** $x = -2$ **9.** $x = 10$ **10.** $x = -8$ **11.** $0.12(x + 3,000) = 4,200$; $32,000

Independent Practice

13. a. $x + 14$ **b.** Joey's age in 5 years: $x + 5$; Martina's age in 5 years: $x + 19$ **c.** $3(x + 5) = x + 19$ **d.** Joey: 2 years old; Martina: 16 years old **15.** It is not necessary. In this case, distributing the fractions directly results in whole number coefficients and constants. **17.** Table first row: 0.25, 0.25x; table second row: 100 − x, 0.15, 0.15(100 − x); table third row: 0.19, 19 **a.** The milliliters of acid in the 25% solution plus the milliliters of acid in the 15% solution equals the milliliters of acid in the mixture. **b.** $0.25x + 0.15(100 - x) = 19$ **c.** The chemist used 40 ml of the 25% solution and 60 ml of the 15% solution. **19.** Use the Distributive Property to distribute both 3 and 2 inside the square parentheses on the left side. Combine like terms inside the square parentheses. Then use the Distributive Property again to distribute 5. Combine like terms on the left side and use inverse operations to solve the equation. $x = 1$

LESSON 15.4

Your Turn

2. True **3.** True **4.** False **6.** one solution **7.** infinitely many solutions **8.** Sample answer: 6; Any number except 1 will yield no solution. **9.** 4

Guided Practice

1. 9x; 25; + 2; + 2; 9; 27; 9; 27; 9; 9; $x = 3$; true **2.** 2x − 2; 1; 2x; 2x; −4 = 1; false **3.** none **4.** Any value of x will result in a true statement; infinitely many solutions **5.** true; same variable; same constant; like; 10; $10 + x$; $10 + x + 5$; $15 + x = 15 + x$

Independent Practice

7. $0 = 0$; infinitely many solutions **9.** Sample answer: 5 **11.** $x + 1$ **13. a.** Yes; because the perimeters are equal, you get the equation $(2x - 2) + (x + 1) + x + (x + 1) = (2x - 9) + (x + 1) + (x + 8) + x$, or $5x = 5x$. Since $5x = 5x$ is a true statement, there are an infinite number of values for x. **b.** The condition was that the two perimeters are to be equal. However, a specific number was not given, so there are an infinite number of possible perimeters. **c.** 12; Sample answer: I used the trapezoid and wrote the equation $(2x - 2) + (x + 1) + x + (x + 1) = 60$. Solving this gives $x = 12$. **15.** No; setting the expressions equal to each other and solving gives $100 + 35x = 50 + 35x$, or $100 = 50$, which is false. **17.** Matt is incorrect. He applied the Distributive Property to the right side incorrectly. Correctly simplified, the equation is $0 = -7$, which is false, meaning no solution.

Selected Answers

MODULE **16**

LESSON 16.1

Your Turn

3. (−1, 3)

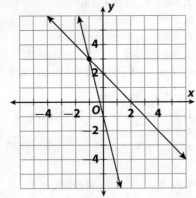

4. (1, 3)

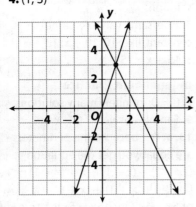

6a. $x + y = 6$ and $2x + 4y = 20$;
$y = -x + 8$ and $y = -0.5x + 5$

b.

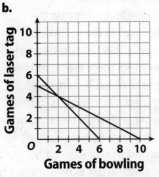

c. Marquis will bowl 2 games and play 4 games of laser tag.

Guided Practice
1. (3, 5)

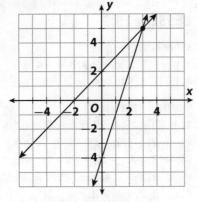

2. infinitely many solutions

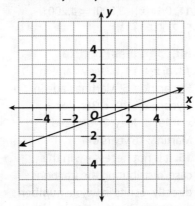

3a. $y = -x + 15$ **b.** $y = -0.5x + 10$

c.

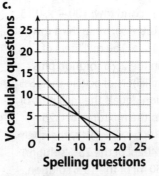

d. 10 spelling questions and 5 vocabulary questions

Independent Practice
5. system of equations
7a. $y = 2.50x + 2$; $y = 2x + 4$
b. The solution is (4, 12). The cost at both alleys will be the same for 4 games bowled, $12.

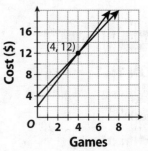

Cost of Bowling

11. Infinitely many; Rearranging the left side of the 2nd equation and subtracting $3a$ from both sides gives $-ax + ay = -3a$. Dividing both sides by $-a$ gives $x - y = 3$. The equations describe the same line.

LESSON 16.2

Your Turn
4. (2, 5) **5.** (−6, 4) **6.** (−9, −7)
7.

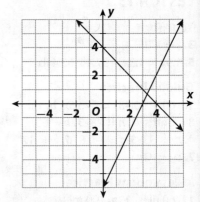

Estimate: (3, 1)
Solution: $\left(\frac{10}{3}, \frac{2}{3}\right)$
The solution is reasonable because $\frac{10}{3}$ is close to the estimate of 3 and $\frac{2}{3}$ is close to the estimate of 1.
8. Carlos: $4x + 160y = 120$
Vanessa: $x + 240y = 80$
(20, 0.25); 20 represents the cost per day: $20; 0.25 represents the cost per mile: $0.25

Guided Practice
1. (5, 3) **2.** (3, −1) **3.** (2, 1) **4.** (4, 1)
5. Estimate: (2, −5);
Solution: $\left(\frac{7}{5}, -\frac{22}{5}\right)$

6. Estimate: $(-1, 5)$;
Solution: $\left(-1, \frac{9}{2}\right)$
7. Estimate: $(3, -6)$;
Solution: $\left(\frac{13}{4}, -\frac{23}{4}\right)$
8. Estimate: $(-1, 1)$;
Solution: $\left(-\frac{3}{4}, \frac{1}{2}\right)$
9. a. Henson's cost: $3x + y = 163$;
Garcia's cost: $2x + 3y = 174$
b. adult ticket price: $45; child ticket price: $28

Independent Practice
11.

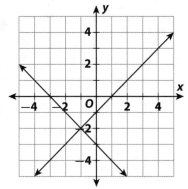

The graph shows that the
x-coordinate of the solution is
negative, so Zach's solution is not
reasonable.
13. 120 nickels and 80 dimes
15. $\left(\frac{8}{3}, -\frac{10}{3}\right)$
17. The substitution method has
the advantage of always giving an
exact answer. Graphing produces
an exact answer only if the
solution is an ordered pair whose
coordinates are integers.

LESSON 16.3

Your Turn
3. $(3, -4)$ **4.** $(2, -3)$ **5.** $(-1, 2)$
8. $(0, -2)$ **9.** $(7, -3)$ **10.** $\left(7, \frac{1}{2}\right)$
11. hot dog: $1.95; juice drink:
$1.25

Guided Practice
1. Step 1: 0; -10; y; -10; -2; 5.
Step 2: 3; $(-2, 3)$ **2.** $(2, -2)$
3. $(6, 5)$ **4.** $(7, -7)$ **5.** $(-3, 8)$
6. $(2, 3)$ **7.** $(-5, -2)$
8. a. Tony: $2x + 3.5y = 355$;
Rae: $2x + 3y = 320$
b. Minimum speed limit: 55 mi/h;
maximum speed limit: 70 mi/h

Independent Practice
11. Guppy: 3 inches; platy:
2 inches
13. Labor fee: $14.95; quart of oil:
$1.50
15. 407 adult tickets; 839 student
tickets
17. a. Jenny substituted her
expression for y into the same
equation she used to find y. She
should substitute her expression
into the other equation. **b.** Yes;
adding the equations would have
resulted in $3x = 9$, easily giving
$x = 3$ after dividing each side by 3.
Substitution requires many more
steps.

LESSON 16.4

Your Turn
4. $(-8, 15)$ **5.** $(-1, 5)$ **6.** $\left(\frac{1}{2}, -1\right)$
7. $(3, 1)$ **8.** $(-4, -1)$
9. $\left(\frac{1}{3}, 6\right)$ **10.** Contestants run
0.75 hour and bike 0.5 hour.

Guided Practice
1. Step 1: 12; 4; 32; 20; y; 2; 10.
Step 2: -2; $(2, -2)$ **2.** $(6, -1)$
3. $(-3, 8)$ **4.** $\left(\frac{7}{2}, \frac{7}{4}\right)$ **5.** $(3, -3)$
6. $(4, -1)$ **7.** $(-2, 4)$
8. a. First store: $0.64x + 0.45y = 5.26$; second store: $0.32x + 0.39y = 3.62$ **b.** Number of apples:
4; number of pears: 6

Independent Practice
11. a. $\begin{cases} 79x + 149y = 1,456 \\ x + y = 14 \end{cases}$
b. Multiply the second equation
by 79. Subtract the new equation
from the first one and solve
the resulting equation for y.
c. Solve the second equation for
x. Substitute the expression for x
in the first equation and solve the
resulting equation for y.
d. 9 polyester-fill, 5 down-fill
13. 21 pies, 16 jars of applesauce
15. a. Multiply the first equation
by 1.5 and subtract. This would
be less than ideal because you
would introduce decimals into the
solution process. **b.** Yes; multiply
the first equation by 3 and the

second equation by 2. Both x-term
coefficients would be 6. Solve
by eliminating the x-terms using
subtraction. **c.** $(9, -4)$

LESSON 16.5

Your Turn
6. no solution **7.** $(10, -2)$; one
solution **8.** infinitely many
solutions

Guided Practice
1. Step 1: are parallel; intersect; are
the same line Step 2: one; no; an
infinite number of Step 3: no, no;
1, $(1, 5)$; an infinite number of, All
2. infinitely many solutions **3.** no
solution **4.** $(-3, -4)$; one solution

Independent Practice
7.

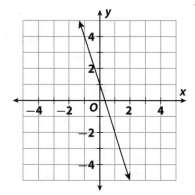

infinitely many solutions
9. one solution **11.** one solution
13. one solution
15. No; although the lines do
not intersect on the graph, they
intersect at a point that is not on
the graph. To prove that a system
has no solution, you must do so
algebraically.
17. No; both Juan and Tory run
at the same rate, so the lines
representing the distances each
has run are parallel. There is no
solution to the system.
19. A, B, and C must all be the
same multiple of 3, 5, and 8,
respectively. The two equations
represent a single line, so the
coefficients and constants of one
equation must be a multiple of
the other.

MODULE 17

LESSON 17.1

Your Turn

4.

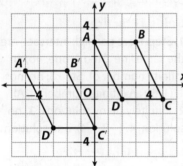

Guided Practice

1. transformation **2.** preimage; image **3.** The orientation will be the same. **4.** They are congruent.

5.

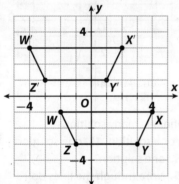

Independent Practice

7a.

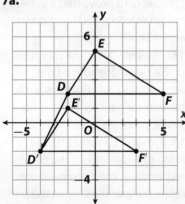

b. The translation moved the triangle 2 units to the left and 4 units down. **c.** They are congruent.

9.

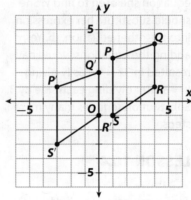

11. The hot air balloon was translated 4 units to the right and 5 units up.

13a.–c.

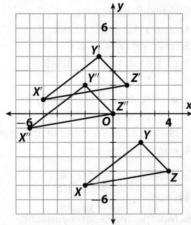

d. The original triangle was translated 4 units up and 4 units to the left.

LESSON 17.2

Your Turn

4.

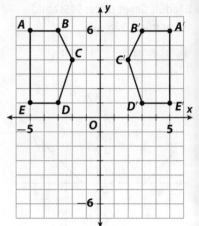

Guided Practice

1. line of reflection

2a.

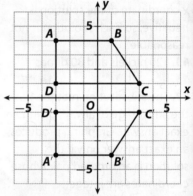

b. They are congruent. **c.** The orientation would be reversed horizontally: the figure from left to right in the preimage would match the figure from right to left in the image.

Independent Practice

5. *C* and *D* **7.** Sample answer: Since each triangle is either a reflection or translation of triangle *C*, they are all congruent. **9.** Yes; if the point lies on the line of reflection, then the image and the preimage will be the same point.

11a.–c.

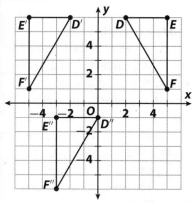

d. Sample answer: Translate triangle *DEF* 7 units down and 2 units to the left. Then reflect the image across the *y*-axis.

LESSON 17.3

Your Turn

6.–7.

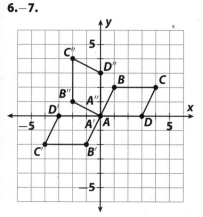

8. $(2, -4)$

Guided Practice

1. point **2.** The triangle is turned 90° to the left about vertex *E*.
3. Yes, the figures are congruent.
4.

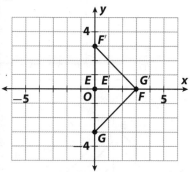

5.

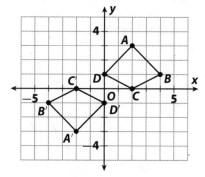

Independent Practice

7a. *ABC* was rotated 90° counterclockwise. **b.** $A'(3, 1)$; $B'(2, 3)$; $C'(-1, 4)$ **9.** 180° rotation
11. 90° clockwise **13.** 90° clockwise

15.

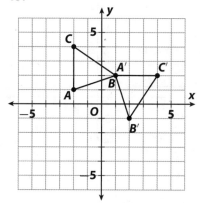

17. 2 times; 1 time; 4 times
19. Sample answer: If *A* is at the origin, then so is *A'* for any rotation about the origin. Otherwise, *A'* is on the *x*-axis for 90° and 270° rotations and on the *y*-axis for a 180° rotation.

LESSON 17.4

Your Turn

1. $(-6, -5)$, $(-6, 0)$, $(-3, -5)$, and $(-3, 0)$; the rectangle is translated 6 units to the left and 3 units down. **2.** $A'(-2, -6)$, $B'(0, -5)$, and $C'(3, 1)$ **4.** $J'(4, -2)$, $K'(-5, 1)$, and $L'(-2, 2)$

Guided Practice

1. $X'(3, -2)$, $Y'(5, 0)$, and $Z'(7, -6)$

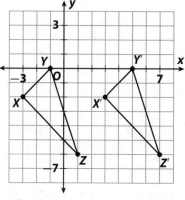

2. The *x*-coordinate remains the same, while the *y*-coordinate changes sign. **3.** The triangle is rotated 90° clockwise.

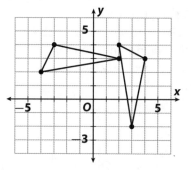

Independent Practice

5. $(x, y) \rightarrow (x + 5, y - 2)$; translation of 2 units to the left and 5 units down **7.** $(x, y) \rightarrow (x - 3.2, y + 1)$; $Y'(4.3, 6)$, $Z'(4.8, 5)$
9. The rectangle is translated 2 units to the left and 4 units down.

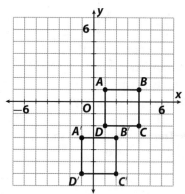

11. $(x, y) \rightarrow (x + 0.5, y - 0.25)$
13a. $(-5, -5)$; *x* and *y* are equal, so switching *x* and *y* has no effect on the coordinates. **b.** $y = x$ **c.** The triangle is reflected across the line $y = x$.

UNIT 8 Selected Answers *(cont'd)*

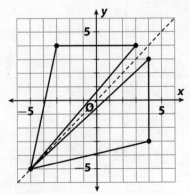

15a. $A''(1, 0)$, $B''(0, 3)$, and $C''(4, 3)$
b. $(x, y) \rightarrow (x + 3, y + 2)$

LESSON 17.5

Your Turn

3. Rotation 90° clockwise about the origin, translation 5 units down; $(x, y) \rightarrow (y, -x)$, $(x, y) \rightarrow (x, y - 5)$

Guided Practice

1.

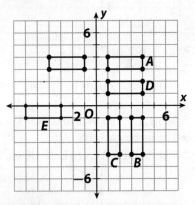

2. reflection across the y-axis
3. translation 3 units right and 4 units down
4. $(x, y) \rightarrow (-x, y)$, $(x, y) \rightarrow (x + 3, y - 4)$
5. The figures have the same size and the same shape.

Independent Practice

7.

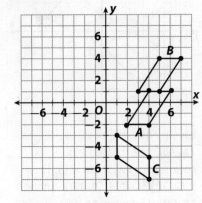

Different orientation

9.

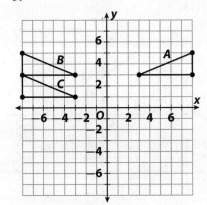

Different orientation
11. Sample answer: translation 2 units right and 4 units down, reflection across y-axis; size: no; orientation: yes
13. No; the point $(1, 2)$ translated 2 units to the right becomes $(3, 2)$, then rotated 90° clockwise about the origin, it becomes $(2, -3)$. The point $(1, 2)$ rotated 90° clockwise around the origin becomes $(2, -1)$, then translated 2 units to the right, it becomes $(4, -1)$, which is not the same.

MODULE 18

LESSON 18.1

Your Turn
5. The scale factor is 0.5.

Guided Practice
1. 2; 2 **2.** equal; equal **3.** 2
4. congruent **5.** 2

Independent Practice

7. No; the ratios of the lengths of the corresponding sides are not equal. **9.** Yes; a dilation produces an image similar to the original figure. **11.** Yes; each coordinate of triangle $U'V'W'$ is $\frac{3}{4}$ times the corresponding coordinate of triangle UVW. **13.** changed; same; same **15.** same; changed; same
17. 3 **19.** Locate the corresponding vertices of the triangles, and draw lines connecting each pair. The lines will intersect at the center of dilation.

LESSON 18.2

Your Turn
5. $(x, y) \rightarrow \left(\frac{1}{3}x, \frac{1}{3}y\right)$

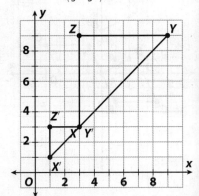

Guided Practice
1.

PreImage	Image
(2, 0)	(3, 0)
(0, 2)	(0, 3)
(−2, 0)	(−3, 0)
(0, −2)	(0, −3)

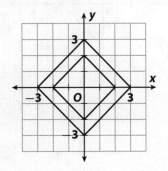

2.

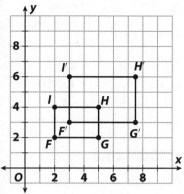

$(x, y) \rightarrow (1.5x, 1.5y)$

3.

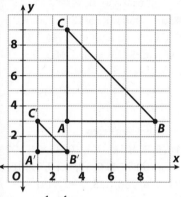

$(x, y) \rightarrow (\frac{1}{3}x, \frac{1}{3}y)$

Independent Practice
5. Green square: $(x, y) \rightarrow (2x, 2y)$; Purple square $(x, y) \rightarrow (\frac{1}{2}x, \frac{1}{2}y)$
7. $(x, y) \rightarrow (\frac{2}{3}x, \frac{2}{3}y)$ **9a.** The scale factor is 48. **b.** 48 inches or 4 feet **c.** $(x, y) \rightarrow (48x, 48y)$

---

d. $Q'(2.5, 2.5)$, $R'(8.75, 2.5)$, $S'(8.75, 6.25)$, and $T'(2.5, 6.25)$
e. Dimensions on blueprint: 6.25 in. by 3.75 in. Dimensions in house: 25 ft by 15 ft **11.** The crewmember's calculation is incorrect. The scale factor is $\frac{1}{20}$, not $\frac{1}{12}$. **13.** The figure is dilated by a factor of 2, but the orientation of the figure is rotated 180°.

LESSON 18.3

Your Turn
3. Sample answer: $(x, y) \rightarrow (x + 7, y - 12)$; rotation 90° counterclockwise about the origin; $(x, y) \rightarrow (x + 5, y + 3)$; $(x, y) \rightarrow (3x, 3y)$

Guided Practice
1.

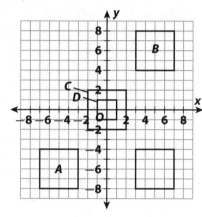

---

2. $(x, y) \rightarrow (x, -y)$; $(x, y) \rightarrow (x + 5, y - 6)$
3. $(x, y) \rightarrow (x, y + 6)$; rotate 90° counterclockwise
4. $(x, y) \rightarrow (1.5x, 1.5y)$; $(x, y) \rightarrow (x + 3, y + 5)$

Independent Practice
7. Dilate the image by a scale factor of $\frac{1}{3}$ and reflect it back across the x-axis; $(x, y) \rightarrow (\frac{1}{3}x, \frac{1}{3}y)$, $(x, y) \rightarrow (x, -y)$.
9. Rotate the image 90° counterclockwise and dilate it by a factor of $\frac{1}{5}$; $(x, y) \rightarrow (-y, x)$, $(x, y) \rightarrow (\frac{1}{5}x, \frac{1}{5}y)$.
11. There can be an even number of dilations in pairs where each has the opposite effect.
13. No; dilate first: $(0, 0) \rightarrow (0, 0) \rightarrow (0, 5)$ and $(1, 1) \rightarrow (3, 3) \rightarrow (3, 8)$, so $y = x + 5$; translate first: $(0, 0) \rightarrow (0, 5) \rightarrow (0, 15)$ and $(1, 1) \rightarrow (1, 6) \rightarrow (3, 18)$, so $y = x + 15$.

UNIT 9 Selected Answers

LESSON 19.1

Your Turn
5. 72° **6.** 108° **7.** 108°

Guided Practice
1. ∠VWZ **2.** alternate interior
3. 80° **4.** 100° **5.** same-side interior

Independent Practice
7. ∠1 and ∠5, ∠2 and ∠6, ∠3 and ∠7, ∠4 and ∠8 **9.** alternate interior angles **11.** 30°
13. 110° **15.** 78° **17.** 132°; the 48° angle is supplementary to the larger angle because the two angles are same-side interior angles. **19.** ∠6 and ∠2 are corr., so m∠2 = 125°. ∠6 and ∠3 are alt. int., so m∠3 = 125°. ∠3 and ∠7 are corr., so m∠7 = 125°. ∠6 and ∠4 are same-side int., so m∠4 = 180° − 125°, or 55°. ∠4 and ∠8 are corr., so m∠8 = 55°. ∠4 and ∠5 are alt. int., so m∠5 = 55°. ∠1 and ∠5 are corr., so m∠1 = 55°.
21. 3 angles; 4 angles; no

LESSON 19.2

Your Turn
4. 53° **5.** 90° **8.** 78°; 68°

Guided Practice
1. 71° **2.** 30° **3.** 88°; 29°; 63°
4. 90°; 45°; 45° **5.** 40°; 76°; 64°
6. 129°; 32°; 19°

Independent Practice
9. 60°; 30° **11.** 98°; 55°; 27°
13. 60°; 90°; 30°; 150° **15.** No; the measure of an obtuse angle is greater than 90°. If a triangle had two obtuse angles, the sum of their measures would be greater than 180°, the sum of the angle measures of a triangle. **17a.** 360° **b.** The sum of the angle measures of a quadrilateral is 360°.

Sample answer: Any quadrilateral can be divided into two triangles, so the sum of its angle measures is 2 × 180° = 360°.

LESSON 19.3

Your Turn
3. The triangles are not similar because only one angle is congruent. The angle measures of the triangles are 70°, 58°, and 52° and 70°, 61°, and 49°. **5.** 8 inches
6. 21 ft

Guided Practice
1. 41°, 109°, and 30°; 41°, 109°, and 30°; two angles; two angles; similar **2.** 7.5; 23.5; 17.2
3. congruent; alternate interior angles; congruent; alternate interior angles; AA Similarity; similar

Independent Practice
5. m∠B = 42°, m∠F = 69°, m∠H = 64°, m∠K = 53° **7.** ∠J ≅ ∠A, ∠L ≅ ∠B, and ∠K ≅ ∠C **9.** 25 feet
11. In the first line, Ryan should have added 19.5 and 6.5 to get a denominator of 26 for the expression on the right side to get the correct value of 13.6 cm for h.

MODULE 20

LESSON 20.1

Your Turn
4. 50 ft **5.** 9 in. **6.** $r = \sqrt{228}$, so the greatest length is 15 in.

Guided Practice
1. 10^2, 676, 26 **2a.** 1700
2b. 41.2 in.; yes

Independent Practice
5. 11.5 in. **7.** 14.1 in. **9.** 12 feet
11. 52.8 ft; $12^2 + 39^2 = c^2$, so 144 + 1521 = c^2, 1665 = c^2, and 40.8 ≈ c. Adding this to the height of the

bottom of the tree: 40.8 + 12 = 52.8 ft. **13.** $\sqrt{x^2 + x^2}$ (or $\sqrt{2x^2}$ or $x\sqrt{2}$); if $a = x$ and $b = x$, then $x^2 + x^2 = c^2$. Thus, $c = \sqrt{x^2 + x^2}$.

LESSON 20.2

Your Turn
2. not a right triangle **3.** right triangle **4.** right triangle **5.** not a right triangle **6.** Yes; $140^2 + 480^2 = 250,000$; $500^2 = 250,000$; $250,000 = 250,000$ **7.** No; $18^2 + 19^2 = 685$, $25^2 = 625$, 685 ≠ 625 **8.** No; there are no pairs of whole numbers whose squares add to $12^2 = 144$.

Guided Practice
1a. 6; 8, 10 **b.** 6, 8, 10; 36, 64, 100; 100, 100; is **2.** 9, 12, 16; 9, 12, 16; 81, 144, 256; 225, 256; is not
3. Yes; $2.5^2 + 6^2 = 42.25$, $6.5^2 = 42.25$, 42.25 = 42.25

Independent Practice
5. right triangle **7.** not a right triangle **9.** not a right triangle
11. right triangle **13.** not a right triangle **15.** No; $13^2 + 14^2 = 365$, $15^2 = 225$, and 365 ≠ 225.
17. No; $6^2 + 10^2 = 136$, $12^2 = 144$, and 136 ≠ 144. **19.** Yes; since $0.75^2 + 1^2 = 1.25^2$, the triangles are right triangles. Adjoining them at their hypotenuses will form a rectangle with sides 1 m and 0.75 m. **21.** Yes **23.** The diagonals should measure $\sqrt{90^2 + 48^2} = 102$ yards if the sides of the field meet at right angles.

LESSON 20.3

Your Turn
1. 6.4 units **4.** approximately 214.7 meters

Guided Practice
1. 5.8 units **2.** 13 units
3. 103.6 miles

Independent Practice

7a. $ET = \sqrt{113}$ units **b.** Let (x_1, y_1) $= (-3, 4)$ and $(x_2, y_2) = (4, -4)$. Substitute the coordinates into the Distance Formula and then simplify. **9.** (5, 0), (4, 3), (3, 4), (0, 5), (−3, 4), (−4, 3), (−5, 0), (−4, −3), (−3, −4), (0, −5), (3, −4), (4, −3); The points would form a circle.

11.

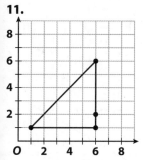

Let $(x_1, y_1) = (6, 6)$, and $(x_2, y_2) = (1, 1)$. Use the Distance Formula to show that hypotenuse $= \sqrt{50} \approx 7.1$.

LESSON 21.1

Your Turn

4. 471 in³ **5.** 602.9 ft³ **6.** 452.2 in³

Guided Practice

1. two congruent circles that lie in parallel planes **2.** Sample answer: 427 in³; there are 61 cubes on the bottom of the cylinder. The height is 7 cubes. $V = 61 \times 7 = 427$ in³ **3.** 6; 15; 36; 15; 1695.6; 1695.6 **4.** 1.35; 15.5

Independent Practice

7. 1205.8 in³ **9.** 942 in³ **11.** 803.8 m³ **13.** 6838.9 in³ **15.** 339,120 m³ **17.** 57.7 in³ **19.** Divide the diameter by 2 to find the radius. Substitute the volume and radius in $V = \pi r^2 h$ and solve for h.

LESSON 21.2

Your Turn

4. 942 cm³ **5.** 12.6 ft³ **6.** about 19,300,000 m³

Guided Practice

1. 45; 10; 450; 450; 150; 150 **2.** 54 m³; the volume of a cylinder is 3 times the volume of a cone with a congruent base and height. **3.** 65.9 ft³ **4.** 113,982 in³ **5.** 141.3 in³ **6.** 13,083.3 m³

Independent Practice

9. 25.1 in³ **11.** 94.2 m³ **13.** 167.5 in³ **15.** 628 in³ **17.** 6 cm **19a.** either the diameter or the radius of the base **b.** No; the cone is tapered from top to bottom. An equal volume of sand has a smaller radius and a greater height as the sand rises. **21.** Since the radius and height of the cones and cylinder are the same, it will take 3 cones to equal the volume of the cylinder.

LESSON 21.3

Your Turn

2. 4186.7 cm³ **3.** 20.6 m³ **6.** 904.3 in³

Guided Practice

1. the same distance **2.** radius **3.** 4.2 in³ **4.** 4,186.7 cm³ **5.** 14.1 ft³ **6.** 4.2 yd³ **7.** 12.8 in³ **8.** 435 in³ **9a.** $\frac{1}{3}$; the ball takes up $\frac{2}{3}$ of the space, so $\frac{1}{3}$ is empty. **b.** $(2r)^3 = 8r^3$ **c.** Almost $\frac{1}{2}$; the empty space is $8r^3 - \frac{4}{3}\pi r^3$, or about $3.81r^3$, and $\frac{3.81}{8} \approx 0.48$.

Independent Practice

11. 124.7 m³ **13.** 904.3 in³ **15.** 5572.5 cm³ **17.** 5389 cm³ **19.** 1766.3 in³ **21.** Divide $V = \frac{4}{3}\pi r^3$ by 2 to find the volume of the hemisphere: $V = \frac{2}{3}\pi r^3$. Add the volume of the cylinder, $V = \pi r^2 h = \pi r^3 : V = \frac{2}{3}\pi r^3 + \pi r^3 = \frac{5}{3}\pi r^3$. **23.** 12.3 in³ **25.** The cylindrical glass; the cylinder has a volume of πr^3, the hemisphere's volume is $\frac{2}{3}\pi r^3$, and the cone's volume is $\frac{1}{3}\pi r^3$. **27.** About 16 feet; 136 is 8 times 17, so the volume must be 8 times as big. Because $2^3 = 8$, this means the radius, and thus the diameter, must be twice as big.

Glossary/Glosario

ENGLISH	SPANISH	EXAMPLES
absolute value The distance of a number from zero on a number line; shown by | |.	**valor absoluto** Distancia a la que está un número de 0 en una recta numérica. El símbolo del valor absoluto es | |.	$\|-5\| = 5$
accuracy The closeness of a given measurement or value to the actual measurement or value.	**exactitud** Cercanía de una medida o un valor a la medida o el valor real.	
acute angle An angle that measures greater than 0° and less than 90°.	**ángulo agudo** Ángulo que mide mas de 0° y menos de 90°.	
acute triangle A triangle with all angles measuring less than 90°.	**triángulo acutángulo** Triángulo en el que todos los ángulos miden menos de 90°.	
Addition Property of Equality The property that states that if you add the same number to both sides of an equation, the new equation will have the same solution.	**Propiedad de igualdad de la suma** Propiedad que establece que puedes sumar el mismo número a ambos lados de una ecuación y la nueva ecuación tendrá la misma solución.	$14 - 6 = 8$ $\underline{+6 \quad +6}$ $14 = 14$
Addition Property of Opposites The property that states that the sum of a number and its opposite equals zero.	**Propiedad de la suma de los opuestos** Propiedad que establece que la suma de un número y su opuesto es cero.	$12 + (-12) = 0$
additive inverse The opposite of a number.	**inverso aditivo** El opuesto de un número.	The additive inverse of 5 is -5.
adjacent angles Angles in the same plane that have a common vertex and a common side.	**ángulos adyacentes** Ángulos en el mismo plano que comparten un vértice y un lado.	
algebraic expression An expression that contains at least one variable.	**expresión algebraica** Expresión que contiene al menos una variable.	$x + 8$ $4(m - b)$
algebraic inequality An inequality that contains at least one variable.	**desigualdad algebraica** Desigualdad que contiene al menos una variable.	$x + 3 > 10$ $5a > b + 3$

alternate exterior angles For two lines intersected by a transversal, a pair of angles that lie on opposite sides of the transversal and outside the other two lines.

ángulos alternos externos Dadas dos rectas cortadas por una transversal, par de ángulos no adyacentes ubicados en los lados opuestos de la transversal y fuera de las otras dos rectas.

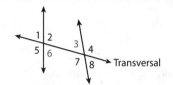

∠4 and ∠5 are alternate exterior angles.

---

alternate interior angles For two lines intersected by a transversal, a pair of nonadjacent angles that lie on opposite sides of the transversal and between the other two lines.

ángulos alternos internos Dadas dos rectas cortadas por una transversal, par de ángulos no adyacentes ubicados en los lados opuestos de la transversal y entre de las otras dos rectas.

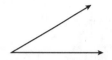

∠3 and ∠6 are alternate interior angles.

---

angle A figure formed by two rays with a common endpoint called the vertex.

ángulo Figura formada por dos rayos con un extremo común llamado vértice.

---

angle bisector A line, segment, or ray that divides an angle into two congruent angles.

bisectriz de un ángulo Línea, segmento o rayo que divide un ángulo en dos ángulos congruentes.

$\overrightarrow{MP}$ is an angle bisector.

---

arc An unbroken part of a circle.

arco Parte continua de un círculo.

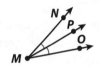

---

area The number of square units needed to cover a given surface.

área El número de unidades cuadradas que se necesitan para cubrir una superficie dada.

---

arithmetic sequence An ordered list of numbers in which the difference between consecutive terms is always the same.

sucesión aritmética Lista ordenada de números en la que la diferencia entre términos consecutivos es siempre la misma.

The sequence 2, 5, 8, 11, 14 ... is an arithmetic sequence.

---

association A description of how data sets are related.

asociación Descripción de cómo se relaciona un conjunto de datos.

Associative Property (of Addition) The property that states that for all real numbers a, b, and c, the sum is always the same, regardless of their grouping.

Propiedad asociativa (de la suma) Propiedad que establece que para todos los números reales a, b y c, la suma siempre es la misma sin importar cómo se agrupen.

$a + b + c = (a + b) + c = a + (b + c)$

Glossary/Glosario

Associative Property (of Multiplication) The property that states that for all real numbers *a, b,* and *c,* their product is always the same, regardless of their grouping.

Propiedad asociativa (de la multiplicación) Propiedad que establece que para todos los números reales *a, b* y *c,* el producto siempre es el mismo, sin importar cómo se agrupen.

$a \cdot b \cdot c = (a \cdot b) \cdot c = a \cdot (b \cdot c)$

---

asymmetry Not identical on either side of a central line; not symmetrical.

asimetría Ocurre cuando dos lados separados por una línea central no son idénticos; falta de simetría.

The quadrilateral has asymmetry.

---

average The sum of a set of data divided by the number of items in the data set; also called *mean.*

promedio La suma de los elementos de un conjunto de datos dividida entre el número de elementos del conjunto. También se llama media.

Data set: 4, 6, 7, 8, 10

Average: $\frac{4+6+7+8+10}{5}$

$= \frac{35}{5} = 7$

---

back-to-back stem-and-leaf plot A stem-and-leaf plot that compares two sets of data by displaying one set of data to the left of the stem and the other to the right.

diagrama doble de tallo y hojas Diagrama de tallo y hojas que compara dos conjuntos de datos presentando uno de ellos a la izquierda del tallo y el otro a la derecha.

Data set A: 9, 12, 14, 16, 23, 27
Data set B: 6, 8, 10, 13, 15, 16, 21

Set A		Set B
9	0	6 8
6 4 2	1	0 3 5 6
7 3	2	1

Key: |2| 1 means 21
7 |2| means 27

---

bar graph A graph that uses vertical or horizontal bars to display data.

gráfica de barras Gráfica en la que se usan barras verticales u horizontales para presentar datos.

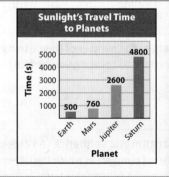

---

base When a number is raised to a power, the number that is used as a factor is the base.

base Cuando un número es elevado a una potencia, el número que se usa como factor es la base.

$3^5 = 3 \cdot 3 \cdot 3 \cdot 3 \cdot 3$; 3 is the base.

---

base (of a polygon or three-dimensional figure) A side of a polygon; a face of a three-dimensional figure by which the figure is measured or classified.

base (de un polígono o figura tridimensional) Lado de un polígono; cara de una figura tridimensional según la cual se mide o se clasifica la figura.

Bases of a cylinder

Bases of a prism

Base of a cone

Base of a pyramid

Glossary/Glosario

ENGLISH	SPANISH	EXAMPLES
biased question A question that leads people to give a certain answer.	**pregunta tendenciosa** pregunta que lleva a las personas a dar una respuesta determinada	
biased sample A sample that does not fairly represent the population.	**muestra no representativa** Muestra que no representa adecuadamente la población.	
binomial A polynomial with two terms.	**binomio** Polinomio con dos términos.	$x + y$ $2a^2 - 3$ $4m^3n^2 + 6mn^4$
bisect To divide into two congruent parts.	**trazar una bisectriz** Dividir en dos partes congruentes.	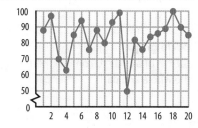$\overrightarrow{JK}$ bisects $\angle LJM$.
bivariate data A set of data that is made of two paired variables.	**datos bivariados** Conjunto de datos compuesto de dos variables apareadas.	
boundary line The set of points where the two sides of a two-variable linear inequality are equal.	**línea de límite** Conjunto de puntos donde los dos lados de una desigualdad lineal con dos variables son iguales.	
box-and-whisker plot A graph that shows how data are distributed by using the median, quartiles, least value, and greatest value; also called a *box plot*.	**gráfica de mediana y rango** Gráfica para demostrar la distribución de datos utilizando la mediana, los cuartiles y los valores menos y más grande; también llamado gráfica de caja.	
break (graph) A zigzag on a horizontal or vertical scale of a graph that indicates that some of the numbers on the scale have been omitted.	**discontinuidad (gráfica)** Zig-zag en la escala horizontal o vertical de una gráfica que indica la omisión de algunos de los números de la escala.	

ENGLISH	SPANISH	EXAMPLES
capacity The amount a container can hold when filled.	**capacidad** Cantidad que cabe en un recipiente cuando se llena.	A large milk container has a capacity of 1 gallon.
Celsius A metric scale for measuring temperature in which 0 °C is the freezing point of water and 100 °C is the boiling point of water; also called *centigrade*.	**Celsius** Escala métrica para medir la temperatura, en la que 0 °C es el punto de congelación del agua y 100 °C es el punto de ebullición. También se llama *centígrado*.	

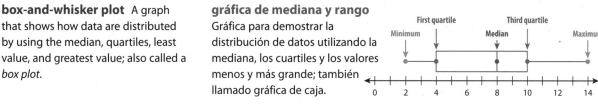

center (of a circle) The point inside a circle that is the same distance from all the points on the circle.

centro (de un círculo) Punto interior de un círculo que se encuentra a la misma distancia de todos los puntos de la circunferencia.

---

center of dilation The point of intersection of lines through each pair of corresponding vertices in a dilation.

centro de una dilatación Punto de intersección de las líneas que pasan a través de cada par de vértices correspondientes en una dilatación.

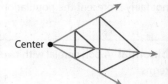

Center

---

center of rotation The point about which a figure is rotated.

centro de una rotación Punto alrededor del cual se hace girar una figura.

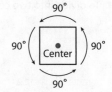

90° 90° Center 90° 90°

---

central angle An angle formed by two radii with its vertex at the center of a circle.

ángulo central de un círculo Ángulo formado por dos radios cuyo vértice se encuentra en el centro de un círculo.

---

certain (probability) Sure to happen; having a probability of 1.

seguro (probabilidad) Que con seguridad sucederá. Representa una probabilidad de 1.

---

chord A segment with its endpoints on a circle.

cuerda Segmento de recta cuyos extremos forman parte de un círculo.

A Chord B

---

circle The set of all points in a plane that are the same distance from a given point called the center.

círculo Conjunto de todos los puntos en un plano que se encuentran a la misma distancia de un punto dado llamado centro.

---

circle graph A graph that uses sectors of a circle to compare parts to the whole and parts to other parts.

gráfica circular Gráfica que usa secciones de un círculo para comparar partes con el todo y con otras partes.

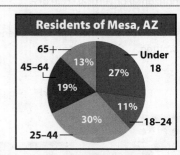

Residents of Mesa, AZ

65+ 13%, Under 18 27%, 45–64, 19%, 18–24 11%, 25–44, 30%

---

circuit A path in a graph that begins and ends at the same vertex.

circuito Una trayectoria en una gráfica que empieza y termina en el mismo vértice.

---

circumference The distance around a circle.

circunferencia Distancia alrededor de un círculo.

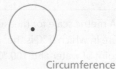

Circumference

ENGLISH	SPANISH	EXAMPLES
clockwise A circular movement in the direction shown.	**en el sentido de las manecillas del reloj** Movimiento circular en la dirección que se indica.	
cluster A set of closely grouped data.	**agrupación** Conjunto de datos bien agrupados.	
clustering A condition that occurs when data points in a scatter plot are grouped more in one part of the graph than another.	**arracimando** Una condición que ocurre cuando los datos están apiñando en una parte de una diagrama de dispersión mas que en otras partes.	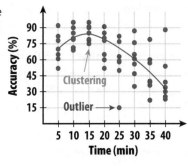
coefficient The number that is multiplied by the variable in an algebraic expression.	**coeficiente** Número que se multiplica por la variable en una expresión algebraica.	5 is the coefficient in 5*b*.
combination An arrangement of items or events in which order does not matter.	**combinación** Agrupación de objetos o sucesos en la que el orden no es importante.	For objects *A, B, C,* and *D,* there are 6 different combinations of 2 objects: *AB, AC, AD, BC, BD, CD.*
commission A fee paid to a person for making a sale.	**comisión** Pago que recibe una persona por realizar una venta.	
commission rate The fee paid to a person who makes a sale expressed as a percent of the selling price.	**tasa de comisión** Pago que recibe una persona por hacer una venta, expresado como un porcentaje del precio de venta.	A commission rate of 5% on a sale of $10,000 results in a commission of $500.
common denominator A denominator that is the same in two or more fractions.	**denominador común** Denominador que es común a dos o más fracciones.	The common denominator of $\frac{5}{8}$ and $\frac{2}{8}$ is 8.
common difference In an arithmetic sequence, the nonzero constant difference of any term and the previous term.	**diferencia común** En una sucesión aritmética, diferencia constante distinta de cero entre cualquier término y el término anterior.	In the arithmetic sequence 3, 5, 7, 9, 11, …, the common difference is 2.
common factor A number that is a factor of two or more numbers.	**factor común** Número que es factor de dos o más números.	8 is a common factor of 16 and 40.
common multiple A number that is a multiple of each of two or more numbers.	**múltiplo común** Número que es múltiplo de dos o más números.	15 is a common multiple of 3 and 5.
common ratio The ratio each term is multiplied by to produce the next term in a geometric sequence.	**razón común** Razón por la que se multiplica cada término para obtener el siguiente término de una sucesión geométrica.	In the geometric sequence 32, 16, 8, 4, 2, …, the common ratio is $\frac{1}{2}$.

Glossary/Glosario

Commutative Property (of Addition) The property that states that two or more numbers can be added in any order without changing the sum.

Propiedad conmutativa (de la suma) Propiedad que establece que sumar dos o más números en cualquier orden no altera la suma.

$8 + 20 = 20 + 8; a + b = b + a$

Commutative Property (of Multiplication) The property that states that two or more numbers can be multiplied in any order without changing the product.

Propiedad conmutativa (de la multiplicación) Propiedad que establece que multiplicar dos o más números en cualquier orden no altera el producto.

$6 \cdot 12 = 12 \cdot 6; a \cdot b = b \cdot a$

---

compatible numbers Numbers that are close to the given numbers that make estimation or mental calculation easier.

números compatibles Números que están cerca de los números dados y hacen más fácil la estimación o el cálculo mental.

To estimate $7,957 + 5,009$, use the compatible numbers 8,000 and 5,000:
$8,000 + 5,000 = 13,000$

---

complement The set of all outcomes in the sample space that are not the event.

complemento La serie de resultados que no están en el suceso.

Experiment: rolling a number cube
Sample space: {1, 2, 3, 4, 5, 6}
Event: rolling a 1, 3, 4, or 6
Complement: rolling a 2 or 5

---

complementary angles Two angles whose measures add to 90°.

ángulos complementarios Dos ángulos cuyas medidas suman 90°.

The complement of a 53° angle is a 37° angle.

---

composite figure A figure made up of simple geometric shapes.

figura compuesta Figura formada por figuras geométricas simples.

---

composite number A number greater than 1 that has more than two whole-number factors.

número compuesto Número mayor que 1 que tiene más de dos factores que son números cabales.

4, 6, 8, and 9 are composite numbers.

---

compound event An event made up of two or more simple events.

suceso compuesto Suceso que consista de dos o más sucesos simples.

Rolling a 3 on a number cube and spinning a 2 on a spinner is a compound event.

---

compound inequality A combination of more than one inequality.

desigualdad compuesta Combinación de dos o más desigualdades.

$-2 \le x < 10$

---

compound interest Interest earned or paid on principal and previously earned or paid interest.

interés compuesto Interés que se gana o se paga sobre el capital y los intereses previamente ganados o pagados.

If $100 is put into an account with an interest rate of 5% compounded monthly, then after 2 years, the account will have $100\left(1 + \frac{0.05}{12}\right)^{12 \cdot 2} = \$110.49$

ENGLISH	SPANISH	EXAMPLES

conditional relative frequency The ratio of a joint relative frequency to a related marginal relative frequency in a two-way table.

frecuencia relativa condicional Razón de una frecuencia relativa conjunta a una frecuencia relativa marginal en una tabla de doble entrada.

---

cone A three-dimensional figure with one vertex and one circular base.

cono Figura tridimensional con un vértice y una base circular.

---

congruence transformation A transformation that results in an image that is the same shape and the same size as the original figure.

transformación de congruencia Una transformación que resulta en una imagen que tiene la misma forma y el mismo tamaño como la figura original.

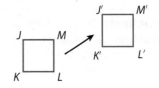

---

congruent Having the same size and shape; the symbol for congruent is ≅.

congruentes Que tienen la misma forma y el mismo tamaño expresado por ≅.

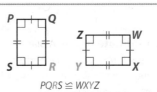

$PQRS \cong WXYZ$

---

congruent angles Angles that have the same measure.

ángulos congruentes Ángulos que tienen la misma medida.

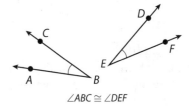

$\angle ABC \cong \angle DEF$

---

congruent figures See *congruent*.

figuras congruentes Vea *congruentes*.

---

congruent segments Segments that have the same length.

segmentos congruentes Segmentos que tienen la misma longitud.

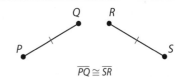

$\overline{PQ} \cong \overline{SR}$

---

conjecture A statement believed to be true.

conjetura Enunciado que se supone verdadero.

---

constant A value that does not change.

constante Valor que no cambia.

$3, 0, \pi$

---

constant of variation The constant k in direct and inverse variation equations.

constante de variación La constante k en ecuaciones de variación directa e inversa.

$y = 5x$
↑
Constant of variation

---

continuous graph A graph made up of connected lines or curves.

gráfica continua Gráfica compuesta por líneas rectas o curvas conectadas.

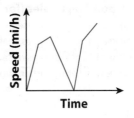

ENGLISH	SPANISH	EXAMPLES
convenience sample A sample based on members of the population that are readily available.	**muestra de conveniencia** Una muestra basada en miembros de la población que están fácilmente disponibles.	
conversion factor A fraction whose numerator and denominator represent the same quantity but use different units; the fraction is equal to 1 because the numerator and denominator are equal.	**factor de conversión** Fracción cuyo numerador y denominador representan la misma cantidad pero con unidades distintas; la fracción es igual a 1 porque el numerador y el denominador son iguales.	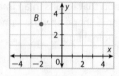
coordinate One of the numbers of an ordered pair that locate a point on a coordinate graph.	**coordenada** Uno de los números de un par ordenado que ubica un punto en una gráfica de coordenadas.	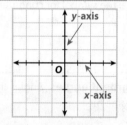 The coordinates of *B* are (−2, 3).
coordinate plane A plane formed by the intersection of a horizontal number line called the *x*-axis and a vertical number line called the *y*-axis.	**plano cartesiano** Plano formado por la intersección de una recta numérica horizontal llamada eje *x* y otra vertical llamada eje *y*.	
correlation The description of the relationship between two data sets.	**correlación** Descripción de la relación entre dos conjuntos de datos.	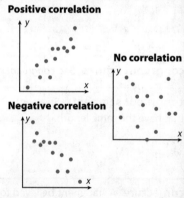
correspondence The relationship between two or more objects that are matched.	**correspondencia** La relación entre dos o más objetos que coinciden.	∠*A* and ∠*D* are corresponding angles. $\overline{AB}$ and $\overline{DE}$ are corresponding sides.
corresponding angles (for lines) For two lines intersected by a transversal, a pair of angles that lie on the same side of the transversal and on the same sides of the other two lines.	**ángulos correspondientes (en líneas)** Dadas dos rectas cortadas por una transversal, el par de ángulos ubicados en el mismo lado de la transversal y en los mismos lados de las otras dos rectas.	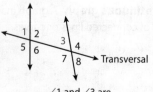 ∠1 and ∠3 are corresponding angles.

ENGLISH	SPANISH	EXAMPLES

corresponding angles (of polygons) Angles in the same relative position in polygons with an equal number of sides.

ángulos correspondientes (en polígonos) Ángulos en la misma posición formaron cuando una tercera línea interseca dos líneas.

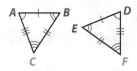

∠*A* and ∠*D* are corresponding angles.

---

corresponding sides Matching sides of two or more polygons.

lados correspondientes Lados que se ubican en la misma posición relativa en dos o más polígonos.

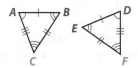

$\overline{AB}$ and $\overline{DE}$ are corresponding sides.

---

counterclockwise A circular movement in the direction shown.

en sentido contrario a las manecillas del reloj Movimiento circular en la dirección que se indica.

---

counterexample An example that proves that a conjecture or statement is false.

contraejemplo Ejemplo que demuestra que una conjetura o enunciado es falso.

---

cross section The intersection of a three-dimensional figure and a plane.

sección transversal Intersección de una figura tridimensional y un plano.

---

cube (geometric figure) A rectangular prism with six congruent square faces.

cubo (figura geométrica) Prisma rectangular con seis caras cuadradas congruentes.

---

cube (in numeration) A number raised to the third power.

cubo (en numeración) Número elevado a la tercera potencia.

$2^3 = 2 \cdot 2 \cdot 2 = 8$
8 is the cube of 2.

---

cube root A number, written as $\sqrt[3]{x}$, whose cube is *x*.

raíz cúbica Número, expresado como $\sqrt[3]{x}$, cuyo cubo es *x*.

$\sqrt[3]{8} = \sqrt[3]{2 \cdot 2 \cdot 2} = 2$
2 is the cube root of 8.

---

cumulative frequency The sum of successive data items.

frecuencia acumulativa La suma de datos sucesivos.

---

customary system of measurement The measurement system often used in the United States.

sistema usual de medidas El sistema de medidas que se usa comúnmente en Estados Unidos.

inches, feet, miles, ounces, pounds, tons, cups, quarts, gallons

---

cylinder A three-dimensional figure with two parallel, congruent circular bases connected by a curved lateral surface.

cilindro Figura tridimensional con dos bases circulares paralelas y congruentes, unidas por una superficie lateral curva.

decagon A polygon with ten sides.

decágono Polígono de diez lados.

---

deductive reasoning Using logic to show that a statement is true.

razonamiento deductivo Uso de la lógica para demostrar que un enunciado es verdadero.

---

degree The unit of measure for angles or temperature.

grado Unidad de medida para ángulos y temperaturas.

---

degree of a polynomial The highest power of the variable in a polynomial.

grado de un polinomio La potencia más alta de la variable en un polinomio.

The polynomial $4x^5 - 6x^2 + 7$ has degree 5.

---

denominator The bottom number of a fraction that tells how many equal parts are in the whole.

denominador Número que está abajo en una fracción y que indica en cuántas partes iguales se divide el entero.

In the fraction $\frac{2}{5}$, 5 is the denominator.

Density Property The property that states that between any two real numbers there is always another real number.

Propiedad de densidad Propiedad según la cual entre dos números reales cualesquiera siempre hay otro número real.

---

dependent events Events for which the outcome of one event affects the probability of the other.

sucesos dependientes Dos sucesos son dependientes si el resultado de uno afecta la probabilidad del otro.

A bag contains 3 red marbles and 2 blue marbles. Drawing a red marble and then drawing a blue marble without replacing the first marble is an example of dependent events.

---

dependent variable The output of a function; a variable whose value depends on the value of the input, or independent variable.

variable dependiente Salida de una función; variable cuyo valor depende del valor de la entrada, o variable independiente.

For $y = 2x + 1$, y is the dependent variable.
input: x output: y

---

diagonal A line segment that connects two nonadjacent vertices of a polygon.

diagonal Segmento de recta que une dos vértices no adyacentes de un polígono.

---

diameter A line segment that passes through the center of a circle and has endpoints on the circle, or the length of that segment.

diámetro Segmento de recta que pasa por el centro de un círculo y tiene sus extremos en la circunferencia, o bien la longitud de ese segmento.

---

dilation A transformation that enlarges or reduces a figure.

dilatación Transformación que agranda o reduce una figura.

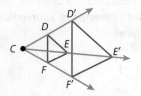

ENGLISH	SPANISH	EXAMPLES
dimensions (geometry) The length, width, or height of a figure.	**dimensiones (geometría)** Longitud, ancho o altura de una figura.	
dimensions (of a matrix) The number of horizontal rows and vertical columns in a matrix.	**dimensiones (de una matriz)** Número de filas y columnas que hay en una matriz.	
direct variation A linear relationship between two variables, x and y, that can be written in the form $y = kx$, where k is a nonzero constant.	**variación directa** Relación lineal entre dos variables, x e y, que puede expresarse en la forma $y = kx$, donde k es una constante distinta de cero.	$y = 2x$
discount The amount by which the original price is reduced.	**descuento** Cantidad que se resta del precio original de un artículo.	
discrete graph A graph made up of unconnected points.	**gráfica discreta** Gráfica compuesta de puntos no conectados.	**Cost of Photo Printing**
disjoint events See *mutually exclusive*.	**sucesos disjuntos** Vea *mutuamente excluyentes*.	
Distributive Property For all real numbers a, b, and c, $a(b + c) = ab + ac$, and $a(b - c) = ab - ac$.	**Propiedad distributiva** Dados los números reales a, b, y c, $a(b + c) = ab + ac$, y $a(b - c) = ab - ac$.	$5 \cdot 21 = 5(20 + 1) = (5 \cdot 20) + (5 \cdot 1)$
dividend The number to be divided in a division problem.	**dividendo** Número que se divide en un problema de división.	In $8 \div 4 = 2$, 8 is the dividend.
divisible Can be divided by a number without leaving a remainder.	**divisible** Que se puede dividir entre un número sin dejar residuo.	18 is divisible by 3.
Division Property of Equality The property that states that if you divide both sides of an equation by the same nonzero number, the new equation will have the same solution.	**Propiedad de igualdad de la división** Propiedad que establece que puedes dividir ambos lados de una ecuación entre el mismo número distinto de cero, y la nueva ecuación tendrá la misma solución.	
divisor The number you are dividing by in a division problem.	**divisor** El número entre el que se divide en un problema de división.	In $8 \div 4 = 2$, 4 is the divisor.
dodecahedron A polyhedron with 12 faces.	**dodecaedro** Poliedro de 12 caras.	

ENGLISH	SPANISH	EXAMPLES
domain The set of all possible input values of a function.	**dominio** Conjunto de todos los posibles valores de entrada de una función.	The domain of the function $y = x^2 + 1$ is all real numbers.
double-bar graph A bar graph that compares two related sets of data.	**gráfica de doble barra** Gráfica de barras que compara dos conjuntos de datos relacionados.	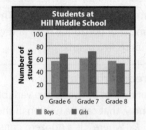
double-line graph A line graph that shows how two related sets of data change over time.	**gráfica de doble línea** Gráfica lineal que muestra cómo cambian con el tiempo dos conjuntos de datos relacionados.	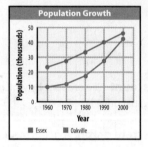

E

edge The line segment along which two faces of a polyhedron intersect.	**arista** Segmento de recta donde se intersecan dos caras de un poliedro.	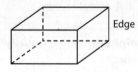
endpoint A point at the end of a line segment or ray.	**extremo** Un punto ubicado al final de un segmento de recta o rayo.	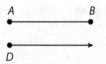
enlargement An increase in size of all dimensions in the same proportions.	**agrandamiento** Aumento de tamaño de todas las dimensiones en las mismas proporciones.	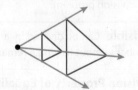
entries (of a matrix) Individual entries in a matrix.	**elementos (de una matriz)** Entradas individuales de una matriz.	
equally likely Outcomes that have the same probability.	**resultados igualmente probables** Resultados que tienen la misma probabilidad de ocurrir.	When tossing a coin, the outcomes "heads" and "tails" are equally likely.
equation A mathematical sentence that shows that two expressions are equivalent.	**ecuación** Enunciado matemático que indica que dos expresiones son equivalentes.	$x + 4 = 7$ $6 + 1 = 10 - 3$

equilateral triangle A triangle with three congruent sides.

triángulo equilátero Triángulo con tres lados congruentes.

---

equivalent Having the same value.

equivalentes Que tienen el mismo valor.

---

equivalent expressions Expressions that have the same value for all values of the variables.

expresiones equivalentes Las expresiones equivalentes tienen el mismo valor para todos los valores de las variables.

$4x + 5x$ and $9x$ are equivalent expressions.

---

equivalent fractions Fractions that name the same amount or part.

fracciones equivalentes Fracciones que representan la misma cantidad o parte.

$\frac{1}{2}$ and $\frac{2}{4}$ are equivalent fractions.

---

equivalent ratios Ratios that name the same comparison.

razones equivalentes Razones que representan la misma comparación.

$\frac{1}{2}$ and $\frac{2}{4}$ are equivalent ratios.

---

estimate (n) An answer that is close to the exact answer and is found by rounding or other methods. **(v)** To find such an answer.

estimación Una solución aproximada a la respuesta exacta que se halla mediante el redondeo u otros métodos.
estimar Hallar una solución aproximada a la respuesta exacta.

500 is an estimate for the sum $98 + 287 + 104$.

---

evaluate To find the value of a numerical or algebraic expression.

evaluar Hallar el valor de una expresión numérica o algebraica.

Evaluate $2x + 7$ for $x = 3$.
$2x + 7$
$2(3) + 7$
$6 + 7$
13

---

event An outcome or set of outcomes of an experiment or situation.

suceso Un resultado o una serie de resultados de un experimento o una situación.

When rolling a number cube, the event "an odd number" consists of the outcomes 1, 3, and 5.

---

expanded form A number written as the sum of the values of its digits.

forma desarrollada Número escrito como suma de los valores de sus dígitos.

236,536 written in expanded form is $200,000 + 30,000 + 6,000 + 500 + 30 + 6$.

---

experiment (probability) In probability, any activity based on chance (such as tossing a coin).

experimento (probabilidad) En probabilidad, cualquier actividad basada en la posibilidad, como lanzar una moneda.

Tossing a coin 10 times and noting the number of "heads"

---

experimental probability The ratio of the number of times an event occurs to the total number of trials, or times that the activity is performed.

probabilidad experimental Razón del número de veces que ocurre un suceso al número total de pruebas o al número de que se realiza el experimento.

Kendra attempted 27 free throws and made 16 of them. Her experimental probability of making a free throw is

$\frac{\text{number made}}{\text{number attempted}} = \frac{16}{27} \approx 0.59$.

---

exponent The number that indicates how many times the base is used as a factor.

exponente Número que indica cuántas veces se usa la base como factor.

$2^3 = 2 \times 2 \times 2 = 8$;
3 is the exponent.

---

exponential decay An exponential function of the form $f(x) = a \cdot r^x$ in which $0 < r < 1$.

decremento exponencial Función exponencial del tipo $f(x) = a \cdot r^x$ en la cual $0 < r < 1$.

Glossary/Glosario

ENGLISH	SPANISH	EXAMPLES
exponential form A number written with a base and an exponent.	**forma exponencial** Se dice que un número está en forma exponencial cuando se escribe con una base y un exponente.	4^2 is the exponential form for $4 \cdot 4$.
exponential function A nonlinear function in which the variable is in the exponent.	**función exponencial** Función no lineal en la que la variable está en el exponente.	$f(x) = 4^x$
exponential growth An exponential function of the form $f(x) = a \cdot r^x$ in which $r > 1$.	**crecimiento exponencial** Función exponencial del tipo $f(x) = a \cdot r^x$ en la cual $r > 1$.	
expression A mathematical phrase that contains operations, numbers, and/or variables.	**expresión** Enunciado matemático que contiene operaciones, números y/o variables.	$6x + 1$
exterior angle (of a polygon) An angle formed by one side of a polygon and the extension of an adjacent side.	**ángulo extreno de un polígono** Ángulo formado por un lado de un polígono y la prolongación del lado adyacente.	

F

face A flat surface of a polyhedron.	**cara** Superficie plana de un poliedro.	Face
factor A number that is multiplied by another number to get a product.	**factor** Número que se multiplica por otro para hallar un producto.	7 is a factor of 21 since $7 \cdot 3 = 21$.
factorial The product of all whole numbers except zero that are less than or equal to a number.	**factorial** El producto de todos los números cabales, excepto cero, que son menores que o iguales a un número.	4 factorial $= 4! = 4 \cdot 3 \cdot 2 \cdot 1$
Fahrenheit A temperature scale in which 32 °F is the freezing point of water and 212 °F is the boiling point of water.	**Fahrenheit** Escala de temperatura en la que 32° F es el punto de congelación del agua y 212° F es el punto de ebullición.	
fair When all outcomes of an experiment are equally likely, the experiment is said to be fair.	**justo** Se dice de un experimento donde todos los resultados posibles son igualmente probables.	When tossing a coin, heads and tails are equally likely, so it is a fair experiment.
Fibonacci sequence The infinite sequence of numbers (1, 1, 2, 3, 5, 8, 13,…); starting with the third term, each number is the sum of the two previous numbers; it is named after the thirteenth-century mathematician Leonardo Fibonacci.	**sucesión de Fibonacci** La sucesión infinita de números (1, 1, 2, 3, 5, 8, 13…); a partir del tercer término, cada número es la suma de los dos anteriores. Esta sucesión lleva el nombre de Leonardo Fibonacci, un matemático del siglo XIII.	1, 1, 2, 3, 5, 8, 13, . . .
first differences A sequence formed by subtracting each term of a sequence from the next term.	**primeras diferencias** Sucesión que se forma al restar cada término de una sucesión del término siguiente.	For the sequence 4, 7, 10, 13, 16, . . ., the first differences are all 3.

ENGLISH	SPANISH	EXAMPLES

first quartile The median of the lower half of a set of data; also called *lower quartile*.

primer cuartil La mediana de la mitad inferior de un conjunto de datos. También se llama *cuartil inferior*.

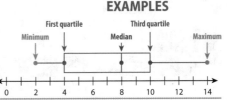

FOIL An acronym for the terms used when multiplying two binomials: the First, Outer, Inner, and Last terms.

FOIL Sigla en inglés de los términos que se usan al multiplicar dos binomios: los primeros, los externos, los internos y los últimos (First, Outer, Inner, Last).

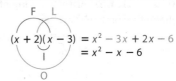

$(x + 2)(x - 3) = x^2 - 3x + 2x - 6$
$= x^2 - x - 6$

---

formula A rule showing relationships among quantities.

fórmula Regla que muestra relaciones entre cantidades.

$A = \ell w$ is the formula for the area of a rectangle.

---

fractal A structure with repeating patterns containing shapes that are like the whole but are of different sizes throughout.

fractal Estructura con patrones repetidos que contiene figuras similares al patrón general pero de diferente tamaño.

---

fraction A number in the form $\frac{a}{b}$, where $b \neq 0$.

fracción Número escrito en la forma $\frac{a}{b}$, donde $b \neq 0$.

$\frac{2}{3}$

---

frequency The number of times the value appears in the data set.

frecuencia Cantidad de veces que aparece el valor en un conjunto de datos.

Data set: 5, 6, 6, 7, 8, 9
The data value 6 has a frequency of 2.

---

frequency table A table that lists items together according to the number of times, or frequency, that the items occur.

tabla de frecuencia Una tabla en la que se organizan los datos de acuerdo con el número de veces que aparece cada valor (o la frecuencia).

Data set: 1, 1, 2, 2, 3, 5, 5, 5
Frequency table:

Data	Frequency
1	2
2	2
3	1

---

function An input-output relationship that has exactly one output for each input.

función Regla que relaciona dos candidates de forma que a cada valor de entrada corresponde exactamente un valor de salida.

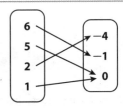

---

function notation The notation used to describe a function.

notación de función Notación que se usa para describir una función.

Equation: $y = 2x$
Function notation: $f(x) = 2x$

---

function table A table of ordered pairs that represent solutions of a function.

tabla de función Tabla de pares ordenados que representan soluciones de una función.

x	3	4	5	6
y	7	9	11	13

Fundamental Counting Principle If one event has m possible outcomes and a second event has n possible outcomes after the first event has occurred, then there are $m \cdot n$ total possible outcomes for the two events.

Principio fundamental de conteo Si un suceso tiene m resultados posibles y otro suceso tiene n resultados posibles después de ocurrido el primer suceso, entonces hay $m \cdot n$ resultados posibles en total para los dos sucesos.

There are 4 colors of shirts and 3 colors of pants. There are $4 \cdot 3 = 12$ possible outfits.

geometric probability A form of theoretical probability determined by a ratio of geometric measures such as lengths, areas, or volumes.

probabilidad geométrica Método para calcular probabilidades basado en una medida geométrica como la longitud o el área.

The probability of the pointer landing on red is $\frac{80}{360}$, or $\frac{2}{9}$.

geometric sequence An ordered list of numbers that has a common ratio between consecutive terms.

sucesión geométrica Lista ordenada de números que tiene una razón común entre términos consecutivos.

The sequence 2, 4, 8, 16 . . . is a geometric sequence.

graph of an equation A graph of the set of ordered pairs that are solutions of the equation.

gráfica de una ecuación Gráfica del conjunto de pares ordenados que son soluciones de la ecuación.

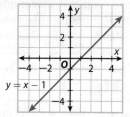

$y = x - 1$

great circle A circle on a sphere such that the plane containing the circle passes through the center of the sphere.

círculo máximo Círculo de una esfera tal que el plano que contiene el círculo pasa por el centro de la esfera.

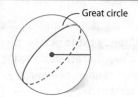

Great circle

greatest common factor (GCF) The largest common factor of two or more given numbers.

máximo común divisor (MCD) El mayor de los factores comunes compartidos por dos o más números dados.

The GCF of 27 and 45 is 9.

height In a pyramid or cone, the perpendicular distance from the base to the opposite vertex.

altura En una pirámide o cono, la distancia perpendicular desde la base al vértice opuesto.

In a triangle or quadrilateral, the perpendicular distance from the base to the opposite vertex or side.

En un triángulo o cuadrilátero, la distancia perpendicular desde la base de la figura al vértice o lado opuesto.

In a prism or cylinder, the perpendicular distance between the bases.

En un prisma o cilindro, la distancia perpendicular entre las bases.

ENGLISH	SPANISH	EXAMPLES

hemisphere A half of a sphere.

hemisferio La mitad de una esfera.

heptagon A seven-sided polygon.

heptágono Polígono de siete lados.

hexagon A six-sided polygon.

hexágono Polígono de seis lados.

histogram A bar graph that shows the frequency of data within equal intervals.

histograma Gráfica de barras que muestra la frecuencia de los datos en intervalos iguales.

hypotenuse In a right triangle, the side opposite the right angle.

hipotenusa En un triángulo rectángulo, el lado opuesto al ángulo recto.

Identity Property of Addition
The property that states the sum of zero and any number is that number.

Propiedad de identidad de la suma
Propiedad que establece que la suma de cero y cualquier número es ese número.

$4 + 0 = 4$
$-3 + 0 = -3$

Identity Property of Multiplication
The property that states that the product of 1 and any number is that number.

Propiedad de identidad de la multiplicación Propiedad que establece que el producto de 1 y cualquier número es ese número.

$4 \cdot 1 = 4$
$-3 \cdot 1 = -3$

image A figure resulting from a transformation.

imagen Figura que resulta de una transformación.

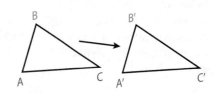

$A'B'C'$ is the image of ABC.

impossible (probability) Can never happen; having a probability of 0.

imposible (en probabilidad) Que no puede ocurrir. Suceso cuya probabilidad de ocurrir es 0.

ENGLISH	SPANISH	EXAMPLES
improper fraction A fraction in which the numerator is greater than or equal to the denominator.	**fracción impropia** Fracción cuyo numerador es mayor que o igual al denominador.	$\frac{17}{5}, \frac{3}{3}$
independent events Events for which the outcome of one event does not affect the probability of the other.	**sucesos independientes** Dos sucesos son independientes si el resultado de uno no afecta la probabilidad del otro.	A bag contains 3 red marbles and 2 blue marbles. Drawing a red marble, replacing it, and then drawing a blue marble is an example of independent events.
independent variable The input of a function; a variable whose value determines the value of the output, or dependent variable.	**variable independiente** Entrada de una función; variable cuyo valor determina el valor de la salida, o variable dependiente.	For $y = 2x + 1$, x is the independent variable. input: x output: y
indirect measurement The technique of using similar figures and proportions to find a measure.	**medición indirecta** La técnica de usar figuras semejantes y proporciones para hallar una medida.	
inductive reasoning Using a pattern to make a conclusion.	**razonamiento inductivo** Uso de un patrón para sacar una conclusión.	
inequality A mathematical sentence that shows the relationship between quantities that are not equivalent.	**desigualdad** Enunciado matemático que muestra una relación entre cantidades que no son equivalentes.	$5 < 8$ $5x + 2 \geq 12$
input The value substituted into an expression or function.	**valor de entrada** Valor que se usa para sustituir una variable en una expresión o función.	For the function $y = 6x$, the input 4 produces an output of 24.
inscribed angle An angle formed by two chords with its vertex on a circle.	**ángulo inscrito** Ángulo formado por dos cuerdas cuyo vértice está en un círculo.	
integers The set of whole numbers and their opposites.	**enteros** Conjunto de todos los números cabales y sus opuestos.	$\ldots -3, -2, -1, 0, 1, 2, 3, \ldots$
interest The amount of money charged for borrowing or using money.	**interés** Cantidad de dinero que se cobra por el préstamo o uso del dinero.	
interior angles Angles on the inner sides of two lines cut by a transversal.	**ángulos internos** Ángulos en los lados internos de dos líneas intersecadas por una transversal.	
interquartile range (IQR) The difference of the third (upper) and first (lower) quartiles in a data set, representing the middle half of the data.	**rango intercuartil (RIC)** Diferencia entre el tercer cuartil (superior) y el primer cuartil (inferior) de un conjunto de datos, que representa la mitad central de los datos.	 Interquartile range: $36 - 23 = 13$
intersecting lines Lines that cross at exactly one point.	**líneas secantes** Líneas que se cruzan en un solo punto.	

ENGLISH	SPANISH	EXAMPLES
interval The space between marked values on a number line or the scale of a graph.	**intervalo** El espacio entre los valores marcados en una recta numérica o en la escala de una gráfica.	
inverse operations Operations that undo each other: addition and subtraction, or multiplication and division.	**operaciones inversas** Operaciones que se cancelan mutuamente: suma y resta, o multiplicación y división.	Addition and subtraction are inverse operations: $5 + 3 = 8; 8 - 3 = 5$ Multiplication and division are inverse operations: $2 \cdot 3 = 6; 6 \div 3 = 2$
inverse variation A relationship in which one variable quantity increases as another variable quantity decreases; the product of the variables is a constant.	**variación inversa** Relación en la que una cantidad variable aumenta a medida que otra cantidad variable disminuye; el producto de las variables es una constante.	$xy = 7, y = \frac{7}{x}$
irrational number A number that cannot be expressed as a ratio of two integers or as a repeating or terminating decimal.	**número irracional** Número que no se puede expresar como una razón de dos enteros ni como un decimal periódico o finito.	$\sqrt{2}, \pi$
isolate the variable To get a variable alone on one side of an equation or inequality in order to solve the equation or inequality.	**despejar la variable** Dejar sola la variable en un lado de una ecuación o desigualdad para resolverla.	$x + 7 = 22$ $\frac{-7 \quad -7}{x \quad\;\; = 15}$ $\quad\frac{12}{3} = \frac{3x}{3}$ $\quad 4 = x$
isometric drawing A representation of a three-dimensional figure that is drawn on a grid of equilateral triangles.	**dibujo isométrico** Representación de una figura tridimensional que se dibuja sobre una cuadrícula de triángulos equiláteros.	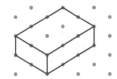
isosceles triangle A triangle with at least two congruent sides.	**triángulo isósceles** Triángulo que tiene al menos dos lados congruentes.	

joint relative frequency The ratio of the frequency in a particular category divided by the total number of data values.	**frecuencia relativa conjunta** La razón de la frecuencia en una determinada categoría dividida entre el número total de valores.	

lateral area The sum of the areas of the lateral faces of a prism or pyramid, or the area of the lateral surface of a cylinder or cone.	**área lateral** Suma de las áreas de las caras laterales de un prisma o pirámide, o área de la superficie lateral de un cilindro o cono.	

Lateral area = area of the 5 rectangular faces

Glossary/Glosario

lateral face In a prism or a pyramid, a face that is not a base.

cara lateral En un prisma o pirámide, una cara que no es la base.

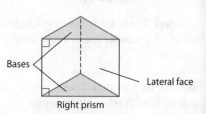

lateral surface In a cylinder, the curved surface connecting the circular bases; in a cone, the curved surface that is not a base.

superficie lateral En un cilindro, superficie curva que une las bases circulares; en un cono, la superficie curva que no es la base.

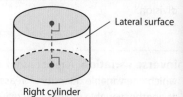

least common denominator (LCD) The least common multiple of two or more denominators.

mínimo común denominador (mcd) El mínimo común múltiplo más pequeño de dos o más denominadores.

The LCD of $\frac{3}{4}$ and $\frac{5}{6}$ is 12.

least common multiple (LCM) The smallest whole number, other than zero, that is a multiple of two or more given numbers.

mínimo común múltiplo (mcm) El menor de los números cabales, distinto de cero, que es múltiplo de dos o más números dados.

The LCM of 6 and 10 is 30.

legs In a right triangle, the sides that include the right angle; in an isosceles triangle, the pair of congruent sides.

catetos En un triángulo rectángulo, los lados adyacentes al ángulo recto. En un triángulo isósceles, el par de lados congruentes.

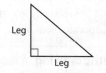

like fractions Fractions that have the same denominator.

fracciones semejantes Fracciones que tienen el mismo denominador.

$\frac{5}{12}$ and $\frac{7}{12}$ are like fractions.

like terms Terms that have the same variable raised to the same exponents.

términos semejantes Términos que contienen las mismas variables elevada a las mismas exponentes.

In the expression $3a^2 + 5b + 12a^2$, $3a^2$ and $12a^2$ are like terms.

line A straight path that has no thickness and extends forever.

línea Un trazo recto que no tiene grosor y se extiende infinitamente.

line graph A graph that uses line segments to show how data changes.

gráfica lineal Gráfica que muestra cómo cambian los datos mediante segmentos de recta.

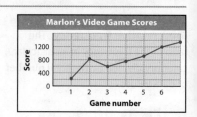

line of best fit A straight line that comes closest to the points on a scatter plot.

línea de mejor ajuste La línea recta que más se aproxima a los puntos de un diagrama de dispersión.

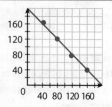

ENGLISH	SPANISH	EXAMPLES
line of reflection A line that a figure is flipped across to create a mirror image of the original figure.	**línea de reflexión** Línea sobre la cual se invierte una figura para crear una imagen reflejada de la figura original.	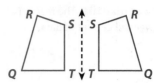
line of symmetry A line that divides a figure into two congruent reflected halves.	**eje de simetría** Línea que divide una figura en dos mitades reflejas.	
line plot A number line with marks or dots that show frequency.	**diagrama de acumulación** Recta numérica con marcas o puntos que indican la frecuencia.	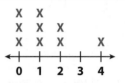
line segment A part of a line consisting of two endpoints and all points between them.	**segmento de recta** Parte de una línea que consiste en dos extremos y todos los puntos entre éstos.	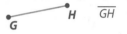
line symmetry A figure has line symmetry if one half is a mirror image of the other half.	**simetría axial** Una figura tiene simetría axial si una de sus mitades es la imagen reflejada de la otra.	
linear equation An equation whose solutions form a straight line on a coordinate plane.	**ecuación lineal** Ecuación cuyas soluciones forman una línea recta en un plano cartesiano.	$y = 2x + 1$
linear function A function whose graph is a straight line.	**función lineal** Función cuya gráfica es una línea recta.	$y = x - 1$ 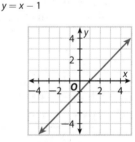
linear inequality A mathematical sentence using $<$, $>$, $\le$, or $\ge$ whose graph is a region with a straight-line boundary.	**desigualdad lineal** Enunciado matemático en que se usan los símbolos $<$, $>$, $\le$, o $\ge$ y cuya gráfica es una región con una línea de límite recta.	
linear relationship A relationship between two quantities in which one variable changes by a constant amount as the other variable changes by a constant amount.	**relación lineal** Relación entre dos cantidades en la cual una variable cambia según una cantidad constante y la otra variable también cambia según una cantidad constante.	
literal equation An equation that contains two or more variables.	**ecuación literal** Ecuación que contiene dos o más variables.	$d = rt$ $A = bh$

ENGLISH	SPANISH	EXAMPLES
lower quartile The median of the lower half of a set of data.	**cuartil inferior** La mediana de la mitad inferior de un conjunto de datos.	Lower half Upper half 18, (23), 28, 29, 36, 42 ↑ Lower quartile

ENGLISH	SPANISH	EXAMPLES
major arc An arc that is more than half of a circle.	**arco mayor** Arco que es más de la mitad de un círculo.	 $\overset{\frown}{ADC}$ is a major arc of the circle.
marginal relative frequency The sum of the joint relative frequencies in a row or column of a two-way table.	**frecuencia relativa marginal** La suma de las frecuencias relativas conjuntas en una fila o columna de una tabla de doble entrada.	
matrix A rectangular arrangement of data enclosed in brackets.	**matriz** Arreglo rectangular de datos encerrado entre corchetes.	$\begin{bmatrix} 1 & 0 & 3 \\ -2 & 2 & -5 \\ 7 & -6 & 3 \end{bmatrix}$
mean The sum of a set of data divided by the number of items in the data set; also called *average*.	**media** La suma de todos los elementos de un conjunto de datos dividida entre el número de elementos del conjunto. También se llama promedio.	Data set: 4, 6, 7, 8, 10 Mean: $\frac{4+6+7+8+10}{5} = \frac{35}{5} = 7$
mean absolute deviation (MAD) The mean distance between each data value and the mean of the data set.	**desviación absoluta media (DAM)** Distancia media entre cada dato y la media del conjunto de datos.	
measure of center A measure used to describe the middle of a data set; the mean, median, and mode are measures of center. Also called *measure of central tendency*.	**medida de tendencia dominante** Medida que describe la parte media de un conjunto de datos; la media, la mediana y la moda son medidas de tendencia dominante.	
median The middle number, or the mean (average) of the two middle numbers, in an ordered set of data.	**mediana** El número intermedio o la media (el promedio) de los dos números intermedios en un conjunto ordenado de datos.	Data set: 4, 6, 7, 8, 10 Median: 7
metric system of measurement A decimal system of weights and measures that is used universally in science and commonly throughout the world.	**sistema métrico de medición** Sistema decimal de pesos y medidas empleado universalmente en las ciencias y de uso común en todo el mundo.	centimeters, meters, kilometers, grams, kilograms, milliliters, liters
midpoint The point that divides a line segment into two congruent line segments.	**punto medio** El punto que divide un segmento de recta en dos segmentos de recta congruentes.	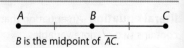 B is the midpoint of $\overline{AC}$.

ENGLISH	SPANISH	EXAMPLES
minor arc An arc that is less than half of a circle.	**arco menor** Arco que es menor que la mitad de un círculo.	$\overset{\frown}{AC}$ is the minor arc of the circle.
mixed number A number made up of a whole number that is not zero and a fraction.	**número mixto** Número compuesto por un número cabal distinto de cero y una fracción.	$4\frac{1}{8}$
mode The number or numbers that occur most frequently in a set of data; when all numbers occur with the same frequency, we say there is no mode.	**moda** Número o números más frecuentes en un conjunto de datos; si todos los números aparecen con la misma frecuencia, no hay moda.	Data set: 3, 5, 8, 8, 10 Mode: 8
monomial A number or a product of numbers and variables with exponents that are whole numbers.	**monomio** Un número o un producto de números y variables con exponentes que son números cabales.	$3x^2y^4$
multiple The product of any number and a nonzero whole number is a multiple of that number.	**múltiplo** El producto de cualquier número y un número cabal distinto de cero es un múltiplo de ese número.	
Multiplication Property of Equality The property that states that if you multiply both sides of an equation by the same number, the new equation will have the same solution.	**Propiedad de igualdad de la multiplicación** Propiedad que establece que puedes multiplicar ambos lados de una ecuación por el mismo número y la nueva ecuación tendrá la misma solución.	$3 \cdot 4 = 12$ $3 \cdot 4 \cdot 2 = 12 \cdot 2$ $24 = 24$
Multiplication Property of Zero The property that states that for all real numbers $a, a \cdot 0 = 0$ and $0 \cdot a = 0$.	**Propiedad de multiplicación del cero** Propiedad que establece que para todos los números reales $a, a \cdot 0 = 0$ y $0 \cdot a = 0$.	
multiplicative inverse A number times its multiplicative inverse is equal to 1; also called *reciprocal*.	**inverso multiplicativo** Un número multiplicado por su inverso multiplicativo es igual a 1. También se llama *recíproco*.	The multiplicative inverse of $\frac{4}{5}$ is $\frac{5}{4}$.
mutually exclusive Two events are mutually exclusive if they cannot occur in the same trial of an experiment.	**mutuamente excluyentes** Dos sucesos son mutuamente excluyentes cuando no pueden ocurrir en la misma prueba de un experimento.	When rolling a number cube once, rolling a 3 and rolling an even number are mutually exclusive events.

N

negative correlation Two data sets have a negative correlation if one set of data values increases while the other decreases.	**correlación negativa** Dos conjuntos de datos tienen correlación negativa si los valores de un conjunto aumentan a medida que los valores del otro conjunto disminuyen.	

negative integer An integer less than zero.

entero negativo Entero menor que cero.

−2 is a negative integer.
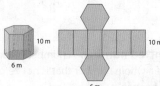

---

net An arrangement of two-dimensional figures that can be folded to form a polyhedron.

plantilla Arreglo de figuras bidimensionales que se doblan para formar un poliedro.

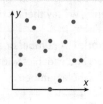

---

network A set of points and the line segments or arcs that connect the points.

red Conjunto de puntos y los segmentos de recta o arcos que los conectan.

---

no correlation Two data sets have no correlation when there is no relationship between their data values.

sin correlación Caso en que los valores de dos conjuntos no muestran ninguna relación.

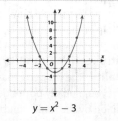

---

nonlinear function A function whose graph is not a straight line.

función no lineal Función cuya gráfica no es una línea recta.

$y = x^2 - 3$

---

nonlinear relationship A relationship between two variables in which the data do not increase or decrease together at the same rate.

relación no lineal Relación entre dos variables en la cual los datos no aumentan o disminuyen al mismo tiempo a una tasa constante.

---

nonterminating decimal A decimal that never ends.

decimal infinito Decimal que nunca termina.

$0.\overline{3}$

---

numerator The top number of a fraction that tells how many parts of a whole are being considered.

numerador El número de arriba de una fracción; indica cuántas partes de un entero se consideran.

$\frac{4}{5}$ ← numerator

---

numerical expression An expression that contains only numbers and operations.

expresión numérica Expresión que incluye sólo números y operaciones.

$(2 \cdot 3) + 1$

obtuse angle An angle whose measure is greater than 90° but less than 180°.

ángulo obtuso Ángulo que mide más de 90° y menos de 180°.

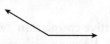

---

obtuse triangle A triangle containing one obtuse angle.

triángulo obtusángulo Triángulo que tiene un ángulo obtuso.

Glossary/Glosario

ENGLISH	SPANISH	EXAMPLES
octagon An eight-sided polygon.	**octágono** Polígono de ocho lados.	
odds A comparison of the number of ways an event can occur and the number of ways an event can *not* occur.	**probabilidades** Comparación del número de las maneras que puede ocurrir un suceso y el número de maneras que no puede ocurrir el suceso.	
odds against The ratio of the number of unfavorable outcomes to the number of favorable outcomes.	**probabilidades en contra** Razón del número de resultados no favorables al número de resultados favorables.	The odds against rolling a 3 on a number cube are 5:1.
odds in favor The ratio of the number of favorable outcomes to the number of unfavorable outcomes.	**probabilidades a favor** Razón del número de resultados favorables al número de resultados no favorables.	The odds in favor of rolling a 3 on a number cube are 1:5.
opposites Two numbers that are an equal distance from zero on a number line; also called *additive inverse*.	**opuestos** Dos números que están a la misma distancia de cero en una recta numérica. También se llaman *inversos aditivos*.	5 and −5 are opposites. 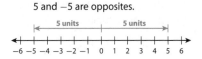
order of operations A rule for evaluating expressions: First perform the operations in parentheses, then compute powers and roots, then perform all multiplication and division from left to right, and then perform all addition and subtraction from left to right.	**orden de las operaciones** Regla para evaluar expresiones: primero se hacen las operaciones entre paréntesis, luego se hallan las potencias y raíces, después todas las multiplicaciones y divisiones de izquierda a derecha, y por último, todas las sumas y restas de izquierda a derecha.	$4^2 + 8 \div 2$ Evaluate the power. $16 + 8 \div 2$ Divide. $16 + 4$ Add. 20
ordered pair A pair of numbers that can be used to locate a point on a coordinate plane.	**par ordenado** Par de números que sirven para ubicar un punto en un plano cartesiano.	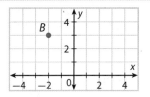 The coordinates of *B* are (−2, 3).
origin The point where the *x*-axis and *y*-axis intersect on the coordinate plane; (0, 0).	**origen** Punto de intersección entre el eje *x* y el eje *y* en un plano cartesiano: (0, 0).	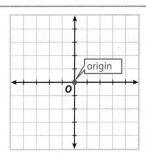

ENGLISH	SPANISH	EXAMPLES
orthogonal views A drawing that shows the top, bottom, front, back, and side views of a three-dimensional object.	**vista ortogonal** Un dibujo que muestra la vista superior, inferior, frontal, posterior y lateral de un objeto de tres dimensiones.	

ENGLISH	SPANISH	EXAMPLES
outcome (probability) A possible result of a probability experiment.	**resultado (en probabilidad)** Posible resultado de un experimento de probabilidad.	When rolling a number cube, the possible outcomes are 1, 2, 3, 4, 5, and 6.
outlier A value much greater or much less than the others in a data set.	**valor extremo** Un valor mucho mayor o menor que los demás valores de un conjunto de datos.	Most of data Mean Outlier
output The value that results from the substitution of a given input into an expression or function.	**valor de salida** Valor que resulta después de sustituir una variable por un valor de entrada determinado en una expresión o función.	For the function $y = 6x$, the input 4 produces an output of 24.
overestimate An estimate that is greater than the exact answer.	**estimación alta** Estimación mayor que la respuesta exacta.	100 is an overestimate for the sum $23 + 24 + 21 + 22$.

P

ENGLISH	SPANISH	EXAMPLES
parabola The graph of a quadratic function.	**parábola** Gráfica de una función cuadrática.	
parallel lines Lines in a plane that do not intersect.	**líneas paralelas** Líneas que se encuentran en el mismo plano pero que nunca se intersecan.	r s
parallelogram A quadrilateral with two pairs of parallel sides.	**paralelogramo** Cuadrilátero con dos pares de lados paralelos.	
pentagon A five-sided polygon.	**pentágono** Polígono de cinco lados.	
percent A ratio comparing a number to 100.	**porcentaje** Razón que compara un número con el número 100.	$45\% = \frac{45}{100}$
percent change The amount stated as a percent that a number increases or decreases.	**porcentaje de cambio** Cantidad en que un número aumenta o disminuye, expresada como un porcentaje.	
percent decrease A percent change describing a decrease in a quantity.	**porcentaje de disminución** Porcentaje de cambio en que una cantidad disminuye.	An item that costs $8 is marked down to $6. The amount of the decrease is $2, and the percent decrease is $\frac{2}{8} = 0.25 = 25\%$.

ENGLISH	SPANISH	EXAMPLES
percent increase A percent change describing an increase in a quantity.	**porcentaje de incremento** Porcentaje de cambio en que una cantidad aumenta.	The price of an item increases from $8 to $12. The amount of the increase is $4, and the percent increase is $\frac{4}{8} = 0.5 = 50\%$.
perfect cube A cube of a whole number.	**cubo perfecto** El cubo de un número cabal.	$2^3 = 8$, so 8 is a perfect cube.
perfect square A square of a whole number.	**cuadrado perfecto** El cuadrado de un número cabal.	$5^2 = 25$, so 25 is a perfect square.
perimeter The distance around a polygon.	**perímetro** Distancia alrededor de un polígono.	18 ft 6 ft perimeter $= 18 + 6 + 18 + 6 = 48$ ft
permutation An arrangement of items or events in which order is important.	**permutación** Arreglo de objetos o sucesos en el que el orden es importante.	For objects *A*, *B*, and *C*, there are 6 different permutations: *ABC*, *ACB*, *BAC*, *BCA*, *CAB*, *CBA*.
perpendicular bisector A line that intersects a segment at its midpoint and is perpendicular to the segment.	**mediatriz** Línea que cruza un segmento en su punto medio y es perpendicular al segmento.	ℓ *A* *B*
perpendicular lines Lines that intersect to form right angles.	**líneas perpendiculares** Líneas que al intersecarse forman ángulos rectos.	*n* *m*
pi (π) The ratio of the circumference of a circle to the length of its diameter; $\pi \approx 3.14$ or $\frac{22}{7}$.	**pi** (π) Razón de la circunferencia de un círculo a la longitud de su diámetro; $\pi \approx 3.14$ ó $\frac{22}{7}$.	
plane A flat surface that has no thickness and extends forever.	**plano** Superficie plana que no tiene ningún grueso y que se extiende por siempre.	*A* *C* $\mathcal{R}$ *B*
point An exact location that has no size.	**punto** Ubicación exacta que no tiene ningún tamaño.	*P.*
point-slope form The equation of a line in the form of $y - y_1 = m(x - x_1)$, where *m* is the slope and (x_1, y_1) is a specific point on the line.	**forma de punto y pendiente** Ecuación lineal del tipo $y - y_1 = m(x - x_1)$, donde *m* es la pendiente y (x_1, y_1) es un punto específico de la línea.	$y - 3 = 2(x - 3)$
polygon A closed plane figure formed by three or more line segments that intersect only at their endpoints (vertices).	**polígono** Figura plana cerrada, formada por tres o más segmentos de recta que se intersecan sólo en sus extremos (vértices).	

ENGLISH	SPANISH	EXAMPLES
polyhedron A three-dimensional figure in which all the surfaces or faces are polygons.	**poliedro** Figura tridimensional cuyas superficies o caras tiene forma de polígonos.	
polynomial One monomial or the sum or difference of monomials.	**polinomio** Un monomio o la suma o la diferencia de monomios.	$2x^2 + 3xy - 7y^2$
population The entire group of objects or individuals considered for a survey.	**población** Grupo completo de objetos o individuos que se desea estudiar.	In a survey about study habits of middle school students, the population is all middle school students.
positive correlation Two data sets have a positive correlation when their data values increase or decrease together.	**correlación positiva** Dos conjuntos de datos tienen una correlación positiva cuando los valores de ambos conjuntos aumentan o disminuyen al mismo tiempo.	
positive integer An integer greater than zero.	**entero positivo** Entero mayor que cero.	2 is a positive integer.
power A number produced by raising a base to an exponent.	**potencia** Número que resulta al elevar una base a un exponente.	$2^3 = 8$, so 2 to the 3rd power is 8.
prediction Something you can reasonably expect to happen in the future.	**predicción** Algo que se puede razonablemente esperar suceder en el futuro.	
preimage The original figure in a transformation.	**imagen original** Figura original en una transformación.	
prime factorization A number written as the product of its prime factors.	**factorización prima** Un número escrito como el producto de sus factores primos.	$10 = 2 \cdot 5$, $24 = 2^3 \cdot 3$
prime number A whole number greater than 1 that has exactly two factors, itself and 1.	**número primo** Número cabal mayor que 1 que sólo es divisible entre 1 y él mismo.	5 is prime because its only factors are 5 and 1.
principal The initial amount of money borrowed or saved.	**principal** Cantidad inicial de dinero depositada o recibida en préstamo.	
principal square root The nonnegative square root of a number.	**raíz cuadrada principal** Raíz cuadrada no negativa de un número.	$\sqrt{25} = 5$; the principal square root of 25 is 5.
prism A polyhedron that has two congruent, polygon-shaped bases and other faces that are all parallelograms.	**prisma** Poliedro con dos bases congruentes con forma de polígono y caras con forma de paralelogramo.	
probability A number from 0 to 1 (or 0% to 100%) that describes how likely an event is to occur.	**probabilidad** Un número entre 0 y 1 (ó 0% y 100%) que describe qué tan probable es un suceso.	A bag contains 3 red marbles and 4 blue marbles. The probability of randomly choosing a red marble is $\frac{3}{7}$.

ENGLISH	SPANISH	EXAMPLES
proper fraction A fraction in which the numerator is less than the denominator.	**fracción propia** Fracción en la que el numerador es menor que el denominador.	$\frac{3}{4}, \frac{1}{12}, \frac{7}{8}$
proportion An equation that states that two ratios are equivalent.	**proporción** Ecuación que establece que dos razones son equivalentes.	$\frac{2}{3} = \frac{4}{6}$
proportional relationship A relationship between two quantities in which the ratio of one quantity to the other quantity is constant.	**relación proporcional** Relación entre dos cantidades en que la razón de una cantidad a la otra es constante.	
protractor A tool for measuring angles.	**transportador** Instrumento para medir ángulos.	
pyramid A polyhedron with a polygon base and triangular sides that all meet at a common vertex.	**pirámide** Poliedro cuya base es un polígono; tiene caras triangulares que se juntan en un vértice común.	
Pythagorean Theorem In a right triangle, the square of the length of the hypotenuse is equal to the sum of the squares of the lengths of the legs.	**Teorema de Pitágoras** En un triángulo rectángulo, la suma de los cuadrados de los catetos es igual al cuadrado de la hipotenusa.	13 cm, 5 cm, 12 cm $5^2 + 12^2 = 13^2$ $25 + 144 = 169$
Pythagorean triple A set of three positive integers a, b, and c such that $a^2 + b^2 = c^2$.	**Tripleta de Pitágoras** Conjunto de tres números enteros positivos de cero a, b y c tal que $a^2 + b^2 = c^2$.	3, 4, 5 because $3^2 + 4^2 = 5^2$

Q

quadrant The x- and y-axes divide the coordinate plane into four regions. Each region is called a quadrant.	**cuadrante** El eje x y el eje y dividen el plano cartesiano en cuatro regiones. Cada región recibe el nombre de cuadrante.	Quadrant II, Quadrant I, 0, Quadrant III, Quadrant IV
quadratic function A function of the form $y = ax^2 + bx + c$, where $a \neq 0$.	**función cuadrática** Función del tipo $y = ax^2 + bx + c$, donde $a \neq 0$.	$y = x^2 - 6x + 8$
quadrilateral A four-sided polygon.	**cuadrilátero** Polígono de cuatro lados.	
quarterly Four times a year.	**trimestral** Cuatro veces al año.	

ENGLISH	SPANISH	EXAMPLES
quartile Three values, one of which is the median, that divide a data set into fourths.	**cuartil** Cada uno de tres valores, uno de los cuales es la mediana, que dividen en cuartos un conjunto de datos.	
quotient The result when one number is divided by another.	**cociente** Resultado de dividir un número entre otro.	In $8 \div 4 = 2$, 2 is the quotient.

radical symbol The symbol $\sqrt{}$ used to represent the nonnegative square root of a number.	**símbolo de radical** El símbolo $\sqrt{}$ con que se representa la raíz cuadrada no negativa de un número.	
radius A line segment with one endpoint at the center of the circle and the other endpoint on the circle, or the length of that segment.	**radio** Segmento de recta con un extremo en el centro de un círculo y el otro en la circunferencia, o bien se llama radio a la longitud de ese segmento.	Radius
random numbers In a set of random numbers, each number has an equal chance of appearing.	**muestra aleatoria** Muestra en la que cada individuo u objeto de la población tiene la misma posibilidad de ser elegido.	
random sample A sample in which each individual or object in the entire population has an equal chance of being selected.	**números aleatorios** En un conjunto de números aleatorios, todos los números tienen la misma probabilidad de ser seleccionados.	
range (in statistics) The difference between the greatest and least values in a data set.	**rango (en estadística)** Diferencia entre los valores máximo y mínimo de un conjunto de datos.	Data set: 3, 5, 7, 7, 12 Range: $12 - 3 = 9$
range (of a function) The set of all possible output values of a function.	**rango (en una función)** El conjunto de todos los valores posibles de una función.	The range of $y = \|x\|$ is $y \geq 0$.
rate A ratio that compares two quantities measured in different units.	**tasa** Una razón que compara dos cantidades medidas en diferentes unidades.	The speed limit is 55 miles per hour or 55 mi/h.
rate of change A ratio that compares the amount of change in a dependent variable to the amount of change in an independent variable.	**tasa de cambio** Razón que compara la cantidad de cambio de la variable dependiente con la cantidad de cambio de la variable independiente.	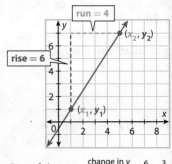

Rate of change $= \dfrac{\text{change in } y}{\text{change in } x} = \dfrac{6}{4} = \dfrac{3}{2}$

ENGLISH	SPANISH	EXAMPLES
rate of interest The percent charged or earned on an amount of money; see *simple interest*.	**tasa de interés** Porcentaje que se cobra por una cantidad de dinero prestada o que se gana por una cantidad de dinero ahorrada; ver *interés simple*.	
ratio A comparison of two quantities by division.	**razón** Comparación de dos cantidades mediante una división.	12 to 25, 12:25, $\frac{12}{25}$
rational number Any number that can be expressed as a ratio of two integers.	**número racional** Número que se puede escribir como una razón de dos enteros.	6 can be expressed as $\frac{6}{1}$. 0.5 can be expressed as $\frac{1}{2}$.
ray A part of a line that starts at one endpoint and extends forever in one direction.	**rayo** Parte de una línea que comienza en un extremo y se extiende de manera infinitamente en una dirección.	
real number A rational or irrational number.	**número real** Número racional o irracional.	
reciprocal One of two numbers whose product is 1; also called *multiplicative inverse*.	**recíproco** Uno de dos números cuyo producto es igual a 1. También se llama *inverso multiplicativo*.	The reciprocal of $\frac{2}{3}$ is $\frac{3}{2}$.
rectangle A parallelogram with four right angles.	**rectángulo** Paralelogramo con cuatro ángulos rectos.	
rectangular prism A polyhedron whose bases are rectangles and whose other faces are parallelograms.	**prisma rectangular** Poliedro cuyas bases son rectángulos y cuyas caras tienen forma de paralelogramo.	
reduction A decrease in the size of all dimensions.	**reducción** Disminución de tamaño en todas las dimensiones de una figura.	
reflection A transformation of a figure that flips the figure across a line.	**reflexión** Transformación que ocurre cuando se invierte una figura sobre una línea.	
regular polygon A polygon with congruent sides and angles.	**polígono regular** Polígono con lados y ángulos congruentes.	
regular pyramid A pyramid whose base is a regular polygon and whose lateral faces are all congruent.	**pirámide regular** Pirámide que tiene un polígono regular como base y caras laterales congruentes.	
relation A set of ordered pairs.	**relación** Conjunto de pares ordenados.	(0, 5), (0, 4), (2, 3), (4, 0)

relative frequency The frequency of a specific data value divided by the total number of data values in the set.

frecuencia relativa La frecuencia de un valor dividido por el número total de los valores en el conjunto.

---

relatively prime Two numbers are relatively prime if their greatest common factor (GCF) is 1.

primo relativo Dos números son primos relativos si su máximo común divisor (MCD) es 1.

8 and 15 are relatively prime.

---

remote interior angle An interior angle of a polygon that is not adjacent to the exterior angle.

ángulo interno remoto Ángulo interno de un polígono que no es adyacente al ángulo externo.

---

repeating decimal A decimal in which one or more digits repeat infinitely.

decimal periódico Decimal en el que uno o más dígitos se repiten infinitamente.

$0.757575\ldots = 0.\overline{75}$

---

rhombus A parallelogram with all sides congruent.

rombo Paralelogramo en el que todos los lados son congruentes.

---

right angle An angle that measures 90°.

ángulo recto Ángulo que mide exactamente 90°.

---

right cone A cone in which a perpendicular line drawn from the base to the tip (vertex) passes through the center of the base.

cono regular Cono en el que una línea perpendicular trazada de la base a la punta (vértice) pasa por el centro de la base.

Right cone

---

right triangle A triangle containing a right angle.

triángulo rectángulo Triángulo que tiene un ángulo recto.

---

rise The vertical change when the slope of a line is expressed as the ratio $\frac{rise}{run}$, or "rise over run."

distancia vertical El cambio vertical cuando la pendiente de una línea se expresa como la razón $\frac{distancia\ vertical}{distancia\ horizontal}$, o "distancia vertical sobre distancia horizontal".

For the points $(3, -1)$ and $(6, 5)$, the rise is $5 - (-1) = 6$.

---

rotation A transformation in which a figure is turned around a point.

rotación Transformación que ocurre cuando una figura gira alrededor de un punto.

---

rotational symmetry A figure has rotational symmetry if it can be rotated less than 360° around a central point and coincide with the original figure.

simetría de rotación Ocurre cuando una figura gira menos de 360° alrededor de un punto central sin dejar de ser congruente con la figura original.

90°   90°   90°   90°

Glossary/Glosario

ENGLISH	SPANISH	EXAMPLES
rounding Replacing a number with an estimate of that number to a given place value.	**redondear** Sustituir un número por una estimación de ese número hasta cierto valor posicional.	2,354 rounded to the nearest thousand is 2,000, and 2,354 rounded to the nearest 100 is 2,400.
run The horizontal change when the slope of a line is expressed as the ratio $\frac{rise}{run}$, or "rise over run."	**distancia horizontal** El cambio horizontal cuando la pendiente de una línea se expresa como la razón $\frac{distancia\ vertical}{distancia\ horizontal}$, o "distancia vertical sobre distancia horizontal".	For the points $(3, -1)$ and $(6, 5)$, the run is $6 - 3 = 3$.

S

ENGLISH	SPANISH	EXAMPLES
sales tax A percent of the cost of an item that is charged by governments to raise money.	**impuesto sobre la venta** Porcentaje del costo de un artículo que los gobiernos cobran para recaudar fondos.	
same-side interior angles A pair of angles on the same side of a transversal and between two lines intersected by the transversal.	**ángulo internos del mismo lado** Dadas dos rectas cortadas por una transversal, par de ángulos ubicados en el mismo lado de la transversal y entre las dos rectas.	
sample A part of the population.	**muestra** Una parte de la población.	
sample space All possible outcomes of an experiment.	**espacio muestral** Conjunto de todos los resultados posibles de un experimento.	When rolling a number cube, the sample space is 1, 2, 3, 4, 5, 6.
scale The ratio between two sets of measurements.	**escala** La razón entre dos conjuntos de medidas.	1 cm : 5 mi
scale drawing A drawing that uses a scale to make an object smaller than (a reduction) or larger than (an enlargement) the real object.	**dibujo a escala** Dibujo en el que se usa una escala para que un objeto se vea menor (reducción) o mayor (agrandamiento) que el objeto real al que representa.	A blueprint is an example of a scale drawing.
scale factor The ratio used to enlarge or reduce similar figures.	**factor de escala** Razón empleada para agrandar o reducir figuras semejantes.	
scale model A proportional model of a three-dimensional object.	**modelo a escala** Modelo proporcional de un objeto tridimensional.	
scalene triangle A triangle with no congruent sides.	**triángulo escaleno** Triángulo que no tiene lados congruentes.	

ENGLISH	SPANISH	EXAMPLES
scatter plot A graph with points plotted to show a possible relationship between two sets of data.	**diagrama de dispersión** Gráfica de puntos que muestra una posible relación entre dos conjuntos de datos.	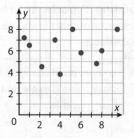
scientific notation A method of writing very large or very small numbers by using powers of 10.	**notación científica** Método que se usa para escribir números muy grandes o muy pequeños mediante potencias de 10.	$12{,}560{,}000{,}000{,}000 = 1.256 \times 10^{13}$
second quartile The median of a set of data.	**segundo cuartil** Mediana de un conjunto de datos.	Data set: 4, 6, 7, 8, 10 Second quartile: 7
sector A region enclosed by two radii and the arc joining their endpoints.	**sector** Región encerrada por dos radios y el arco que une sus extremos.	
sector (data) A section of a circle graph representing part of the data set.	**sector (datos)** Sección de una gráfica circular que representa una parte del conjunto de datos.	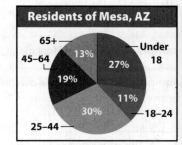 The circle graph has 5 sectors.
segment A part of a line between two endpoints.	**segmento** Parte de una línea entre dos extremos.	
self-selected sample A sample in which members choose to be in the sample.	**muestra auto-seleccionada** Una muestra en la que los miembros eligen participar.	A store provides survey cards for customers who choose to fill them out.
sequence An ordered list of numbers.	**sucesión** Lista ordenada de números.	2, 4, 6, 8, 10, …
set A group of terms.	**conjunto** Un grupo de elementos.	
side A line bounding a geometric figure; one of the faces forming the outside of an object.	**lado** Línea que delimita las figuras geométricas; una de las caras que forman la parte exterior de un objeto.	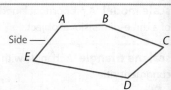
similar Figures with the same shape but not necessarily the same size.	**semejantes** Figuras que tienen la misma forma, pero no necesariamente el mismo tamaño.	

	ENGLISH	SPANISH	EXAMPLES

similarity transformation A transformation that results in an image that is the same shape, but not necessarily the same size, as the original figure.

transformación de semejanza Una transformación que resulta en una imagen que tiene la misma forma, pero no necesariamente el mismo tamaño como la figura original.

---

simple event An event consisting of only one outcome.

suceso simple Suceso que tiene sólo un resultado.

In the experiment of rolling a number cube, the event consisting of the outcome 3 is a simple event.

---

simple interest A fixed percent of the principal. It is found using the formula $I = Prt$, where P represents the principal, r the rate of interest, and t the time.

interés simple Un porcentaje fijo del capital. Se calcula con la fórmula $I = Cit$, donde C representa el capital, i, la tasa de interés y t, el tiempo.

$100 is put into an account with a simple interest rate of 5%. After 2 years, the account will have earned $I = 100 \cdot 0.05 \cdot 2 = \$10$.

---

simplest form A fraction in which the numerator and denominator have no common factors other than 1.

mínima expresión Una fracción está en su mínima expresión cuando el numerador y el denominador no tienen más factor común que 1.

Fraction: $\frac{8}{12}$

Simplest form: $\frac{2}{3}$

---

simplify To write a fraction or expression in simplest form.

simplificar Escribir una fracción o expresión numérica en su mínima expresión.

---

simulation A model of an experiment, often one that would be too difficult or too time-consuming to actually perform.

simulación Representación de un experimento, por lo general, de uno cuya realización sería demasiado difícil o llevaría mucho tiempo.

---

skew lines Lines that lie in different planes that are neither parallel nor intersecting.

líneas oblicuas Líneas que se encuentran en planos distintos, por eso no se intersecan ni son paralelas.

$\overleftrightarrow{AB}$ and $\overleftrightarrow{CG}$ are skew lines.

---

slant height (of a regular pyramid) The distance from the vertex of a regular pyramid to the midpoint of an edge of the base.

altura inclinada (de una pirámide) Distancia desde el vértice de una pirámide hasta el punto medio de una arista de la base.

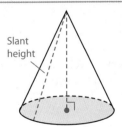

Slant height

Regular pyramid

---

slant height (of a right cone) The distance from the vertex of a right cone to a point on the edge of the base.

altura inclinada (de un cono recto) Distancia desde el vértice de un cono recto hasta un punto en el borde de la base.

Slant height

ENGLISH	SPANISH	EXAMPLES
slope A measure of the steepness of a line on a graph; the rise divided by the run.	**pendiente** Medida de la inclinación de una línea en una gráfica. Razón de la distancia vertical a la distancia horizontal.	Slope $= \frac{\text{rise}}{\text{run}} = \frac{3}{4}$ 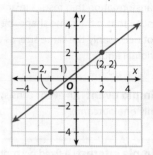
slope-intercept form A linear equation written in the form $y = mx + b$, where m represents slope and b represents the y-intercept.	**forma de pendiente-intersección** Ecuación lineal escrita en la forma $y = mx + b$, donde m es la pendiente y b es la intersección con el eje y.	$y = 6x - 3$
solid figure A three-dimensional figure.	**cuerpo geométrico** Figura tridimensional.	
solution of an equation A value or values that make an equation true.	**solución de una ecuación** Valor o valores que hacen verdadera una ecuación.	Equation: $x + 2 = 6$ Solution: $x = 4$
solution of an inequality A value or values that make an inequality true.	**solución de una desigualdad** Valor o valores que hacen verdadera una desigualdad.	Inequality: $x + 3 \geq 10$ Solution: $x \geq 7$
solution of a system of equations A set of values that make all equations in a system true.	**solución de un sistema de ecuaciones** Conjunto de valores que hacen verdaderas todas las ecuaciones de un sistema.	System: $\begin{cases} x + y = -1 \\ -x + y = -3 \end{cases}$ Solution: $(1, -2)$
solution set The set of values that make a statement true.	**conjunto solución** Conjunto de valores que hacen verdadero un enunciado.	Inequality: $x + 3 \geq 5$ Solution set: $x \geq 2$ 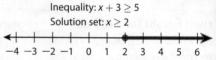
solve To find an answer or a solution.	**resolver** Hallar una respuesta o solución.	
sphere A three-dimensional figure with all points the same distance from the center.	**esfera** Figura tridimensional en la que todos los puntos están a la misma distancia del centro.	
square A rectangle with four congruent sides.	**cuadrado** Rectángulo con cuatro lados congruentes.	

ENGLISH	SPANISH	EXAMPLES

square (numeration) A number raised to the second power.

cuadrado (en numeración) Número elevado a la segunda potencia.

In 5^2, the number 5 is squared.

---

square root A number that is multiplied by itself to form a product is called a square root of that product.

raíz cuadrada El número que se multiplica por sí mismo para formar un producto se denomina la raíz cuadrada de ese producto.

A square root of 16 is 4, because $4^2 = 4 \cdot 4 = 16$.
Another square root of 16 is -4 because $(-4)^2 = (-4)(-4) = 16$.

---

stem-and-leaf plot A graph used to organize and display data so that the frequencies can be compared.

diagrama de tallo y hojas Gráfica que muestra y ordena los datos, y que sirve para comparar las frecuencias.

Stem	Leaves
3	2 3 4 4 7 9
4	0 1 5 7 7 7 8
5	1 2 2 3

Key: 3|2 means 3.2

---

straight angle An angle that measures 180°.

ángulo llano Ángulo que mide exactamente 180°.

---

subset A set contained within another set.

subconjunto Conjunto que pertenece a otro conjunto.

---

substitute To replace a variable with a number or another expression in an algebraic expression.

sustituir Reemplazar una variable por un número u otra expresión en una expresión algebraica.

Substituting 3 for m in the expression $5m - 2$ gives $5(3) - 2 = 15 - 2 = 13$.

Subtraction Property of Equality The property that states that if you subtract the same number from both sides of an equation, the new equation will have the same solution.

Propiedad de igualdad de la resta Propiedad que establece que puedes restar el mismo número de ambos lados de una ecuación y la nueva ecuación tendrá la misma solución.

$$\begin{aligned} 14 - 6 &= \ \ 8 \\ -6 &= -6 \\ \hline 14 - 12 &= \ \ 2 \end{aligned}$$

---

supplementary angles Two angles whose measures have a sum of 180°.

ángulos suplementarios Dos ángulos cuyas medidas suman 180°.

30° 150°

---

surface area The sum of the areas of the faces, or surfaces, of a three-dimensional figure.

área total Suma de las áreas de las caras, o superficies, de una figura tridimensional.

12 cm
6 cm
8 cm
Surface area $= 2(8)(12) + 2(8)(6) + 2(12)(6) = 432\text{ cm}^2$

---

system of equations A set of two or more equations that contain two or more variables.

sistema de ecuaciones Conjunto de dos o más ecuaciones que contienen dos o más variables.

$$\begin{cases} x + y = -1 \\ -x + y = -3 \end{cases}$$

---

systematic sample A sample of a population that has been selected using a pattern.

muestra sistemática Muestra de una población, que ha sido elegida mediante un patrón.

To conduct a phone survey, every tenth name is chosen from the phone book.

term (in an expression) A part of an expression that is added or subtracted.

término (en una expresión) Las partes de una expresión que se suman o se restan.

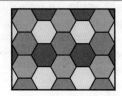

$$3x^2 \quad + \quad 6x \quad - \quad 8$$

Term   Term   Term

---

term (in a sequence) An element or number in a sequence.

término (en una sucesión) Elemento o número de una sucesión.

5 is the third term in the sequence 1, 3, 5, 7, 9, …

---

terminating decimal A decimal number that ends, or terminates.

decimal finito Decimal con un número determinado de posiciones decimales.

6.75

---

tessellation A repeating pattern of plane figures that completely cover a plane with no gaps or overlaps.

teselado Patrón repetido de figuras planas que cubren totalmente un plano sin superponerse ni dejar huecos.

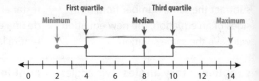

---

theoretical probability The ratio of the number of ways an event can occur to the number of equally likely outcomes.

probabilidad teórica Razón del número de las maneras que puede ocurrir un suceso al numero total de resultados igualmente probables.

When rolling a number cube, the theoretical probability of rolling a 4 is $\frac{1}{6}$.

---

third quartile The median of the upper half of a set of data; also called *upper quartile*.

tercer cuartil La mediana de la mitad superior de un conjunto de datos. También se llama *cuartil superior*.

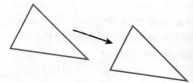

---

transformation A change in the size or position of a figure.

transformación Cambio en el tamaño o la posición de una figura.

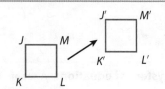

---

translation A movement (slide) of a figure along a straight line.

traslación Desplazamiento de una figura a lo largo de una línea recta.

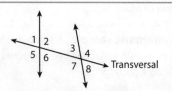

---

transversal A line that intersects two or more lines.

transversal Línea que cruza dos o más líneas.

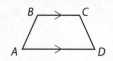

---

trapezoid A quadrilateral with at least one pair of parallel sides.

trapecio Cuadrilátero con al menos un par de lados paralelos.

ENGLISH	SPANISH	EXAMPLES

tree diagram A branching diagram that shows all possible combinations or outcomes of an event.

diagrama de árbol Diagrama ramificado que muestra todas las posibles combinaciones o resultados de un suceso.

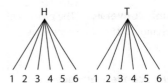

---

trend line A line on a scatter plot that helps show the correlation between data sets more clearly.

línea de tendencia Línea en un diagrama de dispersión que sirve para mostrar la correlación entre conjuntos de datos más claramente. *ver también* línea de mejor ajuste.

---

trial Each repetition or observation of an experiment.

prueba Una sola repetición u observación de un experimento.

When rolling a number cube, each roll is one trial.

Triangle Inequality Theorem The theorem that states that the sum of the lengths of any two sides of a triangle is greater than the length of the third side.

Teorema de desigualdad de triángulos El teorema dice que la suma de cualquier dos lados de un triangulo es mayor que la longitud del lado tercero.

Can form a triangle   Cannot form a triangle

Triangle Sum Theorem The theorem that states that the measures of the angles in a triangle add up to 180°.

Teorema de la suma del triángulo Teorema que establece que las medidas de los ángulos de un triángulo suman 180°.

---

triangular prism A polyhedron whose bases are triangles and whose other faces are parallelograms.

prisma triangular Poliedro cuyas bases son triángulos y cuyas demás caras tienen forma de paralelogramo.

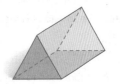

---

trinomial A polynomial with three terms.

trinomio Polinomio con tres términos.

$4x^2 + 3xy - 5y^2$

---

two-way relative frequency table A two-way table that displays relative frequencies.

tabla de frecuencia relativa de doble entrada Una tabla de doble entrada que muestran las frecuencias relativas.

---

two-way table A table that displays two-variable data by organizing it into rows and columns.

tabla de doble entrada Una tabla que muestran los datos de dos variables por organizándolos en columnas y filas.

		Preference		
		Inside	**Outside**	*Total*
Pet	**Cats**	35	15	50
	Dogs	20	30	50
	Total	55	45	100

---

underestimate An estimate that is less than the exact answer.

estimación baja Estimación menor que la respuesta exacta.

ENGLISH	SPANISH	EXAMPLES
unit conversion The process of changing one unit of measure to another.	**conversión de unidades** Proceso que consiste en cambiar una unidad de medida por otra.	
unit conversion factor A fraction used in unit conversion in which the numerator and denominator represent the same amount but are in different units.	**factor de conversión de unidades** Fracción que se usa para la conversión de unidades, donde el numerador y el denominador representan la misma cantidad pero están en unidades distintas.	$\frac{60 \text{ min}}{1 \text{ h}}$ or $\frac{1 \text{ h}}{60 \text{ min}}$
unit price A unit rate used to compare prices.	**precio unitario** Tasa unitaria que sirve para comparar precios.	Cereal costs $0.23 per ounce.
unit rate A rate in which the second quantity in the comparison is one unit.	**tasa unitaria** Una tasa en la que la segunda cantidad de la comparación es la unidad.	10 cm per minute
upper quartile The median of the upper half of a set of data.	**cuartil superior** La mediana de la mitad superior de un conjunto de datos.	Lower half Upper half 18, 23, 28, 29, (36,) 42 ↑ Upper quartile

V

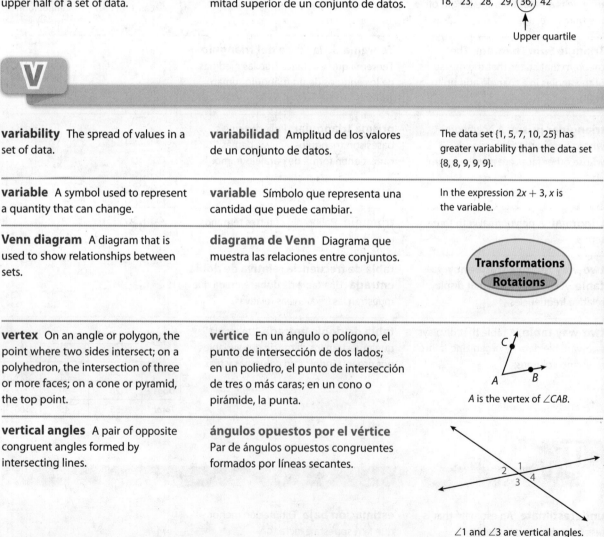

ENGLISH	SPANISH	EXAMPLES
variability The spread of values in a set of data.	**variabilidad** Amplitud de los valores de un conjunto de datos.	The data set {1, 5, 7, 10, 25} has greater variability than the data set {8, 8, 9, 9, 9}.
variable A symbol used to represent a quantity that can change.	**variable** Símbolo que representa una cantidad que puede cambiar.	In the expression $2x + 3$, x is the variable.
Venn diagram A diagram that is used to show relationships between sets.	**diagrama de Venn** Diagrama que muestra las relaciones entre conjuntos.	Transformations / Rotations
vertex On an angle or polygon, the point where two sides intersect; on a polyhedron, the intersection of three or more faces; on a cone or pyramid, the top point.	**vértice** En un ángulo o polígono, el punto de intersección de dos lados; en un poliedro, el punto de intersección de tres o más caras; en un cono o pirámide, la punta.	A is the vertex of $\angle CAB$.
vertical angles A pair of opposite congruent angles formed by intersecting lines.	**ángulos opuestos por el vértice** Par de ángulos opuestos congruentes formados por líneas secantes.	$\angle 1$ and $\angle 3$ are vertical angles.

ENGLISH	SPANISH	EXAMPLES

vertical line test A test used to determine whether a relation is a function. If any vertical line crosses the graph of a relation more than once, the relation is not a function.

prueba de la línea vertical Prueba utilizada para determinar si una relación es una función. Si una línea vertical corta la gráfica de una relación más de una vez, la relación no es una función.

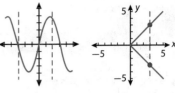

Function   Not a function

---

volume The number of cubic units needed to fill a given space.

volumen Número de unidades cúbicas que se necesitan para llenar un espacio.

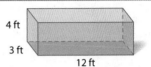

Volume = $3 \cdot 4 \cdot 12 = 144$ ft^3

weighted average A mean that is calculated by multiplying each data value by a weight, and dividing the sum of these products by the sum of the weights.

promedio ponderado Promedio que se calcula por multiplicando cada valor de datos por un peso, y dividiendo la suma de estos productos por la suma de los pesos.

If the data values 0, 5, and 10 are assigned the weights 0.1, 0.2, and 0.7, respectively, the weighted average is:
$$\frac{0(0.1) + 5(0.2) + 10(0.7)}{0.1 + 0.2 + 0.7} = \frac{8}{1}$$

x-axis The horizontal axis on a coordinate plane.

eje x El eje horizontal del plano cartesiano.

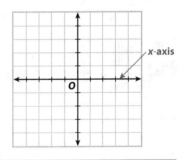

x-axis

---

x-coordinate The first number in an ordered pair; it tells the distance to move right or left from the origin (0, 0).

coordenada x El primer número de un par ordenado; indica la distancia que debes moverte hacia la izquierda o la derecha desde el origen, (0, 0).

5 is the x-coordinate in (5, 3).

---

x-intercept The x-coordinate of the point where the graph of a line crosses the x-axis.

intersección con el eje x Coordenada x del punto donde la gráfica de una línea cruza el eje x.

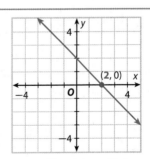

The x-intercept is 2.

ENGLISH	SPANISH	EXAMPLES

y-axis The vertical axis on a coordinate plane.

eje y El eje vertical del plano cartesiano.

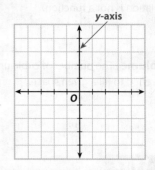

y-coordinate The second number in an ordered pair; it tells the distance to move up or down from the origin (0, 0).

coordenada y El segundo número de un par ordenado; indica la distancia que debes avanzar hacia arriba o hacia abajo desde el origen, (0, 0).

3 is the y-coordinate in (5, 3).

y-intercept The y-coordinate of the point where the graph of a line crosses the y-axis.

intersección con el eje y Coordenada y del punto donde la gráfica de una línea cruza el eje y.

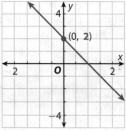

The y-intercept is 2.

zero pair A number and its opposite, which add to 0.

par nulo Un número y su opuesto, cuya suma es 0.

18 and −18

Glossary/Glosario

Index

Index

Index (left margin)

Index

Index

Index

ASSESSMENT REFERENCE SHEET

TABLE OF MEASURES

Length

1 inch = 2.54 centimeters

1 meter ≈ 39.37 inches

1 mile = 5,280 feet

1 mile = 1,760 yards

1 mile ≈ 1.609 kilometers

1 kilometer ≈ 0.62 mile

Mass/Weight

1 pound = 16 ounces

1 pound ≈ 0.454 kilogram

1 kilogram ≈ 2.2 pounds

1 ton = 2,000 pounds

Capacity

1 cup = 8 fluid ounces

1 pint = 2 cups

1 quart = 2 pints

1 gallon = 4 quarts

1 gallon ≈ 3.785 liters

1 liter ≈ 0.264 gallon

1 liter = 1000 cubic centimeters

FORMULAS

Area

Parallelogram	$A = bh$
Circle	$A = \pi r^2$
Triangle	$A = \frac{1}{2} bh$

Volume

General Prisms	$V = Bh$
Cylinder	$V = \pi r^2 h$
Sphere	$V = \frac{4}{3} \pi r^3$
Cone	$V = \frac{1}{3} \pi r^2 h$

Circumference

Circle	$C = \pi d$ or $C = 2\pi r$

Other

Pythagorean Theorem	$a^2 + b^2 = c^2$